ROUTLEDGE HANDBOOK OF THE BELT AND ROAD

Chinese President Xi Jinping announced the Belt and Road Initiative (BRI) in 2013, a development strategy involving infrastructure development and investments in countries in Europe, Asia and Africa. It has rapidly turned into action, reflected in the establishment of a series of international cooperation mechanisms, landing of cooperation projects and harvest of some early results. The influence is huge, and controversy is not unexpected. As one of the most frequently mentioned concepts in the official media, how does the "bid to enhance regional connectivity" construct a unified large market through cultural exchange and integration in practice? What is the status quo of building an innovative pattern with capital inflows, talent pool and technology database?

Routledge Handbook of the Belt and Road is an initial review of the theory and practice of BRI, and is the first handbook of its kind. Contributors are leading subject researchers, aiming to reflect the original intentions and principles, history and current situation, basic knowledge and latest studies. A total of 117 entries related to the BRI have been included, organised into 12 clear parts covering the following key topics:

- China's reform and opening-up and formation of the BRI
- Backstory, concept and framework
- The five roads and six economic corridors
- Foreign affairs with Chinese characteristics
- International action plans relevant and similar to the BRI
- Case studies of the BRI implementation and promotion

Routledge Handbook of the Belt and Road is an essential guide for researchers, practitioners and observers involved in the BRI construction. Global think tanks, media practitioners and universities will also find the book a useful reference.

Cai Fang is Professor of Economics, Vice President of the Chinese Academy of Social Sciences, and President of National Institute for Global Strategy (NIGS), China.

Peter Nolan is Professor of Chinese Development and Director of the Centre of Development Studies, University of Cambridge, UK.

Routledge International Handbooks

The Routledge Handbook of Latin American Development
Edited by Julie Cupples, Marcela Palomina-Schalscha and Manuel Prieto

The Routledge International Handbook of Embodied Perspectives in Psychotherapy: Approaches from Dance Movement and Body Psychotherapies
Edited by Helen Payne, Sabine Koch, Jennifer Tantia and Thomas Fuchs

The Routledge Handbook of Teaching Landscape
Edited by Elke Mertens, Nilgül Karadeniz, Karsten Jørgensen, Richard Stiles

The Routledge International Handbook of Spirituality in Society and the Professions
Edited by Laszlo Flanagan and Bernadette Flanagan

The Routledge International Handbook of Language Education Policy in Asia
Edited by Andy Kirkpatrick and Anthony J. Liddicoat

Routledge International Handbook of Migration Studies 2e
Edited by Steven J. Gold and Stephanie J. Nawyn

Routledge Handbook of Contemporary Feminism
Edited by Tasha Oren and Andrea Press

Routledge Handbook of the Belt and Road
Edited by Cai Fang and Peter Nolan

Routledge Handbook of Language Acquisition
Edited by Jessica S. Horst and Janne von Koss Torkildsen

For more information about this series, please visit: www.routledge.com/Routledge-International-Handbooks/book-series/RIHAND

ROUTLEDGE HANDBOOK OF THE BELT AND ROAD

Edited by Cai Fang and Peter Nolan

This book is published with financial support from the Chinese Fund for the Humanities and Social Sciences.

First published in English 2019
by Routledge
2 Park Square, Milton Park, Abingdon, Oxon OX14 4RN

and by Routledge
52 Vanderbilt Avenue, New York, NY 10017

Routledge is an imprint of the Taylor & Francis Group, an informa business

© 2019 selection and editorial matter, Cai Fang and Peter Nolan; individual chapters, the contributors

Executive editors: Wang Linggui, Zhao Jianglin

Translated by Fu Yili

The right of Cai Fang and Peter Nolan to be identified as the authors of the editorial material, and of the authors for their individual chapters, has been asserted in accordance with sections 77 and 78 of the Copyright, Designs and Patents Act 1988.

All rights reserved. No part of this book may be reprinted or reproduced or utilised in any form or by any electronic, mechanical, or other means, now known or hereafter invented, including photocopying and recording, or in any information storage or retrieval system, without permission in writing from the publishers.

Trademark notice: Product or corporate names may be trademarks or registered trademarks, and are used only for identification and explanation without intent to infringe.

English version by permission of China Social Sciences Press.

British Library Cataloguing-in-Publication Data
A catalogue record for this book is available from the British Library

Library of Congress Cataloging-in-Publication Data
Names: Cai, Fang, editor. | Nolan, Peter, 1949–
Title: Routledge handbook of the belt and road / edited by Cai Fang and Peter Nolan.
Other titles: Yi dai yi lu shou ce. English.
Description: Abingdon, Oxon ; New York, NY : Routledge, 2019. |
Series: Routledge international handbooks
Identifiers: LCCN 2018058029 (print) | LCCN 2019003441 (ebook) |
ISBN 9780429203039 (ebook) | ISBN 9780367195267 (hardcover)
Subjects: LCSH: China–Commerce. | China–Commercial policy. |
China–Foreign economic relations. | Economic development–Developing countries.
Classification: LCC HF3836.5 (ebook) |
LCC HF3836.5 .Y53613 2019 (print) | DDC 381.0951–dc23
LC record available at https://lccn.loc.gov/2018058029

ISBN: 978-0-367-19526-7 (hbk)
ISBN: 978-0-429-20303-9 (ebk)

Typeset in Bembo
by Newgen Publishing UK

 Printed in the United Kingdom
by Henry Ling Limited

CONTENTS

List of contributors   xv
Foreword   xviii
Preface: the Silk Road by land and sea   xxi

PART I
Contribution of China's reform and opening up to the world and formation of the Belt and Road Initiative   1

1. The historic contribution of China's reform and opening up to the world   3
   Zhou Fangye

2. Developing an open economy and the Belt and Road   9
   Zhou Fangye

3. China's economic restructuring and the Belt and Road   15
   Zhou Fangye

4. Innovation-driven development and the Belt and Road   21
   Zhou Fangye

5. Responsibilities of China as a major country and the Belt and Road   27
   Zhou Fangye

6. Confidence of a major country and the Belt and Road   33
   Zhou Fangye

7. Deficit in development and the Belt and Road   38
   Xu Liping

8	Deficit in peace and the Belt and Road *Yang Xiaoping*	43
9	Deficit in governance and the Belt and Road *Wang Xiaoling*	47

PART II
Historic inheritance   51

10	Naming of the Silk Road *Dong Xiangrong*	53
11	A brief history of the Silk Road *Dong Xiangrong*	57
12	The Overland Silk Road *Dong Xiangrong*	63
13	The Maritime Silk Road *Dong Xiangrong*	68
14	Silk road and exchanges among different countries *Dong Xiangrong*	74
15	The Silk Road spirit *Dong Xiangrong*	80

PART III
Formation and framework of the concept   87

16	Process for proposing the concept *Wang Yuzhu*	89
17	Background *Wang Yuzhu*	94
18	The Belt and Road Initiative framework *Wang Yuzhu and Li Shicheng*	99
19	Basic contents *Xu Juan and Wang Yuzhu*	106
20	Basic principles *Wang Yuzhu and Jiang Fangfei*	111

21	Partners *Xu Juan and Wang Yuzhu*	116
22	General ideas *Wang Yuzhu and Jiang Fangfei*	123
23	Directions of cooperation *Fu Jingjun*	127
24	Cooperation mechanisms *Ge Cheng*	131
25	Organisational structure *Liu Junsheng*	136

PART IV
The five roads — 143

26	The Belt and Road Initiative and the Road of Peace *Xie Laihui*	145
27	The Belt and Road Initiative and the Road of Prosperity *Xie Laihui*	150
28	The Belt and Road Initiative and the Road of Openness *Xie Laihui*	155
29	The Belt and Road Initiative and the Road of Innovation *Xie Laihui*	160
30	The Belt and Road Initiative and the Road Connecting Different Civilisations *Xie Laihui*	165

PART V
Five types of connectivity — 171

31	Policy coordination *Qin Sheng*	173
32	Connectivity of infrastructure *Li Tianguo*	178

33	Unimpeded trade *Shen Minghui*	182
34	Financial integration *Shen Minghui*	186
35	Understanding between people *Qin Sheng*	190

PART VI
The six economic corridors — 195

36	The China–Mongolia–Russia Economic Corridor *Wang Jinbo*	197
37	The New Eurasian Continental Bridge Economic Corridor *Wang Jinbo*	202
38	The China–Central Asia–West Asia Economic Corridor *Wang Jinbo*	207
39	The China–Indochina Peninsula Economic Corridor *Wang Jinbo*	213
40	The China–Pakistan Economic Corridor *Wang Jinbo*	218
41	BCIM Economic Corridor *Wang Jinbo*	223

PART VII
Theories and concepts of the foreign affairs with Chinese characteristics — 229

42	Major-country diplomacy with Chinese characteristics *Zhong Feiteng*	231
43	New-type international relations *Zhong Feiteng*	236
44	New-type major-country relations *Zhong Feiteng*	241
45	The community with a shared future for mankind *Li Zhifei*	246

46	Two Centenary Goals *Yang Danzhi*	252
47	Win–win cooperation *Yang Danzhi*	257
48	Regional Comprehensive Economic Partnership *Liu Junsheng*	263
49	The approach of upholding justice while pursuing shared interests *Yang Danzhi*	267
50	Amity, sincerity, mutual benefit and inclusiveness *Li Zhifei*	272
51	Sincerity, practical results, affinity and good faith *Yang Danzhi*	277

PART VIII
Core concepts — 283

52	Bridge development strategies *Xu Xiujun*	285
53	Asian Infrastructure Investment Bank *Xu Xiujun*	290
54	Silk Road Fund *Xu Xiujun*	294
55	New Development Bank *Xu Xiujun*	300
56	China–ASEAN Cooperation Fund *Xu Xiujun*	306
57	Production capacity cooperation *Xu Xiujun*	310
58	Cross-border industrial parks *Xu Xiujun*	315
59	Free trade area in China *Tian Feng*	319

60	Free trade ports *Zhang Zhongyuan*	323
61	Bilateral and Multilateral Cooperation Dialogue Mechanism for Macroeconomic Policies *Feng Weijiang*	327
62	New industrial innovation cooperation *Tian Feng*	332
63	Promoting the international infrastructure network *Tian Feng*	337
64	Standard setting and institutional building for international infrastructure *Tian Feng*	341
65	Global value chain development and supply chain *Tian Feng*	346
66	Promoting renewable energy and energy efficiency cooperation *Wang Yongzhong*	351
67	Tackle climate change *Tian Huifang*	355
68	Sustainable development *Tian Huifang*	360
69	Trade and investment facilitation *Feng Weijiang*	364
70	People-to-people exchanges and cooperation *Xiao He*	368
71	Exchanges and mutual learning among civilisations *Xue Li*	372

PART IX
Belt and Road Forum for International Cooperation — 379

72	Belt and Road Forum for International Cooperation *Ding Gong*	381

73	Thematic Session on Connectivity of Development Policies and Strategies *Ding Gong*	386
74	Thematic Session on Infrastructure Connectivity *Ding Gong*	390
75	Thematic Session on Trade Connectivity *Ding Gong*	394
76	Thematic Session on Financial Connectivity *Qu Caiyun*	398
77	Thematic Session on People-to-People Connectivity *Qu Caiyun*	403
78	Thematic Session on Think-Tank Exchanges *Qu Caiyun*	408

PART X
International action plans relevant to the Belt and Road Initiative 413

79	The Sustainable Development of the 2030 Agenda with the Belt and Road Initiative *Tian Huifang*	415
80	Addis Ababa Action Agenda with the Belt and Road Initiative *Liu Wei*	420
81	African Agenda 2063 with the Belt and Road Initiative *Xiao He*	425
82	Ancient Civilisations Forum with the Belt and Road Initiative *Xiao He*	430
83	Connectivity blueprint of Asia–Pacific Economic Cooperation with the Belt and Road Initiative *Liu Wei*	435
84	ASEAN Community Vision 2025 with the Belt and Road Initiative *Xue Li and Liu Tianyi*	439

85	Asia–Europe Meeting and its connectivity working group with the Belt and Road Initiative Liu Wei	443
86	Cooperation between China and Central and Eastern European Countries with the Belt and Road Initiative Tian Feng	448
87	China–Europe Land–Sea Express Route with the Belt and Road Initiative Xue Li	453
88	Middle Corridor Initiative with the Belt and Road Initiative Xue Li	457
89	China–EU Connectivity Platform (Juncker Plan) with the Belt and Road Initiative Liu Wei and Wei Siying	462
90	Eastern Partnership with the Belt and Road Initiative Xiao He	467
91	Eurasian Partnership Plan based on equal, open and transparent principles with the Belt and Road Initiative Feng Weijiang	472
92	Initiative for Integration of the Regional Infrastructure in South America with the Belt and Road Initiative Xiao He	476
93	The Master Plan on ASEAN Connectivity 2025 with the Belt and Road Initiative Xue Li and Liu Tianyi	480
94	The Paris Agreement with the Belt and Road Initiative Tian Huifang	483
95	Trans-European Transport Networks with the Belt and Road Initiative Feng Weijiang	488
96	Western Balkan 6 Connectivity Agenda with the Belt and Road Initiative Xiao He	492

97	Trade Facilitation Agreement of WTO with the Belt and Road Initiative *Feng Weijiang*	497

PART XI
International plans similar to the Belt and Road Initiative 501

98	Silk Road Tourism Programme (United Nations) *Wei Siying*	503
99	New Silk Road Plan (USA) *Wei Siying*	508
100	Eurasian Economic Union (Russia) *Tian Guangqiang and Liu Wei*	512
101	Quality Infrastructure Partnership Plan (Japan) *Liu Jingye*	517
102	Project Mausam Plan (India) *Wu Zhaoli*	521
103	Global Maritime Axis Strategy (Indonesia) *Liu Jingye*	526
104	Northern Australia Development Plan (Australia) *Pang Jiaxin*	530
105	Amber Railway Freight Corridor (Poland) *Pang Jiaxin*	535
106	Suez Canal Economic Corridor (Egypt) *Tian Guangqiang*	540
107	Lamu Port–South Sudan–Ethiopia Transportation Corridor (Kenya) *Pang Jiaxin*	544
108	Two-corridor and one-ring plan (Vietnam) *Liu Jingye*	549
109	Steppe Road Plan (Mongolia) *Tian Guangqiang*	554

110 Bright Road Plan (Kazakhstan) *Pang Jiaxin*	559
111 New Northward Expansion Policy (South Korea) *Pang Jiaxin*	564

PART XII
Case studies of BRI implementation and promotion   569

112 Case studies of infrastructure connectivity building *Zhang Zhongyuan*	571
113 Case studies of production capacity cooperation *Zhang Zhongyuan*	577
114 Case studies of trade and investment facilitation *Zhang Zhongyuan*	582
115 Case studies of financial cooperation *Zhang Zhongyuan*	587
116 Case studies of people-to-people exchanges *Zhang Zhongyuan*	593
117 The China International Import Expo *Zhang Zhongyuan*	598

Index   604

LIST OF CONTRIBUTORS

丁工 **Ding Gong** is an Assistant Research Fellow, National Institute of International Strategy, Chinese Academy of Social Sciences.

董向荣 **Dong Xiangrong** is a Senior Research Fellow, National Institute of International Strategy, Chinese Academy of Social Sciences.

冯维江 **Feng Weijiang** is a Senior Research Fellow, Institute of World Economics and Politics, Chinese Academy of Social Sciences.

富景筠 **Fu Jingyun** is an Associate Research Fellow, National Institute of International Strategy, Chinese Academy of Social Sciences.

葛成 **Ge Cheng** is an Assistant Research Fellow, National Institute of International Strategy, Chinese Academy of Social Sciences.

蒋芳菲 **Jiang Fangfei** is a PhD Candidate, National Institute of International Strategy, Chinese Academy of Social Sciences.

李嗜成 **Li Shicheng** is a PhD Candidate, National Institute of International Strategy, Chinese Academy of Social Sciences.

李天国 **Li Tianguo** is an Assistant Research Fellow, National Institute of International Strategy, Chinese Academy of Social Sciences.

李志斐 **Li Zhifei** is an Associate Research Fellow, National Institute of International Strategy, Chinese Academy of Social Sciences.

刘静烨 **Liu Jingye** is an Assistant Research Fellow, Institute of Chinese Borderland Studies, Chinese Academy of Social Sciences.

List of contributors

刘均胜 **Liu Junsheng** is an Associate Research Fellow, National Institute of International Strategy, Chinese Academy of Social Sciences.

刘天一 **Liu Tianyi** is a PhD Candidate, National Institute of International Strategy, Chinese Academy of Social Sciences.

刘玮 **Liu Wei** is an Assistant Research Fellow, Institute of World Economics and Politics, Chinese Academy of Social Sciences.

庞佳欣 **Pang Jiaxin** is a PhD Candidate, National Institute of International Strategy, Chinese Academy of Social Sciences.

秦升 **Qin Sheng** is an Assistant Research Fellow, National Institute of International Strategy, Chinese Academy of Social Sciences.

屈彩云 **Qu Caiyun** is an Assistant Research Fellow, National Institute of International Strategy, Chinese Academy of Social Sciences.

沈铭辉 **Shen Minghui** is a Senior Research Fellow, National Institute of International Strategy, Chinese Academy of Social Sciences.

田丰 **Tian Feng** is a Senior Research Fellow, Institute of World Economics and Politics, Chinese Academy of Social Sciences.

田光强 **Tian Guangqiang** is an Assistant Research Fellow, National Institute of International Strategy, Chinese Academy of Social Sciences.

田慧芳 **Tian Huifang** is an Associate Research Fellow, Institute of World Economics and Politics, Chinese Academy of Social Sciences.

王金波 **Wang Jinbo** is an Associate Research Fellow, National Institute of International Strategy, Chinese Academy of Social Sciences.

王灵桂 **Wang Linggui**, Executive Editor, is a Senior Research Fellow, the Executive Vice Chairman of the Board of Directors and the Secretary General of the National Institute for Global Strategy (NIGS), Chinese Academy of Social Sciences.

王晓玲 **Wang Xiaoling** is an Associate Research Fellow, National Institute of International Strategy, Chinese Academy of Social Sciences.

王永中 **Wang Yongzhong** is a Senior Research Fellow, Institute of World Economics and Politics, Chinese Academy of Social Sciences.

王玉主 **Wang Yuzhu** is a Senior Research Fellow, National Institute of International Strategy, Chinese Academy of Social Sciences.

魏斯莹 **Wei Siying** is a Postdoctoral Researcher, National Institute of International Strategy, Chinese Academy of Social Sciences.

List of contributors

吴兆礼 **Wu Zhaoli** is an Associate Research Fellow, National Institute of International Strategy, Chinese Academy of Social Sciences.

肖河 **Xiao He** is an Associate Research Fellow, Institute of World Economics and Politics, Chinese Academy of Social Sciences.

谢来辉 **Xie Laihui** is an Associate Research Fellow, National Institute of International Strategy, Chinese Academy of Social Sciences.

许娟 **Xu Juan** is a Postdoctoral Researcher, National Institute of International Strategy, Chinese Academy of Social Sciences.

许利平 **Xu Liping** is a Senior Research Fellow, National Institute of International Strategy, Chinese Academy of Social Sciences.

徐秀军 **Xu Xiujun** is a Senior Research Fellow, Institute of World Economics and Politics, Chinese Academy of Social Sciences.

薛力 **Xue Li** is a Senior Research Fellow, Institute of World Economics and Politics, Chinese Academy of Social Sciences.

杨丹志 **Yang Danzhi** is an Assistant Research Fellow, National Institute of International Strategy, Chinese Academy of Social Sciences.

杨晓萍 **Yang Xiaoping** is an Assistant Research Fellow, National Institute of International Strategy, Chinese Academy of Social Sciences.

张中元 **Zhang Zhongyuan** is an Associate Research Fellow, National Institute of International Strategy, Chinese Academy of Social Sciences.

赵江林 **Zhao Jianglin**, Executive Editor, is a Senior Research Fellow, National Institute for Global Strategy, Chinese Academy of Social Sciences.

钟飞腾 **Zhong Feiteng** is a Senior Research Fellow, National Institute of International Strategy, Chinese Academy of Social Sciences.

周方冶 **Zhou Fangye** is an Associate Research Fellow, National Institute of International Strategy, Chinese Academy of Social Sciences.

FOREWORD

The countries of the world are at different stages of development and have their own different histories and cultures, but the people of all countries share a common desire for peace and development. It is also the goal and constant commitment of the ruler of every country to raise the country's economic and social development level with a view to bringing people out of poverty and improving their quality of life. Meanwhile, people tend to agree that a country should also accommodate the legitimate concerns of others when seeking its own development and the common development of all countries is the only way for a country to achieve its sustainable development. Since Comrade Xi Jinping was elected the president of China in 2013, he has consistently advocated and made profound interpretations of the idea of building a community of shared future for mankind, which has quickly gained widespread recognition from the international community. The idea itself has also been recorded in a series of UN resolutions.

A desire for common development does not mean the pursuit of a single path, nor does it entail a single model. Instead, it allows diversified and localised development paths that keep abreast with the times. However, all countries also face common obstacles in their development, such as a bottleneck of capital accumulation, inequality in international economic and trade relations, low infrastructure capacity, difficulties in cultivating human capital, and low mobilisation capability and inefficient allocation of human resources. Therefore, while acknowledging and encouraging diversified models, all countries around the world, especially the developing countries, are also desperate for a strategic framework for development that not only helps to create the necessary conditions for development, breaking the bottlenecks in key areas and learning from success or failure, but also gives each country an adequate space of choice. The Belt and Road Initiative proposed by Chinese President Xi Jinping in 2013 is such an open framework.

First of all, the basic ideas of the Belt and Road Initiative have been verified by China's development and shared experience during its reform and opening up. China's development course in the past 40 years has provided a successful case in economic history for making the pie of shared interests even bigger and sharing it among all participators. During the period from 1978 to 2015, China's real total GDP and per-capita GDP increased by 29 times and 20 times, respectively, and along with economic growth, employment expanded continuously, the income of urban and rural residents greatly increased, and the real consumption level increased by 16 times and generally synchronised with labour productivity (which increased by 16.7 times during this period as measured by GDP per worker). Since the beginning of the twenty-first century, the implementation of the regional development strategies, such as the Great Western Development Strategy and the Strategy for the Rise of Central China, has improved the traffic conditions, infrastructure conditions, support capability of basic public services and human capital levels in the central and western regions. As the investment and development environments have been improved significantly, the ability of the central and western regions to take on manufacturing transfer has improved.

Second, the Belt and Road Initiative adheres to the principle of achieving shared growth through discussion and collaboration. The Initiative has deeper historical connotation and inspiration rather than simply borrowing the symbol of the ancient continental and Maritime Silk Road. From a greater historical depth, this symbol implies a negation of the traditional Western centralism and lays more emphasis on the role of connectivity and mutual learning between Eastern and Western civilisations in the history of human development. From a broader historical perspective, this symbol also implies how to break the content and model of supply of global public goods centring on the traditional hegemons and pays more attention to the new idea of eradicating global poverty through the participation of all countries.

Third, the Belt and Road Initiative has identified infrastructure construction as the critical constraint that all countries face. In almost all the countries along and involved in the Belt and Road, there are bottleneck problems brought by poor infrastructure in transportation, energy and other areas, which have long restricted investment efficiency and industrial development and prevented many countries from fully enjoying the dividends of economic globalisation. China has initiated and took the lead in investing in these countries. With the assistance of the Asian Infrastructure Investment Bank (AIIB), BRICS New Development Bank, the Silk Road Fund and other financing institutions, China has cooperated with relevant countries and regions in building infrastructure construction capabilities. As demonstrated by China's Great Western Development Strategy that has already been implemented, it is expected that the Belt and Road Initiative will greatly improve the infrastructure conditions in the developing countries.

Finally, the Belt and Road Initiative provides countries with a sufficient space to explore their own development models that suit their national conditions. To lift itself out of poverty and move towards modernisation, a country eventually needs to proceed from its national conditions and rely on its internal determination and efforts to eradicate various existing obstacles in development and institutional environment. If outsiders can do something meaningful (regardless of whether they can be called international public goods), it is undoubtedly to provide useful knowledge, including successful experiences acquired and lessons drawn from other environments, necessary assistance in software and hardware infrastructure construction, as well as effective market investment opportunities. The Belt and Road is such a joint construction and sharing initiative that runs parallel without interfering with the needs and efforts of all countries.

Since being proposed by Chinese President Xi Jinping in 2013, the Belt and Road Initiative has rapidly become an action, reflected in the establishment of a series of international cooperation mechanisms and projects and the achievement of some early results. However, people still have different understandings, doubts, misunderstandings and even intentional distortions of this Initiative. This is not unexpected. After all, as any activity in human society will inevitably undergo a process of continuous exploration and recognition and any cooperation undertaken needs all parties involved to mutually adapt, the Belt and Road Initiative is inherently open-ended, so it also needs to accumulate experience, improve ideas and enhance mutual understanding during its implementation. Therefore, in every stage of practice of the Initiative, it is necessary to summarise the progress that has been made, evaluate the existing experience and confirm the consensuses that have been formed.

Foreword

  The Handbook can be regarded as a phased summary of the preliminary results of the theory and practice of the Belt and Road. The authors of this Handbook include researchers in related fields, and it tries to reflect the original intentions and principles, history and status quo, basic knowledge and latest research results related to the ideas and practice of the Belt and Road. The editors of the Handbook do not extravagantly hope that it can act as a guidance document for theory and practice, but expect that it can serve as a guide for readers and be of benefit to researchers, practitioners and observers involved in the construction of the Belt and Road Initiative and ordinary readers. The contents in the Handbook may not reflect the latest progress, and there might be some mistakes. The authors and editors are sincerely welcoming of comments and criticisms from readers.

Cai Fang
Vice President and Member of the Chinese Academy of Social Sciences
President of National Institute for Global Strategy (NIGS),
Chinese Academy of Social Sciences
April 25, 2018

PREFACE

The Silk Road by land and sea[1]
Yi Dai Yi Lu
（一带一路）

> *In 1987, 20 exquisite pieces of colored glaze were excavated at the underground chamber of Famen Temple in Shaanxi, China. These East Roman and Islamic relics were brought into China during the Tang Dynasty. Marvelling at these exotic relics, I thought hard and concluded that as we approach the world's different civilizations, we should not limit ourselves to just admiring the exquisiteness of the objects involved. Rather, we should try to learn and appreciate the cultural significance behind them. Instead of only satisfying ourselves with their artistic presentation of people's life in the past, we should do our best to breathe new life into their inherent spirit.*
> (President Xi, Jinping, Speech at the UNESCO headquarters, March 28, 2014)

In 2011/12 the United States announced a major shift of strategic direction towards an emphasis on the Asia-Pacific region: "US economic and security interests are inextricably linked to developments in the arc extending from the Western Pacific and East Asia into the Indian Ocean region and South Asia, creating a mix of evolving challenges and opportunities. Accordingly, while the US military will continue to contribute to security globally, *we will of necessity rebalance toward the Asia-Pacific region*" (US Department of Defense, 2012: 2). US Secretary of State, Hillary Clinton affirmed that "the 21st century will be America's Pacific century, just like previous centuries have been" (Clinton, 2012). She enlarged on the shift in US strategic direction: 'The future of politics will be decided in Asia, not Afghanistan or Iraq and the United States will be right at the centre of the action…One of the most important tasks of American statecraft over the next decade will therefore be to lock in substantially increased investment – diplomatic, economic, strategic, and otherwise – in the Asia Pacific region" (Clinton, 2011).

Constructing a network of Asian political and military alliances is a critically important part of US international relations strategy in the decades ahead. The United States believes that its renewed involvement in Asia is vital to the region's future: "The region is eager for our leadership and our business – perhaps more than at any time in modern history. We are the only power with a network of strong alliances in the region, no territorial ambitions, and a long record of providing for the common good…Our challenge now is to build a web of relationships across the Pacific that is as durable and as consistent with American interests and values as the web we have built across the Atlantic" (Clinton, 2011).

Until around 200 years ago Europe's knowledge of Central Asia and South East Asia, as well as China itself, was extremely limited, and mainly acquired second-hand through the intermediary of trade with East Asia via the Silk Road by Land and Sea. When Captain Cook made his famous voyages of exploration between 1768 and 1779 the Asia-Pacific region was hardly known to Europeans. When Britain's North American colonies announced their independence from Britain in 1776, the United States consisted of a small group of colonial settlers huddled together in the eastern fringes of the vast continent of North America.[2] The West coast state of California, which looks out on the Pacific Ocean, only became part of the "United States" in 1850.

China's President Xi Jinping has made the policy of "The New Silk Road by Land and Sea", which connects China with the West, a key part of China's international relations. On 7 September 2013, President Xi proposed to build a "Silk Road Economic Belt" during his speech at Kazakhstan's Nazarbayev University. On 3rd October 2013, he proposed to build a '21st Century Maritime Silk Road' during his speech at the Indonesian House of Representatives. For over 2000 years China has had a deep inter-relationship with the surrounding regions of Asia. China has had deep long-term trade and cultural interactions with Central Asia through Xinjiang and with Southeast Asia through the Southern Sea (Nan Hai). Xinjiang and the Southern Sea constitute China's "doorway" into Central and South East Asia respectively.

In 2013 President Xi visited Central Asia, including Uzbekistan, Turkmenistan, Kyrgyzstan and Kazakhstan. The visit was especially significant, as no US president has visited the post-Soviet states of Central Asia. President Xi also visited Southeast Asia, including Malaysia and Indonesia. In spring 2014 he visited Europe. In a sequence of speeches during these visits he clarified China's conception of the bridge between China and Europe along the New Silk Road by Land and Sea. He paid close attention to the importance of infrastructure development, including ports, airports, roads, rail, water, electricity, and telecommunications. These are vital in order to stimulate commercial relations, which are the foundation of enhanced mutual understanding.

In each of his visits President Xi Jinping stressed the importance of an appreciation of history for mutual understanding: "For any country in the world, the past always holds the key to the present and the present is always rooted in the past. Only when we know where a country has come from, could we possibly understand why the country is what it is today, and only then could we realize in which direction it is heading" (Xi Jinping, 2014b). He emphasised the contribution that commercial relations make to cultural inter-action and peaceful development. He repeatedly drew attention to the importance of enhanced mutual understanding of culture for peaceful development: "History tells us that only by interacting with and learning from others can a civilization enjoy full vitality. If all civilizations can uphold inclusiveness, the so-called "clash of civilizations" will be out of the question and the harmony of civilizations will become reality" (Xi Jinping, 2014a).

China and Europe stand at either end of the New Silk Road. His speeches drew attention to the long connections between China and Europe from ancient times along both the land and the sea routes: "We need to build a bridge of common cultural prosperity linking the two major civilizations of China and Europe. China represents in an important way the Eastern civilization, while Europe is the birthplace of the Western civilization" (Xi Jinping, 2014a). In his visit he emphasised the contribution that the spread of ideas from China along the Silk Road had made to European development: "China's Four Great Inventions, namely, papermaking, gunpowder, movable-type printing and compass, led to changes in the world, including the

European Renaissance. China's philosophy, literature, medicine, silk, porcelain and tea reached the West and became part of people's daily life. *The Travels of Marco Polo* generated a widespread interest in China" ((Xi Jinping, 2014a).

President Xi stressed the importance of Central Asia and South East Asia as bridges to link China and Europe: "A bridge not only makes life more convenient; it could also be a symbol of communication, understanding and friendship. I have come to Europe to build, together with our European friends, a bridge of friendship and cooperation across the Eurasian continent" (Xi Jinping, 2014b).

The Chinese government's policy of the "New Silk Road by Land and Sea" has the development of infrastructure and commercial relationships at its core. Infrastructure building in order to support commerce and foster social stability was a foundation-stone of China's own long-term prosperity over the course of more than 2000 years. China's traditional international trade was tiny in comparison with the vast volume of internal trade. However, it was highly significant in terms of the deep inter-connections between China and the regions immediately around it to the West and the South. Mainly through trade relations, a deep long-term symbiotic, two-way flow of culture took place between China and these regions, which helped to weave them together in a complex cultural tapestry.

Peter Nolan, CBE
Chong Hua Professor of Chinese Development (Emeritus)
Founding Director, Centre of Development Studies,
University of Cambridge
and
Director, China Centre,
Jesus College,
Cambridge

Notes

1 A short version of this paper was delivered at the China Development Forum in March 2014. A longer version was prepared for the conference on 'The historical heritage of scientists and thinkers of the Medieval East, and its role and significance for the modern civilisation' (Samarkand, 15–16 May 2014). I am grateful to Tim Clissold, Stephen Perry and Zhang Jin for their comments on this paper.
2 In 1780 the United States consisted of just thirteen states on the extreme eastern fringe of the continent. The population was 2.8 million, of whom 2.2 million were white people, mainly from Britain, and 0.6 million were black people, mainly slaves.

Bibliography

Clinton, H., 2011, America's Pacific Century, *Foreign Affairs*, November
Clinton, H., 2012, Forestal Lecture, Naval Academy, Annapolis, January
US Department of Defense, 2012, *Sustaining US Global Leadership: Priorities for 21st Century Defense*, January, Washington DC
Xi, Jinping, 2014a, Speech at the UNESCO headquarters, 28 March
Xi, Jinping, 2014b, Speech at the College of Europe, 1 April

PART I

Contribution of China's reform and opening up to the world and formation of the Belt and Road Initiative

1
THE HISTORIC CONTRIBUTION OF CHINA'S REFORM AND OPENING UP TO THE WORLD

Zhou Fangye

The development process of China's reform and opening up

Since 1978, China has adhered to the basic state policy of "carrying out domestic reforms and opening to the outside world". Reform and opening up complement and promote each other. The Party has firmly promoted reforms in the country's economic, political, cultural, social, and ecological systems, as well as in the system of Party building. China's opening up has also been promoted continuously, and the achievements have drawn the attention of the world. During the years from 1978 to 2017, China's GDP increased from RMB 367.8 billion to RMB 82.7 trillion, an increase of 225 times, firmly occupying the position as the second largest economy in the world; its per-capita GDP increased from RMB 385 to RMB 59,500, an increase of 155 times, entering the ranks of middle-income countries; its total foreign trade increased from US$20.6 billion to US$4.12 trillion, a 200-fold increase, becoming the world's largest exporter; its foreign exchange reserves (forex reserves) increased from US$167 million to US$3.14 trillion, putting China at the top of the list of forex reserve holders worldwide.

The development process of reform and opening up can be divided into three historical stages. The first stage was a comprehensive exploration state from 1978 to 1992. In 1978, the Party made the historic decision of shifting the focus of work of the Party and state to economic development and initiating the reform and opening-up drive at the 3rd Plenary Session of the 11th CPC Central Committee. The reform started with implementing the household contract responsibility system in rural areas and delegating more decision-making power to enterprises and implementing the enterprise-contracting system in urban areas, and comprehensive and specific reforms were carried out on a trial basis. In the mid to late 1980s, the focus of reforms shifted from rural areas to urban areas, from the economic field to the realms of politics, science, technology, and education, as well as other areas of social life, and remarkable results were achieved. In 1992, the Communist Party of China clearly proclaimed establishing the socialist market economic system as the goal of its economic reform at its 14th national congress, based on the famous statement made by Deng Xiaoping in his talk during his inspection tour to south China that a market economy is not capitalism, there are markets under socialism too.

In terms of opening up to the outside world, from 1979 when the special economic zone was launched on a trial basis to 1984 when some coastal cities were opened up, to 1985 when the three delta areas along the Yangtze River and the Pearl River and in the southern part of Fujian province and the Bohai Rim were selected as the open coastal economic areas, to 1990 when Pudong New District in Shanghai was opened up, an opening-up pattern in coastal areas has, by and large, taken shape in China as the opening-up policy was advanced step by step from south to north.

The second stage is the stage of comprehensive advancement from 1992 to 2013.

In terms of domestic reforms, we were able to turn a highly concentrated, planned economy into a vigorous, socialist market economy. To set up and improve the socialist market economic system, we installed a two-tier management system based on the household contracting system and features an integration of unified management with separate management. A basic economic system was established, with public ownership as the pillar and all forms of ownership developing together. A distribution system was installed mainly on the principle of distribution according to work, while allowing other modes of distribution. An economic management system has taken shape, enabling the market to play the basic role in resource allocation under the macro-regulation of the government. Along with deepening reform of the economic system, we have reformed political, cultural, and social institutions, creating flourishing entities to suit China's actual circumstances.[1]

In terms of opening up to the outside world, 13 cities along the border, 6 cities along the Yangtze River, and 18 inland capital cities were opened up in the 1990s upon the approval of the government, and 32 national-level economic and technological development zones, 52 high-tech development zones, 13 bonded zones, and 34 ports were opened up, forming a multi-level and all-directional opening-up pattern in the areas along the coast, along the river, along the border, and in inland areas. After 15 years of tough negotiations, China joined the WTO in 2001. China's opening up has shifted from policy-oriented opening up to a pattern of omnidirectional, multi-level, and wide-ranging opening-up under the legal framework, and has successfully achieved a great historical change from a closed and semi-closed economy to an all-around open one.[2]

The third stage is the comprehensive deepening stage since 2013.

In terms of domestic reforms, the 3rd Plenary Session of the 18th CPC Central Committee in November 2013 adopted the *Decision of the Central Committee of the Communist Party of China on Some Major Issues Concerning Comprehensively Deepening the Reform*, which proposed that the overall goal of deepening the reform comprehensively is to improve and develop socialism with Chinese characteristics, and to promote the modernisation of the national governance system and capacity; economic system reform is the focus of deepening the reform comprehensively; the underlying issue is how to strike a balance between the role of the government and that of the market, and let the market play the decisive role in allocating resources and let the government play its functions better. Specifically, the contents of comprehensively deepening the reform mainly include adhering to and improving the basic economic system, accelerating the improvement of the modern market system, accelerating the transformation of government functions, deepening the reform of the fiscal and taxation systems, improving mechanisms and institutions for integrated development of urban and rural areas, building a new open economic system, strengthening the building of the socialist democratic system, promoting the rule of law, strengthening the check and oversight system of exercise of power, promoting innovation in cultural systems and mechanisms, promoting the reform and innovation of social undertakings, making innovations in the social governance system, accelerating ecological progress, deepening the reform of national defence and armed forces, and strengthening and improving the Party's leadership in the course of comprehensively deepening the reform.[3]

In terms of opening up to the outside world, we will promote the formation of a new pattern of all-round opening up. On the one hand, we will continue to cultivate a business environment that is law-based, internationalised and business-friendly and continue to strengthen efforts in "bringing in"; on the other hand, we will promote the construction of the Belt and Road, strengthen international capacity cooperation and fully participate in global economic cooperation and competition to meet the development need of domestic enterprises and industries to "go global".

The historic contribution of China's reform and opening up

First, China's development pattern provides the developing countries with a new alternative development path. The most important result of reform and opening up is that we have created and developed socialism with Chinese characteristics, which has provided a powerful impetus and strong guarantee for the socialist modernisation drive.[4] The road of building socialism with Chinese characteristics and related theories, systems, and culture have continued to develop, expanding the channels for developing countries to move towards modernisation and providing new choices for countries and nations in the world that want to accelerate their development and maintain their independence.[5]

For developing countries, the path of building socialism with Chinese characteristics provides a successful practice different from the Western path: economically, the government's "visible hand" and the market's "invisible hand" are combined, the plan and the market are combined, the state-owned economy and the private economy are combined through the socialist market economy to avoid the disadvantages of "market fundamentalism"; politically, selection and election are organically combined through socialist democratic politics, and innovations are made from the perspective of contents and results, changing the formal and procedural dogma and stereotype of "democratic fundamentalism"; socially, it has promoted comprehensive social governance, advanced social consultations and dialogues, established positive interactions between the societies and the countries, and bridged the inner tension of the Western societies and countries.[6]

More importantly, China's path adheres to the concept of keeping abreast with the times and asserts that the development of practice, the emancipation of the mind, and the reform and opening up know no boundary. China's path advocates "diversification" and thus is fundamentally different from the stagnating and conservative "centralised" Western path. It helps developing countries to actively explore the development path that suits their national conditions on the basis of drawing on China's experience and avoid repeating and copying the mistakes of the Western path.

Second, China's development path has broken the traditional shackle that "a strong country is bound to seek hegemony" and provides an important guarantee for world peace and stability. As the second largest economy in the world, China's road to revival is a peaceful development road that has stepped out of the historical cycle of Western hegemonic conflicts. In short, China should develop itself by upholding world peace and should contribute to world peace through its own development. It should achieve development with its own efforts and by carrying out reform and innovation. At the same time, it should open itself to the outside and learn from other countries. It should seek mutual benefit and common development with other countries in keeping with the trend of economic globalisation, and it should work together with other countries to build a harmonious world of durable peace and common prosperity.[7]

China has chosen the path of peaceful development because China has a peace-loving cultural tradition. There's no gene for invasion and seeking global hegemony in the blood of Chinese people. China does not subscribe to the outdated logic that "a strong country is bound to seek hegemony". The Chinese people want, more than anything else, to live in peace and harmony with the people of other countries, and to work with them to promote, defend, and share peace together.[8]

On the other hand, it depends on the peace and development demands of reform and opening up. Through domestic reforms, China carries out reform and innovation for economic and social development through its own efforts, and does not shift problems and difficulties onto other countries. Through opening up to the outside, China both pursues independent development and takes part in economic globalisation and both carries forward the fine traditions of the Chinese nation and draws on all the fine achievements of other civilisations. It combines both the domestic and foreign markets and uses both domestic and foreign resources. China integrates itself with the rest of the world with an open attitude, expands and deepens the opening-up strategy, and strengthens exchanges and cooperation with other countries in a bid to build a new system of open economy that is diversified, balanced, safe, and efficient, and that brings about mutual benefits and win–win outcomes.[9] Thus, China needs not follow the same old disastrous road of seeking hegemony as the Western powers did, and has an incentive to proactively safeguard world peace and stability.

Third, China will contribute its wisdom and solutions to help solve human problems. Since the beginning of the twenty-first century, China has actively solved the common problems faced by human society and has provided an important direction for cooperation among all countries in the world. In 2015, on the basis of inheriting the Millennium Development Goals, the United Nations further proposed the 2030 Agenda for Sustainable Development, which advocates to end poverty and hunger everywhere; to combat inequalities within and among countries; to build peaceful, just, and inclusive societies; to protect human rights and promote gender equality and the empowerment of women and girls; and to ensure the lasting protection of the planet and its natural resources.[10]

To solve the common problems for mankind such as poverty reduction and environmental protection, China always adheres to the major strategic judgement that development is still the key to solving all problems in China during its reform and opening up and takes economic construction as our central task. We will deepen social structural reform by concentrating on safeguarding and improving the people's well-being and promoting social fairness and justice. We will reform the income distribution system and promote common prosperity. We will promote system innovation in the social sector, promote equal access to basic public services, and step up efforts to form a scientific and effective social management system so that our society is not only full of vigour, but is also harmonious and orderly. We will deepen ecological environment management reform by concentrating on building a beautiful China. We will accelerate system building to promote ecological progress, improve institutions and mechanisms for developing geographical space, conserving resources and protecting the ecological environment and promoting modernisation featuring harmonious development between man and nature.[11]

Through reform and opening up, China has not only submitted a high-quality answer sheet for the UN Millennium Development Goals, but has also taken the lead in the implementation of the 2030 Agenda for Sustainable Development and made significant achievements, particularly in reducing poverty. The number of people below the poverty line in rural areas in China fell from 770 million in 1978 to 43.35 million in 2016. The poverty incidence rate dropped from 97.5% in 2015 to 4.5% in the same period, thus making a positive contribution to the great cause of poverty eradication in human society.[12]

More importantly, China's development experience in the process of domestic reforms, especially its experience in poverty reduction, will provide China's wisdom and solutions for other countries facing a daunting task in development. Meanwhile, in the process of opening up to the outside, China has actively advocated inclusive economic development through bilateral and multilateral cooperation and strived to create conditions and provide assistance for developing countries to learn from China's development experience, effectively promoting the historical process of poverty eradication in the world.

Fourth, China provides new impetus for the development of globalisation. Economic globalisation is an objective requirement of development of social productive forces and an inevitable result of scientific and technological progress. It provides a strong driving force for economic growth in the world and promotes the flow of commodities and capital, the advancement of science and technology, the progress of human civilisation and people-to-people exchanges among all countries. The long-term rapid development of China's social economy has largely benefited from the constant adaptation and integration into the process of globalisation through reform and opening up.

However, globalisation is not always a bed of roses. Since the international financial and economic crisis in 2008, the global economy has remained sluggish for a long time, and the three critical issues in the economic sphere have not been effectively addressed: lack of robust driving forces for global growth makes it difficult to sustain the steady growth of the global economy; inadequate global economic governance makes it difficult to adapt to new developments in the global economy; and uneven global development makes it difficult to meet people's expectations for better lives.[13] In response to the practical problems of globalisation, China is firmly committed to the policy of reform and opening up and will continue its efforts to safeguard world peace, and contribute to global development and uphold the international order. China will assume the historic task of promoting to build a community of a shared future for mankind.[14]

Through domestic reforms, China has steadily strengthened the innovation capacity and competitiveness of its economy. We must put quality first and give priority to performance. We should pursue supply-side structural reform as our main task, and work hard for better-quality, higher-efficiency, and more robust drivers of economic growth through reform. We need to raise total factor productivity and accelerate the building of an industrial system that promotes coordinated development of the real economy with technological innovation, modern finance, and human resources. We should endeavour to develop an economy with more effective market mechanisms, dynamic micro-entities, and sound macro-regulation. As the world's second-largest economy, China has contributed more than 30% of global economic growth annually since the international financial crisis and thus has provided strong momentum for the sustained and stable growth of the world economy.

Through opening up to the outside world, China has achieved interactive development with a large number of countries. We should pursue the Belt and Road Initiative as a priority, give equal emphasis to "bringing in" and "going global", follow the principle of achieving shared growth through discussion and collaboration, and increase openness and cooperation in building innovation capacity. With these efforts, we hope to make new ground in opening China further through links running eastward and westward, across land and over sea. This will make global economic development more balanced and more inclusive, providing favourable conditions for the further improvement of global economic governance.

Notes

1 "Speech by Hu Jintao at the 30th Anniversary of the Convening of the Third Plenary Session of the 11th Central Committee of the Communist Party of China," Xinhua News Agency, Beijing, December 18, 2008.
2 Chang Jian, "The Historical Process of China's Opening to the Outside World," *Proceedings of the 6th China Forum on Modernization Research*, 2008, pp. 301–304.

3 *Decision of the Central Committee of the Communist Party of China on Some Major Issues Concerning Comprehensively Deepening the Reform*, adopted at the Third Plenary Session of the 18th Central Committee of the Communist Party of China on November 12, 2013.
4 Ibid.
5 *Secure a Decisive Victory in Building a Moderately Prosperous Society in All Respects and Strive for the Great Success of Socialism with Chinese Characteristics for a New Era*, Xi Jinping's report to the 19th National Congress of the Communist Party of China on October 18, 2017.
6 Zhang Weiwei, "The Transcendence of the Chinese Path to the Western Model," *People's Daily*, 5th ed., October 23, 2016.
7 *White Paper on China's Peaceful Development Information*, Office of the State Council, September 6, 2011.
8 "Speech by President Xi Jinping at China International Friendship Conference in Commemoration of the 60th Anniversary of the Chinese People's Association for Friendship with Foreign Countries," Xinhua News Agency, Beijing, May 15, 2014.
9 *White Paper on China's Peaceful Development Information*, Office of the State Council, September 6, 2011.
10 *Transforming our world: the 2030 Agenda for Sustainable Development*, the United Nations, 2016.
11 *Decision of the Central Committee of the Communist Party of China on Some Major Issues Concerning Comprehensively Deepening the Reform*, adopted at the Third Plenary Session of the 18th Central Committee of the Communist Party of China on November 12, 2013.
12 *China's Progress Report on the Implementation of the 2030 Agenda for Sustainable Development*, the Ministry of Foreign Affairs of the People's Republic of China, August 2017, p. 5.
13 "Keynote Speech by Xi Jinping at the Opening Ceremony of the 2017 Annual Conference of the World Economic Forum," Xinhua News Agency, Davos, Switzerland, January 17, 2017.
14 *Secure a Decisive Victory in Building a Moderately Prosperous Society in All Respects and Strive for the Great Success of Socialism with Chinese Characteristics for a New Era*, Xi Jinping's report to the 19th National Congress of the Communist Party of China on October 18, 2017.

2
DEVELOPING AN OPEN ECONOMY AND THE BELT AND ROAD

Zhou Fangye

The formation and development of an open economy

An open economy is an important concept that has been continuously enriched and improved in the process of China's reform and opening up. It covers major theoretical topics such as economic systems and structures, open strategies, participation in global economic governance, and formation of new advantages in participating in international economic competition and cooperation.[1] In 1993, the 3rd Plenary Session of the 14th CPC Central Committee put forward the concept of "an open economy" for the first time and required that "we should make the best use of both domestic and international markets and resources so as to optimize the allocation of resources".[2] The main contents include: first, geologically, all-round opening up is stressed, and apart from advancing special economic zones and opening up of coastal areas, we must also focus on advancing the opening up of cities along the border and rivers and inland cities; second, we must deepen the reform of foreign trade system, and accelerate the conversion of foreign operation system for various types of enterprises; third, we must further actively introduce foreign capital, technologies, talents, and management experience.

In the report to the 15th CPC National Congress in 1997, the Party further proposed that "We will improve the pattern of omnidirectional, multilevel and wide-ranging opening-up and develop an open economy".[3] The report added some new contents, including expanding trade in services, actively participating in regional economic cooperation and the global multilateral trading system, promoting the opening up of service industries step by step, encouraging outward foreign investments that could leverage China's comparative advantages, and making best use of both domestic and foreign markets and resources, etc. The 5th Plenary Session of the 15th CPC Central Committee held in 2000 emphasised that "we will further expand the areas of opening up and develop an open economy".[4] It proposed for the first time the "going global" strategy and required making best use of the development opportunities brought by the accession to the WTO and striving to make new breakthroughs in utilising both domestic and international markets and resources.

While highly praising the achievements in developing an open economy, the report to the 16th CPC National Congress in 2002 clearly stated that the key to further promoting the development of an open economy was to adhere to the integration of "bringing in" and "going global".[5] The 5th Plenary Session of the 16th CPC Central Committee held in 2005 clearly proposed to advance "the development of an open economy to a new level" and proposed for the first time to promote the liberalisation and facilitation of global trade and investment and implement a mutually beneficial, win–win strategy for opening up.[6]

The report to the 17th CPC National Congress in 2007 proposed for the first time the concept of "an open economic system" and required that "we should expand the areas of opening up, optimize its structure, raise its quality, and turn our open economy into one in which domestic development and opening to the outside world interact and Chinese businesses and their foreign counterparts engage in win–win cooperation, and one that features security and efficiency".[7] The 5th Plenary Session of the 17th CPC Central Committee in 2010 further proposed that "we will improve an institutional mechanism that better suits the requirements of developing an open economy" and put forward for the first time that "we will actively participate in global economic governance and regional cooperation" and "promote the reform of the international economic system".[8]

The report to the 18th CPC National Congress in 2012 further clarified that "we will promote all-around improvements to China's open economy. In response to new developments in economic globalization, we must implement a more proactive opening up strategy and improve the open economy so that it promotes mutual benefit and is diversified, balanced, secure and efficient".[9] Therefore, it has identified the new positioning and requirements for building an open economy. The report to the 19th CPC National Congress in 2017 further clearly stated that "We must actively participate in and promote economic globalization and develop an open economy of higher standards" and includes the new concept of "promoting the development of an open global economy" into the scope of building an open economy.[10]

Achievements and prospects of building an open economy

After nearly 40 years of exploration and practice of reform and opening up, China has made significant progress in the development of an open economy. First, remarkable results have been made in foreign trade. China has become the world's largest trader in goods, the second largest trader in services and the second largest service outsourcing provider. Foreign trade has made significant contributions to the economy, and the total number of jobs created, directly or indirectly, was 180 million, which was roughly 23% of the number of all jobs in the country. Second, remarkable results have been made in "bringing in". In 2016, China actually introduced 844.4 billion yuan of foreign investment, ranking first among developing countries for 25 consecutive years. Foreign investment has made significant contribution to the economy. In 2016, foreign-funded enterprises accounted for 43.7% of the country's total exports, 18.3% of total tax payment, 9.9% of total employment in urban areas and 25.2% of total profits of industrial enterprises above designated size. Third, the scale of "going out" was expanded. In 2016, China ranked second in the world by the flow of outward foreign investment and became a net exporter of capital in strict sense. China's stock of outward foreign direct investment exceeded US$1.3 trillion, and its total amount of oversea assets was nearly US$5 trillion.[11]

As the world is moving further towards multi-polarisation and economic globalisation, the international political and economic environments are undergoing profound changes, and China's reform and opening up is now at a new historical starting point. Under the guidance of Xi Jinping's Thoughts on Socialist Economy with Chinese Characteristics for the New Era, the open economy has also entered a new stage of development. In 2013, the *Decision of the Central Committee of the Communist Party of China on Some Major Issues Concerning Comprehensively Deepening the Reform* adopted at the 3rd Plenary Session of the 18th Central CPC Committee proposed the main direction of developing an open economy. In 2015, *Several Opinions of the*

CPC Central Committee and the State Council on Developing a New System of Open Economy clearly specified the objectives and contents of a new system of open economy. The *Outline of the 13th Five-Year Plan for the National Economic and Social Development of the People's Republic of China* further proposed the work programme for the development of an open economy. So far, the development layout for building an open economy in the new era has taken shape.[12]

Starting from the reform of the economic system, the *Decision of the Central Committee of the Communist Party of China on Some Major Issues Concerning Comprehensively Deepening the Reform* has made important arrangements for the development of an open economy and proposed the development requirements, such as nurturing new advantages for comprehensive industrial competition, new advantages for all-round opening up, new advantages for creating stable, transparent and predictable business environment, and new advantages for participating in and leading the formulation of international rules and standards so as to create new advantages for participating in and leading international economic cooperation in fierce international competition.[13]

Several Opinions on Developing a New System of Open Economy proposed the overall objectives to be achieved in developing a new system of open economy: to nurture new advantages for international cooperation and competition at a quicker pace; to more actively promote the balance between domestic and external demand, import and export, and the attraction of foreign investment into China and outbound investment by Chinese enterprises; to progressively realise the overall balance of international payments; to form a new pattern of all-round opening up; to modernise open economic governance systems and governance capabilities; to uphold justice while pursuing shared interests in opening wider to the rest of the world; to earnestly safeguard national interests and maintain national security; and to promote the common development of China and other countries in the world, and build a new system of open economy that is diversified, balanced, safe, and efficient, and that brings about mutual benefits and win–win outcomes. On this basis, four concrete objectives are further broken down: a new mechanism for market allocation of resources shall be established; a new model for economic operation and management shall be formed; a new pattern of all-round opening-up shall take shape; and new advantages shall be developed for international cooperation and competition. The document has also specified the contents of 10 categories of 46 work items: foreign investment management regime shall be innovated; a new regime facilitating the implementation of the "going global" strategy shall be established; a new mechanism for the sustainable development of foreign trade shall be created; the regional distribution of opening up shall be optimised; the implementation of the Belt and Road Initiative shall be accelerated; the new space of international economic cooperation shall be expanded; an open and safe financial system shall be established; a stable, fair, transparent and predictable business environment shall be created; the support for the establishment of security mechanism shall be strengthened; and a security assurance system for the open economy shall be established and steadily improved. These have provided an action guide and roadmap for an open economy.[14]

The *Outline of the 13th Five-Year Plan for National Economic and Social Development of the People's Republic of China* emphasises that "Opening up is the path China must take to achieve prosperity and development". The Outline stated that in adapting to China's ever-deepening integration into the world economy, we would pursue a mutually beneficial strategy of opening up, coordinate the role of domestic and foreign demand in stimulating growth, balance imports and exports, stress the importance of both bringing in and going global, and work simultaneously to attract foreign investment, technology, and talent; we would achieve a higher level of openness within our economy, participate actively in global economic governance and global supply of public goods, seek a greater say in the institutions for global economic governance, and look to build more international communities of interests. On this basis, it proposed the corresponding specific plans and work programmes in the five key areas, i.e. to improve the strategic layout of opening up, to improve the new system of opening up, to promote the implementation of the Belt and Road Initiative, to actively participate in global economic governance, and to actively assume international responsibilities and obligations.[15]

The Belt and Road Initiative promotes the development of an open economy

Developing an open economy has a close logic relationship with the Belt and Road Initiative. On the one hand, developing an open economy is the intrinsic requirement and prerequisite condition of the Belt and Road Initiative. As the initiator and responsible practitioner of the Belt and Road Initiative, China must set a positive example in opening up to the outside world. Only in this way can China play a leading role in promoting the Belt and Road Initiative and ensure its vitality. On the other hand, the Belt and Road Initiative is an important platform and an effective means for developing an open economy, and it helps to integrate domestic and foreign resources and promotes the development of an open economy that is diversified, balanced, safe, and efficient and that brings about mutual benefits and win–win outcomes.

First, the Belt and Road Initiative helps to ensure that the development of an open economy brings about mutual benefits and win–win outcomes. The basic requirement of an open economy is free flow of goods, capital, personnel, technology, and other factors so as to rationalise allocation of resources and maximise production efficiency. However, compared with the concept of free economy advocated in the Western countries, the most significant difference of an open economy to be developed under the guidance of Xi Jinping's Thoughts on Socialist Economy with Chinese Characteristics for the New Era is that it insists on bringing about mutual benefit and win–win outcomes. That is, China will strive to promote the common development of China and other countries in the process of opening up to the outside world so as to fundamentally change the unreasonable and unfair international system of industrial division of labour and effectively curb the hegemonic behaviour of "neo-colonialism".

The Belt and Road Initiative carries forward the Silk Road spirit of seeking mutual benefit and win–win cooperation and pursues the principle that all countries, big or small, rich or poor, can participate on an equal footing. China is willing to combine the experience and foundations of its own development with the development will and comparative strengths of all countries, and use the Belt and Road Initiative as an important opportunity and a cooperation platform to promote economic policy coordination among various countries, improve connectivity, foster bilateral and multilateral cooperation with a broader scope and at a higher and deeper level, and build a new cooperation framework that is open, inclusive, balanced, and mutually beneficial. The Belt and Road Initiative, characterised by equality and inclusiveness and grounded in realism, manifests the common interests of countries along the routes, including China.

At the end of 2017, China had signed 100 cooperation agreements with 86 countries and international organisations on jointly building the Belt and Road Initiative, covering a broad range of fields that include connectivity, production capacity, investment, economy and trade, finance, science and technology, society, humanities, quality of life, and marine issues. Meanwhile, while actively fulfilling its international responsibilities, China has advanced its cooperation with relevant international organisations in the Belt and Road framework. It has signed cooperation documents on jointly building the Belt and Road with the United Nations Development Programme, United Nations Economic and Social Commission for Asia and the Pacific, and the World Health Organisation.[16] This provides a strong guarantee for the mutually beneficial and win–win direction of China's open economy.

Second, the Belt and Road Initiative helps to promote the development of a multilateral yet balanced structure of an open economy. In the new stage of development of an open economy, China has clearly put forward the principle of maintaining a multilateral yet balanced structure of an open economy and called for changing the long-standing imbalance in development. Through building the Belt and Road Initiative, we will be able to make new ground in opening China further through links running eastwards and westwards, across land and over sea. This will help to effectively improve the problem of unbalanced development between bringing in and going global and between the eastern and western regions and southern and northern regions in China during the new round of China's reform and opening up.

First, the unbalanced development between bringing in and going global. Since the beginning of the twenty-first century, China has actively promoted the strategy of going global and has achieved remarkable results, but there is still a significant gap compared to the bringing-in strategy. The Belt and Road Initiative focuses on promoting policy coordination, connectivity of infrastructure, unimpeded trade, financial integration, and understanding between people, which will effectively improve the external environment for the strategy of going global and help to adhere to the principle of laying equal emphasis on bringing in and going global and effectively strike a balance between internality and external conditions of the Chinese economy, especially a balance between internal and external demands.

Second, the imbalanced development between the eastern and western regions in China. There is a large development gap between the eastern and western regions in China after the reform and opening up, and the openness and development achievements of the central and western regions lag far behind those of the eastern coastal areas. The six major international economic cooperation corridors proposed under the Belt and Road Initiative—including the China–Mongolia–Russia Economic Corridor, the New Eurasian Land Bridge Economic Corridor, the China–Central Asia–West Asia Economic Corridor, the China–Indochina Peninsula Economic Corridor, the China–Pakistan Economic Corridor, and the Bangladesh–China–India–Myanmar Economic Corridor—have paved the way for the opening up of the central and western regions and thus enable China to implement the overall strategies for regional development, including the Great Western Development Strategy, the Northeast Revitalisation Strategy, the Strategy for the Rise of Central China, etc.

Third, the imbalanced development between the northern and southern regions in China. The Western developed countries have traditionally mainly been important economic and trade partners of China, while South–South cooperation is relatively weak. The Belt and Road Initiative provides sustained new momentum for China's economic and trade cooperation with the countries along the routes, especially the developing countries. In recent years, the trade between China and the countries along the Belt and Road has become a new and persistent growth point of China's foreign trade. In 2017, China's imports and exports with the countries along the Belt and Road accounted for 26.5% of its total foreign trade.

Third, the Belt and Road Initiative will help increase the level of safety and efficiency in developing an open economy. On the one hand, while developing an open economy, we should pay attention to safe institutional construction and prevent the impact of external risk. On the other hand, we must also remove unreasonable institutional barriers, promote the flow of transnational factors and improve cooperation efficiency. The Belt and Road aims to build a new system of global economic governance based on the principles of extensive consultation, joint contribution and shared benefits. This will not only help promote a reasonable allocation of global resources and markets, but will effectively reduce the likelihood of global economic and financial crisis, reduce barriers to trade and investment among countries, and help all countries to avoid taking irrational measures to shift their risks on to others. In November 2016, the 193 member states of the UN unanimously adopted a resolution, which welcomes the establishment of the Belt and Road Initiative and other economic cooperation initiatives and calls on the international community to provide a safe and secure environment for the Belt and Road Initiative. On March 17, 2017, the UN Security Council unanimously adopted Resolution 2344, calling on the international community to strengthen regional economic cooperation through the Belt and Road Initiative. This has created a favourable international environment for China's open economy.

Notes

1 Pei Changhong, "Outline of the Research on the Open Economy Theory with Chinese Characteristics," *Economic Research Journal*, Issue 4, 2016.
2 *Decision of the CPC Central Committee on Some Issues Concerning the Establishment of a Socialist Market Economic Structure*, adopted at the Third Plenary Session of the 14th Central Committee of the Communist Party of China on November 14, 1993.
3 *Hold High the Great Banner of Deng Xiaoping Theory for an All-round Advancement of the Cause of Building Socialism with Chinese Characteristics to the 21st Century*, Jiang Zemin's Report to the 15th National Congress of the Communist Party of China on September 12, 1997.
4 "Suggestions of the CCCPC on Formulating the Tenth Five-Year Plan for National Economic and Social Development," adopted at the Fifth Plenary Session of the 15th Central Committee of the Communist Party of China on October 11, 2000.
5 *Build a Well-off Society in an All-Round Way and Create a New Situation in Building Socialism with Chinese Characteristics*, Jiang Zemin's Report to the 16th National Congress of the Communist Party of China on November 8, 2002.
6 "Suggestions of the CCCPC on Formulating the Eleventh Five-Year Plan for National Economic and Social Development," adopted at the Sixth Plenary Session of the Central Committee of the Communist Party of China on October 11, 2005.
7 *Hold High the Great Banner of Socialism with Chinese Characteristics and Strive for New Victories in Building a Moderately Prosperous Society in all Respects*, Hu Jintao's Report to the 17th National Congress of the Communist Party of China on October 15, 2007.
8 "Suggestions of the CCCPC on Formulating the 12th Five-Year Plan for National Economic and Social Development," adopted the Fifth Plenary Session of the 17th Central Committee of the Communist Party of China on October 18, 2010.
9 *Firmly March on the Path of Socialism with Chinese Characteristics and Strive to Complete the Building of A Moderately Prosperous Society in All Respects*, Hu Jintao's Report to the 18th National Congress of the Communist Party of China on November 8, 2012.
10 *Secure a Decisive Victory in Building a Moderately Prosperous Society in All Respects and Strive for the Great Success of Socialism with Chinese Characteristics for a New Era*, Xi Jinping's report to the 19th National Congress of the Communist Party of China on October 18, 2017.
11 The Party Group of the Ministry of Commerce of the People's Republic of China, "The Comprehensive Improvement of the Level of China's Open Economy since the 18th National Congress of the Communist Party of China," *Seeking Truth*, Issue 20, 2017, p. 26.
12 Sheng Bin & Li Feng, "What Are the 'New Characteristics' of the New System of China's Open Economy?" *International Economic Review*, Issue 1, 2017, p. 134.
13 Wang Yang, "Building a New System of Open Economy," *People's Daily*, 6th ed., November 22, 2013.
14 *Several Opinions of the CPC Central Committee and the State Council on Developing a New System of Open Economy*, issued on May 5, 2015, Xinhua News Agency, Beijing, September 17.
15 "Outline of the 13th Five-Year Plan for the National Economic and Social Development of the People's Republic of China," Xinhua News Agency, Beijing, March 17, 2016.
16 "Building the Belt and Road: Concept, Practice and China's Contribution," Office of the Leading Group for the Belt and Road Initiative, May 10, 2017.

3
CHINA'S ECONOMIC RESTRUCTURING AND THE BELT AND ROAD

Zhou Fangye

Characteristics and process of China's economic restructuring

In the initial stage of reform and opening up, China's economic restructuring mainly refers to the transition of economic system, i.e. the transition from the planned economy to the socialist market economy. In 1995, the CPC Central Committee officially employed the phrase "change the pattern of economic growth" for the first time in the Party's document and proposed to "implement two fundamental changes". According to the document, while transforming the economic system, we should promote the transition from an extensive pattern of economic growth to the intensive one, and China's economic restructuring began to exhibit the characteristics of "double transition", namely, institutional transition and development transition.

As the first five-year plan under the conditions of the socialist market economy, the 9th Five-Year Plan (1996–2000) explicitly proposed to implement "two fundamental changes that have holistic significance".[1] However, following the outbreak of the Asian financial crisis in 1997, China adopted some policy measures to cope with the crisis, such as expanding domestic demands, issuing government bonds, increasing investments in infrastructure such as highways, water conservancy and cities, expanding the scale of enrolment in higher education, and accelerating the reform of housing marketisation. As a result, the pattern of economic growth did not change substantially during the 9th Five-Year Plan period.

The 10th Five-Year Plan (2001–2005) pointed out that "China's economy had already reached the point where we could not further develop the economy without making structural adjustments. Under the old economic structure and its crude manner of growth, products would not be marketable, and it would be impossible to sustain resources and preserve the environment."[2] The plan also proposed to make a proactive and all-round strategic adjustment of economic structure and combine the adjustment of the patterns of economic development between different industries, between different regions, and between urban and rural areas, with emphasis on the industrial structure.[3] With China's accession to the WTO in 2001, the Chinese economy once again entered a double-digit rapid growth period driven by foreign trade. However, under the export- and investment-led development pattern, the imbalance between internal and external demand structure and investment and consumption structure has further intensified.

The 11th Five-Year Plan (2006–2010) stated that China's "rapid development had caused some serious problems: uncoordinated relationship between investment and consumption, blind expansion of some industries, overcapacity, slow transition of the mode of economic growth, excessive energy and resource consumption and worsening environmental pollution". The plan called for propelling three transitions in the mode of economic growth: the transition from relying mainly on investment and export to relying on a well-coordinated combination of consumption, investment, domestic demand, and foreign demand, the transition from mainly relying on industries and quantity expansion to primary, secondary, and tertiary industries jointly driving economic growth and optimisation and upgrading of industrial structure, and the transition from relying heavily on increase in input of resources to relying mainly on improvement in resource utilisation efficiency.[4] In 2007, the report to the 17th CPC National Congress changed "the transition of economic growth mode" to "the transition of economic development mode" and explicitly specified the new requirements for "accelerating the transition of economic development mode".[5]

During the 11th Five-Year Plan period, China's economy grew at an average annual rate of 11.3%, and China overtook the United Kingdom to become the world's fourth largest economy in 2006, overtook Germany to become the world's third largest economy in 2007, and overtook Japan to become the world's second largest economy in 2009. In 2010, China overtook the United States to become the world's largest manufacturer. China has achieved in several decades what took developed countries centuries to achieve and created a miracle in global economic development.[6] However, China's economic transition failed to achieve the desired results under the influence of the global financial crisis in 2008. China's launch of a large-scale bail-out plan on the one hand has prevented drastic economic downturn, but on the other hand it has also caused negative effects such as excessive production capacity and inventory and high leverage ratios.

During the 12th Five-Year Plan period (2011–2015), China's economy showed an L-shaped development trend under the influence of structural factors at home and abroad. The growth rate had been declining year by year since 2011, falling below the record low set in 1991. In this regard, Xi Jinping has made a judgement that a significant characteristic of China's economic development is that it has entered a state of "new normal" and clearly pointed out that:

> the economy should shift gear from the previous high speed to a medium-to-high speed growth, from an extensive mode that emphasized scale and speed to a more intensive one emphasizing quality and efficiency; the economic structure is shifting from increment-and-capacity expansion to one with simultaneous stock adjustment and increment optimization; the new driver for the economy is shifting from being driven by input of factors such as resource and low-cost labor to being driven by innovation.

Xi Jinping also stressed that "a new normal period is a stage that China must endure if it is to upgrade and optimize its economy", which points out the direction for the deepening of China's economic restructuring.[7]

The path and effectiveness of China's economic restructuring

The report to the 19th CPC National Congress held in 2017 stated that "China's economy has been transitioning from a phase of rapid growth to a stage of high-quality development. This is a pivotal stage for transforming our growth model, improving our economic structure, and fostering new drivers of growth". The report also proposed the path for transitioning economic development. That is, "We should pursue supply-side structural reform as our main task, and work hard for better quality, higher efficiency, and more robust drivers of economic growth through reform. We need to raise total factor productivity".[8]

Supply-side structural reform will focus on unleashing and developing productive forces, advancing structural adjustment through reforms, reducing ineffective and low-end supply of goods and services, expanding effective and mid-to-high-end supply, enhancing the adaptability and flexibility of the supply structure to demand changes, and improving total factor productivity.[9] Its main tasks are "cutting overcapacity, destocking, deleveraging, reducing corporate costs and shoring up weak spots": (1) cutting overcapacity: eliminating backward excessive capacity, especially steel and coal production capacity; (2) destocking: reducing real estate inventory, especially in the third- and fourth-tier cities; (3) deleveraging: reducing the debt level of governments, enterprises and individuals; (4) reducing costs: reducing social costs, especially corporate costs; (5) shoring up weak spots: shoring up weak spots in public services, infrastructure and institutions.

It is necessary to understand the supply-side structural reform from the following aspects.[10]

First, there is a fundamental difference between supply-side structural reforms and Western supply-side economics. Supply-side economics emphasises tax cuts, overemphasises the role of tax rates, and has a relatively absolute ideological approach. It focuses only on supply but neglects demand, and focuses only on market functions while neglecting the role of the government. Supply-side structural reform involves not only the issues of taxes and tax rates, but also aims to address a series of problems in the supply side of China's economy through a series of policy measures, particularly the policy measures to promote scientific and technological innovation, to develop the real economy and guarantee and improve people's living standards. The reform not only emphasises supply but also pays close attention to demand and highlights both the development of productive forces and the improvement of relations of production. The reform enables the market to play a decisive role in resource allocation, gives better play to the governmental role, and needs to both focus on the present and look ahead to the future. From the perspective of political economics, the fundamentality of supply-side structural reform is to make China's supply capacity better meet the ever-increasing and ever-escalating individualised material, cultural, and ecological needs of the broad masses of people so as to achieve the goal of socialist production.

Second, supply-side structural reform is an inherent requirement for rebalancing of supply and demand. At present and in a coming period, China will face "four declines and one increase" in its economic development, namely decline in economic growth rate, decline in the prices of industrial products, decline in profitability of enterprises, decline in fiscal revenue, and increase in probability of economic risks. The main contradiction of these problems is not cyclical but structural, and the supply structure mismatch problem is serious. Meanwhile, the principle aspect of the contradiction is on the supply side rather than on the demand side. The main problem in China is not that there is insufficient demand or no demand, but that the demand has changed while the supply of products has not changed, and the quality and services fail to keep up with the pace of change. The shortage of effective supply capacity has caused a serious outflow of spending power.

As it is difficult to solve the structural contradictions such as overcapacity by relying solely on stimulating domestic demand, we should give priority to improving the supply-side structure and focus on effectively addressing overcapacity from the production side, promoting the optimisation and reorganisation of industries, reducing the costs of enterprises, developing the emerging industries of strategic importance and modern service industries, increasing the supply of public goods and services, and improving the adaptability and flexibility of the supply structure to changes in demand so as to realise a leap from a low-level balance between supply and demand to a high-level balance between supply and demand.

Third, the supply-side structural reform provides the endogenous power for sustained and healthy economic development. Since the beginning of the 13th Five-Year Plan period (2016–2020), China has continued to deepen the supply-side reform and achieved initial results in economic restructuring and upgrading. The continuous decline of China's economic growth in the previous six years ended in 2017, and China's GDP exceeded the threshold of 80 trillion yuan for the first time; the economic profits continued to increase, the total profits of the enterprises under the Central Government exceeded 1.4 trillion yuan for the first time, the increment and growth rate of economic profits hit the best level in five years, the unemployment rate fell to its lowest point in five years, and the ex-factory prices of industrial producers turned from negative to positive for the first time in five years; the conversion of the impetus for economic growth was accelerated, the contribution rate of consumer spending to economic growth reached 58.8%, an increase of nearly 4% compared with 5 years ago, and the added value of the service industry accounted for 60% of the GDP, an increase of 5% compared with 5 years ago; the export structure has been continuously optimised, and the main forces for export have changed from labour-intensive industries to technology-intensive industries, high-speed rail, marine equipments, nuclear power equipments and satellites have become new competitive industries for export; and the industrial structure is moving towards the mid-to-high end in a quicker pace. According to the *Global Innovation Index* of the World Intellectual Property Organisation, the China Innovation Index has risen from 34th in 2012 to 22nd in 2017.[11]

China's economic restructuring and the Belt and Road complement each other

On the one hand, China's economic restructuring will provide a sustainable driving force for the Belt and Road Initiative. Conceptually, the Belt and Road Initiative pursues the principle that all countries, big or small, rich or poor, can participate on an equal footing. However, in terms of responsibility, as the largest developing country and the second largest economy in the world, especially as the initiator of the Belt and Road Initiative, China will inevitably have to shoulder more historical responsibilities in the initial stage to ensure that the Belt and Road Initiative will enter a virtuous cycle in the context of a weak global economic recovery. This imposes stricter requirements on the "locomotive" role of China's economic growth. As efforts to supply-side structural reform are beginning to deliver results, the endogenous power of China's economic restructuring will be further enhanced, thus providing a sustainable driving force for the Belt and Road Initiative.[12] On the other hand, the Belt and Road Initiative will provide a favourable external environment for China's economic restructuring. First, it helps transform and upgrade the manufacturing industry. The Belt and Road Initiative will promote construction of infrastructure and transnational and inter-regional connectivity. This will not only increase the effective demand for building materials such as iron, steel, and cement in the countries along the Belt and Road and alleviate the problem of overcapacity in traditional Chinese industries, but also sharply increase the demand for various types of complete sets of equipments through cooperation in major projects for high-speed railways, ports, electricity, oil and gas, and communications, thus expanding overseas markets for the development of China's high-end manufacturing industries.

More importantly, the Belt and Road Initiative promotes trade facilitation on the basis of connectivity, which will effectively promote the trade between China and other countries, thus providing a broader space for the transition and upgrading of China's manufacturing industry under the unfavourable conditions of weak global trade growth.[13] In 2017, China's trade volume with the countries involved in the Belt and Road Initiative reached 7.4 trillion yuan, a year-on-year increase of 17.8%, which was 3.6% higher than China's foreign trade growth rate.[14]

Second, it helps promote innovation and development of the service industry. China is the second largest trader in services in the world. In 2016, China's total trade in services was US$657.5 billion, second only to the United States. However, China has set the goal of economic restructuring and upgrading that "By 2020, the amount of imported and exported services shall exceed US$100 million; the proportion of trade in services to foreign trade shall be further enhanced; and the global proportion of our trade in services shall be increased year by year".[15] Meanwhile, we should also actively exploit the emerging markets, especially the service industry market with broad prospects in the countries along the Belt and Road.

More importantly, China is strengthening financial cooperation with the countries along the routes under the Belt and Road framework and promoting unimpeded currency circulation and financial integration. A network of financial institutions and services is spreading out to support the Belt and Road Initiative through innovative financing mechanisms. China supports cultural exchanges and cooperation in various fields and at different levels to promote understanding between people. This will provide financial convenience and humanistic advantages for China's service industry to "go global" and effectively improve the service industry's innovation capability and international competitiveness.

Third, it is conducive to the optimisation and remodelling of the international labour division system. The global financial crisis in 2008 broke the grand global economic cycle in which the developed economies in Europe and the United States spent by borrowing, East Asian areas provided high savings, cheap labour and products, and Russia, the Middle East, Latin America and other countries provided energy and resources, and it prompted the rapid adjustment of the pattern of global division of labour and cross-border reallocation of capital. All the major economies in the world have sought to improve their position in the division of labour through structural adjustments and strive for a more favourable position in division of labour.

China is willing to use the Belt and Road Initiative as a cooperation platform to promote economic policy coordination among various countries, improve the level of connectivity, foster bilateral and multilateral cooperation with a broader scope and at a higher and deeper level, and build a new cooperation framework that is open, inclusive, balanced, and mutually beneficial. This helps China and other countries along the routes to raise their positions in the international division of labour in the process of optimising and reshaping the international division of labour system and the global value chain, and prevents the developed countries' long-term "low-end lock-in" of developing countries by relying on their technology and capital advantages so as to effectively ensure a good international environment for China's economic restructuring.

Notes

1 "The Ninth-Five-Year Plan of the People's Republic of China on National Economic and Social Development and Outlines of Objectives in Perspective of the Year 2010," adopted at the Fourth Session of the Eighth National People's Congress on March 17, 1996.
2 "Report on the Outline of the Tenth Five-Year Plan for National Economic and Social Development," adopted at the Fourth Session of the Ninth National People's Congress on March 15, 2001.
3 Ibid.

4 "The Outline of 11th Five-Year Plan for National Economic and Social Development of the People's Republic of China," adopted at the Fourth Session of the Tenth National People's Congress on March 14, 2006.
5 *Hold High the Great Banner of Socialism with Chinese Characteristics and Strive for New Victories in Building a Moderately Prosperous Society in all Respects*, Hu Jintao's report to the 17th National Congress of the Communist Party of China on October 15, 2007.
6 "Speech by Xi Jinping at the Symposium Attended by Senior Provincial and Ministerial Officials for Studying and Implementing the Spirit of the Fifth Plenary Session of the 18th CPC Central Committee," January 18, 2016, *People's Daily*, 2nd ed., May 10, 2016.
7 Ibid.
8 *Secure a Decisive Victory in Building a Moderately Prosperous Society in All Respects and Strive for the Great Success of Socialism with Chinese Characteristics for a New Era*, Xi Jinping's report to the 19th National Congress of the Communist Party of China on October 18, 2017.
9 "Speech by Xi Jinping at the Symposium Attended by Senior Provincial and Ministerial Officials for Studying and Implementing the Spirit of the Fifth Plenary Session of the 18th CPC Central Committee," January 18, 2016, *People's Daily*, 2nd ed., May 10, 2016.
10 Ibid.
11 Hu Angang & Zhang Xin, "A Big Step in High-quality Development: Highlights of China's Economy in 2017," *People's Daily*, 7th ed., January 22, 2018.
12 Wang Jun, "China Contribution in the Steady Recovery of the World Economy," *Economic Daily*, 4th ed., January 25, 2018.
13 Fang Honglin, "The Significance of the Belt and Road to China's Economic Transformation," *Guangming Daily*, 15th ed., October 28, 2015.
14 "The Remarkable Achievements in Comprehensive and Pragmatic Cooperation of the Belt and Road," *People's Daily*, 1st ed., January 26, 2018.
15 *Several Opinions of the State Council on Accelerating the Development of Service Trade*, Guofa [2015] No. 8, January 28, 2015.

4

INNOVATION-DRIVEN DEVELOPMENT AND THE BELT AND ROAD

Zhou Fangye

Concepts and features of innovation-driven development

Innovation-driven development is the core element of China's new development concepts and is at the top of the five development concepts of "innovation, coordination, green development, opening up, and sharing". Innovation-driven development means that innovation becomes the primary impetus for development, and scientific and technological innovation combines with institutional innovation, administration innovation, commercial mode innovation, format innovation, and cultural innovation, facilitating the transition of development mode to ongoing accumulation of knowledge, technological progress and improvement of labour force quality, and promoting the economy to progress to the stage of more advanced form, more delicate division of labour and more reasonable structure.[1]

First, innovation-driven development is centred on scientific and technological innovation. A nation thrives when its science and technology thrive; a nation is powerful when its science and technology are powerful.[2] The Communist Party of China has been adhering to the important thought of Marxism regarding "socially productive force of labor is above all the power of science"[3] and is committed to promoting the innovative development of science and technology. In this regard, Mao Tse-Tung clearly pointed out: "We cannot just follow the beaten track traversed by other countries in the development of technology and trail behind them at a snail's pace. We must break away from conventions and do our utmost to adopt advanced techniques in order to make China a powerful modern socialist country in not too long a historical period".[4]

Since the reform and opening up, the Chinese Communist Party has constantly put forward new ideas for scientific and technological innovation. From Deng Xiaoping's statement that "Science and technology constitute a primary productive force"[5] to Jiang Zemin's proposal of "invigorating China through science and education", to Hu Jintao's statement that "we must keep to the path of independent innovation with Chinese characteristics", and then to Xi Jinping's statement that "to implement the innovation-driven development strategy, we must firmly grasp this 'bull nose' of scientific and technological innovation",[6] the Communist Party of China has conducted long-term exploration and practice.

Second, innovation-driven development is a systematic project of all-round innovation. Innovation-driven development is a complex social systematic project involving all areas of economy and society.[7] Scientific and technological achievements should meet the needs of the state, the requirements of the people, and the market demands, and accomplish the three-step jump from scientific research to experimental development and finally to promotional application. Only in this way can they realise the true value of innovation and innovation-driven development.[8] Therefore, to promote innovation-driven development, we should step up efforts to improve the innovation mechanism, establish a national innovation system, and build an ecosystem featuring close coordination and interaction among various innovation entities as well as unimpeded flow and efficient allocation of innovation factors, and bring about the carriers, institutional arrangements and safeguards for achieving innovation-driven development.[9] We should promote scientific and technological innovation, enterprise innovation, product innovation, market innovation and brand innovation in an all-round way, accelerate the transformation of scientific and technological achievements into practical productivity and promote close integration of science and technology with economic development.[10]

Third, the starting point and standpoint of innovation-driven development is "putting people first". To promote innovation-driven development, China adheres to the basic standpoint of "putting people first" and has proposed the development goal of "mass entrepreneurship and innovation".[11] As far as the starting point is concerned, the fundamental driving force for innovation-driven development comes from the people's innovation. This is different from innovation by a small number of people such as experts, scientists, engineers, and so on. It is the real innovation by the people and all-involvement innovation. Each innovator is not only the subject of innovation, but also the beneficiary, communicator, and sharer of innovation activities and innovative ideas. The micro-innovation of hundreds of millions of innovators and entrepreneurs every day and every minute will surely converge into a continuous gathering of ideas, knowledge and technologies, inducing an exponential growth of social innovation and eventually making it the largest innovation in the world. The fundamental purpose of innovation-driven development is to stimulate the vitality of the people, which is an important condition for accelerating innovation-led and innovation-driven development in China.[12]

Fourth, innovation-driven development is independent innovation with an open international vision. Innovation-driven development adheres to independent innovation with Chinese characteristics because "only by firmly holding core technologies in our own hands can we truly seize the initiative in competition and development and fundamentally guarantee national economic security, national defense security and other securities".[13] Therefore, we must give to play the superiority of socialism, pool resources to undertake major national initiatives, focus on major issues, grasp cutting-edge technologies, adopt an "asymmetric" catch-up strategy, and seize the commanding heights for technological competition and future development. However, we cannot possibly pursue independent innovation behind closed doors. Under the grand background of deepening economic globalisation, the flow of innovation resources are accelerating around the world, and the economic and technological ties among different countries are becoming closer. No country can solve all innovation problems by solely relying on its own efforts.[14] Therefore, to promote innovation-driven development, we must adhere to the combination of bringing in and going global, integrate into the global innovation network with a more proactive attitude, absorb global innovation resources with a more open mind, adopt a more active strategy to promote the output of technologies and standards and build an open innovation mechanism at a higher level.[15]

Path and achievements in innovation-driven development

Since the "innovation-driven development strategy" was formally launched at the 18th CPC National Congress in 2012, the Party and state leaders have repeatedly emphasised the importance of innovation-driven development and successively promulgated various decisions and arrangements to implement the innovation-driven development strategies and build an innovation-oriented country and create a world power in science and technology. In 2015, the CPC Central Committee and the State Council issued *Several Opinions of the CPC Central Committee and the State Council on Deepening the Reform of Systems and Mechanisms to Accelerate the Implementation of Innovation-driven Development Strategies*, which introduced the plan for deepening the science and technology system reform and the pilot plan for promoting comprehensive innovation and reform. In 2016, the CPC Central Committee and the State Council issued the *Outline of the National Strategy of Innovation-Driven Development*, which specified the strategic background and requirements of the innovation-driven development strategy, proposed the strategic deployment and strategic tasks and identified the strategic guarantees and organisational implementation. In the same year, the State Council issued the *13th Five-Year Plan on National Scientific and Technological Innovation*, which specified the general ideas, development goals, major tasks, and major measures for scientific and technological innovation during the 13th Five-Year Plan period.

The *Outline* proposed the three-step goals for innovation-driven development. Step 1, China should become an innovation-oriented country by 2020 and basically establish a national innovation system with Chinese characteristics to give strong support for building a moderately prosperous society in all respects. Step 2, China should move to the forefront of innovation-oriented countries by 2030, realise fundamental transformation of the driving force for development and greatly improve the level of economic and social development and international competitiveness to lay a solid foundation for building China into a major economic power and a society of common prosperity. Step 3, China should become an innovation power and a major world centre for science and innovation by 2050 to support the building of a prosperous, strong, democratic, culturally advanced, harmonious, modern socialist country and the realisation of the Chinese dream of national renewal.

The *Outline* stressed the importance of promoting six transformations to achieve innovation-driven development: transformation in the model of development from an inefficient model focusing on scale expansion to a more sustainable one focusing on quality and efficiency; transformation in the driving force of development from traditional factors to innovation factors; transformation in the industrial sector from the lower-to-medium end of the value chain to the medium-to-higher end; transformation in the status of innovation capability from being "behind, on a par with or ahead of" other countries at the same time but mostly "behind" to being "on a par with" or "ahead of" other countries; transformation in the allocation of resources from focusing on R&D to a balanced distribution along the industrial chain, innovation chain and capital chain; and transformation in innovation entity from an "elite group" of science and technology professionals to the interaction between the "elite group" and the general public involving innovation and entrepreneurship.

In recent years, the quantity and quality of China's S&T input and output have both significantly increased, and it is now an important period to shift from quantitative growth to qualitative improvement. In terms of input, China's total spending on research and development reached 1567.67 billion yuan in 2016, accounting for 2.11% of its GDP, and China's total spending on research and development exceeded the average of the EU's 15 countries; the full-time equivalent of research and development personnel was 3.878 million person-years, the full-time equivalent of research and development personnel per 10,000 population was 28.1 person-years, and China ranked first in total number of research and development personnel in the world.

In terms of quantity and quality of output, the number of domestic patent applications accepted in China was 3.281 million in 2016, including 1.193 million invention patents, which was an increase of 74% and 128.1%, respectively, over 2012. The number of international patent applications filed under the *Patent Cooperation Treaty* by Chinese inventors reached 43,168, ranking third in the world for 4 consecutive years; scientific papers published by Chinese scholars in international journals ranked second in the world, the times papers were cited rose to fourth place, and the proportion of papers from China published in the Science Citation Index journals to the world's total rose from 3.2% in 2000 to 16.3% in 2015. Meanwhile, major advances have been made in science and technology, including the successful launch of the Tiangong-2 space lab, the commissioning of the deep-sea manned submersible *Jiaolong* and of the 500-metre aperture spherical telescope (FAST) Tianyan, the launch of the dark matter probe satellite Wukong and the quantum science satellite Mozi, and the test flight of the airliner C919.[16]

In 2017, the report to the 19th CPC National Congress once again clearly set the development requirement of "making China an innovation-oriented country" and put forward four development priorities. First, we should aim to reach frontier areas of science and technology, strengthen basic research, and make major breakthroughs in pioneering basic research and path-breaking and original innovations. We will strengthen basic research in applied sciences, launch major national science and technology projects, and prioritise innovation in key generic technologies, cutting-edge frontier technologies, modern engineering technologies, and disruptive technologies. These efforts will provide powerful support for building China's strength in science and technology, product quality, aerospace, cyberspace, and transportation and for building a digital China and a smart society. Second, we should give a role to resource allocation in a market economy and develop a market-oriented system for technological innovation in which enterprises are the main players and synergy is created through the joint efforts of enterprises, universities, and research institutes. Third, we should put people first, fully mobilise their enthusiasm, initiative, and creativity, attach equal importance to achievements and talent cultivation, and combine the results of scientific research with talent cultivation. Fourth, we should foster a culture of innovation, and strengthen the creation, protection, and application of intellectual property to create a good atmosphere and guarantee for innovation-driven development.

Innovation-driven development leads the building of the Belt and Road

Innovation-driven development and the Belt and Road Initiative complement each other. Xi Jinping pointed out that "we should build the Belt and Road into a road of innovation. Innovation is an important force powering development. The Belt and Road Initiative is new by nature and we need to encourage innovation in pursuing this initiative".[17]

On the one hand, innovation-driven development is the fundamental driving force of the Belt and Road Initiative. In the initial stage, the driving force of development of the Belt and Road Initiative mainly stems from the free flow of natural resources, labour, capital, and other production factors. By relying on policy coordination, connectivity of infrastructure, unimpeded trade, financial integration and understanding between people, it breaks down trade and investment barriers across countries and explores the economic growth potential of the countries along the routes, especially the developing countries, so as to inject new vitality into the global economic recovery. However, in the medium to long term, the driving force of the development of the Belt and Road Initiative will ultimately depend on comprehensive innovation with scientific and technological innovation at the core.

Developing countries will face mounting population, resource, and environmental pressures, and the old path of fighting for investment, resources, and environment will lead the country nowhere. Only through innovation-driven development will developing countries be able to enhance their total factor productivity and international competitiveness in the process of building the Belt and Road and build a fairer and more rational global industrial division of labour system to ensure that the countries along the routes can have a more favourable development position in global value chains.

On the other hand, the Belt and Road Initiative provides an important platform for innovation-driven development. First, it is a cooperation platform for technological innovation. With the further development of globalisation, information technologies and the Internet, innovation elements are more open and flowable and we cannot possibly pursue innovation behind closed doors.[18] The Belt and Road Initiative helps to improve China's ability to allocate global innovative resources; it helps enterprises deploy their global innovation networks, establish overseas R&D centres, merge and acquire foreign innovative enterprises and R&D institutions or carry out cooperation with them in the form of joint venture or equity participation based on international rules, and improve their ability to operate intellectual property rights abroad; it encourages foreign investors to invest in emerging industries of strategic importance, high-tech industries and modern service industries, and supports multinational enterprises to set up R&D centres in China to realise the combination of attracting investment and introducing talents and technologies; it encourages and guides internationally renowned scientific research institutions to jointly establish international science and technology centres in China, and attracts international innovative talents to work in China and participate and undertake the national science and technology programmes so as to make better use of both domestic and foreign innovation resources.

Second, the Belt and Road Initiative provides a platform for transformation of innovation achievements. The main characteristics of today's global technological revolution are the transformation from "science" to "technology". The basic requirement is to industrialise major basic research achievements.[19] This requires acting in response to the major needs of economic and social development and strives to open up the channels through which technologies are transformed into practical productive forces.[20] The Belt and Road Initiative helps deepen the reform in the field of intellectual property, improve the ability to create, use, protect, and manage intellectual properties, and establish the international investigation and oversea right protection mechanisms to fight against infringement on intellectual property rights; it helps raise the level of China's standards, strengthens the development of basic and generic standards, improves the interactive support mechanism for technological innovation, patent protection and standardisation, encourages enterprises, alliances, and associations to participate in or lead the development of international standards and promote China's superior technologies and standards to become international standards; it helps promote the establishment of Chinese brands and an international mutual recognition brand evaluation system and promotes the internationalisation of high-quality Chinese brands, thus creating a favourable international environment for transforming innovation results into real industrial activities at the institutional and institutional level.

Third, the Belt and Road Initiative provides an incubation platform for "mass entrepreneurship and innovation". The achievements in innovation-driven development depend not only on the height of technological innovation, but also on the breadth and depth of "mass entrepreneurship and innovation". The Belt and Road Initiative helps to broaden the international vision of entrepreneurs, cultivates innovative entrepreneurs who are bold in making innovations and taking risks, and creates a specialised, market-oriented and internationalised team of professional managers; it helps foster innovative small and micro-enterprises, promotes distributed and networked innovation in the countries along the routes, explores business-model innovations, and encourages small and micro-enterprises to increase their capacity to turn out products that are new, distinctive, specialised, and sophisticated; it helps induce creative inspirations, encourages different cultures in the countries along the routes to exchange or dialogue with each other, and develops creative products with stronger breath of life and vitality with the help of local wisdom of each country. This will further strengthen the "people-oriented" social foundation for innovation and development.

Notes

1 *The Outline of National Strategy of Innovation-Driven Development*, Gazette of State Council No. 15, 2016, Xinhua News Agency, Beijing, May 19, 2016.
2 "Speech by Xi Jinping at the 9th Group Study Session of Members of the Politburo of the 18th CPC Central Committee," September 30, 2013.
3 Central Compilation & Translation Bureau, *Karl Marx and Frederick Engels* (Vol. 46), Beijing: People's Publishing House, 1995, pp. 211–217.
4 Party Literature Research Center of the CPC Central Committee, *Collected Writings of Mao Tse-Tung* (Vol. 8), Beijing: People's Publishing House, 1999, p. 341.
5 Editorial Committee on Party Literature of the CPC Central Committee: *Selected Works of Deng Xiaoping* (Vol. 3), Beijing: People's Publishing House, 1993, p. 274.
6 "Speech by Xi Jinping at the 7th Meeting of the Central Leading Group for Financial and Economic Affairs," August 18, 2014.
7 "Speech by Xi Jinping at the Symposium Attended by Senior Provincial and Ministerial Officials for Studying and Implementing the Spirit of the Fifth Plenary Session of the 18th CPC Central Committee," January 18, 2016, *People's Daily*, 2nd ed., May 10, 2016.
8 "Speech by Xi Jinping at the Seventeenth Academician Meeting of the Chinese Academy of Sciences and the Twelfth Academician Conference of the Chinese Academy of Engineering," June 9, 2014.
9 *The Outline of National Strategy of Innovation-Driven Development*, Gazette of State Council No. 15, 2016, Xinhua News Agency, Beijing, May 19, 2016.
10 "Speech by Xi Jinping in the Inspection Tour in Guangdong," December 7–11, 2012.
11 *The Outline of National Strategy of Innovation-Driven Development*, Gazette of State Council No. 15, 2016, Xinhua News Agency, Beijing, May 19, 2016.
12 Hu Angang & Zhang Xin, "Innovative Development: The Core of the National Development," *Journal of the Party School of the CPC Central Committee*, Issue 2, 2016, p. 109.
13 "Speech by Xi Jinping at the Group Discussion of Members from China Association for Science and Technology and the Scientific Research Community at the 1st Session of the 12th National Committee of the Chinese People's Political Consultative Conference," March 4, 2013.
14 "Speech by Xi Jinping at the 9th Group Study Session of Members of the Politburo of the 18th CPC Central Committee," September 30, 2013.
15 *Several Opinions of the CPC Central Committee and the State Council on Deepening the Reform of Systems and Mechanisms to Accelerate the Implementation of Innovation-driven Development Strategies*, Gazette of State Council No. 10, 2015, Xinhua News Agency, Beijing, March 23, 2015.
16 Mu Rongping, "Strengthening the First Motive Force of Innovation and Adding New Momentum to Drive Sustained Development," *People's Tribune*, S2, 2017.
17 "Work Together to Build the Silk Road Economic Belt and The 21st Century Maritime Silk Road—Speech by Xi Jinping President of the People's Republic of China at the Opening Ceremony of the Belt and Road Forum for International Cooperation," Xinhua News Agency, Beijing, May 14, 2017.
18 "Speech by Xi Jinping at the 7th Meeting of the Central Leading Group for Financial and Economic Affairs," August 18, 2014.
19 "Speech by Xi Jinping at the 7th Meeting of the Central Leading Group for Financial and Economic Affairs," August 18, 2014.
20 *Several Opinions of the CPC Central Committee and the State Council on Deepening the Reform of Systems and Mechanisms to Accelerate the Implementation of Innovation-driven Development Strategies*, Gazette of State Council No. 10, 2015, Xinhua News Agency, Beijing, March 23, 2015.

5
RESPONSIBILITIES OF CHINA AS A MAJOR COUNTRY AND THE BELT AND ROAD

Zhou Fangye

Principles and position of responsibilities and accountabilities of China as a major country

From the 1950s to the 1970s, China was "a socialist country" and "a national independent country" whose diplomatic task was mainly to safeguard national sovereignty, win international recognition, and support national liberation movements and just struggles in other Asian and African countries.[1] At that time, by supporting the independence and development of the Third World, China could not only fend off the growing diplomatic isolation, but also mobilise as many international forces as possible to fight against imperialism and hegemonism, reflecting a high degree of unity of patriotism (self-interest) and internationalism (international obligations).[2] Thanks to the joint efforts of China and Asian and African countries, Asian-African nations had successively gained political independence and effectively safeguarded their national sovereignty. This has markedly enhanced the overall position of the Third World in the international system on the basis of South–South Cooperation.

After the reform and opening up in 1978, China began to emphasise its identity as the "largest developing country", changed its views on the mainstream international systems, actively "participated in" and "integrated in" the mainstream international systems, and transformed the previous stages of struggle into mutually beneficial and win–win cooperation platforms. According to statistics, China had joined 33 international conventions from 1949 to 1978 and 240 international conventions from 1979 to 2003.[3] Since the late 1990s, China has clearly stated that it would be "a responsible major country" in the international community and began to participate more actively in international affairs. Since the beginning of the twenty-first century, with the rise of China's overall national strength, there are growing expectations of the international community for China to exert a greater global role. Since the 18th CPC National Congress in 2012, facing the complex international situation, China has formed and established Xi Jinping's thought on major-country diplomacy with Chinese characteristics for the new era, which has thus pointed out the direction for deepening the development of Chinese socialist cause.

First, guiding the reform of the international system is the fundamental position of China as a responsible major country. Judging from the historical experience, the international system has been continuously developed and improved in the process of alternation of old and new forces, especially the interaction of major countries. Regarding the current international system, China upholds its reform stand. On the one hand, China has been integrating itself into the international community through reform and opening up and has become a beneficiary of the current international system. Xi Jinping pointed out that "As far as the existing international system is concerned, China has been a participant, builder and contributor. We stand firmly for the international order and system that is based on the purposes and principles of the *UN Charter*". On the other hand, there are also many injustices and unreasonable phenomena need to be adjusted in the current international system. In this regard, Xi Jinping stressed that "A great number of countries, especially developing countries, want to see a more just and equitable international system, but it doesn't mean they want to unravel the entire system or start all over again. Rather, what they want is to reform and improve the system to keep up with the times".[4] In order to promote the development and improvement of the international system, China has successively proposed a series of important reform concepts, including the new security concept featuring "mutual trust, mutual benefit, equality and cooperation", the initiative of promoting democracy in international relations based on the multi-polar development trend, the solemn commitment to adherence to a peaceful development path, and the advocacy of "fostering a new form of major-country relations featuring no conflict or confrontation, mutual respect and win–win cooperation". In 2017, the report to the 19th CPC National Congress further proposed to "foster a new form of international relations" based on the following core principles. First, mutual respect. Countries of different size, strength or wealth, and with diverse systems, religions, and civilisations, are all equals. Second, fairness and justice. The law of the jungle which puts the weak at the mercy of the strong must be rejected, and the legitimate rights and interests of all countries, in particular the developing countries, should be upheld. Third, win–win cooperation. The outdated mindset of zero-sum game or winner-takes-all should be replaced with a new approach of working for common development and shared benefits.[5]

Second, enhancing the common interests of all mankind is an important goal of China as a responsible major country. As a world we are now facing growing uncertainties and destabilising factors. Global economic growth lacks energy; the gap between rich and poor continues to widen; hotspot issues often arise in some regions; and unconventional security threats like terrorism, cyber-insecurity, major infectious diseases, and climate change continue to spread. As human beings we have many common challenges to face. We are in urgent need of feasible solutions to solve various global problems. In response, China has proposed the initiative of "building of a community of a shared future for mankind" so as to build an open, inclusive, clean, and beautiful world that enjoys lasting peace, universal security, and common prosperity. Its contents include: we should take a new approach to developing state-to-state relations with communication, not confrontation, and with partnership, not alliance; we should commit to settling disputes through dialogue and resolving differences through discussion, coordinate responses to traditional and non-traditional threats, and oppose terrorism in all its forms; we should make economic globalisation more open, inclusive, and balanced so that its benefits are shared by all; we should work together to facilitate exchanges and mutual learning among civilisations; we should be good friends to the environment and cooperate to tackle climate change.[6]

Third, doing everything within our capacity and keeping the parity of authority and responsibility is the basic principle of China as a responsible major country. China ranks second in the world by total economic output, but it is in a position below 70th by per-capita income. According to the standards set by the United Nations, China still has a poverty-stricken population of more than 100 million. This shows that unbalanced development is still China's basic national condition, and a large developing country is still the basic identity of China. Therefore, on the one hand, China should actively assume the responsibilities of a major country, providing more public goods for the world on the basis of continuous development of national strength, and on the other hand, we must also bear in mind the basic national conditions of China as a developing country to avoid assuming responsibilities and obligations that exceed its bearing capacity.[7] Meanwhile, as far as global governance is concerned, authority is the legal condition and prerequisite for fulfilling responsibilities. Responsibility is the obligation and expense for enjoying authority. As an emerging power, China needs to shoulder greater responsibilities and obligations in the governance of global issues. It should also gain more say and influence so as to gain a more favourable international environment for sustainable development of China.[8]

Fields and contributions of responsibilities and obligations of China as a responsible major country

The *Outline of 13th Five-Year Plan for National Economic and Social Development of the People's Republic of China* promulgated in 2016 elaborated on the issue regarding "actively assuming international responsibilities and obligations". China has sent to the outside world the clear information that it will more proactively play a constructive role in the international community and provide public products. Specifically, the responsibilities and obligations of China as a major country in the new era are mainly reflected in the following areas.[9]

First, further strengthening foreign assistance. From 1950 to 2016, China provided more than 400 billion yuan of assistance to more than 160 countries and international organisations in accordance with the principles of "mutual respect, equality, keeping promise, mutual benefits and win–win", built more than 2700 complete-set engineering projects, and trained nearly 12 million talents of various types, having become a model for South–South Cooperation.

Under the new situation, foreign assistance is an important manifestation of China's role as a responsible major country. China will further expand its scale of foreign aid, improve its foreign aid methods, provide more free training for developing countries in human resources, development plans and economic policies, expand foreign cooperation and assistance in scientific and technological education, medical and health care, disaster prevention and reduction, environmental governance, wild animal and plant protection, poverty alleviation and other aspects, and strengthen efforts in humanitarian assistance.

Second, actively responding to North–South development imbalances. China is an important participant and contributor to global development cooperation. It has actively implemented the UN Millennium Development Goals and made remarkable achievements in poverty reduction, health, education, and other fields. It has also provided important support and help to more than 120 developing countries to help them realise the UN Millennium Development Goals. In 2015, Xi Jinping announced at the UN Summit on Sustainable Development that China would set up a South–South Cooperation Assistance Fund with an initial contribution of US$2 billion, to support South–South cooperation and assist developing countries in implementing their post-2015 development agenda. China would also do its best to raise its investment in the least developed countries (LDCs) to US$12 billion by 2030. In addition, China would exempt the debt of the outstanding intergovernmental interest-free loans due by the end of 2015 owed by relevant LDCs, land-locked developing countries, and small island developing countries.[10]

Third, actively responding to global climate change. China attaches great importance to the issue of climate change. China is actively implementing the relevant national strategies for combating climate change and has submitted *Enhanced Actions on Climate Change: China's*

Intended Nationally Determined Contributions to the secretariat of the United Nations Framework Convention on Climate Change (UNFCCC), making an important contribution to coping with global climate change. China has always actively participated in the relevant negotiations under the framework convention and is committed to promoting the establishment of a fair and reasonable global climate governance system. China also advocates that the system should adhere to the principles of equity and common but differentiated responsibilities and respective capabilities, and take into account differentiated historical responsibilities and distinct national circumstances, development stages and capabilities of developed and developing countries. It should reflect all elements in a comprehensive and balanced way, including mitigation, adaptation, finance, technology development and transfer, capacity building, and transparency of action and support.

Fourth, actively maintaining the international public safety. China is firmly opposed to all forms of terrorism, actively carries out international anti-terrorism cooperation, and has established anti-terrorism policy dialogue mechanisms with nearly 20 countries. It is also deeply involved in anti-terrorist cooperation under the framework of multilateral mechanisms such as the UN, APEC, and the Global Anti-Terrorism Forum to curb the spread of terrorism.

China has always actively supported UN peacekeeping operations. It has participated in peacekeeping operations for nearly 30 years and has sent more than 30,000 peacekeepers to various countries and regions. It is a permanent member of the Security Council and has sent the most peacekeepers. China is often among the top 10 of all contributors and has committed the most troops out of all the permanent UN Security Council members.

China is always opposed to proliferation of weapons of mass destruction (WMDs) and their means of delivery. It calls for adopting political and diplomatic means to achieve non-proliferation goals, giving full play to the core role of the United Nations and other international organisations and handling the relationship between non-proliferation and peaceful use in a balanced way, and is opposed to discriminatory measures and double standards. China has participated in all international treaties and related international organisations in the field of non-proliferation and will continue to participate fully in international arms control, disarmament and non-proliferation affairs, conscientiously fulfil its treaty obligations, actively participate in international cooperation in non-proliferation and formulation of international rules, and strive to safeguard the seriousness and authority of the international arms control and non-proliferation system.

China has actively pushed for political solutions to sensitive international and regional hotspot issues. China has insisted on resolving conflicts of territorial claims and disputes over maritime rights and interests with its neighbours through peaceful means. So far, it has solved the land boundary issue with 12 of the 14 countries that border China. China has advocated the "dual track" approach in handling the South China Sea issue. China will continue to uphold fairness and justice and insist on proper control and resolution of sensitive hotspot issues through dialogue and consultation.

Based on the principles of peace, sovereignty, co-governance, and universal benefits, China advocates building a cyber space featuring peace, security, openness, and cooperation and building a multilateral, democratic, and transparent Internet governance system. China has established dialogue mechanisms on network affairs with relevant countries and participated in multilateral network dialogues and cooperation. It is committed to promoting the development of the International Code of Conduct for Information Security within the framework of the United Nations, helps developing countries bridge the "digital divide", and supports the international community to jointly combat cybercrime and cyber hacking.

Responsibilities and obligations of China for the Belt and Road

The Belt and Road is an important channel for China to fulfil its responsibilities and obligations as a responsible major country. In today's world, global growth requires new drivers, development needs to be more inclusive and balanced, and the gap between the rich and the poor needs to be narrowed. Hotspots in some regions are causing instability and terrorism is rampant. Deficits in peace, development, and governance pose a daunting challenge to mankind. The Belt and Road Initiative is an effective solution imbued with China's wisdom and accountabilities that China has proposed with its identity as a responsible large developing country.

The Belt and Road is a road for peace, a road of prosperity, a road of opening-up, a road of innovation, a road connecting different civilisations, and a road of greenness. It helps to fundamentally solve many real challenges that the world is facing, particularly security issues, development issues, and climate issues. However, to advance the Belt and Road Initiative, we need to strengthen extensive consultation and joint contribution and share benefits among countries along the routes, and more importantly, it is necessary for the major countries to assume important responsibilities in maintaining security, promoting cooperation, and assisting development.

China is not only the initiator but also the responsible practitioner of the Belt and Road Initiative.[11] China emphasises that the pursuit of the Belt and Road Initiative is not meant to reinvent the wheel. Rather, it aims to complement the development strategies of the countries involved by leveraging their comparative strengths. We should foster a new form of international relations featuring win–win cooperation; we should foster partnership of dialogue with no confrontation and friendship rather than alliance; we should work to resolve hotspot issues through political means, and promote mediation in the spirit of justice; we should intensify counter-terrorism efforts, address both its symptoms and root causes, and strive to eradicate poverty, backwardness, and social injustice.

At the Belt and Road Forum for International Cooperation in 2017, China clearly committed that we would scale up financing support for the Belt and Road Initiative and encourage cooperation in infrastructure, production capacity, and finance; offer short-term research visits to China for young foreign scientists, train foreign scientists, engineers and managers, and set up joint laboratories; we would set up a big data service platform on ecological and environmental protection; we proposed establishing an international coalition for green development under the Belt and Road, and would provide support to related countries in adapting to climate change; and we would launch more projects to improve people's well-being.[12]

As China has demonstrated its commitment as a responsible major country, the Belt and Road Initiative has gained the understanding and recognition of the international community in a short period of time. In November 2016, the 193 member states of the UN unanimously adopted a resolution, which welcomes the establishment of the Belt and Road Initiative and other economic cooperation initiatives and calls on the international community to provide a safe and secure environment for the Belt and Road Initiative. In March 2017, the UN Security Council unanimously adopted Resolution 2344, calling on the international community to strengthen regional economic cooperation through the Belt and Road Initiative. So far, remarkable results have been achieved in the building of the Belt and Road. However, in the medium to long term, its development remains a long and arduous task, and China needs to continue to assume its responsibilities as a major country and escort for the building of the Belt and Road.

Notes

1 Xie Yixian, Editor-in-Chief, *China's Diplomatic History (the Period of the People's Republic of China 1949–1979)*, Zhengzhou: Henan People's Publishing House, 1998 ed., p. 11.

2 Zhou Hong, "Thirty Years of China's Foreign Aid and Reform and Opening-up," *World Economics and Politics*, Issue 11, 2008.
3 "List of China's Participation in International Conventions (1875–2003)," official website of the Ministry of Foreign Affairs of the People's Republic of China, searched on February 5, 2018.
4 "Speech by Xi Jinping at the Welcome Banquet in Seattle," Xinhua News Agency, Seattle, September 22, 2015.
5 Wang Yi, "New Look, New Accomplishments and New Role—China's Diplomacy in a New Era," *Global Times*, 7th ed., December 11, 2017.
6 "Work Together to Build a Community of Shared Future for Mankind—Speech by Xi Jinping at the United Nations Office at Geneva," Xinhua News Agency, Geneva, January 18, 2017.
7 Luo Jianbo, "A Responsible Major Developing Country: China's Identity and Its Responsibilities As A Major Country," *West Asia and Africa*, Issue 5, 2014, pp. 42–43.
8 Lin Yueqin, "Global Governance Innovation and the Responsibilities of Emerging Powers," *Social Sciences in Nanjing*, Issue 10, 2016, p. 1.
9 Yang Jiechi, "Actively Assume International Responsibilities and Obligations," *People's Daily*, 6th ed., November 23, 2015.
10 "Towards a Mutually Beneficial Partnership for Sustainable Development—Speech by Xi Jinping at the UN Sustainable Development Summit," Xinhua News Agency, United Nations, September 26, 2015.
11 Office of the Leading Group for the Belt and Road Initiative, "Building the Belt and Road: Concept, Practice and China's Contribution," May 10, 2017.
12 "Work Together to Build the Silk Road Economic Belt and The 21st Century Maritime Silk Road—Speech by Xi Jinping President of the People's Republic of China at the Opening Ceremony of the Belt and Road Forum for International Cooperation," Xinhua News Agency, Beijing, May 14, 2017.

6

CONFIDENCE OF A MAJOR COUNTRY AND THE BELT AND ROAD

Zhou Fangye

From the "three aspects of confidence" to "four aspects of confidences"

Since the reform and opening-up policy was launched in 1978, China has maintained its overall social stability and rapid economic development for a long period of time. It has become the world's second largest economy and the world's largest manufacturer, and its incidence of rural poverty has fallen from over 30% to below 4%. The two goals—ensuring that people's basic needs are met and that their lives are generally decent—have been accomplished ahead of time and a great achievement known as the "Chinese miracle" has been made.

On the basis of previous development, China has also proposed two new "Centenary Goals". That is, we will surely complete the building of a moderately prosperous society in all respects by 2021 when the Communist Party of China celebrates its centennial, basically realise socialist modernisation by 2035, and turn China into a modern socialist country that is prosperous, strong, democratic, culturally advanced, and harmonious when the People's Republic of China celebrates its centennial by the middle of the twenty-first century.

In 2011, Hu Jintao's Speech at the Meeting Commemorating the 90th Anniversary of the Founding of the Communist Party of China systematically summarised for the first time the scientific connotation of socialism with Chinese characteristics from the three aspects of roads, theoretical systems, and institutions.[1] In 2012, the report to the 18th CPC National Congress further emphasised that the path, guiding theories and system of socialism with Chinese characteristics function as an integral whole in the great practice of building socialism with Chinese characteristics, and proposed for the first time that the entire Party must have firm confidence in the path, guiding theories, system, and culture of socialism with Chinese characteristics.[2]

At the 33rd Group Study Session of Members of the Politburo of the CPC Central Committee in 2016, Xi Jinping introduced the confidence in culture together with the "three aspects of confidence" for the first time and required that the whole Party should have confidence in the path, guiding theories, and system, and most importantly, confidence in our culture. In 2016, Xi Jinping stated in his speech at the Meeting Commemorating the 90th Anniversary of the Founding of the Communist Party of China that: "Of all the political parties, countries, and peoples in the world today, none have as much cause to be confident as the CPC, the People's Republic of China, and the Chinese people" and stressed that "The CPC and Chinese people have every confidence in their ability to provide a Chinese solution to aid the exploration of a better social system for humanity".

First, confidence in the path. Taking the path of socialism with Chinese characteristics means we must, under the leadership of the Communist Party of China and basing ourselves on China's realities, take economic development as the central task and adhere to the four cardinal principles and the policy of reform and opening up. It means we must unleash and develop the productive forces, develop the socialist market economy, socialist democracy, an advanced socialist culture and a harmonious socialist society, and promote socialist ecological progress. It also means we must promote well-rounded development of the person, achieve prosperity for all over time, and make China a modern socialist country that is prosperous, strong, democratic, culturally advanced, and harmonious.

Second, confidence in guiding theories. The system of theories of socialism with Chinese characteristics is a system of scientific theories that includes Deng Xiaoping Theory, the important thought of Three Represents, the Scientific Outlook on Development and Xi Jinping's Thought on Socialism with Chinese Characteristics for the New Era. This system represents the Party's adherence to and development of Marxism–Leninism and Mao Tse-Tung Thought.

Third, confidence in the system. The socialist system with Chinese characteristics includes the following: the fundamental political system—the system of people's congresses; the basic political systems—the system of multiparty cooperation and political consultation under the leadership of the Communist Party of China, the system of regional ethnic autonomy, and the system of community-level self-governance; the socialist system of laws with Chinese characteristics; the basic economic system in which public ownership is the mainstay and economic entities of diverse ownership develop together; and the specific economic, political, cultural, and social institutions based on these systems.

Fourth, confidence in culture. Socialist culture with Chinese characteristics is derived from China's fine traditional culture, which was born of the Chinese civilisation and nurtured over more than 5000 years; it has grown out of the revolutionary and advanced socialist culture that developed over the course of the Chinese people's revolution, construction, and reform under the Party's leadership; and it is rooted in the great practice of socialism with Chinese characteristics.

The confidence in the path, guiding theories, system, and culture of socialism with Chinese characteristics is an organic unity. They are both relatively independent and complementary to each other. Among them, the path of socialism with Chinese characteristics is the only path to socialist modernisation and a better life for the people. The theories of socialism with Chinese characteristics are the right theories to guide the Party and people to realise national rejuvenation. The system of socialism with Chinese characteristics provides the fundamental institutional guarantee for progress and development in contemporary China. The culture of socialism with Chinese characteristics is a powerful source of strength that inspires all members of the Party and the people of all ethnic groups in China.[3] The "four aspects of confidence" are unified in the great practice of socialism with Chinese characteristics.

The confidence of a major country must be based on confidence in culture

Confidence in culture is the foundation that supports confidence in the path, confidence in guiding theories and confidence in the system. It permeates into confidence in the path, confidence in guiding theory, and confidence in the system. Without confidence in culture, confidence in the path, confidence in guiding theories and confidence in the system can hardly support the cause of socialism with Chinese characteristics.

The confidence of a major country should be based on the confidence in culture. In 2016, Xi Jinping pointed out at the Forum on Philosophy and Social Sciences that "To have firm confidence in the path, guiding theories and system is after all to have firm cultural confidence. Cultural confidence represents a fundamental and profound force that sustains the development of a country and a nation".[4] In 2017, the Party's report to the 19th CPC National Congress clearly stated that "We must building stronger cultural confidence and help socialist culture to flourish" and requires that we should develop a socialist culture for our nation—a culture that is sound and people-oriented, that embraces modernisation, the world, and the future, and that both promotes socialist material well-being and raises socialist cultural–ethical standards. In developing this culture, we must follow the guidance of Marxism, base our efforts on Chinese culture, and take into account the realities of contemporary China and the conditions of the present era.

First, the great rejuvenation of the Chinese nation requires the prosperity of Chinese culture. Having gone through over 5000 years of vicissitudes, Chinese civilisation has always kept to its original root. As the unique cultural identity of the Chinese nation, it contains our most profound cultural pursuits and provides us with abundant nourishment for existence and development.[5] The Chinese people have strong confidence in the path, theories, and system with Chinese characteristics, with their confidence in Chinese culture as the essence, because China is a country with a civilisation over 5000 years old.[6] The Chinese dream will be realised through balanced development and mutual reinforcement of material and cultural progress. Without the continuation and development of civilisation or the promotion and prosperity of culture, the Chinese dream will not come true. The realisation of the Chinese dream is a process of both material and cultural development. As China continues to make economic and social progress, Chinese civilisation will keep pace with the times and acquire greater vitality.[7]

Second, we must consolidate the guiding position of Marxism and hold firmly the leading position in ideological work. Ideology determines the direction a culture should take and the path it should follow as it develops. In 2013, Xi Jinping pointed out at the National Conference on Propaganda and Ideological Work that: whether or not it is possible to do ideological work well relates to the future destiny of the Party, relates to the long-term peace and order of the country, and relates to the cohesion and centripetal force of the nation. To have firm cultural confidence, we must continue to adapt Marxism to China's conditions, keep it up-to-date, and enhance its popular appeal. We will develop socialist ideology that has the ability to unite and the power to inspire the people to embrace shared ideals, convictions, values, and moral standards.[8]

Third, we must nurture and practice core socialist values and raise the ideological and moral standards of the entire nation. The core values of socialism with Chinese characteristics is to "promote prosperity, democracy, civility, and harmony, uphold freedom, equality, justice and the rule of law and advocate patriotism, dedication, integrity, and friendship". This is a concentrated embodiment of the contemporary Chinese spirit and the ideological and moral foundation that boosts national cohesion. To have firm confidence in culture, we must continuously strengthen the building of the system of socialist core values, make fostering and promoting socialist core values a basic project for spiritual cohesion and foundation consolidation, and implement it in a practical way. We should do more to foster a Chinese spirit, Chinese values, and Chinese strength to provide an endless source of spiritual power and moral nourishment for the cause of Socialism with Chinese Characteristics.

Fourth, we must promote advanced socialist culture and improve the country's cultural soft power. Cultural soft power represents the cohesion and vitality of a country based on culture, and the resulting attractiveness and influence. From a historical point of view, the development process of any major country is not only the process of raising hard power such as economic aggregates and military power, but also the process of raising the soft power such as values, ideology, and culture.

For China, raising the country's cultural soft power relates to the realisation of the "Two Centenary Goals" and the Chinese dream of the great rejuvenation of the Chinese nation. Therefore, to have firm cultural confidence, we must promote advanced socialist culture, deepen the reform of the cultural system, create a new surge in promoting socialist culture and bring about its great development and enrichment, inspire the cultural creativity of the whole nation, promote rapid development and all-around flourishing of the cultural industry and cultural services, constantly enrich people's cultural life and enhance their moral strength, continuously enhance the overall strength and international competitiveness of Chinese culture, and strive to meet the grand goal of developing a strong socialist culture in China.[9]

The Belt and Road highlights the confidence of China as a major country

The Belt and Road Initiative is a Chinese proposal whose aim is to promote peaceful cooperation and common development throughout the world. It helps China to demonstrate its confidence in actively responding to global governance problems and portray itself as a civilised country featuring rich history, ethnic unity, and cultural diversity; as an oriental power with good government, developed economy, cultural prosperity, social stability, national unity, and beautiful mountains and rivers; as a responsible country that advocates peaceful and common development, safeguards international justice, and makes contributions to humanity; and as a socialist country which is open, amicable, promising, and vibrant. It will enhance the understanding and recognition of China by countries along the Belt and Road.

As a road of prosperity, the Belt and Road is a platform for extensive consultation, joint contribution and shared benefits for all countries along the routes. We are ready to share the practices of development with other countries, but we have no intention to interfere in other countries' internal affairs, export our own social system and model of development, or impose our own will on others.[10] However, through promoting policy coordination, connectivity of infrastructure, unimpeded trade, financial integration, and understanding between people, the Belt and Road demonstrates the path, guiding theories, system and culture of socialism with Chinese characteristics to the countries along the routes and thus provide references for all these countries, especially developing countries, to explore their own development path. Meanwhile, during the hard time when we are witnessing a backlash against globalisation by Western countries, especially the United States, China's confidence in actively promoting globalisation will also help encourage the countries along the Belt and Road to participate more actively in cooperation and work together to build a global economy that is more invigorated, more open, more stable, more sustainable, and more inclusive.

As a road connecting different civilisations, in pursuing the Belt and Road Initiative, we should ensure that when it comes to different civilisations, exchange will replace estrangement, mutual learning will replace clashes, and coexistence will replace a sense of superiority. This will boost mutual understanding, mutual respect, and mutual trust among different countries. The Chinese nation has always been a peace-loving nation.[11] As an important part of Chinese culture, the concept of harmony has a long history and strong appeal. We believe in unity between man and nature, peace among countries, the approach of "agree to disagree", and the good nature of people. In China's 5000-year history, the Chinese nation has pursued and maintained the philosophy of peace, friendship, and harmony. Peace is most precious; treat others with kindness; don't do to others what you don't want others to do to you. These ideas have passed from generation to generation and taken root in the mentality of the Chinese and are reflected in their behaviour.[12] This will provide important guidance for the countries along the Belt and Road to put into action the Silk Road spirit of "peace and cooperation, openness and inclusiveness, mutual learning and mutual benefit" and will help to effectively avoid the exclusive praise or belittling of one particular civilisation, thus enriching the colours of various civilisations and the cultural life of people, and opening up still greater alternatives in the future. Meanwhile, China will also fully draw on the beneficial results of the world's civilisations in the process of building the Belt and Road to further develop and improve the socialist culture with Chinese characteristics. On this basis, China will guide the people to develop an accurate understanding of history, ethnicity, country, and culture and enhance the spine and confidence of the Chinese people and build stronger cultural confidence in the construction of socialism with Chinese characteristics.

Notes

1 "Speech by Hu Jintao at the Celebration of the 90th Anniversary of the Founding of the Communist Party of China," Xinhua News Agency, Beijing, July 1, 2011.
2 *Firmly March on the Path of Socialism with Chinese Characteristics and Strive to Complete the Building of A Moderately Prosperous Society in All Respects*, Hu Jintao's report to the 18th National Congress of the Communist Party of China on November 8, 2012.
3 *Secure a Decisive Victory in Building a Moderately Prosperous Society in All Respects and Strive for the Great Success of Socialism with Chinese Characteristics for a New Era*, Xi Jinping's report to the 19th National Congress of the Communist Party of China on October 18, 2017.
4 "Speech by Xi Jinping at the Symposium on Philosophy and Social Sciences," Xinhua News Agency, Beijing, May 18, 2016.
5 "Speech by Xi Jinping at UNESCO Headquarters," Xinhuanet Paris, March 27, 2014.
6 "Remarks by Xi Jinping about Cultural Confidence," *People's Daily* Overseas Edition, 12th ed., July 13, 2016.
7 "Speech by Xi Jinping at UNESCO Headquarters," Xinhuanet Paris, March 27, 2014.
8 "Remarks by Xi Jinping about Cultural Confidence," *People's Daily* Overseas Edition, 12th ed., July 13, 2016.
9 "Xi Jinping Presided over the 12th Group Study Session of Members of the Politburo of the CPC Central Committee and Delivered A Keynoted Speech," Xinhuanet Beijing, December 31, 2013.
10 "Work Together to Build the Silk Road Economic Belt and The 21st Century Maritime Silk Road—Speech by President Xi Jinping of the People's Republic of China at the Opening Ceremony of the Belt and Road Forum for International Cooperation," Xinhua News Agency, Beijing, May 14, 2017.
11 Ibid.
12 "Speech by Chinese President Xi Jinping at China International Friendship Conference in Commemoration of the 60th Anniversary of the Chinese People's Association for Friendship with Foreign Countries," Xinhua News Agency, Beijing, May 15, 2014.

7

DEFICIT IN DEVELOPMENT AND THE BELT AND ROAD

Xu Liping

Deficit in development is mainly manifested in development imbalance between the North and the South, loss of control over the gap between the rich and the poor, and loss of harmony between man and nature.

The imbalance between the South and the North means that the gap between developing countries and developed countries is growing wider, and the fundamental balance point between them has been lost. Since the beginning of the twenty-first century, with the rise of emerging economies, the focus of the world economy has begun to shift from traditional developed countries to emerging economies. The share of developed countries led by the United States in the world economy has gradually decreased, but they still take the dominant position in the world economic rules and agendas and occupy the centre of the world economy. There is no fundamental change in the macro situation of imbalance between the North and the South. According to the statistics of the International Monetary Fund over the years, by comparing the three indicators of GDP per capita, human development index, and Engel's coefficient, the development gap between the developing countries and the developed countries is continuously widening.

The loss of control over the gap between the rich and the poor means that global issues such as poverty, unemployment, and income inequality are increasingly serious. The rate of return on capital is higher than the rate of economic growth and even higher than labour productivity, which is manifested as mismatch between personal wealth and distributed income and extreme disparity between the rich and the poor. The Gini coefficient is an index that measures the degree of income equality of residents, and it is also an important reference index for measuring the disparity between the rich and the poor in a country. In September 2016, President Xi Jinping clearly stated at the 11th G20 Summit that "Gini coefficient has reached around 0.7, higher than the recognized alarm level which stands at 0.6. This is something we must pay great attention to".[1]

The loss of harmony between man and nature means that with rapid development of global industrialisation and urbanisation, human beings have overly exploited and utilised natural resources, causing ecological damage to the global natural environment, which is mainly manifested in unsustainable development. According to the *2013 Human Development Report* issued by the United Nations, the inaction in the aspects of environmental changes, deforestation, and water and air pollution may cause the world's poorest countries and regions to lose more than what they gain. Humans need to focus more efforts on environmental issues. Climate changes have exacerbated long-term climate disasters. The lack of ecosystems has limited the survival and development opportunities for humans, especially the poor.

At the opening ceremony of the Belt and Road Forum for International Cooperation in 2017, President Xi Jinping stated that: "we should build the Belt and Road into a road of prosperity. Development holds the master key to solving all problems. In pursuing the Belt and Road Initiative, we should focus on the fundamental issue of development, release the growth potential of various countries and achieve economic integration and interconnected development and deliver benefits to all".[2]

Unlike other regional economic cooperation mechanisms that are rule-oriented, the Belt and Road is oriented towards development and aims to crack down on the global problem of deficit in development. In response to the imbalance between the North and the South in deficit in development, the building of the Belt and Road has taken addressing the development issue for the developing countries as its core objective, aiming at promoting new types of South–South cooperation. The participating countries of the Belt and Road are numerous and vary greatly, so it is unrealistic to presuppose a unified cooperation mechanism. Therefore, the building of the Belt and Road has always been proceeded from the actual needs of the development of all countries, and it has pursued a diversified cooperation mechanism in accordance with the principles of extensive consultation, joint contribution and shared benefits and is committed to building a community of shared future for mankind based on the community of shared interests and responsibility. For example, it regards connectivity of infrastructure as a priority area because the backwardness of infrastructure is a bottleneck for the development of many developing countries. In practice, it can not only synergise the development strategies of various countries, but also complement with the current regional economic cooperation mechanisms and will effectively promote the development of countries along the routes and even the world.

The Belt and Road Initiative has provided opportunities for many developing countries to participate in regional economic cooperation on an equal footing. It will help bring into play the existing comparative advantages of various countries and help them to form new comparative advantages, and make economic globalisation more open, inclusive, balanced, and beneficial to all. In 2016, China's direct investment in countries along the Belt and Road reached US$14.5 billion. Chinese enterprises have already established 56 economic and trade cooperation zones in more than 20 countries along the routes, which involve a total investment of US$18.5 billion, and added nearly US$1.1 billion in taxes and 180,000 jobs for the host countries.

China proposed the new concepts of "innovative, coordinated, green, open and inclusive" development to provide a new path for the building of the Belt and Road Initiative.

The concept of innovative development (or innovation-driven development) is the core of new development concepts and it emphasises that innovation is the primary driving force for development. The driving force for development determines the speed, effectiveness, and sustainability of development. Innovation is the primary driving force for the development in the new normal and the vitality and source of promoting coordinated development, green development, open development and shared development. The concept of innovative development emphasises all-round innovation in theory, system, science and technology, and culture, with particular emphasis on innovation in science and technology. Xi Jinping stated that innovation was a complex social systematic project involving all areas of economy and society. Various areas are closely linked to each other, so it is necessary to break the constraints and obstacles in an all-around and systematic way and carry out multi-dimensional innovation. Among them, innovation in science and technology is the key and core part. Science and technology constitute a primary productive force and are an important lever and fundamental driving force for economic and social development.

The concept of coordinated development emphasises that we should avoid preference for unitary development, break path dependence, and pursue coordinated development in all aspects and links such as balance of the relations between production and productivity forces and between the superstructure and the economic base, expand the development space in various fields, and strengthen coordinated, integrated, and systematic development to promote the smooth development of socialist cause with Chinese characteristics and build a well-off society in all respects. The concept of coordinated development stresses that we should seriously handle the major relations in development, address the issue of development imbalance, and form a balanced new structure. China adheres to coordinated regional development and is adjusting its economic structure and spatial structure and adopting a new model of optimised development in densely populated areas and an intensive economic growth model. China insists on balanced urban and rural development and promotes the simultaneous advancement of new industrialisation, IT application, urbanisation, and agricultural modernisation to realise the integration of urban and rural development. China fosters both material progress and cultural and ethical (cultural and ideological) progress, improves people's material and spiritual life, and enhances the material and spiritual strength of construction of the socialist cause with Chinese characteristics.

The concept of coordinated development emphasises cooperation, development, mutual benefits, and win–win outcomes. China enhances coordinated development in all areas and has launched the development strategies to encourage the government, enterprises and non-government organisations to carry out comprehensive cooperation in politics, economy, culture, and ecology. China enhances cooperation with various countries in the world, puts aside cooperation barriers and disputes and works hard to seek interest integration points and economic balance to achieve mutual benefits and win–win outcomes.

The concept of coordinated development emphasises the establishment of an equal and balanced global development relationship to achieve common development and common progress. Due to the uneven development in today's world, it is necessary to eliminate imbalanced and inequitable development burdens and political attachment conditions, expand the integration of economic interests, narrow the development gap between countries, allow countries and people of all ranks in society to share development dividends, and promote all countries to achieve different levels of development and eventually achieve common prosperity.

How to realise the harmonious coexistence of man and nature is unarguably a pressing issue that all countries in the world should ponder over and address. The concept of "green development" advocated by China is precisely the scientific outlook on development that promotes sustainable development of human society. Green development advocates green productive forces, aims to achieve mutual benefit and integration in productive force development, ecological development and social development, and pursues the dialectical unity of development and environmental protection. Green development advocates the concept of green nature, emphasises that mankind is a part of the natural environment, respects and protects nature, pursues the harmony between man and nature, and opposes the confrontation between man and nature. The development of human society has experienced agricultural civilisation, industrial civilisation, and even the current post-industrial civilisation era. Particularly, the wave of industrialisation in the modern world has brought about positive effects to humankind. Meanwhile, it has also brought a lot of negative effects and resulted in waste of resources, environmental destruction, ecological imbalance, and eternal swelling of people's materialism and hedonism. Such a mode of development at the expense of destroying mankind's own living conditions does not serve the overall interests and long-term interests of mankind. Green development advocates green development modes, optimises the economic production structure, transforms the modes of economic growth and development, and seeks new growth points that can achieve both economic and ecological benefits. Green development emphasises the relationship between poverty, development, and the environment and advocates comprehensive, all-around and equitable development. It is a concept of sustainable development different from the traditional concept of development and a mode of development that is subject to assessment, constraints and regulations. Green development advocates environmental protection awareness and value orientation and insists that that everyone has the responsibility and obligation to take care of and protect the environment. Everyone should start from small things and from everyday life and work together to build a beautiful homeland for mankind. Green development is not only a rational response and choice made by human society after deep reflections on the ever-increasing contradiction between population, economy, environment, and resources, but it is also an internationally recognised economic ethical norm. It is also a criterion and value-oriented guidance for regulating and restricting the behaviours of human beings in the process of coordination between mankind and nature.

The concept of open development emphasises that we should implement a more proactive opening-up strategy, raise the quality of opening up, and improve the open economy so that it promotes mutual benefit and is diversified, balanced, secure, and efficient. China will continuously improve its foreign trade and foreign investment structure, deepen its all-around opening-up to the outside world, develop an open economy of higher standards, establish an open socialist economic system with Chinese characteristics, further integrate itself into global economic development, make full use of advanced scientific and technological achievements and useful management experience created by the human society, and strive to enter the middle and upper ends of the global industrial value chain and take a favourable position in the international division of labour so as to continuously inject new vitality for socialist modernisation. Open development emphasises emancipating the mind, enhancing confidence in opening up, and expanding awareness of opening up. China has always adhered to the ideology of emancipating the mind and opening up to the outside world, and will strive to build a pattern of opening up and international environment conducive to China's economic development and continuous rise.

The concept of shared development adheres to the principle of development for the people, by the people and to the benefit of the people so that all our people have a greater sense of fulfillment as they contribute to and gain from development and the people of the world can share China's contributions. China's development has benefited from the international community, and it is willing to share its own development experience and opportunities with other countries. China welcomes all countries to ride on its development and share the achievements of its reform and opening up.

The concept of shared development emphasises on ensuring that the achievements and fruits of reform and opening up benefit all people and that China's programmes and contributions benefit the people of all countries. Ever since the reform and opening up, China has made material and non-material achievements in the fields of economy, politics, society, culture, science and technology, education, health care, and ecology. These achievements have not only met the material needs of people such as food, clothing, shelter, etc., but also satisfied people's spiritual needs for the pursuit of their own values, their sense of fulfillment, and their sense of well-being. These achievements should bring benefits to all people. Meanwhile, the active explorations made by China and the development models forming in the process of its reform and opening up are all of great significance and value. For the world, they are all shared results that can play a positive role and effect.

The concept of shared development emphasises reducing poverty, narrowing the gap between the rich and the poor, and pursuing fairness and justice. Without fairness and justice, it is impossible to realise shared development. Shared development objectively requires that all fruits of reform and development should be distributed in a fair and reasonable manner among all people, and that we should achieve shared benefits while making joint contribution and promotes joint contribution while achieving shared benefits. Strengthening efforts in reducing poverty, narrowing the gap between the rich and the poor, and safeguarding the rights and interests of the disadvantaged groups in society is an important issue we are facing in shared development. We should establish an institutional guarantee system to safeguard the rights of people in equal participation and development, which is an important guarantee for achieving shared benefits.

The concept of shared development advocates common development and pursues common prosperity. Xi Jinping once stated that a self-perpetuating divide between the haves and have-nots was not acceptable. True happiness should be shared and enjoyed by all. Shared development is to eliminate the disparity and polarisation between the rich and the poor, realise the common development of the Chinese people, share the benefits, and create a better life and ultimately achieve common prosperity for everyone so as to realise the ideal state of common development and common prosperity of China and the rest of the world.

Notes

1 Xi Jinping, "Implementing the 2030 Agenda for Sustainable Development to Promote Inclusive Development," Xinhuanet, September 4, 2016, www.xinhuanet.com/world/2016-09/04/c_129268985.htm
2 "Xi Jinping Made Five Comments on Promoting the Building of the Belt and Road," Xinhuanet, May 14, 2017, www.xinhuanet.com/world/2017-05/14/c_129604239.htm

8
DEFICIT IN PEACE AND THE BELT AND ROAD

Yang Xiaoping

Elaboration on the concept of "deficit in peace" and development

On May 14, 2017, President Xi Jinping of the People's Republic of China attended the Belt and Road Forum for International Cooperation and delivered a keynote speech. He pointed out that: "Deficit in peace, development and governance poses a daunting challenge to mankind. This is the issue that has always been on my mind".

At present, the world is experiencing major development, transformation, and adjustment. The world is not peaceful, and the security environment in which we are living is still highly uncertain. There are signs of increasing hegemonism, power politics and neo-interventionism, and the dangers of war still exist. Local turmoils and conflicts and confrontations caused by territorial disputes and resource contention have occurred frequently. Terrorism is rampant, and there are increasing terrorist attacks in both developed and developing countries. All of these have seriously threatened or impacted the peace and stability of people's production and living environment and reduced people's perception of safety.

As traditional security actors, all countries are increasingly closely linked today, so it is difficult for a country to deal with these security issues alone by relying on its own strength. Almost all countries are plagued by deficit in peace, and no country is immune from it. In 2014, China proposed the new Asian security concept for the first time, whose core purpose is "Common, Integrated, Cooperative, and Sustainable". At the Belt and Road Forum for International Cooperation hosted by China in May 2017, President Xi employed this concept of security to the building of the Belt and Road Initiative. He stated that we should foster a new form of international relations featuring win–win cooperation; we should foster partnership of dialogue with no confrontation and friendship rather than alliance. At the 9th BRICS Summit held in September 2017, all participating countries frankly stated that there are incessant conflicts in some parts of the world and hotspot issues, and the intertwined threats of terrorism and lack of cyber security, among others, are posing huge "deficit" challenges to world peace.

The so-called "deficit in peace" means that there is a large gap between the realistic security environment we are facing and the ideal security environment, and we are paying a greater price for this gap. "Deficit in peace" stems from the following factors. (1) The problems left over by history, which are re-emerging and evolving under new backgrounds, and driven by various factors. (2) Interference from external forces. For whatever consideration, geopolitics, monopoly of resources and markets or values, if a preventive or punitive attack is launched without truly respecting a regional country and understanding the regional issues, this will inevitably cause great hidden dangers to regional security and become the main external source of regional political turmoil. (3) The failure of a country in its domestic democratisation transition and modernisation-seeking efforts can lead to the malfunction of the government, the rise of local powerful forces, or the seizure of power by military dictatorships, and the chaotic situation has become a trigger for a civil war or racial slaughter. Such civil strife may also extend beyond the borders of a country and become a source of instability in the entire region.

Therefore, the BRICS mechanism has tentatively decided to respond to "deficit in peace" by strengthening political security cooperation and work together to address the peace issue we are facing in global development. Specifically, the BRICS countries have established multi-level and multi-field dialogue channels, including the Meeting of BRICS High Representatives for Security Issues and the Meeting of BRICS Ministers of Foreign Affairs/International Relations, and have put in place the regular meeting mechanism for the permanent representatives to the multilateral institutions, convened the Foreign Policy Planning Dialogue, the Meeting of the Counter-Terrorism Working Group, the Meeting of the Cybersecurity Working Group, and the Consultation on Peacekeeping Operations, and strengthened communication and coordination on major international and regional issues.

China's new contributions to the world in response to a "deficit in peace"

Starting from building a community of a shared future for mankind, China is committed to fostering a new form of international relations featuring win–win cooperation. This is an attempt to build a world of lasting peace and is of great significance to world peace and development. It is reflected as follows.

First, we should weaken the "competition" and "zero-sum" attributes of current security issues. China proposes that mankind is a community of a shared future, advocates to foster partnership of dialogue with no confrontation and friendship rather than alliance, and pursues common, comprehensive, cooperative, and sustainable security. China proposes that major powers should respect each other's core interests and major concerns, keep their differences under control and foster a new form of relations featuring non-conflict, non-confrontation, mutual respect, and win–win cooperation. Big countries should treat smaller ones as equals instead of acting as a hegemon, imposing their will on others; no country should willfully wage wars or undermine the international rule of law. Nuclear weapons should be completely prohibited and thoroughly destroyed over time to make the world free of nuclear weapons. Guided by the principle of peace, sovereignty, inclusiveness, and shared governance, we should turn the deep sea, the polar regions, the outer space, and the Internet into new frontiers for cooperation rather than a wrestling ground for competition. We must be aware of the nature and prospects of the community of a shared future for mankind, and a country should gain its security on ensuring the security of others and world peace and create a security architecture featuring joint contribution and shared benefits.

Second, China will seize the opportunity provided by the Initiative, explore new opportunities, seek new drivers, expand new space for development, and actively provide public goods for world peace. At present, the Chinese government has established the "Five Principles of Peaceful Coexistence Friendship Award" and the "Five Principles of Peaceful Coexistence Scholarship of Excellence" to recognise and encourage more people and groups to uphold and promote the Five Principles of Peaceful Coexistence. China has vigorously urged the Shanghai Cooperation Organisation, the BRICS countries, and other cooperation mechanisms to play a role in security dialogue and cooperation, established a law enforcement security cooperation mechanism for the Mekong River Basin, launched the International Law Enforcement Cooperation Forum on Secure Corridor of the New Eurasian Land Bridge, and discussed the establishment of a new framework for international security cooperation. Meanwhile, China believes that multilateralism is an effective way to preserve peace and has established the China–UN Peace and Development Fund to support projects that are conducive to peaceful development. China has provided US$60 million of grant to support the building and operation of the African Standby Force and the African Capacity for the Immediate Response to Crisis. China is also the permanent member of the Security Council that has sent the most troops and peacekeepers. The Chinese people have contributed sweat and even precious lives for the world's peacekeeping.

Finally, with an open mind, China has actively enhanced synergies with other countries to jointly build the Belt and Road Initiative through consultation to meet the interests of all and cope with the deficit in peace through cooperation. At present, many countries have introduced their own economic development plans or visions, such as the Eurasian Economic Union of Russia, the Master Plan on ASEAN Connectivity proposed by ASEAN, and the Middle Corridor proposed by Turkey. China is advancing cooperation with many countries through promoting connectivity to produce "one plus one is greater than two" effects.

The significance of coping with a "deficit in peace" through the Belt and Road Initiative

A "deficit in peace" poses a daunting challenge to mankind. Facing the chaos in the world, the international community is "treating the symptoms rather than getting to the root of the problem". China proposes to jointly cope with this "deficit in peace" through the Belt and Road Initiative. This is China's solution for world peace and a Chinese voice sent to the international community.

China sticks to peaceful development as its strategic choice, follows the principle of seeking win–win cooperation, regards global partnerships as the best path, and takes the right approach to justice and interests. China has launched the Belt and Road Initiative as a practice to achieve shared growth through consultation and collaboration, to seek new drivers for development, to create new space for development, and to move towards the goal of building a community of a shared future for mankind. China is fully displaying the major country diplomacy with Chinese characteristics, Chinese styles, and in the Chinese way.

The development of China needs the world and the prosperity of the world needs China. At present, China's economic aggregate and relatively rapid growth rate determines that its contribution to world economic growth far exceeds the sum of developed countries and is the main driving force for world economic growth. China is determined and has the strength to steer a new round of globalisation. With "a community of a shared future for mankind" as its core concept, the Belt and Road Initiative as its strategic layout and overall path, and international financial innovations such as the AIIB as its tools, China will steer globalisation into a new stage of connotation reconstruction and joint participation of North and South.

"Expanding South–South cooperation" and "promoting North–South cooperation" advocated by China go hand in hand and let the world understand that developing countries should unite and cooperate and developing countries and developed countries are also an interconnected whole for development. The concept of "a community with shared future for mankind" is a new value guide. It advocates abandoning the hegemonic policies, rises above the old approach of zero-sum games, negates the law of the jungle, and opens up new roads for the development of civilisation through joint contribution and win–win cooperation. This is a great creation to change the world. Since 2017, this major concept has been successively written into the resolutions of the UN, the Security Council, and the Human Rights Council. It has become an important part of the discourse system of global governance, indicating that it has been universally recognised by UN member states and demonstrates China's great contribution to global governance.

The premise for China to jointly cope with the "deficit in peace" through the pursuit of the Belt and Road Initiative is to affirm and respect the characteristics and differences between countries. China advocates seeking harmony but not uniformity and rejects the old thinking of a strong country being bound to seek hegemony, winners-take-all, and alliance and confrontation. China strives to step over the estrangement of ideology and geopolitics, foster a new form of major-country relations featuring no conflict or confrontation, mutual respect and win–win cooperation, build a new form of international relations featuring mutual respect, fairness and justice, and win–win cooperation, and take the initiative to foster global partnerships. Win–win cooperation has become the logical starting point and core element of China's new logic in fostering international relations. It is not only the logic of the relationship between China and the world, but also the universal logic of international relations. It is also the innovation and transcendence of contemporary theories on international relations.

9
DEFICIT IN GOVERNANCE AND THE BELT AND ROAD

Wang Xiaoling

The meaning and presentation of a global "deficit in governance"

"Global governance" refers to the settlement of global issues through binding international rules in order to maintain a normal international political and economic order. On May 14, 2017, Xi Jinping stated in a keynote speech at the Belt and Road Forum for International Cooperation that "Deficit in peace, development and governance poses a daunting challenge to mankind".[1] The "deficit in governance" proposed by Xi Jinping vividly depicts the phenomenon that more and more global problems are emerging, but the global governance capacity of the existing international order and the existing global governance aspirations of major countries are declining.

As globalisation is deepening and more and more global problems are emerging, it is getting harder for the global governance ability of a single hegemonic power to meet real-world needs. Nevertheless, the emerging economies represented by the five BRICS countries are developing rapidly, and their contribution to global economic growth has exceeded 70%. The prevailing global governance rules fail to reflect such changes in power. Therefore, the prevailing governance rules are no longer applicable to the current global issues and changes in world power.

In 2016, when Donald Trump was elected as president of the United States, he announced the "America first" principle. The United Kingdom also announced it's intention to withdraw from the European Union. The core of the Western world has set off a wave of "counter globalisation" which has weakened the foundation of global governance. Ever since President Trump took office, he has not only threatened to withdraw from the multilateral trading system, but also threatened to withdraw from the existing regional economic cooperation mechanisms or renegotiate them. In June 2017, the United States announced its withdrawal from the Paris Agreement, and in December 2017, it announced significant cuts in its United Nations budget obligations. The most powerful country in the world has taken a passive or retreat attitude in global governance, which has greatly weakened the effectiveness of the existing global governance system.

The Western international political theories set out from "individuals" and believe that all individuals should pursue their own survival and prosperity and thus deduce that the initial state of the international community is the "Hobbes Forest where the strong prey on the weak". In line with such judgement, the international community would not be an organic whole but just a dynamic equilibrium formed by the constant games between individuals. When some emerging countries are rising and the balance of power is broken, the "Thucydides Trap" will emerge. After the two world wars, mankind had seriously pondered over the Thucydides Trap phenomenon, and on this basis, various international organisations and institutional arrangements had been developed to safeguard world peace. As all major powers in the world have possessed nuclear weapons and economic globalisation is deepening, the Western theories on international relations have also begun to develop towards "neoliberalism" and "constructivism". Even realism no longer sees the world as a simple world where the strong prey on the weak. However, as long as the "nation-state" is regarded as the basic unit of analysis in international relations and enhancing the interests of a nation-state is regarded as the rule of conduct of the international community, then competition and confrontation are the most basic international relations.

Under the hegemonic order, individuals do not have the moral consciousness to safeguard the overall interests of the international community. There has always been a tense relationship between individuals and between the interests of individuals and the interests of the international community. Egoistic behaviours are believed to be reasonable, even if they undermine the interests of the international community as a whole. Based on such judgement, when a hegemonic power feels that its own interests cannot be safeguarded, it will choose to jump off the "global governance" and "globalisation" ships. Also based on such judgement, the hegemonic power will establish a hierarchical system of alliances to safeguard its own interests, identify who its friends and enemies are, and suppress and discriminate against those who hold different views. Therefore, the global governance dominated by a hegemonic power can never achieve "fairness and justice" and "mutual benefit and win–win outcomes".

The wisdom of China and Chinese concept for the international order

To solve the "deficit in governance", we need to introduce a new concept for the international order, and the wisdom of China can provide references for the world. At present, the United States and other Western powers are losing their enthusiasm to deal with global governance, and many small countries also lack the capacity to respond to it. In such a case, the international community more than ever needs the wisdom of China. The Chinese leaders have proposed the concept of "a community of a shared future for mankind" for the international order and launched the Belt and Road Initiative.

From the perspective of relation, the world view of traditional Chinese culture sees the world as an organic whole. Different countries are harmonious yet different, interdependent and mutually symbiotic. From the perspective of "relation", "zero-sum game" is irrational while "mutual benefit and win–win" are rational.

The Chinese culture has never been dominated by a particular religion. It has experienced long-term mutual integration among different ethnic groups and has a compatible and inclusive attitude towards other cultures. In the traditional Chinese culture, there is no need to eradicate the "heretics", and instead we regard diversity as an opportunity for development. The Chinese culture has unshakable self-confidence, and does not pursue expansion, but follows the principle of "not restricting others by etiquettes". Meanwhile, the Chinese culture pursues practical values, emphasises practice, and is open to the solution of problems. Precisely because of this, China respects the diversity and particularity of the world cultures and respects each country's own choice of road.

In the early years after the founding of the PRC, the world was in the shadow of the Cold War. Although China was not recognised by the capitalist world, it had never given up expanding its diplomatic relations. In 1953, China proposed the "Five Principles of Peaceful

Coexistence", which for the first time explained to the world the Chinese expected international order: mutual respect for sovereignty and territorial integrity, mutual non-aggression, non-interference in each other's internal affairs, equality and mutual benefit, and peaceful coexistence. Just because China pursued "peace and development" and believed the world would move towards "peace and development", China resolutely embarked on the road to reform and opening up in the 1970s and actively carried out economic cooperation with Western developed countries. China pursued the non-alignment and non-confrontation diplomatic policy and creatively proposed "one country, two systems" on the issue of Hong Kong. China proposed "shelving disputes and seeking joint development" on the issue of the Diaoyu Islands. When China had international disputes with other countries, it consistently called for dialogue to solve problems.[2] After the end of the Cold War, China adopted proactive and meticulous diplomatic efforts and had determined the legal borders with neighbouring countries in a peaceful way. At that time, the United States had united with Western countries to impose sanctions on China. China had always adhered to the principle of "non-confrontation" and "seeking cooperation". It has established "partnership" with more and more countries and has actively participated in many international cooperation mechanisms.[3] Since the beginning of the twenty-first century, China gradually moved towards the centre of the world stage and began to elaborate on China's concepts for the international order. We proposed the concept of "a harmonious world" and introduced to the world its historical and cultural traditions of "upholding harmony" and opposing "wantonly engaging in military aggression". China has introduced to the world the Chinese wisdom of "seeking harmony but not uniformity" and "harmony generates vitality".[4]

Nowadays, China's concept for the international order has the following characteristics: first, we believe that cooperation and mutual benefit is the core of international relations. With the deepening of economic globalisation, more and more global problems are emerging, and the basic way to solve global problems is cooperation. Cooperation and mutual benefit are two sides of a coin: the purpose of cooperation is to achieve mutual benefit, and mutual benefit is the foundation of cooperation. Second, we regard sharing responsibility and interest as the basic code of conduct for the international community. Sharing responsibility and interest does not mean that the responsibilities and interests of all countries are evenly distributed, because there are differences in interest demands between big and small countries and between developed and developing countries, and there are differences in their ability to assume international responsibilities. We must accommodate the interests of different types of countries and their global governance capabilities and promote the democratisation of the international community. Third, we must take common and sustainable comprehensive development as our goal. Development is a comprehensive indicator, which apart from economic growth also involves contents such as education, employment, medical care, pensions, relatively fair income distribution, and environmental sustainability. In developing countries, development issues are mainly reflected as poverty, disease, environmental degradation, and so on. In developed countries, development issues are largely reflected as uneven income distribution. On global scale, development issues are mainly reflected as failure of many developing countries to obtain development opportunities.[5]

The Belt and Road Initiative makes up for deficit in global governance

At the World Economic Forum Annual Meeting in 2017, Xi Jinping proposed four major models of global governance: "we should develop a dynamic, innovation-driven growth model; we should pursue a well-coordinated and interconnected approach to develop a model of open and win–win cooperation; we should develop a model of fair and equitable governance in keeping with the trend of the times; we should develop a balanced, equitable and inclusive development model". If, so to speak, "a community of a shared future for mankind" is a good way to deal with a deficit in governance, then the Belt and Road is the most important practice of this concept.

The Belt and Road Initiative provides the world with public infrastructure, helps the countries along the routes to achieve connectivity of infrastructure and further promotes the integration of developing countries into economic globalisation. The "going global" of Chinese enterprises has facilitated the economic cooperation between China and the host countries and related regions. New multilateral financial institutions under the Belt and Road Initiative such as AIIB have also promoted interconnected global growth. With the Belt and Road Initiative as a platform, China has actively organised the international forums such as the Belt and Road Forum for International Cooperation to amplify the voice of cooperation and peace in the "counter-globalisation" trend.

What the Belt and Road contributes to global governance goes far beyond providing the above-mentioned public goods. More importantly, it demonstrates a new concept for the international order and a new rule for international governance. Under the Belt and Road Initiative, we have established the mechanism for jointly building through consultation to meet the interests of all. China will not seek hegemony even though it is becoming more and more powerful and will only act as the initiator rather than the head of the countries along the routes. We will reject dominance by just one or several countries and will not indulge in self-aggrandisement or bully the weak. We emphasise that all countries have equal say in international affairs. For example, China has advocated the establishment of the AIIB but did not seek "one-vote veto power". The Belt and Road Initiative attaches importance to open cooperation but will not seek alliance; it emphasises communication but not confrontation; and insists on mutual assistance, cooperation, and win–win development. In the pursuit of the Belt and Road Initiative, China emphasises following the right approach to justice and interests, encourages "altruistic behaviours" and takes the lead in doing so, assumes responsibilities that match China's capability, and accumulates social capital for the international community. In the pursuit of the Belt and Road Initiative, we practice a new path for global governance and insist on acting as the "ameliorator" of the current international system to send out Chinese voices, add Chinese elements and propose China's solutions for governance cooperation in a gentle and flexible way. For example, the AIIB, which is identified as a supplement to the existing international financial system, will work closely with the World Bank and the Asian Development Bank and has won widespread recognition from the international community.

Notes

1 Xi Jinping, "The Severe Challenge Facing All Human Beings Is the Issue I Have Been Thinking about", Xinhuanet, May 14, 2017.
2 Chen Shuisheng, "'Harmonism': A Probe into the Theory of International Relations with Chinese Characteristics," *Public Diplomacy Quarterly*, Issue 3, 2015, p. 20.
3 Zhang Yunling, "China and Its Relations with Surrounding Countries: The Logic of the Community of Destiny," *People's Tribune*, February 2014, pp. 36–37.
4 Jin Yingzhong, "From 'Harmonious Culture' to the Concept of Emerging International Relations," *Social Science*, Issue 11, 2015, p. 20.
5 Li Xiangyang, "The Value of the Times of the Concept of Community of Shared Future for Mankind," *People's Daily*, March 8, 2017.

PART II

Historic inheritance

10
NAMING OF THE SILK ROAD

Dong Xiangrong

In the ancient Eurasian and African continents, several separate and self-contained civilisations had gradually formed after thousands of years of social evolution on the basis of agricultural production, mainly including the ancient Chinese civilisation in the valleys of the Yellow River and the Yangtze River, the Mesopotamian civilisation on the Tigris and Euphrates rivers in Mesopotamia in Western Asia, the Indus Valley civilisation, and the ancient Egyptian civilisation on the Nile River Valley in Northern Africa. These centres of civilisation, distributed on the Old Continent, were separated by mountains, deserts, and oceans. For example, the Qinghai–Tibet Plateau, the birthplace of the Yellow River and the Yangtze River, known as the "roof of the world", separates China from India. Located in the hinterland of Asia, the Taklimakan Desert stretches more than 1000 kilometres from east to west and more than 400 kilometres from north to south. In the untraversed desert, severe wind and dust storms occur frequently, and the weather is either scorching hot or freezing cold. The complicated landforms and climatic conditions limited the depth, breadth, and frequency of exchanges between these centres of ancient civilisation, especially exchanges between China and other centres of civilisation. Most of the limited exchanges took place along the edges of the plateaus and the deserts, which had led to the formation of several routes for personnel exchanges and goods circulation. This is the basic background for the formation of the Silk Road. For thousands of years, people on the Eurasian continent exchanged needed goods on these roads, starting the historical journey of mutual learning among the civilisations.

During the ancient Greek period in the first century AD, these land-based trade routes between China and Central Asia, Western Asia, and even Europe and Africa had already appeared in the Western literatures. It was reported that the ancient Chinese discovered earlier that wild silkworms could spin silk to make cocoons and that filaments taken from silkworm cocoons could be used as raw materials for making fabrics. The Chinese domesticated wild silkworms and made fine fabrics with silk. Silk fabrics in ancient China were introduced to Europe very early. Europe used to call China with the name of the country that originated from the word "silk". Some scholars who have carried out textual source research for this word argued that the ancient Greeks and Romans translated the word "silk" into "Ser" and called China "Seres" (meaning "silk country"). In the major languages of later Europe, the words expressing "silk" all stemmed from "Ser", such as "Silk" in English, "Soie" in French and "Seide" in German.¹ Roughly at the end of the first century, the ancient Greek geographer, Marinos of Tyre, recorded a road heading to the country of Seres. To traffic in silk, the merchants set out from the Euphrates River, passed through the Stone Tower, and finally arrived in Sera (Luoyang), capital of the state of Seres. The documents which Marinos's writings were based on were from the Macedonian businessman Maes Titianos, who had sent his subordinates to the country of Seres to do business. The ancient Greek geographer Claudius Ptolemaeus (Ptolemy) (around 90–168 AD) wrote the *Geography* around 150 AD and included the commercial routes recorded by Marinos in the book.² Ptolemy's records of the Silk Road had a great influence on the later studies of Orientalism in Europe. He revised some of Marinos's statements, such as the distance from the course of the Euphrates River to the Stone Tower and then to Sera City. Ptolemy also mentioned in *Geography* that "the later journey was carried out under the protection provided by the king of the region to all travelers" and the journey from the Stone Pagoda to Sera City was "accompanied by a severe storm". Marinos himself also mentioned that "they stayed repeatedly on the way due to the wind storms".³ Roman writer Pliny the Elder wrote in his book *Natural History* in 77 AD that the Seres were "famous for the wool they produced in the forests. They sprinkle water on the leaves of certain trees to wash down the white villus, and then their wives complete the two processes of spinning and weaving. As the people of remote areas have performed the complex work, it is possible for Roman noblewomen to appear in the public in transparent dress". He also mentioned in the book that the Seres "did not communicate with other peoples and waited for deals at the door … By the lowest reckoning, India, Seres and the Arabian peninsula take from our Empire 100 millions of sesterces every year: that is how much our luxuries and women cost us … In all kinds of iron, the iron from Seres was at the top of the list. The Seres also exported iron while exporting clothing and leather goods".⁴ Thus, the Europeans at the time just picked up what had been heard on the way about how the Chinese raised silkworms and did spinning and weaving. However, some descriptions were close to the harsh climatic conditions and the social environment where banditries and robberies were rampant on the Silk Road from Central Asia to the Central Plains of China.

In the period under the reign of the King of Great Qin called Andun in the second century, Pausanias stated in *Description of Greece* that the silks used by the Seres to make clothes were not extracted from the bark but from a kind of insect the Greeks called "Ser". They could "create a kind of filaments wrapping around their feet".⁵ It seems that it was not until the second century AD that Europeans had a basic understanding of silk.

As there were more exchanges between the East and the West and more extant documents became available, the West had an increasingly better understanding of the East. In 1271, the 17-year-old Italian traveler Marco Polo (1254–1324) visited China with his father and left China in 1291. In the 1298 sea war, Marco Polo was captured and sent to prison. In prison, he dictated the stories of his travels to a cellmate, Rustichello da Pisa, who later became an Italian litterateur. Rustichello da Pisa wrote down the stories told by Marco Polo and they both completed *The Travels of Marco Polo* (also known as *The Description of the World*, *The Marvels of the World*, *Oriente Poliano*, etc.), which records his oriental travelogues in detail. This book was very popular in Europe, greatly enriching the Europeans' understanding of the East and provoking European navigators' obsession with the East in the fifteenth century. It was said various manuscripts of the book, including Italian edition, French edition and Latin edition, were circulating in Europe in the early fourteenth century when Marco Polo was still alive. At the end of the fifteenth century, before the advent and spread of movable-type printing to Europe, there had been at least 138 manuscripts, and these manuscripts have been preserved so far.⁶ After the advent of European-style printing, the first printed German edition of the book was published in 1477, and its second printed Latin edition was published in 1485. According to relevant documents, the navigator Columbus had a Latin edition of Marco Polo's *The Travels of Marco Polo* printed in 1485. He often read the book and made 264 side notes in a total of 475 lines.[7] Although some scholars have questioned whether Marco Polo had ever been to China,[8] the influence of *The Travels of Marco Polo* on future generations is beyond doubt. It is an important document of European historics and geography, and especially compared with the concise descriptions and speculations in previous European documents on the East, the descriptions of the Oriental World in *The Travels of Marco Polo* are rich and colourful, making a historic contribution to promoting the exchanges between Europe and Asia.

Since the beginning of the modern times, European scholars have begun to show their interest in China. These "orientalists" had an interest in all aspects of China, including western China. Among the orientalists in the nineteenth century, the British geographer Henry Yule focused his study on the history of communications between China and the West. He devoted substantive attention to the study of the early manuscripts of *The Travels of Marco Polo* and the archives concerning the activities of ancient Italian missionaries and travellers in China and Central Asia and had written a two-volume book entitled *Cathay and the Way Thither: Being a Collection of Medieval Notices of China*, which was published in 1866. The first volume of the book has also studied various records of ancient Greece and Rome about the state of Seres. An excerpt from Ptolemy's *Geography* is an appendix to the book. Although Yule did not use words like "Silk Road" in his book, he first conducted detailed textual criticism and research on "the Road to Seres". In 1871, Yule published his two-volume annotated edition of *The Travels of Marco Polo* in London, the title of which was literally translated as *The Book of Ser Marco Polo, the Venetian: Concerning the Kingdoms and Marvels of the East*.

Yule's *Cathay and the Way Thither: Being a Collection of Medieval Notices of China* and his annotated edition of *The Travels of Marco Polo* had a great influence on the German historical geographer Ferdinand von Richthofen. Von Richthofen made 7 expeditions to China from 1868 to 1872, leaving footprints in East China, North China, Central China, South China, Northeast China, Southwest China, and Shaanxi Province in the northwestern region. He made a field trip to the transport routes in Central and West China described in *Cathay and the Way Thither: Being a Collection of Medieval Notices of China*. After finishing his expeditions in China, von Richthofen returned to Germany in 1872 and served as Professor of Geology at the University of Bonn in 1875. Von Richthofen devoted himself to composing the results of his expeditions in China into a book entitled *China: The Results of My Travels and the Studies Based Thereon*. The first volume of *China* was published in Berlin in 1877. In Volume 1 of *China*, von Richthofen again discussed Ptolemy's *Geography* according to Yule's book *Cathay and the Way Thither: Being a Collection of Medieval Notices of China* and discussed "the road to Seres" as recorded by Marinos. In the first volume of *China*, von Richthofen mentioned Siedenstrasse des Marinus, which was the first time in history that the term *Seidenstrasse* (Silk Road) was used. The term *Seidenstrasse* was a new word coined by von Richthofen by combining the German words *Seiden* (silk) and *Strasse* (road). Its Chinese translation is "Silk Road".[9]

When Volume 1 of *China* was published, it shocked Western geographers and orientalists. In 1878, the Royal Geographical Society of London awarded von Lichhofen with the most prestigious medal of the society, the Founder's Medal. Von Richthofen published Volume 2 of *China* in 1882 and Volume 4 of *China* in 1883 when he was alive. In 1905, von Richthofen died in Berlin, and Volume 3 (1912) and Volume 5 (1911) of *China* were collated, edited, and published later after his death. *China*, a five-volume masterpiece, laid the foundation for von Richthofen's important position in the Chinese geographic world in the nineteenth century. *Ferdinand von Richthofen's Travel in China (Ferdinand von Richthofen's Tagebücher aus China)* is a compilation of his diaries, manuscripts, and a large number of personal letters written by him during his expeditions in China. The German edition of the book was published in Berlin in 1907, and its Chinese translated edition was published by the Commercial Press in 2016, enabling Chinese readers to get a full understanding of China in the nineteenth century from the eyes of a foreigner and fully know the real intention of von Richthofen's expeditions in China.

In Volume 1 of *China*, von Richthofen defined the "the Silk Road" as the network of trade and communication routes linking China to Central Asia and India along which silks were traded from 114 BC to 127 AD. After the term "Silk Road" was coined, it was widely accepted by academic circles and gradually translated from German into the languages of various countries in the world, such as "Silk Road (Silk Route)" in English, "Routes de la Soie" in French, and "絹の道" in Japanese. Regarding the communication network between ancient China and the outside world, because different goods were traded, some researchers also called it "the Road to China", "the Fur Road", "the Road of Silk and Spice", "the Road to Belief", and "the Slave Road". Some scholars gave other names based on the means of transportation or the regions they passed through, such as "the Camel Road", "the Desert Road", "the Oasis Road", "the Steppe Road", "the Ancient Tea-Horse Road", etc. These names are also reasonable. However, only the wording of "the Silk Road" had spread most widely, becoming a synonym for economic and cultural exchanges between ancient Eastern and Western countries. After the wording of "the Silk Road" was widely accepted, its time span, connotation, and extension have all undergone great changes. It is largely used to broadly refer to the routes for Eastern and Western economic and cultural exchanges between ancient China and the African and Eurasian continents.

Notes

1 Wang Jiqing, "The Origin of the Phrase 'Silk Road,'" *Journal of Dunhuang Studies*, Issue 2, 2015.
2 Ibid.
3 Coedes, G. ed., Geng Sheng trans., *A Collection of Works on Far East of Greek Latin Writers*, Zhonghua Book Company, 1987, pp. 19–21.
4 Coedes, G. ed., Geng Sheng trans., *A Collection of Works on Far East of Greek Latin Writers*, Zhonghua Book Company, 1987, pp. 9–13.
5 Coedes, G. ed., Geng Sheng trans., *A Collection of Works on Far East of Greek Latin Writers*, Zhonghua Book Company, 1987, pp. 53–54.
6 Boies Penrose, *Travel and Discovery in the Renaissance*, 1420–1620, Harvard University Press, Cambridge, 1952, p. 22. Cited indirectly from Zhang Jian's "Marco Polo and Geographical Discovery," *World History*, Issue 4, 1994, pp. 51–56.
7 Henry Yule, Henri Cordier, *The Book of Sir Marco Polo*, Vol. 2, London, 1926, p. 558. Cited indirectly from Zhang Jian's "Marco Polo and Geographical Discovery," *World History*, Issue 4, 1994, pp. 51–56.
8 For example, Frances Wood, *Did Marco Polo go to China?* Secker & Warburg, London, 1995.
9 Wang Jiqing, "The Origin of the Phrase 'Silk Road,'" *Journal of Dunhuang Studies*, Issue 2, 2015, pp. 21–26.

11

A BRIEF HISTORY OF THE SILK ROAD

Dong Xiangrong

The prehistory of the Silk Road

In the history of China, the Silk Road was closely related to the Western Regions. The term "Western Regions" or "Xiyu" (西域) first appeared in *The Book of Han Chronicle on the Western Regions*. In the Western Han Dynasty, the term "Western Regions", in a narrow sense, referred to the vast region to the west of Yumenguan and Yangguan, to the east of Congling (the Pamir Plateau), to the north of the Kunlun Mountains and to the south of Lake Balkhash, i.e. the region under the jurisdiction of the General-Governor Office for the Western Regions in the Han Dynasty. In a broader sense, it covered Central Asia, Western Asia, India, the Caucasus, and the countries along the Black Sea to the west of Congling, including the areas now known as Afghanistan, Iran, Uzbekistan, and the countries along the Mediterranean Sea, and even Eastern and Southern Europe. The Western Regions were divided into two parts by Mount Tianshan; most of the habitants lived around the Tarim Basin. In the early years of the Western Han Dynasty, there were "thirty-six states and kingdoms": on the southern edge, there were Loulan (now known as Shanshan County near Lop Nor), Guqiang, Qiemo, Yutian (now known as Hetian in Xinjiang Province), and Shache etc., which were habitually referred to as "the southern countries"; on the northern edge, there were Gushi (now known as Anterior Cheshi and Posterior Cheshi in Turpan Basin), Weili, Yanqi, Qiuci (now known as Kuqa), Wensu, Gumo (now known as Aksu in Xinjing Provine), Shule (now known as Kashgar), etc., which were called "the northern countries".

The *Records of the Grand Historian Treatise on the Dayuan* says that "However, this kind of exchanges was initiated by Zhang Qian, so the emissaries who were sent to various countries in the Western Regions later were all called the Marquess of Bowang". The Grand Historian (Taishi Gong 太史公) honored Zhang Qian's journey to the Western Regions in the Western Han Dynasty as "opening an overland route linking the East and the West" because he thought highly of Zhang Qian's role as an explorer in the exchanges between the Central Plains and the Western Regions. In fact, many archaeological discoveries have proved that the cultural pathways connecting the Central Plains and the outer regions via the northwest regions had been opened before Zhang Qian's diplomatic mission to the Western Regions. These pathways played a role of commodity circulation and cultural dissemination. The Eastern and Western cultures in prehistoric times bore many similarities, thus people had speculated the existence of exchanges between the East and the West based on cultural similarities.

Before the Silk Road was formed, several jade transport routes were extending in Eurasia. Hetian jade was produced in Yutian under the Kunlun Mountains, and Qinghai was rich in Kunlun jade. The jade produced here was transported eastwards to the Central Plains and westwards to Europe. A large number of Hetian jade devices have been unearthed in the northern Red Mountain cultural site with a history of over 6000 years and in the southern Liangzhu cultural site. In the documents of the pre-Qin period, there are a large number of records on the legends of interactions between the kingdom of Queen Mother of the West and the hinterland based on the medium of Kunlun jade. For example, it is recorded in the *Biography of King Mu* that after seeing the Queen Mother of the West, King Mu of Zhou returned with "three chariots of jade plates and ten thousand jade articles". Hetian jade was exported westwards to the countries in West Asia, and the jade used in ancient artefacts unearthed in Babylon and Syria, and the jade used in the Stone Age wares unearthed in European countries were all products of Yutian. The tribes and geographical names in the Western Regions recorded in *The Classic of Mountains and Seas*, *Guanzi* and *Huainanzi* show to varying degrees that the economic and cultural exchanges between the Central Plains and the countries in the Western Regions in the pre-Han period had occurred long ago.

According to historians' textual research, from the remote ages to the pre-Qin period, some land routes to the West had gradually been formed. There were three main routes in the east section. The first route started in the north from Guanzhong (now known as Henan), went across the Yin Mountains in Monan to Juyanhai Oasis, to the northern and southern foot of Mount Tianshan and extended to the Western Regions. It is the so-called "Juyan Road" or "Steppe Road". The second route started from Guanzhong, went across Mount Lushan, passed through the Hexi Corridor and extended to the Western Regions. It is the so-called "Hexi Road". The third route started from the south foot of Mount Qilian and extended to Qinghai Lake along the Huangshui River, then went across the Qaidam Basin and extended to Ruoqiang in Xinjiang. It is the so-called "Qinghai Road".[1] The Qinghai Road went across Mount Kunlun, which was rich in jade, and via this route, a large amount of Kunlun jade was transported to the hinterland, West Asia, and even Europe. It became "the Jade Road", connecting ancient Chinese and Western civilisations. After the Qin and Han Dynasties, with the development of Chinese silks and textiles, silk gradually replaced jade and became the main medium for economic and cultural exchanges between China and the West. In a sense, the ancient Jade Road was the forerunner of the Silk Road.

Zhang Qian's journey to the Western Regions and the Silk Road

The national security and diplomacy of the Han Dynasty to a large extent centred on how to deal with the nomadic Xiongnu Empire in the northern grasslands. The objective of Zhang Qian's first mission was to seek a military alliance with the Greater Yuezhi (月氏) (modern Tajikistan) so as to execute a cooperative attack against the Huns (Xiongnu). Zhang Qian made his second journey to the Western Regions with the aim to ally with Wusun against the Huns. Although Zhang Qian failed to finish the major missions in his two expeditions, he obtained a great deal of information about the Western Regions, which aroused the interest of Emperor Wu of the Han Dynasty in the Western Regions. A large number of emissaries began to travel back and forth between the Central Plains and the Western Regions, greatly promoting the exchanges between the Central Plains and the Western Regions. From the perspective of the size of transport before and after Zhang Qian's missions to the Western Regions, it is not an exaggeration to say that Zhang Qian had "opened the road" to the Western Region.

The *Records of the Grand Historian Treatise on the Dayuan* recorded in detail the process of Zhang Xi's expeditions to the Western Regions. In the first year of his reign, Emperor Wu of the Han Dynasty intended to ally with the Greater Yuezhi to fight against the Huns and Zhang Qian was enlisted to serve as the emissary. In 138 BC, Zhang Qian left Chang'an and later departed from Longxi with a delegation of over 100, accompanied by a Xiongnu guide named Ganfu (甘父). Unfortunately, Zhang Qian and the delegation were captured by the Huns when they reached the Hexi Corridor. The famous archeologist Pei Wenzhong stated that "Gansu was an important area in the northwest regions, bordering on the Central Plains of China, and it was the base of Chinese culture's westward advancement. This area also served as a traffic artery for the introduction of Western cultures into China. Such was the case in the historic times and also in the prehistoric period. It was actually a necessary phenomenon resulting from the geographical conditions".² This is also the reason why Zhang Qian made his departure to the Western Regions from Longxi. After Zhang Qian was captured, he was escorted to see the Chanyu (Xiongnu chief). After learning that Zhang Qian was heading towards Yuezhi, the Chanyu said: "Yuezhi is on our northern side, is it possible from the Han court to send its emissaries to Yuezhi? If we want to send emissaries to Nanyue (南越), will the Han court allow us to do so?" Obviously, the Huns were deeply sceptical of Zhang Qian's act and even the Han court's intention, but they did not regard it as a completely hostile act. Ten years later, Zhang Qian was eventually able to escape after the Huns relaxed surveillance over him. Zhang Qian and his men made their way westwards to Dayuan, went through Kangju, and eventually arrived at the land of the Greater Yuezhi. However, after learning the intention of the Han court, the Greater Yuezhi had almost no desire to make an alliance against the Huns. Zhang Qian failed to finish the mission to make a military alliance with the Greater Yuezhi and had to begin his return trip. On the way back, Zhang Qian followed a southern route, but was again captured by the Huns and detained for more than a year. In the Third Year of Yuanshuo (126 BC), a riot broke out among the Huns, providing Zhang Qian an opportunity to escape and return to Han. This trip lasted as long as 13 years.

Although he failed to finish the mission to make a military alliance with the Greater Yuezhi in his first expedition, Zhang Qian brought back a great deal of first-hand information on the Western Regions, which greatly enriched the Han Empire's knowledge of the Western Regions. Emperor Wu of the Han Dynasty rewarded him and conferred him the title Tai Zong Dai Fu (太中大夫). Afterwards, in the sixth year of Yuanshuo, Zhang Qian followed General Wei Qing in a major military raid against the Huns. As he knew where the army should stop to rest, the army was able to avoid exhaustion, and Zhang Qian was therefore conferred the title of the Marquess of Bowang by the Emperor. In the seventh year of Yuanshuo, Zhang Qian served as a chamberlain for the palace garrison (Weiwei) and departed from the right side of Peking together with General Li Guang to fight against the Huns. General Li Guang's troops suffered heavy casualties. Zhang Qian was sentenced to death because he could not arrive on schedule. He had to atone for his misdeeds and became a civilian. Later, Emperor Wu of the Han Dynasty often asked Zhang Qian the situation in Daxia (Bactria) and other regions. Zhang Qian mainly introduced the conflicts between Wusun and the Huns after Wusun reached the side of the Yili River and suggested that Emperor Wu should summon Wusun to return to Dunhuang and ally with the Han to fight against the Huns. This is the famous strategy of "cutting the right arm of the Huns". Meanwhile, Zhang Qian also proposed that after allying with Wusun, Han should make other small countries in the Western Regions into its vassal states. Emperor Wu of Han took on board his proposals. In 119 BC, Emperor Wu of Han dispatched Zhang Qian to the Western Regions for the second time in an attempt to persuade Wusun to return to the old land of Hexi and fight against the Huns together with

Han. Zhang Qian led a group of about 300 people and took a great number of cows and sheep and a lot of silks as presents to the King of Wusun. Zhang Qian himself directly arrived in Wusun, and his deputy emissaries arrived in Kangju, Dayuan, and the Grester Yueshi. In the second year of Yuanding (115 BC), Zhang Qian returned to Chang'an and was conferred the title of "Da Hang Ling" (foreign minister), which was among the Nine Ministers (九卿). He died the next year. Although Wusun did not want to relocate to the old land, he sent emissaries to accompany Zhang Qian to the Han Empire and presented Wusun horses to the Han Empire. After Zhang Qian's diplomatic missions, there were frequent exchanges between the Central Plains and Dayuan.

Zhang Qian's missions to the Western Regions produced remarkable demonstrative effects, so he gathered many followers. According to the *Records of the Grand Historian*, since the Marquess of Bowang was conferred a high social status and great wealth for opening up the road heading to foreign countries, the bureaucrats and soldiers who followed the emissaries all scrambled to submit letters to elaborate the precious things, weird things, and matters of greatest importance in foreign countries and required to serve as emissaries. Emperor Wu of Han believed that foreign countries were very far away and not everyone was willing to go there, so he accepted their requests, gave them tallies (with two halves, made of wood, bamboo, jade, metal, issued by a ruler to generals, envoys, etc., as credentials in ancient China), recruited officials and ordinary people without asking them their origins, provided them with assistants and dispatched them on diplomatic missions to expand communication with foreign countries. In order to expand these trade routes, Emperor Wu of Han actively dispatched these emissaries to foreign countries. To keep the Silk Road unimpeded, the Han army defeated Loulan, besieged Wusun and Dayuan by riding on the wave of strong military might of victory, and extended Han's mountain passes to Yumenguan.

In general, the Han Empire began contact with the Western Regions for military reasons, but it had more than just military influence after the road to the Western Regions was opened up. It blazed a road in the Western Han Dynasty that originated from Dunhuang, ran through Yumenguan, extended to Xinjiang and then linked Xinjiang with Central Asia and West Asia. In a few centuries, it played the role of a major land pathway connecting the East and the West. Silk was only one of many commodities that were transported through this pathway. Besides commodity trade, these routes played a more important role in technological and cultural exchanges. The species originally native to the Western Regions, such as alfalfa, walnut, grape, pomegranate, horse bean, etc., were grown in the Central Plains. Songs and musical instruments like the urheen of the Western Regions enriched the cultural life of the Han people. The Han army based in Shanshan and Cheshi used karez to open up the wasteland, which was promoted gradually in these regions. At that time, the countries ranging from Dayuan to Anxi did not produce silk or cast iron, and these skills were introduced by the emissaries and soldiers of the Han Dynasty to these countries later. The western spread of silk and iron metallurgy greatly promoted the development of human civilisation.

The prosperity of the Silk Road during the Sui and Tang Dynasties

The Silk Road defined by von Richthofen was almost the Silk Road in its narrowest sense. In the view of the time line, it refers to the period from 114 BC to 127 AD. In the view of space, it refers to the space from China of the Han Dynasty to Central Asia and India. After the term Silk Road was accepted, few people have ever defined the Silk Road in such a strict sense, but instead the ancient network of communication routes that connected China and the outside world has generally been referred to in a broader sense as the "Silk Road".

The Silk Road flourished during the Sui and Tang Dynasties. Emperor Yang of Sui embarked on a western tour to reclaim wasteland and held a grand gathering on the steppe under Mount Yanzhi (in today's Shandan County, Gansu) in Zhangye. The grand gathering was recorded in *Comprehensive Mirror for Aid in Government*: "The emissaries from the remaining aboriginal tribes of more than 20 countries attended the feast in the company of Their Royal Highnesses". Merchants and emissaries from various countries gathered in unprecedented numbers. Emperor Yang of Sui issued an imperial edict to set up the four prefectures of Xihai, Heyuan, Shanshan and Qiemuo. The Silk Road in the Tang Dynasty was also very active. Delegations and business travellers arrived at Chang'an via the Silk Road. American scholar James A. Millward said, "At that time, Chang'an, the capital of the Tang Empire, was inhabited by various monks and merchant groups from Persia, India, Central Asia, South East Asia and Northeast Asia, including Christians, Buddhists, Manichaeans and Muslims. In the first half of the Tang Dynasty, the Chinese people were pleased to accept various articles and cultures from the broad world, and they were so open-minded that no one could match them in hundreds of years afterwards".[3]

The decline and rejuvenation of the Silk Road

The Overland Silk Road was greatly affected by the arrival of the era of ocean navigation. After the sailboats of Spain, the Netherlands, the United Kingdom, and other countries began to sail across the oceans, the importance of the Overland Silk Road where horses and camels were the commonly used means of transport had greatly diminished. Compared with land-borne trade, long-distance, sea-borne trade had remarkable cost advantages. Although the trade and exchanges on the Overland Silk Road were not completely terminated, their importance was greatly reduced. The southern Marine Silk Road was increasingly active. China's ships set sail from coastal ports such as Guangzhou, Quanzhou, and Xuwen to the Malay Archipelago, to the Arabian Sea, and even to Africa's east coast. The Maritime Silk Road had become the main route for exchange between China and the outside world. Zheng He in the Ming Dynasty made seven voyages to the Western oceans and had travelled to more than 30 countries, further expanding the route of the Maritime Silk Road. With the implementation of the ban on maritime trade during the Ming and Qing Dynasties, the development of China's sea routes had also stagnated.

After the beginning of the twenty-first century, the rise of China has brought about changes in geopolitics and economic structure. How East Asia, as the engine of world economy, is closely linked with South East Asia, Central Asia, Europe, and Africa has become a new epochal topic. The timeliness of railway and highway transport, the improvement of the security situation along the routes, and the expansion of trade demands among countries along the routes have all laid the foundation for Silk Road to thrive again. When Chinese President Xi Jinping visited Central and South East Asia in 2013, he proposed the initiative of jointly building the Silk Road Economic Belt and the 21st-Century Maritime Silk Road, which have attracted close attention from all over the world. The British scholar Frankopan stated that President Xi Jinping "is recalling people's memories of prosperity that they had been long been familiar with. His ideas on promoting trade development, investing in overland and sea routes and establishing cooperative relations with various countries are based on common knowledge. That is, today's criss-crossing traffic trunk lines in Asia that connect China with Europe, the Caspian Sea, the Caucasus Mountains, the Persian Gulf, and every corner of South East Asia follow exactly the footprints of travellers and sages who rushed about with their goods and their beliefs in those years". Undoubtedly, the difference lies in speed—the speed of our travels, the speed of bulk trades, and the speed with which we communicate and learn.[4]

Notes

1 Zhang Dezu, "The Ancient Jade Stone Road and the Qinghai Route of the Silk Road," *Journal of Qinghai Normal University* (Philosophy and Social Sciences Edition), Issue 5, 2008, pp. 56–59.
2 Pei Wenzhong, *The Northwest Regions in the Prehistoric Times*, Shanxi People's Publishing House, 2015, p. 26.
3 James A. Millward, Ma Rui trans., *The Silk Road*, Yilin Press, 2017, p. 33.
4 Peter Frankopan, Shao Xudong, and Sun Fang trans., *The Silk Roads: A New History of the World*, Zhejiang University Press, 2016, Chinese version of the Preface, p. 6.

12
THE OVERLAND SILK ROAD

Dong Xiangrong

In Volume 1 of *China: The Results of My Travels and the Studies Based Thereon* published in 1877, the German geographer von Richthofen defined the "the Silk Road" as the network of trade and communication routes linking China to Central Asia and India on which silks were traded from 114 BC to 127 AD. Von Richthofen's definition of "the Silk Road" was widespread. On this basis, the connotation of this term was constantly expanding. It is generally used to refer to the network of overland communication routes linking ancient China and West Asia, South Africa, and even Europe through the hinterland of Asia.

The Overland Silk Road was not a fixed route but a communication network consisting of a number of trunk and branch routes. These routes changed continuously along with changes in historical geography and social environment. The Overland Silk Road mainly consisted of three routes: one is the route related to Zhang Qian's expeditions to the Western Regions, also known as the Desert Silk Road; the second route is the Steppe Silk Road; and the third route is the Southern Silk Road, which mainly refers to the southwestern overland route linking China to the outside world.

The basic trend of the Desert Silk Road

In *A General History of China*, Chinese historian Bai Shouyi stated that

> in order to develop contacts with countries in Central Asia, West Asia and South Asia, the Han Empire built roads to the west of Lingju (now known as Yongdeng in Gansu) and set up pavilions and posts to facilitate business trips. According to historical records, the road to the Western Regions at that time roughly ran through the four counties of Hexi, passed through Yumenguan or Yangguan and Bailongdui and reached Loulan (i.e. Shanshan) from which it was divided into two parts: the northern route and the southern route. The northern route headed westwards from here, extended along the Peacock River to Quli (now known as Korla in Xinjiang), Wulei and Luntai, then passed through Qiuci (now known as Kuqa in Xinjiang), Gumo (now known as Aksu in Xinjiang) and reached Shule (now known as Kashgar in Xinjiang). The southern route originated from Yuni City in Shanshan, ran southwestwards along

the Qarqan River, passed through Qiemo, Yumi, Yutian (now known as Hetian in Xinjiang), Pishan and Shache and reached Shule. It extended westwards from Shule, ran through Congling, extended southwestwards to the Greater Yuezhi (mainly in Afghanistan), further westwards to Anxi (Parthia in Iran), to Tiaozhi (now known as Iraq), and finally reached Daqin (east of the Roman Empire). Starting from Shule and crossing Congling, it could reach Dayuan (Fergana of the former Soviet Union) and Kangju (Samarkand of the former Soviet Union). In the Eastern Han Dynasty, the Han Empire waged a series of military battles against the northern Huns, forcing the northern Huns to move westwards, and the Han Empire thus opened up a new northern road. This new road headed northwards from Dunhuang to Yiwu, then ran through Liuzhong, Gaochangbi, the City of Jiaohe of Anterior Cheshi (now known as Turpan in Xinjiang) in the west, passed Yanqi and reached Qiuci via Mount Tianshan, and then ran along the former northern route to Shule. These important routes facilitating the communication between China and the West are the well-known Silk Road.[1]

During the Sui Dynasty, Turk occupied a vast area between the Western Regions and the Caspian Sea. Tuyuhun in today's Qinghai Province also invaded and harassed the Hexi Corridor. The official and non-governmental exchanges between China and the Western Regions and even Europe were greatly hindered. However, the exchanges between the Sui Empire and the peoples of the countries along the Silk Road were not seriously affected. Emperor Yang of Sui summoned merchants from the Western Regions to promote continuous mutual trade in Zhangye City. According to the preface to *History of Sui Dynasty Records of the Western Regions*, during the reign of Emperor Yang of Sui, he sent Weijie and Du Hangman to the countries in the Western Regions, and they got agate cups when arriving in Ji Bin (an area near Tashkent now), Buddhist scriptures when arriving in Rajagaha, and 10 dancers, lion skins, and fire rat fur when arriving in the state of Shi (史国).

The Overland Silk Road in the Tang Dynasty experienced its peak and rapid decline. Emperor Taizong of Tang, also known as his original name Li Shimin, defeated the East Turkic Tuyuhun and made the southern and northern areas of the Gobi Desert surrendered. Emperor Gaozong of Tang, Li Zhi, also destroyed the Western Turks and set up the two Protector-Generals in Anxi and Beiting. The territory of the Great Tang Empire stretched from the Korean coast in the east to Dachangshui in the west. In the Tang Dynasty, official and private contacts in which the Tazi Empire served a bridge between the East and the West were fully expanded through the Silk Road. In the eastern section of the Silk Road, the northern and southern areas of the Gobi Desert and various countries in the Western Regions built a large number of branches to the Silk Road, which were also known as "the Cantian Khan Road". Tazi (大食, the Arab Empire) and the Eastern Roman Empire also sent emissaries to Chang'an to communicate with China. The places such as Dunhuang, Yangguan and Yumen became the "overland sea markets". After the Anshi Rebellion, the Tang Empire began to decline. Tufan (吐蕃) crossed the Kunlun Mountains and occupied most of the Western Regions, and the Overland Silk Road gradually declined. Coupled with the rise of the Maritime Silk Road, the cost to performance ratio of trade and exchanges by sea was higher, and Guangzhou, Quanzhou, and other places were emerging as the core areas of foreign exchanges. Although business travellers from some Western countries still travelled via Central Asia and the Western Regions on land, the role of the Overland Silk Road was significantly reduced compared with that of the Maritime Silk Road.

The Overland Silk Road

The Steppe Silk Road

The Steppe Silk Road is also known as "the Northern Silk Road", "the Fur Road", "the Tea Road", "the China Road", and "the Ironware Road". Chinese scholar Geng Sheng believes that in terms of the time when the Silk Road was opened, the Northern Steppe Silk Road and the Northwest Gobi and Oasis Silk Road basically existed in the same period. As far back as the seventh to second centuries BC, the communication trunk routes crossing the Eurasian continent were not the Gobi and Oasis Silk Road but the Steppe Silk Road.[2]

The Steppe Silk Road originated from the Hetao area of the Yellow River in China and gradually extended northwestwards through the Mongolian steppes. It crossed the Altai Mountains, extended northwards along the Irtysh River valley, ran through the southern Siberian steppes, reached the Scythians on the northern shore of the Black Sea and then stretched to Central Asia and Europe. On the Steppe Silk Road, the Mongolian steppes and the Altay area in Xinjiang played a pivotal role. Zhang Qian's expeditions to the Western Regions promoted the prosperity of the Gobi and Oasis Silk Road, while the Steppe Silk Road was snubbed. However, after the Maritime Silk Road was opened in the fifteenth and sixteenth centuries, the Northwestern Silk Road was declining, but the Steppe Silk Road was not completely replaced by the sea routes. From the end of the nineteenth century to the beginning of the twentieth century, the trade in tea, fur, porcelain, and Chinese herbal medicines between China and Russia through the northern Steppe Silk Road still flourished. Until the middle of the twentieth century, due to the dramatic changes in the situation in China and Russia and the Cold War, the northern Steppe Silk Road began to become sluggish. In terms of the geographical areas and ethnic groups covered by the Steppe Silk Road, it partially overlapped with the Gobi and Oasis Silk Road to the Western Regions in the west, intersected with it in the north and had unique areas in the east.[3]

The Southern Silk Road

According to *Records of the Grand Historian Treatise on the Dayuan*, Zhang Qian said that "When I was in Daxia (Bactria), I saw Qiong bamboo rods and Shu cloth. 'Where did you get these things?' I asked. The people of Daxia State said, 'Our merchants bought them from the State of Yuandu (now known as India). The state is several thousand miles southeast of Daxia'." Zhang Qian saw Qiong bamboo rods and Shu cloth in Daxia, indicating that a lot of cargo from southwestern China had already been introduced to other countries via the State of Yuandu. The southwestern route of the Silk Road was expanded by the Han Empire originally because the former route that ran through the Hexi Corridor to Daxia was dangerous and the Qiang people and the Huns were important obstacles to the above route. But "heading from the Shu area, there might be a straight road along which there were no intruders". Emperor Wu of Han had two measures: sending the army to repel the Huns and ensure the unimpeded flow on the Northern Silk Road; dispatching emissaries to set off in four directions to explore the routes from the Shu area to the Southwestern Yi (Southwest China). According to *Records of the Grand Historian Treatise on the Dayuan*, the four routes were: "one route originated from Mang (駹), one from Ran (冉), one from Xi and one from Qiongbo (邛、僰), each of which ran one or two thousand miles". It was far from a smooth process to blaze the southwestern routes. On the northern route, travellers might be stopped by the Di (氐) and Zuo (笮) peoples, and on the southern route, they might be stopped by the Xi (巂) and Kunming (昆明) people. The ethnic minority groups in Kunming and its surrounding areas did not have monarchs. They were fond of robbing and stealing and always killed and robbed the emissaries of the Han Empire, and no one had ever successfully passed through these routes. However, during this process, it was said that there was a state called Dianyue that was over 1000 miles to the west, and the merchants of the Shu area had ever sold their goods there, so the Han Empire began contact with the state of Dianyue.

Chinese scholar Luo Erhu believes that the Southwestern Silk Road had existed before the middle of the Western Han Dynasty, but the Han Empire did not open up the whole length of this road until the twelfth year of the reign of Emperor Yongping in the Eastern Han Dynasty (69 AD). It headed south from Chengdu and ran through Yongchang Prefecture (today's western Yunnan) to reach Yuandu (身毒) (now known as India) and beyond. At that time, many roads heading to this ancient road were built, as were prefecture- and county-level administrative offices and various transportation and communication facilities, there was a large number of immigrants, and troops were stationed to ensure smooth traffic flow on the roads and efficient mail and message delivery.[4]

After the southwestern pathway was expanded in the Han Dynasty, three major routes were gradually formed.[5] The first one was the "Shu–Yuandu Route" heading to Myanmar and India. It consisted of the eastern and western branches. The western branch, known as the Lingguan Road or the Old Yak Route (gu maoniu dao, 古旄牛道), extended westwards from Chengdu to Qionglai and ran southwards through Mingshan–Ya'an–Yingjing–Hanyuan–Ganluo–Yuexi–Xide–Mianning–Xichang–Dechang–Miyi–Huili–Panzhihua–Yongren, Yunnan–Dayao–Dali. The eastern branch, known as the Wuchi Route, originated from Chengdu, extended southwards along the Minjiang River and ran through Leshan–Qianwei–Yibin–Wuchidao–Daguan, Yunnan–Weining, Guizhou–Zhaotong, Yunnan–Qujing–Kunming–Chuxiong–Dali. The western and eastern branches combined into one in Dali, ran westwards to Baoshan–Tengchong–Myitkyina, Myanmar (or ran southwards from Boshan to Ruili and entered Bhamo, Myanmar), and then ran through Assam in northeast India to the Indus–Ganges River Plain and reached Central Asia and West Asia via Pakistan and Afghanistan.

The second route was the river–land route to Vietnam. Its eastern section, known as the Jinsang Road, extended from Shu to Central Yunnan, crossed the Nanpanjiang River via Mile, ran through Wenshan and southeast Yunnan, followed the Panlong River and reached Hanoi via Ha Giang and Tuyen Quang. Its western section, known as the Butou Road, headed from Shu to Dali in western Yunnan, followed the Red River to Hanoi, Vietnam, and entered the sea from Hanoi. It was the oldest waterway connecting Yunnan and the Indo-China Peninsula. Compared with "the Shu–Yuandu Route", the trend of the river–land route to Vietnam in southwestern China could be easily identified because it covered fewer areas and there were waterways connecting the cross-border ethnic groups.

The third route is the Ancient Tea-Horse Road connecting China with Nepal and India, which covered the Sichuan–Tibet Road from Sichuan to Tibet, i.e. Chengdu–Ya'an–Kangding–Tibet–Changdu–Nepal–India, and the Yunnan–Tibet Road from Yunnan to Tibet, i.e. Pu'er – Dali–Lijiang–Shangri-la–Bangda–Changdu–Nepal–India. In the territory of China, it basically overlapped with the routes of today's Sichuan–Yunnan Railway and Yunnan–Tibet Highway. The Ancient Tea-Horse Road was an important route in the Tibetan areas of southwest China connecting Sichuan and Yunnan with South Asian and Central Asia and the outside world. Domestically, the Ancient Tea-Horse Road was a pathway for business and trade, and internationally, it was an important passage for foreign trade with India and South Asia, playing an important role in business exchanges between southwest China and South Asia.

The historical significance of the Overland Silk Road

Before Zhang Qian's missions to the Western Regions in the Han Dynasty, there had been direct or indirect commodity exchanges and people-to-people exchanges between China and Central Asia, West Asia, South Asia, and Western Europe. After Zhang Qian's missions to the Western Regions, the Silk Road, as an important official road, was opened and became a major pathway for exchanges between official missions and commercial groups. In over 1000 years from the Han and Tang Dynasties to the Song and Yuan Dynasties, the Silk Road had been an important official pathway for China to strengthen contacts and conduct economic and cultural exchanges with the countries and peoples of Central Asia, West Asia, South Asia, and Europe. Exotic music, dancing, painting, sculpture, architecture and other arts, astronomy, calendar calculation, medicine and other scientific and technological knowledge, Buddhism, Mazdaizm, Manichaeism, Nestorianism, Islam and other religions were introduced to China through the Silk Road; China's textile, paper-making, printing, gunpowder, compass, porcelain and other techniques, as well as Confucian and Taoist thoughts, also spread to the West through the Silk Road. The Silk Road linked China with the two distant civilisations of India and Western Europe. While enabling commodity exchanges, it had promoted the spread of cultural knowledge and also made people's values and beliefs more diversified. For a long period of time, the Overland Silk Road was the main link between China and the outside world and had special significance, especially in early cultural exchanges.

Meanwhile, it is noteworthy that in the pre-industrial society when camels, horses, and manpower were used as the main means of transportation, commodities that could be traded on the Overland Silk Road were limited due to geographical and meteorological conditions such as mountains, deserts and winds, as well as social and environmental conditions such as the presence of many small countries and rampant banditry along the way. Because of this, when evaluating the historical role of the Silk Road, the famous historian Li Bozhong said that "Generally speaking, from the time the Silk Road was opened in the reign of Emperor Wu of Han until the establishment of the Ming Dynasty, except in the first half of the Tang Dynasty and the Yuan Dynasty, this Silk Road was actually in a half-opened and half-closed state during most of the times, and it was basically closed in the Eastern Han Dynasty and the Song Dynasty. This also proves that it was not economically significant".[6]

Notes

1 Bai Shouyi, Editor-in-Chief, *A General History of China*, Vol. 4, Shanghai People's Publishing House, 1995, pp. 403–404. Cited indirectly from *The History of Guangdong Maritime Silk Road*, Huang Qichen ed., Guangdong Economic Publishing House, 2003, Preface, pp. 2–3.
2 Geng Sheng, "The Frenchman Who Inspected the Steppe Silk Road", *Journal of North Minzu University* (Philosophy and Social Sciences), Issue 6, 2009, pp. 18–28.
3 Ibid.
4 Luo Erhu, "China's Southwestern Silk Road in the Han and Jin Dynasties," *Journal of Sichuan University* (Philosophy and Social Sciences), 2000, Issue 1, pp. 84–105.
5 Qu Xiaoling, "Southwest China and Ancient Roads: A Brief Introduction of the Southern Silk Road and Its Studies," *North West Ethno-national Studies*, Issue 1, 2011, pp. 172–179.
6 Li Bozhong, *Fire Guns and Books of Accounts: China and East Asia in the Era of Early Economic Globalization*, Joint Publishing Company, 2017, p. 38.

13

THE MARITIME SILK ROAD

Dong Xiangrong

The Overland Silk Road was not a route but a communication network. Similarly, the Maritime Silk Road was not merely a route, but a network consisting of multiple sea routes. Geographically, it mainly included the Eastern Maritime Silk Road and the Southern Maritime Silk Road. The Eastern Maritime Silk Road was developed earlier, while the Southern Maritime Silk Road was of greater importance.

The Eastern Maritime Silk Road

The Eastern Maritime Silk Road was originally a maritime pathway for disseminating the Central Plain culture between mainland China and the Korean Peninsula and the Japanese archipelago. According to *Records of the Grand Historian House of Song Wei Zi* and *Records of the Grand Historian Annals of Zhou*, Jizi (箕子) exhorted Emperor Zhou of Shang to be attentive with state affairs, but Emperor Zhou of Shang did not listen. Jizi pretended to be mad to express his frustration and worry about the empire under the rule of Emperor Zhou of Shang. Emperor Zhou of Shang mistook that Jizi was really crazy, so he imprisoned Jizi and demoted him into a slave. After Emperor Wu of the Western Zhou Dynasty conquered Emperor Zhou of the late Shang Dynasty, he released Jizi and enfeoffed Jizi as the ruler of Chaoxian (朝鲜), historically called "Jizi Chaoxian". According to the *Book of Han Treatise on Geography*, when Emperor Wu of the Western Zhou Dynasty enfeoffed Jizi as the ruler of Chaoxian, he "educated his people propriety and justice, as well as silkworms growing and silk weaving". Thus, it can be seen that since the Shang Dynasty, the silk-weaving culture of the Central Plains had begun to spread to the Korean Peninsula. During the Qin and Han Dynasties, the port of Dengzhou in Shandong was ever an important port from which Qin Shi Huang, the first emperor of the Qin Dynasty, and Emperor Wu of Han set sail for sea cruises and prayed for god-blessing. According to *Records of the Grand Historian*, *Book of Han*, and *Comprehensive Mirror for Aid in Government*, Emperor Wu of Han made 8 sea cruises to Donglai. Frequent sea cruises and god-blessing activities had promoted the development of local shipbuilding, navigation and port industries and created conditions for non-governmental trade and exchanges between the Central Plains and the Korean Peninsula and Japan. Archeological discoveries show that a large amount of Chinese silk fabrics were unearthed from more than 1000 Han tombs in Rakrang District, Pyongyang, North Korea.

These are important tangible evidence that Chinese silk fabrics were introduced to North Korea in large quantities in the Han Dynasty.

According to Volume 8 of the *Chronicles of Japan* in the eighth year of the reign of Emperor Chuai (199 AD), someone who claimed to be a descendant of the eleventh generation of Qin Shihuang introduced silkworms from the east of Baekje on the Korean peninsula to Japan. This was roughly close to the time when "the state of Wa (ancient Japan) produced hemp and mulberries and found the solution for weaving fine fabrics" as recorded in *Records of the Three Kingdoms Records of Wei*. This was the time when the expertise for silkworm raising and silk production began to be introduced from China to Japan.[1] In 238 AD, Queen Himiko of Yamataikoku in the state of Wa (ancient Japan) sent emissaries to Luoyang, the capital of Wei, via the Korean Peninsula to present gifts such as Banbu. Emperor Ming of Wei bestowed upon her the title "Queen of Wa Friendly to Wei" along with the gifts including exquisite silk fabrics: 5 pieces of crimson brocade with dragon designs, 10 pieces of crimson tapestry with dappled pattern, 50 lengths of bluish-red fabric, 50 lengths of dark blue fabric, 3 pieces of blue brocade with interwoven characters, and 50 lengths of white silk, etc. This is the earliest document recording the introduction of various kinds of Chinese silk fabrics to Japan as diplomatic gifts.[2] During the Southern Dynasty, China sent silk-weaving and tailoring women workers, Han Zhi, Wu Zhi, Xiong Yuan, and Yu Yuan, to Japan to pass on skills and techniques, thus promoting the development of the Japanese silk industry.

According to *The New History of the Tang Dynasty Geography Records*, an important route of the Eastern Maritime Silk Road "sailed from Dengzhou to Goryeo and the Bohai Course". It was the route of the Maritime Silk Road that headed from Dengzhou Port to the Korean peninsula and Japan. The maritime route had two branches: one headed from Dengzhou Port, crossed the Bohai Straits to Lushunkou in Liaoning, then ran along the Liaodong Peninsula to the mouth of the Yalu River, then ran southwards along the Korean Peninsula, and crossed the Tsushima Strait to Japan. The other branch started from Dengzhou Port, passed Bajiao and Zhifu, crossed the Yellow Sea to Incheon in North Korea, then ran southwards along the Korean Peninsula, and crossed the Tsushima Strait to Japan.[3] The Tang Dynasty opened a southern route that directly crossed the sea from the regions south of the Yangtze River to Japan without passing through the Korean Peninsula. It headed directly to Japan from Yangzhou, Chuzhou, Suzhou, and Mingzhou (now known as Ningbo), and the voyage was greatly shortened. During the Southern and Northern Song Dynasties, the northern regions were occupied by Liao and Jin, and the political and economic centre moved from the south to the north. The silk industry flourished in Jiangsu and Zhejiang, shipbuilding and navigation were also well developed, so Mingzhou had gradually developed into an important trading port along the Eastern Maritime Route.

During the Tang and Song Dynasties, China's silk and shipbuilding industries developed rapidly, creating favourable conditions for overseas trade exchanges through the Maritime Silk Road. The maritime trade and exchanges between the Tang Empire and Japan and North Korea were more frequent than previously. Japan sent its emissaries to the Tang Empire to nominally present diplomatic tributes, and the Tang Empire bestowed upon them gifts in return, but these were actually official trade in a disguised form. In addition to official trade, the folk exchanges between China and Japan were also very active. After the arrival of the Great Navigation Age, the volume of trade between China and Japan also increased significantly. Historian Li Bozhong stated that "in the 16th and 17th centuries, China was the main supplier of silk and silk products in world trade, and Japan, Portugal and the Netherlands were the main buyers. China was the main supplier of ceramics, and Japan, Portugal, Spain and the Netherlands were the main buyers. China was the main supplier of sugar, and Japan, the Netherlands and the United Kingdom were the main buyers".[4] Zheng Ruozeng, a military strategist in the period of reign of Emperor

Jiajing of the Ming Dynasty, made outstanding contributions in resisting the Wa pirates. His works included *An Illustrated Compendium on Maritime Security* (*Chou Hai Tu Bian*), *Compilation of Maps of Japan* (*Ri Ben Tu Zuan*) and *The Jiangnan Strategies* (*Jiang Nan Jing Lue*). With regard to Japan's demand for raw silk from China, Zheng Ruozeng once stated that "silk is used for weaving cloth with unique patterns in the country. When there was a court meeting or a banquet, the people there would weave cloth by themselves for their own use. Chinese silk cloth is only used for inner clothes. If foreign ships are not accessible, there will be no silk to weave cloth".[5] This shows that the industrial chain of the silk industry had been formed between China and Japan at that time.

The Southern Maritime Silk Road

The Southern Maritime Silk Road was a main transport route for travelling from mainland China to South East Asia, South Asia, and even Europe and Africa by sea. According to Volume 28 of *Book of Han Treatise on Geography*, in the period of the reign of Emperor Wu of Han, Chinese sea boats carrying onboard gold and silk fabrics departed from the Leizhou Peninsula, and made a long voyage to Kanchipuram in the southern part of the Indian peninsula in the Indian Ocean via Vietnam, Thailand, Malaysia, and Myanmar to exchange for pearls, gems, and other specialties. Then they returned from Sri Lanka. This is the earliest record of Chinese silk being introducing as a commodity to the above-mentioned countries.[6] In the following millennium, silk became an important gift presented in return to the diplomatic ambassadors from different countries in tribute trade and international exchanges. According to Volume 28 of *The Book of the Later Han Biography of Daqin*, "In the trade between Daqin and Anxi and Tianzhu on the sea, there were 10 times of profits … The emperor of Daqin wanted to send emissaries to the Han Empire to carry out direct trade with Han. But Anxi wanted to sell color fabrics from the Han Empire to Da Qin, so it intentionally blocked the route". Some scholars have pointed out that Chinese silk was introduced to the West through the Silk Road in the Western Regions, but because Anxi tried to monopolise the silk trade, it blocked this traditional Silk Road, forcing China (where the silk was produced) and Rome (where silk was the most widely consumed) to open up the sea route.[7] In fact, the maritime route was opened probably not just for the sake of Anxi. More likely, the maritime route itself was more cost-effective than the overland route when navigation technologies had developed sufficiently. On the Maritime Silk Road, porcelain became an important commodity. It is hard to imagine how such heavy-weight, fragile products like porcelains could travel along the Overland Silk Road in large quantities.

Ports such as Guangzhou, Quanzhou, and Xuwen played an important role in the Southern Maritime Silk Road. According to *The New History of the Tang Dynasty Geography Records*, there was a sea route that was referred to by Jia Dan as "the sea route from Guangzhou to foreign countries". During the Tang Dynasty, there were two major routes from China to West Asia and eastern Africa: one started from Guangzhou, ran through the central and southern coastal areas of Vietnam and the nearby islands, crossed the Singapore Strait, passed through the Java Island, the Sumatra Island and the Nicobar Islands to Sihaladipa (now known as Sri Lanka), then ran along the west coast of the Indian Peninsula to Ubullah at the mouth of the Euphrates River via the Persian Gulf, and stretched from here overland to its termination—the city of Baghdad in Iraq. The second route was the other extension of the first one. After the above route reached the west coast of the Indian peninsula, it crossed the Indian Ocean to Sanlam (now known as Tanzania) in the eastern part of Africa, went north through dozens of small countries to Ubullah and finally converged with the first route. The sea route to foreign countries connected China with South East Asia, South Asia, Western Europe and even Africa. In addition to silk and other

Chinese products, technologies including the compass, gunpowder, paper-making and movable type printing were also spread to foreign countries. Therefore, the Maritime Silk Road was an important passage for cultural exchanges between China and Western countries.

In the mid-Tang Dynasty, the proportion of foreign trade in silk through the sea route increased. The appointment of the official who was usually set in Guangzhou to specially manage city ship business implied that the importance of private commerce in the silk trade had risen. Especially in the Tang and Song Dynasties, with the development of shipbuilding and navigation technologies, the trade along the Maritime Silk Road flourished even further. The great ships such as "Yu Da Niang" and "Cang Bo" were well-known in the Tang Dynasty. The large ships made in the Song Dynasty were longer and could carry hundreds of people and food for use in one year. The ships also carried onboard the most advanced navigation equipment in the world at that time and began to navigate with a compass. The Yuan Dynasty government actively promoted the trade policy in which "the imperial court built ships and provided ships and capital to the merchants it has selected to carry out the trade of goods. The imperial court takes 70% of the profits, and the merchants take 30%". It went a step further than the practice in the Song Dynasty that rewarded the development of overseas trade. The Yuan Empire established the city ship transport department in Quanzhou and Hangzhou and the city ship management department in Qingyuan (Ningbo), Shanghai, Ganpu, Wenzhou, and Guangzhou. At that time, Quanzhou became a world-famous commercial port. China's silk, porcelains, and other commodities were exported to North Korea, Japan, South East Asia, and South Asia and even to West Europe and Africa. Medicinal materials, sand gold, brass, spices, jewelry, ivory, rhinoceros and other commodities were constantly shipped from these countries to China.

The Ming Dynasty played a unique role in the development of the Maritime Silk Road. First, the great navigator Zheng He's voyages to the Western oceans in the Ming Dynasty created the greatest feat in the history of Chinese navigation. Second, the Ming Dynasty began to impose the sea ban and chose to close its door on the occasion of the arrival of the world's major aviation era, throwing China from the regional centre to the margin of the world system.

Between 1405 and 1433, Zheng He led seven long voyages to more than 30 countries and reached the ports on the east coast of Africa and along the Red Sea. When arriving in each place, Zheng He exchanged porcelain, silk and other items for local products, or presented them to the local kings. On his return trips, he invited the ambassadors of different countries to visit China. In this way, more and more ambassadors came to China. By the time of the fifth return, the ambassadors from as many as 17 countries had accompanied the fleet to China. In 1413, Calicut in India dispatched more than 1200 ambassadors and entourages to China, which was the first time in history. This was also rare in the history of Sino-foreign relations. The ambassadors brought all kinds of special products from their countries as gifts, and the gifts presented by China in return were nothing more than silk. In order to reward foreign ambassadors, large quantities of silk were once transported from Nanjing to Beijing for later use. According to the relevant records, "on the day of Gengyin in August of the 3rd year of the reign of Emperor Xuande (1428), Zheng He and Wang Jinghong et al., the guardian eunuchs of the emperor's temporary palace in Nanjing, were ordered to store 100,000 bolts of silk and 230,000 bolts of cotton cloth in the imperial storehouse, and the officials of the Board of Revenue and Population were ordered to send them to Beijing".[8]

In addition to the official trade carried out by Zheng He's fleets in the Ming Dynasty, the coastal merchants in Fujian and Guangdong still travelled to South East Asia by raft to do business, despite the sea ban. After the ban was lifted in 1567, the greatest number of maritime merchants from Fujian went to the Luzon Island to do business, and they established many Chinese communities overseas. In the Philippines occupied by the Spanish colonists, there was a specific Chinese district called "Jiannei", meaning "raw silk market". Merchant ships from China's coastal ports such as Zhangzhou and Quanzhou were loaded with all kinds of raw silk and silk fabrics, Chinese merchants exchanged them for silver coins from Spanish colonists in Manila and other places, while Spanish colonists transported Chinese silk and other goods to Mexico and carried silver coins from Mexico when they returned to the Philippines, or sold Chinese silk and other commodities in Spain. It is estimated that between 1565 and 1820, Mexico delivered 400 million pesos of silver to Manila, most of which had flowed to China. China was originally a country with insufficient silver output. Since Spain occupied Manila in 1571, China imported "Eagle Ocean" (Mexican silver coins) that weighed 26.856 g each from Mexico through Manila, and these silver coins circulated in parallel with the Chinese-made silver coins, becoming the legal standard currency. This played an important role in the social economy and currency circulation since the Ming and Qing dynasties.[9]

The sea ban and the decline of the dominant power of the Maritime Silk Road

At the end of the Yuan Dynasty and the beginning of the Ming Dynasty, Japan was divided into several separatist vassal regimes that attacked each other. The feudal lords who failed in the war organised warriors, merchants, and rogues (i.e. the Wa pirates) to carry out armed smuggling, robbery, and harassment in the Korean peninsula and coastal areas of China. In response to this, during the reign of Emperor Hongwu, Zhu Yuanzhang ordered to imposeprohibition on private foreign trade (the sea ban) in order to prevent the nuisance of coastal warlords and pirates. In the beginning, the sea ban was targeted at commercial intercourses (commercial ban), which prohibited the Chinese from going abroad for doing business and also restricted foreign merchants from trading in China (except paying tributes). During the reign of Emperor Yongle in the Ming Dynasty, despite the feat of Zheng He's voyages to the West, only certain countries or tribes were allowed to trade with China in a tributary form, and no other private overseas trade was allowed. Later, as the Wa pirates were rampant, the sea ban policy became more stringent. Although playing a role of self-protection, it greatly hindered the development of Sino-foreign exchange. During the reign of Emperor Longqing, the Ming government adjusted its policies and allowed people to go abroad for business, which was called historically "Longqing's Opening to Foreign Trade". After the lifting of the sea ban, Chinese–foreign trade and exchange entered a new phase. After the Qing Dynasty, in order to ban and cut the ties between the anti-Qing forces on the southeast coast and foreign countries, the Qing court issued 5 bans in 1655, 1656, 1662, 1666, and 1675, prohibiting private overseas trade. It was not until the Qing army occupied Taiwan in 1683 that Emperor Kangxi accepted the request of officials from the southeast coast and stopped the Qing government's sea ban policy of the previous period. In the twenty-third year of the reign of Emperor Kangxi (1684), the Qing government officially opened the coastal areas of Guangdong, Fujian, Zhejiang, and Jiangsu to foreign trade and set up 4 customs offices in Guangzhou, Zhangzhou, Ningbo, and Yuntaishan. This was the period of the "Four Customs Clearance System". Although the sea ban was lifted, Kangxi did not encourage the Chinese people to go abroad and trade with the West. In his view, "China will probably be invaded by the foreign countries, such as the Western countries, after thousands of years. This is my inference". In the twenty-second year of his reign (1757), Emperor Qianlong ordered to close the ports of Ningbo, Zhangzhou, and Yuntaishan and only opened the port of Guangzhou. This was the period of the "Single Port Commerce System".

After the implementation of the "Single Port Commerce System", the import and export trade between the Qing Empire and other countries continued to grow year by year. From the late Qianlong era to the outbreak of the Opium War, the British trade in Guangzhou increased by 80%, while the United States' trade almost tripled. At that time, Guangzhou, thanks to its booming foreign trade, showed a very prosperous scene.

Historian Liu Yingsheng once stated that "Zheng He's voyages to the Western Oceans were the peak but also the last performance in ancient Chinese marine undertakings. It can even be called the swan song of ancient Chinese navigation which later witnessed a cliff-like fall".[10] In fact, the so-called "decline of the Maritime Silk Road" does not mean a decline in the volume of trade between China and other countries through the sea routes, but the decline of the dominant power of the Silk Road. That is to say, due to the repeated sea bans in the Ming and Qing Dynasties, China lost the opportunity to master the dominant power of international trade in the great navigation era, and it was unable to withstand the Western hardships and canons while striving to close its door. This was the background of the outbreak of the Opium War.

Notes

1. Chen Yan, "A Brief Analysis of the 'Maritime Silk Road,'" *Historical Research*, Issue 3, 1982, pp. 161–177.
2. *Records of the Three Kingdoms Records of Wei*. Vol. 30, Chronicle of East Yi, cited indirectly from Chen Yan's "A Brief Analysis of the 'Maritime Silk Road,'" *Historical Research*, Issue 3, 1982, pp. 161–177.
3. The Chronicles Compilation Committee of the History of Penglai City, Shandong Province, *Chronicle of Penglai County* [M], Jinan: Qilu Press Co., Ltd, 1995, p. 377. Cited indirectly from Zhu Long and Dong Yuhua's "Dengzhou Port and the Oriental Maritime Silk Road," *Journal of Ocean University of China* (Social Science), Issue 4, 2004, pp. 19–23.
4. Li Bozhong, *Fire Guns and Books of Accounts: China and East Asia in the Era of Early Economic Globalization*, Joint Publishing Company, 2017, pp. 58–61.
5. *An Illustrated Compendium on Maritime Security*, Vol. 2, Complete Library in the Four Branches of Literature, pp. 51–55. http://blog.sina.com.cn/s/blog_4943247e0102dv81.html. "A Study of Fujian Silk Industry in the Ming Dynasty" (omitted).
6. Chen Yan, "A Brief Analysis of the Maritime Silk Road," *Historical Research*, Issue 3, 1982, pp. 161–177.
7. Ibid.
8. Ibid.
9. Ibid.
10. Liu Yingsheng, "The Apocalypse of the Silk Road: Lessons and Implications of the Decline of Ancient Silk Roads," *Reference News*, May 3, 2017.

14

SILK ROAD AND EXCHANGES AMONG DIFFERENT COUNTRIES

Dong Xiangrong

In Sima Qian's *Records of the Grand Historian The Biographies of Merchants*, there is a proverb that says "You don't go a hundred miles to peddle firewood; you don't go a thousand miles to deal in grain". On the long, ancient commercial roads that were blocked by mountains, what kind of cargos were worth being transported thousands of miles away for trading? These items must meet the following conditions. First, they were luxury goods with high values or high profits or some irreplaceable necessities; second, they could be kept for a long time and be easily transported. Based on the historic records, the main goods traded on the Silk Road include: silk, jade, spices, tea, horses, salt, medicinal herbs, porcelain, etc. The exchanges of goods and people naturally led to exchanges of technical knowledge, animal and plant species, religious beliefs, literature and art with goods and people as carriers. In fact, to a large extent, the latter is more significant than the former.

Commodity exchanges on the Silk Road

The continental Silk Road connected the civilisation rims that were blocked by mountains and deserts in East Asia, West Asia, South Asia, North Africa, and Europe. The differences in these civilisation rims were mainly due to the differences in wild animals and plants domesticated by humans. The American scholar Jared has pointed out 5 regions that had successfully domesticated wild animals and plants in the early days of mankind, including: Southwest Asia, also known as the Near East or Fertile Crescent; China; Mesoamerica; the Andes of South America, and possibly the adjacent Amazon Basin as well; and the eastern United States. It is said that in Southwest Asia, wheat, pea, olive, sheep, goat, and other plants and animals had been domesticated by around 8500 BC. China had domesticated rice, millet, pig, silkworm, and other plants and animals by 7500 BC. In the Indus Valley region of the Indian subcontinent, "the earliest farming communities there in the seventh millennium B.C. utilized wheat, barley, and other crops that had been previously domesticated in the Fertile Crescent and that evidently spread to the Indus Valley through Iran … In Egypt as well, food production began in the sixth millennium B.C. with the arrival of Southwest Asian crops".[1] As early as thousands of years ago, there had been exchanges among the major civilisation rims. These exchanges are of great significance for promoting global agricultural development and evolution of civilisation.

Two important items that supported the exchanges on the continental Silk Road were silk and horses. China was the first region in the world to domesticate silkworms. China was the supplier of silk, and Europe was the demander of silk. China was the demander of horses, and Central Asia was the supplier of horses.

At the western end of the Silk Road, Roman aristocrats had a strong demand for silk, which even caused the Roman Empire to fall into serious fiscal deficit. Roman writer Pliny the Elder (Gaius Plinius Secundus) stated in *Natural History* in 77 AD that as the people of remote Seres had performed the complex spinning and weaving work, "it is possible for Roman noblewomen to appear in the public in transparent dress ... By the lowest reckoning, India, Seres [China] and the Arabian peninsula take from our Empire 100 millions of sesterces every year: that is how much our luxuries and women cost us".[2]

In the Era of Cold Weapons (no gunpowder, explosives or other burners), war horses were an important means for military mobile operations. Similarly, before the Industrial Revolution, horses were also the most important means of transportation in the Central Plains. The fondness of ancient Chinese emperors for war horses can be seen from Emperor Qin's terracotta warriors and horses. In the ancient Central Plains, horses were largely Mongolian horses. Mongolian horses were hard-working, short and small in size and ran at a low speed. Dayuan horses and Wusun horses in Central Asia had a good figure and ran at a fast pace. After Zhang Qian in the Han Dynasty was dispatched on a diplomatic mission to the Western Regions, he described that "there are many prized horses (in Dayuan), these horses shed sweat like blood, and their ancestors are the sons of heavenly horses", which aroused great interest of Emperor Wu of Han. According to the *Records of the Grand Historian*,

> The emperors of the Han Dynasty were fond of Dayuan horses, so the emissaries were dispatched continuously to Dayuan. Each group of emissaries who were dispatched abroad consisted of over a hundred to several hundred members, and the things that each emissary carried were roughly the same as those brought by the Marquess of Bowang. Since then, it has became a common practice to send emissaries abroad for a diplomatic mission. So, fewer emissaries were sent abroad later on. Roughly ten groups of emissaries at most and five or six groups of emissaries at least were sent abroad by the emperors of the Han Dynasty in one year. In the places far away, the emissaries could not return until eight or nine years later. In the places nearby, they could return in a few years.

To take possession of Dayuan horses, Emperor Wu of Han sent emissaries carrying a great deal of money and gold horses to Dayuan to exchange horses, but this ended in failure. After the Kingdom of Dayuan executed the emissaries of the Han Dynasty, Emperor Wu of Han was furious and commissioned Li Guangli as a general to direct the war against Dayuan. Finally, Li Guangli brought back dozens of prized horses and more than 3000 horses at the middle level and below. The *Records of the Grand Historian* also records that "The king of Wusun married a girl of the Han Dynasty with a thousand horses as betrothal gifts". Some scholars stated that "Ever since this era, the 'silk trade relationship' between Central Asia and the Central Plains has been formally established".[3] It is said that the horses imported from Central Asia had improved the horse varieties in the Central Plains. Archeologists have discovered that the figures of Chinese war horses after the Han Dynasty were obviously different from the past.

In the Tang Dynasty, horses were mainly acquired from the Northern and Western Regions through trade and diplomatic donations. American scholar James A. Millward once pointed out that after the An Shi Rebellion, "the rulers of the Tang Dynasty had to purchase horses at a high price from the nomadic Uighur tribes to which the Tang Dynasty had once gave assistance. The price of each horse is about 40 pieces of silk".[4] The horses imported to the Central Plains mainly aimed to meet the needs of the emperors and noblemen. The love of noblemen of the Tang Dynasty for hunting and polo had further promoted the "trade of silk and horses". In addition to silk and horses, along with the exchanges among people on the Silk Road, the seeds of crops such as alfalfa, grapes, and walnuts and related cultivation techniques had also spread from west to east along the Silk Road.

From the perspective of goods transportation, the goods transported by the Northern Grassland Silk Road were unique. Apart from silk, these goods mainly included tea, fur, and wool products, as well as porcelains, iron wares, and Chinese herbal medicines, and their quantities were considerable. In terms of cultural exchanges beyond material exchanges, the Northern Grassland Silk Road had spread Buddhism (mainly Lamaism or Tibetan Buddhism), Shamanism, Zoroastrianism, Islam, Manichaeism, Christianity (Nestorianism and Catholic Franciscans), as well as various native wizardries and totem worships. It has communicated and integrated the Chinese civilisation with the Greek–Roman civilisation, the Central Asian Muslim civilisation, the desert oasis civilisation, the grassland civilisation, the Slavic civilisation, and other civilisations in the Far East, thus making indelible contribution to the development of Chinese and Western cultural and material exchanges.[5]

On the southwestern continental Silk Road, Shu clothes and tea took a large proportion.

Likewise, although it was called "the Maritime Silk Road", the goods traded on these sea routes were far more than silk. With the development of foreign trade, the Maritime Silk Road spread the ancient Chinese inventions such as the compass, gunpowder, paper-making and movable type printing as well as porcelains and medicinal herbs to other places throughout the world. Particularly, through ocean transportation, Chinese porcelains were brought to different parts of the world in large quantities. It is said that a large ship that sank on the Indonesian coast in the ninth century was loaded with more than 70,000 pieces of porcelain.[6] This was only a small part of the massive amount of porcelains and silk imported by the Abbasid empire. It is hard to imagine how many camel and horse teams would be required to ship so many porcelains if they were transported by land rather than through the Maritime Silk Road. In the meanwhile, the Maritime Silk Road also introduced foreign commodities and animal and plant species to China, such as pearls, precious stones, spices, cotton, longan, corn, sweet potatoes, tobacco, peanuts, sunflowers, potatoes, and tomatoes. The mutual exchange of inventions and production technologies greatly promoted the development of social productive forces in different places and progress in human history.

Frequent flow of people on the Silk Road

Judging from the sources of the diplomatic corps of the Han Dynasty on the Silk Road in the Han Dynasty, only a small number of people who were driven by fame and fortune at that time asked for a diplomatic mission to the Western Regions, and Emperor Wu of Han thought that the road was long and dangerous, so he said yes to all the requests. Due to the hardships and risks en route, few ordinary traders and people in the Central Plains went back and forth between the Central Plains and the Western Regions. Moreover, the passengers on the Silk Road did not travel continuously from Luoyang to Rome, or from Rome to Luoyang, but stopped somewhere and carried out exchanges. Therefore, besides the emissaries of the empires of the Central Plains that were active on the Silk Road, who were the main travellers on the road?

American scholar James A. Millward once said that in the sixth to tenth centuries AD, the most active travelers on the Silk Road were people who spoke various Iranian languages: the merchants of the Sassanian Empire (226–651 AD) dominated the trade by seaway not only in the places near the Persian Gulf, but also in the Arabian Sea, the eastern coast of Africa, the Indian coast and Sri Lanka, and as far as in Malaysia and southern China. Persian merchants lived in the specific areas in Guangzhou. Sogdian merchants set off from the land route to Armenia and the entire Asia, passed through northern China and even reached China's northeastern regions and Korea at the farthest end. It is the dominance of these merchant groups that made Persian a common language for business and communication on the Silk Road.[7]

The Old Book of Tang Records of the Western Regions records that the Sogdian people "were good at doing business and scrambled even for mere interests". If a covetous Sogdian person had a son, he would feed him with "stone honey" and apply glue on his palms, hoping that he would be good at sweet talk and get rich when he grew up. At the age of 20, men would leave their hometowns and go far away to do business, and they would reach any place where they found they could make money. According to Chinese scholar Rong Xinjiang's archaeological discoveries and the interpretation of Sogdian documents,

Gongyue on the northern grassland road, the Hongzha valley in southern India, Kepantuo on the Congling plateau and Shenshanbao in the Tarim Basin had all become the trade centers, goods distribution centers and even the settlements of the Sogdian people. The Sogdian merchants did not always sell gems and spices from the west to the east, and they also transported gold, silver and silk from the east to the west with the cities in the Central Plains like Chang'an and Wuwei as their bases. However, whether eastward or westward, the towns of the above-mentioned kingdoms in the Western Regions inevitably became the middle stations for the Sogdian people and had also obtained substantial benefits from the Silk Road trade.[8]

Pliny the Elder, mentioned above, claimed that Roman silver coins were taken away by Seres and other countries. However, almost no Roman silver coins belonging to the first century AD have ever been found in any ancient site in China. Where did these coins go? Some scholars stated that "this money was mostly earned by the Sogdian merchants as middlemen on the Silk Road".[9] The archaeologist Xia Naiconducted in-depth research on the silver coins of the Persian Sassanian Dynasty unearthed in China. He believes that in the Sassanian era, the "Silk Road" that linked the two countries' transport routes was unimpeded. China's silk and other goods flowed endlessly to the West along this "Silk Road", and the goods exported to China by the Western countries such as Persia also included a certain number of Sassanian silver coins besides glassware, spices, gems, silverwares, wool fabrics, etc. According to the information available at that time, 1174 Sassanian silver coins were discovered in China and were unearthed in 12 places (counties), including Turpan, Kuche, Gaochang, Xining, Taiyuan, Dingxian, Luoyang, Xian, and Yingde and Qujiang in Guangdong. Linking these areas together, we can outline the rough route of the Silk Road in China at that time. According to the number of unearthed silver coins and other documents, Xia Nai speculated that the peoples of China and Iran had had frequent and friendly exchanges since the second century BC (the mid-Western Han Dynasty), and that "at the end of the fourth century to the seventh century, Xining was on the transport channel between China and the West. This transport route that was slightly southerly may be as significant as the Hexi Corridor in some period (the fifth century)". Xia Nai also believes that "the circulation and use of silver coins of the Western Regions in some northwestern regions of China during the Northern Zhou Dynasty and the early Tang Dynasty were recorded in our country's historical records".[10] Thus, it can be seen that Sassanian silver coins might play the role of circulation currency on the Silk Road in certain periods.

The Grassland Silk Road almost involved all ethnic groups of the Altai family of languages: the ethnic groups speaking Mongolian, Turkic, and Tungusic languages; many ethnic groups of the Di and Hu families in ancient northern China, especially the Huns; many ethnic groups speaking the ancient Indo-European languages, such as Scythians, Kushans, Sakas, Ephthalites, etc.; many native peoples and tribes of Southern Siberia; some Slavic peoples. Although the northern Grassland Silk Road did not encompass vast areas like the Western Silk Road, it still formed, supported, and promoted a contact network for different regions and ethnic groups.[11]

On the Maritime Silk Road, the earliest active travelers were the official diplomatic corps of the countries involved in the tributary trade. With the development of European navigation technology and the establishment of Asian colonies, the trading activities on the Maritime Silk Road were dominated by Europeans. For example, on the Macau–Malacca–Goa–Lisbon sea route established in the sixteenth century, the Portuguese traded goods in many places. The Spaniards created the Spain–South America–Manila–Spain global sea route.

> These voyages of European navigators established the direct sea routes between the major continents, allowing the traditionally existing east-to-west maritime Silk Road from the Far East to the Red Sea to extend eastwards to the Americas and to expand globally, linking Asia with Europe from the eastern and western directions. The distances between various regions and countries in the world were shortened, the international economic links became unprecedentedly close, and the world market began to take shape. Apart from the three old colonial countries of Portugal, Spain and the Netherlands, the European countries competing for business in Asia also included Britain, France and Russia.[12]

Jared once pointed out that "One of them (the areas mentioned above) is western and central Europe, where food production arose with the arrival of Southwest Asian crops and animals between 6000 and 3500 B.C., but at least one plant (the poppy) was then domesticated locally".[13] The world's history is strange in that China traded silk and porcelains with Europe, but European products found no market in China, so it was the poppy and the resulting Opium War that had opened up the door of China.

Notes

1 Jared Diamond, *Guns, Germs, and Steel: the Fates of Human Societies* (revised edition), W.W. Norton & Company, Inc., 2005, Xie Yanguang trans., Shanghai Translation Publishing House, 2016, pp. 87–91.
2 [France] G. Coedès, ed., Geng Sheng, trans., *Texts of Greek and Latin Authors on the Far East*, Zhonghua Book Company, 1987, pp. 10–12.
3 Liu Yingsheng, *The Silk Road*, Jiangsu People's Publishing House, 2014, p. 60.
4 James A. Millward, Ma Rui trans., *The Silk Road*, Yilin Press, 2017, p. 51.
5 Geng Sheng, "The French Who Investigated the Grassland Silk Road," *Journal of North Minzu University* (Philosophy and Social Sciences), 2009, Issue 6, pp. 18–28.
6 J. Stargardt, "Indian Ocean Trade in the Ninth and Tenth Centuries: Demand, Distance, and Profit," *South Asian Studies*, 30.1 (2014), p. 37.
7 James A. Millward, Ma Rui trans., *The Silk Road*, Yilin Press, 2017, p. 31.
8 Rong Xinjiang, "Retrieving and Studying the Settlements of the Sogdian Migrants in the Western Regions," *The Western Regions Studies*, Issue 2, 2005, pp. 1–11.

9 Lin Meicun, "Sogdian Contract for Buying a Tablet and Slave Girl Trade on the Silk Road," *Chinese Cultural Relics*, Issue 9, 1992, pp. 49–54.
10 Xia Nai, "An Overview of the Persian Sasadian Silver Coins Unearthed in China," *Journal of Archaeology*, Issue 1, 1974, pp. 91–110.
11 Geng Sheng, "The French Who Investigated the Grassland Silk Road," *Journal of North Minzu University* (Philosophy and Social Sciences), 2009, Issue 6, pp. 18–28.
12 Liu Yingsheng, *The Silk Road*, Jiangsu People's Publishing House, 2014, p. 557.
13 Jared Diamond, *Guns, Germs, and Steel: the Fates of Human Societies* (revised edition), W.W. Norton & Company, Inc., 2005, Xie Yanguang trans., Shanghai Translation Publishing House, 2016, pp. 89–90.

15

THE SILK ROAD SPIRIT

Dong Xiangrong

What is the Silk Road spirit?

In history, the Silk Road was an important pathway connecting the three ancient civilisation rims in Asia, Europe and Africa, and it consisted of the maritime and overland routes connecting China with the outside world. Archaeological findings indicate that European aristocrats had used silk from China as early as the sixth century BC. Economic and trade exchanges between Europe, Central Asia and China's Central Plains region had promoted cultural exchanges among these regions. In the Han Dynasty, Zhang Qian led a delegation to the Western Regions twice in 138 BC and 119 BC, and the exchanges on the Silk Road became increasingly extensive. The Chinese culture spread along the Silk Road to the Western Regions, and grape, alfalfa, pomegranate, flax, sesame and other crops in the Western Regions were also introduced to the Central Plains. Frequent people-to-people exchanges between the Central Plains and the Western Regions led to the exchanges of ideas and the spread of beliefs. The prosperity of the Silk Road made positive contributions to the development of the Central Plains and Central Asia.

On September 7, 2013, Chinese President Xi Jinping delivered a speech entitled "Promote Friendship Between Our People and Work Together to Build a Bright Future" at Nazarbayev University in Kazakhstan. In the speech, President Xi Jinping stated that:

> Throughout the millennia, the people of various countries along the ancient Silk Road have jointly written a chapter of friendship that has been passed on to this very day. The over 2,000-year history of exchanges demonstrates that on the basis of solidarity, mutual trust, equality, inclusiveness, mutual learning and win–win cooperation, countries of different races, beliefs and cultural backgrounds are fully capable of sharing peace and development. This is the valuable inspiration we have drawn from the ancient Silk Road.

On October 3, 2013, Xi Jinping stated in his speech to the People's Representative Council of Indonesia that:

> Southeast Asia has since ancient times been an important hub along the ancient Maritime Silk Road. China will strengthen maritime cooperation with ASEAN

countries to make good use of the China–ASEAN Maritime Cooperation Fund set up by the Chinese government and vigorously develop maritime partnership in a joint effort to build the Maritime Silk Road of the 21st century. China is ready to expand its practical cooperation with ASEAN countries across the board, supplying each other's needs and complementing each other's strength, with a view to jointly seizing opportunities and meeting challenges for the benefit of common development and prosperity.

After the major initiative of "Jointly Building Silk Road Economic Belt and 21st-Century Maritime Silk Road" was proposed, it has attracted close attention from all over the world and will bring new vigour and vitality to the traditional Silk Road.

On April 29, 2016, General Secretary Xi Jinping stated in his speech at the thirty-first group study session of members of the Politburo of the CPC Central Committee that "the Belt and Road Initiative evokes the historical memory of the countries along the route. The ancient Silk Road was more a road of friendship than a road of trade. In friendly exchanges with other nations, the Chinese nation formed the Silk Road Spirit featuring peace and cooperation, openness and inclusiveness, mutual learning and mutual benefit". This is the summary of the Silk Road spirit.

The content of the Silk Road spirit

Peace and cooperation means that all countries should abandon the use of military force, adopt peaceful means, carry out active foreign cooperation and exchanges, and give full play to their respective comparative advantages to achieve win–win cooperation. Historically, there were conflicts and cooperation among the countries along the Silk Road, while cooperation was the mainstream part. The Chinese civilisation originated from the mainland's farming civilisation, and advocates stability and harmony, stresses the relationship between man and nature and attaches importance to the ethics of family and state. It is embodied as a spiritual core of respecting order, loving peace, promoting mutual assistance and cooperating and restraining. It emphasises the unity of nature and harmony and treasures harmonious relations. *Mencius Teng Wen Gong (Vol. 1)* said, "On occasions of death, or removal from one dwelling to another, there will be no quitting the district. In the fields of a district, those who belong to the same nine squares render all friendly offices to one another in their going out and coming in, aid one another in keeping watch and ward, and sustain one another in sickness. Thus the people are brought to live in affection and harmony". Under the background of global economic integration and intertwined global affairs, no country can exist in isolation. In this global village, no one can leave this village and it will be a "community of a shared future". In this community, we should render all friendly offices to one another in their going out and coming in and aid one another in keeping watch and ward. We should not only support each other in terms of safety, we must do our best to help each other in sickness or distress. President Xi Jinping has repeatedly stressed that the international community must advocate mutual assistance, build a community of a shared future for mankind, and lead a new trend in international relations in the new era. The Belt and Road Initiative advocated by China is the embodiment of China's emphasis on the spirit of peace and cooperation.

Openness and inclusiveness means that in the process of opening up, all countries in the world should incorporate things of diverse nature and learn widely from others' strong points to achieve common development based on the principle of pursuing inclusiveness and seeking a common ground while reserving differences. There are many independent political and economic entities along the long Silk Road. These countries have different political systems and different economic development paths, and their peoples have different religious beliefs. The Silk Road was able to become an international pathway for economic and cultural exchanges between ancient China and foreign countries because the countries along the routes took an open and inclusive attitude, respected the diversity of world civilisations and development paths, and respected and safeguarded the rights of people of different countries to choose their own development paths to achieve coexistence and common prosperity. On June 28, 2014, President Xi Jinping stated at the Conference Marking the 60th anniversary of the Five Principles of Peaceful Co-existence that "Countries should align their own interests with those of other countries and expand areas of converging interests. Instead of undercutting each other's efforts, countries should reinforce each other's endeavor and make greater common progress".[1] In his speech, President Xi Jinping quoted the famous saying of Chinese sociologist Fei Xiaotong, "Countries should respect others' interests while pursuing their own and advance common interests of all", which expresses the expectation of coexistence and co-prosperity with the open and inclusive attitude of all countries in the world.

Mutual learning means that we should respect the diversity of civilisations and pursue common progress through mutual learning and drawing on each other's strength. President Xi Jinping stated in his speech at UNESCO Headquarters that:

> The Tang Dynasty saw dynamic interactions between China and other countries. According to historical documents, the dynasty exchanged envoys with over 70 countries, and Chang'an, the capital of Tang, bustled with envoys, merchants and students from other countries. Exchanges of such a magnitude helped the spread of the Chinese culture to the rest of the world and the introduction into China of the cultures and products from other countries. In the early 15th century, Zheng He, the famous navigator of China's Ming Dynasty, made seven expeditions to the Western Seas, reaching many Southeast Asian countries and even Kenya on the east coast of Africa. These trips left behind many stories of friendly exchanges between the people of China and countries along the route. In late Ming Dynasty and early Qing Dynasty, the Chinese people began to learn modern science and technology with great zeal, as the European knowledge of astronomy, medicine, mathematics, geometry and geography were being introduced into China, which helped broaden the horizon of the Chinese people. Thereafter, exchanges and mutual learning between the Chinese civilization and other civilizations became more frequent. There were indeed conflicts, frictions, bewilderment and denial in this process. But the more dominant features of the period were learning, digestion, integration and innovation.[2]

In the 40 years of reform and opening up, China has embarked on a successful road that can be characterised by the well-known Chinese proverb, "If you want to be rich, you must first build roads". China is well aware of the strong demand for infrastructure construction in the less-developed Asian regions and also well aware that the existing international organisations in the international community are unable to meet this demand. Therefore, under the Belt and Road Initiative, China proposed to establish the AIIB, which provides an opportunity for regional economic development and has received strong support from Asian countries and many countries outside the region.

Mutual benefit means that countries and regions with different dominant ethnic groups and different religious and cultural traditions can work together to cope with threats and challenges through mutually beneficial cooperation, and strive for benefits and well-being to achieve mutually beneficial and win–win development. The Silk Road is a network of communication routes connecting China and the West and connecting Europe and Asia. Peoples of different countries exchange their needed goods, and such exchanges and cooperation have promoted the prosperity and development of Europe, Asia and Africa. China actively advocates that we should champion a new vision of win–win outcomes for all and reject the obsolete notion of a zero-sum game or winner-taking-all, and we should seek common development of all countries along the Silk Road. Mencius said in *Mencius Jin Xin* that:

> Honoring virtues and being delight in rightness, you may always be perfectly satisfied. Therefore, in times of hardship, one should not go against the moral standards; in times of success, he should not lose a sense of righteousness. In times of hardship, if you do not go against the moral standards, you can be self-satisfied; in times of success, if you do not lose a sense of righteousness, you won't make the populace disappointed. In times of hardship, one should treasure himself solely; in times of success, he should benefit the others concurrently.

The concept of "benefiting the others concurrently" reflects traditional Chinese values, and it is also the original intention that China proposed the Belt and Road Initiative to promote the common development of all countries along the Silk Road and build a community of a shared future for mankind. Professor Zheng Yongnian once pointed out that China, as a major country, has never planned to build its own international relations in the same way as Western countries did. The formation of China's international relations is a natural order formed by China and its neighbouring countries in dealing with each other according to their mutual needs. What China considers is how to govern this naturally formed order. From this perspective, China has unarguably always been "keeping a low profile". The core of diplomacy is always trade, and it rarely involves the use of state power and conquest. However, economy and trade, in today's words, have a win–win and reciprocal relationship.[3]

How to promote the Silk Road spirit

In the new era of globalisation, countries are more interdependent on one another This interdependent relationship goes far beyond the era of the ancient Silk Road. In today's society, technological development changes with each passing day. This speed is far from what people in the era of the ancient Silk Road could imagine. The development of the world today needs peace and cooperation more than ever before, and peoples from all countries need to join hands to build a better future more than ever before.

To carry forward the Silk Road spirit, we need to promote mutual learning among civilisations. No one civilisation can be judged superior to another, and civilisations have become richer and more colourful with equal exchanges. As an old Chinese saying goes, "Different colours bring out the best in each other and the ensemble of musical notes makes for the song of harmony". To promote the Silk Road spirit, we need to respect the development path independently embarked upon by a country. "People don't need to wear the same shoes; they should find what suit their feet. Governments don't have to adopt the same model of governance; they should find what benefits their people." It is the people of a country that are best placed to judge whether the development path they have chosen for themselves is suitable. Just as we should not require that all flowers should become violets, we should not require that all countries with different cultural traditions, different historical encounters and different real national conditions should adopt the same development model. Otherwise, the world would be too monotonous. To carry forward the Silk Road spirit, we should persist in win–win cooperation. China is pursuing common development. We should pursue a good life for ourselves, and wish others a good life as well. To promote the Silk Road spirit, we should promote dialogue and peace. China will participate in regional affairs in a constructive manner, adhere to principles and uphold justice, and work together with the Arab countries to find the greatest common divisor for the concerns of all through dialogue, and provide more public goods for properly addressing regional hotspot issues.[4]

The Belt and Road Initiative proposed by China aims to inherit and carry forward the Silk Road spirit and link China's development with the development of other countries along the route, and the Chinese dream with the dreams of the people in those countries. It imbues the ancient Silk Road with a new spirit of the times. China has proposed to adopt "five types of connectivity" to promote the cooperation of the countries along the Silk Road. First, we need to step up policy coordination. Countries should have full discussions on development strategies and policy response, work out plans and measures for advancing regional cooperation through consultation in the spirit of seeking common ground while reserving differences and give the policy and legal "green light" to regional economic integration. Second, we need to improve road connectivity. The Shanghai Cooperation Organisation (SCO) is working on an agreement on transportation facilitation. If signed and implemented at an early date, it will open up a major transportation route connecting the Pacific and the Baltic Sea. Building on that, we will actively discuss the best way to improve cross-border transportation infrastructure and work towards a transportation network connecting East Asia, West Asia and South Asia to facilitate economic development and travel in the region. Third, we need to promote unimpeded trade. The proposed "economic belt along the Silk Road" is inhabited by close to 3 billion people and represents the biggest market in the world with unparalleled potential. The potential for trade and investment cooperation between the relevant countries is enormous. We should discuss a proper arrangement for trade and investment facilitation, remove trade barriers, reduce trade and investment cost, increase the speed and quality of regional economic flows and achieve win–win progress in the region. Fourth, we need to enhance monetary circulation. China and Russia have already had sound cooperation on settling trade in local currencies, and have gained gratifying results and rich experience. There is no reason not to share this good practice with others in the region. If our region can realise local currency convertibility and settlement under current and capital accounts, it will significantly lower circulation cost, increase our ability to fend off financial risks and make our region more competitive economically in the world. Fifth, we need to increase understanding between our people. Amity between the people holds the key to good relations between states. To have productive cooperation in the above-mentioned areas, we need the support of our people. We should encourage more friendly exchanges between our people to enhance mutual understanding and traditional friendship and build strong public support and a solid social foundation for regional cooperation.

As President Xi Jinping has stated, "China will work with countries along the routes to build the mutually beneficial cooperation network of the Belt and Road, develop an innovative cooperation model, establish a platform for diversified cooperation, promote projects in key areas, and work together to build the Belt and Road that is green, healthy, intelligent and peaceful to benefit the countries and people along the routes".[5]

Notes

1 "Speech by Xi Jinping at the Conference Marking the 60th anniversary of the Five Principles of Peaceful Co-existence," June 28, 2014.
2 "Speech by Xi Jinping at UNESCO Headquarters," March 27, 2014.
3 Zheng Yongnian, "The Silk Road and China's Spirit of the Times," *Lianhe Zaobao*, June 10, 2014.
4 "Speech by Xi Jinping at the Opening Ceremony of the Sixth Ministerial Conference of the China–Arab States Cooperation Forum," June 5, 2014.
5 The congratulatory letter sent by Xi Jinping to the 2016 Media Cooperation Forum on the Belt and Road on July 25, 2016.

PART III

Formation and framework of the concept

PART III

Formation and framework of the concept

16

PROCESS FOR PROPOSING THE CONCEPT

Wang Yuzhu

The ideas of the Belt and Road were first proposed by President Xi Jinping, but they are also the products of the collective wisdom of the new generation of Chinese central leadership on how to carry out international cooperation in the new era.

President Xi Jinping took the lead in issuing the Initiative

In September 2013, President Xi Jinping visited Kazakhstan. On September 7, President Xi delivered an important speech entitled "Promote Friendship between Our People and Work Together to Build a Bright Future" at Nazarbayev University. In the speech, President Xi proposed that to forge closer economic ties, deepen cooperation and expand development space in the Eurasian region, we should take an innovative approach and jointly build an "economic belt along the Silk Road". This will be a great undertaking benefitting the people of all countries along the route. To turn this into a reality, we may start with work in individual areas and link them up over time to cover the whole region. President Xi Jinping emphasised the importance of connectivity as an approach for strengthening cooperation and specifically analysed the connectivity in five aspects. First, we need to step up policy communication. Countries should have full discussions on development strategies and policy response and work out plans and measures for advancing regional cooperation through consultation. Second, we need to improve road connectivity. We will open up a major transportation route connecting the Pacific and the Baltic Sea and work towards a transportation network connecting East Asia, West Asia and South Asia. Third, we need to promote unimpeded trade. We should discuss a proper arrangement for trade and investment facilitation. Fourth, we need to enhance monetary circulation. We should promote local currency convertibility and settlement to increase our ability to fend off financial risks and make our region more competitive economically in the world. Fifth, we need to increase understanding between our people. We should encourage more friendly exchanges between our people to enhance mutual understanding and traditional friendship.

Later, in October 2013, President Xi Jinping visited Indonesia. In the speech delivered by President Xi to the People's Representative Council of Indonesia on October 3, he expounded the importance of China–ASEAN win–win cooperation and clearly proposed the Initiative to jointly build the 21st Century Maritime Silk Road with ASEAN. In his speech, Xi Jinping said that:

China is ready to open itself wider to ASEAN countries on the basis of equality and mutual benefit to enable ASEAN countries to benefit more from China's development. China is prepared to elevate the level of China–ASEAN Free Trade Area and strive to expand two-way trade to one trillion U.S. dollars by 2020. China is committed to greater connectivity with ASEAN countries and has proposed to establish an Asian infrastructure investment bank that would support infrastructure connectivity between ASEAN countries as well as other developing countries in the region. Southeast Asia has since ancient times been an important hub along the ancient Maritime Silk Road. China will strengthen maritime cooperation with ASEAN countries to make good use of the China–ASEAN Maritime Cooperation Fund set up by the Chinese government and vigorously develop maritime partnership in a joint effort to build the Maritime Silk Road of the 21st century. China is ready to expand its practical cooperation with ASEAN countries across the board, supplying each other's needs and complementing each other's strength, with a view to jointly seizing opportunities and meeting challenges for the benefit of common development and prosperity.

After the two initiatives were proposed, they caused tremendous repercussions in China. Most people did not realise at that time that the two cooperation initiatives proposed separately would be subsequently integrated into what we now call the Belt and Road Initiative. This is because from the perspective of specific environments in which the two initiatives were proposed, the Silk Road Economic Belt is oriented towards Asian and European countries, while the 21st Century Maritime Silk Road seems to gravitate towards cooperation between China and ASEAN. Because the two initiatives were aimed in two different directions, the feedback from public opinion at the beginning did not link them together. However, one thing is clear to everyone: that the CPC Central Committee attaches great importance to these two initiatives. The *Decision of the Central Committee of the Communist Party of China on Some Major Issues Concerning Comprehensively Deepening the Reform* adopted by the 3rd Plenary Session of the 18th CPC Central Committee on November 12, 2013 clearly stated that "We will set up development-oriented financial institutions, accelerate the construction of infrastructure connecting China with neighboring countries and regions, and work hard to build a Silk Road Economic Belt and a Maritime Silk Road, so as to form a new pattern of all-round opening".

The Initiative was included in the *Decision* adopted at the 3rd Plenary Session of the 18th CPC Central Committee, which means that it has become the collective consensus of the central government. Moreover, at the Central Economic Work Conference held about a month later in December 2013, President Xi Jinping proposed six major tasks for economic work in 2014: "we should promote the building of the Silk Road Economic Belt, formulate strategic plans and strengthen infrastructure connectivity. We should build the 21st Century Maritime Silk Road, strengthen the connectivity of sea routes and more closely intertwine the interests of the countries". These are the tasks of continuously deepening opening-up. In the 2014 government work report, as a result of the implementation of the decision of the central government, Premier Li Keqiang proposed that "We will intensify the planning and building of a Silk Road economic belt and a 21st century maritime Silk Road, and promote the building of the Bangladesh–China–India–Myanmar Economic Corridor and the China–Pakistan Economic Corridor. By launching a number of major projects, we will speed up infrastructure connectivity with our neighbors, and open up new space for enhancing international economic and technologic cooperation".

Thus it can be seen that the central government has closely linked the two initiatives with China's opening up, and has reflected such perception from the central decision-making level to the government work level. However, in the above-mentioned documents, the two initiatives were still expressed separately. It was still not clear then whether these two initiatives would be integrated into the Belt and Road Initiative.

Promulgation of the *Vision and Actions*

Many specific details of the Belt and Road Initiative were announced when *Vision and Actions on Jointly Building the Silk Road Economic Belt and the 21st Century Maritime Silk Road* was promulgated in March 2015, especially in which the two initiatives were clearly referred to as the Belt and Road. However, if you sort out the reports on relevant activities of the central leadership, you will find that the Chinese government had begun to use the phrase "Belt and Road" before the release of the *Vision and Actions*. According to Xinhua News Agency, Vice Premier Zhang Gaoli presided over a symposium to promote the building of the Belt and Road in Xi'an on October 10, 2014, and at that meeting, Vice Premier Zhang Gaoli repeatedly used the Belt and Road as the short form to refer to the two initiatives of Silk Road Economic Belt and 21st Century Maritime Silk Road. In November 2014, President Xi Jinping attended the 22nd APEC Informal Leaders' Meeting and announced that China would commit US$40 billion to the establishment of a Silk Road Fund. During that event, President Xi Jinping emphasised that the Belt and Road Initiative and the connectivity endeavour were compatible and mutually reinforcing. Although these two initiatives were expressed separately in the previous important documents of the central government, the speeches of President Xi and Vice Premier Zhang Gaoli showed that the Belt and the Road had been integrated into one at the central level.

To strengthen the implementation of the Belt and Road Initiative, the Leading Group for the Belt and Road Initiative led by Vice Premier Zhang Gaoli was established in February 2015. According to the information released later, Vice Premier of the State Council Zhang Gaoli was named the leader of the Leading Group, and the deputy leaders of the Leading Group included Wang Huning, director of the Policy Research Office of the CPC Central Committee, Wang Yang, Vice Premier of the State Council, State Councillor Yang Jing and State Councillor Yang Jiechi. The Office of the Leading Group is located on the National Development and Reform Commission. In March 2015, authorised by the State Council, the National Development and Reform Commission, the Ministry of Foreign Affairs and the Ministry of Commerce jointly issued the *Vision and Actions on Jointly Building the Silk Road Economic Belt and the 21st Century Maritime Silk Road*. This is the first document in which the "Belt and Road" was explicitly used as the short form to refer to the initiatives of Silk Road Economic Belt and 21st Century Maritime Silk Road. At that time, it had been nearly a year and a half since the Initiative was first proposed by President Xi. Therefore, although the *Vision and Actions* also clearly states that the English translation of the Initiative is "the Belt and Road Initiative (BRI)", the phrase "One Belt One Road (OBOR)" translated directly previously had already become popular in the international community.

Continual evolution of the ideas of the Belt and Road

It was nearly a year and a half from the ideas of "Belt and Road" being proposed by President Xi in his two speeches to the Chinese government's promulgation of the *Vision and Actions*. This shows that ideas of "Belt and Road" are in the process of continuous improvement. This changing process is partially undergoing self-improvement and adjustment, and largely it is a response to the international community's cognition. Without doubt, the opinions and suggestions raised by the governments, industries and universities on promoting the Belt and Road construction have also been widely adopted.

The change in the expression of the "five types of connectivity" is a good example. The Belt and Road Initiative attaches great importance to improving connectivity, and President Xi has proposed the concept of "five types of connectivity". In the *Vision and Actions*, the "five types of connectivity" refer to policy coordination, connectivity of infrastructure, unimpeded trade, financial integration and understanding between people. However, what was referred to the "five types of connectivity" by President Xi in his speech at Nazarbayev University in Kazakhstan was "policy coordination, road connectivity, unimpeded trade, monetary circulation, and understanding between people". In October 2014, when Vice Premier Zhang Gaoli presided over the symposium to promote the building of the Belt and Road, he still used the version as mentioned by Xi Jinping in his speech at Nazarbayev University in Kazakhstan. However, in the *Vision and Actions*, "road connectivity" and "monetary circulation" were changed to "connectivity of infrastructure" and "financial integration", and the "five types of connectivity" was identified as the top priority in cooperation under the Belt and Road.

Connectivity was originally a term in the field of network communications. The *Master Plan on ASEAN Connectivity* released in 2010 proposed to strengthen connectivity and defined "connectivity" as "physical, institutional and people-to-people linkages". The "five types of connectivity" proposed by President Xi expanded ASEAN's definition of connectivity, but "road connectivity" originally proposed did not cover the energy network and communication network in the infrastructure construction under the Belt and Road, so it was changed to "infrastructure connectivity" to cover more areas of infrastructure construction. Similarly, "monetary circulation" originally proposed by President Xi focused only on monetary risks in the trade field. However, in the pursuit of the Belt and Road Initiative, financing is an issue of equal and even greater interest, which is why China has not only established unilaterally the $40 billion Silk Road Fund, but has also promoted the international community to jointly establish the AIIB. The proposal of "financial integration" is in response to this important concern in building the Belt and Road.

In addition, the geographical scope of the Belt and Road has also been changing. As mentioned earlier, when President Xi proposed the Silk Road Economic Belt, its goal was to strengthen Asia–Europe cooperation, while the 21st Century Maritime Silk Road focused more on China–ASEAN cooperation. In the *Vision and Actions* promulgated in 2015, the Belt and Road was described as follows: The Belt and Road routes run through the continents of Asia, Europe and Africa, connecting the vibrant East Asia economic circle at one end and developed European economic circle at the other, and encompassing countries with huge potential for economic development. The Silk Road Economic Belt focuses on bringing together China, Central Asia, Russia and Europe (the Baltic); linking China with the Persian Gulf and the Mediterranean Sea through Central Asia and West Asia; and connecting China with South East Asia, South Asia and the Indian Ocean. The 21st Century Maritime Silk Road is designed to go from China's coast to Europe through the South China Sea and the Indian Ocean in one route, and from China's coast through the South China Sea to the South Pacific in the other. It is also based on such descriptions that the Belt and Road was originally identified to cover 65 countries along the routes.

With the establishment of the AIIB, the number of participating countries quickly increased from the initial 57 to 70, and this figure increased further later. In addition, some countries along the routes that were originally not included in the initial planning have begun to participate in the Belt and Road projects. More importantly, the promising prospects of the cooperation through the Belt and Road Initiative have attracted many developing countries. As more countries not along the routes have joined the Belt and Road, the concept of countries along the Belt and Road routes has begun to blur, and the Belt and Road has begun to transform into an international cooperation platform. In the report to the 18th CPC National Congress held in 2017, President Xi proposed to actively promote international cooperation through the Belt and Road Initiative, indicating that the Belt and Road has surpassed its original geographical scope and become an international cooperation platform for all friendly countries.

In this process of evolution, China has gradually clarified the similarities and differences between the Belt and Road and the Marshall Plan, responded to public doubt about China's attempt to construct its central system, and carefully analysed criticisms towards China's outward foreign direct investment. The process of advancing the Initiative over the past 5 years is arguably also a process in which China has actively responded to various challenges and criticisms, and accepted and adopted many excellent suggestions.

The Belt and Road is an initiative proposed by the new generation of Chinese leadership to accelerate opening up in the context of constant change in the international environment. This idea began with President Xi's two cooperation initiatives, but it soon rose to become the national will and has been self-evolving, self-improving, expanding and deepening in the later practice through drawing on the opinions and suggestions of many domestic and foreign international institutions and non-governmental organisations in an open and inclusive attitude. Presently, in the pursuit of the Belt and Road Initiative, we will still encounter new challenges, and will inevitably continue to make adjustments to cope with the challenges. The Belt and Road is essentially a strategy adopted by China to accelerate opening up in the current stage in response to environmental changes and directly serve the grand goal of China's economic development, and most countries welcome the opportunities brought by the Belt and Road Initiative, but some countries have seen competition and threats. For example, experts at the Centre for Strategic and International Studies (CSIS) believe that if the Belt and Road Initiative is successfully implemented, it will bring China to the centre of the world stage, which originally belonged to the United States. Such challenging understanding shows that to realise the goal of "building the Belt and Road into a road for peace, a road of prosperity, a road of opening up, a road of innovation and a road connecting different civilizations" as proposed by Xi Jinping at the Belt and Road Forum for International Cooperation, the idea of the Belt and Road also needs continuous evolution during its implementation process.

17

BACKGROUND

Wang Yuzhu

President Xi Jinping's proposal to build the Belt and Road is a choice to follow the trend of the times and the general trend of international and domestic development. The first part of the *Vision and Actions on Jointly Building Silk Road Economic Belt and 21st Century Maritime Silk Road* (hereinafter referred to as the *Vision and Actions*) promulgated in March 2015 explained the triple historic background under which the Belt and Road Initiative was proposed: on the global scale, the world economy is recovering slowly and global development is uneven, so it is necessary to seek a new model of global governance; on the regional scale, a complex interconnected network necessary for deep integration has not yet been established, and regional cooperation needs new breakthroughs to support regional win–win cooperation among different countries; as far as China itself is concerned, after more than 40 years of reform and opening up, the Chinese economy is now deeply integrated with the world economy, but to achieve the "Two Centenary Goals",[1] China needs to continue to open up and deepen cooperation with countries around the world.

Global background of building the Belt and Road

Complex and profound changes are taking place in the world. The underlying impact of the international financial crisis keeps emerging; the world economy is recovering slowly, and global development is uneven; the international trade and investment landscape and rules for multilateral trade and investment are undergoing major adjustments; and countries still face big challenges to their development. The Initiative to jointly build the Belt and Road, embracing the trend towards a multi-polar world, economic globalisation, cultural diversity and greater IT application, is designed to uphold the global free trade regime and the open world economy in the spirit of open regional cooperation. Jointly building the Belt and Road is in the interests of the world community. Reflecting the common ideals and pursuit of human societies, it is a positive endeavour to seek new models of international cooperation and global governance, and will inject new positive energy into world peace and development. This passage of the *Vision and Actions* elaborates the judgement of the Chinese leadership on the overall development trend of the world.

Since the beginning of the twenty-first century, the economic development level of many developing countries, such as China, India and other BRICS countries, has increased substantially. China, particularly, has become the second largest economy in the world after promoting innovation-driven development through reform and opening up in just 40 years and more. With the rise of the international standing of developing countries, developed countries have been in a relative decline—their previous huge advantages have been shrinking. Even American defenders like Joseph Nye have to admit the great achievements of developing countries such as China. Facing relative decline, the United States began to turn to conservatism, and especially a series of policies adopted by Trump after he was elected president of the United States, including the launch of the Trans-Pacific Partnership (TPP) and the renegotiation of the North American Free Trade Area, have caused a widely shared concern in the international community. The counter-globalisation trend has therefore become a fashion. Such changes have unarguably posed challenges to the post-war international investment and trade pattern and the multilateral investment and trade rules. Based on its own development practices, China believes that maintaining the multilateral trading system is in the interests of developing countries. The Belt and Road Initiative is therefore a firm force for maintaining the open world economic system.

Moreover, another characteristic of post-war world economic development is that in the process of common development, the development gap between many developing countries and developed countries has not really been narrowed, and many developing economies are facing challenges in the current context while the developed economies have entered a stage of low-speed growth. China, as the largest developing country in the world, has explored a development model with distinct characteristics in the past 40 years of practice. In the current diversified world economy, China hopes to provide a new model of development for countries around the world with Chinese experience. Without doubt, China will not force other countries to learn the Chinese model, because China will never accept the model that others impose on China.

Regional background of building the Belt and Road

Although the Belt and Road Initiative does not lack international visions and global care, it can be seen from President Xi Jinping's speech on the Belt and Road Initiative that regional cooperation is its direct pursuit. In Kazakhstan, President Xi said that "To forge closer economic ties, deepen cooperation and expand development space in the Eurasian region, we should take an innovative approach and jointly build an 'economic belt along the Silk Road'".[2] In Indonesia, President Xi said that "Southeast Asia has since ancient times been an important hub along the ancient Maritime Silk Road. China will strengthen maritime cooperation with ASEAN countries … in a joint effort to build the Maritime Silk Road of the 21st century. China is ready to expand its practical cooperation with ASEAN countries across the board, supplying each other's needs and complementing each other's strength, with a view to jointly seizing opportunities and meeting challenges for the benefit of common development and prosperity".[3] However, we find that most developing countries, especially China's neighboring countries and regions with which China is trying to seek win–win cooperation, generally have backward infrastructure conditions, so connectivity has become an important bottleneck for deepening cooperation. The regional integration path with institutionalisation as the main goal has not been able to effectively exert its welfare effects in these areas. Therefore, in practice, the economic ties between these regions are mainly externally oriented. Especially in developed countries and regions with developed markets and abundant funds, there is a relatively weak horizontal linkage between the economies within the regions, which limits their development potential through adopting regional cooperation. Meanwhile, the economic development of those regions with low connectivity level has lagged behind for a long time, resulting in long-term development imbalance in these regions. Therefore, President Xi Jinping proposed to strengthen policy coordination, road connectivity, unimpeded trade, monetary circulation and understanding between people,[4] which is in response to the connectivity constraints faced by developing countries in regional cooperation. Therefore, the *Vision and Actions* released in 2015 made the following statements: "The Belt and Road Initiative aims to promote the connectivity of Asian, European and African continents and their adjacent seas, establish and strengthen partnerships among the countries along the Belt and Road, set up all-dimensional, multi-tiered and composite connectivity networks, and realize diversified, independent, balanced and sustainable development in these countries".

Domestic background of building the Belt and Road

The Belt and Road Initiative is a product of China's perception of the world, but China's policies have always been rooted in China's reality. It is based on the keen understanding that "China cannot develop itself in isolation of the world, and the world also needs China for its development".[5] In other words, China's Belt and Road Initiative is not a product of altruism, but a platform for pursuing cooperation and mutual benefit. It serves the grand goal of long-term stable development of China's economy and the Chinese people pursuing a better life. Undoubtedly, while advancing China's development, the Belt and Road clearly pursues the goal of building a community of a shared future for mankind.

China's achievements since the reform and opening up have attracted worldwide attention and even led to extensive discussions on the transfer of international power. Some international organisations and development experts predict that China's economy will surpass the United States as the world's largest economy in the near future. Indeed, starting from "abject poverty", China has moved up from per-capita GDP of a few hundred US dollars to nearly $9,000 under the leadership of the Communist Party of China. Its total GDP has rapidly surpassed that of most developed countries and close to that of the United States. However, while being proud of the great achievements that have been made in reform and opening up, China also has an objective and clear understanding of the challenges in its future development. Although China's per-capita GDP is close to $9,000, it is still lagging behind many countries, and is still a major developing country. Like most developing countries, China still needs to continuously maintain a relatively high economic growth rate to create jobs and narrow the gap with developed countries. Unlike ordinary developing countries, similar problems are more difficult to solve in China than in other developing countries due to its size. The same development achievements will have different international influences and thus trigger completely different international responses. These differences mean that China's solution to development problems sometimes becomes a political issue, and China's development will therefore carry political burdens.

From a development perspective, China's largest pressure lies in the transition from "a world factory" to "a world market". Over 40 years and more of reform and opening up, China has promoted industrial development through the introduction of external direct investment, and has formed huge advantages in the manufacturing sector, becoming a manufacturing power and "a world factory". However, China's huge production capacity requires a corresponding market to consume its products. When the economy of developed countries goes down, China is facing not only market pressure in the "new normal", but also complaints from other developing countries about competition in the third-party market. Therefore, China inevitably seeks to transform from "a world factory" to "a world market" after its economic level has been improved and to contribute to world economic growth by providing new product consumer markets to countries around the world. At present, China's import capacity is growing.[6] However, it will inevitably take a long time for China to turn itself into "a world market". In this process, China must speed up the pace of reform to gradually optimise its industrial structure, and meanwhile, we must try our best to keep a high economic growth rate to create jobs. This requires active and effective capacity cooperation with developing countries to on the one hand expand the developing markets and on the other hand to promote industrial transfer. Promoting the building of the Belt and Road is not only China's the need to expand and deepen its opening up, but also the need to strengthen mutually beneficial cooperation with Asia, Europe and the rest of the world.

Some misunderstandings about the Belt and Road Initiative

At present, China's economy is coming under pressure to phase out excess capacity to optimise the industrial structure. In this regard, some observers believe that China will export the eliminated production capacity to some less-developed countries through cooperation under the Belt and Road. In the early days of the Initiative, some Chinese scholars had even put forward such suggestions. With the advancement of cooperation under the Belt and Road, all parties have seen that China's real outputs are superior production capacity, because cooperation under the Belt and Road follows the principles of "extensive consultation, joint contribution and shared benefits", so China will never shift out its eliminated capacity arbitrarily, and capacity cooperation projects must only be carried out smoothly under the premise of fully respecting the wishes and interests of both parties. In fact, at the beginning, many people worried that China would output its excess capacity and pollutants through cooperation under the Belt and Road, but this has not occurred. Those who blamed China for this issue have long been speechless. However, as mentioned earlier, the Belt and Road Initiative proposed by China focuses on the international economic landscape and aims to solve its own development issues. However, China is a big country, and its development has a global impact. This is also the historic and political background the Belt and Road Initiative cannot escape. This is why, until now, some people have been hyping up fears about China's geopolitical ambitions in the launch of the Belt and Road Initiative. For the United States, which has been striving to maintain its global hegemony, the success of cooperation under the Belt and Road will further enhance the economic standing of developing countries, especially China, intensify the global multi-polarisation that is already in progress, and even enhance China's potential to challenge its dominance. Therefore, the United States does not want to see the success of cooperation under the Belt and Road, blaming China for trying to create a China-centred regional order through cooperation under the Belt and Road or for rebuilding the past "tributary system" as its cheap tool. We believe that with the deepening of cooperation under the Belt and Road, more and more cooperative participators will benefit from cooperation and understand China's cooperation intentions. They will be gradually aware that some misunderstandings of the Belt and Road Initiative are caused by lack of current knowledge about the Initiative, some are the product of a special international political background in this era, and some are deliberate.

China has created an economic miracle in the process of integration with the world, so China will continue to choose to embrace the world under the backdrop of counter-globalisation. Based on China's development reality, the Belt and Road Initiative proceeds from the welfare of 1.3 billion Chinese people and from realising the "Chinese Dream" of great rejuvenation of the Chinese nation and turns its eyes to the developing countries. The Belt and Road Initiative is a product of a major developing country's understanding of the requirements of the times and its understanding of its own responsibilities. The Initiative is designed with the objective of building a community of a shared future for mankind, which is the great pursuit of our time and the grand background under which the Initiative was proposed.

Notes

1 The "Two Centenary Goals" were first proposed in the report to the 15th CPC National Congress: the first Centenary Goal is to comprehensively build a moderately prosperous society by 2021 to celebrate the centenary of the Communist Party of China; the second Centenary Goal is to build a modern socialist country that is prosperous, strong, democratic, culturally advanced and harmonious by 2049 to celebrate the centenary of New China. The report to the 19th CPC National Congress states that "based on a comprehensive analysis of the international and domestic environments and the conditions for China's development, we have drawn up a two-stage development plan for the period from 2020 to the middle of this century. From 2020 to 2035, we will build on the foundation created by the moderately prosperous society with a further 15 years of hard work to see that socialist modernization is basically realized. From 2035 to the middle of the 21st century, we will, building on having basically achieved modernization, work hard for a further 15 years and develop China into a great modern socialist country that is prosperous, strong, democratic, culturally advanced, harmonious, and beautiful".
2 "Promote Friendship Between Our People and Work Together to Build a Bright Future—Speech by Xi Jinping at Nazarbayev University in Kazakhstan," September 7, 2013.
3 "Work together to Build a China–ASEAN Community of Shared Destiny—Speech by Xi Jinping President of the People's Republic of China at the People's Representative Council of Indonesia," October 3, 2013.
4 "Promote Friendship Between Our People and Work Together to Build a Bright Future—Speech by Xi Jinping at Nazarbayev University in Kazakhstan", September 7, 2013.
5 "Work together to Build a China–ASEAN Community of Shared Destiny—Speech by Xi Jinping President of the People's Republic of China at the People's Representative Council of Indonesia," October 3, 2013.
6 President Xi Jinping said at the Sixth Ministerial Conference of the China–Arab States Cooperation Forum that China plans to import goods worth over $10 trillion in the next 5 years. According to the news of the Chinese Ministry of Commerce, China will also import more than $2.2 trillion worth of services from the world in the next 5 years.

18

THE BELT AND ROAD INITIATIVE FRAMEWORK

Wang Yuzhu and Li Shicheng

The Belt and Road Initiative is a way for win–win cooperation that promotes common development and prosperity and a road towards peace and friendship by enhancing mutual understanding and trust and strengthening all round exchanges. The Belt and Road Initiative is a development initiative, a cooperative initiative and an open initiative to share China's development opportunities and promote common prosperity with countries along the routes.

Upholding four concepts and building three communities

The Belt and Road Initiative upholds the concepts of peace and cooperation, openness and inclusiveness, mutual learning and mutual benefit. It is based on the "five types of connectivity", namely, policy coordination, infrastructure connectivity, unimpeded trade, financial integration and understanding between people. It promotes practical cooperation in all fields, and works to build a community of shared interests, destiny and responsibility featuring mutual political trust, economic integration and cultural inclusiveness.

The concepts of "peace and cooperation, openness and inclusiveness, mutual learning and mutual benefit" are not only the inheritance of the spirit of the ancient Silk Road, but also the innovation of the development concepts. Inclusiveness is a typical feature of the Belt and Road Initiative that distinguishes it from other cooperative organisations or mechanisms. The building of the Belt and Road is open and inclusive. We welcome all countries and international and regional organisations to take an active part in cooperation under the Belt and Road, strengthen dialogues, and seek common ground while reserving differences to achieve shared growth through consultations and enable more regions to benefit from the fruits of cooperation.

The Initiative emphasises mutual benefit, rises above the old mentality of global governance and replaces the zero-sum game with win–win cooperation. All countries can participate on an equal footing and work together to advance its implementation. It accommodates interests and concerns, reflects the wisdom and creativity and gives full play to strengths and potentials of all parties involved, and helps to nurture new competitive edges. It seeks mutual benefit and a conjunction of interests and the "biggest common denominator" for cooperation, and makes economic globalisation more open, inclusive and balanced so that its benefits can be shared by all.

The Belt and Road Initiative upholds the general principle of building a community of shared interests. As a major initiative that benefits all parties, the Belt and Road Initiative strikes a chord of building a cross-border community of shared interests. It will rely on wide-ranging international economic cooperation to promote connectivity and facilitate trade and investment. It envisions a world of new economic growth, where win–win strategies are favoured. Individual countries along the routes—most of which are developing countries—each have their own natural resources, infrastructure and historical experiences; such differences, among other factors, have led to different levels of development. In a joint effort to build the Belt and Road, each country's comparative strengths can be better exploited, and economic complementarities can be better transformed into new drivers of development. It promotes interconnected development of countries along the routes and deepens economic integration. In this process, countries will forge a community of shared interests for common development and prosperity, thus laying the foundation for building the community of a shared future.

The Belt and Road Initiative regards it as part of its corporate responsibility to build a community of shared responsibility. The Initiative helps to promote rapid development of developing countries, maintain regional stability and promote cultural exchanges. Building an Afro-Eurasia and even a world of durable peace and common prosperity is the common aspiration of all countries along the routes. The Belt and Road connects different civilisations through a new mode of cooperation, promotes the harmonious coexistence and mutual learning of different countries and their peoples and urges different countries to jointly shoulder the responsibility for solving international problems. This is a major contribution made by countries of different races, different faiths and different cultural backgrounds to the development of human civilisation in the new era.

Under the Belt and Road Initiative, a community of a shared future can only be built on the basis of shared interests and responsibility. To build a community of a shared future, we must abandon the "zero-sum" mentality, reject exclusive interests, adhere to equal consultations, accommodate the comfort level of all parties, promote mutual trust through cooperation and promote mutual cooperation through mutual trust to finally achieve a community of a shared future called for by all parties. To build a community of a shared future, we must respect each other and treat each other as equals, seek win–win cooperation and common development, and ensure inclusiveness and mutual learning among civilisations. To build a community of a shared future, we must also strengthen cooperation in non-economic areas, mainly including ensuring the safety of transport pathways, especially ocean transport pathways, strengthening counter-terrorism cooperation at the regional level, establishing territorial and maritime delimitation dispute settlement mechanisms, promoting joint development of marine resources and cooperation in environmental protection.

Building four major Silk Roads

The Belt and Road focuses on building the four Silk Roads together with the countries along the routes: the Silk Road of Green Development, the Silk Road of Health Cooperation, the Silk Road of Intelligence and the Silk Road of Peace. With the spirit of driving nails, we will steadily advance the Belt and Road Initiative to benefit the peoples along the routes. President Xi Jinping stressed in his speech to the Legislative Chamber of the Supreme Assembly of Uzbekistan on June 22, 2016 that we must deepen environmental protection cooperation, practice the concept of green development, step up efforts in ecological environmental protection, and work together to build a "Silk Road of Green Development"; we must strengthen mutually beneficial cooperation in medical and health services, notification of infectious disease and epidemic situation, disease prevention and control, medical rescue and traditional medicine, and work together to build a "Silk Road of Health Cooperation"; we must strengthen cooperation in talent cultivation, and work together to build a "Silk Road of Intelligence"; we must strengthen security cooperation, uphold a vision on common, comprehensive, cooperative and sustainable security in Asia, promote the construction of a safe governance model with Asian characteristics, and work together to build a "Silk Road of Peace".[1]

Upholding the principles of extensive consultation, joint contribution and shared benefits

China will uphold the principles of extensive consultation, joint contribution and shared benefits in promoting the building of the Belt and Road with countries along the routes. In his speech entitled "Work Together to Build the Silk Road Economic Belt and The 21st Century Maritime Silk Road", President Xi Jinping emphasised that "The pursuit of this initiative is based on extensive consultation and its benefits will be shared by us all".[2] The Belt and Road is an undertaking shared by China and all participating countries. We will uphold the principles of extensive consultation, joint contribution and shared benefits, pursue equality and mutual benefit, strengthen friendly dialogues and consultation with the participating countries, and synergise China's Belt and Road Initiative with the development strategies of other countries in the region, and we welcome all parties to take a free ride on China's fast development in an open and inclusive attitude and share the achievements and experience of China's development.[3] We will support the participating countries to actively develop an open economy based on their own national conditions, participate in global governance and supply of public goods, work together to build a wide-covering community of shared interests and establish an open cooperation platform to maintain and develop an open world economy, which is specifically embodied in the following aspects.

First, the Belt and Road Initiative is in line with the purposes and principles of the UN Charter. It upholds the Five Principles of Peaceful Coexistence: mutual respect for each other's sovereignty and territorial integrity, mutual non-aggression, mutual non-interference in each other's internal affairs, equality and mutual benefit and peaceful coexistence.

Second, the Initiative is open for cooperation. It covers, but is not limited to, the area of the ancient Silk Road. It is open to all countries and international and regional organisations for engagement, so that the results of the concerted efforts will benefit wider areas.

Third, the Initiative is harmonious and inclusive. It advocates tolerance among civilisations, respects the paths and modes of development chosen by different countries, and supports dialogues among different civilisations on the principles of seeking common ground while shelving differences and drawing on each other's strengths, so that all countries can coexist in peace for common prosperity.

Fourth, the Initiative follows market operation. It will abide by market rules and international norms, give play to the decisive role of the market in resource allocation and the primary role of enterprises, and let the governments perform their due functions.

Fifth, the Initiative seeks mutual benefit. It accommodates the interests and concerns of all parties involved, and seeks a conjunction of interests and the "biggest common denominator" for cooperation so as to give full play to the wisdom and creativity, strengths and potentials of all parties.

Five key cooperation directions

The Belt and Road routes run through the continents of Asia, Europe and Africa, connecting the vibrant East Asia economic circle at one end and developed European economic circle at the other, and encompassing countries with huge potential for economic development. Based on the proposal from President Xi and the need to promote international cooperation, and taking into consideration the routes of the ancient land and sea Silk Roads, China has identified five routes for the Belt and Road. The Silk Road Economic Belt has three routes: one from Northwest China and Northeast China to Europe and the Baltic Sea via Central Asia and Russia; one from Northwest China to the Persian Gulf and the Mediterranean Sea, passing through Central Asia and West Asia; and one from Southwest China through the Indochina Peninsula to the Indian Ocean. The 21st Century Maritime Silk Road has two major routes: one starts from coastal ports of China, crosses the South China Sea, passes through the Malacca Strait, and reaches the Indian Ocean, extending to Europe; the other starts from coastal ports of China, crosses the South China Sea, and extends to the South Pacific.[4]

A framework including six corridors, six means of communication, multiple countries and multiple ports

Based on the above five routes, as well as the cooperation priorities and spatial distribution of the Belt and Road, China has proposed a framework including six corridors, six means of communication, multiple countries and multiple ports. The "six corridors" are: the New Eurasian Land Bridge Economic Corridor, the China–Mongolia–Russia Economic Corridor, the China–Central Asia–West Asia Economic Corridor, the China–Indochina Peninsula Economic Corridor, the China–Pakistan Economic Corridor and the Bangladesh–China–India–Myanmar Economic Corridor. The "six means of communication" are rail, highways, seagoing transport, aviation, pipelines and aerospace integrated information network, which comprise the main targets of infrastructure connectivity. "Multiple countries" refer to a number of countries along the Belt and Road that first joined the Initiative, and China will cooperate with them on the basis of equality and mutual benefit. However, pragmatism requires a need to cooperate first with a number of particular countries, and try to achieve results with them that have a demonstrative impact and embody the concept of the Belt and Road, so that more countries will be attracted to participate in the initiative. "Multiple ports" refer to a number of ports that ensure safe and smooth sea passages. By building a number of important ports and key cities with countries along the Belt and Road, China works to promote maritime cooperation. The cooperation framework is the framework for joint building of the Belt and Road, giving a clear direction for countries involved to participate in the initiative.

The "five types of connectivity"

Countries along the Belt and Road have their own resource advantages and their economies are mutually complementary. Therefore, there is a great potential and space for cooperation. They should promote policy coordination, infrastructure connectivity, unimpeded trade, financial integration and understanding between people as their five major goals, and strengthen cooperation in the following key areas.

Enhancing policy coordination is an important guarantee for implementing the Initiative. We should promote intergovernmental cooperation, build a multi-level intergovernmental macro policy exchange and communication mechanism, expand shared interests, enhance mutual political trust and build new cooperation consensus. Countries along the Belt and Road may fully coordinate their economic development strategies and policies, work out plans and measures for regional cooperation, negotiate to solve cooperation-related issues, and jointly provide policy support for the implementation of practical cooperation and large-scale projects.

Infrastructure connectivity is a priority area for implementing the Initiative. On the basis of respecting each other's sovereignty and security concerns, countries along the Belt and

Road should improve the connectivity of their infrastructure construction plans and technical standard systems, jointly push forward the construction of international trunk passageways, and form an infrastructure network connecting all subregions in Asia, and between Asia, Europe and Africa step by step. At the same time, efforts should be made to promote green and low-carbon infrastructure construction and operation management, taking into full account the impact of climate change on the construction.

Promoting unimpeded trade is a major task in building the Belt and Road. We should strive to improve investment and trade facilitation, and remove investment and trade barriers for the creation of a sound business environment within the region and in all related countries. We will discuss with countries and regions along the Belt and Road on opening free trade areas so as to unleash the potential for expanded cooperation.

Financial integration is an important underpinning for implementing the Belt and Road Initiative. We should deepen financial cooperation, and make more efforts in building a currency stability system, investment and financing system and credit information system in Asia. We should expand the scope and scale of bilateral currency swap and settlement with other countries along the Belt and Road, open and develop the bond market in Asia, make joint efforts to establish the Asian Infrastructure Investment Bank and BRICS New Development Bank, conduct negotiation among related parties on establishing Shanghai Cooperation Organisation (SCO) financing institution, and set up and put into operation the Silk Road Fund as early as possible. We should strengthen practical cooperation of China–ASEAN Interbank Association and SCO Interbank Association, and carry out multilateral financial cooperation in the form of syndicated loans and bank credit. We will support the efforts of governments of the countries along the Belt and Road and their companies and financial institutions with good credit rating to issue Renminbi bonds in China. Qualified Chinese financial institutions and companies are encouraged to issue bonds in both Renminbi and foreign currencies outside China, and use the funds thus collected in countries along the Belt and Road.

Peoples' mutual understanding provides the public support for implementing the Initiative. We should carry forward the spirit of friendly cooperation of the Silk Road by promoting extensive cultural and academic exchanges, personnel exchanges and cooperation, media cooperation, youth and women exchanges and volunteer services, so as to win public support for deepening bilateral and multilateral cooperation.

Cooperation mechanisms

The world economic integration is accelerating and regional cooperation is on the upswing. China will take full advantage of the existing bilateral and multilateral cooperation mechanisms to push forward the building of the Belt and Road and to promote the development of regional cooperation.

We should strengthen bilateral cooperation, and promote comprehensive development of bilateral relations through multi-level and multi-channel communication and consultation. We should encourage the signing of cooperation memorandums of understanding (MOUs) or plans, and develop a number of bilateral cooperation pilot projects. We should establish and improve bilateral joint working mechanisms, and draw up implementation plans and roadmaps for advancing the Belt and Road Initiative. In addition, we should give full play to the existing bilateral mechanisms such as joint committee, mixed committee, coordinating committee, steering committee and management committee to coordinate and promote the implementation of cooperation projects.

We should enhance the role of multilateral cooperation mechanisms, and make full use of existing mechanisms such as the SCO, ASEAN Plus China (10+1), Asia–Pacific Economic

Cooperation (APEC), Asia–Europe Meeting (ASEM), Asia Cooperation Dialogue (ACD), Conference on Interaction and Confidence-Building Measures in Asia (CICA), China–Arab States Cooperation Forum (CASCF), China–Gulf Cooperation Council (GCC) Strategic Dialogue, Greater Mekong Subregion (GMS) Economic Cooperation, and Central Asia Regional Economic Cooperation (CAREC) to strengthen communication with relevant countries and attract more countries and regions to participate in the Belt and Road Initiative.

We should continue to encourage the constructive role of the international forums and exhibitions at regional and subregional levels hosted by countries along the Belt and Road, as well as such platforms as Boao Forum for Asia, China–ASEAN Expo, China–Eurasia Expo, Euro-Asia Economic Forum, China International Fair for Investment and Trade, China–South Asia Expo, China–Arab States Expo, Western China International Fair, China–Russia Expo and Qianhai Cooperation Forum. We should support the local authorities and general public of countries along the Belt and Road to explore the historical and cultural heritage of the Belt and Road, jointly hold investment, trade and cultural exchange activities, and ensure the success of the Silk Road (Dunhuang) International Culture Expo, Silk Road International Film Festival and Silk Road International Book Fair. We propose to set up an international summit forum on the Belt and Road Initiative.

Organisational guarantee of the Belt and Road

Implementing the Belt and Road Initiative is a massive undertaking involving a wide range of areas, a long span of time and arduous construction tasks. Integrated planning and guidance are essential. Therefore, a leading group for the Belt and Road Initiative has thus been established at the national level to provide guidance and coordination in the implementation of the Initiative. The Office of the Leading Group is located in the National Development and Reform Commission and is responsible for the routine work of the Leading Group. China will join other countries along the Belt and Road to substantiate and improve the contents and mode of cooperation under the Belt and Road, work out relevant timetables and road maps, align national development programmes and regional cooperation plans and sign cooperation framework agreements and memoranda. China will work with countries along the Belt and Road to carry out joint research, forums and fairs, personnel training, exchanges and visits under the framework of existing bilateral, multilateral, regional and subregional cooperation mechanisms, so that they will gain a better understanding and recognition of the contents, objectives and tasks of the Belt and Road Initiative. China will work with countries along the Belt and Road to steadily advance demonstration projects, jointly identify programmes that accommodate bilateral and multilateral interests and accelerate the launching of programmes that are agreed upon by parties and ready for implementation, so as to ensure early harvests and bring benefits to the local people.

Promoting the formation of a new pattern of regional economic integration

The Initiative is an ambitious economic vision of the opening-up of and cooperation among the countries along the Belt and Road. Countries should work in concert and move towards the objectives of mutual benefit and common security. To be specific, they need to improve the region's infrastructure, and put in place a secure and efficient network of land, sea and air passages, lifting their connectivity to a higher level; further enhance trade and investment facilitation, establish a network of free trade areas that meet high standards, maintain closer economic ties and deepen political trust; enhance cultural exchanges; encourage different civilisations to learn from each other and flourish together; and promote mutual understanding, peace and friendship among people of all countries.

Notes

1 "Speech by Xi Jinping to the Legislative Chamber of the Supreme Assembly of Uzbekistan (full text)," Xinhuanet, www.xinhuanet.com/politics/2016-06/23/c_1119094900.htm
2 "Work together to Promote the Building of the Belt and Road," renminnet, http://world.people.com.cn/n1/2017/0515/c1002-29274975.html
3 "Promote the Building of the Belt and Road to Build A Community of A Shared Future for Mankind—In-depth Study of the Important Arguments of Vol. 2 of *The Governance of China* about the Building of the Belt and Road," people.com.cn, www.cssn.cn/zx/201801/t20180129_3831068_2.shtml
4 "Vision and Actions on Jointly Building Silk Road Economic Belt and 21st-Century Maritime Silk Road," www.yidaiyilu.gov.cn. www.yidaiyilu.gov.cn/yw/qwfb/604.htm

19
BASIC CONTENTS

Xu Juan and Wang Yuzhu

The Belt and Road, which should be jointly built through consultation to meet the interests of all, aims to connect Asian, European and African countries as well as Latin American countries more closely in new forms by integrating the historical symbolism of the ancient Silk Road to provide China's solutions and proposals to maintain an open world economic system.

The basic content of the Silk Road Economic Belt

The Silk Road Economic Belt is a new economic development zone formed on the concept of the ancient Silk Road. In the Western Han Dynasty more than 2000 years ago, Zhang Qian's missions to the Western Regions opened up a roadway, with Chang'an (now known as Xi'an) as the starting point, from China via the Guanzhong Plain, the Hexi Corridor and the Tarim Basin to Central Asia, Iran and the Mediterranean countries. This land-based trade passage was known as the most important trade artery in the world. With the passage of time, trade and investment on this ancient Silk Road became active again in the early 21st century. Under the background of rapid development of modern transportation and information industries and globalisation, promoting the development and cooperation in various areas of economic and trade along the Silk Road is not only the inheritance of history and culture, but also the exploitation of great development potential in the region. On September 7, 2013, Chinese President Xi Jinping made an important speech at Nazarbayev University in Kazakhstan and proposed to jointly build the Silk Road Economic Belt. To forge closer economic ties, deepen cooperation and expand development space in the Eurasian region, we should take an innovative approach and jointly build an "economic belt along the Silk Road".[1]

The Silk Road Economic Belt stretches over 7000 kilometres across Asia and Europe, passes through many countries and covers areas with a total population of nearly 3 billion. The Silk Road Economic Belt connects the Asia–Pacific Economic Circle in the east and the European Economic Circle in the west. Most countries along the routes are in the "collapse zone" between the two engines, and the terrain of the region is "high on both sides and low in the middle". The Silk Road Economic Belt is considered to be "the longest and most promising economic corridor in the world". The Silk Road Economic Belt is first of all a concept of "economic belt", and it embodies the idea of concentrated and coordinated development of cities on the Economic Belt.[2]

The Silk Road Economic Belt has initially formed three routes in spatial extending direction, namely the northern route mainly composed of the Eurasian Continental Bridge, the middle route mainly composed of oil and gas pipelines, and the southern route mainly composed of transnational highways. At present, the development plans for the three main routes of the economic belt are being formulated. The regions involved within the territory of China currently include the five northwestern provinces, Chongqing, Sichuan, Inner Mongolia and Xinjiang Construction Corps, and will further expand to other provinces and regions in China in the future.

The basic content of the 21st Century Maritime Silk Road

The 21st Century Maritime Silk Road was also inherited from the ancient Maritime Silk Road. The ancient Maritime Silk Road ran along the southeast coast of China, passed through the Indo-China Peninsula and the countries surrounding the South China Sea, crossed the Indian Ocean and extended to the Red Sea, East Africa and finally Europe, becoming a large-scale, ocean-going passage for trade and cultural exchange between China and foreign countries and promoting common development of countries along the route. After entering the twenty-first century, vigour and vitality were instilled into the Maritime Silk Road. General Secretary Xi Jinping proposed the strategic concept of the 21st Century Maritime Silk Road during his visit to ASEAN in October 2013. The strategic partners of the 21st Century Maritime Silk Road are not limited to ASEAN. Starting with the launch of individual projects that are expected to help spur a wider range of cooperative activities, it envisions a network of interconnected markets linking the ASEAN countries, South Asia, West Africa, North Africa and Europe, and a strategic partnership for the South China Sea and the Pacific and Indian oceans. Its long-term development goal is to promote economic and trade integration in Asia, Europe and Africa. At the crossroads and as a necessary part of the Maritime Silk Road, ASEAN is the primary development goal of the 21st Century Maritime Silk Road strategy.

The 21st Century Maritime Silk Road has two main routes: one connects China and Europe via the South China Sea and the Indian Ocean; the other connects China and the South Pacific through the South China Sea. Constructing the ports along the sea routes is an essential part of the 21st Century Maritime Silk Road. Capacity expansion and industrial agglomeration can be achieved in port cities by strengthening connectivity of infrastructures such as roads and railways. Priority should be given to building port fulcrums to drive the economic development of the hinterlands of the fulcrum countries so as to forge a bilateral and multilateral cooperative economic belt.

The 21st Century Maritime Silk Road aims to strengthen China's positive spillovers to the external economy, and solve the imbalance or hindrance of resource allocation in the process of interaction between both sides. Meanwhile, by providing funds and assistance in infrastructure, technology and other fields to developing countries, we can promote the effective allocation of production materials in China and regions and countries along the route. On the basis of consolidating cooperation with the existing surrounding natural economic regions, we can further develop new transboundary regional economic cooperation in the potential geo-economic space to create more economic consortiums and market communities.[3]

The basic content of the Belt and Road

First, the Belt and Road Initiative is a road towards friendship by enhancing mutual understanding and trust, a way for win–win cooperation that promotes common development and prosperity and a way that is open and inclusive for all countries. The Belt and Road inherits and carries forward the spirit of the ancient Silk Road. Although proposed and advocated by the Chinese government, the Initiative works to build a community of shared interests, destiny and responsibility featuring mutual political trust, economic integration and cultural inclusiveness. The Belt and Road Initiative is not an aid programme, a security alliance or a Chinese version of the "Marshall Plan". It is a concept and initiative that adheres to cooperative development and aims to promote multilateral cooperation between China and the rest of the world. The Belt and Road emphasises joint participation and mutual assistance, contribution and promotion. It adheres to promoting government guidance, enterprise participation and market operation, and gives play to the advantages of all countries in capital, technology, market, etc. to achieve complementarities, make the cake of common interests bigger and achieve win–win outcomes. In cooperation, China has always insisted on friendly consultations and lays stress on improving people's livelihood without any political strings attached. The Belt and Road Initiative has no threshold requirements and is not targeted at any third party or any existing international cooperation mechanism. All countries can be participants, builders and beneficiaries of the Belt and Road Initiative.[4] The Belt and Road Initiative is not a closed regional economic cooperation mechanism. The Belt and Road Initiative is open and inclusive in space. Its geographical scope is not limited to Eurasia and its adjacent oceans. It is a platform for cooperation that welcomes all countries willing to cooperate with China to achieve win–win outcomes.

Second, the Belt and Road Initiative is a road that will be built by all participants based on its guiding principles of extensive consultation, joint contribution and shared benefits. "Extensive consultation" means that all participating countries should strengthen exchanges and mutual trust and jointly resolve international political disputes and economic contradictions through consultations. China follows the trend of the world, respects the sovereignty of all countries and advocates that countries of different size, strength or wealth are all equal. All countries along the routes should reach political consensus and seek common interests through consultations, which is conducive to building a new type of international relations with win–win cooperation as the core and conducive to building a community of a shared future for mankind. "Joint contribution" means that all countries along the routes will jointly participate in the building of the Belt and Road, share development opportunities and expand common interests, thus forming a mutually beneficial and win–win community of shared interests. The Belt and Road is a Chinese solution to promote global common development. It is not a solo for China itself but a real chorus comprising all countries along the routes. It aims to realise complementary advantages and pursues mutual benefit through cooperation. "Shared benefit" means that all countries along the routes will pursue equal development and share interests so that every country and its people in the world can enjoy equal opportunities for development and share the fruits of world economic development. The Belt and Road aims to seek common interests of the countries concerned and share interests in win–win cooperation through economic integration and development interaction.[5]

Third, the Belt and Road is a road to achieve coordinated and interactive development of land and sea. The Belt and Road Initiative has two major dimensions: land and sea. The two complement each other, and each has its own emphasis. The Belt focuses on opening to the West and establishing a land-based passage from western China to Central Asia, Russia, West Asia, Africa and finally Europe. It strengthens physical connectivity between countries and reduces the costs of freight transportation. The Road focuses on opening up from the east to the west via the sea, building an ocean-going passage from South East Asia, South Asia to the Indian Ocean and Europe. It strengthens rational use and development of marine resources and deepens cooperation in the fields of maritime environment protection, navigation safety, maritime search and rescue and marine technology. The Belt and Road Initiative will break the long-standing pattern that land power and sea power are opposite, and promote the connectivity of Eurasia and the Pacific Ocean, the Indian Ocean and the Atlantic Ocean and the integration of land and sea, forming a safe and efficient sea–land transport network and building a new pattern of all-round opening-up through coordinated sea and land transport.

Fourth, the Belt and Road Initiative is a new model of global governance and international cooperation. Global governance is a major issue facing the world, and it is also a major issue facing China. Under the international background of rising counter-globalisation and populism, China's innovative global governance thinking and model enable the rest of the world to share the successful experience of China's reform and opening up and provide "global public goods" with Chinese characteristics for global governance. China hopes to drive common development with its partners through the Belt and Road Initiative, especially for the developing countries, to jointly promote infrastructure construction, improve the level of industrialisation and solve the imbalance of world economic development. The Belt and Road emphasises "mutual aid between the East and the West", "North–South cooperation" and "South–South cooperation". While striving to maintain the international order, China will work with developing countries to build an international political and economic order that is fairer and more just and reasonable.

Fifth, the Belt and Road Initiative aims to improve connectivity across Asia, Europe and Africa. If the Belt and Road are likened to the two wings of a soaring Asia, then connectivity is like their arteries and veins. Only by opening up the arteries and veins can we ensure the circulation of personnel, funds and goods, and truly promote the building of the Belt and Road.[6] In the address at the Dialogue on Strengthening Connectivity Partnership held in November 2014, Chinese President Xi Jinping defined "connectivity" as "a three-way combination of infrastructure, institutions and people-to-people exchanges", "a five-way progress in policy communication, infrastructure connectivity, trade link, capital flow, and understanding among peoples" and "a wide-ranging, multi-dimensional, vibrant and open connectivity network that pools talent and resources from all stakeholders".[7] On the basis of respecting each other's sovereignty and security concerns, countries along the Belt and Road should improve the connectivity of their infrastructure construction plans and technical standard systems, jointly push forward the construction of international trunk passageways, improve the coordination of development plans and technical standards in land, water, aviation, energy and communications, and form an infrastructure network connecting all subregions in Asia, and between Asia, Europe and Africa step by step.

Sixth, the Belt and Road Initiative focuses on economic cooperation. The Belt and Road Initiative aims to enhance the level of economic and trade cooperation, promote cooperation in production capacity and investment and expand financial cooperation space by relying on the key economic industrial parks as cooperation platforms. The Belt and Road Initiative will focus on building the six major economic corridors: the New Eurasian Land Bridge, the China–Mongolia–Russia Economic Corridor (CMREC), the China–Pakistan Economic Corridor (CPEC), the China–Central and Western Asia Economic Corridor, the China–Indochina Peninsula Economic Corridor, the Bangladesh–China–India–Myanmar Economic Corridor (BCIMEC). It is funded by the AIIB and the Silk Road Fund. We should embrace the outside world with an open mind, uphold the multilateral trading regime, advance the building of free trade areas and promote liberalisation and facilitation of trade and investment. The implementation of the Belt and Road Initiative will advance cooperation in transnational industrial chains and promote the construction of various industrial parks such as overseas economic and trade cooperation zones and cross-border economic cooperation zones. In accordance with the market-oriented operation mode, we will promote the construction of industrial parks in countries along the Belt and Road. According to the development needs of enterprises, combined with the resource advantages and the strategies for improving people's livelihood and development of the relevant countries, it will promote the economic development and industrial upgrading in these countries. One of the priority cooperation directions for building the Belt and Road is to promote cooperation in international production capacity and equipment manufacturing and expand mutual investment. Meanwhile, it will strengthen various forms of financial cooperation between China and the participating countries and relevant institutions, promote the networking of financial institutions and financial services and innovate financing mechanisms.

Seventh, understanding between people provides the public support for implementing the Initiative. The Belt and Road will promote cultural exchanges between different countries, nations, religions and cultures, eliminate each other's barriers and suspicions, enhance friendship and cultural integration and jointly promote the prosperity and development of human civilisation. The Belt and Road Initiative inherits and promotes the Silk Road spirit of friendly cooperation, and extensively carries out cultural exchanges, academic exchanges, talent exchanges and cooperation, media cooperation, youth and women's exchanges, volunteer services, etc. laying a solid foundation of public opinions for deepening bilateral and multilateral cooperation. While promoting economic and trade cooperation, the Belt and Road also emphasises exchanges and cooperation between universities, think tanks, research institutions, enterprises and personnel of all countries along the routes. While having confidence in Chinese culture and path, we will maintain respect for the culture, religion and traditions of countries along the route.

Eighth, the Belt and Road Initiative aims to achieve mutual benefit and common security. The basic content of the Belt and Road is very rich, involving economics, culture, politics, diplomacy and security. The Belt and Road Initiative will uphold the Silk Road Spirit of "peace and cooperation, openness and inclusiveness, mutual learning and mutual benefit". Security of all countries is inter-related and will affect each other. We must abandon the narrow security concept of acting as a hegemon imposing our will on others, benefiting ourselves at other people's cost or shifting our risks on to others. We regard mutually beneficial cooperation as the only choice to promote common security among all countries.[8]

Notes

1 "Speech by Xi Jinping at Nazarbayev University in Kazakhstan," cpc.people.com.cn, http://cpc.people.com.cn/n/2013/0908/c64094-22843681.html.
2 "Comprehensive Interpretation of the Silk Road Economic Belt," Xinhuanet, http://travel.news.cn/2015-06/15/c_127917660.htm.
3 Pan Zhongqi & Huang Renwei, "China's Geo-Economic Strategy," in *Journal of Tsinghua University* (Philosophy and Social Sciences), 2008, Issue 5, p. 122.
4 "Building the Belt and Road: Content, Significance and Think Tank Mission," Xinhuanet, www.xinhuanet.com/politics/2015-06/01/c_127865670.htm
5 Chen Jianzhong, "Global Governance through Wide Consultation, Joint Contribution and Shared Benefits Has Profound Significance," http://theory.people.com.cn/n1/2017/0912/c40531-29529079.html.
6 "Xi Jinping's 'Belt and Road' Footprints," cpc.people, http://cpc.people.com.cn/xuexi/n1/2016/0906/c385474-28694919-2.html.
7 "Infrastructure Connectivity Is the Foundation of Connectivity of Policies, Rules and Standards," the website of the Development Research Center of the State Council, www.drc.gov.cn/xsyzcfx/20141128/1-1243-2885207.htm
8 "China's Solution to Promote Global Security Governance", Xinhuanet, www.xinhuanet.com/mrdx/2017-09/27/c_136641202.htm

20
BASIC PRINCIPLES

Wang Yuzhu and Jiang Fangfei

Proposal of the principles of "extensive consultation, joint contribution and shared benefits"

"Extensive consultation, joint contribution and shared benefits" is an important part of the thought on major-country diplomacy with Chinese characteristics for the new era. It is the basic principle for China to build the Belt and Road and participate in global governance, and an effective way to build a community of a shared future for mankind. The principles of "extensive consultation, joint contribution and shared benefits" were proposed based on the status quo of global governance failure in the post-financial crisis era. It is based on China's dual identity as the largest developing country and an emerging power, reflecting the attitude of China as a responsible major country towards actively participating in global governance and promoting international win–win cooperation.

In March 2015, the Chinese government issued the *Vision and Actions on Jointly Building the Silk Road Economic Belt and the 21st Century Maritime Silk Road*, which proposed promoting policy coordination, infrastructure connectivity, unimpeded trade, financial integration, and understanding between people and adhering to the principle of achieving shared growth through discussion and collaboration in actively propelling the Belt and Road construction.

In September 2015, the 2015 Media Cooperation Forum on the Belt and Road with the theme "Common Destiny and New Patterns of Cooperation" was held in Beijing. Wang Jiarui, vice chairman of the National Committee of the Chinese People's Political Consultative Conference and Minister of the International Liaison Department of the CPC Central Committee, said in his speech at the forum that President Xi Jinping had repeatedly stressed that China's pursuit of the Belt and Road was to promote the mutual benefit and common development of countries along the routes and even in the world. In the pursuit of the Belt and Road, we must uphold the principle of extensive consultation, joint contribution and shared benefits. This is also the core content of the Belt and Road Initiative.

In October 2015, Xi Jinping presided over the 27th group study session of members of the Politburo of the CPC Central Committee. He stressed that "we should promote innovative development of visions on global governance, actively seek the point of resonance between the positive ways of life and governance in Chinese culture and today's world, continue to enrich the ideas of building a community of a shared future for mankind, and promote the principle of achieving shared growth through discussion and collaboration in engaging in global governance".

In May 2017, Xi Jinping emphasised in the closing ceremony of the Belt and Road Forum for International Cooperation that all parties will adhere to the principle of extensive consultation, joint contribution and shared benefits, respect each other, make joint decisions through democratic consultation, and promote the cooperation under the Belt and Road to continuously make new progress and inject strong impetus into building a community of a shared future for mankind. In October 2017, the report to the 19th National Congress clearly states that China will follow the principle of achieving shared growth through discussion and collaboration in engaging in global governance.

The content and internal logic of the principles of "extensive consultation, joint contribution and shared benefits"

As the basic principle and core content of the Belt and Road Initiative, the principles of "extensive consultation, joint contribution and shared benefits" integrate Western civilisation with Eastern wisdom, combines a world vision with Chinese characteristics and advocates that developed countries and developing countries should jointly discuss the major plans for development, solve problems together, jointly build cooperation mechanisms and share a bright future.

"Extensive consultation" means that all participating countries should strengthen exchanges and mutual trust and jointly resolve international political disputes and economic contradictions through consultations. The Initiative accommodates the interests and concerns of all parties involved, and seeks a conjunction of interests and the "biggest common denominator" for cooperation so as to give full play to the wisdom and creativity, strengths and potentials of all parties. It highlights "collective beauty" and "goodness of dialogue". The essence of the principle of "extensive consultation" is equality and respect. The sovereignty and dignity of all countries, whether big or small, strong or weak, rich or poor, must be respected. This principle means that the Belt and Road Initiative advocates harmony and inclusiveness, fully respects the paths and modes of development chosen by different countries, and advocates dialogues among civilisations on the principles of seeking common ground while shelving differences and drawing on each other's strengths, so that all countries can coexist in peace for common prosperity.

"Joint contribution" means that all countries should participate in and cooperate with each other so as to give full play to the wisdom and creativity, strengths and potentials of all parties in the process of building the Belt and Road, and work together to build a peaceful, open, inclusive, prosperous and green community of a shared future for mankind. The essence of "joint contribution" is cooperation and responsibility. The building of the Belt and Road should not rely solely on the strength of China, but should pool the strength of all parties and needs active participation of all parties to jointly create more opportunities for development. This principle means that the Belt and Road Initiative advocates open cooperation. On the one hand, it covers, but is not limited to, the area of the ancient Silk Road. It is open to all countries, and international and regional organisations for engagement. On the other hand, China attaches great importance to the role of various market players, including enterprises, governments and individuals, in the building of the Belt and Road.

"Shared benefits" means that all countries along the routes enjoy equal access to development opportunities and development benefits, and in this way the achievements of joint contribution will benefit more regions. The principle of "shared benefits" is committed to ensuring that the fruits of the Belt and Road benefit all participants more equitably and the achievements of joint contribution benefit more regions. The essence of "shared benefits" lies in inclusiveness and mutual benefit. This means that the Belt and Road Initiative advocated by China is not a "zero-sum game" at the expense of damaging or sacrificing the interests of other countries. China will not "monopolise" the fruits of the Belt and Road construction. Instead, with an inclusive and open mind, China expects to enhance synergies with other countries to jointly build the Belt and Road Initiative through consultation to meet the interests of all.

Theoretical and practical significance of the principles of "extensive consultation, joint contribution and shared benefits"

The principles of "extensive consultation, joint contribution and shared benefits" are new principles, new ideas and new concepts proposed by the Chinese leaders to solve the common problems faced by today's human society after the financial crisis, and to instill vigour and vitality to the Belt and Road and the community of a shared future for mankind, which has profound theoretical significance and remarkable practical significance.

First, the principles of "extensive consultation, joint contribution and shared benefits" provide China's wisdom for updating Western ideas on global governance. The principles of "extensive consultation, joint contribution and shared benefits" emphasises the diversification and equalisation of global governance subjects, opposes hegemonism and power politics, emphasises common interests and interdependence between countries, and advocates easing conflicts and contradictions through consultations to achieve mutual benefit through joint contribution in building the Belt and Road and sharing contribution achievements. Fundamentally speaking, "extensive consultation, joint contribution and shared benefits" is an innovation of ideas on global governance. It abandons the law of the jungle and zero-sum mentality, gets rid of the shackles of realist theoretical logic and embodies the equality, openness, cooperation, win–win thinking and values advocated by China.

Second, the principles of "extensive consultation, joint contribution and shared benefits" provide a Chinese solution for improving the global governance system. After World War II, the global governance system led by the United States and the international rules formulated under the leadership of the United States have played an important role in regulating the post-war international order, safeguarding world peace and promoting world economic development. After the Cold War, the original global governance system has lagged behind the changes in the international situation, and the imbalance, inequity and under-representation of the system are the important reasons for global governance failure. The principles of "extensive consultation, joint contribution and shared benefits" help to guide the establishment of a more representative, inclusive, open and fair global governance system and guide equal consultation between developed and developing countries to encourage developing countries to actively participate in the formulation and implementation of international rules. In this way, they help to further improve the existing international institutional system to guarantee that and the achievements of global governance benefit more countries.

Third, the principles of "extensive consultation, joint contribution and shared benefits" provide the direction of action for building a community of a shared future for mankind. All countries of the world today have become a community of a shared future in which all are bound together for good or ill. The fundamental aim of the Belt and Road Initiative is to protect and promote the common interests of all mankind, and its ultimate goal is to build the community of a shared future for mankind, which are the essential characteristics that distinguish the Initiative from other international cooperation mechanisms. The principles of "extensive consultation, joint contribution and shared benefits" give the direction of action for realising a community of a shared future for mankind. The principles of "extensive consultation, joint contribution and shared benefits" help to nurture a habit of interaction and a cultural atmosphere of mutual respect, dialogue and cooperation among countries, which is conducive to forging a new type of international relationship. Meanwhile, by guiding countries to work to build a community of shared interests, destiny and responsibility featuring mutual political trust, economic integration and cultural inclusiveness, they facilitate the establishment of a new international political and economic order that is peaceful, safe, fair, rational and open to fundamentally solve the problem of global governance failure.

Fourth, the principles of "extensive consultation, joint contribution and shared benefits" provide the prerequisite and guarantee for the smooth and effective implementation of the Belt and Road. An important feature of the Belt and Road Initiative is the "diversification" of participants. It covers, but is not limited to, the area of the ancient Silk Road. It is open to all countries, and international and regional organisations for engagement. There are no threshold requirements, so any country or region can become a participant, builder and beneficiary so long as it is willing to do so. Mutual benefit is the fundamental driving force for the building of the Belt and Road. The principles of "extensive consultation, joint contribution and shared benefits" facilitate the reflection of the interests of all parties involved in a fairer and more balanced manner, and guide all parties involved to actively participate in the building of the Belt and Road, not to engage in zero-sum game, not to pursue mercantilism or shift their risks on to others, not to dump their products. They encourage all participants to make use of their complementary advantages to achieve benefit sharing and common development so as to build the Belt and Road into a road to mutual respect and mutual trust, a road to cooperation for mutual benefit and a road to mutual learning between cultures.

Upholding the principles of "extensive consultation, joint contribution and shared benefits"

The idea of a great initiative will be a feat only after it is put into practice and tested by practice. Therefore, the reform of the global governance system and the realisation of a community of a shared future for mankind depend on upholding the principles of "extensive consultation, joint contribution and shared benefits". In the pursuit of the Belt and Road, upholding the principles of "extensive consultation, joint contribution and shared benefits" will be the only way to build a community of a shared future for mankind. To uphold these principles, we should meet the following requirements.

First, we should strengthen policy coordination and development strategy integration, build more cooperation consensuses, seek a balance of concerns and strive to achieve coordinated development. We should further strengthen the coordination of macroeconomic policies in the fields of economy, finance, trade, investment, etc.; further promote trade and investment liberalisation and facilitation and effectively synergise development and cooperation plans to complement each other's advantages. We should strengthen policy coordination among all parties in non-traditional security and pool global forces to cope with global crises.

Second, we will pragmatically promote pragmatic cooperation in various fields, continue to make the pie of shared interests even bigger and strive to achieve new results. All parties should continue to strengthen connectivity, build infrastructure networks and actively promote the construction of economic corridors to achieve better and faster development of the real economy. We should adhere to market operations, attach importance to investment and financing cooperation, support further opening up of financial market, and strive to build a stable, sustainable and risk-controlled financial security system. We should make full use of existing bilateral and multilateral cooperation mechanisms, give to play a constructive role of relevant regional and subregional platforms of all countries and subregions and coordinate the implementation of cooperation projects. We should further deepen and expand cultural cooperation and facilitate people-to-people exchanges among all countries. We should strengthen pragmatic cooperation in the areas of environmental protection, climate change, anti-corruption, refugee crisis, and anti-terrorism.

Third, we should pragmatically enhance the "institutional discourse power" of developing countries in global governance and international rule-making, strive to build a platform for dialogue and cooperation between the North and the South, create a "sharing" atmosphere, and make the global governance system fairer and more rational, inclusive and open to radiate world development achievements and global governance outcomes to benefit more regions and countries.

21
PARTNERS

Xu Juan and Wang Yuzhu

The Belt and Road Initiative, which shoulders the mission of the new era and integrates the content of the new era, is rooted in the historical soil of the ancient Silk Road, although it covers, but is not limited to, the area of the ancient Silk Road. In order to adapt to the development of the times and changes in the international situation, the Chinese government is striving to build the Belt and Road into an open cooperation platform, which adheres to the Silk Road spirit of "peace and cooperation, openness and inclusiveness, mutual learning and mutual benefit", upholds the principles of "extensive consultation, joint contribution and shared benefits" and aims to create carriers, build channels, bridge geographical, civilised, economic and social development gaps, promote common development and harmonious development of all countries in the world and build a community of a shared future for mankind.

Categories of partners of the Belt and Road Initiative

The Belt and Road Initiative involves a large number of partners that can be categorised from the following perspectives.

(1) *International relation actors*

The Belt and Road Initiative opens its doors to all sovereign countries in the world and promotes exchanges and cooperation between governments, political parties and parliaments of all countries. Meanwhile, the Belt and Road Initiative has actively attracted international intergovernmental organisations, non-governmental organisations, multinational corporations, academic groups, think tanks, media and civil societies, including the United Nations, APEC, ASEAN, the South Asian Association for Regional Cooperation (SAARC), the European Union (EU) and the African Union (AU). The Belt and Road not only emphasises the one-track cooperation among governments, but also promotes two-track private cooperation. In this way, while exerting the leading role of governments, it can also mobilise the subjective initiative of the general public. Moreover, the Belt and Road Initiative not only emphasises communication and cooperation at the central government level, but also attaches importance to communication and interaction at the local government level. The Chinese government hopes to build a more dynamic, open, stable, sustainable and inclusive global economy through the Belt and Road cooperation platform, so that the achievements of joint contribution will benefit all corners of the world. The Belt and Road Initiative strives to form a cooperative mode combining governments, markets and societies and a three-dimensional government-led pattern that encourages enterprise participation and private investment.

(2) Principal status

China is the proposer and promoter of the Belt and Road Initiative, but China will never give a one-man show, practice the dictatorial rule or reinvent the wheel. Instead, China strives to combine the experience and achievements of China's development with the development willingness and comparative advantages of other countries, strengthen policy coordination of all countries, improve the level of connectivity and exchanges, and foster bilateral and multilateral cooperation with a broader scope and at a deeper level. Cooperation under the Belt and Road framework is something in which all countries, big or small, rich or poor, can participate on an equal footing. In the cooperation under the Belt and Road, there are neither the leader and the led nor the dominator and the dominated,

(3) Development level

The Belt and Road Initiative emphasises cooperation among developing countries and actively promotes cooperation between developing and developed countries. In addition, third-party cooperation is an important part of building the Belt and Road Initiative. The Belt and Road Initiative is an open and transparent cooperation initiative. China is ready to work with relevant developed countries to leverage complementary advantages in technology, capital, production capacity and market and carry out third-party cooperation with countries along the routes to promote mutual benefit and win–win results in accordance with the principles of "extensive consultation, joint contribution and shared benefits" and the laws of the market.

(4) Geographical coverage

Geologically, whether from Asia, Europe, Africa or the Americas, all can be partners in building the Belt and Road. Among them, the Eurasian Continent is one of the major engines of global economic growth as well as the main region under the Belt and Road Initiative. Africa is a key partner of the Belt and Road Initiative. China and Africa have deep traditional friendship and close bilateral relations. China welcomes the participation of Latin America and the Caribbean in the construction of the Belt and Road. China is committed to aligning its development strategy with those of the countries concerned in Latin America and the Caribbean. Oceania is a region covered by the southerly extension of the 21st Century Maritime Silk Road.[1]

Paths to participate in the Belt and Road

China sincerely welcomes all countries, international and regional organisations, enterprises and civil societies to take an active part in the open cooperation platform of the Belt and Road. The Chinese government provides diversified, convenient, flexible, open and fair ways for all parties to join the Initiative.

First, to sign bilateral cooperation agreements. The Chinese government is ready to sign cooperation framework agreements, memoranda and medium- and long-term development plans with legal effects, align the construction plans and quality and technology systems, facilitate transportation facilitation, promote project construction, connect energy facilities, and build information networks. Through consultations and agreements, a number of bilateral cooperation demonstration projects will be built to seek early harvest.

Second, to rely on multilateral cooperation mechanisms. China welcomes governments of all countries to actively join the AIIB, Silk Road Fund, China–Europe Cooperation Fund, China–Eurasia Economic Cooperation Fund, China–ASEAN Maritime Cooperation Fund, China–ASEAN Investment Cooperation Fund and surrounding friendly exchange professional funds, etc. to add to prosperity of the Belt and Road. Meanwhile, China hopes to work with all parties to seek a consensus on cooperation by hosting the Belt and Road Forum for International Cooperation. In addition, China will actively give to play the role of existing multilateral cooperation mechanisms, such as Shanghai Cooperation Organisation, ASEAN Plus China (10+1) Summit, APEC, ASEM, Asia Cooperation Dialogue, CICA, CASCF, China-GCC Strategic Dialogue, Great Mekong Subregion Cooperation and CAREC, to attract more countries and regions to participate in the Belt and Road Initiative. China is warmly welcoming governments, enterprises and individuals to actively participate in large-scale exhibitions and related activities such as China–ASEAN Expo, China–Asia–Europe Expo, China–Arab Expo, China–South Asia Expo and China–CEEC Investment and Trade Expo.

Third, to achieve cooperation through projects. Cooperation under the Belt and Road is not limited to textual agreements and verbal statements. Instead, cooperation is reached through the implementation of concrete projects. Through the Belt and Road cooperation platform, the Chinese government hopes to provide help to relevant countries in infrastructure construction, people's livelihood improvement, scientific and technological capacity building, and sustainable development.

Fourth, to establish or join a cooperative alliance. The Chinese government encourages all parties to actively establish think-tank alliances, university alliances, industrial association alliances, enterprise alliances and civil society alliances related to the Belt and Road. We will conduct joint consultation and discussion, pool the wisdom and efforts of all parties, strengthen cooperation among all parties, and integrate resources of all parties to jointly promote the building of the Belt and Road.

Partners whose strategies are aligned with the Belt and Road Initiative or partners with cooperation intention

No "membership" will be formed in cooperation under the Belt and Road Initiative. With an open mind, China welcomes the participation of any like-minded country and organisation so long as it is interested in it. As of December 2017, China has signed 100 cooperation agreements under the Belt and Road Initiative with 86 countries and international organisations.[2] In the following parts, we will list the countries, international organisations and civil society groups that are carrying out or intend to carry out cooperation with China under the Belt and Road Initiative.

(1) Sovereign countries

Northeast Asian countries

South Korea: We are willing to actively participate in the China-proposed Belt and Road Initiative and hope that the idea of the Belt and Road will bring new economic growth opportunities to the Asian regions including South Korea.

Japan: We will study each specific project, and Japan will seriously participate in it whenever possible.

North Korea: We have sent a delegation to participate in the 2017 Belt and Road Forum for International Cooperation.

South East Asian countries

Indonesia: We will deepen cooperation under the framework of the China-proposed Belt and Road to improve the level of economic and trade investment.

Cambodia: We will accelerate a more effective alignment between China's Belt and Road Initiative and the 13th Five-Year Plan of China and Cambodia's national development strategy and Industrial Development Policy 2015–2025.

Philippines: We have realised the potential of the Belt and Road Initiative and the Philippines's development plan, as well as its synergy with the Master Plan on ASEAN Connectivity.

Laos: We will effectively synergise the China-proposed Belt and Road Initiative with Laos' strategy for "transition from a land-locked country into a land-linked country".

Vietnam: We are willing to work with China to implement the cooperation documents for jointly building the Belt and Road and "Two Corridors plus One Ring" that have been signed by both sides.

Malaysia: We welcome the Belt and Road Initiative for cooperation, and both sides have agreed to strengthen the alignment of development strategy under this framework.

Myanmar: We support the Belt and Road Initiative, and are ready to speed up the process of building the Belt and Road with China.

Thailand: We believe that the strategy of the Eastern Economic Corridor of Thailand is highly compatible with the Belt and Road Initiative.

Singapore: We fully support the Belt and Road Initiative.

East Timor: We have signed with China the *Memorandum of Understanding on the Building of the Belt and Road*.

South Asian countries

Maldives: We actively support and participate in the Belt and Road.

Afghanistan: We welcome the Silk Road Economic Belt Initiative.

Nepal: We are ready to synergise our strategies with the Belt and Road Initiative.

Sri Lanka: We will actively participate in the China-proposed Belt and Road Initiative.

Pakistan: We have signed with China the *Memorandum of Understanding on Cooperation for the Long-term Plan on China–Pakistan Economic Corridor Between the Government of the People's Republic of China and the Government of the Islamic Republic of Pakistan*, the *Outline of Long-term Plan for China–Pakistan Economic Corridor* and other important agreements.

Bangladesh: We are ready to actively participate in the construction of the Belt and Road and support the construction of the Bangladesh–China–India–Myanmar Economic Corridor.

India: India is an important participant in the AIIB and the Bangladesh–China–India–Myanmar Economic Corridor.

Central Asian countries

Mongolia: We will accelerate an effective alignment between the China-led Belt and Road Initiative and Mongolia's Development Road Strategy.

Russia: We will continue to actively promote an effective alignment between the China-led Belt and Road Initiative and the Eurasian Economic Union.

Kyrgyzstan: We will deeply promote cooperation under the Belt and Road and exert the potential of cross-border transportation of the two countries.

Tajikistan: We will promote cooperation and synergise the Belt and Road Initiative with Tajikistan's National Development Strategy for the period up to 2030.

Kazakhstan: We will synergise the Silk Road Initiative with Kazakhstan's Bright Road Initiative.

Uzbekistan: We will fully support the construction of the Silk Road Economic Belt.

Belarus: We will synergise the Belt and Road Initiative with the development strategy of Belarus.

Middle East countries

United Arab Emirates: We have signed a number of agreements with China including the *Framework Agreement on Strengthening Capacity and Investment Cooperation*.

Israel: We are ready to strengthen bilateral and third-party innovative cooperation in infrastructure in the framework of the Belt and Road Initiative and the AIIB, in which Israel is a founding member.

Qatar: We are ready to work together to build the Silk Road Economic Belt and the 21st Century Maritime Silk Road.

Iran: We have signed with China the *Memorandum of Understanding on the Belt and Road Initiative* and other cooperation agreements.

Egypt: We support the Belt and Road Initiative, and both sides agreed to strengthen cooperation within the framework of the Initiative.

Saudi Arabia: We are ready to jointly promote the construction of the Belt and Road.

Iraq: We are ready to actively participate in the construction of the Belt and Road.

Jordan: We are discussing cooperation with China under the framework of the Belt and Road Initiative.

Lebanon: We have signed with China the documents such as the *Executive Programme of Cultural Agreement for the Years 2017–2020*.

Tunisia: We have signed with China the *Agreement on the Reciprocal Establishment of Cultural Centres* and other documents.

European countries

France: We welcome the Belt and Road Initiative.

Italy: Both sides will jointly fulfil the relevant bilateral agreements.

Britain: We agree to strengthen cooperation under the Belt and Road Initiative on the basis of "extensive consultation, joint contribution and shared benefits". We recognise the synergic effects between the Belt and Road Initiative and Britain's regional development strategies including the Northern Powerhouse in the north of England.

Germany: We will promote two-way investment and third-party market cooperation under the Belt and Road framework, and recommend synergising "China Made 2025" with Germany's "Industry 4.0" Strategy.

Hungary: We will promote cooperation under the Belt and Road Initiative and Hungary's Eastern Opening strategy.

Poland: We will promote cooperation under the Belt and Road Initiative and Poland's Sustainable Development Plan.

Switzerland: We will actively support the China-proposed Belt and Road Initiative and have taken the lead in joining the AIIB among European countries.

Netherlands: We will actively participate in relevant cooperation and support to synergise the Belt and Road Initiative with the European investment plan.

Norway: We have actively responded to the China-proposed Belt and Road Initiative, and Norway is a founding member of the AIIB.

African countries

African countries such as South Africa, Kenya, Tanzania, Mozambique and Ethiopia are looking forward to synergising their development strategies with China's strategy for cooperation under the Belt and Road, and they are committed to strengthening policy coordination, infrastructure connectivity, unimpeded trade, financial integration and understanding between people. Hisense South Africa Industrial Park, Beiqi Group South Africa Plant, Addis Ababa–Djibouti Standard Gauge Railway and the industrial belts along the route, Mombasa–Nairobi Standard Gauge Railway and the industrial belts along the routes, Mombasa Special Economic Zone and other major China–Africa capacity cooperation and industrial projects are progressing steadily and have achieved early harvest.

Latin American and Caribbean countries

Many countries in Latin America are looking forward to promoting their own development through international cooperation under the Belt and Road and pushing China–Latin America relations to a higher level. The heads of state of Argentina and Chile and many high-level representatives of Latin American countries came to China in May 2017 to attend the first the Belt and Road Forum for International Cooperation. Panama and China have issued a joint statement expressing its willingness to participate in building the Belt and Road.

Oceanian countries

New Zealand: We have signed with China the *Memorandum of Understanding on Strengthening the Cooperation* under the Belt and Road Initiative.

(2) International organisations

The Chinese government departments have signed the documents for cooperation under the Belt and Road with a number of international organisations, including the United Nations Development Programme, the United Nations Industrial Development Organisation, the United Nations Human Settlements Programme, the United Nations Children's Fund, the United Nations Population Fund, the United Nations Conference on Trade and Development, the World Health Organisation, the World Intellectual Property Organisation, the International Criminal Police Organisation, the United Nations Economic Commission for Europe, the World Economic Forum, the International Road Transport Union, the International Trade Centre, the International Telecommunication Union, the International Civil Aviation Organisation, the United Nations Alliance of Civilisations, the International Development Law Organisation, the World Meteorological Organisation and the International Maritime Organisation. On March 17, 2017, the Belt and Road was also written into a joint resolution. In addition, regional cooperation mechanisms such as ASEAN, EU, AU, Cooperation between China and Central and Eastern European Countries, and SCO has actively carried out cooperation under the Belt and Road Initiative.

In terms of energy cooperation, the Global Energy Interconnection Development and Cooperation Organisation initiated by State Grid Corporation of China has signed the memorandum of cooperation in the energy sector with the United Nations Department of Economic and Social Affairs, the United Nations Economic and Social Commission for Asia and the Pacific, the League of Arab States, the African Union and the Interconnection Power Grid Authority of the Gulf Cooperation Council.

In terms of financial cooperation, China has initiated and established the AIIB. As of June 2018, the number of AIIB members has increased to 87.

In terms of input in people's livelihood, the Chinese government has signed assistance agreements with the United Nations World Food Programme, the United Nations International Organisation for Migration, the United Nations International Children's Fund, the United Nations High Commission for Refugees, the World Health Organisation, the International Committee of the Red Cross, the United Nations Development Programme, the United Nations Industrial Development Organisation, the World Trade Organisation, the International Civil Aviation Organisation, the United Nations Population Fund, the United Nations Conference on Trade and Development, the International Trade Centre and the United Nations Educational, Scientific and Cultural Organisation.

(3) NGOs

China NGO Network for International Exchanges and over 80 Chinese NGOs have jointly launched the Chinese Social Organisations' Action Plan for Stronger People-to-People Connectivity along the Belt and Road (2017–20). China NGO Network for International Exchanges and over 150 civil organisations have jointly set up the Silk Road NGO Cooperation Network. The Silk Road Think Tank Association (SRTA) has launched the International Think Tank Cooperation Programme on Enhancing People-to-People Connectivity along the Belt and Road.

Notes

1 "Building the Belt and Road: Concept, Practice and China's Contribution," www.yidaiyilu.gov.cn, www.yidaiyilu.gov.cn/zchj/qwfb/12658.htm
2 "China has signed 100 cooperation agreements under the Belt and Road Initiative with 86 countries and international organizations," Xinhuanet, www.xinhuanet.com/fortune/2017-12/22/c_1122155143.htm

22
GENERAL IDEAS

Wang Yuzhu and Jiang Fangfei

Basic positioning and main purposes of the Belt and Road

The Belt and Road Initiative is an initiative proposed by the Chinese leadership to promote connectivity and mutually beneficial cooperation between China and countries in Asia, Europe, Africa and the rest of the world based on the observation of and reflection on the situation of the world and after taking both domestic and international situations into consideration. In terms of international layout, the Silk Road Economic Belt focuses on building the six economic corridors and aims to bring together China, Central Asia, Russia and Europe (the Baltic), thereby linking China with the Persian Gulf and the Mediterranean Sea through Central Asia and West Asia and connecting China with South East Asia, South Asia and the Indian Ocean. The 21st Century Maritime Silk Road is designed to go from the coast of China to Europe through the South China Sea and the Indian Ocean in one route, and from the coast of China through the South China Sea to the South Pacific in the other direction. In terms of domestic layout, the Belt and Road has identified 18 key provinces and formed a pattern of comprehensive advancement with coordinated land and marine development from east to west.

The Belt and Road Initiative covers a vast population of 4.4 billion and an economic output of $21 trillion in more than 60 countries in Asia, Europe and Africa. It is an unprecedented transcontinental cooperation initiative. The Initiative involves not only China's own opening up, but also the practice of China's diplomatic philosophy and China's relations with neighbouring countries and countries along the routes. It also involves the development process of regional cooperation and the economic development of countries around the world. These factors together constitute the basic positioning and main purposes of the Belt and Road.

First, the Belt and Road is a major move of China to comprehensively deepen reform and opening up in the new era. It aims to inject new impetus to China's economic development by promoting open cooperation between China's central and western regions and neighbouring countries. With the gradual disappearance of China's demographic dividend, the dividend of opening up brought about by China's accession to the WTO has basically been realised. China's economy has been transitioning from a phase of rapid growth to a stage of high-quality development. This is a pivotal stage for transforming our growth model, improving our economic structure and fostering new drivers of growth. In the meantime, the Chinese economy is undergoing a new round of opening up, and there are strong appeals for promoting domestic reform through opening up. In the past, China's opening up was mainly concentrated in the southeastern coastal regions, and the degree of openness in the central and western regions was seriously lagging behind. This is an important reason for the imbalance of economic development in the eastern and western regions of China. Therefore, the new round of opening up needs to extend as far as possible to the vast inland areas of the central and western regions so as to make new ground in opening China further through links running eastward and westward, across land and over sea.

Second, the Belt and Road is an important platform for China to pursue the principles of "amity, sincerity, mutual benefit and inclusiveness" in diplomacy with neighbouring countries and to practice major-country diplomacy with Chinese characteristics in the new era. It aims to build a new form of international relations featuring mutual respect, fairness and justice and win–win cooperation with all countries in the world. In 2013, at the neighbourhood diplomacy work conference, President Xi Jinping established the principles of "amity, sincerity, mutual benefit and inclusiveness" in diplomacy with neighbouring countries. The report to the 19th CPC National Congress clearly stated that "China has actively developed global partnerships and expanded the convergence of interests with other countries. China will promote coordination and cooperation with other major countries and work to build a framework for major country relations featuring overall stability and balanced development. China will deepen relations with its neighbors in accordance with the principles of amity, sincerity, mutual benefit, and inclusiveness and the policy of forging friendship and partnership with its neighbors. China will, guided by the principle of upholding justice while pursuing shared interests and the principle of sincerity, honesty, affinity, and good faith, work to strengthen solidarity and cooperation with other developing countries". The Belt and Road upholds the Silk Road spirit of "peace and cooperation, openness and inclusiveness, mutual learning and mutual benefit" and adheres to the principle of achieving shared growth through discussion and collaboration, which are highly compatible with the principles of "amity, sincerity, mutual benefit and inclusiveness". In addition, the Belt and Road is committed to enhancing connectivity of Asia, Europe and Africa and nearby oceans, which has a high degree of internal consistency with China's pursuit of a new form of international relations.

Third, the Belt and Road Initiative is a new mechanism and a new model for China to actively participate in regional cooperation. It is aimed at promoting orderly and free flow of economic factors, highly efficient allocation of resources and deep integration of markets; encouraging the countries along the Belt and Road to achieve economic policy coordination and carry out broader and more in-depth regional cooperation of higher standards; and jointly creating an open, inclusive and balanced regional economic cooperation architecture that benefits all. Affected by historical and natural factors and attracted by external markets and investment, regional cooperation in Asia has shown a clear "enclave" phenomenon. So far, no horizontal integration has been formed, and the degree of Asian integration is still at a low level. The Belt and Road will adhere to open regionalism, and build a multilateral regional cooperation mechanism that mutually complements and promotes with other regional cooperation mechanisms by fully relying on the existing dual multilateral mechanisms between China and relevant countries and the existing and effective regional cooperation platforms so as to forge closer economic ties among countries, deepen regional cooperation, create a more innovative cooperation model, and foster more diversified cooperators. To turn this into a reality, we may start with work in individual areas and link them up over time to promote integration of regional economy.

Fourth, the Belt and Road is an effective way to realise economic complementarities between China and other countries and solve the underlying problems of economic growth of China and countries along the routes. It aims to promote greater connectivity and synergise the development strategies of individual countries along the routes to instill new impetus for common sustainable development. China welcomes neighbouring countries to take a free ride on China's fast economic development. It also hopes to continuously explore the market potential of countries in the region through the connectivity projects under the Belt and Road, promote consumption and investment, create demands and jobs and promote common prosperity. The Belt and Road will unleash superior production capacity of China, deepen its integration into the world economic system, provide historic opportunities for developing countries to realise their own industrialisation and modernisation, and provide a new platform for promoting the wide-ranging South–South cooperation, enhancing North–South dialogue and promoting North–South cooperation.

The ultimate goal of the Belt and Road

In May 2017, President Xi Jinping stressed in his opening speech at the Leaders Roundtable of the Belt and Road Forum for International Cooperation that:

> In pursuing international cooperation and the Belt and Road Initiative, the parties follow the principle of extensive consultation, joint contribution and shared benefits, and join hands to meet global economic challenges. Aiming to draw on each other's strength and deliver win–win results, the Parties will explore new opportunities, seek new drivers and expand new space for development, moving closer towards a community of shared future for mankind. This is what I had in mind when I first put forward the Belt and Road Initiative. It is also the ultimate goal of this Initiative.

First, a community of shared future for mankind and the Belt and Road are rooted in history, but based on reality. They are the inheritance and development of ancient wisdom and excellent traditional culture of Chinese civilisation. A community of shared future for mankind fully embodies China's traditional philosophical values of "harmony between man and nature" and "world unity" and the cultural ideas of "all living beings are equal", "harmony between things and ego" and "yin–yang balance". All countries of the world today have forged a relationship in which all are bound together for good or ill. China and the rest of the world belong to an organic whole with a balance of yin and yang. The interests of all countries are highly integrated, and problems in any link may cause the break of the global interest chain. Therefore, in the pursuit of the Belt and Road, we will draw on the wisdom and strength from China's more than 5000 years of historical civilisation and the ancient Silk Road, pursue the Silk Road spirit of peace and cooperation, openness and inclusiveness, mutual learning and mutual benefit, adhere to the civilised cultural outlook of equality, inclusiveness and mutual learning, uphold the right approach to justice and interests with a priority to justice, seek the greatest degree of common interests and effectively resolve conflicts and contradictions, and seek win–win cooperation while pursuing "harmony but not uniformity".

Second, both a community of shared future for mankind and the Belt and Road originate from China, but belong to the world. They are Chinese solutions to cope with global challenges and break through the dilemma of human development. In a world of growing interdependence and challenges, no country can tackle the challenges or solve the world's problems on its own. Individual countries need to coordinate national policies and make good use of economic factors and development resources on a greater global scale. Only in this way can we build synergy and promote peace, stability and common development in the world. In this grand context, the Belt and Road Initiative proposed by China will help all countries involved to explore new opportunities, seek new drivers and expand new space for development, enabling the international community to join hands to meet global challenges and build development synergies.

Third, both a community of shared future for mankind and the Belt and Road Initiative focus on the present, but look into the future. Both actively advocate establishing a new international order that is more peaceful, just, rational, equal and open. Under the current international pattern of "only super power and multi-great powers", although the world is in a relatively peaceful and stable international environment, conflicts, contradictions and even wars arising from imbalances in economic and social development between regions and countries have occurred from time to time, which is not conducive to sustainable development of human society. The key to solving these problems lies in the establishment of a new international political and economic order that is more peaceful, just, reasonable, equal and open on the basis of the old political and economic structure, thus creating a more peaceful and stable international environment for building consensus and seeking common development. Unlike the traditional Western concepts of "the strong preying on the weak", "zero-sum game" and "vying for global hegemony", the Belt and Road pursues the basic concept that "all countries, large and small, should be equal", focuses on common development and win–win cooperation and follows the principles of extensive consultation, joint contribution and shared benefits. It is open to all like-minded friends, and does not exclude or target any party. It actively contributes to promoting the development of countries and regions along the routes, strengthening political mutual trust between countries and maintaining world peace.

The ultimate goal of a community of a shared future for mankind demonstrates the holistic view and sense of responsibility of China as a world power. China is ready to do its utmost to shoulder more international responsibilities and obligations so as to make greater contributions to the peaceful development of mankind. Meanwhile, a community of a shared future for mankind has also endowed the Belt and Road with a sense of mission and direction. In pursuing the Belt and Road Initiative, China will hold high the banner of peace, development, cooperation and mutual benefit, uphold the spirit of peace and cooperation, openness and inclusiveness, mutual learning and mutual benefit, promote pragmatic cooperation in all aspects, and work together to build a community of shared interests, destiny and responsibility featuring mutual political trust, economic integration and cultural inclusiveness.

23
DIRECTIONS OF COOPERATION

Fu Jingjun

In September and October 2013, Chinese President Xi Jinping successively proposed the Silk Road Economic Belt and the 21st Century Maritime Silk Road, which have attracted considerable attention from the international community and won a positive response from the countries involved. China adheres to the Silk Road spirit of "peace and cooperation, openness and inclusiveness, mutual learning and mutual benefit", follows the principle of extensive consultation, joint contribution and shared benefits, and constantly expands cooperation consensus with countries along the routes to promote the transformation of the Belt and Road from a plan and design to concerted actions involving all parties. The Initiative aims to promote infrastructure development and greater connectivity, synergise the development policies and strategies of individual countries, deepen practical cooperation, encourage coordinated and interconnected development and bring about common prosperity.[1]

Specific contents of cooperation

Based on the proposal from President Xi and the need to promote international cooperation under the new situation, and taking into consideration the routes of the ancient land and sea Silk Roads, China has identified five routes for the Belt and Road. The Silk Road Economic Belt has three routes: one from Northwest China and Northeast China to Europe and the Baltic Sea via Central Asia and Russia; one from Northwest China to the Persian Gulf and the Mediterranean Sea, passing through Central Asia and West Asia; and one from Southwest China through the Indochina Peninsula to the Indian Ocean. The 21st Century Maritime Silk Road has two major routes: one starts from coastal ports of China, crosses the South China Sea, passes through the Malacca Strait and reaches the Indian Ocean, extending to Europe; the other starts from coastal ports of China, crosses the South China Sea and extends to the South Pacific.

The Belt and Road runs through the three continents of Asia, Europe and Africa. Among them, the two regions of Western Europe and Eastern Asia are the starting points. The regions and seas covered include Central Asia, Russia, West Asia, Persian Gulf, Mediterranean Sea, South East Asia, South Asia, Indian Ocean, Africa, etc. The ways to achieve connectivity of these regions are the Economic Belt and the Maritime Silk Road, and the two are connected through Central Asia, the Middle East and the Persian Gulf.

Based on the focus of cooperation and spatial distribution for building the Belt and Road, China has proposed a framework including six corridors, six means of communication, multiple countries and multiple ports. The "six corridors" are: the New Eurasian Land Bridge Economic Corridor, the China–Mongolia–Russia Economic Corridor, the China–Central Asia–West Asia Economic Corridor, the China–Indochina Peninsula Economic Corridor, the China–Pakistan Economic Corridor and the Bangladesh–China–India–Myanmar Economic Corridor. The "six means of communication" are rail, highways, seagoing transport, aviation, pipelines and aerospace integrated information network, which comprise the main targets of infrastructure connectivity. "Multiple countries" refers to a number of countries along the Belt and Road that first joined the Initiative, and China will cooperate with them on the basis of equality and mutual benefit. However, pragmatism requires a need to cooperate first with a number of particular countries, and try to achieve results with them that have a demonstrative impact and embody the concept of the Belt and Road, so that more countries will be attracted to participate in the initiative. "Multiple ports" refers to a number of ports that ensure safe and smooth sea passages. By building a number of important ports and key cities with countries along the Belt and Road, China works to promote maritime cooperation. The cooperation framework is the framework for joint building of the Belt and Road, giving a clear direction for countries involved to participate in the initiative.[2]

Background for proposing the cooperation directions

Around the world today, economic globalisation and regional integration has stimulated strong potential for economic activity. However, a considerable number of countries suffer from inadequate infrastructure, and regional and subregional development faces numerous constraints. We recognise that stronger cooperation is the fundamental solution. It is for this reason that China has proposed the Belt and Road Initiative.

China is willing to combine the experience and foundations of its own development with the development will and comparative strengths of all countries, and use the Belt and Road as an important opportunity and a cooperation platform to promote economic policy coordination among various countries, improve connectivity, foster bilateral and multilateral cooperation with a broader scope and at a higher and deeper level and build a new cooperation framework that is open, inclusive, balanced and mutually beneficial. The Belt and Road Initiative, characterised by equality and inclusiveness, and grounded in realism, manifests the common interests of countries along the routes, including China, and is a new future-oriented consensus for international cooperation. It showcases a positive vision that the Chinese Dream is interconnected with the world dream and all countries work together to build a human community of shared destiny.[3]

The Initiative is an ambitious economic vision of the opening-up of and cooperation among the countries along the Belt and Road. Countries should work in concert and move towards the objectives of mutual benefit and common security. It integrates the historical symbolism of the ancient Silk Road with the new requirements of today. The initiative is a Chinese programme whose goal is to maintain an open world economic system, and achieve diversified, independent, balanced and sustainable development, and also a Chinese proposal intended to advance regional cooperation, strengthen communications between civilisations and safeguard world peace and stability. It showcases the fact that China, as the largest developing country and the world's second largest economy, shoulders its wider responsibilities in promoting international economic governance towards a fair, just and rational system.[4]

Directions of cooperation

The role of cooperation direction in the Belt and Road

The Silk Road Economic Belt covers economic integration in South East Asia and economic integration in Northeast Asia, and eventually merges into one heading to Europe to form a major trend of economic integration in Eurasia. The 21st Century Maritime Silk Road connects the three continents of Europe, Asia and Africa through the sea and forms a closed land-based and ocean-going loop together with the Silk Road Economic Belt.

The Silk Road Economic Belt and the 21st Century Maritime Silk Road are strip zones that can promote the development of countries along the routes. The Economic Belt, starting with individual projects, is expected to help spur larger-scale regional cooperative development.[5] By blazing railways, highways and air routes, the Economic Belt will drive population migration, resource development and urbanisation along the routes and nearby areas, thereby promoting a cluster-like development trend in countries or regions along the routes. The Maritime Silk Road can also promote the development of coastal areas through construction and operation of ports, waterways and sea transportation.

There is a mutual promotion and mutual transformation relationship between the Economic Belt and the Maritime Silk Road. The foundation for their transformation is the connectivity projects under the Belt and Road that connect them together. The projects under the Belt and Road will be embedded into the existing or planned infrastructure networks of countries along the routes. The building of the Belt and Road will be a part of the Transcontinental Development Corridor, which will eventually drive balanced development of countries and regions along the routes. Through connecting with other bridges or corridors in the world, the Belt and Road can be expanded to not only radiate the three continents of Asia, Europe and Africa, but may even connect with the infrastructures in North America and Australia. Connected by "roads, belts, corridors and bridges", the Belt and Road will give full play to the functions of mutual ocean–land nourishing and promoting the well-being of mankind and eventually connect the whole world through individual projects.[6]

External influence of cooperation directions

The Belt and Road runs through the continents of Asia, Europe and Africa, connecting the vibrant East Asia economic circle at one end and developed European economic circle at the other, and encompassing countries with huge potential for economic development. The New Eurasian Land Bridge Economic Corridor, China–Mongolia–Russia Economic Corridor and China–Central Asia–West Asia Economic Corridor run through central and eastern Eurasia, connecting the economically dynamic East Asian economic circle and the developed European economic circle, while also building a smooth cooperation channel from the Persian Gulf to the Mediterranean and the Baltic Sea. They make it possible for establishing an efficient and smooth Eurasian market, and create opportunities of development for countries in the hinterland of Eurasia and along the Belt and Road. The New Eurasian Land Bridge Economic Corridor extends westward from the eastern coast of China to Central and Eastern Europe, passing through the northwestern part of China, Central Asia and Russia. Construction of this corridor is based on a modern international logistics system including China–Europe rail services, with focus on economic and trade development and production capacity cooperation, expansion of cooperation in energy and other resources and establishment of a highly efficient regional market.[7] The integration of the Silk Road Economic Belt with the Eurasian Economic Union and the Mongolian Prairie Road Initiative will form the China–Mongolia–Russia Economic Corridor and open up the common economic space of the entire Eurasia.[8]

The China–Indochina Peninsula Economic Corridor, the China–Pakistan Economic Corridor and the BCIM Economic Corridor run through the eastern and southern parts of Asia, the most densely populated regions in the world, and connect major cities, densely populated areas and industrial clusters along the routes. The Lancang–Mekong River International Waterway and the railways, highways and oil and gas networks under construction will link the Silk Road Economic Belt with the 21st Century Maritime Silk Road, and the economic effects will radiate to South Asia, South East Asia, the Indian Ocean and the South Pacific. The China–Indochina Economic Corridor, starting from southwest China and connecting China and Indo-China Peninsula Countries, is an important carrier that can expand cooperation between China and ASEAN. The China–Pakistan Economic Corridor is the flagship project for the building of the Belt and Road. The BCIM Economic Corridor connects the three major subregions of East Asia, South Asia and South East Asia, and links the Pacific Ocean and the Indian Ocean.[9]

Notes

1 "Opening Speech by Xi Jinping President at the Leaders Roundtable of the Belt and Road Forum for International Cooperation," renminnet, http://jhsjk.people.cn/article/29277193, May 16, 2017.
2 "Building the Belt and Road: Concept, Practice and China's Contribution," Xinhua News Agency, www.scio.gov.cn/m/31773/35507/htws35512/Document/1551506/1551506.htm, May 11, 2017.
3 "Building the Belt and Road: Concept, Practice and China's Contribution," Xinhua News Agency, www.scio.gov.cn/m/31773/35507/htws35512/Document/1551506/1551506.htm, May 11, 2017.
4 "Vision and Actions on Jointly Building Silk Road Economic Belt and 21st-Century Maritime Silk Road," the Ministry of Foreign Affairs, www.yidaiyilu.gov.cn/yw/qwfb/604.htm, March 29, 2015.
5 "Promote Friendship Between Our People and Work Together to Build a Bright Future—Speech by Xi Jinping at Nazarbayev University in Kazakhstan," in *People's Daily*, September 8, 2013.
6 Zeng Xianghong, "Geopolitical Imagination and Regional Cooperation of the Belt and Road," in *World Economics and Politics*, Issue 1, 2016, p. 54.
7 "Vision and Actions on Jointly Building Silk Road Economic Belt and 21st-Century Maritime Silk Road," the Ministry of Foreign Affairs, www.yidaiyilu.gov.cn/yw/qwfb/604.htm, March 29, 2015.
8 "Outline of the Plan for Building the China–Mongolia–Russia Economic Corridor," the National Development and Reform Commission, www.yidaiyilu.gov.cn/yw/qwfb/633.htm, September 14, 2016.
9 "Building the Belt and Road: Concept, Practice and China's Contribution," Xinhua News Agency, www.scio.gov.cn/m/31773/35507/htws35512/Document/1551506/1551506.htm, May 11, 2017.

24
COOPERATION MECHANISMS

Ge Cheng

After several years of practice, the cooperation mechanisms under the Belt and Road are mainly the dialogue mechanisms at different levels, complemented by (trade) treaty mechanisms. These cooperation mechanisms widely intersect with the existing development strategies, initiatives and agendas of the countries along the routes and international organisations. They are parallel with the existing multilateral and bilateral dialogues and treaty mechanisms and highlight the principle of inclusiveness. At different levels, the top-level cooperation mechanisms, strategic synergy, multilateral cooperation and bilateral cooperation mechanisms are compatible with each other and will be gradually improved.

After having been discussed at a series of bilateral and multilateral leaders' meetings in recent years, the top-level cooperation mechanism has been launched at the Belt and Road Forum for International Cooperation. The forum consists of a leaders' roundtable and a number of high-level parallel thematic sessions. The forum outlines the cooperation mechanism for the Belt and Road Initiative and shows the direction for cooperation from the top-level perspective.[1] Strategic synergy reflects China's efforts to effectively synergise the Belt and Road Initiative with the development strategies of the countries along routes, and seek the "biggest common denominator" for cooperation in an equal, open and inclusive approach. It reflects the spirit that all countries along the routes will jointly build the Belt and Road through consultations and the fruits will be shared by all. The multilateral cooperation mechanisms include SCO, ASEAN Plus China (10+1), APEC, CICA and other multilateral dialogue mechanisms. The countries involved should strengthen communication and broaden the areas of cooperation in building Belt and Road. Bilateral cooperation constitutes the foundation of the Belt and Road construction, and is achieved through multi-level and multi-channel communication and consultation mechanisms. We will promote all-round development of bilateral relations between China and countries along the routes, speed up the signing of cooperation memorandums or cooperation plans, build bilateral cooperation demonstration projects, establish and improve bilateral joint work mechanisms and explore the implementation plans and action roadmaps for advancing the Belt and Road.

Top-level cooperation mechanisms

The top-level cooperation mechanisms include the Belt and Road Forum for International Cooperation as well as various types of leaders' dialogues, providing a strong political driving force for jointly building the Belt and Road. Since the Belt and Road Initiative was proposed, Chinese President Xi Jinping, Premier Li Keqiang and other state leaders have visited many regions along the Belt and Road, including Central Asia, South East Asia, South Asia and Central and Eastern Europe. At the APEC Leaders' Summit, the East Asia Summit, and the G20 Summit, promoting the building of the Belt and Road became an important content, and won positive response from the countries involved and international organisations, yielding fruitful results including building consensus for cooperation, signing cooperation agreements, promoting the construction of major projects and expanding exchanges and cooperation in various fields. On this basis, the Belt and Road Forum for International Cooperation was successfully held in Beijing on May 14, 2017, becoming the highest-level and largest international conference within the Belt and Road framework. The theme of the forum is "Work Together to Build the Silk Road Economic Belt and The 21st Century Maritime Silk Road". The forum consists of three parts: the Opening Ceremony, the Leaders Roundtable, and the High-level Meeting. About 1500 representatives from more than 130 countries and more than 70 international organisations, including 29 foreign heads of state and government, attended the summit.

The top-level cooperation mechanisms represented by the Belt and Road Forum for International Cooperation show the direction and provide strong policy support for the Belt and Road Initiative. The Leaders Roundtable has established the political basis for cooperation. The government departments are carrying out research on policy synergy, and financial institutions, trade institutions, research institutions, and non-government organisations all will take their seats and fulfil respective cooperation contents. With the establishment of this mechanism, significant progress has been made in improving the connectivity. China is synergising its policies and plans with those of the countries involved and has signed cooperation agreements with more than 40 countries and international organisations, and carried out institutionalised capacity cooperation with more than 30 countries. A complex infrastructure network has gradually formed and the financial cooperation network has begun to take shape. Cooperation in science, education, culture, health and people-to-people exchanges has been widely carried out.

Synergy with other development strategies

An effective synergy with existing development strategies, initiatives and agendas of countries along the routes and international organisations is an important realisation mechanism for advancing the Belt and Road. *Building the Belt and Road: Concept, Practice and China's Contribution* states that "China is striving to promote an effective synergy of the Belt and Road Initiative with the development strategies of the countries along the routes, and seek the 'biggest common denominator' for cooperation".[2] The *Vision and Actions on Jointly Building Silk Road Economic Belt and 21st-Century Maritime Silk Road* states that "opportunities can be created by communication and coordination among other global, regional and national frameworks and initiatives for promoting cooperation in connectivity and sustainable development".

To synergise the Belt and Road Initiative with global, regional and national cooperation initiatives, we must first realise synergy of relevant concepts. The Belt and Road Initiative and the above-mentioned cooperation initiatives are highly overlapped in concepts and goals, and all are committed to promoting inclusive and sustainable economic growth and social development. For example, unimpeded trade and investment facilitation are both core elements of the Belt and Road Initiative and the UN's 2030 Agenda for Sustainable Development, both of which emphasise the irreplaceable role of infrastructure in achieving sustainable development. Therefore, strengthening the principle of inclusive and interconnected development is the foundation for an effective synergy of the Belt and Road Initiative with other cooperation initiatives.

Second, we must seek synergy of policy. Enhancing policy coordination is an important guarantee for implementing the Initiative. We should promote intergovernmental cooperation, establish a multi-level intergovernmental macro policy exchange and communication mechanism, and build new consensus on cooperation through full exchanges of economic development strategies and counter-measures. The successful holding of the 2017 Belt and Road Forum for International Cooperation marks a significant achievement in the efforts for strong policy coordination. The political foundation of synergy of the Belt and Road Initiative with other cooperation initiatives has been established.

Third, we should strengthen the synergy of platforms. Taking the financing platforms, for example, the AIIB and the Silk Road Fund are the core supporting mechanisms for the Belt and Road Initiative, and they are also the financing platforms for northern and southern countries to jointly participate in the development of the Initiative.[3] The projects financed by the two institutions have covered energy, transportation and urban development in Indonesia, Tajikistan, Pakistan, Bangladesh and other regions, as well as infrastructure construction, resource utilisation, capacity cooperation and other fields in Russia, Mongolia and Central Asia, South Asia and South East Asia. In addition, the Chinese government has proposed to set up a China–CEEC coordinated investment and financing cooperation framework, in which multiple financing mechanisms, including the US$10 billion special credit line and the Central and Eastern European Investment Cooperation Fund, will jointly provide financing support for Central and Eastern Europe. Industrial and Commercial Bank of China has spearheaded the founding of Sino-CEEF Holding Company Limited and initiated a Sino-CEE fund. In the future, China will continue to support North–South Cooperation to exert its role as a main financing channel for international development. Meanwhile, we should focus on building and operating the financing institutions within the framework of the Belt and Road Initiative, such as AIIB and Silk Road Fund, to synergise them with existing international financing platforms.

Multilateral cooperation mechanisms

China has always attached importance to the maintenance and promotion of the role of multilateral mechanisms. Within the framework of the Belt and Road Initiative, the role of multilateral cooperation and dialogue mechanisms has been further enhanced. We should make full use of existing mechanisms such as SCO, ASEAN Plus China (10+1), APEC, ASEM, ACD, CICA, CASCF, China–GCC strategic dialogue, China–Pacific Island Countries Economic Development and Cooperation Forum, Greater Mekong Subregion (GMS) Economic Cooperation, Pan-Beibu Gulf Economic Cooperation Forum, CAREC and other dialogue mechanisms to introduce and promote the Belt and Road Initiative to the countries involved and attract more countries to participate in the Belt and Road Initiative.

Meanwhile, we should continue to give to play the constructive role of regional and subregional international forums and exhibitions in countries along the routes, such as the Boao Forum for Asia, China–ASEAN Expo, China–Asia–Europe Expo, Eurasian Economic Forum, China International Fair for Investment & Trade, and China–South Asia Expo, China–Arab Expo, Western China International Fair and China–Russia Expo, to broaden the exchanges among business and academic circles and people-to-people exchanges outside the policy mechanism. We should support local and non-government organisations along the routes to explore the historical and cultural heritages of the Belt and Road, jointly organise special investment, trade and cultural exchange activities and stage successfully the Silk Road (Dunhuang) International Cultural Expo, the Silk Road International Film Festival and the Book Fair.

In practice, forging a new subregional cooperation mechanism is an important way to achieve multilateralisation of cooperation mechanisms. New subregional cooperation mechanisms involve fewer members, which is conducive to a faster consensus, and can be more easily accepted by other members of the Belt and Road than bilateral cooperation mechanisms, which is conducive to further promoting the cooperation mechanisms that have proved effective in practice. For example, the new subregional cooperation mechanism jointly launched by the six countries of China, Cambodia, Laos, Myanmar, Thailand and Vietnam around the Lancang–Mekong River Basin has entered a new stage of comprehensive implementation, mechanism construction and pragmatic cooperation have made positive progress, and Lancang–Mekong cooperation will be built into an important platform for the Belt and Road Initiative.

Bilateral cooperation mechanisms

Bilateral cooperation mechanisms, especially the bilateral mechanisms established by the fulcrum countries along the Belt and Road, are the important foundation for advancing the Belt and Road Initiative. In the keynote speech at the opening ceremony of the Belt and Road Forum for International Cooperation, President Xi Jinping stated that China would enhance friendship and cooperation with all countries involved in the Belt and Road Initiative on the basis of the Five Principles of Peaceful Coexistence. We are ready to share practices of development with other countries. What we hope to achieve is a new model of win–win cooperation. What we hope to create is a big family of harmonious coexistence. The *Vision and Actions on Jointly Building Silk Road Economic Belt and 21st-Century Maritime Silk Road* stated that we should strengthen bilateral cooperation and promote comprehensive development of bilateral relations through multi-level and multi-channel communication and consultation. We should encourage the signing of cooperation MOUs or plans, and develop a number of bilateral cooperation pilot projects. We should establish and improve bilateral joint working mechanisms and draw up implementation plans and roadmaps for advancing the Belt and Road Initiative.

Presently, China and the countries along the Belt and Road have established relatively sound cooperation mechanisms on the basis of mutual respect and mutual trust. Bilateral dialogue has become the major means of communication. China and the countries involved have continuously strengthened the role of bilateral mechanisms and cooperation in the key areas of building the Belt and Road such as service connectivity, trade and investment, capacity and cultural exchanges. By strengthening strategic synergy, financial support, infrastructure connectivity and direct assistance, the bilateral cooperation mechanisms with fulcrum countries will be strengthened to form the arteries and veins of the Belt and Road Initiative. For example, bilateral cooperation between China and Greece, Kenya, Pakistan and other countries within the framework of the Belt and Road has remarkable fulcrum significance.

Meanwhile, China and other countries along the Belt and Road have conducted exchanges and cooperation in diverse forms between political parties, parliaments and localities as well as NGOs to enhance mutual understanding between peoples of different countries and build extensive consensus on Belt and Road cooperation. In addition, we should give full play to the existing bilateral mechanisms such as joint committee, mixed committee, coordinating committee, steering committee and management committee to coordinate and promote the implementation of cooperation projects. For countries that want to learn the development model with Chinese characteristics, China will fully provide channels for people-to-people exchanges and communication, such as the Institute of South–South Cooperation and Development established by Peking University, the Research Centre for Developing Countries established by Beijing Normal University, the Silk Road Think Tank Network (SILKS) jointly sponsored by the Development Research Centre of the State Council of China and relevant international think tanks, etc. By relying on these platform resources, China will share the experience on governance with the developing countries, promote exchanges in entrepreneurship and employment for women and young people and other fields, cultivate administrative talents at all levels, and build an international think-tank cooperation platform and a cooperation network to broaden communication channels, create a favourable foundation of public support and provide intellectual support for the Belt and Road.

Among all the cooperation mechanisms under the Belt and Road Initiative, the top-level dialogue has established the principle and direction for the development of the Belt and Road Initiative. Strategic synergy, multilateral cooperation and bilateral cooperation, in which the concepts of openness and sharing are deeply embedded, will play a critical role in building the Belt and Road. All these show the direction for the development and evolution of the Belt and Road.

Notes

1 "The Leaders Roundtable of the Belt and Road Forum for International Cooperation, www.beltandroadforum.org, www.beltandroadforum.org/n100/2017/0514/c24-414.html
2 "Building the Belt and Road: Concept, Practice and China's Contribution," Xinhuanet, www.xinhuanet.com/politics/2017-05/10/c_1120951928.htm
3 "Guiding Principles on Financing the Development of the Belt and Road," www.yidaiyilu.gov.cn, www.yidaiyilu.gov.cn/zchj/qwfb/13767.htm

25
ORGANISATIONAL STRUCTURE

Liu Junsheng

Content and basic organisational structure

The Belt and Road Initiative is a Chinese solution for promoting global peace, cooperation and common development. The Initiative is unprecedented in terms of geographical scope, membership, construction period and arduous tasks. Therefore, it is necessary to form a strong organisational structure for overall planning and management of the implementation of this huge systematic project.

In February 2015, the central government established the Leading Group for the Belt and Road Initiative (hereinafter referred to as the Leading Group), marking the official formation of the organisational structure for the Belt and Road. Vice Premier of the State Council Zhang Gaoli was named the leader of the Leading Group, and the four deputy leaders of the Leading Group included Wang Huning, director of the Policy Research Office of the CPC Central Committee, Wang Yang, a member of the Political Bureau of the CPC Central Committee and Vice Premier of the State Council, Yang Jing, Secretary of the Secretariat of the CPC Central Committee, State Councillor and Secretary General of the State Council and State Councillor Yang Jiechi.[1] The office of the Leading Group is located in the National Development and Reform Commission. In September 2016, Xu Shaoshi, director of the National Development and Reform Commission, was concurrently appointed the director of the Office of the Leading Group. Up to now, the working mechanism has been formed, in which the Leading Group plays a leading role, the Office is responsible for overall planning and coordination, local departments are responsible for their respective parts and enterprises are main players.

In October 2015, the *Notice on Strengthening and Regulating the Review of the Foreign Exchange Platforms for the Belt and Road* was issued. In July 2017, the Leading Group issued through Xinhua News Agency a notice to resolutely prevent making ill use of the Belt and Road concept to collect wealth by unfair means. The authority of the Leading Group for management of the Belt and Road was established. In the report entitled *Building the Belt and Road: Concept, Practice and China's Contribution* released at the Belt and Road Forum for International Cooperation in Beijing in May 2017, it was clearly stated that "the Chinese government attaches great importance to the Belt and Road Initiative and has established a leading group for advancing the Initiative". Moreover, the report was endorsed by the Leading Group. The Belt and Road Forum for International Cooperation in Beijing is a major international event to comprehensively promote pragmatic cooperation under the Belt and Road Initiative. It is the highest-profile event under the Belt and Road framework. By organising forums and publishing keynote reports, the Leading Group has become better known at home and abroad.

Position of the organisational structure in the strategic decisions of the central government and its tasks

Zhang Gaoli, leader of the Leading Group, is also the deputy leader of the Central Leading Group for Comprehensively Deepening Reforms. Wang Huning is the director of the office of the Central Leading Group for Comprehensively Deepening Reforms, which is responsible for promoting a new round of comprehensive reforms and opening up in China. General Secretary Xi Jinping is the leader of the Central Leading Group for Comprehensively Deepening Reforms. As shown above, the leaders of the Leading Group for the Belt and Road as the key part of comprehensively deepening reforms are members of the Central Leading Group for Comprehensively Deepening Reforms that is directly led by General Secretary Xi Jinping.[2] Xi Jinping was the proposer of the Belt and Road Initiative. He proposed to build the Silk Road Economic Belt during his visit to Kazakhstan in September 2013, and then proposed to build the 21st Century Maritime Silk Road when visiting Indonesia. In October 2013, Xi Jinping placed side by side the Economic Belt and the Maritime Silk Road for the first time at the neighbourhood diplomacy work conference, held for the first since the founding of the People's Republic of China. He said that "we must work together with relevant countries to speed up infrastructure connectivity and build the Silk Road Economic Belt and the 21st Century Maritime Silk Road". It was the first time that the concept of the Belt and Road appeared.[3] The Belt and Road, the Beijing–Tianjin–Hebei Coordinated Development Programme and the Yangtze River Economic Belt are the three major strategies for future development, and the Belt and Road ranks first among them. From the perspective of opening up to the outside world, the Belt and Road has more significance than the latter two strategies. From the perspective of the relationship between the strategy for comprehensively deepening reforms and the Belt and Road, the strategy for comprehensively deepening reforms covers the building of the Belt and Road and provides the domestic environment, institutional foundation and power resources for the latter. The Belt and Road optimises the international environment and seeks institutional alignment for comprehensively deepening reforms. More importantly, it provides forced power for upgrading the overall national strategy. In this sense, Xi Jinping and other top leaders regard the Belt and Road as the priority of future neighbourhood diplomacy, the purpose of which is to promote the coordination and development of other aspects of work so as to improve the overall capacity and effectiveness of the system and thus force the reform of China's diplomatic policy.

At the 1st Plenary Session of the 19th CPC Central Committee, Wang Yang and Wang Huning, both deputy leaders of the Leading Group, were elected members of the Standing Committee of the Political Bureau of the CPC Central Committee, thus ensuring the continuity of the Belt and Road in organisation and policy. Wang Huning has long been working at the Central Policy Research Office of the CPC Central Committee for a long time and has been widely seen as "a top brain in Zhongnanhai". Given that the Belt and Road needs to coordinate and take into consideration both the domestic and international situations, the high-profile personnel arrangement of the Leading Group makes it possible to handle various contradictions in advancing the Belt and Road such as development and security, responsibilities and contribution, history and reality, and tradition and modernity from the perspective of reform and opening up in the new era.

Before the establishment of the Leading Group, the Belt and Road was mainly promoted by the external propaganda by the Chinese leaders, the relevant meetings at the central level and the ministries and commissions under the State Council. After the establishment of the Leading Group, the building of the Belt and Road has entered the stage of authoritative interpretation, comprehensive deployment and orderly advancement.

On February 1, 2015, Vice Premier Zhang Gaoli presided over the work conference on advancing the Belt and Road Initiative. An important content of the conference was to conscientiously study and implement the important speeches and guiding spirit of General Secretary Xi Jinping on the building of the Belt and Road and study the requirements of the instructions of the leaders of the central government such as Premier Li Keqiang. The conference has also comprehensively discussed the nature, purpose, tasks, contents, security and executors of the Belt and Road. At the conference, the major issues and key tasks for the building of the Belt and Road in 2015 and later were arranged.

Zhang Gaoli, leader of the Leading Group, urged all localities and departments to strengthen organiaational guidance and coordination, fully mobiliae the enthusiasm of localities, departments and market entities and give full play to the enthusiasm of the governments and peoples along the routes to create a strong synergy for building the Belt and Road. In response to the request of the Leading Group, the governments of most provinces have listed the Belt and Road as the policy priority in their government work reports to the National People's Congress and the Chinese People's Political Consultative Conference, and expressed that they would take an active part in the building of the Belt and Road.[4]

On March 28, 2015, the National Development and Reform Commission, the Ministry of Foreign Affairs, and the Ministry of Commerce jointly issued the *Vision and Actions on Jointly Building the Silk Road Economic Belt and the 21st Century Maritime Silk Road*, which comprehensively discussed the Belt and Road from the eight aspects of "background, principles, framework, cooperation mechanisms, China's regions in pursuing opening up, China in action, and embracing a bright future together", which show the direction for its future development.[5]

In October 2015, the Office of the Leading Group issued the *Notice on Strengthening and Regulating the Review of the Foreign Exchange Platforms for the Belt and Road*, stating that the Office of the Leading Group is responsible for issuing its review opinions on the foreign exchange platforms that were established in the name of the Belt and Road and have been approved by the CPC Central Committee and the State Council, and promoting the orderly construction of foreign exchange platforms by strengthening and standardising the review work. The Notice sets the requirements for properly handling the relevant matters. First, we should support the foreign exchange platforms identified by the *National Strategic Plan* to play a constructive role; second, in principle, we should no longer support the establishment any new foreign exchange platform; third, we should strictly abide by the relevant provisions on the participation of party and government agencies in the activities of foreign exchange platforms.[6]

On September 7, 2016, Xu Shaoshi, director of the National Development and Reform Commission, made a public appearance as the director of the Office of the Leading Group for the Belt and Road Initiative. In advancing the Belt and Road in the future, Xu Shaoshi asked all localities and departments to further study and understand the eight practical advancements clearly proposed by General Secretary Xi Jinping: practically advance the unity of thought; practically advance the implementation of plans; practically advance overall coordination; practically advance the implementation of key projects; practically advance financial innovation; practically advance people-to-people (P2P) ties; practically advance public opinions and propaganda; and practically advance security guarantee. The Office of the Leading Group will promote the building of the Belt and Road in a more powerful, orderly and effective manner in accordance with the guiding principles from the speeches of General Secretary Xi Jinping.[7]

In May 2017, the Belt and Road Forum for International Cooperation was held in Beijing, and the thematic report of the forum entitled *Building the Belt and Road: Concept, Practice and China's Contribution* was issued in the name of the Office of the Leading Group for the Belt and Road Initiative. The report systematically expounds the Belt and Road Initiative from the five aspects of "Call of the Times: From Concept to Blueprint; Cooperation Framework: From Plan to Practice; Areas of Cooperation: Economy and Culture; Diverse Cooperative Mechanisms; and A Future Vision Based on Reality Conclusion", and demonstrates the fruitful achievements of jointly building the Belt and Road, enhancing the understanding of the Belt and Road by the international community and strategic mutual trust and dialogue and cooperation among the countries involved. The Belt and Road Forum for International Cooperation held in Beijing is a major international event after the Belt and Road Initiative has entered the stage of comprehensive advancement of pragmatic cooperation. It is so far the highest-profile event within the Belt and Road framework.[8]

In July 2017, the Leading Group issued through Xinhua News Agency a notice to resolutely prevent making ill use of the Belt and Road concept to collect wealth by unfair means. The Notice states that there are chaotic phenomena in the society that the concept of the Belt and Road has been generalised and used for improper purposes, and even the Belt and Road is used as a facade to collect wealth by unfair means. For example, some P2P wealth management products and investment funds were sold in the name of commemorative coins of the Belt and Road, and the so-called "Belt and Road" alliance organisations, research associations, regional working groups, etc. were randomly set up without registration or filing. These chaotic phenomena have impaired the seriousness and authority of the concept of the Belt and Road and produced serious negative social impacts. The Notice stresses that we should resolutely prevent the spread and rampancy of the chaotic phenomena of gathering wealth by unfair means in the disguise of the Belt and Road, and identify and seriously investigate and punish illegal acts according to the law.[9]

On January 16, 2018, the Conference to Promote the Construction of the Belt and Road was held in Beijing, which required that we should thoroughly study and put into practice the guiding principles from the 19th CPC National Congress and the Central Economic Work Conference, put into practice the guiding principles from General Secretary Xi Jinping's major speeches, and summarise the work progress and arrange the work priorities for building the Belt and Road in the next step.[10]

Zhang Gaoli, leader of the Leading Group, stressed that we should build broader consensus on cooperation, enhance the international appeal of building the Belt and Road, and strengthen connectivity cooperation; advance "hard connectivity" of infrastructure and "soft connectivity" of policies and rules; improve the level of economic and trade investment cooperation and deepen international production capacity cooperation; innovate financial products and improve the level of financial services; expand cultural exchanges and cooperation, and cement the public opinion foundation; actively fulfil social responsibilities and strengthen ecological environmental protection; do a good job in risk assessment and emergency response and strengthen the safety guarantee in building the Belt and Road.

Innovative working mechanism and concept of the Leading Group in the new stage of deepening reform and opening up

To advance the Belt and Road Initiative, we should not only coordinate the resources in the domestic and international markets, but also coordinate the relationship among domestic ministries and commissions. In the top-level design of the Belt and Road, a more thorough ministry and commission coordination mechanism rather than the original, commonly used inter-ministerial joint meeting mechanism has been adopted. This is a great attempt for innovation of working mechanism under the background of reform and opening up in the new era.

The ministries and commissions related to the building of the Belt and Road mainly include two categories that are engaged in economic and diplomatic affairs. The former include the National Development and Reform Commission, the Ministry of Commerce, the Ministry of Finance, and the Central Bank. The latter is mainly the Ministry of Foreign Affairs. The National Development and Reform Commission is a functional agency under the State Council. It is responsible for comprehensively studying and formulating economic and social development policies, and conducting aggregate balance and macroeconomic regulation. The connectivity of infrastructure is a priority for implementing the Belt and Road Initiative, and the overall plans of the National Development and Reform Commission are indispensable for the large-scale infrastructure projects. At the Central Work Conference in December 2014, Xi Jinping stated that to promote the building the Belt and Road, we should concentrate resources on the key landmark projects, help the countries along the routes to carry out planning of transportation, electricity and communication infrastructures, advance the projects that have undergone pre-research and propose a list of projects that can accommodate bilateral and multilateral interests. The Ministry of Commerce is a department under the State Council that is responsible for domestic and international trade and international economic cooperation. The Belt and Road is a new type of economic cooperation mechanism covering free trade areas (FTAs), cross-border economic cooperation, economic corridors, infrastructure, financial investment and foreign aid, etc., many of which involve the functions of the Ministry of Commerce. Financial support is indispensable for the building of the Belt and Road, and the Ministry of Finance and the Central Bank are responsible for managing foreign exchange reserves and developmental financial institutions in China. The *Decision of the Central Committee of the Communist Party of China on Some Major Issues Concerning Comprehensively Deepening the Reform* adopted at the 3rd Plenary Session of the 18th CPC Central Committee on November 12, 2013 clearly stated that "We will set up development-oriented financial institutions, accelerate the construction of infrastructure connecting China with neighboring countries and regions, and work hard to build a Silk Road Economic Belt and a Maritime Silk Road, so as to form a new pattern of all-round opening".[11] In October 2014, the signing ceremony for the Memorandum of Understanding for the AIIB was held in Beijing, and 21 prospective founding members jointly decided to establish the AIIB. On November 8, Xi Jinping stated at the Dialogue on Strengthening Connectivity Partnership that China would contribute US$40 billion to set up a Silk Road fund to provide investment and financing support for projects in infrastructure and resource development and industrial cooperation in countries along the Belt and Road. The Silk Road Fund is open and welcomes the active participation of investors within and outside Asia.[12] These two major financing institutions were established with the support of the Ministry of Finance and the Central Bank, and they provide a strong guarantee for the building of the Belt and Road and the internationalisation of RMB. The Ministry of Foreign Affairs is responsible for managing foreign affairs and implementing China's overall foreign policies, and more importantly, it safeguards national interests from a political perspective.

Notes

1 "The Name list of the Leaders of the Leading Group for the Road and Road Initiative Was Published, and the Top Brain Wang Huning Has Made His Appearance on the Stage from behind the Scenes", in Singapore's Lianhe Zaobao, April 4, 2015.

Organisational structure

2 "The Namelist of the Leaders of the Leading Group for the Belt and Road Initiative Was Disclosed for the First Time," finance.ifeng.com, http://finance.ifeng.com/a/20150405/13609326_0.shtml.
3 "Speech by Xi Jinping at the Neighborhood Diplomacy Work Conference," http://politics.people.com.cn/n/2013/1025/c1024-23332318.html.
4 "Zhang Gaoli Presided Over the Conference to Promote the Construction of the Belt and Road," reminnet, http://finance.people.com.cn/n/2015/0202/c1004-26488088.html.
5 "Vision and Actions on Jointly Building the Silk Road Economic Belt and the 21st Century Maritime Silk Road," jointly issued by the National Development and Reform Commission, the Ministry of Foreign Affairs, and the Ministry of Commerce on March 28, 2015, www.yidaiyilu.gov.cn, www.yidaiyilu.gov.cn/yw/qwfb/604.html
6 "Notice on Strengthening and Regulating the Review of the Foreign Exchange Platforms for the Belt and Road," issued by the Office of the Leading Group for the Belt and Road Initiative," www.yidaiyilu.gov.cn, www.yidaiyilu.gov.cn/yw/qwfb/2161.html
7 "Xu Shaoshi was appointed the Director of the Office of the Leading Group for the Belt and Road Initiative," money.163.com, http://money.163.com/16/0909/14/C0HE0M7F002581PP.html
8 "Building the Belt and Road: Concept, Practice and China's Contribution," Xinhuanet, www.xinhuanet.com/politics/2017-05/10/c_1120951928.html
9 "Resolutely Prevent Making Ill Use of the Concept of the Belt and Road for Collecting Wealth," Xinhuanet, www.xinhuanet.com/fortune/2017-06/30/c_1121244403.html
10 "The Conference to Promote the Construction of the Belt and Road was held in Beijing," www.yidaiyilu.gov.cn, www.yidaiyilu.gov.cn/xwzx/xgcdt/44344.html
11 *Decision of the Central Committee of the Communist Party of China on Some Major Issues Concerning Comprehensively Deepening the Reform,*" dazhongnet, www.dzwww.com/2013/gghl/jd/
12 "Connectivity Spearheads Development and Partnership Enables Cooperation—Speech by Xi Jinping at the Dialogue on Strengthening Connectivity Partnership," *People's Daily*, November 9, 2014.

PART IV

The five roads

26
THE BELT AND ROAD INITIATIVE AND THE ROAD OF PEACE

Xie Laihui

Concept and origin of the Road of Peace

At the Belt and Road Forum for International Cooperation held on May 14, 2017 in Beijing, President Xi Jinping delivered a keynote speech entitled *Work Together to Build the Silk Road Economic Belt and The 21st Century Maritime Silk Road*. Xi pointed out that a solid first step has been taken in pursuing the Belt and Road Initiative, and we should build on the sound momentum generated to steer the Belt and Road Initiative towards greater success. It was against such backdrop that President Xi proposed to build the Belt and Road into a road of peace, prosperity, openness and innovation and a road connecting different civilisations.[1]

As President Xi views it, building the Road of Peace remains the priority in enhancing the prospect of the Belt and Road Initiative. Peace is the fundamental principle and goal of the Belt and Road Initiative as well as the prerequisite to exchange, cooperation, development and prosperity. Only in a peaceful and stable environment can we fulfil this vision and bring benefits to people of all countries.

Xi pointed out that the ancient silk routes thrived in times of peace, but lost vigour in times of war. Some regions along the ancient Silk Road used to be "a land of milk and honey". Yet today, these places are often associated with conflict, turbulence, crisis and challenge. Owing to factors relating history, religion and culture, some countries and regions alongside the ancient Silk Road have been through turbulence and instability for a long time, with the geopolitical crisis being deepened by the emerging extremism, terrorism and separatism. Some countries and regions are still being plagued by frequent war and conflicts, with its economy on the brink of collapse, people displaced in imminent danger of death and their lives and properties at risk. These could all be attributed to the lack of peace.

Xi held that such a state of affairs should not be allowed to continue, for the pursuit of the Belt and Road Initiative requires a peaceful and stable environment. It is stressed by Xi that those pioneers of the ancient silk routes won their place in history not as conquerors with warships, guns or swords. Rather, they are remembered as friendly emissaries leading camel caravans and sailing treasure-loaded ships. Generation after generation, the silk routes travellers have built a bridge for peace and East–West cooperation.

Spirit of the Road of Peace reflected in the Belt and Road Initiative

First, the Belt and Road Initiative will foster a new type of international relations featuring mutual respect, fairness, justice and win–win cooperation and forge partnerships of dialogue with no confrontation and of friendship rather than alliance.

China looks forward to enhancing friendship and cooperation with all countries involved in the Belt and Road Initiative on the basis of the Five Principles of Peaceful Coexistence. We are ready to share practices of development with other countries, but we have no intention to interfere in other countries' internal affairs, export our own social system and model of development, or impose our own will on others. "In pursuing the Belt and Road Initiative, we will not resort to outdated geopolitical maneuvering. What we hope to achieve is a new model of win–win cooperation. We have no intention to form a small group detrimental to stability, what we hope to create is a big family of harmonious co-existence". "All countries should respect each other's sovereignty, dignity and territorial integrity, each other's development paths and social systems, and each other's core interests and major concerns".

Guided by the principle of seeking benefits through extensive consultation and collaboration, the BRI countries will conduct cooperation on the basis of respect to each country's will and choice. Chinese Foreign Minister Wang Yi emphasised that the Belt and Road Initiative is a product of inclusive cooperation, not a tool of geopolitics, and must not be viewed with the outdated Cold War mentality. In promoting this initiative, China will follow the principle of wide consultation, joint contribution and shared benefits and respect the independent choice of other countries in cooperation. We will be sensitive to the comfort level of other parties, ensure transparency and openness, align the initiative with the development strategies of other participants, and create synergy with the existing regional cooperation mechanisms. The vision of this initiative is common development and its goal is win–win progress through cooperation. If we may use a musical metaphor, the BRI is not China's solo, but a symphony performed by all relevant countries.[2]

Secondly, the BRI aims to foster the vision of common, comprehensive, cooperative and sustainable security and create a security environment built and shared by all. As President Xi addressed in his speech at the United Nations Office at Geneva, "No country in the world can enjoy absolute security. A country cannot have security while others are in turmoil, as threats facing other countries may haunt it also. When neighbors are in trouble, instead of tightening his own fences, one should extend a helping hand to them. As a saying goes, 'United we stand, divided we fall.' All countries should pursue common, comprehensive, cooperative and sustainable security".[3]

Thirdly, China is firmly committed to the path of peaceful development and has gained the trust of the Belt and Road countries. In September 2011, the Chinese State Council published a white paper entitled *China's Peaceful Development Road*, noting that after suffering from war and poverty in late modern times, the Chinese people have learned to their cost the importance of cherishing peace and pursuing development. It is believed that only in a peaceful environment can people live and work in peace and contentment, and only through development can people improve their well-being. China looks forward to working with other countries to promote, defend and share peace.[4]

China remains unchanged in its commitment to uphold world peace. For several millennia, peace has been in the blood of us Chinese and a part of our DNA. Chinese people firmly believe that peace and stability is the only way to development and prosperity. China has grown from a poor and weak country to the world's second largest economy not by committing military expansion or colonial plunder, but through the hard work of its people and our efforts to uphold peace. As President Xi addressed in his speech at the UN Headquarters in New York, "China will never waver in its pursuit of peaceful development. No matter how strong its economy grows, China will never seek hegemony, expansion or sphere of influence".[5]

This commitment was stressed again in Xi's speech at the United Nations Office at Geneva in 2017. "China will never waver in its pursuit of peaceful development. No matter how strong its economy grows, China will never seek hegemony, expansion or sphere of influence. History has borne this out and will continue to do so". Xi notes,

> Countries should foster partnerships based on dialogue, non-confrontation and non-alliance. Major Powers should respect each other's core interests and major concerns, keep their differences under control and build a new model of relations featuring non-conflict, non-confrontation, mutual respect and win–win cooperation. As long as we maintain communication and treat each other with sincerity, the "Thucydides trap" can be avoided. Big countries should treat smaller ones as equals instead of acting as a hegemony imposing their will on others. No country should open the Pandora's Box by willfully waging wars or undermining the international rule of law. Nuclear weapons, the Sword of Damocles that hangs over mankind, should be completely prohibited and thoroughly destroyed over time to make the world free of nuclear weapons.[6]

On November 17, 2016, 193 UN members adopted a resolution by consensus, embracing economic cooperation initiatives including the Belt and Road Initiative while calling on the international community to provide a secure environment for the construction of the Belt and Road. On March 17, 2017, the UN Security Council unanimously adopted Resolution 2344, calling on the international community to strengthen regional economic cooperation through the Belt and Road Initiative.

Fourthly, China has made positive contributions to the building of the Road of Peace, helping the Belt and Road countries achieve peace and stability. To promote the Belt and Road Initiative, China proposes to "work to resolve hotspot issues through political means, and promote mediation in the spirit of justice. We should intensify counter-terrorism efforts, address both its symptoms and root causes, and strive to eradicate poverty, backwardness and social injustice".

In recent years, China has actively participated in dialogue and negotiations on hotspot issues like the Korean Peninsula nuclear issue, the Iranian nuclear issue, the Israeli–Palestinian conflict, the issues of Syria, South Sudan and Afghanistan, the Rohingya issue of Myanmar as well as regional counter-terrorism, contributing its share to promoting political settlement. In January 2017, President Xi Jinping announced at the United Nations Office in Geneva that China had decided to provide an additional RMB200 million of humanitarian assistance for refugees and the displaced of Syria. At the Belt and Road Forum for International Cooperation on May 14, 2017, President Xi made a solemn promise to the world that in the coming three years, China would provide assistance worth RMB60 billion to developing countries and international organisations participating in the Belt and Road Initiative to launch more projects to improve people's well-being.

Contribution of the Road of Peace to the world

It is the common aspiration of China and the Belt and Road countries to build this initiative into a Road of Peace, which also underpins the smooth implementation of the Belt and Road

Initiative. With a view to intensifying regional cooperation, the Belt and Road Initiative will mainly strengthen cultural exchanges and mutual accommodation and promote the peace and stability of the world.

First of all, building the Road of Peace together will make significant contributions to the peace and stability of the world. Covering wide areas of Asia, Europe, Africa and Latin America and a large spread of population, the Belt and Road Initiative will contribute significantly to the global security situation if peace and stability are to be achieved. The Belt and Road countries are mainly developing countries, with many of them faced with complex geopolitical landscapes. Especially in some regions of the Middle East, South and Central Asia and Africa, conflict and turbulence still exist. More importantly, many of these regions have become a hotbed and source of religious extremism and terrorism, posing great threats to world peace and stability.

The Belt and Road Initiative upholds the principle of seeking shared benefits through consultation and collaboration, with an aim to complement different countries' development strategies to achieve common development. It forges a community of common interest, same responsibilities and a shared future, so as to eradicate the root of conflict and war plaguing certain regions. The principle and practice of the Road of Peace will bring benefits to the relevant countries and its peoples as well as to the whole world.

Second, the Road of Peace is underpinned by a new type of international relations and the vision of common, comprehensive, cooperative and sustainable security, which could reduce deficit in peace across the world. China advocates a new type of international relations featuring mutual respect, justice and fairness and mutual benefit and a common, comprehensive, cooperative and sustainable security concept. All countries, big or small, shall be treated equally, and disputes shall be resolved through political and diplomatic negotiation rather than the resort to the use of force. These new ideas have risen above the hegemonism and power politics that have long dominated the world and served as important guidance for making political and economic order more fair and equitable and achieving real peace and stability in the long run.

Furthermore, the Road of Peace embraces the principle of promoting peace and stability through common development, which is helpful in building a peaceful and prosperous world free from crisis. Underdevelopment and imbalanced development is the root of chaos and turbulence. And imbalanced global growth, inequality in income distribution and uneven development space are of great concern. This is the biggest challenge facing the world today. It is also what is behind the social turmoil in some countries. Over 700 million people in the world are still suffering from extreme poverty, with most of them living in Asia and Africa, which are also the main areas covered by the Belt and Road Initiative. The Belt and Road Initiative focus on resolving underdevelopment and unbalanced development and advancing North–South, South–South cooperation, in order to jointly safeguard world peace and stability and promote common development.

The governance solution represented by the Road of Peace is to promote the coordinated development of all social sectors through economic advancement and to seek peace through development. For the developing nations which constitute the majority of the Belt and Road countries, economic development and prosperity hold the master key to solving all problems. As stated by President Xi at the UN Sustainable Development Summit 2015, "At the global level, peace and development remain the dominant themes of the times. To properly address the range of global challenges we face, including the recent refugee crisis in Europe, there is no fundamental solution other than the pursuit of peace and development. Confronted by such a multiplicity of challenges and difficulties, we must hold fast to development as our master key, for only through development can we resolve the root cause of conflicts, safeguard the basic rights of the people, and meet the ardent hopes of people for a better future". Guided by this very principle, China stays committed to promoting the development of the Belt and Road countries and addressing the security problems brought by poverty, backwardness and conflicts on development interest, so as to eradicate the social economic breeding ground for extremism and terrorism.[7]

Notes

1. Xi Jinping, "Work Together to Build the Silk Road Economic Belt and The 21st Century Maritime Silk Road—Speech at the Opening Ceremony of The Belt and Road Forum for International Cooperation on 14 May 2017," *Xi Jinping: The Governance of China*, Foreign Language Press, 2017, pp. 506–517.
2. "Wang Yi: the BRI is not China's solo but a symphony performed by all relevant countries," *China News*, March 8, 2015, www.chinanews.com/gn/2015/03-08/7110383.shtml
3. Xi Jinping, "Work Together to Build a Community of Shared Future for Mankind," quoted in Xi Jinping: *The Governance of China* (Volume 2), 2017, pp. 542.
4. "Information Office of the State Council: China's peaceful development", September 11, 2011, Chinese Government, www.scio.gov.cn/zxbd/nd/2011/Document/1006416/1006416.htm
5. Xi Jinping, "Working Together to Create a New Mutually Beneficial Partnership and Community of Shared Future for Mankind," quoted in Xi Jinping: *The Governance of China* (Volume 2), Beijing: Foreign Languages Press, 2017, p. 525.
6. Xi Jinping, "Work Together to Build a Community of Shared Future for Mankind," quoted in Xi Jinping: *The Governance of China* (Volume 2), Beijing: Foreign Languages Press, 2017, p. 541.
7. Xi Jinping, "Towards a Mutually Beneficial Partnership for Sustainable Development—Speech at the UN Sustainable Development Summit," September 26, 2015, *People's Daily*, China, http://politics.people.com.cn/n/2015/0927/c1024-27638350.html

27

THE BELT AND ROAD INITIATIVE AND THE ROAD OF PROSPERITY

Xie Laihui

Concept and origin of the Road of Prosperity

At the Belt and Road Forum for International Cooperation held on May 14, 2017 in Beijing, President Xi Jinping delivered a keynote speech entitled *Work Together to Build the Silk Road Economic Belt and the 21st Century Maritime Silk Road*. Xi pointed out that a solid first step has been taken in pursuing the Belt and Road Initiative. And we should build on the sound momentum generated to steer the Belt and Road Initiative towards greater success. It was against such backdrop that President Xi proposed in his speech to build the Belt and Road into a road of peace, prosperity, openness and innovation and a road connecting different civilisations.[1]

On the Road of Prosperity, Xi emphasised that development holds the master key to solving all problems. In pursuing the Belt and Road Initiative, we should focus on the fundamental issue of development, release the growth potential of various countries and achieve economic integration and interconnected development and deliver benefits to all.

Spirit of the Road of Prosperity reflected in the Belt and Road Initiative

Building the Road of Prosperity is the fundamental goal of the Belt and Road Initiative, which seeks for connectivity of policy, infrastructure, trade and finance.

The Belt and Road Initiative is, in final analysis, an economic cooperation initiative, with its core functions being achieving common development between China and other Belt and Road countries. This initiative will lead both China and other Belt and Road countries to common development, shared prosperity and win–win outcome.

By working together to forge the international cooperation platform for the Belt and Road Initiative, China will deliver significant development opportunities to countries involved with its advantages in areas of overcapacity, applicable technology, building capacity of major projects, reliable source of financing and the large scale of market. Great impetus will also be given to the Belt and Road countries in their effort to improve infrastructure, speed up industrialisation, expand external trade, attract foreign investment and promote economic and social development.

The Road of Prosperity in the Belt and Road Initiative could be built in following ways.

First, in advancing the Belt and Road Initiative, we should deepen industrial cooperation so that industrial development plans of different countries will complement and reinforce each other. Focus should be put on launching major projects. We should strengthen international cooperation on production capacity and equipment manufacturing, and seize new development opportunities presented by the new industrial revolution to foster new businesses and maintain dynamic growth.

Second, we should establish a stable and sustainable financial safeguard system that keeps risks under control, create new models of investment and financing, encourage greater cooperation between government and private capital and build a diversified financing system and a multi-tiered capital market. We should also develop inclusive finance and improve financial services networks.

Third, infrastructure connectivity is the foundation of development through cooperation. We should promote land, maritime, air and cyberspace connectivity, concentrate our efforts on key passageways, cities and projects and connect networks of highways, railways and sea ports. And steady progress should be made to build six major economic corridors under the Belt and Road Initiative.

Fourth, we need to seize opportunities presented by the new round of change in energy mix and the revolution in energy technologies to develop global energy interconnection and achieve green and low-carbon development. Meanwhile, the trans-regional logistics network should also be improved.

Fifth, we should promote connectivity of policies, rules and standards so as to provide institutional guarantee for enhancing connectivity.

In building the Road of Prosperity, we have achieved progress in some areas so far.

First, Belt and Road countries have become important destinations of China's outbound investment. In 2016, China invested US$14.5 billion in these countries, accounting for 8.5% of its total investment abroad. It signed new overseas engineering contracts worth US$126 billion, up 36% year on year. The process of talks on bilateral investment protection treaties has been stepped up. By the end of 2016, China had signed bilateral investment treaties with 53 Belt and Road countries, and established mechanisms for promoting economic and trade and investment cooperation with most countries. China has also signed double taxation avoidance agreements with 54 Belt and Road countries.

Second, positive progress has been made in international cooperation on production capacity. By the end of 2016, China had signed production capacity cooperation documents with Kazakhstan, Ethiopia and 25 other countries, published the "Joint Statement Between ASEAN and China on Production Capacity Cooperation" with 10 ASEAN member states and the "Joint Statement on Production Capacity Cooperation Among Lancang–Mekong Countries" with five countries along this river, which would facilitate alignment and cooperation in their planning, policy, information and project management. The China–Russia Investment Cooperation Committee was set up under the mechanism of regular meeting of premiers to coordinate investment in non-energy industries.

Having invested about more than US$18.5 billion, Chinese enterprises are working to set up 56 economic and trade cooperation zones in 20 Belt and Road countries and intensifying investment and cooperation as well as sharing Chinese practices of development. Notable achievements have been made in external industrial parks like China–Belarus Industrial Park in Minsk of Belarus, Thai–China Industrial Park in Rayong of Thailand and the Suez Economic Zone in Egypt. And these serve as a testament to the going global of the Chinese enterprises cluster and the friendship and cooperation with its foreign counterparts.

Third, solid progress has been made in improving financial safeguard system and establishing a financial services network that covers all areas. The Chinese government encourages development and policy-based finance institutions to take part in Belt and Road financial cooperation activities. Since the Initiative was proposed, the China Development Bank has signed off more than 100 projects in the Belt and Road countries, to a value surpassing US$40 billion, with US$30 billion issued in loans. The Export–Import Bank of China has signed 1100 projects, valued at US$100 billion, in the Belt and Road countries, issuing US$80 billion in loans. China Export & Credit Insurance Corporation has insured more than US$320 billion of export and investment projects in the Belt and Road countries. By the end of 2016, 9 Chinese-funded banks had set up 62 primary branches in 26 Belt and Road countries, and 54 banks from 20 Belt and Road countries had opened 6 subsidiaries, 20 branches and 40 offices in China.

As stated by President Xi at the Belt and Road Forum for International Cooperation in May 2017, China would scale up financing support for the Belt and Road Initiative by contributing an additional RMB100 billion to the Silk Road Fund, and we encourage financial institutions to conduct overseas RMB fund business with an estimated amount of about RMB300 billion. The China Development Bank and the Export–Import Bank of China will set up special lending schemes worth RMB250 billion equivalents and RMB130 billion equivalents, respectively, to support Belt and Road cooperation on infrastructure, industrial capacity and financing.

As of now, China has signed currency swap agreements with 22 Belt and Road countries and regions, with a total value of RMB982.2 billion. Local currency settlement agreements were signed between China and Vietnam, Mongolia, Laos and Kyrgyzstan in border trade, and agreements on general trade and local currency settlement in investment were signed between China and Russia, Kazakhstan, Belarus and Nepal.

China promotes memorandums of understanding (MOUs) to support cooperation on financial supervision, in an effort to establish an efficient supervision and coordination mechanism in the region, improve the framework of financial crisis management and response, and enhance the capacity of jointly addressing financial risks. By the end of 2016, the People's Bank of China has signed MOUs with 42 overseas anti-money laundering institutions; the China Banking Regulatory Commission has signed MOUs or exchanged notes on cooperation with the financial regulators in 29 Belt and Road countries; and the China Insurance Regulatory Commission is negotiating the signing of MOUs with Belt and Road countries and has founded the Asian Forum of Insurance Regulators.

Fourth, we have stepped up pace in enhancing the connectivity of facilities at both physical and institutional levels. A large number of connectivity projects have been planned and implemented by China with relevant countries, including the building of the Jakarta–Bandung high-speed railway, the China–Laos railway, the Addis Ababa–Djibouti railway and the Hungary–Serbia railway, and upgraded Gwadar and Piraeus ports. Today, a multi-dimensional infrastructure network is taking shape, one that is underpinned by economic corridors such as China–Pakistan Economic Corridor, China–Mongolia–Russia Economic Corridor and the New Eurasian Continental Bridge, featuring land–sea–air transportation routes and information expressway and supported by major railway, port and pipeline projects.

China and 15 Belt and Road countries have signed 16 bilateral or multilateral agreements on facilitation of transport, including the "Intergovernmental Agreement of the SCO Member States on the Facilitation of International Road Transport" and the "Intergovernmental Agreement on International Road Transport Along the Asian Highway Network", adopted the measures outlined in the "Greater Mekong Sub-region Cross-Border Transport Facilitation Agreement", and opened 356 international transport routes running through 73 land ports. China has signed 38 bilateral or regional ocean shipment agreements with 47 Belt and Road countries, and bilateral intergovernmental aviation transport agreements with 62 countries. Direct civil flights now reach 43 countries. The Chinese government has issued "Guidelines on the Implementation of Promoting International Road Transport Facilitation in the Context of the Belt and Road Initiative", in an aim to align the connectivity-related regulations and systems of relevant countries for better "soft connectivity".[2]

Contribution of the Road of Prosperity to the world

The Belt and Road initiative originated in China, but it has delivered benefits well beyond its borders. The Silk Road Economic Belt and 21st Century Maritime Silk Road Initiative presents opportunities for both China and the rest of the world. It will deliver shared benefits to the Belt and Road countries as well as others.

First, thanks to the complementarities between China and the Belt and Road countries, building the Road of Prosperity will promote international cooperation on production capacity and infrastructure construction, which creates new effective demand for the world economy. By improving the connectivity between different countries, the Belt and Road Initiative will intensify cooperation in trade and investment as well as cooperation on international production capacity and manufacturing. Therefore, it is essentially the increase of effective supply that helps give a new boost to demand and rebalance the world economy. Especially in the face of the lasting sluggishness of the world economy, China's tremendous production and building capacity could meet the urgent need of Belt and Road countries for advancing industrialisation, modernisation and infrastructure construction, which is significant for a stable world economy.[3] As the largest developing country and the second largest economy in the world, China bears considerable responsibility for ensuring the stability of the global economic growth. Since the 2008 international financial crisis, China has contributed to over 30% of global growth each year on average.

Second, the connectivity of the Road of Prosperity will largely reduce the logistic cost and inject new impetus to economic globalisation. One of the most prominent features of the Belt and Road Initiative is the connectivity focused on infrastructure construction. The Belt and Road Initiative, Asian Infrastructure Investment Bank and the Silk Road Fund have just in time met the demand for investment and cooperation on regional infrastructure construction. At the Boao Forum for Asia in 2015, many representatives of developing countries made clear that the purpose of their participation in the Asian investment Bank was to follow the right trend for development rather than siding with China. The benefits of the connectivity of the BRI will flow not only into the Belt and Road countries but also to the world at large. According to an article published on the *Forbes Magazine* website in February 2017, the Belt and Road Initiative would bring benefits to western companies in many aspects. Particularly worth mentioning is that western transnational corporations will be able to tap the labour force market in Central Asia, South East Asia and Africa and reshape the global supply and value chain with the support of relevant railway networks. Meanwhile, they can also board the express railway of the Belt and Road Initiative to explore new consumer markets within these regions. Western logistics companies can also benefit from it by cutting cost and transport time.[4]

Third, the Road of prosperity will help build a more balanced and equitable world that delivers benefits for all. Social and economic developments in many Belt and Road countries are still relatively backward, and Asia and Africa are still home to most of the poor population. In this sense, these regions are the weak links in economic globalisation and world development. However, building the Road of Prosperity can effectively reduce poverty within these regions and improve the living standards of the bottom across the world, correcting the imbalance of the global growth. Such significance was also highlighted in President Xi's keynote speech at the Global Poverty Reduction and Development Forum held on October 16, 2015. Xi said,

Upholding and developing an open economy, establishing an international financial system that is fair, just, inclusive and orderly, and fostering a favorable external environment for the developing countries is an important priority for reducing poverty. China has proposed to build the Silk Road Economic Belt and 21st Century Maritime Silk Road, initiated the Asian Infrastructure Investment Bank, and set up the Silk Road Fund. With the purpose to support developing countries in cooperating on infrastructure development and helping them strengthen self-generated development, we encourage those countries to get more integrated into global supply chain, industrial chain and value chain and inject more vitality to this global agenda.[5]

Fourth, the Road of Prosperity embodies the principles and purposes enshrined in the UN Charter and play an important role in upholding multilateralism. In May 2016, on behalf of the Asia–Pacific Economic and Social Council, the United Nations Deputy Secretary-General and UN Economic and Social Commission for Asia and the Pacific (ESCAP) Executive Secretary Shamshad Akhtar signed letter of Intent with the Chinese side on advancing connectivity and the Belt and Road Initiative. According to Dr Akhtar, "Seamless Connectivity" is our common language; The Belt and Road Initiative presents a historic opportunity for the connectivity of infrastructure construction as well as institutional building in the Asia–Pacific region. She held that the Belt and Road Initiative has strengthened multilateralism both in theory and practice. And it not only carries forward the principle and purpose of UN Charter but also serves as international public goods.[6]

Notes

1 Xi Jinping, "Make the Belt and Road Initiative Deliver Greater Benefits to People of Countries Involved," quoted in Xi Jinping: *The Governance of China* (Volume 2), Beijing: Foreign Languages Press, 2017, p. 504.
2 Office of the Leading Group for the Belt and Road Initiative, "Building the Belt and Road: Concept, Practice and China's Contribution," May 10, 2017, www.xinhuanet.com/politics/2017-05/10/c_1120951928.htm
3 Xi Jinping, "Make the Belt and Road Initiative Deliver Greater Benefits to People of Countries Involved," quoted in Xi Jinping: *The Governance of China* (Volume 2), Beijing: Foreign Languages Press, 2017, p. 504.
4 Alex Capri, "Here Are 5 Ways China's New Silk Road Is Good For Western Companies," *Forbes*, February 9, 2017, www.forbes.com/sites/alexcapri/2017/02/09/here-are-5-ways-chinas-new-silk-road-is-good-for-western-companies
5 Xi Jinping, "Work Together to Eradicate Poverty and Promote Common Development—Keynote Speech at the 2015 Global Poverty Reduction and Development Forum," quoted in *People's Daily*, 2nd edition, October 17, 2015.
6 "Belt and Road Initiative a game changer in Asia–Pacific: UNESCAP," May 19, 2016, www.xinhuanet.com/english/2016-05/19/c_135369770.htm

28
THE BELT AND ROAD INITIATIVE AND THE ROAD OF OPENNESS

Xie Laihui

Concept and origin of the Road of Openness

At the Belt and Road Forum for International Cooperation held on May 14, 2017 in Beijing, Chinese President Xi Jinping delivered a keynote speech entitled *Work Together to Build the Silk Road Economic Belt and the 21st Century Maritime Silk Road*. Xi pointed out that a solid first step has been taken in pursuing the Belt and Road Initiative, and we should build on the sound momentum generated to steer the Belt and Road Initiative towards greater success. It was against such backdrop that President Xi proposed in his speech to build the Belt and Road into a road of peace, prosperity, openness and innovation and a road connecting different civilisations.[1]

On the Road of Openness, President Xi stressed, "Opening up brings progress while isolation results in backwardness"; "Civilization thrives with openness and nations prosper through exchange". The Belt and Road Initiative should be an open one that will achieve both economic growth and balanced development.

Spirit of the Road of Openness reflected in the Belt and Road Initiative

The Belt and Road Initiative is an open platform for economic cooperation, with its principle as seeking shared benefits through consultation and collaboration and its vision establishing a global community of shared future.

The Belt and Road Initiative is proposed by China, but is shared by all as a global public good. The Belt and Road Initiative embraces the spirit of openness, inclusiveness, cooperation and mutual benefit, and it calls for pursuing joint development and sharing benefits on the basis of equality and mutual benefit. In his speech, President Xi highlighted the openness of the Belt and Road Initiative in particular. Xi said that the Belt and Road Initiative is rooted in the ancient Silk Road. It focuses on the Asian, European and African continents, but is also open to all other countries. All countries, from Asia, Europe, Africa or the Americas, can be international cooperation partners of the Belt and Road Initiative. The pursuit of this initiative is based on extensive consultation and its benefits will be shared by us all.[2]

Building the Road of Openness has laid foundation for the Belt and Road Initiative to become a global proposal. Any developed country, be it along the Belt and Road or not, can participate in this initiative as a third-party state and enjoy opportunities and outcomes brought by the Belt and Road Initiative. The Chinese government stressed that the initiative is an open and transparent channel for cooperation. Guided by the principle of achieving shared growth through discussion and collaboration and in line with the law of the market, China looks forward to working with relevant developed countries to give more play to each one's complementarities in technology, capital, production capacity and market. And it will carry out third-party cooperation among the Belt and Road countries so as to promote mutual benefit and win–win outcome.[3]

In his speech at the Belt and Road Forum for International Cooperation, President Xi set out the specific principles and charted the course of action on building the Road of Openness.

First, the Road of Openness is about building an open platform of cooperation and upholding and grows an open world economy. We should jointly create an environment that will facilitate opening up and development, establish a fair, equitable and transparent system of international trade and investment rules and boost the orderly flow of production factors, efficient resources allocation and full market integration.

Second, in advancing the Belt and Road Initiative, we should uphold the multilateral trading regime, advance the building of free trade areas and promote liberalisation and facilitation of trade and investment.

Lastly, we should also focus on resolving issues such as imbalances in development, difficulties in governance, digital divide and income disparity and make economic globalisation open, inclusive, balanced and beneficial to all. China welcomes efforts made by other countries to grow open economies based on their national conditions, participate in global governance and provide public goods. Together, we can build a broad community of shared interests.

Our efforts in building the Road of Openness have paid off in the following areas.

First of all, many countries, both within and without the Belt and Road Initiative, and multiple international organisations have signed a number of cooperation agreements within the framework of Belt and Road Initiative. Four years on, over 100 countries and international organisations have supported and become involved in this initiative. China has signed cooperation agreements with over 40 countries and international organisations and carried out framework cooperation on production capacity with more than 30 countries. During the forum, the Ministry of Commerce of China and the relevant agencies of more than 60 countries and international organisations jointly issued the Initiative on Promoting Unimpeded Trade Cooperation along the Belt and Road. At the second ministerial meeting of the Forum of China and the Community of Latin American and Caribbean States held on January 24, 2018, the Foreign Ministers issued a special declaration on supporting and participating in the Belt and Road Initiative. The participation of over 30 Latin American countries in building the Silk Road Economic Belt on the Pacific Ocean is a further testament to the Road of Openness.

Additionally, China has maintained close economic and trade ties with the Belt and Road countries in recent years, which has greatly boosted the local economies and industrial development. Against a backdrop of sluggish global trade, in 2016 China's total trade volume with the Belt and Road countries reached US$947.8 billion, accounting for 25.7% of its imports and exports of goods. The volume of service imports and exports with these countries stood at US$122.2 billion, accounting for 15.2% of its total, up 3.4 percentage points from 2015.[4]

Driven by industrial transformation and upgrading, increasing domestic demand, and upgrading of consumption, China's huge market offers plenty of economic and trade opportunities for these countries. In addition, while addressing the Belt and Road Forum for International Cooperation, President Xi also announced that the first China International Import Expo will be held in Shanghai in 2018 so as to promote the exports of Belt and Road countries with China.

China is an advocate of more inclusive free trade, and has conducted talks on trade agreements with the economies along the Belt and Road, in an effort to build the Belt and Road free trade areas network. The China–ASEAN Free Trade Area has been upgraded, and the China–Georgia free trade talks have been completed. Real progress has been achieved in the talks on the Regional Comprehensive Economic Partnership (RCEP), and breakthroughs have been made in the talks on the China–Maldives Free Trade Area. Talks on the China–Gulf Cooperation Council Free Trade Area, the China–Israel Free Trade Area, the China–Sri Lanka Free Trade Area and phase II of the China–Pakistan Free Trade Area are progressing. Joint research on the feasibility of the China–Nepal Free Trade Area, the China–Bangladesh Free Trade Area and the China–Moldova free trade agreement is making progress as well.

With a view to facilitating trade, China and the Belt and Road countries will cooperate on their customs clearance systems and realise exchanges of information, mutual recognition of their respective customs regulations and mutual help in law enforcement. "Single-window" trials have been launched in international trade, and the introduction of integrated procedures for customs clearance and inspection and quarantine work has been stepped up, which will realise "rapid clearance procedures for import and export". Fast-track customs clearance has been opened at Chinese ports for farm produce imported from Kazakhstan, Kyrgyzstan and Tajikistan. Relevant countries and organisations along the Belt and Road have released such documents as "Joint Statement of Strengthening Cooperation on Animal and Plant Quarantine, Facilitating Economic and Trade Development" (Chongqing Joint Statement), "Joint Statement on the Belt and Road Food Safety Cooperation" and "Joint Statement of the Fifth China–ASEAN Ministerial Meeting on Quality Supervision, Inspection and Quarantine". As of April 2017, China has signed 78 documents on cooperation with Belt and Road countries and regions, to promote their work and mechanism alignment, technological standards coordination, mutual recognition of inspection results and networking of electronic certificates.[5]

Contribution of the Road of Openness to the world

First, the Road of Openness embodies the spirit of openness, inclusive, cooperation and mutual benefit and opposes exclusive regional cooperation, which is conducive to promoting global economic integration and shared interests of the whole world. Traditional regional economic cooperation like European Union (EU), North American Free Trade Agreement (NAFTA) and Trans-Pacific Economic Partnership (TPP) are closed and exclusive platforms. While bringing trade creation effects to its member states, those frameworks also create trade diversion effects, undermining the interests of the countries outside. Therefore, such regional economic cooperation frameworks might go against the liberalisation of Trade and Investment in multilateralism. However, as a new type of economic cooperation, the Belt and Road Initiative embraces the principle of achieving shared growth through discussion and collaboration, acts on the core values of openness, inclusiveness, cooperation and mutual benefit and welcomes the participation of all countries and its peoples in this cause so as to enjoy its shared benefits. Because of this, the Belt and Road Initiative has gained endorsement from UN and multiple international organisations and has been incorporated by the UN General Assembly and the UN Security Council in their relevant resolutions and documents.

Second, building the Road of Openness is of great significance to promoting economic globalisation. Since the 2008 international financial crisis, there have been skepticisms over economic globalisation and multilateralism in many western countries, with trade protectionism on the rise and the world on the brink of recession.

Against such a backdrop, the Belt and Road Initiative has actually supported economic globalisation and liberalisation of trade and investment in a practical manner. President Xi addressed at the World Economic Forum in Davos in January 2017 that we must redouble efforts to develop global connectivity to enable all countries to achieve interconnected growth and share prosperity. We must remain committed to developing global free trade and investment; promote trade and investment liberalisation and facilitation through opening up; and say no to protectionism.

The Belt and Road Initiative has now become a primary effort for China to build an open world economy. As President Xi stressed once again in his report at the 19th CPC National Congress,

> China adheres to the fundamental national policy of opening up and pursues development with its doors open wide. China will actively promote international cooperation through the Belt and Road Initiative. In doing so, we hope to achieve policy, infrastructure, trade, financial, and people-to-people connectivity and thus build a new platform for international cooperation to create new drivers of shared development. China will increase assistance to other developing countries, especially the least developed countries, and do its part to reduce the North–South development gap. China will support multilateral trade regimes and work to facilitate the establishment of free trade areas and build an open world economy.[6]

Lastly, the Road of Openness will be focused on resolving issues such as imbalances in development, difficulties in governance, digital divide and income disparity, which will help improve inclusive global development. Following the 2008 international financial crisis, with deeper understanding of the problem of development imbalances and income inequalities, more and more international organisations give priority to achieving inclusive development, in an attempt to deliver the shared benefits of economic globalisation to countries and peoples at all levels.

China is among the countries that were first to propose and advocate the concept of inclusive development. On a particular note, in his speech at the Asian–African Summit in April 2015, President Xi stated that:

> Developing countries in their large numbers are all faced with the common mission of accelerating development and improving people's lives. They ought to look to one another for comfort and come to each other's aid in times of difficulty. And they should actively carry out cooperation across the board to realize their respective development blueprints. Helping developing countries to achieve development so as to close the North–South gap is the bounden responsibility and obligation of the developed countries. It is important to prod developed countries to earnestly deliver on their ODA commitments, step up their support for developing countries with no political strings attached, and build a more fair and balanced new global development partnership by strengthening the developing countries' capacity for independent development. It is also important to uphold and promote an open world economy, build fair, equitable, inclusive and rules-based international economic and financial systems, and create a sound external environment favorable for the development of developing countries.[7]

Building the Belt and Road Initiative into the Road of Openness is an embodiment of China's adherence to promoting inclusive development and a new type of globalisation. By delivering shared prosperity with common development to both China and the Belt and Road countries, especially the developing countries, the Belt and Road Initiative will significantly bridge the development gap between different countries and generate more globalisation dividends for all its peoples, so as to strongly promote inclusive development across the world.

Notes

1. Xi Jinping, "Working Together to Create a New Mutually Beneficial Partnership and Community of Shared Future for Mankind—keynote speech at the opening ceremony of the Belt and Road Forum for International Cooperation," quoted in Xi Jinping: *the Governance of China* (Volume 2), Beijing: Foreign Languages Press, 2017, pp. 506–517.
2. Xi Jinping, "Working Together to Create a New Mutually Beneficial Partnership and Community of Shared Future for Mankind—keynote speech at the opening ceremony of the Belt and Road Forum for International Cooperation," quoted in Xi Jinping: *the Governance of China* (Volume 2), Beijing: Foreign Languages Press, 2017, p. 516.
3. Office of the Leading Group for the Belt and Road Initiative, "Building the Belt and Road: Concept, Practice and China's Contribution," Chinese Government, May 10, 2017, www.sdpc.gov.cn/gzdt/201705/t20170511_847228.html
4. Ibid.
5. Ibid.
6. Xi Jinping, "Secure a Decisive Victory in Building a Moderately Prosperous Society in All Respects and Strive for the Great Success of Socialism with Chinese Characteristics for a New Era—Delivered at the 19th National Congress of the Communist Party of China," October 18, 2017.
7. Xi Jinping, "Carry Forward the Bandung Spirit for Win–Win Cooperation—Remarks at the Asian–African Summit Jakarta," quoted in *People's Daily*, 2nd edition, April 22, 2015.

29
THE BELT AND ROAD INITIATIVE AND THE ROAD OF INNOVATION

Xie Laihui

Concept and origin of the Road of Innovation

At the Belt and Road Forum for International Cooperation held on May 14, 2017 in Beijing, President Xi Jinping delivered a keynote speech entitled *Work Together to Build the Silk Road Economic Belt and the 21st Century Maritime Silk Road*. Xi pointed out that a solid first step has been taken in pursuing the Belt and Road Initiative and we should build on the sound momentum generated to steer the Belt and Road Initiative towards greater success. It was against such a backdrop that President Xi proposed in his speech to build the Belt and Road into a road of peace, prosperity, openness and innovation and a road connecting different civilisations.[1]

On the Road of Innovation, President Xi stressed that "Innovation is an important force powering development". "The Belt and Road Initiative is new by nature and we need to encourage innovation in pursuing this initiative".

Spirit of the Road of Innovation reflected in the Belt and Road Initiative

The Belt and Road Initiative is in itself a ground-breaking effort and a testament to the spirit of innovation.

Building on the historical achievement of the Ancient Silk Routes, the Belt and Road Initiative takes on new implications from the trend of our time. The Belt and Road Initiative is a new type of cooperation model that embraces the principle of seeking benefits through consultation and collaboration. With the complementarities between development strategies of the Belt and Road countries and the trend of trade and investment liberalisation and facilitation, the Initiative bases its effort on physical connectivity, production capacity cooperation, people-to-people exchanges and mutually beneficial cooperation in finance so as to promote more bilateral and regional cooperation.

China cooperates with other Belt and Road countries on the basis of building a new type of international relations featuring mutual respect, fairness, justice and win–win cooperation, and works to establish economic and trade partnership of mutual benefit and win–win outcome with countries involved in this initiative. As of the end of 2016, more than 100 countries have expressed their support and willingness to participate in the initiative. China has signed 46 cooperation agreements with 39 countries and international organisations, covering a broad range of fields that include connectivity, production capacity, investment, economy and trade, finance, science and technology, society, humanities, quality of life and marine issues.²

The Belt and Road Initiative has explored new ways to strengthen financing mechanism and has introduced many new systems, platforms and norms. To support the initiative financially, besides the existing policy-based financial institutions, China has set up the Silk Road Fund and made full use of some newly established platforms such as the Asian Infrastructure Investment Bank and the BRICS New Development Bank. China also works with the World Bank and other multilateral development institutions to support the projects related to the Belt and Road Initiative.

With a commitment to innovation-driven development, the BRI aims to forge a dynamic growth model and tap new driving forces powering the world economy. In his speech entitled *Work Together to Build the Silk Road Economic Belt and the 21st Century Maritime Silk Road* at the Belt and Road Forum for International Cooperation, President Xi charted the course of action on building the Road of Innovation. First of all, we should pursue innovation-driven development and intensify cooperation in frontier areas such as digital economy, artificial intelligence, nanotechnology and quantum computing. And we should advance the development of big data, cloud computing and smart cities so as to turn them into a digital silk road of the twenty-first century. Second, we should spur the full integration of science and technology into industries and finance, improve the environment for innovation and pool resources for innovation. Third, we should create space and platforms for young people of various countries to pursue their dreams in the age of the internet. Fourth, we should pursue the new vision of green development and a way of life and work that is green, low-carbon, circular and sustainable. Efforts should be made to strengthen cooperation in ecological and environmental protection and build a sound ecosystem so as to realise the goals set by the 2030 Agenda for Sustainable Development. In the future, we will launch the Belt and Road Science, Technology and Innovation Cooperation Action Plan, which consists of the Science and Technology People-to-People Exchange Initiative, the Joint Laboratory Initiative, the Science Park Cooperation Initiative and the Technology Transfer Initiative.

Over the past 4 years, we have achieved a series of important outcomes in building the Road of Innovation.

First, progress has been made in scientific and cultural exchanges and scientific and technological training. China supports the Belt and Road countries in sending young scientists to China for scientific research, helps them train tens of thousands of scientific talents and management personnel and offers various technical training courses in relevant countries. In 2013, the Talents Import Plan for the Outstanding Young Scientists in Asian and African Countries was launched by the Ministry of Science and Technology in an effort to attract more Asian and African scientists under the age of 45 to work in China. As of now, more than 200 young scientists have come to China for scientific research in various fields. From 2011 to 2016, the Ministry of Science and Technology offered more than 200 technical training courses for around 5000 students in developing countries. In the coming 5 years, China will offer 2500 short-term research visits to China for young foreign scientists, train 5000 foreign scientists, engineers and managers and set up 50 joint laboratories.

Second, intergovernmental cooperation on innovation has been enhanced. The Chinese government has signed 46 intergovernmental agreements on scientific and technological cooperation with the Belt and Road countries and has together launched a set of innovation programmes, including the China–ASEAN Science and Technology Partnership Programme, the China–South Asia Science and Technology Partnership Programme and the China–Arab States Scientific and Technological partnership programme.³ The Special Plan on Advancing

Cooperation of Science and Technology Innovation in the Belt and Road Construction was released by the Ministry of Science and Technology, the National Development and Reform Commission, Ministry of Foreign Affairs and Ministry of Commerce on September 8, 2016, setting out a series of positive measures for innovation cooperation of the Belt and Road Initiative. As set out in the Plan, together with the Belt and Road countries, China will build a number of research laboratories, research centres, technology transfer centres and advanced technology demonstration and promotion bases. This is aimed to promote the interconnectivity and sharing of scientific research data and resources and strengthen the application of new technologies in the fields of smart grid, information communication network, traffic detection systems of railway and highway and improve infrastructure along the Belt and Road so as to upgrade their innovation capacity.

Third, China has already carried out various forms of financial cooperation with the Belt and Road countries and other interested parties. A network of financial institutions and services is spreading out to support the Belt and Road Initiative through innovative financing mechanisms.

On December 25, 2015, the China-proposed Asian Infrastructure Investment Bank (AIIB) was officially launched, with a legal capital of US$100 billion and focusing on regional connectivity and industrial development. By the end of 2016, the AIIB had provided US$1.7 billion in loans to 9 projects in fields such as energy, transport and urban development in Indonesia, Tajikistan, Pakistan and Bangladesh. China also injected US$40 billion in starting capital in the Silk Road Fund, with an initial registered capital of US$10 billion, which finances the Belt and Road Initiative through equity stakes and other forms of financing. By the end of 2016, the Fund had signed 15 projects, with an estimated investment value of US$6 billion. The projects cover such areas as infrastructure, energy utilisation and production capacity and finance cooperation in Russia, Mongolia, Central Asia, South Asia and South East Asia. The Fund also allocated US$2 billion to start the China–Kazakhstan Production Capacity Cooperation Fund. China proposed the China–CEE Joint Investment and Financing Framework, including a US$10 billion special loan, the China–CEE Investment Cooperation Fund and other mechanisms to provide financing support to Central and Eastern Europe. The Industrial and Commercial Bank of China took the lead in founding China–CEE Financial Holdings Ltd, which launched the China–CEE Fund.

Fourth, good progress has been achieved in building a Green Silk Road, providing a strong guidance for the cooperation on the BRI. The Chinese government has issued "The Guidance on Promoting Green Belt and Road" to promote ecological progress in the cooperation with foreign countries. China has put in place an ecological protection system for the Belt and Road Initiative, and developed policies and guidelines for green industrial development, thus providing an institutional guarantee for the Green Silk Road. In forging multiple cooperation platforms centred on the Green Silk Road, China has signed the Memorandum of Understanding between the United Nations Environment Programme and Ministry of Environmental Protection of the People's Republic of China on Building a Green "Belt and Road" and established bodies such as the Centre for Belt and Road Environmental Technology Exchange and Transfer in an effort to promote international exchange and application of advanced technologies in environmental protection. China has signed 35 forestry cooperation agreements with the Belt and Road countries and founded the China–ASEAN and China–CEE forestry cooperation mechanisms in an effort to promote the sustainable development of forestry and protect forest resources. It organised the Ministerial-level Meeting on Forestry in Greater Central Asia, the China–ASEAN Forestry Cooperation Forum and the China–Russia Forestry Investment Policy Forum, and published "The One Belt and One Road Joint Action to Combating Desertification Initiative".

China actively promotes South–South cooperation in addressing climate change, by providing energy-efficient, low-carbon and renewable energy materials to the Belt and Road countries, launching cooperation projects on solar energy, wind energy, methane gas, hydroelectric power and clean cooking stoves, organising dialogues and exchanges on energy efficiency, energy saving and environmental protection and offering training to address climate change. China will set up a big data service platform on ecological and environmental protection. We propose the establishment of an international coalition for green development on the Belt and Road, and we will assist related countries in adapting to climate change.

The contribution of the Road of Innovation to the world

First of all, the Road of Innovation will explore new ways for economic cooperation, which is beneficial for promoting an economic globalisation that is open, inclusive, reciprocal, balanced and mutually beneficial. As a new model of economic cooperation, the Belt and Road Initiative will make the international order more just and equitable. The majority of the Belt and Road participants are developing countries that are weak in economic development, social systems, foreign investment and the necessary infrastructure. Therefore, these countries are often able to benefit from globalisation dividends. Against such a backdrop, we proposed in the Belt and Road Initiative that our efforts should be focused on resolving issues such as imbalances in development, difficulties in governance, digital divide and income disparity and make economic globalisation open, inclusive, balanced and beneficial to all.[4]

Second, the Road of Innovation will blaze a new path for growth and instil new dynamism into the world economy. With a view to developing new growth models, we should seize opportunities presented by the new round of industrial revolution and digital economy. We should meet the challenges of environmental resource limits and climate change. We should address the negative impact of IT application and automation on jobs. When cultivating new industries and new forms models of business models, we should create new jobs and restore confidence and hope of the people of Belt and Road countries.

Therefore, the Road of Innovation is extremely critical to solving the problem of the lack of driving force and imbalance economic growth. With this in mind, G20 leaders reached an important consensus at the Hangzhou Summit in 2016 and adopted the *G20 Blueprint on Innovative Growth*, stressing that we should take innovation as a key driver and foster new driving force of growth for both individual countries and the global economy. As pointed out by President Xi at the World Economic Forum in January 2017, "The fundamental issue plaguing the global economy is the lack of driving force for growth. Innovation is the primary force guiding development. Unlike the previous industrial revolutions, the fourth industrial revolution is unfolding at an exponential rather than linear pace. We need to relentlessly pursue innovation. Only with the courage to innovate and reform can we remove bottlenecks blocking global growth and development ... We should develop a new development philosophy, adopt new policy instruments and advance structural reform to create more space for growth and sustain its momentum".

Third, the Road of Innovation will put in practice the new philosophy of green development so as to help achieve the goals set out by the 2030 Agenda for Sustainable Development. The Green Silk Road is a highlight of the Belt and Road Initiative. As announced in the Vision and Actions on Jointly Building Silk Road Economic Belt and 21st Century Maritime Silk Road released in March 2015, "We should promote ecological progress in conducting investment and trade, increase cooperation in conserving eco-environment, protecting biodiversity, and tackling climate change, and join hands to make the Silk Road an environment-friendly one".

It is made clear that achieving the 2030 Agenda for Sustainable Development remains one of the goals in building the Green Silk Road. On September 26, 2015, President Xi made a pledge at the UN Summit for Sustainable Development that we will join our own efforts with those of other countries in a concerted drive to realise the Post-2015 Development Agenda. In his speech, Xi made clear an important line of efforts, "China is ready to work with other parties concerned to make continuous efforts towards this end".[5] As pointed out by President Xi, in advancing the Belt and Road Initiative, we should pursue the new vision of green development and a way of life and work that is green, low-carbon, circular and sustainable. Efforts should be made to strengthen cooperation in ecological and environmental protection and build a sound ecosystem so as to realise the goals set by the 2030 Agenda for Sustainable Development.

Notes

1 Xi Jinping, "Working Together to Create a New Mutually Beneficial Partnership and Community of Shared Future for Mankind—keynote speech at the opening ceremony of the Belt and Road Forum for International Cooperation," quoted in Xi Jinping: *The Governance of China* (Volume 2), Beijing: Foreign Languages Press, 2017, pp. 506–517.
2 Office of the Leading Group for the Belt and Road Initiative, "Building the Belt and Road: Concept, Practice and China's Contribution," May 10, 2017, www.xinhuanet.com/politics/2017-05/10/c_1120951928.htm
3 Vice Minister of Chinese Ministry of Science and Technology, Yin Hejun, "Making Solid Progress in Advancing Innovation Cooperation of the Belt and Road Initiative," December 12, 2017, www.stdaily.com/zhuanti01/pjlt/2017-12/12/content_607487.shtml
4 Xi Jinping, "Working Together to Create a New Mutually Beneficial Partnership and Community of Shared Future for Mankind—keynote speech at the opening ceremony of the Belt and Road Forum for International Cooperation," quoted in Xi Jinping: *The Governance of China* (Volume 2), Beijing: Foreign Languages Press, 2017, p. 513.
5 Xi Jinping, "Towards a Mutually Beneficial Partnership for Sustainable Development—Speech at the UN Sustainable Development Summit," September 26, 2015, *People's Daily*, http://politics.people.com.cn/n/2015/0927/c1024-27638350.html

30
THE BELT AND ROAD INITIATIVE AND THE ROAD CONNECTING DIFFERENT CIVILISATIONS

Xie Laihui

Concept and origin of the Road Connecting Different Civilisations

At the Belt and Road Forum for International Cooperation held on May 14, 2017 in Beijing, President Xi Jinping delivered a keynote speech entitled *Work Together to Build the Silk Road Economic Belt and the 21st Century Maritime Silk Road*. Xi pointed out that a solid first step has been taken in pursuing the Belt and Road Initiative and we should build on the sound momentum generated to steer the Belt and Road Initiative towards greater success. It was against such a backdrop that President Xi proposed in his speech to build the Belt and Road into a road of peace, prosperity, openness and innovation and a road connecting different civilisations.[1]

On building the Road Connecting Different Civilisations, Xi stressed that when it comes to different civilisations, exchange shall replace estrangement, mutual learning shall replace clashes, and coexistence shall replace a sense of superiority. This will boost mutual understanding, mutual respect and mutual trust among different countries.

The spirit of the Road Connecting Different Civilisations reflected in the Belt and Road Initiative

As an important part of the Belt and Road Initiative, people-to-people bonds will lay out social foundation for implementing the Belt and Road Initiative. Xi holds that in order to promote the Belt and Road Initiative, we must foster an environment where people from Belt and Road countries can appreciate, understand and respect each other. People-to-people bonds also serve as the foundation of cultural exchanges. We should advance both economic cooperation and cultural exchanges and give more emphasis to people-to-people exchange with full respect to history, cultures and social customs of different countries. With that, we can strengthen friendly relationships with the peoples of the Belt and Road countries and build extensive social foundations for implementing the Initiative.

As pointed out by President Xi at the 6th Ministerial Meeting of China–Arab States Cooperation Forum in June 2014, with an open and inclusive mind, China chooses dialogue and exchange over conflict and confrontation and achieves harmony among countries with different social systems, religions and cultural traditions. China will continue to unswervingly support Arabian countries in protecting national and cultural traditions and oppose all forms of discrimination and prejudice against any certain ethnic groups and religions. We should work together to uphold cultural and religious tolerance so as to prevent extremism from creating gaps among civilisations.[2]

In his speech at the Belt and Road Forum for International Cooperation, President Xi charted the course of action on building the Road Connecting Different Civilisation.

First, we should establish a multi-tiered mechanism for cultural and people-to-people exchanges, build more cooperation platforms and open more cooperation channels. Second, educational cooperation should be boosted, more exchange students should be encouraged and the performance of cooperatively run schools should be enhanced. Third, think tanks should play a better role and efforts should be made to establish think-tank networks and partnerships. Fourth, in the cultural, sports and health sectors, new cooperation models should be created to facilitate projects with concrete benefits. Fifth, historical and cultural heritage should be fully tapped to jointly develop tourist products and protect heritage in ways that preserve the distinctive features of the Silk Road. Sixth, we should strengthen exchanges between parliaments, political parties and non-governmental organisations of different countries as well as between women, youths and people with disabilities with a view to achieving inclusive development. Seventh, we should also strengthen international counter-corruption cooperation so that the Belt and Road will be a road with high ethical standards.

Over the past 4 years, we have made important achievements in cultural exchanges and cooperation in various fields and at different levels.[3]

- Educational and cultural cooperation. China follows the "Education Action Plan for Jointly Building the Belt and Road", and has provided government scholarships for 10,000 students from countries along the Belt and Road each year. Since the launch of the Belt and Road Initiative, China has held 20 cultural exchange events such as "Cultural Years" with countries along the Belt and Road and signed 43 action plans on cultural exchanges or other intergovernmental cooperation agreements. By the end of 2016, China had built 30 Chinese culture centres and set up Confucius Institutes in countries along the Belt and Road. China has held important events such as the Silk Road (Dunhuang) International Cultural Expo, Silk Road International Arts Festival and Maritime Silk Road International Arts Festival. China, Kazakhstan and Kyrgyzstan jointly applied and succeeded in listing "Silk Roads: the Routes Network of Chang'an–Tianshan Corridor" on UNESCO's World Cultural Heritage. In foreign aid, China has restored cultural sites such as Ta Keo Temple of Angkor, Cambodia, Itchan Kala, the Ancient City of Khiva, Khorazm in Uzbekistan and provided aid for post-quake restoration of cultural relics in Nepal and Myanmar. It has also applied to have the Maritime Silk Road listed as an item of World Cultural Heritage and promoted the Mazu marine culture.
- Cooperation on science and technology. The Chinese government has signed 46 intergovernmental agreements on scientific and technological cooperation with countries along the Belt and Road, covering various fields such as agriculture, life science, information technology, environmental protection, new energy, aerospace, policies for scientific and technological development and innovation management. China has built platforms to boost innovation cooperation, including joint laboratories, international technology transfer centres and science parks. With the goal of facilitating the building of the Belt and Road with science and technology, China has built the China–ASEAN Mariculture Technology Joint Research and Promotion Centre, the China–South Asia Technology Transfer Centre and the China–Arab Nations Technology Transfer Centre. The country has also improved

the mechanism for scientific, technological and cultural exchanges. In 2016 alone, more than 100 researchers from India, Pakistan, Bangladesh, Myanmar, Mongolia, Thailand, Sri Lanka, Nepal, Egypt and Syria conducted scientific research in China through the Talented Young Scientist Programme.
- Cooperation on tourism. To scale-up tourist cooperation, China is holding Tourist Year events with countries along the Belt and Road, and conducting tourist promotion and exchanges. By holding events such as the World Conference on the Development of Tourism, the Tourism Ministerial Meeting of Countries Along the Silk Road Economic Belt, the China–South Asian Countries Tourism Ministerial Meeting, the China–Russia–Mongolia Tourism Ministerial Meeting and the China–ASEAN Senior Tourist Officials' Meeting, China and the related countries have formed a tourist cooperation mechanism under the Belt and Road Initiative at different levels and in different regions. To promote tourist brands, China has held the Silk Road Tourism Year for the last 3 years, founded the China Alliance for Silk Road Tourism Promotion, the Maritime Silk Road Tourism Promotion Alliance, and the China–Russia–Mongolia "Tea Road" International Tourism Alliance. Cooperation on sports is also booming.
- Cooperation on health care. Under the Belt and Road Initiative, China attaches importance to promoting cooperation among the related countries in the prevention and control of contagious diseases, medical system and policies, health care capacity building, personnel training and exchange and traditional medicine. China and the related countries have published the "China–Central and Eastern European (CEE) Countries Prague Declaration on Health Cooperation and Development", the "Suzhou Joint Communique on the Second Health Ministers Meeting between China and CEEC" and the "Nanning Declaration on China–ASEAN Health Cooperation and Development" and implemented 41 programmes including the China–Africa Cooperation Plan on Public Health and the China–ASEAN Plan on Training One Hundred Health Professionals. China has promoted exchanges and cooperation on traditional medicine with countries along the Belt and Road, founded 16 overseas Traditional Chinese Medicine centres, including one in the Czech Republic, and signed Chinese medicine cooperation agreements with 15 countries. The Chinese government signed the "Memorandum of Understanding on Health Sector Cooperation under the Belt and Road Initiative" with the World Health Organisation, so as to build a healthy Silk Road. China has also set up a Medical Centre for the Silk Road Economic Belt in Xinjiang Uygur Autonomous Region to provide medical services to surrounding countries in Central Asia.
- Disaster relief, aid and poverty reduction. China has participated in humanitarian operations organised by the UN, the WHO and other organisations in Syria, and over the years has dispatched medical teams to provide aid to its surrounding countries and countries in Africa. It has actively participated in international disaster prevention and relief actions, sent the national rescue team and medical team to provide earthquake relief in Nepal, and provided emergency relief aid to countries including Maldives, the Federated States of Micronesia, Vanuatu and Fiji. It has provided emergency food assistance to drought-stricken African countries influenced by El Niño, replenished water for the Mekong River as part of emergency drought relief for countries along the river and provided technical support for flood prevention to countries such as Thailand and Myanmar. China has also carried out programmes such as the China–Africa Cooperation Plan for Poverty Reduction and People's Benefit and the East Asia Poverty Reduction Pilot to provide aid in the fields of poverty reduction, agriculture, education, health care and environmental protection. China's social organisations have played an active role in various undertakings to improve

the lives of populations along the Belt and Road, and carried out many public welfare programmes.
- People-to-people exchanges. China has concluded reciprocal visa-free agreements with 55 countries along the Belt and Road, including Pakistan, Russia, the Philippines and Serbia, and concluded 19 agreements (or made arrangements) on simplifying visa procedures with 15 countries including Kazakhstan, the Czech Republic and Nepal. Twenty-two countries such as the United Arab Emirates, Iran and Thailand have provided Chinese citizens with the privilege of visa-free entry or visa on arrival.[4]

The contribution of the Road of Civilisation to the World

First, in building the Road Connecting Different Civilisations, we embrace mutual learning and exchange between different civilisations, for it drives the human progress and underpins the creation of new ideas. Xi noted in his speech at the United Nations Office at Geneva on January 18, 2017 that:

> Diversity of civilizations is a basic feature of human society, and an important driving force for the progress of mankind. The world has more than two hundred countries and areas, and more than two thousand five hundred nationalities and various religions. Different histories, national conditions, ethnic groups and customs give birth to different civilizations and make the world a colorful one. There is no such thing as a superior or inferior civilization, and civilizations are different only in identity and location. Every civilization, with its own appeal and root, is a human treasure. Diverse civilizations should draw on each other to achieve common progress. We should make exchanges among civilizations a source of inspiration for advancing human society.[5]

The Belt and Road Forum for International Cooperation held in May this year is an example in point. More than 1500 representatives from over 130 countries attended the forum for joint discussion on cooperation. By engaging in full exchanges of views, all parties contributed to pursuing the Belt and Road Initiative, a project of the century, so that it will benefit people across the world.

Second, in building the Road Connecting Different Civilisations, we appreciate the diversity of civilisations, and the Road could serve as a bond that keeps the world in peace. The Road Connecting Different Civilisations will promote mutual learning and accommodation between different civilisations and integration and innovation of different cultures, building a community of peace and development, where people from different cultures learn from each other, blend with each other, understand each other and appreciate each other's qualities. Diversity of civilisations should not be a source of global conflict. The so-called clash of civilisations is not inevitable. For thousands of years, people of different countries, ethnic groups and religions along the Ancient Silk Routes have maintained friendly exchanges. As long as there is mutual respect and openness and inclusiveness among different civilisations, cooperation and coexistence can be achieved.

By enhancing the complementarities of development strategies of different Belt and Road countries, the Belt and Road Initiative could meet people's common aspiration for a better life. Through enhanced dialogue and cooperation among civilisations, the Road Connecting Different Civilisations will bridge the gaps, defuse conflicts and help promote understanding and reach consensus, so as to be a bond that keeps the world in peace.

Third, in building the Road Connecting Different Civilisations, we should highlight the importance of mutual learning, which is significant for the prosperity and development of the world. Mutual respect and learning between different civilisations will boost economic cooperation and common development. In spite of the different development paths in line with its own national conditions, any country can join the Belt and Road Initiative in resource allocation and mutual exchange so as to achieve common development and prosperity.

In building the Road Connecting Different Civilisations, we call on all parties to share governance experience and draw strengths from each other's culture, history and development courses. The pursuit of the Belt and Road Initiative is not meant to reinvent the wheel. Rather, it aims to complement the development strategies of countries involved by leveraging their comparative strengths. With connectivity in areas such as policy, infrastructure, finance and trade, we can multiply the effects and achieve win–win outcomes.

In building the Road Connecting Different Civilisations, we propose to enhance people-to-people exchanges, encourage educational exchange and cooperation, promote the flow of talents, support scientific and technological exchanges and research cooperation and expand cooperation in tourism and cultural industries and in health care and disaster prevention and mitigation. These are conducive to promoting innovation, dissemination and application of knowledge and ensuring rational allocation of production factors such as talents and technologies, which will all the way boost the world economy.

Notes

1 Xi Jinping, "Working Together to Create a New Mutually Beneficial Partnership and Community of Shared Future for Mankind—keynote speech at the opening ceremony of the Belt and Road Forum for International Cooperation," quoted in Xi Jinping: *The Governance of China* (Volume 2), Beijing: Foreign Languages Press, 2017, pp. 506–517.
2 Xi Jinping, Speech at the Opening Ceremony of the Sixth Ministerial Conference of the Forum on China–Africa Cooperation, quoted in *People's Daily*, 2nd edition, June 6, 2014.
3 Office of the Leading Group for the Belt and Road Initiative, "Building the Belt and Road: Concept, Practice and China's Contribution," May 10, 2017, www.xinhuanet.com/politics/2017-05/10/c_1120951928.htm
4 Ibid.
5 Xi Jinping, "Work Together to Build a Community of Shared Future for Mankind," quoted in Xi Jinping: *The Governance of China* (Volume 2), 2017, p. 544.

PART V

Five types of connectivity

31
POLICY COORDINATION

Qin Sheng

The concept of policy coordination

Policy coordination is the main point of the "Belt and Road Initiative" and ranks the first among five types of connectivity. In March 2015, China's State Council authorised the release of *Vision and Actions on Jointly Building Silk Road Economic Belt and 21st Century Maritime Silk Road*, which places special focus on policy coordination, connectivity of infrastructure, unimpeded trade, financial integration and understanding between people. Enhancing policy coordination is an important guarantee for implementing the Initiative. We should takes as our chief means of enhancing policy coordination by promoting intergovernmental cooperation and building a multi-level intergovernmental macro policy exchange and communication mechanism; we should take as our primary objective to expand shared interests, enhance mutual political trust, and reach new cooperation consensus; we should take as our main principle that countries along the Belt and Road may fully coordinate their economic development strategies and policies, work out plans and measures for regional cooperation, negotiate to solve cooperation-related issues and jointly provide policy support for the implementation of practical cooperation and large-scale projects.

Although the Initiative aims at global development, its participating countries diverge greatly on political systems, economic development levels, historical culture as well as religious beliefs. Therefore, it is of vital importance to enhance political mutual trust and reach consensuses on cooperation and development, in a way to facilitate its implementation and long-term development. The purpose of policy coordination is to maintain good communication with participating countries by way of dialogue mechanisms and institutional arrangements at different levels, to fully respect their development characteristics and stages and explore their development potentials and to bridge differences, innovate ways of cooperation and seek the greatest common divisor for development amidst constant collision of ideas and policy consultations. In the trend of multipolarisation, economic globalisation, cultural diversity and social informatisation, countries could keep step with the times, form consensus on development, accumulate joint forces for development and jointly promote the building of the Belt and Road only through adequate, timely and continuous policy coordination.

Policy coordination is a process of state interactions in an attempt to establish mutual political trust, promote strategic cooperation, complete institutional integration and achieve economic win–win situations. The primary task of policy coordination is to eliminate all aspects of interference, establish mutual political trust, focus on development issues and reach a consensus on the concept, model and direction of development through top-level design. Its secondary task is, on the basis of a wide consensus and under the premise of adherence to diversity, inclusiveness as well as respect for each country's national conditions, encourage greater synergy between their respective development strategy and the Initiative, establish an all-directional, multi-layered and wide-ranging cooperation mechanism, and enlarge the depth and breadth of institutional integration. Finally, the goal of institutional integration is to reduce the cost of trade and investment, improve corresponding laws and regulations, explore the market potentials of participating countries, enhance the efficiency and effectiveness of economic cooperation and truly realise a virtuous cycle of extensive consultation, joint contribution and shared benefits.

Governments play a principal role in the process of policy coordination, but it is the broad masses of the people, companies, as well as investment and financing institutions of the participating countries that push forward coordination progress and test its effects. Therefore, as the focal point of the Initiative, policy coordination requires us not only to remain committed to our mission, but to advance with the times; not only to realise the goals of green, sustainable and win–win development, take concrete actions to allow more countries and people to share development dividends, but to innovate the ways, approaches and ideas of policy coordination and achieve even more ambitious goals by way of embracing the mission of building a human community with shared destiny.

Practical significance of policy coordination

Policy communication is the top priority of the Initiative. It is the precondition and foundation for facilities connectivity, unimpeded trade, financial integration and understanding between people, and runs through the entire process of seeking consensuses, bridging differences, resolving conflicts and developing side by side.

Policy coordination guides the direction of facilities connectivity. The Belt and Road Initiative aims to promote the connectivity among countries in Eurasia and from the Indian Ocean to the Pacific, and is devoted to establishing and strengthening partnerships among countries along the Belt and Road, setting up all-dimensional, multi-tiered and composite connectivity networks, and realising diversified, independent, balanced and sustainable development in these countries. Infrastructure construction is the foothold and starting point of the Initiative at the current stage; it is also a new growth point for the economic development of participating countries. However, transnational infrastructure construction is not ordinary market-oriented investment or production behaviour. It is usually based on national development strategies and international cooperation, and requires detailed planning, huge investment, a long construction and return period, as well as concerted efforts of the international community. Each participating country, as the main body in building the Belt and Road, should conduct active and effective policy communication, so that they can play a coordinating role in infrastructure planning, construction and financing, lead the direction of construction, share construction costs, and improve construction efficiency.

Policy coordination is the first step of unimpeded trade. The main purpose of unimpeded trade is to improve trade liberalisation and facilitation, remove investment and trade barriers and create a sound business environment within the region and in all related countries. Policy coordination plays an important role in the following three aspects. First, it is the first step towards the establishment of a free trade zone after negotiations among participating countries; the negotiation process on a free trade agreement is, in essence, communication of different investment and trade policies. Second, whether to expand the areas of investment and trade and whether to deepen industrial cooperation depend on the judgment of different countries about their own industrial development trends and economic development advantages; continuous and targeted policy communication can strengthen mutual understanding, help innovate trade forms, foster new growth points of trade and promote trade balance. Third, foreign trade concerns all aspects of a country's economy, involves domestic and foreign laws and regulations at all levels and in all fields; adequate policy communication will guarantee the legitimacy of transnational investment and trade, reduce trade disputes, and provide preconditions for all participating countries to achieve mutual benefit and win–win situation.

Policy coordination is the core part of financial integration. The focus of the Belt and Road Initiative is put on large-scale infrastructure construction across borders, across continents and across the oceans, which requires huge capital investment. Policy communication among governments will provide strong support for deepening financial cooperation between different economies, giving full play to the role of the Silk Road Fund and that of sovereign wealth funds of countries along the Belt and Road. Thus, it is the key to the successful implementation of major projects. In addition, financial integration has another important mission, that is, to strengthen financial regulation cooperation, maintain the stability of the Asian monetary system, establish an efficient regulation coordination mechanism in the region, and contribute to the establishment of a stable and fair international financial system. In today's world, with the deepening of financial globalisation, both capital regulation and currency stability need more governmental communication, consensus and collaboration than ever before. Only by strengthening communication and working together can the international financial system be used for the Belt and Road Initiative and contribute positive energy to economic cooperation.

Policy coordination helps strengthen understanding between people. People-to-people friendship provides a solid, stable public opinion foundation for the Initiative as well as bilateral and multilateral cooperation. The ways of exchanges include: cultural exchange, academic exchange, talent exchange, media cooperation, youth and women's interactions and volunteer services. The key to sound understanding between people lies in "amity" developed mainly through people-to-people contacts and exchanges. Policy coordination provides important, systemic support for understanding between people, as shown in two respects: first, policy communication between countries facilitates bilateral and multilateral exchanges by way of administrative means, establishes exchange platforms through various cooperation agreements and frameworks and acts as an important bridge, so that it will be more convenient for people to conduct in-depth exchanges; second, governments, as a powerful backing for the people, provide support and funding from different ways and at varying levels, so that people-to-people exchanges will keep unceasing and ongoing.

Implementation progress of policy coordination

Since the Belt and Road Initiative was put forward, top-level design and summit diplomacy have become the highlights of policy coordination, with multilateral frameworks and cooperation mechanisms as the main platforms.

In terms of top-level design, two programmatic documents, namely the *Strategic Plan on the Building of the Silk Road Economic Belt and the 21st Century Maritime Silk Road* and the *Vision and Actions on Jointly Building Silk Road Economic Belt and 21st Century Maritime Silk Road*, were issued in December 2014 and March 2015, respectively, and served as a guide for pursuing the Belt and Road Initiative. In February 2015, a steering group for the Belt and Road Initiative was formally established at the national level, which lays a solid foundation towards realising the blueprint of the Initiative. In May 2017, the first Belt and Road Forum for International Cooperation was successfully held in Beijing, during which the *List of Deliverables of the Belt and Road Forum for International Cooperation* and the *Joint Communiqué of the Leaders Roundtable of the Belt and Road Forum for International Cooperation* were released. The Forum provides an important opportunity for world leaders and international organisation to push forward the Initiative on a larger scope, with higher standards and at deeper levels, and to work out common solutions to major global economic challenges. In October 2017, the Belt and Road Initiative was written into the Constitution of the Communist Party of China, linking the Initiative with the Party's cause. The above top-level design embodies the innovative and pioneering spirit of Chinese leaders.

In terms of summit diplomacy, Chinese leaders take the lead in policy communication, make unremitting efforts to facilitate policy coordination by way of major-country diplomacy, continuously enhance political mutual trust and reach new consensuses on cooperation, in an effort to build a human community with shared destiny. In January 2016, President Xi Jinping paid a state visit to the Middle East. During the visit, China signed a MOU, respectively, with Saudi Arabia, Egypt and Iran, as a manifestation of their common desire for mutual development. In March 2016, President Xi Jinping held talks with his Czech counterpart Milos Zeman. During the talks, the two sides agreed to align the Initiative with the Czech development strategy. In October 2016, during President Xi Jinping's visit to South East Asia, China, Cambodia and Bangladesh agreed to enhance coordination of their development strategies, to deepen pragmatic cooperation, to formulate and implement the Guideline for Plan on Cooperation on the Building of the Belt and Road; Nepal and Sri Lanka expressed support and willingness to actively participate in the Initiative. In November 2016, President Xi Jinping attended the APEC Summit in Lima and visited three Latin American countries. He once again introduced the Belt and Road Initiative to the world, and welcomed all parties to participate in the cooperation, share opportunities, meet challenges and seek common development. In May 2017, China successfully hosted the Belt and Road Forum for International Cooperation (BRF) in Beijing. The BRF is the highest-level and largest international conference proposed and hosted by China since the founding of new China. It was attended by Heads of State and Government from 29 countries, and more than 1500 representatives from over 130 countries and 70 international organisations. The BRF achieved fruitful results with a list of major deliverables, which includes 76 items comprising more than 270 concrete results in 5 key areas. In June 2017, when meeting with Prime Minister of Luxembourg Xavier Bettel, President Xi Jinping proposed the concept of "Aerial Silk Road" and stated that China supports the construction of an "Aerial Silk Road" from Zhengzhou to Luxembourg. In July 2017, during his state visit to Russia, President Xi Jinping responded positively to the "invitation" to the construction of an Arctic sea route, hoping that the two sides will jointly develop and use sea passages, especially the Arctic waterways, to build a "Polar Silk Road". In November 2017, President Xi Jinping was invited to pay a state visit to Vietnam and attend the 25th APEC Economic Leader' Meeting. The leaders of the two countries jointly witnessed the signing of an MOU on the Building of the "Belt and Road" and "Two Corridors and One Ring".

With multilateral frameworks and multilateral cooperation mechanisms as the platform, policy coordination has enlarged the friend circle and influence of countries along the Belt and Road, and thus nurtured a seedbed for the far-reaching development of the Initiative. In recent years, China has made full use of existing mechanisms such as the Shanghai Cooperation Organisation (SCO), ASEAN Plus China (10+1), Asia–Pacific Economic Cooperation (APEC), Asia–Europe Meeting (ASEM), Asia Cooperation Dialogue (ACD), Conference on Interaction and Confidence-Building Measures in Asia (CICA), China–Arab States Cooperation Forum

Policy coordination

(CASCF), China–Gulf Cooperation Council Strategic Dialogue, Greater Mekong Subregion (GMS) Economic Cooperation and Central Asia Regional Economic Cooperation (CAREC) to strengthen communication with relevant countries and organisations and attract more countries and regions to participate in the Belt and Road Initiative. We make constant efforts to improve policy communication tools, align the Belt and Road Initiative with other international initiatives as well as cooperation frameworks and enhance coordination with development strategies of other countries, in order to bring opportunities for interconnection and sustainable development. On March 17, 2017, the UN Security Council unanimously adopted Resolution 2344 on Afghanistan with 15 favourable votes, calling for a consensus on assisting Afghanistan and urging the international community to strengthen regional economic cooperation through the Belt and Road Initiative and the like. The Resolution urges all parties to provide security safeguard for the Belt and Road Initiative, strengthen synergy of development strategies and push forward cooperation on connectivity. This is a major achievement of policy coordination, showing that the Belt and Road Initiative is universally recognised by the international community and will embrace promising developments.

32
CONNECTIVITY OF INFRASTRUCTURE

Li Tianguo

The concept of "facilities connectivity"[1]

Infrastructure usually includes transportation, post and telecommunications, water and power supply, commercial services, scientific research and technical services, landscaping, environmental protection, culture and education, health and other municipal utilities as well as public living service facilities. Facilities connectivity is a major direction, and also the priority area for implementing the Initiative. The *Vision and Actions on Jointly Building Silk Road Economic Belt and 21st Century Maritime Silk Road* issued by China's government proposes that, "on the basis of respecting each other's sovereignty and security concerns, countries along the Belt and Road should improve the connectivity of their infrastructure construction plans and technical standard systems, jointly push forward the construction of international trunk passageways, and form an infrastructure network connecting all sub-regions in Asia, and between Asia, Europe and Africa step by step".

Connectivity is not just flat or linear connection like road or bridge building; it is a combination of infrastructure, regulations and personnel exchanges. It is an integral whole consisting of policy coordination, facilities connectivity, unimpeded trade, financial integration and understanding between people. Among them, the interconnection of infrastructure lays the basis, and it is also the weakest link that restricts further cooperation among countries along the Belt and Road. We should give priority to linking up unconnected road sections, removing transport bottlenecks, and improving road connectivity, so that transport networks connecting Asian regions and between Asia, Africa and Europe will be gradually established and contribute to bilateral and multilateral economic cooperation under the Initiative.

Infrastructure construction emphasises green and low-carbon planning to break through the restrictions of traditional ecological protection, to integrate construction and operation at the regional, district and community levels, and to achieve a coordinated and sustainable development of ecology, society and economy. Green and low-carbon infrastructure construction is a complex system that can bring a variety of benefits, reflecting new concepts of green living environment. A scientific and rational use of clean energies like hydropower, wind power, solar energy and nuclear power will help maintain biodiversity and ecological environment during the process of infrastructure construction. Enterprises involved should take their social responsibility to protect and supervise various ecosystems and to enhance the systematisation and synergy of protection efforts, while carrying out construction in line with requirements on the protection of mountain, water, forest, cropland and lake.

In infrastructure construction, the building of key passageways and junctions is conducive to removing transport bottlenecks and revitalising the entire transportation network. Thus, we will focus on key projects for key passageways and prioritise linking up unconnected road sections to improve road network connectivity. In addition, a cross-border transportation coordination mechanism is also an indispensable institutional guarantee. We need to build a unified coordination mechanism for whole-course transportation to realise efficient, seamless connectivity of multimodal transport and establish an unimpeded international transport network.

Energy and resource cooperation is an important carrier for infrastructure connectivity. Energy is the foundation of social development and economic growth; therefore, infrastructure construction cannot be separated from the construction of energy thoroughfares. Energy infrastructure is the basis of modern economic, logistics, industrial and social service systems. Countries along the Belt and Road differ greatly in their resource and energy endowment; thus, there are huge potentials for energy supply and demand growth. Participating countries should work in concert to ensure the security of oil and gas pipelines and other transport routes, build cross-border power grids, promote the interconnection and upgrading of these grids, thereby reducing the cost of energy supply, optimising energy structure and improving energy security.

The telecommunications industry is one of the major engines for economic development and social advancement. The Belt and Road Initiative will contribute to the overall improvement of the telecommunications level. Despite major achievements in global telecommunications, the level of regional development is imbalanced. There is still much room for the improvement of international telecommunications connectivity. We should advance the construction of regional cross-border cable networks and other communications trunk line networks at a quicker pace, plan transcontinental submarine optical cable projects, and improve satellite information passageways to promote global information exchanges and cooperation.

Practical significance of facilities connectivity

Infrastructure plays a key role in maintaining the upward momentum of the national and regional economy and it is the basis and prerequisite for economic and social development. An important reason for the slow economic growth of many developing countries is their stagnant infrastructure development and existing construction bottlenecks. In recent years, although the infrastructure situation in countries along the Belt and Road has improved a lot, investment has failed to keep pace with the infrastructure demand brought by rapid economic growth. In particular, the lack of engineering infrastructure is considered to be the root cause of poverty. Infrastructure development will remain the most basic and urgent need for participating countries. It is an important prerequisite for sustaining the healthy development of economy.

The upgrading and expansion of the infrastructure network has a "multiplier effect" that can create social demand and national income several times the amount of investment. Experiences of other countries show that the return on investment in transportation, energy and telecommunications infrastructure is far more than that of other types of investment. Some Asian countries have achieved unimaginable returns through huge infrastructure investment in their early stage of industrialisation, thereby laying an important foundation for economic take-off. Infrastructure upgrading will not only benefit the economic growth of one specific country, but also that of other countries in the region. Every country in the regional supply chain will gain advantage from the improvement of infrastructure networks during the flow of goods and people. Therefore, improved infrastructure by each country will contribute to the overall trade and economic growth in the whole region. Concerted efforts from member countries in the region to connect national power grids, oil and gas pipelines and to develop natural resources will help reduce trade costs and transportation costs, ensure energy security and supply, and achieve a win–win situation.

Due to the current sluggish growth of global economy, infrastructure development will help create social demand and job opportunities, and provide an impetus for economic growth. As the global economy is on a downtrend, materials and other costs for infrastructure construction are reduced accordingly, so that countries will be able to better their infrastructure even with a limited amount of funds. As a result, the cross-border flow of goods and people will be more cost-saving and convenient, international connectivity will be enhanced, and a more favourable environment will be provided for domestic economic growth.

The Belt and Road Initiative fully considers infrastructure transformation and upgrading as an urgent concern of developing countries, and sees insufficient funding in this respect. According to reports released by the Asian Development Bank, from 2010 to 2020, the total amount of infrastructure investment needed by Asian countries will reach $8 trillion, 68% of which will be spent on newly added capacity and 32% on maintaining and replacing existing infrastructure. Thus, the annual investment demand is about $730 billion, with electricity and highway accounting for, respectively, 51% and 29%. The total demand of East Asia and Pacific Island countries is $4.67 trillion, that of South Asia $2.87 trillion and that of Central Asia $460 billion.[2] Similarly, according to research by the World Bank, the annual infrastructure investment needed by African countries is $93 billion.[3]

Sufficient funding is essential to infrastructure development. However, due to the risks and uncertainties involved, it is difficult for the private sector to undertake such heavy responsibilities. Therefore, most infrastructure projects need motivation and support from the government. On the other hand, in order to improve the construction efficiency of infrastructure projects, it is necessary to introduce private funds and operational capabilities. The Belt and Road Initiative also actively encourages private funds and personnel to participate in government-sponsored projects.

Implementation progress of facilities connectivity

Initiated and promoted by China, with the positive response of neighbouring countries, the Belt and Road Initiative has been widely endorsed and welcomed by the international community. Committed to the principles of extensive consultation, joint contribution and shared benefits, relying on infrastructure projects, China is now actively studying how to better utilise existing bilateral and multilateral cooperation mechanisms to deepen cooperation with neighbouring countries in railway, highway, waterway, civil aviation, postal service and other areas.

First, a series of major infrastructure projects in countries along the Belt and Road have entered the construction stage. Economic corridor development is making steady progress; an interconnected infrastructure network is taking shape; trade and investment have increased significantly; key project cooperation is underway. China has achieved a lot of achievements in infrastructure interconnection with neighbouring countries, signed a series of construction agreements and many major projects have gradually been implemented. According to the *Belt and Road Infrastructure Development Index Report 2017*, the infrastructure growth rate and passion for cross-border infrastructure projects are soaring, as proven by a skyrocketing number and value of new infrastructure contracts. According to statistics, the new contract value experienced a sudden 150% year-on-year spurt in 2015 and remained high in 2016 despite a slight fall over the previous year. Some ASEAN and South Asian countries have been the hotspots for cross-border infrastructure projects. Under the guidance of the Initiative, China's engineering companies are actively cooperating with their counterparts in overseas countries. In 2016, China's accomplished business revenue through foreign contracted projects was $159.4 billion, up by 3.5% on the previous year. $76 billion, namely 47.7% of the total, are from projects conducted in Belt and Road countries, with a growth of 9.7%. A number of international capacity cooperation projects and infrastructure interconnection projects, including the China–Pakistan Economic Corridor and the Ethiopia–Djibouti railway, have been successfully implemented. In the first 11 months of 2017, the contractual volume of newly signed foreign contracted projects in Belt and Road countries totalled $113.52 billion, accounting for 54.1% of the total, up by 13.1%; the accomplished business revenue was $65.39 billion, accounting for 48.7% of the total, up by 6.1%.[4]

Second, transportation, power and other industries have become the main areas of infrastructure development. Most countries along the Belt and Road are taking transportation projects as the emphasis of construction, concentrating efforts on the upgrading and transformation of railways and highways and making plans to build high-speed railway networks and highway networks. In addition, in the field of energy infrastructure, the power industry has the highest proportion of investment, as it is the most basic and important energy industry in the development of the national economy, and it also has vital bearing on people's livelihood. Consequently, most Belt and Road countries regard electricity as a priority industry in their national economic development strategy, strive to expand power generation and transmission capacity, and increase investments to ensure the continuity of electricity supply. According to plans, Iran will build 9 nuclear power plants by 2025; Vietnam will increase its hydropower generating capacity to 21,600 MW by 2020 and to 24,600 MW by 2025. Saudi Arabia and Pakistan have both launched plans for nuclear power generation.

Third, the adoption of build–operate–transfer (BOT), public–private–partnership (PPP) and other financing models has achieved initial results. Countries along the Belt and Road differ greatly in their economic development level and financial system. When engaged in overseas infrastructure projects, Chinese companies usually adopt the financing model of development financial institutions, the BOT model and the PPP model, and the Asian Infrastructure Investment Bank has been set up.

Notes

1 Lin Yifu, *China's Four Advantages in Promoting Infrastructure Construction under the Belt and Road Initiative*. Retrieved February 3, 2018 from www.chinanews.com/cj/2017/11–30/8389320.shtml.
2 Asian Development Bank Institute, *Infrastructure for a Seamless Asia*, Social Science Academic Press, 2012, p. 111.
3 Lin Yifu, *Infrastructure Investment and Construction from the Perspective of Economic Development*. Retrieved February 2, 2018 from www.rmzxb.com.cn/c/2016-06-14/866496.shtml.
4 Chen Heng, "2050: Building a Major Country in Trade and Economy," *Guangming Daily*, January 2, 2018, p. 14.

33
UNIMPEDED TRADE

Shen Minghui

The concept of unimpeded trade

Unimpeded trade is a major task in building the Belt and Road. The *Vision and Actions on Jointly Building Silk Road Economic Belt and 21st Century Maritime Silk Road* issued by China's government proposes that "we should strive to improve investment and trade facilitation, and remove investment and trade barriers for the creation of a sound business environment within the region and in all related countries. We will discuss with countries and regions along the Belt and Road on opening free trade areas so as to unleash the potential for expanded cooperation".

Due to the important role of unimpeded trade, the *Joint Communiqué of the Leaders Roundtable of the Belt and Road Forum for International Cooperation* appeals for strengthening "the rules-based multilateral trading regime" and urges cooperation among multiple forums to solve poverty, promote employment and support sustainable development. The *Joint Communiqué* further mentions that, "we reaffirm our shared commitment to building open economy, ensuring free and inclusive trade, and opposing all forms of protectionism under the framework of the Belt and Road Initiative. We endeavor to promote a universal, rules-based, open, non-discriminatory and equitable multilateral trading system with WTO at its core".

To realise unimpeded trade, all participating countries are required to comply with the Silk Road spirit, promote trade and investment liberalisation and facilitation through cooperation and win–win and strive to achieve sustainable development that features trade balance and coordination. China has sent the proposal of unimpeded trade to over 60 countries and international organisations. The proposal will help upgrade the scale and level of foreign trade in participating countries, resist the wave of trade protectionism, improve the situation of weak demand in the global market, and promote global trade recovery and growth.

To enhance trade connectivity along the Belt and Road, China would like to put forth the following five moves "with a view to connectivity, efficiency, mutual benefit and development".[1] First, China will hold China International Import Expo in an effort to expand its import, build a multilateral platform for enterprises from all over the world to exhibit their products, and provide more opportunities for exchanges and economic cooperation. Second, China will continue to promote bilateral and multilateral free trade agreement negotiations, expand the level of opening up and embrace mechanisms of free trade. Third, China will sign economic and trade cooperation agreements with countries with the willingness, implement trade and investment promotion projects and maintain the multilateral trading system. Fourth, China will establish economic and trade cooperation zones jointly with countries that have the willingness, so as to promote regional employment, stimulate economic growth and achieve economies of scale. One of the main drivers of unimpeded trade is to promote international manufacturing cooperation by means of establishing industrial parks. China has always supported the WTO-based multilateral trading system and emphasised innovative investment cooperation modes, economic and trade cooperation zones as well as international capacity cooperation. Fifth, China will actively help participating countries to strengthen their ability in economic development, support their economic development by training their personnel and sending Chinese economists and trade experts, jointly promote the implementation of the *UN 2030 Agenda for Sustainable Development*, and support the trade and investment promotion arrangements made by the WTO and UN.

We still need to tap the market potentials of Belt and Road countries and allow more time for nurturing markets for emerging technologies and products. Enterprises willing to do business in these countries should develop, by trial and error, production and marketing strategies that suit different national conditions. China will be devoted to building a new pattern of comprehensive opening up, "promoting connectivity of policies, rules and standards so as to provide institutional safeguards for enhancing connectivity", "accelerating the progress of customs and quarantine inspection cooperation projects"[2] and deepening all-round cooperation with Belt and Road countries in large-scale simplification of customs clearance procedures. China will further simplify relevant procedures to facilitate customs clearance, and improve the logistics network, trade and service economy system; promote foreign trade transformation and upgrading, accelerate new development momentum of foreign trade, support new trade business, actively participate in the formulation of international trade rules and promote the development of open economy.

Practical significance of unimpeded trade

Unimpeded trade meets the need of most developing countries along the Belt and Road for common development. Since the global financial crisis, the world economy has slowed down noticeably. Countries need to strengthen foreign trade and investment in order to get rid of the prolonged economic downturn. Most Belt and Road countries are emerging economies or developing countries. As they are still in the early stage of industrialisation, their national economy encounters various bottlenecks in infrastructure, technology and capital. Thus, they have a strong desire for economic and trade exchanges, and need to remove these bottlenecks through international economic and trade activities. China and countries participating in the Belt and Road Initiative need to rely on their own resource endowments and give play to their comparative advantages, thereby strengthening bilateral and multilateral economic and trade cooperation, achieving trade facilitation and investment liberalisation, and realising a rational allocation of production factors in the region.

Unimpeded trade is conducive to opposing trade protectionism, promoting economic globalisation, and facilitating regional economic cooperation. In recent years, in favour of the interests of their domestic manufacturers, some countries have adopted a series of trade protection measures, including technical trade barriers and trade restrictions, which hinder, to some extent, the development of global trade. Trade and investment protectionism events continue to occur globally, which is disadvantageous to the sustained economic growth through trade development. In the face of trade protectionism, transnational corporations have to undergo grim tests in terms of large-scale overseas investment and trade. Currently, due to the sluggish global economic growth, we need to push the global economy to develop in a more dynamic, inclusive and sustainable way, promote trade and investment liberalisation and facilitation and resist protectionism, while respecting the development goals of different countries. China will unswervingly support economic globalisation, and continuously explore measures of trade liberalisation and investment facilitation through trade connections, so as to promote global trade growth and overall economic recovery.

Implementation progress of unimpeded trade[3]

The Belt and Road Initiative complies with the requirements of the times and the desire of all countries to accelerate development. Countries participating in the Initiative will jointly share achievements through five types of connectivity. The Initiative will bring new highlights and growth points to China and related countries in foreign trade and economy.[4]

First, countries participating in the Initiative will jointly promote trade facilitation, strengthen service trade cooperation and expand trade scale. China will discuss with these countries to find ways to enhance the level of foreign trade liberalisation, e.g. through simplification of customs clearance procedures and signing free trade agreements. As for countries that have signed free trade agreements, China will further expand the opening of service trade and investment, and provide a more relaxed, permissive trade and investment environment for both its own companies and those from related countries.

A network of free trade zones between China and participating countries is taking shape. Currently, China has signed and implemented agreements on free trade with 22 countries and regions, 11 of which are along the Belt and Road. These agreements cover not only commodity trade, but also service trade as well as intellectual property and labour protection. The Chinese government is now enhancing the favourable impact of investment on trade, further protecting the legitimate rights and interests of investors and constantly improving the business environment. According to China's customs statistics, in 2017, China's import and export volume with Belt and Road countries amounted to 7.37 trillion yuan with a year-on-year increase of 17.8%, which was 3.6% higher than the growth rate of China's foreign trade and accounted for 26.5% of China's total foreign trade. The export volume was increased by 12.1% to 4.3 trillion yuan, and the import volume was increased by 26.8% to 3.07 trillion yuan. In 2017, China's FDI (foreign direct investment) flow and stock in Belt and Road countries reached $23.6 billion and $160.3 billion, respectively. China will further open its market, deepen economic and trade cooperation, allow the achievement of the Initiative to serve the economic and social development of more countries and the improvement of people's living standards and promote the continued development of global economy.

Second, in respect of cross-border e-commerce, China has signed with relevant countries international cooperation agreements on the development of e-commerce, including postal transport cooperation agreements, so as to improve customs clearance capacity and efficiency and to make cross-border e-commerce become a new way for promoting trade and economic development. "Internet+" and other innovative trade forms will also provide a more convenient trading and logistics platform for cross-border e-commerce, build a regional marketing network, open up international markets and promote the sustainable development of foreign trade.

At present, there are more than 5000 cross-border platform providers in China, and over 200,000 foreign trade enterprises are engaged in cross-border e-commerce through these platforms. According to the China e-Business Research Centre, in 2016, the market size of cross-border e-commerce reached 6.7 trillion yuan, of which the export volume was 5.5 trillion yuan. The export volume of cross-border business to customer (B2C) e-commerce exceeded

500 billion yuan in 2015, and it is estimated to reach 2 trillion yuan by 2020. The market potentials are huge.[5] The price/performance advantage of China-made products is instantly transmitted to the overseas market through the Internet and wins the favor of consumers. The proportion of cross-border e-commerce in import and export trade increased from 6% in 2010 to 28% in 2016, and it is expected to reach 38% in 2020.[6]

Third, in respect of economic industrial parks, China has established wide-range, multi-purpose industrial parks in neighbouring countries, which have become an important carrier of unimpeded trade. Currently, industrial parks in Belt and Road countries mainly fall into the following types: comprehensive development, trade and logistics, processing and manufacturing, technology research and development, resource utilisation, agricultural industry. According to the Ministry of Commerce of China, as of March 2017, Chinese companies have set up 56 industrial parks in 20 countries along the Belt and Road, with an accumulated investment of over $18 billion, creating tax revenue of more than $1 billion for the host countries as well as more than 160,000 jobs.[7] China's National Development and Reform Commission encourage Chinese enterprises to go global, and support them to set up International Production Capacity Cooperation Enterprise Alliance for their own industry. At present, China has established 10 key industry alliances in construction machinery, electric power, building material, petro chemistry, automobile, textile, non-ferrous metal, light industry, steel and telecommunications, as well as Belt and Road Mining Alliance, Satellite Application Alliance and Industrial Park Alliance. These industrial parks play a very active role in promoting unimpeded investment and trade between China and related countries.

Notes

1. Bu Xin, "Five Moves to Enhance Trade Connectivity under the Belt and Road Initiative," *International Business Daily*, May 15, 2017.
2. *Speech by President Xi Jinping at the Belt and Road Forum for International Cooperation*. Retrieved January 29, 2018 from www.xinhuanet.com/world/2017-05/14/c_1120969677.htm
3. Shi Kai, "The Ministry of Commerce Promotes Unimpeded Trade with the Belt and Road Countries," *International Business Daily*, May 26, 2017.
4. *China's Imports and Exports with the Belt and Road Countries Increased by 17.8% in 2017*. Retrieved February 2, 2018 from http://news.cnstock.com/news,bwkx-201801-4175185.htm
5. *Analysis of China's Export Situation in Cross-border E-commerce*. Retrieved February 3, 2018 from www.chyxx.com/industry/201712/595670.html
6. Ibid.
7. Zhang Xin, "Establishing a New Model of Cooperation and Win–Win Situation for Industrial Parks under the Belt and Road Initiative," *Shanghai Securities News*, May 15, 2017.

34
FINANCIAL INTEGRATION

Shen Minghui

The concept of financial integration

Financial integration is one of the highlights and an important underpinning for implementing the Belt and Road Initiative. In March 2015, China's State Council authorised the release of *Vision and Actions on Jointly Building Silk Road Economic Belt and 21st Century Maritime Silk Road*, which elaborates on financial integration from the aspects of financial cooperation and financial stability.

We should deepen financial cooperation. First, we need to expand the scope and scale of bilateral currency swap and settlement with other countries along the Belt and Road, promote the signing of bilateral currency settlement and cooperation agreements, encourage financial cooperation through dialogues and avoid financial risks. Relying on the internationalisation of RMB, we will promote mutual opening and interconnection of financial markets through payment system cooperation and inclusive finance. Second, we should foster and support the growth of related investment and financing institutions, make joint efforts to establish the Asian Infrastructure Investment Bank and BRICS New Development Bank, conduct negotiation among related parties on establishing Shanghai Cooperation Organisation (SCO) financing institution and set up and put into operation the Silk Road Fund as early as possible; strengthen the practical cooperation of the China–ASEAN Interbank Association and the SCO Interbank Association, carry out multilateral financial cooperation in the form of syndicated loans and bank credit, encourage commercial equity investment funds and private funds to participate in the construction of key projects and provide financing guarantee for infrastructure construction in countries along the Belt and Road. Third, we should encourage financial institutions to set up branches in relevant countries and regions, support the efforts of governments of the countries along the Belt and Road and their companies and financial institutions with good credit-rating to issue RMB bonds in China. Qualified Chinese financial institutions and companies are encouraged to issue bonds in both RMB and foreign currencies outside China, and use the funds thus collected in countries along the Belt and Road.

We should strengthen financial stability. First, with respect to enhancing financial regulation cooperation and resisting financial risks, we should encourage the signing of MOUs on cooperation in bilateral financial regulation and gradually establish an efficient regulation coordination mechanism in the region, improve the system of risk response and crisis management, build a regional financial risk early-warning system and create an exchange and cooperation mechanism for addressing cross-border risks and crisis. Second, with respect to regulating investment and the financing environment, we should promote the building of the Asian currency stability system, investment and financing system and credit system, encourage the opening and development of the Asian bond market, and establish a sound capital and legal environment for investment and financing. Third, with respect to building a credit system, we should increase cross-border exchange and cooperation between credit investigation regulators, credit investigation institutions and credit rating institutions, so as to contribute to building a stable and fair international financial system.

In his speech at the Belt and Road Forum for International Cooperation, President Xi Jinping proposed that, "We should establish a stable and sustainable financial safeguard system that keeps risks under control, create new models of investment and financing, encourage greater cooperation between government and private capital and build a diversified financing system and a multi-tiered capital market. We should also develop inclusive finance and improve financial services networks". His words illustrate the overall requirement for financial integration. First, it is necessary to ensure the stability and security of the financial system, which are the bottom line and also the red line. Second, the Initiative should be taken as an important chance and driving force for financial innovation. We should broaden the financing channels and expand the diversity of the capital market so that finance can maximise its investment and financing functions and serve the development and construction of countries along the Belt and Road. Third, financial integration is not limited to financial support for large-scale projects and programmes; it also serves the financial needs of other sectors of society. The way to develop inclusive finance is to provide affordable and effective financial services to small and micro enterprises, residents, farmers, etc. We will strive to establish a wide-ranging, high-standard financial service network along the Belt and Road.

Practical significance of financial integration

The Belt and Road Initiative first recognises the fundamental role of interconnection and its pushing effect on the economic growth of developing economies, and takes economic corridors and facilities connectivity, including transportation, communications and electricity, as the priority areas of development. Meanwhile, the Initiative focuses on financial integration as a key area of cooperation, fully estimating the huge funding gap that may occur in the process of facilities connectivity.

China has assumed a leading role in the establishment of Asian Infrastructure Investment Bank, the Silk Road Fund, the BRICS Development Bank, the SCO Development Bank and other financial platforms, reflecting China's deep understanding of the financing and investment situation under the Initiative. In the future, what the Initiative needs is not unilateral, unidirectional financial support, but an investment and financing system jointly built by the international community through wide consultations under the principle of sharing responsibilities, risks and benefits. By way of consolidating governmental, social and market forces, the allocation of resources will be optimised, so that the Initiative could obtain the momentum of sustainable development in a long period of time. Traditional multilateral financial institutions, including the Asian Development Bank, the European Bank for Reconstruction and Development, the World Bank and the International Monetary Fund, could work together with Asian Infrastructure Investment Bank and the Silk Road Fund to take advantage of each other's resources, functions and strengths, and to jointly provide investment and financing services for improving the efficiency, level and quality of financial integration under the Initiative.

RMB globalisation, especially a currency swap network among Belt and Road countries, could give full play to the advantages of each country's domestic currency, reduce the intermediate links of financial services and cut down the cost of currency exchange during business operation. On the other hand, efforts should be made to innovate cross-border RMB services and to establish a RMB clearing framework for countries in need, so as to indirectly serve the building of the Belt and Road. In addition, expanding the scale and scope of currency swaps between China and the Belt and Road countries will also mobilise, to the greatest extent, each participating country to use their funds and capital to resist financial risks and maintain financial stability.

Implementation progress of financial integration

With respect to RMB globalisation, on November 30, 2016, IMF officially issued a statement to include RMB as a fifth currency in the SDR basket along with the US dollar, the Euro, the Japanese yen and the British pound sterling. The RMB will have a 10.92% weighting and the new SDR basket will be effective from October 1, 2016. Upon approval of the People's Bank of China, on October 9, 2017, the China Foreign Exchange Trading Centre launched the payment versus payment (PVP) service for Chinese yuan and Russian ruble transaction, relying on the high-value payment system. This signifies that China's foreign exchange market has formally established the PVP system and new progress has been made in the foreign exchange infrastructure. Since 2008, China has signed currency swap agreements with more than 30 countries and regions, 22 of which are along the Belt and Road. China also conducts direct currency transactions with 23 countries, 8 of which are along the Belt and Road, and direct regional currency transactions with 2 of them. Since the second half of 2016, China has successively signed bilateral currency swap agreements with the Bank of Mongolia, the Central Bank of Argentina, the Swiss National Bank and Hong Kong Monetary Authority, involving a total value of 635 billion yuan.

With respect to inter-state cooperation, in Cairo in September 2017, China Development Bank (CDB) and Egypt's SAIBANK signed a contract involving a special loan of 260 million yuan and a special loan of $40 million for small and medium-sized enterprises in Africa, marking the first CDB's Belt and Road Special Load project in Egypt. In September 2017, China Export & Credit Insurance Corporation signed with Georgia's Partnership Fund a "Framework Cooperation Agreement", according to which the two sides will establish a financing and insurance cooperation platform in infrastructure, energy, machinery, logistics, electricity, large-scale complete sets of equipment, etc. In November 2017, the Bank of China signed an agreement with the Philippine government to underwrite the $ 200 million RMB-denominated panda bond issued by the Philippines. On November 27, 2017, H.E. Li Keqiang, Premier of the State Council of the China, attended the Sixth Summit of Heads of Government of China and Central and Eastern European Countries; during the Summit, in order to promote multilateral financial cooperation under the "16+1" cooperation, the China–CEEC Interbank Association, initiated by CDB and financial institutions in central and eastern Europe, was formally established. On December 16, 2017, during the 9th UK–China Economic and Financial Dialogue, the UK formalised its commitment to provide $50 million to the AIIB's "Special Fund for Project Preparation", matching China's commitment of the same. In the meantime, the Standard Chartered Bank announced that it will provide at least $20 billion financing support for Belt and Road projects before the end of 2020.

With respect to project support, in September 2017, the Asian Infrastructure Investment Bank (AIIB) provided $210 million debt financing to an Egyptian solar project, in an attempt to utilise the potentials of renewable energies in Egypt. In September 2017, AIIB approved a $500 million co-financing for Philippines to improve flood control in the Greater Manila region. In September 2017, the Asian Development Bank (ADB) used co-financing with AIIB to provide supplementary funds for a subproject of Indian power transmission network, and the subproject will be connected to the ADB-funded Indian green energy corridor and grid enhancement project. In all, ADB has provided $1 billion financing to the Indian National Power Transmission Corporation and Power Grid Corporation of India. In November 2017, a CDB-based banking consortium passed a $1.5 billion financing plan for the 1320-MW Hub coal power plant in Pakistan. The project, whose total investment is estimated to be $2 billion, is included in China–Pakistan Economic Corridor. In December 2017, AIIB approved a $335 million loan for the subway construction in Bangalore, India. In December 2017, the Kazakhstan Branch of the Bank of China signed with the European Bank for Reconstruction and Development syndicate loan contract in Almaty, southern Kazakhstan to jointly provide loans for the zinc mine reconstruction and expansion project of Shalkiya Zinc NV. This is the first time the two banks have cooperated with each other. The total loan amount is $295 million, with the Bank of China providing $120 million and the European Bank for Reconstruction and Development $175 million.

In respect to financing scale, since 2015, the China Construction Bank (CCB) has provided financial support for 50 major overseas projects in 18 countries along the Belt and Road, including Russia, Pakistan, Singapore, United Arab Emirates, Vietnam, Saudi Arabia and Malaysia, with a total contract amount of $9.8 billion. As of the end of June 2017, the loans granted by CDB in Belt and Road countries aggregated to $170 billion, with a balance of over $110 billion. On December 16, 2017, the China Development Bank Capital, in alliance with Guangxi Investment Group, set up the Guangxi–ASEAN Belt and Road Fund, which totals $50 billion, to invest in key infrastructure and industrial projects in Guangxi and ASEAN countries. On October 16, 2017, the Singapore Branch of CCB successfully issued an S$500 million Belt and Road infrastructure bond. The bond will be listed on the Singapore Exchange. This is the first time the Singapore Branch of the CCB has issued Singapore dollar bonds in the local market; it is also the second phase of the Belt and Road infrastructure bond. By the end of 2017, the Bank of China had supported about 520 major Belt and Road projects, and provided $98 billion credit to relevant countries from 2015 to November 2017. By the end of 2017, AIIB has approved 21 investment projects with a total investment of $3.49 billion. Since its official establishment, AIIB has carried out 24 infrastructure investment projects in 12 member countries with a total loan of $4.2 billion, which will attract $20 billion from public- and private-sector funds. As of the end of 2017, the Silk Road Fund has signed 17 projects and committed itself to investing $7 billion. The supported projects involve a total investment of $80 billion.

35
UNDERSTANDING BETWEEN PEOPLE

Qin Sheng

The concept of understanding between people

Understanding between people provides the public support for implementing the Initiative. In March 2015, China's State Council authorised the release of *Vision and Actions on Jointly Building Silk Road Economic Belt and 21st Century Maritime Silk Road*, which places special focus on policy coordination, facilities connectivity, unimpeded trade, financial integration and understanding between people. Tightening understanding between people has a far-reaching significance: we should carry forward the spirit of friendly cooperation of the Silk Road by promoting extensive cultural and academic exchanges, personnel exchanges and cooperation, media cooperation, youth and women exchanges and volunteer services, so as to win public support for deepening bilateral and multilateral cooperation. Specifically, it includes the following.

First, cultural and academic exchanges. We should send more students to each other's countries and promote cooperation in jointly running schools. China provides 10,000 government scholarships to the countries along the Belt and Road every year. We should hold culture years, arts festivals, film festivals, TV weeks and book fairs in each other's countries; cooperate on the production and translation of fine films, radio and TV programmes; and jointly apply for and protect World Cultural Heritage sites. We should also increase personnel exchange and cooperation between countries along the Belt and Road.

Second, tourism cooperation and sports exchange. We should hold tourism promotion weeks and publicity months in each other's countries to guide and expand the scale of tourism; jointly create competitive international tourist routes and products with Silk Road features; and make it more convenient to apply for tourist visas in countries along the Belt and Road. We should push forward cooperation on the 21st Century Maritime Silk Road cruise tourism programme. We should carry out sports exchanges and support countries along the Belt and Road in their bid for hosting major international sports events.

Third, disease control and medical cooperation. We should strengthen cooperation with neighbouring countries on epidemic information sharing, the exchange of prevention and treatment technologies and the training of medical professionals, and improve our capability to jointly address public health emergencies. We will provide medical assistance and emergency medical aid to relevant countries, and carry out practical cooperation in maternal and child health, disability rehabilitation and major infectious diseases including AIDS, tuberculosis and malaria. We will also expand cooperation on traditional medicine.

Fourth, sci-tech cooperation and personnel training. By way of establishing joint laboratories (or research centres), international technology transfer centres and maritime cooperation centres, we should promote sci-tech personnel exchanges, cooperate in tackling key sci-tech problems, work together to improve sci-tech innovation capability, and enlarge technology spillover effects. We should integrate existing resources to expand and advance practical cooperation between countries along the Belt and Road on youth employment, entrepreneurship training, vocational skill development, social security management, public administration and management and in other areas of common interest.

Fifth, double-track communication between political parties and think tanks. We should give full play to the bridging role of communication between political parties and parliaments and promote friendly exchanges between legislative bodies, major political parties and political organisations of countries along the Belt and Road. We should carry out exchanges and cooperation among cities, encourage major cities in these countries to become sister cities, focus on promoting practical cooperation, particularly cultural and people-to-people exchanges, and create more lively examples of cooperation. We welcome the think tanks in the countries along the Belt and Road to jointly conduct research and hold forums.

Sixth, non-governmental exchanges and media cooperation. We should increase exchanges and cooperation between non-governmental organisations of countries along the Belt and Road, organise public interest activities concerning education, health care, poverty reduction, biodiversity and ecological protection for the benefit of the general public, and improve the production and living conditions of poverty-stricken areas along the Belt and Road. We should enhance international exchanges and cooperation on culture and media, and leverage the positive role of the Internet and new media tools to foster harmonious and friendly cultural environment and public opinion.

Understanding between people aims to strengthening cultural exchanges and non-governmental contacts, deepening practical cooperation in the areas of education, science and technology, sports, health, think tanks, media and capacity building including internship training. We should encourage dialogues and cultural exchanges among civilisations, rely on the wisdom and courage of people in countries along the Belt and Road, maintain the diversity of civilisations and protect the world's cultural and natural heritage.

Practical significance of understanding between people

In January 2016, President Xi Jinping delivered a speech at the Arab League headquarters and stressed that, "Like the diverse species in Mother Nature, cultural diversity gives life to our planet. We should promote dialogue among civilizations in a spirit of inclusiveness and mutual learning and explore together values in our respective cultural tradition that remain relevant today as positive guidance for good relations". He also pointed out that, "the Belt and Road Initiative calls for exchanges between nations and civilizations for mutual understanding, rather than mutual resentment. It is important to remove, rather than erect walls between each other, take dialogue as the golden rule and be good neighbors with each other". We should strengthen people-to-people exchanges in the spirit of respect for differences, inclusiveness, equality, voluntariness and mutual benefit, and strive to reduce suspicion, eliminate misunderstandings, enhance understanding and reach consensus, so as to lay a solid public opinion foundation and social foundation for countries and regions to participate in the Belt and Road Initiative.

China, as the initiator of the Belt and Road Initiative, believes that "telling Chinese stories and spreading Chinese voices" is an important way for strengthening understanding between people. The Confucius Institute is the best carrier. In London in October 2015, when President

Xi Jinping attended the opening ceremony of the UK Confucius Institutes and Confucius Classrooms Annual Conference, he praised the importance of Confucius Institute highly for the spread of Chinese language. He said, "Confucius Institute is an important platform for the world to understand China. Confucius Institutes and Classrooms, as windows and bridges for linguistic and cultural exchanges between China and the world, have played an active role in facilitating people around the world to learn Chinese language and understand its culture. In addition, they have also made important contributions to China's people-to-people exchanges with the world, as well as the development of a diverse and colorful world civilization". Therefore, the popularisation of the Chinese language will enable officials, entrepreneurs and ordinary people in countries along the Belt and Road to gain an in-depth understanding of China's long history, its unique development model, its pluralistic society, its innovative spirit and advanced technology, as well as its contribution to the development of the world economy. "Telling Chinese stories and spreading Chinese voices" is to present a vivid picture of contemporary China to the international community, so that countries participating in the Belt and Road Initiative could appreciate the charm of China as a major country.

The Belt and Road Initiative calls for not only the interconnection of infrastructure, but also the interchange of culture, learning, media, sports, science and technology, talents and historical memory. Facilities connectivity is the realistic basis for understanding between people, as multiple means of connection and reduced costs will make it easier to conduct people-to-people exchanges, which in turn will promote facilities connectivity and make the cooperation between different states, enterprises and people more meaningful and far-reaching. The Initiative covers a wide range of countries with complicated domestic situations and severe geopolitical conflicts; people-to-people exchanges will help eliminate barriers, encourage brotherhood and restore consensus. Thus, understanding between people is the social foundation for the Initiative. Only when participating countries make frequent exchanges, fully respect and understand each other can they work together to build a bright future for mankind.

Implementation progress of understanding between people
Cultural and academic exchanges

In 2016, China's Ministry of Education issued the *Educational Action for Building the Belt and Road*, which stated that concerted efforts should be made to build an education community for countries along the Belt and Road and to cultivate a large number of talents who are urgently needed. As of the end of 2016, China has signed agreements on mutual recognition of degrees and diplomas with 46 countries and regions, 24 of which are countries along the Belt and Road. The Ministry of Education also launched the "Silk Road" Programme for Studying Abroad, and in 2016 selected 226 talents specialised in country and district studies to go to 34 countries. According to the *Annual Report on the Development of Chinese Students Studying Abroad (2017)*, the number of international students studying in China continues to grow, and the countries with the fastest-growing number of students are South Korea, Thailand, India, Pakistan, Indonesia and Laos. Thailand, India, Pakistan, Indonesia and Laos are along the Belt and Road, and the average growth rate of students from these countries is over 20%.

On November 26, 2017, the South China Sea Buddhism Shenzhen Roundtable was held in Shenzhen with the theme of "Building a Community with Shared Future and Moving towards a New Era of the South China Sea"; participants included leaders of Buddhist communities and friendship associations from 10 countries, including China, Thailand, Cambodia, Laos, Sri Lanka, Nepal, Myanmar, Mongolia, Canada and the United States. At the roundtable, a consensus was reached to set up the "South China Sea Silk Road Fund" and to establish "the South China Sea Buddhist Culture Research Institute" and a standing office of South China Sea Buddhism Shenzhen Roundtable.

Tourism cooperation and sports exchanges

Since 2011 when the State Council approved Kazakhstan as an outbound tourism destination for Chinese citizens, their tourism cooperation has taken a big step forward. In December 2015, the two countries signed the *Memorandum of Understanding to Facilitate the Travel of Chinese Citizens to Kazakhstan in the Form of Groups*. In July 2016, the business of Chinese tourist groups to Kazakhstan was officially launched, and their tourism cooperation entered the fast lane. On November 17, 2017, the closing ceremony for the "China–Kazakhstan Year of Tourism" was held in Astana, capital of Kazakhstan. The celebration of the "China–Kazakhstan Year of Tourism" laid a solid foundation for the two countries to deepen cooperation in various fields under the Belt and Road Initiative.

On November 13, 2017, China and ASEAN issued a joint statement on tourism cooperation in Manila, emphasising once again the strategic significance of the tourism industry for closer people-to-people exchanges and sustainable development of society and economy, as well as for enhancing mutual trust and maintaining regional stability. The two sides put forward new goals in the fields of mechanism building, information sharing, joint promotion, service improvement, human resource development and interconnection.

Disease control and medical cooperation

By the end of 2016, China had established 17 Overseas Centres for Traditional Chinese Medicine in countries along the Belt and Road, and set up several hundred traditional Chinese medicine colleges in more than 30 countries and regions. As of the end of 2017, China had signed 86 traditional Chinese medicine cooperation agreements with foreign governments, regions and organisations. Traditional Chinese medicine has become an important part of China's free trade zone negotiations with 14 countries and regions, so as to improve market entry conditions and reduce trade barriers. In 2017, Chinese Red Cross Foundation set up the Silk Road Loving Fund, which aims to serve the Belt and Road Initiative and provide humanitarian services. In just one year, the Fund has funded a number of humanitarian relief projects; 9 groups of 63 people were sent abroad to carry out international assistance projects.

On November 19, 2017, the "Belt and Road Brightness Journey" Programme was conducted in an eye hospital in Sagaing Province, Myanmar. The medical team from China Aier Eye Hospital performed cataract surgery on 200 patients in Myanmar and restored their sight. On November 25, 2017, the China–Sweden Belt & Road Forum on Acupuncture–Moxibustion and Traditional Chinese Medicine was held at the China Cultural Centre in Stockholm. Participants at the Forum exchanged views on the theory, practice, research and industrial standards of acupuncture and moxibustion.

Language cooperation and talent training

In July 2017, the Ministry of Education and the National Language Working Committee released the *White Paper on the Development of Chinese Language in 2017*, which pointed out that 84 Confucius Institutes and Confucius Classrooms at the primary and secondary school level were newly established in 2016. Currently, there are 134 Confucius Institutes and 130 Confucius Classrooms in 51 countries and regions along the Belt and Road, and full coverage has been achieved in all of the 28 countries of the European Union and 16 countries in Central and Eastern Europe.

Double-track exchange between political parties and think tanks

From November 30 to December 3, 2017, China held in Beijing the "CPC in Dialogue with World Political Parties High-Level Meeting". Delegates representing more than 200 political parties and political organisations from over 120 countries conducted extensive and in-depth discussions and interactions under the theme of "Working Together towards a Community with a Shared Future for Mankind and a Better World". On February 5, 2018, the non-governmental "Belt and Road Research Institute" was founded in South Korea. Choi Jae Cheon, chief lawyer of Heritage Law Office, serves as the chairman; Roh Jae Seon, the eldest son of former South Korean President Roh Tae Woo and dean of Korea China Culture Centre, as well as Qu Huan, Korea–China Association for Cultural Exchange, serve as the director.

People-to-people exchange and media cooperation

In August 2016, China International Television Corporation initiated the establishment of the "Belt and Road Media Community". The members of the Community have grown to 41 countries and 68 media organisations. A large number of outstanding Chinese programmes have been successively translated into nearly 20 languages and broadcast in countries and regions along the Belt and Road. On November 21, 2017, with the support of the International Department of the Central Committee of CPC, the First Silk Road NGO Cooperation Network Forum was convened. Up to now, more than 300 NGOs from over 60 countries have joined the cooperation network. During the Forum, the *Beijing Consensus of Silk Road NGO Cooperation Network Forum* was released. In December 2017, the *White Paper on Big Data of Film Industry in Countries alongside Belt and Road (2017)* was released, which includes the data of the film industry in 11 countries including China. By the end of 2017, Star Times, a Chinese company and a digital TV operator, had invested $2.5 billion in over 20 countries in Africa and has 5000 dealers and more than 10 million digital TV users. As a result, the cost for watching digital TV is greatly reduced, and the life of the local people becomes more colourful with an "information highway" connecting them with the outside world.

PART VI

The six economic corridors

36
THE CHINA–MONGOLIA–RUSSIA ECONOMIC CORRIDOR

Wang Jinbo

Concept explanation

The China–Mongolia–Russia Economic Corridor is a shared carrier to implement the synergy of the Belt and Road Initiative (BRI) of China, the Development Road (Prairie Road programme) Initiative of Mongolia and the Eurasian Economic Union Initiative of Russia.

At his meeting with the heads of state of Russia and Mongolia on September 11, 2014, President Xi proposed for the first time that the three neighbours should align the Silk Road Economic Belt with the Russia's Trans-Eurasian Railways and Mongolia's Prairie Road Programme, to build the China–Mongolia–Russia Economic Corridor.[1]

In Moscow on August 8, 2015, China and Russia issued the *Joint Statement of the People's Republic of China and the Russian Federation on Cooperation in the Construction of the Silk Road Economic Belt and the Construction of the Eurasian Economic Union*.

On July 9, 2015, the relevant departments of the three countries signed the *Memorandum of Understanding on Compiling the Outline of the Plan on Establishing the China–Mongolia–Russia Economic Corridor* in Ufa during the meeting of the heads of state of the countries. The Memorandum defined the overall framework and main content of the *Outline of the Plan on Establishing the China–Mongolia–Russia Economic Corridor*.[2]

Heads of state of China, Mongolia and Russia, on June 23rd, 2016 in Tashkent, jointly signed *the Outline of the Plan on Establishing the China–Mongolia–Russia Economic Corridor*, which symbolised the official implementation of the first multilateral cooperation outline under the framework of the BRI and effectively promoted the synergy of development strategies of the three states within the BRI framework.[3]

During the Belt and Road Forum for International Cooperation in May 2017, China and Mongolia reached a consensus to change the Prairie Road Programme into the Development Road Programme and signed the *Memorandum of Understanding on the Synergy of Mongolia's Development Road Programme and China's BRI*, which was to give full play to Mongolia as a bridge and belt connecting Eurasia.[4]

Mongolia's Development Road Programme is composed of multiple projects which account for a total investment of US$50 billion, such as the 997-km expressway connecting China and Russia, the 1100-km electrified railway extension of Trans-Mongolian railway and gas and oil pipelines. The Programme, of which the cooperation contents and spatial distribution are highly consistent with that of the China–Mongolia–Russia Economic Corridor, shares many common interests and cooperation space with the integration process under the framework of Russia's Eurasian Economic Union.

Details

The China–Mongolia–Russia Economic Corridor is a systematic project covering multiple sectors such as infrastructure connectivity, port construction, capacity, investment, trade and economy, civilisation and ecological environmental protection.[5]

First, infrastructure connectivity. Infrastructure connectivity is a priority area of the China–Mongolia–Russia Economic Corridor. Sound infrastructure, such as highway, railway, aviation, haven and port, not only improve the basic condition for promoting connectivity and meet the demand of free influence and integration of factors between China, Mongolia and Russia, but can also bring new historic opportunities for the three countries to improve economic development quality, narrow economic gaps and promote balanced development.

Cooperation between the three countries, including port, international transport corridor, international container train, border infrastructure and cross-border transport organisation, can improve cross-border supply chain quality between the three countries and between Asia and Europe with indexes of infrastructure, customs clearance facilitation, international transport, logistics capability, tracking and tracing, domestic logistics cost and transport time. What's more, cooperation on the energetic infrastructure sector between the three countries, such as the China–Russia crude oil and gas pipelines construction which runs across Mongolian territory, can enhance energy security capability and the level of cooperation of the three countries.

Second, production capacity and investment cooperation. Cooperation in production capacity and equipment manufacturing and mutual investment is another priority area of the China–Mongolia–Russia Economic Corridor, as well as the basic factor in deepening cooperation between the three countries. The three countries enjoy relatively strong complementarities in such fields as resource structure, industrial structure, technological structure and labor force structure. The three countries' cooperation in nuclear energy, hydroelectricity, photovoltaic energy, biomass energy and mineral resources helps enrich and deepen the connotation of China–Russia energy strategic cooperation, thus boosting China–Russia and China–Mongolia–Russia energy cooperation to a new historic level.

Strengthening cooperation between the three countries in manufacturing industry, farming, forestry and animal husbandry brings not only a coordinated industrial development between China, Mongolia and Russia, but also the formation of regional production network and extension of value chain for the three.

Cooperation between the three countries in e-commerce and high-tech is favourable for creating a cluster of production capacity and investment cooperation, and promoting the upgrade and transformation of economic and trade relations between the three countries from inter-industry division to intra-industry division and intra-product division, thereby fostering a new industrial cluster.

Third, economic and trade cooperation. Economic and trade cooperation is of great importance for the China–Mongolia–Russia Economic Corridor. Further expansion of trade scale between the three in fields such as energy mineral resource, building materials, textiles and agricultural products within the framework of the China–Mongolia–Russia Economic Corridor not only taps into comparative advantage and complementary of the three, but also optimises the structure of trade in goods.

Exchanges and cooperation on trade in service, such as finance, logistics, advertising, consultation, culture creativity and tourism between the three countries, help form a new production network.

New vitality is injected into the increasing growth of trade between China, Mongolia and Russia by strengthening cooperation in fields like software R&D, data maintenance, IT, business procedure and technology outsourcing.

In addition, new industry cluster districts and new comparative advantages will take shape under the framework of the China–Mongolia–Russia Economic Corridor on the platform of cross-border economic cooperation zones and outbound industrial parks. The industry clusters and platform effect will further enhance economic and trade cooperation between the three countries.

Fourth, people-to-people exchanges and ecological environmental protection cooperation. Common construction of the China–Mongolia–Russia Economic Corridor cannot be achieved without the support and participation of the people in the three countries. Cooperation in such fields as education, culture, tourism and intellectual property rights can not only promote the facilitation of personnel exchanges, but also expand non-governmental exchanges and communication. Beyond that, cooperation in areas of biodiversity, natural reserve, wetland protection, forest-fire prevention and desertification will create new opportunities for the three countries to co-build a green economic corridor. Cooperation between China and Russia in protection and utilisation of forest resources, border fire prevention and migrant bird protection and cooperation between China and Mongolia in wild species protection, prevention and control of desertification will not only yield huge ecological benefits, but also dig out potential economic benefits for the three countries.

Latest development

Since the initiative of building the China–Mongolia–Russia Economic Corridor was first proposed in 2014, initial achievements have been seen. Trade and investment have enjoyed stable increase with major programmes delivered.

First, infrastructure connectivity projects represented by the Sino-Russian Tongjiang Railway and the Sino-Russia Heihe Bridge began with a smooth start.

Among them, the Tongjiang Railway Bridge, started in 2014, is the first railway bridge across the border between China and Russia, which will greatly improve the trade and transportation conditions between the two countries.

The Sino-Russian Heihe Bridge is the first modern highway bridge between China and Russia and is expected to be open for traffic in 2019. A new international passage will exist with its completion.

In addition, the, survey and design of the 770-km MOSCA-Kazan high-speed rail, which constitutes a pilot project of the Russia (Moscow)–China (Beijing) Eurasian high-speed transport corridor, has been completed. In the same period, infrastructure connectivity construction exemplified by port construction has gained sound momentum. The building of 19 paperless, IT-based and intelligent open ports, including Manchuria and Erenhot, has also lent a strong impetus to the infrastructure connectivity of the China–Mongolia–Russia Economic Corridor.

China's customs statistics show that the largest land port between China and Mongolia—the Erenhot Port saw 15 lines of China–Europe trains in operation, of which the value reached US$2.512 billion in 2017.[6]

The implementation of the above-mentioned infrastructure connectivity priority projects has provided strong support to the China–Mongolia–Russia Economic Corridor construction.

In the field of energy cooperation, the energy cooperation projects represented by the Huadian Teninskaya power Station, the Yamal liquefied natural gas project and the Amur natural gas processing plant have been put into production, and the second China–Russia crude oil pipeline project has formally come into commercial operation. Among them, the Huadian Teninskaya power station, which was put into operation in June 2017, is China's largest electrical energy investment project in Russia at present, and the successful commissioning of the power station marks further deepening of China–Russian cooperation in electrical energy. The Yamal liquefied natural gas project, which was officially put into operation in December 2017, is China's first overseas mega-project following the BRI, and the first whole industrial chain cooperation project between China and Russia in the Arctic Circle.

When completed, the project will be the world's largest liquefied natural project in the Arctic, with 16.5 million tons' production of liquefied natural gas per year.[7] The second China–Russia crude oil pipeline project was officially put into commercial operation on January 1, 2018, from which 30 million tons of Russian oil will enter China per year.[8] The successful operation of these energy projects not only boosts the development of Russia's energy industry, but is also a milestone in deepening Sino-Russian energy and power cooperation within the framework of the China–Mongolia–Russia Economic Corridor.

As to economic, trade and capacity cooperation, since 2014 when China, Mongolia and Russia first proposed the building of the China–Mongolia–Russia Economic Corridor, the capacity cooperation between them has been continuously deepened, and the level of trade and investment has also been greatly improved. Sino-Mongolian and Sino-Russian bilateral trade value reached US$6.347 billion and US$84.03 billion, respectively, in 2017, with a year-on-year growth of 40.31% and 21.05%, respectively, according to Chinese customs agency.[9] China has become the largest trading partner of Mongolia and Russia. Statistics of the Chinese Ministry of Commerce show that China's investment in Mongolia and Russia totalled US$3.84 billion and US$12.98 billion, respectively, by the end of 2016, registering an annual average growth rate of 6.8% and 27.7%, respectively, compared to the years prior to 2012 (in which the BRI was initiated).[10]

In addition, China, Mongolia and Russia have also made great progress in cooperation on such fields as energy, power, mineral and commercial logistics, thanks to the platforms of the Russian Ussuriysk economic and trade cooperation zone, the China Russia Tomsk timber industry and trade cooperation zone in Russian, the China–Russia (Primorsky Krai) agricultural industry cooperation zone, the Russian LongYeu forestry economic cooperation zone, the Suifen River and Heihe River national border economic cooperation zone, and the China–Mongolia Erenhot–ZaminUud cross-border economic cooperation zone.

Industrial and investment cooperation will play an active role in the improving and restructuring of the regional production network, the extension of value chain and supply chain, and the optimal allocation of trade and production factors between China, Mongolia and Russia, and also bring new opportunities for narrowing the economic gap, promoting balanced development within the region, improving people's welfare and achieving sustainable economic growth between the three countries.[11]

Notes

1 Xi Jinping: To build the China–Mongolia–Russia Economic Corridor, Xinhuanet, September 26, 2014. Retrieved January 15, 2018 from www.xinhuanet.com/world/2014-09/12/c_1112448804.html
2 China, Mongolia and Russia signed the *Memorandum of Understanding on Compiling the Outline of the Plan on Establishing the China–Mongolia–Russia Economic Corridor*, website of National Development and Reform Commission of PRC, July 13, 2015. Retrieved July 13, 2015 from www.ndrc.gov.cn/gzdt/201507/t20150713_737154.html

3 "Building the Belt and Road: Concept, Practice and China's Contribution," Xinhuanet, May 10, 2017. Retrieved January 10, 2018 from www.xinhuanet.com/politics/2017-05/10/c_1120951928.html
4 "President Xi Jinping meets with Prime Minister of Mongolia: To deliver results of the synergy between the Belt and Road Initiative and Mongolia's Development Road Program," China News. Retrieved January 10, 2018 from www.chinanews.com/gn/2017/05-12/8222181.shtml
5 "The Outline of the Plan on Establishing the China–Mongolia–Russia Economic Corridor," National Development and Reform Commission of PRC, June 23, 2017. Retrieved January 15, 2018 from www.ndrc.gov.cn/zcfb/zcfbghwb/201609/t20160912_818326.html
6 "China–Mongolia's largest land port has seen over US $2.5 billion goods value produced by China–EU trains in 2017," China news, January 2, 2018. Retrieved January 20, 2018 from www.yidaiyilu.gov.cn/xwzx/dfdt/42031.htm
7 The second China–Russia crude oil pipeline project completed, Xinhuanet, November 1h, 2017. Retrieved January 20, 2018 from www.xinhuanet.com/world/2017-11/12/c_1121943190.htm
8 "Sino-Russian major energy cooperation project of the Yamal liquefied natural gas project is officially put into production," CNR, December 9, 2017. Retrieved Janaury 20, 2018 from http://china.cnr.cn/yaowen/20171209/t20171209_524055590.shtml
9 Source: Global Trade Database (Global Trade Atlas, GTA), www.gtis.com/gta/
10 Ministry of Commerce of the People's Republic of China, National Bureau of Statistics, State Administration of Foreign Exchange: *Statistical bulletin of China's foreign direct investment (FDI) for 2016*, China Statistics Publishing House, first edition, September 2017.
11 Wang Jinbo, *"The Belt and Road" Economic Corridor and Regional Economic Integration: The Formation Mechanism and Function Evolution*. Social Sciences Academic Press, 2017.

37

THE NEW EURASIAN CONTINENTAL BRIDGE ECONOMIC CORRIDOR

Wang Jinbo

Concept explanation

Starting from China's east coast, the New Eurasian Continental Bridge Economic Corridor spans the Eurasian continent (reaching Central and Eastern Europe through China's Northwest, Central Asia and Russia), links the economically dynamic East Asia economic circle to the east, connects the developed European economic circle to the westand covers the two regions of Central and Eastern Europe (CEE) and Central Asia, plus two platforms of the "16+1 cooperation" (China and 16 Central and Eastern European countries) and SCO (Shanghai Cooperation Organisation).[1] Based on modern international logistics system such as the China–Europe Railways, the New Eurasian Continental Bridge Economic Corridor will open up a broader space for cooperation between China and the CEE countries (CEECs), with expanding energy resources cooperation as lead, promoting economic and trade and production capacity cooperation as priority, and building a smooth and efficient regional greater market as objective. It also provides new opportunities for the development of vast countries in the inland of Eurasia.

Since his proposal of the BRI in 2013, President Xi Jinping has repeatedly underscored during meetings with leaders of CEECs that "16+1" cooperation should serve as a major gateway in the further implementation of the BRI in the European economic circle.[2]

In November 2015, President Xi witnessed the signing of memorandums of understanding between China and Poland, China and Serbia, China and the Czech Republic, China and Bulgaria, China and Slovakia, respectively, which aim to jointly promote intergovernmental construction of the BRI.[3] In June 2016 during his visit to Serbia—the first CEEC that has ever established strategic partnership with China—President Xi Jinping mentioned again that "16+1" cooperation should serve as a major gateway in the further implementation of the BRI in the European economic circle. When visiting Poland, President Xi Jinping put forward a 5-point proposal on the BRI, namely making concerted efforts, highlighting the key points, working closely, optimising mechanism and putting intelligence first. In his state visit to Uzbekistan, President Xi Jinping offered to work together to create a "green, healthy, intellectual, and peaceful" 4-pointed Silk Road. In November 2017, China and 16 CEECs issued *the Budapest Outline of China–CEECs Cooperation*, emphasising the will of extensive consultation, joint contribution and shared benefits of the BRI and promoting the initiative to align with major initiatives such as the European Investment Plan and national development plans on the basis of the "16+1" cooperation.[4]

Details

First, infrastructure connectivity. Infrastructure connectivity is a priority of the New Eurasian Continental Bridge Economic Corridor. As an international transportation corridor, the New Eurasian Continental Bridge will bring new historical opportunities for the deepening and upgrading of China's cooperation with the countries along the way.

Based on the modern international logistics system such as the China–Europe Railways, and taking the New Eurasian Continental Bridge Economic Corridor as the lead, taking the land, sea and air passage and information superhighway as skeleton, a compound type of infrastructure network will be formed in Eurasia.[5] This compound type of infrastructure network will further improve the quality of cross-border supply chains between Eurasian countries in terms of infrastructure, customs facilitation, international transportation, logistics capabilities, tracking and tracing, domestic logistics costs, transport time, etc. Moreover, with the New Eurasian Continental Bridge Economic Corridor as the framework and the China–EU interconnection platform as the carrier, the two sides can fully combine the BRI with the Sino-European cooperation, strive for synergy between the "Eurasia Interconnection Blueprint" and the BRI, speed up China–EU interconnection cooperation and expand cooperation in areas such as the Asia–Europe supply chain logistics network compatibility, maritime transport, railway services, logistics, traffic safety, low-carbon and intelligent transportation, and strengthen complementary of traffic technology regulations and standards. Work should be done to maximise the synergy effect of China's opening-up strategy and the EU integration strategy and the "Europe 2020 Strategy".

Second, industrial and investment cooperation. Industrial and investment cooperation is a key area of the New Eurasian Continental Bridge Economic Corridor. Industrial and investment cooperation, taken as the priority and under the framework of the New Eurasian Continental Bridge Economic Corridor, will play an active role in promoting and restructuring regional production networks, broadening value chains, and optimising trade configuration and production factors of China and countries along the Belt and Road, and bring new models and new opportunities for the effective synergy between the BRI and the Juncker Plan. Radiation effects and linkage effects of the New Eurasian Continental Bridge Economic Corridor, measures of trade and investment liberalisation and customs clearance facilitation under the integrated framework will not only play a positive role in expanding value chains between countries along the Belt and Road and provide new impetus to economic endogenous development of the countries along the Belt and Road, especially developing ones, but also provide a new linking paradigm for the countries along the Belt and Road to transform from utilising comparative advantages to creating comparative advantages and from the mode of corridor to integration.[6]

Third, economic and trade cooperation. Economic and trade cooperation is an important part of the New Eurasian Continental Bridge Economic Corridor. Aiming at building a smooth and efficient regional greater market, economic and trade cooperation between China and the countries along the New Eurasian Continental Bridge will be the main driving force behind economic development and innovation. At present, China is negotiating on the Bilateral Investment Treaty (China–EU BIT) with the EU, and exploring the possibility of signing free trade agreements with members of the EU and the SCO, aiming at creating more favourable conditions for the sustainable development of economic and trade relations between China and Europe and between China and the SCO members, and providing institutional security for the sustainable growth of trade and investment between China and the countries along the New Eurasian Continental Bridge Economic Corridor. According to the report of the Centre for European Policy Studies (CEPS), the signing of the FTA will bring an increase of China's GDP by 1.87% and that of EU by 0.76%.[7]

Moreover, as an important part and a useful supplement of China–EU comprehensive strategic partnership, the effective synergy of the "16+1" cooperation and the BRI will lead China–EU relations to a higher level, a wider area and deeper development.

Latest development

First of all, as for infrastructure connection, the infrastructure connection projects of the BRI, represented by the China–Europe Railways, the Hungarian–Serbia Railway and the Greek Piraeus Port, have made significant progress. According to the National Development and Reform Commission's report, since the China–Europe Railways unified brand in June 2016, they have been running across 38 cities domestically, bound for 36 cities in 13 European countries by late 2017, with 23 cities in 5 countries increased compared to 2016 and a total of 61 running lines. The total running time of the China–Europe Railways is shortened from over 20 days in the initial period to 12–14 days, and the overall transportation cost drops by about 40% compared to the beginning.[8]

As an important platform for the construction of the BRI and the New Eurasian Continental Bridge Economic Corridor, the China–Europe Railways will be increased to 5000 per year by 2020, accounting for 80% of the total international intermodal transport of container railways.[9] The Hungarian–Serbia Railway, as the first Chinese railway project entering the EU market, was officially launched on November 24, 2015. On the very same day, China and Hungary signed the *Agreement on Cooperation in Development, Construction and Financing of the Hungarian Section of the Hungarian–Serbia Railway Project* at the Central and Eastern Europe 16+1 meeting. The Hungarian–Serbia Railway, which is 350 km long, starts from Budapest in the north to Belgrade in the south, and east to the Greek Piraeus Port through the projected China–Europe Land–Sea Express Line. When completed, it will be an important transport artery in Central Europe. Greek Piraeus Port is the largest port in Greece and the second largest port in the Mediterranean. China Ocean Shipping Company (COSCO) won the franchise of the port's No. 2 and No. 3 wharfs after the financial crisis in 2008. Thanks to this, the port's throughput has now exceeded 4 million twenty-foot equivalent units (TEUs), which is an increase of over 4 times compared to the 880,000 TEUs in 2010, making its global ranking rise from 93rd in 2008 to 38th in 2016.[10] The Piraeus Port is becoming an important hub port of the Belt and Road and a model of strategic cooperation between China and Greece.

In the area of capacity cooperation, the industrial cooperation projects represented by the China–Belarus Industrial Park, the Hungarian China–Europe Trade Logistics Park, the China–Hungary BorsodChem Trade and Economic Cooperation Zone and the Polish Cross-Border Electric Commerce Industrial Park have achieved remarkable results. Located at the outskirts of Minsk, the capital of Belarus, the China–Belarus Industrial Park is China's largest overseas industrial park, as well as a landmark project of joint construction of the Silk Road Economic Belt between China and Belarus. Since entering a substantive development in 2015, the China–Belarus Industrial Park has seen the completion of the China–Belarus Trade Logistics Park, covering a total area of 100,000 square metres and 25 enterprises. The Hungarian China–Europe Trade Logistics Park is China's first national economic and trade cooperation zone in Europe, and the first national economic and trade cooperation zone featuring trade logistics. The Polish Cross-Border Electric Commerce Industrial Park, launched in June 2016, is China's largest cross-border e-commerce industrial park in Europe. With the overseas industrial parks and economic and trade cooperation zones as the platforms, production capacity cooperation under the framework of the new Eurasian Continental Bridge will lay a new foundation for deepening economic and trade cooperation between China and countries along the bridge, promoting the industrial upgrading of the host countries and improving economic development.

In addition, as a model project of international capacity cooperation between China and CEECs, the resumption of the No. 2 blast furnace at the Smederevo steel plant in Serbia and the completion of the phase I of the Kostolac Power Plant have become the model of industrial cooperation between the two countries under the framework of the BRI and the New Eurasian Continental Bridge Economic Corridor.

Cooperation in trade and investment between China and the countries along the New Eurasian Continental Bridge has seen a rising trend since China put forward the BRI in 2013.

According to Chinese customs' statistics, trade volume between China and CEECs and between China and members of the SCO (excluding India and Pakistan) were US$68.042 billion and US$113.42 billion, respectively, in 2017, a year-on-year growth of 15.5% and 21.0%, higher than China's total foreign trade growth over the same period of 4.3 percentage points and 9.8 percentage points.[11]

With the trade volume between China and the EU of US$640.65 billion (up 14.1% year-on-year), accounting for about 15.7% of China's total foreign trade and about 15.1% of the EU's external total volume, the EU has become China's largest trading partner for 10 consecutive years, and China has been the EU's second largest trading partner since 2003.

According to the Chinese Ministry of Commerce, China's cumulative investment to the 16 CEECs and the SCO members is US$1.667 billion and US$21.874 billion, respectively, by late 2016, with an annual growth of 4.6% and 12% compared to 2012 before the proposal of the BRI. The cumulative direct investment in the EU amounted to US$69.837 billion, a 2.2 times increase compared to that of 2012.

Investment has become an important way to build economic corridor between China and countries along the New Eurasian Continental Bridge.

Apart from direct investment, the China–CEE Investment Cooperation Fund, which was jointly funded by the banking institutions of China, Poland and Hungary, launched its first equity investment project, Grenoble Wind Power Project in Poland in September 2014.

The China–Eurasia Economic Cooperation Fund, jointly sponsored by the EIBC (Export–Import Bank of China) and the Bank of China (BOC), has already provided US$27.1 billion loan quota for the SCO member states, which is mainly invested in agricultural development, logistics, infrastructure, new generation of information technology, manufacturing and other priority development industries in Eurasia.

Notes

1 National Development and Reform Commission (2017), "Building the Belt and Road: Concept, Practice and China's Contribution." Retrieved February 10. 2017 from www.ndrc.gov.cn/gzdt/201705/t20170511_847228.html
2 Zhong Sheng, "Synergizing Development Strategy and accelerating the BRI," *People's Daily*, June 26, 2016.
3 "Xi Jinping meets leaders of 16 countries in Central and Eastern Europe," Xinhuanet, November 27, 2015. Retrieved February 10, 2018 from www.xinhuanet.com/mrdx/2015-11/27/c_134860944.htm
4 "Budapest Outline of China–CEE Countries Cooperation," Ministry of Foreign Affairs of the People's Republic of China, November 28, 2017. Retrieved February 10, 2018 from www.fmprc.gov.cn/web/zyxw/t1514532.shtml
5 "Making Joint Efforts to Promote the B&R Construction—Speech on the Opening Ceremony of the B&R International Cooperation Forum (2017)," Xinhuanet. Retrieved February 10, 2018 from www.xinhuanet.com/politics/2017- 05/14 / c_1120969677.html

6 Wang Jinbo, *Formation Mechanism and Evolution of Function of the B&R Economic Corridor and Regional Economic Integration*. Social Sciences Academic Press, 2017.
7 Center for European Policy Studies (CEPS), "Tomorrow's Silk Road: Assessing an EU–China free Trade agreement," April 2016, www.ceps.eu/system/files/EUCHINA_FTA_Final.pdf.
8 "The number of China–Europe Railways has seen a year-on-year growth of 116% in 2017," Xinhuanet, January 1, 2018). Retrieved February 10, 2018 from www.xinhuanet.com/2018-01/22/c_1122297180.htm
9 "China–Europe Railways Construction and Development Plan (2016–2020)," published on the website of National Railways Administration (October 19, 2016). Retrieved February 10, 2017 from www.nra.gov.cn/jgzf/yxjg/zfdt/201610/t20161027_28807.html
10 "Greek Piraeus Port welcomes its first 20,000 TEUs grade container ship," Xinhunet, February 27, 2018. Retrieved February 28, 2018 from www.xinhuanet.com/photo/2018-02/27/c_129818357.htm
11 Data Source: Global Customs Database (GTA), www.gtis.com/gta/.

38
THE CHINA–CENTRAL ASIA–WEST ASIA ECONOMIC CORRIDOR

Wang Jinbo

Concept explanation

The China–Central Asia–West Asia Economic Corridor extends westward from northwestern China via Central Asia to the Persian Gulf, the Arabian Peninsula and the Mediterranean coast, involving relevant countries in Central Asia, West Asia and North Africa. As the backbone of the ancient Silk Road, the 5 Central Asian countries once occupied an important position on the road. Today, China and the 5 Central Asian countries are still linked by the same mountains and rivers.

Similarly, as the intersection point of the ancient maritime and land Silk Road, West Asia, especially the Middle East Gulf countries, also played a pivotal role in East–West economic, trade and cultural exchanges.

Today, West Asia, the Middle East Gulf countries in particular, has become China's most important oil and gas supplier, while China has already become the largest oil export market of the Middle East Gulf countries.

When Chinese President Xi Jinping visited Kazakhstan in September 2013, he raised the initiative of co-building the Silk Road Economic Belt.

In June 2014, at the sixth ministerial conference of the China–Arab States Cooperation Forum, President Xi proposed the China–Arab "1+2+3" cooperation network, with energy cooperation as the main axis, infrastructure construction and trade and investment facilitation as the two wings and the three high-tech areas of nuclear energy, aerospace satellites and new energy as breakthroughs.[1]

During the G20 Hangzhou Summit in 2016, the leaders of China and Kazakhstan witnessed the signing of the *Cooperation Plan on Dovetailing the Silk Road Economic Belt and NurlyZhol (Bright Road)*. As requested in the plan, the two sides, in the promotion of cooperation on dovetailing the Silk Road Economic Belt and Bright Road, should steadily promote production capacity and investment cooperation, actively develop economic and trade cooperation, deepen energy resources cooperation and expand people-to-people exchanges.[2]

China also signed cooperation documents on building the Silk Road Economic Belt with Tajikistan, Kyrgyzstan, Uzbekistan and other countries, and MOUs on building the Belt and Road with Turkey, Iran, Saudi Arabia, Qatar, Kuwait and other countries.[3]

The signing of the above plan, cooperation documents and memorandums provides a stable institutional guarantee for China and the Central Asian and West Asian countries to jointly build the Belt and Road and the China–Central Asia–West Asia economic corridor.

Details

First, infrastructure connectivity. Infrastructure connectivity is a priority area of the China–Central Asia–West Asia Economic Corridor. The practice of China's reform and opening-up and the experience of developed countries prove that sound infrastructure plays an important role in the growth of a country's economy, the increase of TFP (total factor productivity) and the increase of per-capita income.

According to the Global Competitiveness Report of the World Economic Forum (WEF), in 2017, among countries along the China–Central Asia–West Asia Economic Corridor, infrastructure competitiveness indexes of Qatar (5.8), Saudi Arabia (5.2), Bahrain (5.1), Oman (4.9) Gulf and other Middle East Gulf countries are significantly higher than Kazakhstan (4.2), Tajikistan (3.3) and Kyrgyzstan (3.0) and other Central Asian countries. Qatar, in 13th place, ranked the highest among the 137 countries, while Kyrgyzstan's (109th) position was significantly lower.[4]

According to the World Bank, among countries along the China–Central Asia–West Asia Economic Corridor, electricity convenience index of Tajikistan and Kyrgyzstan is only 35.00 and 44.19, respectively, ranking 171st and 164th in 190 countries and regions globally, significantly lower than the UAE's 99.92 and Uzbekistan's 85.50 (respectively, 1st and 27th).[5]

The above-mentioned reports show that inadequate infrastructure, especially power shortfall, remains an important factor restraining economic development of some countries along the China–Central Asia–West Asia Economic Corridor.

The infrastructure connectivity, under the framework of the China–Central Asia–West Asia Economic Corridor, provides new opportunities for China, Central Asia and West Asia to jointly improve infrastructure and facilitation and achieve a "seamless link" in the supply chain.

Second, energy cooperation. Energy cooperation is an important content of the China–Central Asia–West Asia Economic Corridor. The Middle East has gradually lost its status as the largest oil supplier for Europe and America during the past decade, due to the strategy of diversified supply sources of developed economies in Europe and America and the impact of modularisation of the international oil market. Therefore, looking for long-term stable oil export markets becomes the major concern of the Middle East. In this regard, the rapid growth of China's economy, the rapid increase of its oil demand, the proposal of the BRI and the China–Central Asia–West Asia Economic Corridor all provide a great opportunity for Central Asia and Middle Eastern Gulf countries to solve the security problems of oil and gas exports.

According to British Petroleum (BP), of the total 983 million tons of crude oil exported from Middle East countries, only about 243 million tons went to Europe (153 million tons) and the US (89 million tons) in 2016; while as much as 614 million tons to China (199 million tons), India (154 million tons), Japan (161 million tons) and other Asian countries, accounting for 62.5% of the total Middle East crude oil exports.[6]

As the largest market of the Middle East Gulf countries' crude oil exports, China will enjoy new opportunities and solid guarantee to jointly build the Belt and Road and the China–Central Asia–West Asia Economic Corridor with Central Asia and Middle East Gulf countries, which are brought by the long-term stability of energy cooperation and the consistency of the core interests of both sides—China's energy demand and the security demand for oil exports of Central Asia and the Gulf states.

Third, industrial and investment cooperation. Industrial and investment cooperation is a key area of the China–Central Asia–West Asia Economic Corridor. Because of their different economic development levels and development stages, countries along the China–Central Asia–West Asia Economic Corridor are different from each other in terms of industrial structure, industrial base and international competitiveness.

As the world's largest trade in goods power and manufacturing power,[7] China's advantages in the scale of conventional manufacturing, together with the advantages in resources of Central Asia and West Asia, constitute unique advantages in strengthening industrial and investment cooperation between China and Central Asia and West Asia. Industrial and investment cooperation within the framework of the BRI and the economic corridor not only benefits the value realisation and appreciation of the resource endowment of China and the countries of Central Asia and West Asia, but also promotes the initiation and change of the economic structure between China and the countries in Central Asia and West Asia through the self-reinforcing role of spatial aggregation, and offers a stable dynamic mechanism for the extension of the value chain and the formation of regional production networks in China and the countries in Central Asia and West Asia. Furthermore, according to the Global Customs Database (GTA), China's total value of trade in goods amounted to US$4.07 trillion, with a year-on-year growth of 11.18% in 2017, ranking the world's first in the scale of trade in goods.

Fourth, economic and trade cooperation. Economic and trade cooperation is an important part of the China–Central Asia–West Asia Economic Corridor. The China–Central Asia–West Asia Economic Corridor is first and foremost a trade corridor as it highlights smooth trade as underlined in the BRI. Benefiting from the economic globalisation, production internationalisation and the continuous expansion of global value chain, China and the countries of Central Asia and West Asia have gradually formed a complementary trade pattern over the past few decades. China's trade ties with Kyrgyzstan, Tajikistan, Uzbekistan and other Central Asian countries are gradually strengthened, and the trade bond with the Middle East Gulf countries has been continuously stable.

China has become, to Central Asia and West Asia, an important export destination for energy and resources and an important source of industrial manufactures such as textiles, machinery, electronics, steel, fine chemicals and precision machinery. Sustainable development of bilateral trade is not only conducive to improving economic ties and the interdependence between China and the countries of Central Asia and West Asia, but also significantly improves the welfare of China and its trade partners in Central Asia and West Asia.

Latest development

Since 2013 when Chinese President Xi Jinping proposed the BRI, substantial progress has been made in infrastructure connectivity, energy, industry and investment, economy and trade, and many other fields along the China–Central Asia–West Asia Economic Corridor.

First, in terms of infrastructure connectivity, a number of fruitful results have been achieved in the BRI priority projects represented by the China–Kyrgyzstan–Ukrainian Railway, Turkey's east–west high-speed rail project and the COSCO Shipping Abu Dhabi Wharf. As an important project under the framework of the Silk Road Economic Belt, the China–Kyrgyzstan–Ukrainian Railway which links China with Kyrgyzstan and Uzbekistan has enjoyed a tripartite joint working mechanism since May 2016. When the railway construction is completed, Kyrgyzstan and Uzbekistan will become international transit countries, and see a great improvement in cross-border supply chain quality and in basic conditions for connectivity and a rapid economic development in both countries.

China and Turkey have reached an important consensus on cooperation in the Turkey's east–west high-speed rail project, which is a key line of infrastructure connectivity in the Silk Road Economic Belt, and they have started substantive talks.[8]

The COSCO Shipping Abu Dhabi Wharf, started in November 2017, will be the largest container station in the area, marking new progress in the Belt and Road project construction between China and the UAE.[9]

The China–Egypt railway project signed in August 2017 marks significant results made by pragmatic cooperation between China and Egypt under the BRI.[10]

In addition, infrastructure connection plans and framework agreements of the BRI and the China–Central Asia–West Asia Economic Corridor have been put into effect, including the *Central Asia Regional Transport and Trade Facilitation Strategy (2020)*, the *Agreement on Facilitation of International Road Transport between Governments of SCO Member States*, and the *China–Kazakhstan–Russia International Road Transport of Temporary Transit Goods Agreement*.

As for energy cooperation, remarkable results have been made in energy cooperation projects, which are represented by the Kazakhstan southern gas pipeline project, the Turkmenistan–China gas pipeline project, the China–Kyrgyzstan Bishkek thermal power plant reconstruction project and cooperation between China and Saudi Arabia in petrochemical projects.

The Kazakhstan southern gas pipeline project, as the key project of energy cooperation between the two countries, was completed on April 4, 2017. It provides gas supply not only to southern Kazakhstan and areas along the Belt and Road, but also to China through the China–Kazakhstan gas pipeline in the future.

The Turkmenistan–China gas pipeline project in Tajikistan was started in January 2018, and is predicted to transport 30 billion cubic meters of natural gas to China annually after completion.

The largest energy cooperation project between China and Kyrgyzstan, namely the China–Kyrgyzstan Bishkek thermal power plant reconstruction project, was completed and put into production on August 30, 2017. It will increase the power of the Bishkek thermal power plant from the original 262 million kilowatt-hours to 1.74 billion kilowatt-hours per year, which will help the country achieve self-dependent power generation.[11]

In August 2017, the second meeting of the China–Saudi Arabia joint high-level committee reached a consensus to establish a package of energy cooperation mechanism, and made a list of energy cooperation projects including petrochemical projects.[12]

In industrial and investment cooperation, remarkable results have been achieved in the construction of industrial cooperation platforms exemplified by overseas industrial parks and cross-border economic cooperation zones such as the China–Kazakhstan Horgos International Border Cooperation Centre, the Northern Tajikistan Non-ferrous Metals Industrial Park, China–Oman (Duqm) Industrial Park and China–Egypt Suez Economic and Trade Cooperation Zone.

As China's first cross-border economic and trade zone and investment cooperation centre, the China–Kazakhstan Horgos International Border Cooperation Centre has become an integrated trading zone along the Silk Road Economic Belt of multiple functions such as trade, warehousing and transportation and financial services.

As China's first industrial park in Tajikistan, the China–Tajikistan Industrial Park was upgraded to the Northern Tajikistan Non-ferrous Metals Industrial Park in September 2017.

What's more, the China–Oman (Duqm) industrial park and the China–UAE (Abu Dhabi) Capacity Cooperation Park were started in April 2017 and January 2018, respectively, marking an important step in production capacity cooperation between China and Oman, and between China and the UAE within the framework of the BRI and China–Central Asia–West Asia Economic Corridor.[13]

In economic and trade cooperation, a significant progress has been made in both trade and investment between China and Central Asia and between China and West Asia.

According to China's customs, the trade volume between China and the 5 Central Asian countries and between China and members of the Gulf Cooperation Council (GCC) totalled US$36.29 billion and US$127.66 billion, respectively, and bilateral trade volume between China and Turkey and between China and Egypt amounted to US$21.92 billion and US$10.87 billion, respectively, in 2017.

According to the Chinese Ministry of Commerce, China's investment to China–Central Asia–West Asia major economies—the 5 Central Asian countries, the GCC, Turkey and Egypt—totalled US$9.14 billion, US$9.22 billion, US$1.06 billion and US$0.89 billion, respectively, by the end of 2016.

Foreign investment is becoming an important way for China to promote the construction of the BRI and the China–Central Asia–West Asia Economic Corridor.

In addition, after 9 rounds of negotiation, 9 of 15 topics on the China–GCC Free Trade Zone (FTZ) for discussion have been settled.[14]

Trade liberalisation and investment facilitation under the China–GCC FTZ framework will create new conditions and lay a new foundation for the sustainable development in the economic and trade relations and sustainable growth in trade and investment between China and the GCC countries.

Notes

1 "Promoting the Silk Road Spirit to deepen Sino-Arab Cooperation—speech at the opening ceremony of the sixth ministerial conference of the China–Arab States Cooperation Forum," June 6, 2014. People.cn. Retrieved February 1, 2018 from http://politics.people.com.cn/n/2014/0606/, C1024-25110600.html
2 "China and Kazakhstan signed the Cooperation Plan on Dovetailing the Silk Road Economic Belt and NurlyZhol (Bright Road)," National Development and Reform Commission website, September 5, 2016. Retrieved February 1, 2018 from www.ndrc.gov.cn/gzdt/201609/t20160905_ 817637.html
3 "Jointly build the BRI: Ideas, Practices and China's Contribution," National Development and Reform Commission of the PRC, May 10, 2017. Xinhuanet. Retrieved February 1, 2018 from www.xinhuanet.com/politics/2017-05/10/c_1120951928.htm
4 *The Global Competitiveness Report 2017–2018*. World Economic Forum (WEF), www3.weforum.org/docs/GCR2017-2018/05FullReport/TheGlobalCompetitivenessReport2017-2018.pdf.
5 "Doing Business 2018," World Bank, www.doingbusiness.org/-/media/WBG/DoingBusiness/Documents/Annual-Reports/ English/db2018-full-report.pdf.
6 *Statistical Review of World Energy* (June 2017), BP, www.bp.com/content/dam/bp/en/corporate/pdf/energy-economics/statistical-review-2017/bp-statistical-review-of-world-energy-2017-full-report.pdf.
7 According to the report of the United Nations Statistics Division, China's manufacturing added value amounted to US$3.08 trillion in 2016, higher than US$2.18 trillion of the United States and US$979.2 billion of Japan, ranking the first in the world.
8 Wang Yi and Turkish Foreign Minister Chavush Oulu held the first meeting of China–Turkey Foreign Minister Consultation Mechanism. Ministry of Foreign Affairs website. November 14, 2016. Retrieved February 10, 2018 from www.fmprc.gov.cn/web/zyxw/t1415137.shtml
9 "The COSCO Shipping Abu Dhabi Wharf to start," Xinhuanet, November 6, 2017. Retrieved February 10, 2018 from www.xinhuanet.com/world/2017-11/06/c_129733868.htm
10 "China–Egypt railway project signing ceremony was held in Cairo," *People's Daily*, August 16, 2017.
11 "China–Kyrgyzstan largest energy cooperation project put into production to achieve self-dependent power generation," China Belt and Road Network. August 31, 2017. Retrieved February 10, 2018 from www.yidaiyilu.gov.cn/xwzx/hwxw/25537.htm
12 "China and Saudi Arabia agree to establish energy cooperation mechanism," Phoenix, August 26, 2017. Retrieved February 15, 2018 from http://finance.ifeng.com/a/20170825/15606522_0.shtml

13 "The China–Oman Industrial Park had the first batch of enterprises signed in," Xinhuanet, April 19 2017. Retrieved February 10, 2018 from www.xinhuanet.com/2017-04/19/c_129552534.htm
14 "The China–GCC FTZ ninth round of negotiations closed in Riyadh, Saudi Arabia," China FTZ Service Network, December 22, 2016. Retrieved February 10, 2018 from http://fta.mofcom.gov.cn/article/chinahaihehui/haihehuinews/201612/33882_1.html

39

THE CHINA–INDOCHINA PENINSULA ECONOMIC CORRIDOR

Wang Jinbo

Concept explanation

The China–Indochina Peninsula Economic Corridor, with Nanning, Guangxi (East Line) and Kunming, Yunnan (Western Line) as the starting points and Singapore as the end, passes through the Indochina Peninsula, covering the 6 major ASEAN members—Vietnam, Laos, Cambodia, Thailand, Malaysia and Singapore. It's not only an important carrier for China and ASEAN to further expand and enhance cooperation, but also an important channel and transnational economic corridor connecting the Sea and Land Silk Road, China and South East Asia. The Indochina Peninsula, located between China and the South Asia subcontinent, and between the Indian Ocean and the Pacific Ocean, with unique location advantages and geographical advantages, has historically been the pivot of the Maritime Silk Road. In addition, the Malacca Strait is an international strategic channel as famous as the Panama Canal and the Suez Canal. The Lancang–Mekong International Waterway and the cross-border traffic and oil and gas networks under construction link the Land and Sea Silk Road closely together. As major members of ASEAN, countries of the Indochina Peninsula have played an important role in the process of East Asian integration centred on ASEAN, while ASEAN has become China's third largest trading partner, the fourth largest export market and the second largest source of imports.

During his visit to the South-East Asian countries in 2013, President Xi Jinping for the first time proposed the important initiative of building the 21st Century Maritime Silk Road. Launched in March 2015, the *Vision and Actions on Jointly Building Silk Road Economic Belt and 21st Century Maritime Silk Road* clearly demanded jointly building the China–Indochina Peninsula Economic Corridor, with the cities along the Belt and Road as the support, and the key economic and trade industrial parks as cooperation platforms.[1] Issued on May 26, 2016, the *China–Indochina Peninsula Economic Corridor Proposal* once again proposed building the China–Indochina Peninsula Economic Corridor into an international economic cooperation corridor with Guangxi and Yunnan in China as the main gateway, passing through Vietnam, Laos, Cambodia, Thailand to Malaysia and Singapore.[2] The *Five-Year Plan of Action of the Lancang-Mekong Cooperation (2018–2022)*, issued on January 10, 2018, required that synergy be strengthened between the BRI, the *ASEAN 2025: Forging Ahead Together*, the *Master Plan on ASEAN Connectivity 2025* and other Mekong subregional cooperation mechanisms on the platform of the China–Indochina Peninsula Economic Corridor, and that Lancang–Mekong

Cooperation be built into a new platform and a new subregional cooperation mechanism for the China–Indochina Peninsula Economic Corridor.³

Details

The China–Indochina Peninsula Economic Corridor is a systematic project involving multiple fields, such as trade, investment, finance, energy, industry, transport and infrastructure.

First, unimpeded trade is of great importance to the China–Indochina Peninsula Economic Corridor. Thanks to the complete regional production network in East Asia, the effective industrial division system and the institutional dividend of the China–ASEAN FTA, a complementary trade pattern has been formed between China and the Indochina Peninsula countries. Objectively speaking, among the six major economic corridors along the Belt and Road, China enjoys higher trade integration, foreign direct investment (FDI) intensity and intra-industry trade index with the Indochina Peninsula countries than other corridor countries. The trade creation effect of the China–Indochina Peninsula Economic Corridor can not only help China and the Indochina Peninsula countries to integrate into global value chain and stimulate economic growth, but also give full play to the comparative advantages of the countries along the corridor and promote the welfare effect.

Second, investment is an important way for China and the Indochina Peninsula countries to develop the Belt and Road and the economic corridor. China and the Indochina Peninsula countries have achieved, over the past few decades, improvement in the total factor productivity and sustainable growth in economy to varying degrees, thanks to the continued growth in investment scale and the spillover effects of foreign direct investment, namely the industrial structure effect, technological spillover effect, trade creation effect and institutional change effect.⁴ According to the Chinese Ministry of Commerce, in 2016, China's total investment to the Indochina Peninsula countries amounted to US$8.356 billion, accounting for 4.3% of China's foreign direct investment volume, and the cumulative investment added up to US$61.086 billion, accounting for 4.5% of China's foreign direct investment stock that year.⁵ The investment promotion effect of the Indochina Peninsula Economic Corridor not only benefits the formation of new production networks between China and countries along the Belt and Road, but also injects new vitality to the continued growth of bilateral trade.

Third, industrial cooperation is a key area of the China–Indochina Peninsula Economic Corridor. Industrial cooperation based on overseas industrial parks and cross-border economic cooperation zones is not only conducive to the formation of new production networks between China and the Indochina Peninsula countries, but also creates new conditions for deepening intra-industry or intra-product vertical division of labour and the extension of the value chain between China and the Indochina Peninsula countries, and lays a new foundation for China and the Indochina Peninsula countries to participate in global value chain governance and raise their own voice. Since 2001, the "value chain trade" between China and the Indochina Peninsula countries, with the main characteristics of intra-industry trade or intra-product trade (intermediate goods trade) and offshore manufacturing, has achieved rapid growth.

Fourth, infrastructure connectivity is a priority area and basic foundation of the China–Indochina Peninsula Economic Corridor. Sound infrastructure, especially productive infrastructure, plays an important role in the growth of a country's economy, the improvement of TFP (total factor productivity) and the increase of per-capita income.⁶ According to the Economic Research Institute for ASEAN and East Asia (ERIA), Asia's infrastructure connectivity, including the China–Indochina Peninsula (ASEAN) connectivity, will increase the cumulative GDP of ASEAN countries by 42.08%, and that of the East Asian countries ("10+6") by

5.87% between 2021 and 2030. The reduction of supply chain barriers and non-tariff measures will increase the cumulative GDP of ASEAN countries by 31.19%, and that of the East Asian countries by 7.76%.[7]

Fifth, trade and investment facilitation is an important area of the China–Indochina Peninsula Economic Corridor. Based on the upgraded version of the China–ASEAN Free Trade Area (FTA), with the RCEP negotiation as an opportunity, the process of trade liberalisation and investment facilitation within the framework of the China–Indochina Peninsula Economic Corridor will not only promote the improvement of the production network of East Asia and the construction of regional unified market, but will also provide a new impetus for the endogenous development of the East Asian economy, and give new connotations to and lay a new foundation for the construction of the China–ASEAN community of common destiny and the Maritime Silk Road.[8] In other words, economic returns and welfare effects of the China–Indochina Peninsula Economic Corridor should benefit more from the reduction of non-tariff barriers and the increase of output and factor income of industries with comparative advantage after trade and investment liberalisation. Taking the China–Indochina Peninsula Economic Corridor as the carrier, the process of trade liberalisation and investment facilitation within the framework of the upgraded version of China–ASEAN FTA and RCEP will create conditions and lay the foundation for the sustainable development of economic and trade relations, the sustainable growth of bilateral trade and mutual investment and the extension of value chain and supply chain between China and the Indochina Peninsula countries, and between China and ASEAN, and provide a new link paradigm for the cooperation to transform from utilising comparative advantage to creating comparative advantage between China and the Indochina Peninsula countries, and between China and ASEAN.

Latest development

Since China put forward the initiative of jointly building the Maritime Silk Road in 2013, the China–Indochina Peninsula Economic Corridor has had many substantial results over 4 years of construction.

In the field of infrastructure connectivity, a group of the BRI pilot projects including the China–Thailand Railway, the China–Laos Railway, the Malaysia–Singapore High Speed Rail and the Southern Malaysia Railway has achieved initial results. Among them, the first phase of the China–Thailand Railway project, started on December 21, 2017, is Thailand's first standard-gauge high-speed railway. When completed, it will further enhance Thailand's status as a transportation hub in Indochina and promote effective synergy between the Belt and Road infrastructure connectivity and ASEAN connectivity. The China–Laos Railway, started on November 25, 2016, is expected to open to traffic by the end of 2021. The completion of the China–Laos Railway will effectively promote the synergy between Laos' strategy of transforming itself from a land-locked to a land-linked country and China's BRI, as well as the China–Laos Economic Corridor construction. In addition, the Malaysia East Coast Rail Line (ECRL) Project, started on August 9, 2017, will be the economic and railway transport artery running from east to west in Malaysia. Vietnam's first light rail, which is built by Chinese companies, will also be officially operational in 2018, becoming the first suburban railway in Hanoi and even in Vietnam. As a priority area of the BRI, the successful completion of the above-mentioned infrastructure connectivity projects will not only play an active role in promoting the improvement and reconstruction of regional production networks between China and the Indochina Peninsula countries, the construction of regional unified market, and the optimal allocation of trade and production factors, but also bring new opportunities for the sustainable economic growth of China and the Indochina Peninsula countries.

In the field of capacity cooperation, overseas industrial parks exemplified by the China–Malaysia "Two Countries, Twin Park" (Qinzhou Industrial Park and Guandan Industrial Park), the Thailand–China Rayong Industrial Park, the Cambodia Sihanoukville Special Economic Zone and the Vietnam Longjiang Industrial Park, and cross-border economic cooperation zones exemplified by the China–Vietnam Cross-border Economic Cooperation Zone, the China–Thailand (Chongzuo) Industrial Park and the China–Laos Mohan–Boten Cross-border Economic Cooperation Zone have become important platforms for the China–Indochina Peninsula Economic Corridor to strengthen capacity cooperation and explore new models of cross-border cooperation, involving multiple areas such as industry, technology, energy and environment cooperation. Among them, the Thailand–China Rayong Industrial Park, located at the Eastern Economic Corridor of Thailand, is the first industrial park that China has developed and built in Thailand. The China–Malaysia Qinzhou Industrial Park and the Malaysia–China Guandan Industrial Park have become the model of cooperation between China and Malaysia. The Cambodia Sihanoukville Special Economic Zone has become a model of the win–win cooperation between China and Cambodia. Taking the overseas industrial parks and the cross-border economic zones as platforms, the construction of the China–Indochina Peninsula Economic Corridor can not only extend the value chains and supply chains of enterprises in China and the Indochina Peninsula countries, but also maximise the synergy effect of China's opening-up strategy, the development strategies of the Indochina Peninsula countries and regional and subregional cooperation strategies.

In the field of trade and investment, on the basis of the upgraded China–ASEAN FTA, and with the opportunity of RCEP negotiation, China and the Indochina Peninsula countries have accelerated the process of trade liberalisation and investment facilitation. While reducing the cost of trade and investment, they further enhanced the connectivity of supply chains between China and the Indochina Peninsula countries, and created new conditions for the extension of value chains and the improvement of supply chains between China and the Indochina Peninsula countries. The trade volume between China and the Indochina Peninsula countries has increased from US$30.7 billion in 2001 to US$373.23 billion in 2017 (about 9.2% of China's total foreign trade, accounting for about 74.4% of that between China and ASEAN), with an annual growth of 16.9%, higher than China's annually growth of 3 percentage points of total foreign trade in the same period.[9]

Notes

1 *Vision and Actions on Jointly Building Silk Road Economic Belt and 21st Century Maritime Silk Road*, Xinhuanet, March 28, 2015. Retrieved January 20, 2018 from www.xinhuanet.com/world/2015-03/28/ c_1114793986.htm
2 *China–Indochina Economic Corridor Proposal issued in the Ninth Pan-Beibu Gulf Economic Cooperation Forum*, China News Network, May 26, 2016. Retrieved January 20, 2018 from www.chinanews.com/cj/2016/05-26/7884638.shtml
3 The *Five-Year Plan of Action of the Lancang-Mekong Cooperation (2018–2022)*. The Foreign Ministry Website, January 11, 2018. Retrieved January 20, 2018 from www.fmprc.gov.cn/web/zyxw/t1524881.shtml
4 Wang Jinbo, *The Belt and Road Economic Corridor and Regional Economic Integration: The Formation Mechanism and Function Evolution*. Social Sciences Academic Press, 2016.
5 Data Source: Ministry of Commerce of the People's Republic of China, National Bureau of Statistics, State Administration of Foreign Exchange: *Statistical bulletin of China's foreign direct investment (FDI) for 2016*, China Statistics Publishing House, first edition, September 2017.

6 Wang Jinbo, *From Corridor to Regional Economic Integration: The Formation Mechanism and Function Evolution of Economic Corridor along the B&R*, International Economic Cooperation, 2017.
7 Economic Institute for ASEAN and East Asia (ERIA), The comprehensive Asia Development Plan 2.0 (CADP 2.0): Infrastructure for connectivity and innovation, November 2015. www.eria.org/publications/key_reports/FY2014/No.04.html.
8 Wang Jinbo, *The BRI Construction and the ASEAN FTA Arrangement.* Social Sciences Academic Press, 2015.
9 Global Trade Database (Global Trade Atlas, GTA). Retrieved January 10, 2018 from www.worldtradestatistics.com/gta/

40
THE CHINA–PAKISTAN ECONOMIC CORRIDOR

Wang Jinbo

Concept explanation

"Corridor" is a special economic space form formed by economic factors continually gathering and spreading within a certain geographical area. As the flagship project of the BRI, the China–Pakistan Economic Corridor, north to Kashi, Xinjiang and south to the Gwadar Port, is a growth axis and development belt of complementary advantages and mutual benefits based on cooperation projects in the fields of major infrastructure construction and industry and people's livelihood, with the comprehensive transport corridor and industrial cooperation as the main axis, economic and trade and cultural exchanges as the engine. The Corridor is an important manifestation of the all-weather strategic cooperation between China and Pakistan.

The China–Pakistan Economic Corridor was first proposed by Chinese Premier Li Keqiang during his visit to Pakistan in May 2013, during which the two sides signed the *Memorandum of Understanding on Cooperation for the Long-term Plan on China–Pakistan Economic Corridor*. In March 2015, jointly issued by the National Development and Reform Commission, the Ministry of Foreign Affairs and the Ministry of Commerce, the *Vision and Actions on Jointly Building Silk Road Economic Belt and 21st Century Maritime Silk Road* clearly states that the China–Pakistan Economic Corridor is closely linked to the BRI construction, and cooperation should be further promoted to achieve greater progress.[1] During Chinese President Xi Jinping's visit to Pakistan in April 2015, the two sides signed 51 cooperation agreements and memoranda, of which nearly 40 were related to the construction of the China–Pakistan Economic Corridor, marking the full implementation of the China–Pakistan Economic Corridor. The two sides also agreed to take the China–Pakistan Economic Corridor as the guide and put emphasis on the Gwadar Port, energy, transport infrastructure and industrial cooperation to form the "1+4" economic cooperation layout.[2]

In December 2017, the two countries launched the *Long-term Plan on China–Pakistan Economic Corridor* in Islamabad, which effectively synergised the BRI and the Pakistani "2025 development Vision", marking the China–Pakistan Economic Corridor construction getting into the fast lane. According to the plan, the China–Pakistan Economic Corridor will be spatially divided into the core area and the radiation area with the layout of "one belt, three axes and multiple channels", and functionally divided into five key functional areas.[3] "One belt" refers to the belt area formed by the core area of the corridor, from Kashi in Xinjiang, China to

Gwadar Port in Pakistan. "Three axes" refers to the three east-west development axes—north from the Lahore to Peshawar, north centre from Sukkur to Quetta and south from Karachi to Gwadar Port. "Multiple channels" refers to main lines of railway and highway from Islamabad, capital of Pakistan, to Karachi and Gwadar Port. Five key functional areas, from south to north, are the Xinjiang Foreign Economic Zone, the Northern Border Logistics Trade Channel and Ecological Conservation Area, the Central and Eastern Plain Economic Zone, the Western Logistics channel Trade Area and the Southern Coastal Logistics Trade Area.

Details

The China–Pakistan Economic Corridor is a systematic project, involving many cooperation fields, such as infrastructure connectivity, energy, trade, investment, finance, industry, agricultural development and poverty alleviation, tourism, people's livelihood and people-to-people exchanges, etc.

First, infrastructure connectivity. Infrastructure connectivity is a priority cooperation area of the China–Pakistan Economic Corridor. Sound infrastructure, especially productive infrastructure such as roads, railways, ports, energy, electricity and telecommunications, play a very important role in the growth of a country's economy, total factor productivity and per-capita income. However, at least for now, basic conditions for the promotion of the infrastructure connectivity and cross-border supply chain quality with indicators of infrastructure, customs clearance facilitation, international transport, logistics capabilities, domestic logistics costs and transport time are still unable to meet the requirements of the free flow and integration of factors between the two countries. Inadequate and backward infrastructure is still an important factor restricting Pakistan's economy. Taking infrastructure connectivity as a priority area of the China–Pakistan Economic Corridor will not only help Pakistan raise the level of economic development, enhance productivity and resource allocation efficiency, improve public health, increase quality employment and promote industrial development, but also give full play to the comparative advantages and heterogeneous resource allocation capability of the two countries.

Second, energy. Energy shortage has always been a major problem of economic development of Pakistan, especially inadequate electricity infrastructure and constraints of electric power development. According to the International Energy Agency (IEA), in 2015 the total generating capacity of Pakistan was only 97.8 trillion watt-hours, which not only suffered from a large shortage of power supply, but also had a power loss rate of 17.1%, significantly higher than the world average of 8.1%.[4] According to estimates of the Asian Development Bank, power shortage results in an annual loss of US$13.5 billion in Pakistan, accounting for about 7% of its gross domestic product.[5] Therefore, in order to ease the energy shortage in Pakistan, energy cooperation is listed as the key cooperation area of the China–Pakistan Economic Corridor with over 10 energy and power infrastructure projects launched in the first place to promote Pakistan's economic development and social stability.

Third, economy and trade and industrial parks. Economic and trade and industrial cooperation is the key area of the China–Pakistan Economy Corridor. China and Pakistan complement each other in the fields of trade, investment, raw materials, equipment manufacturing, light industry, clean energy, green environmental protection and high-tech industries. It is exactly the different resource endowment and stages of development that lead to the great promotion of both international trade and investment based on comparative advantages and dynamic transfer of industries or sectors of industry between countries based on scale effect and spillovers effect for the two countries to transform from corridor to regional economic integration and regional infrastructure integration. As the world's largest cargo trade power and manufacturing power,

China's advantages in the scale of conventional manufacture and the regional advantages in the value chain trade and the synergy effect together form the unique advantages of China and Pakistan to jointly build the economic corridor. Trade, investment and capacity cooperation within the framework of the China–Pakistan Economic Corridor will provide conditions and lay foundation for the sustainable development of bilateral economic and trade relations, the sustainable growth of trade and mutual investment and the extension of the value chain and supply chain, thus providing a new link paradigm for the cooperation between China and Pakistan to transform from using comparative advantage to creating comparative advantage.

Latest development

Since April 20, 2015, over 20 early harvest projects have been under construction or completed along the China–Pakistan Economic Corridor, covering energy, transportation, ports and other fields, initially forming the "1+4" cooperation layout with the Gwadar Port, energy, transport infrastructure and industrial cooperation as the focus, thus becoming the BRI model projects.

First, in the field of infrastructure connectivity, early harvest projects of ports and transport infrastructure exemplified by the Gwadar Port, the change and expansion project of Karakoram Highway phase II (the section from Havelian to Thakot), the Peshawar–Karachi Expressway and the Karachi–Lahore Expressway (Sukkur–Multan section) have achieved initial results. Among them, the Gwadar Port, as a starting point of the China–Pakistan Economic Corridor and the flagship project, was officially opened to navigation on November 13, 2016. The Peshawar–Karachi Expressway, as the largest road infrastructure project of the China–Pakistan Economic Corridor, has also been under construction.[6] The change and expansion project of Karakoram Highway phase II was started in April 2016, marking the official launch of the construction of the land channel which runs through the north and south of Pakistan and connects China with Pakistan.

In addition, China and Pakistan also completed the upgrading of the Karachi–Peshawar Railway Line (ML-1) and the joint feasibility study of the Havelian land port construction project. The Karachi–Peshawar Railway Line (ML-1) runs north from Karachi through Lahore and Islamabad to White Sands, with a length of 1726 km. Havelian station is located in the northern end of the railway network in Pakistan, from where the upgraded Karachi–Peshawar Railway Line (ML-1) will run north through the China–Pakistan Khunjerab pass to Kashgar, Xinjiang in China.

Second, in the field of energy, the successful operation of the Karot Hydropower Station, the Karachi Nuclear Power Project, the Sahiwal Coal Fired Power Plant and the Qasim Coal Fired Power Plant, together with the official connection of 300 megawatts of the Punjab Photovoltaic Power Station Phase I to the national power grid, mark the rapid development of energy cooperation of the China–Pakistan Economic Corridor. Among them, Unit 1 of the Sahiwal Coal-Fired Power Plant was officially put into operation in May 2017, and when completed, it will become one of Pakistan's clean coal-fired coal power stations with the largest installed capacity. The Punjab Photovoltaic Power Station, which is invested by ZONERGY with a total investment of more than US$1.5 billion, has a total capacity of 900 MW. The project will be implemented in three phases, and when completed, it will be the largest single photovoltaic power generation project in the world, providing 1.3 billion kilowatt-hours of clean electricity for Pakistan every year. As the first hydropower project of the China–Pakistan Economic Corridor, the construction of the main part of the Karot Hydropower Station was started in October 2016 and is planned to be put into operation in 2020. In addition, the Jhimpir Wind Power Project with an installed capacity of 500 megawatts, the Kohala Hydropower

Project with an installed capacity of 1100 MW, the Sachal Wind Power Project, the Bahawalpur Single Solar Power Plant Project and the DAWOOD Wind Power Project have also begun. The above-mentioned priority projects of the China–Pakistan Economic Corridor, if completed as scheduled, will greatly ease the current state of energy shortages and constraints on Pakistan's economy.

Finally, in the economic and trade and industrial cooperation domain, the construction of overseas parks, which is represented by the Gwadar Port Free Zone, has achieved remarkable results. As a landmark project of the BRI construction, the Gwadar Free Zone Phase I was formally put into operation on January 29, 2018. The completion of the Gwadar Free Zone will strongly promote economic and trade, capacity and investment cooperation between the two countries within the framework of the China–Pakistan Economic Corridor and enhance the level of bilateral economic and trade cooperation. According to the Chinese customs, the bilateral trade between China and Pakistan reached US$20.16 billion in 2017, 14 times of that in 2001 with an average annual growth of 18.1%, making China the largest trade partner of Pakistan.[7] According to the Chinese Ministry of Commerce, by the end of 2016, China's accumulated direct investment to Pakistan has amounted to US$4.759 billion, accounting for 12.2% of total foreign direct investment of Pakistan, twice that in 2012 before the concept of the China–Pakistan Economic Corridor was proposed, with an annual increase of 20.8%. China has become an important source of foreign investment of Pakistan, while investment has already become an important way to build the Belt and Road and the China–Pakistan Economic Corridor.[8] In addition, in order to promote the process of trade liberalisation and investment facilitation of the China–Pakistan Economic Corridor, China and Pakistan launched the second phase of the China–Pakistan FTA negotiations. By September 2017, eight meetings have been held during the second phase of the China–Pakistan FTA negotiations, at which the two sides carried out a series of talks on a wide range of issues on trade in goods, trade in services, investment, inspection and quarantine, electronic data interchange systems, etc. so as to improve bilateral trade liberalisation.[9] The process of trade liberalisation and investment facilitation within the framework of the China–Pakistan FTA will bring a new institutional guarantee for the two countries to deepen economic and trade cooperation.

Notes

1 The *Vision and Actions on Jointly Building Silk Road Economic Belt and 21st Century Maritime Silk Road*. Xinhuanet, March 28, 2015. Retrieved January 20, 2018 from www.xinhuanet.com/world/2015-03/28/ c_1114793986.htm
2 *Joint Statement on Establishing All-weather Strategic Co-operative Partnership between the People's Republic of China and the Islamic Republic of Pakistan*. Ministry of Foreign Affairs website, April 21, 2015. Retrieved January 10, 2018 from www.fmprc.gov.cn/web/ziliao_674904/zt_674979/ Ywzt_675099/2015nzt/xjpcxbjstwlhy_675021/zxxx_675023/t1256274.shtml
3 The *China–Pakistan Economic Corridor entering the fast lane in the new era*. Guangmingnet, December 24, 2017. Retrieved January 10, 2018 from http://news.gmw.cn/2017-12/24/content_27170780.htm
4 International Energy Agency (2015), Electricity Information 2015, IEA Paris, http://dx.doi.org/10.1787/electricity-2015-en
5 Quoted from Li Hui, "Pakistan to Open A New Era of Energy," *China Energy News*, April 27, 2015, 7th edition.
6 "Building the Belt and Road: Concept, Practice and China's Contribution," Xinhuanet, May 10, 2017. Retrieved January 10, 2018 from www.xinhuanet.com/politics/2017-05/10/c_1120951928.html
7 Source: Global Trade Database (Global Trade Atlas, GTA), Retrieved January 20, 2018 from www.worldtradestatistics.com/gta

8 Source: Ministry of Commerce of the People's Republic of China, National Bureau of Statistics, State Administration of Foreign Exchange: *Statistical bulletin of China's foreign direct investment (FDI) for 2016*, China Statistics Publishing House, first edition September 2017.
9 "The eighth round of the second phase of China–Pakistan FTZ negotiations held in Beijing," China FTZ Service Network, September 14, 2017. Retrieved January 20, 2018 from http://fta.mofcom.gov.cn/article/chinahaihehui/haihehuinews/201612/33882_1.html

41

BCIM ECONOMIC CORRIDOR

Wang Jinbo

Concept explanation

The Bangladesh–China–India–Myanmar (BCIM) Economic Corridor starts north from Yunnan, China (Kunming) through Myanmar, India and Bangladesh to the Indian Ocean. The corridor connects the three regions of East Asia, South Asia and South East Asia and links up the Pacific and Indian oceans, possessing unique regional advantages and geographical advantages. Among the countries along the corridor, Myanmar has unique position advantage, located at the junction of the three geopolitical plates of South Asia, South East Asia and East Asia. India is the largest economy in South Asia and China's largest trade partner in this region. Bangladesh is well located at the intersection of the three major economies of China, India and ASEAN. Because Bangladesh, China, India and Myanmar are all developing countries, and Myanmar and Bangladesh belong to the least developed countries, it is necessary for the four countries, especially China and India, to take the opportunity of joint construction of the BCIM Economic Corridor to put comparative advantages, location advantages, energy resources and the demographic dividend into development advantages.

In May 2013, a joint initiative of building the BCIM Economic Corridor of the leaders of China and India got positive responses from the two governments of Bangladesh and Myanmar. In December 2013, the first meeting of the Joint Working Group for the BCIM Economic Corridor took place in Kunming, China. The parties involved signed the minutes of the meeting and a plan on joint research on the corridor, formally launching intergovernmental cooperation.[1] In December 2014, the second meeting of the Joint Working Group for the BCIM Economic Corridor took place in Cox's Bazar, Bangladesh, at which the four countries discussed the prospects, priorities, and development direction for the construction of the corridor.[2] The *Vision and Actions on Jointly Building Silk Road Economic Belt and 21st Century Maritime Silk Road* issued in March 2015 clearly pointed out that the BCIM Economic Corridor and the Belt and Road construction had close ties, and cooperation should be promoted to achieve more progress.[3] In April 2017, the third meeting of the Joint Working Group for the BCIM Economic Corridor was held in Calcutta, India, at which the representatives of the four countries reached a consensus on exchanges and cooperation of key areas, such as connectivity, energy, investment and financing, trade in goods and trade in services, investment facilitation, sustainable development and people-to-people exchanges, and agreed to launch an intergovernmental framework to arrange consultations after the joint research report is completed.[4]

Details

The BCIM Economic Corridor is a systematic project covering multiple fields of infrastructure connectivity, energy, industry and investment, trade and economy, etc.

First, infrastructure connectivity is a priority area of the BCIM Economic Corridor. Sound infrastructure, especially productive infrastructure such as railways, roads, ports, energy, electricity, telecommunications and finance, play a very important role in economic growth, improving total factor productivity and raising per-capita income levels for the BCIM countries.[5] According to the World Economic Forum (WEF) Global Competitiveness Report, in 2017, India and Bangladesh's infrastructure competitiveness index were 4.2 and 2.9 among the BCIM countries, ranking 66th and 111th, respectively, in 137 countries around the world.[6] According to the World Bank, among the BCIM countries, the electricity convenience index of Bangladesh and Myanmar is only 16.97 and 52.52, respectively, ranking 151st and 185th in 190 countries and regions in the world.[7] It shows that inadequate infrastructure, especially inadequate electricity, greatly restricts the economic development and per-capita welfare improvement of Bangladesh and Myanmar. Infrastructure connectivity within the BCIM Economic Corridor framework has brought a good opportunity for the above-mentioned countries to improve their infrastructure.

Second, industrial and investment cooperation is a key area of the BCIM Economic Corridor. Due to their different levels of economic development and stages of development, the four countries are differentiated in industrial structure, industrial base and international competitiveness. The four countries complement each other in the areas of trade in services, investment, high-end manufacturing and infrastructure construction, and there is still a great deal of room for cooperation in improving trade structure and expanding the scale of trade and investment among them. Industrial and investment cooperation between the four countries within the BCIM Economic Corridor framework will provide a good opportunity and platform for China and Myanmar, China and Bangladesh, and China and India to strengthen industrial cooperation and form new production networks. With overseas industrial parks and cross-border economic cooperation zones as the platforms, China's advanced technology and competitive industrial capacity can make up for the industrial development gap of Bangladesh and Myanmar in many areas. Cooperation in areas of service trade and high-end manufacturing between China and India creates new conditions and brings new opportunities for the two countries to continue to participate in international division of labor and improve the position of both countries and emerging economies in the global value chain.

Third, economic and trade cooperation is an important part of the BCIM Economic Corridor construction. The economic and trade cooperation within the framework of the BCIM Economic Corridor between the four countries, which are endowed with abundant resources and unique advantages, can not only transform the comparative advantage, location advantage, resource advantage and demographic dividend of the four countries into development advantages, but also raise the total factor productivity level of the four countries through the technology spillover effect, the trade creation effect and the industrial structure effect of foreign direct investment. Trade liberalisation and investment facilitation between China and India within the RCEP framework will create new conditions and lay a new foundation for the sustainable development in the economic and trade relations, the sustainable growth in bilateral trade and mutual investment and the extension of the value chain and supply chain. According to the United Nations Conference on Trade and Development (UNCTAD), in 2016, the total trade in services of China and India amounted to US$661.502 billion and US$295.555 billion, respectively, together accounting for about 9.89% of total global trade in services.[8] The two countries hold a very important position in regional and global trade in services. However, services trade and investment ties between China and India are much looser than that with other countries in the world, which have gained a good momentum. This asymmetric pattern means that there is still a lot of room for further trade in services and investment between China and India within the framework of the BCIM Economic Corridor.

Latest development

Since 2013 when China proposed the BRI, substantial progress has been made in infrastructure connectivity, energy, industry, economy and trade, investment and many other fields along the BCIM Economic Corridor.

First of all, in the area of infrastructure connectivity, the BRI priority projects represented by the China–Myanmar Crude Oil Pipeline Project, the China–Myanmar International Railway and the Bangladesh Padma Bridge have achieved initial results. The China–Myanmar Crude Oil Pipeline Project was formally put into operation on April 10, 2017. With a total length of 771 km, it is the pilot project of the BRI carried out in Myanmar, as well as the landmark project of infrastructure connectivity along the BCIM Economic Corridor.[9] The last section of the China–Myanmar International Railway in China, namely the Darui (Dali–Ruili) Railway, was put into construction in 2015. Once completed, the China–Myanmar International Railway will become a major international channel for China to connect South East Asia and South Asia, and will also play a positive role in promoting economic and trade cooperation and people-to-people exchanges between China and the BCIM Economic Corridor countries. As a pivot traffic project of the BRI, the Bangladesh Padma Bridge across the Padma River (the Ganges) and the 215-km long rail link project with the bridge as the node were officially signed and started in August 2016. When completed, the bridge will connect Dhaka, the capital with 21 regions in southern Bangladesh, while the railway link will become one of the important channels which connect China with the Pan-Asian Railway.

In the field of energy cooperation, the first independent financing project of the Asian Infrastructure Investment Bank (AIIB), namely the Bangladesh Power Grid Network Strengthening Project, has been officially put into construction, which will benefit more than 12.5 million rural residents when completed.[10] The Payra Coal-Fired Power Plant, the largest coal-fired power plant in Bangladesh built by Chinese enterprises, was started in 2016, with a total installed capacity of 660 megawatts, accounting for 1/10 of total installed capacity of Bangladesh at present. When put into operation in 2019, it will dramatically improve electricity self-sufficiency of Bangladesh.[11] The China–Myanmar joint venture Thaketa Gas-Fired Combined Cycle Power Plant was started in May 2016, marking a new development in China–Myanmar clean energy cooperation.[12] When completed, the power plant will effectively improve the power generation capacity of Yangon and relieve the power shortage in Myanmar. In addition, the Myanmar North–South Backbone Network Connection and Transmission and Transformation Project with a total length of 300 km was started in November 2017 and planned to be put into operation in 2019. As one of the key projects of the BRI, the project will deliver clean energy from north to the Southern Load Centre, effectively solving the problem of energy transmission in Myanmar.[13]

In the field of industrial cooperation, the construction of industrial cooperation platforms represented by the China–Myanmar Border Economic Cooperation Zone and the Chittagong Chinese Economic and Industrial Park in Bangladesh have achieved remarkable results. On May 16, 2017, under the witness of Chinese Prime Minister Li Keqiang and Myanmar State Counsellor Aung San Suu Kyi, China and Myanmar formally signed the *Memorandum* of Understanding Between Ministry of Commerce of the People's Republic of China and Ministry of Commerce of the Republic of the Union of Myanmar On the Establishment of China–Myanmar Border Economic Cooperation Zone, which is China's third bilateral border economic cooperation zone within the framework of the BRI after the China–Kazakhstan Huoerguosi International Border Cooperation Centre and the China–Laos Mohan–Boten Economic Cooperation Zone. "The China–Myanmar Border Economic Cooperation Zone has created a new way of economic and trade cooperation and a new mode of border cooperation between China and Myanmar, which is conducive to deepening China–Myanmar economic and trade cooperation."[14] On November 19, 2017, at a joint press conference with Aung San Suu Kyi, the State Counsellor and the Foreign Minister of Myanmar, Chinese Foreign Minister Wang Yi for the first time proposed that China would like to discuss with Myanmar about building the China–Myanmar Economic Corridor, which is north to Yunnan, China, south to Mandalay, east to Yangon New Town and west to Kyaukpyu Special Economic Zone, blazing a new path for China and Myanmar to jointly build the BCIM Economic Corridor and the Belt and Road.[15] The Chittagong Chinese Economic and Industrial Park in Bangladesh, which is Bangladesh's first special economic park covering chemical, pharmaceutical, clothing, telecommunications, agricultural machinery, electron and electric, information technology and many other industries, will create 100,000 jobs in Bangladesh.[16]

In the field of economic and trade cooperation, the trade and investment between China and the BCIM Economic Corridor countries have been greatly improved since 2013 when China proposed the BRI. According to China Customs, the bilateral trade volume between China and Bangladesh, China and India and China and Burma in 2017 amounted to US$16.109 billion, US$84.439 billion and US$12.389 billion, respectively, increased by 13.8%, 4.9% and 12.2% annually compared with years before 2012 (in which the BRI was initiated).[17] According to the statistics of Chinese Ministry of Commerce, China's investment in Bangladesh, India and Myanmar totalled US$225 million, US$3.108 billion and US$4.62 billion, respectively, by the end of 2016, registering an annual average growth rate of 13.9%, 21.6% and 8.4% compared with years before 2012 (in which the BRI was initiated).[18] Foreign investment is becoming an important way for the four countries to promote the construction of the BRI.

Notes

1 *The first meeting of the Joint Working Group for the BCIM Economic Corridor took place in Kunming.* The Chinese Government website, December 20, 2013. Retrieved February 10, 2018 from www.gov.cn/gzdt/2013-12/20/content_2551850.htm
2 *The Joint Working Group for the BCIM Economic Corridor discuss to strengthen cooperation and connectivity.* The Chinese Government website, December 19, 2014. Retrieved February 10, 2018 from www.gov.cn/xinwen/2014-12/19/content_2794163.htm
3 Authorized Release: *Promote the Vision and Actions on Jointly Building Silk Road Economic Belt and 21st-Century Maritime Silk Road.* Xinhua News Agency, March 28, 2015. Retrieved February 10, 2018 from www.xinhuanet.com/world/2015-03/28/c_1114793986.htm
4 *The third meeting of the Joint Working Group for the BCIM Economic Corridor held in India.* Xinhuanet, April 26, 2017. Retrieved February 10, 2018 from www.xinhuanet.com/world/2017-04/26/c_1120880101.htm
5 Wang Jinbo, "From corridor to regional economic integration: the formation mechanism and function evolution of economic corridor along the B&R," *International Economic Cooperation*, 2017, No. 2, pp. 9–15.
6 *The Global Competitiveness Report 2017–2018.* World Economic Forum (WEF), www3.weforum.org/docs/GCR2017-2018/05FullReport/TheGlobalCompetitivenessReport2017-2018.pdf.
7 *Doing Business 2018.* World Bank, www.doingbusiness.org/~/media/WBG/DoingBusiness/Documents/Annual-Reports/English/db2018-full-report.pdf.

8 Source: UNCTAD, http://unctadstat.unctad.org/wds/ReportFolders/reportFolders.aspxsCS_ChosenLang=en
9 "China–Myanmar Crude Oil Pipeline Project Officially Put Into Operation," Xinhua News Agency, April 10 2017. Retrieved February 1, 2018 from www.xinhuanet.com/2017-04/10/c_1120784084.htm
10 "AIIB to finance the rural Bangladesh millions of new electricity meters," Xinhuanet, January 22, 2018. Retrieved February 1, 2018 from www.xinhuanet.com/2018-01/22/c_129796228.htm
11 "China is our reliable partner on the road of chasing dreams," People.cn, June 15, 2017. Retrieved February 1, 2018 from http://world.people.com.cn/n1/2017/0615/c1002-29340168.html
12 "The China–Myanmar joint venture gas-fired power plant inaugurated in Yangon," People.cn, May 13, 2016. Retrieved February 10, 2018 from http://energy.people.com.cn/n1/2016/0513/c71661-28347628.html
13 "Significant progress achieved in electricity and energy cooperation between China and Myanmar," People.cn, November 11, 2017. Retrieved February 10, 2018 from http://world.people.com.cn/n1/2017/1111/c1002-29640093.html
14 *The Ministry of Commerce of the People's Republic of China and the Ministry of Commerce of the Republic of the Union of Myanmar Signed the Memorandum of Understanding On the Establishment of China–Myanmar Border Economic Cooperation Zone.* China Ministry of Commerce website, May 7, 2017. Retrieved February 10, 2018 from www.mofcom.gov.cn/article/ae/ai/201705/20170502575934.shtml
15 "China proposes the initiative of building the China–Myanmar Economic Corridor," Xinhuanet, November 20, 2017. Retrieved February 10, 2018 from www.xinhuanet.com/silkroad/2017-11/20/c_1121982554.htm
16 *China and Bangladesh signed agreements on industrial parks development.* China Ministry of Commerce website, June 24, 2016. Retrieved February 10, 2018 from http://bd.mofcom.gov.cn/article/jmxw/201606/20160601345559.shtml
17 Data Source: Global Trade Atlas (GTA), www.gtis.com/gta_3d/default.cfm
18 Source: China's Ministry of Commerce, National Bureau of Statistics, State Administration of Foreign Exchange: *Statistical bulletin of China's foreign direct investment (FDI) for 2016.*

PART VII

Theories and concepts of the foreign affairs with Chinese characteristics

42
MAJOR-COUNTRY DIPLOMACY WITH CHINESE CHARACTERISTICS

Zhong Feiteng

Since 2012, especially after the concept of major-country diplomacy with Chinese characteristics initiated at the end of November 2014, Chinese diplomatic ideas and endeavours have been focused on shaping this new kind of relationship. The international community agrees that China has already been an important force in contemporary international community, but many countries are still not clear about how China can use its power. The misunderstanding and misconception of some countries not only result from ideological bias but also, more importantly, from the lack of theoretical knowledge.

The formation of the concept of major-country diplomacy with Chinese characteristics

Since reform and opening up, China's diplomacy has been mainly used to protect three kinds of national interests—national sovereignty, security and development interests. The focus of diplomatic work in each phase has been determined by the major strategic goals of different development stages.

In 2008, the international financial crisis quickly changed the international pattern, and the speed of China's rise was significantly accelerated. All these have promoted the development of China's diplomatic work. At the Eleventh Diplomatic Envoy Conference, President Hu Jintao declared that China "has stood at a new historical starting point" and believed that "at present and in the coming period of time, diplomatic work must focus on responding effectively to the impact of the international financial crisis to maintain a relatively fast economic growth and guaranteeing faster growth, people's well-being and social stability".[1] It is the unprecedented international financial crisis of a hundred years that has made China's leaders realise that China's international status, international responsibilities and national interests are all at their unprecedented level.

The 18th National Congress of the Communist Party of China, held in November 2012, responded to the trend of the time and proposed some new diplomatic ideas, including "the initiation of a community with a shared future" and "the establishment of a long-term, stable, and healthy major-country diplomacy". For the countries that have long lived in the Western-dominated international order, the contents of the two concepts have great significance.

The Great Rejuvenation of the Chinese Nation was the core of the administration after Xi Jinping served as President in China. On November 29, 2012, less than 2 weeks after his visiting the "Revival Road" exhibition, General Secretary Xi Jinping proposed that "the Great Rejuvenation of the Chinese Nation is the greatest dream of the Chinese nation in modern times".[2] On the one hand, Xi Jinping believes that at this time, China is ever closer to the goal of the Great Rejuvenation of the Chinese Nation than any other period in history. The goals are to finish building a moderately prosperous society in all aspects by the time the CPC celebrates its centenary in 2021 and to turn China into a modern socialist country by the time the PRC celebrates its centenary in 2049. On the other hand, Xi Jinping also emphasised that "backwards brings bullying from other countries, and only through development can a country become strong" and we must firmly follow the path of socialism with Chinese characteristics.

At the eve of the Central Conference on Foreign Affairs convened by Xi Jinping, China's international status has changed significantly. In early October 2014, a piece of news from the International Monetary Fund (IMF) went viural among major international media.

According to the prediction of IMF, China's economic gross, measured in terms of "purchasing power parity" (PPP), will reach 17.6 trillion international dollars in 2014, compared with 17.4 trillion of the United States.[3] Although China will overtake the United States in economic venue someday in the future, such a quick speed shocked global public opinion. Xi Jinping pointed out at the Central Conference on Foreign Affairs that "the world's trend to multi-polarization will not change" and China "has entered a crucial stage for the Great Rejuvenation of the Chinese Nation".[4]

At the CPC Central Committee's Foreign Affairs Conference, Xi Jinping proposed that "China must adopt major country diplomacy with its own characteristics".[5] After this assertion was made, it quickly became the core of China's diplomatic works. At the end of October 2013, the CPC Central Committee convened a symposium on peripheral diplomatic works in the new era, laying out the strategic objectives, basic guidelines and overall blueprint for peripheral diplomatic works in the next 5–10 years. The meeting called for more vigorous efforts to promote the peripheral diplomacy. The change from "working hard" on peripheral diplomacy to "major-country diplomacy with Chinese characteristics" shows that China's diplomacy has entered a new stage.

From the peripheral diplomacy of "working hard" to "the diplomacy of a big country with Chinese characteristics", it can be said that China's diplomacy has entered a new stage, and the overall goal of diplomacy has been set to serve the Great Rejuvenation of the Chinese Nation. This goal, obviously, goes far beyond the common goal of serving national development.

The main content of the major-country diplomacy with Chinese characteristics

In China's foreign relations, the ideas of classification among neighbouring countries, developed countries, developing countries have been used since the 1990s. Peripheral diplomacy was a prominent innovation in the 1990s. Soon after the end of Cold War, the relationship between China and the West was at a low, and the collapse of the Soviet Union also brought tremendous changes in China's surroundings. These called for new concepts to coordinate new diplomatic work. At that time, the development of the East Asia region, such as the Asia–Pacific Economic Cooperation (APEC) and ASEAN, was in full swing. These have great influence on the formation of multilateralism in China's diplomacy. The new thinking of the diplomacy of major countries also had new meaning at that stage. In particular, a new type of partnership with Russia was established. It can be said that the tremendous changes of world pattern and the international situation have laid the foundation for the flourishing China to forge a new kind of diplomacy.

At the Central Conference on Foreign Affairs in 2014, major-country diplomacy with Chinese characteristics was embodied in three principles. First, we should uphold the CPC's leadership and socialism with Chinese characteristics. We will stick to our development path, social system, cultural tradition and values. Second, we should continue to follow the independent foreign policy of peace, always pursue the development of the country and the nation by relying on ourselves, and follow our own path unswervingly. While pursuing peaceful development, we will never relinquish our legitimate rights and interests, or allow China's core interests to be impaired. Third, we will promote democracy in international relations, and uphold the Five Principles of Peaceful Coexistence. We are firm in our position that all countries, regardless of their size, strength and level of development, are equal members of the international community and that the destiny of the world should be decided by people of all countries. We will uphold international justice and, in particular, speak up for developing countries.[6] The three "Persistence" not only summed up the relationship among the CPC, socialism and China's diplomacy, but also pointed out that China's diplomacy relies on itself rather than foreign countries. In addition, China still gives high priority to the relationship with developing countries that hold the majority of the world's population and largely remain poor. Theoretically speaking, the goal of a socialist country is to give all people happy lives. If the majority of people remain poor, it is hard to say that there will be real peace and development in this world.

Major-country diplomacy with Chinese characteristics is mainly reflected in two aspects: "Chinese characteristics" and "major-country diplomacy". "Chinese characteristics" refer to the path of socialism with Chinese characteristics under the leadership of the CPC. As for major-country diplomacy, it mainly means the diplomacy carried out by China after being a major country. Although major-country diplomacy was once used to describe China's diplomacy in the past, the concept at that time mainly referred to foreign relations with a certain group of foreign countries, namely major countries, which together with developing countries, neighbouring countries and others form the classification system of China's foreign affairs. Since "major-country diplomacy" was officially proposed, it has become the basic point of all works in China's foreign affairs.

China's major-country diplomacy provides new ideas to the definition of major country and diplomacy. Prominent change has been witnessed in the understanding of the concept of major country. Major country, in China's diplomacy, often refers to a country with a big territory and population. However, the major country raised in 2014 at the Central Conference on Foreign Affairs was not just a territorial and demographic concept. The two concepts were almost constants, which has always been the case since the founding of the PRC. Even when China resumed a permanent member's seat of the UN Security Council back in the 1970s, it did not consider itself to be a major country comparable to the European countries and the United States. However, when Xi Jinping proposed "major-country diplomacy with Chinese characteristics", China's status as a major country reached an unprecedented high; that is, it has moved closer to the Great Rejuvenation of the Chinese Nation and closer to the centre of the world stage. Besides territory and population, China's international influence on the political, economic and military sectors is second only to the United States'.

At the same time, China also increased the number of major countries in its diplomatic practice. In the past, major countries mainly referred to a few developed Western countries. At the Central Foreign Affairs Working Conference, Xi Jinping proposed that "we should manage our relations with other major countries well, build a sound and stable framework of major-country relationship, and expand cooperation with other major countries in the developing world".

In other words, there are now two types of countries in the views of China's major-country diplomacy: the traditional Western developed countries and the major countries in developing world, in this context, referring to a group of rising developing countries represented by the BRICS countries.

In particular, major-country diplomacy with Chinese characteristics attaches great importance to a more balanced approach to upholding principles and pursuing interests. In other words, China is a major country that not only values materialism, but also cherishes morality, responsibility and value to a certain degree. The Great Rejuvenation of the Chinese Nation will not only make the country a top-level major country in economy, military and politics, but also makes new contributions to the progress and development of human society in civilisation and cultural aspects.

The practical and theoretical significance of major-country diplomacy with Chinese characteristics

From the perspective of China's foreign relations, "major-country diplomacy with Chinese characteristics" serves as a blueprint. All diplomatic works that China is committed to should be guided by "major-country diplomacy with Chinese characteristics" to better serve the Great Rejuvenation of the Chinese Nation. Therefore, it is not difficult to understand China's resolve and principle in maintaining its own legitimate rights and interests, in peripheral regions particularly. One important problem is to safeguard China's rights and interests in the South China Sea. The other is to maintain the stability of the Korean Peninsula. To a certain extent, it can be said that "major-country diplomacy with Chinese characteristics" is vividly reflected in the expansion of China's maritime interests and overseas rights and interests.

BRI has become the most vibrant practice of the diplomatic ideology of major-country diplomacy with Chinese characteristics. The Western community initially thought the BRI to be the Chinese version of the "Marshall Plan", indicating that China is trying to seek hegemony in Eurasia. However, the Chinese government repeatedly stated in its general principle of diplomacy that China has no intention for hegemony and will not interfere in the internal affairs of other countries. In May 2017, the first summit of Belt and Road Forum for International Cooperation was held in Beijing, with active support and participation by more than 140 countries and more than 80 international organisations. This shows that BRI, an institutional platform for promoting globalisation and cooperation initiated by China in the new era, has been welcomed by most countries in the world.

Global governance is another diplomacy with widespread impact in practice. The expectation of the major-country diplomacy pushes the Chinese government's active engagement in global governance to take its share of responsibility as a responsible major country. For example, China has played an active role in the reform of the World Bank, IMF and other institutions. On December 25, 2015, the Asian Infrastructure Investment Bank, a new kind of multilateral developing bank initiated by China in the twenty-first century, was formally established featuring professionality, efficiency and probity. On October 1, 2016, the RMB officially joined the IMF's Special Drawing Right (SDR) currency basket. These two events marked the turning point in China's participation in global governance.

Notes

1 Hu Jintao, *Selected Works of Hu Jintao* (the third volume). Beijing: People's Press, 2016, pp. 235, 238–239.
2 Xi Jinping, *The Governance of China*, Beijing: Foreign Language Press, 2014, p. 36.

3 "China surpasses US as world's largest economy based on key measure," October 8, 2014, www.rt.com/business/194264-china-surpass-us-gdp
4 Xi Jinping, *The Governance of China II*, Beijing: Foreign Language Press, 2017, p. 442.
5 Xi Jinping, *The Governance of China II*, Beijing: Foreign Language Press, 2017, pp. 441–444.
6 Xi Jinping: *The Governance of China II*, Beijing: Foreign Language Press, 2017, p. 443.

43
NEW-TYPE INTERNATIONAL RELATIONS

Zhong Feiteng

In October 2017, the report of the 19th CPC National Congress clearly stated that China will "promote the building of new-type international relations featuring mutual respect, fairness and justice, and win–win cooperation". Although this is not the first statement about the "new-type international relations" in an important document, the change in the attributes of "new-type international relations" is still very noticeable. On the one hand, mutual respect, fairness and justice were only used in statements about the relations with a part of countries in a part of China's diplomatic policies in the past. A systematic perception was created this time. On the other hand, after the Party's 18th National Congress, China has repeatedly used "new-type" to summarise the international situation and the new meaning of China's diplomacy. The contrast of China's leading comprehensive national power and US and other Western countries' declining willingness to shoulder international responsibilities raises global concern about the future trend of the international order.

Is China's "new-type international relations" a revolutionary plan? Or is China trying to build a world order with itself at the centre? Or does it mean that other countries also have the opportunity to participate in this emerging new order? All these issues require further understanding.

The formation of the new-type international relations

The Sino-Soviet Treaty of Friendship and Mutual Assistance signed in February 1950 was a legal definition of the new relationship between the two countries. The text of the treaty was very short, but it is very powerful, because it was a treaty of alliance. In addition, Article 5 also stipulates the principles of "equality, mutual benefit, mutual respect for national sovereignty and territorial integrity, and non-interference in other's internal affairs". However, practice shows that even countries with the same social system may not be able to develop relations in accordance with the contents signed in the treaty. In 1979, neither country renewed the treaty after it expired. The development of the Sino-Soviet relations during the Cold War period completely changed the Chinese leaders' views on alliance. Therefore, unlike the United States and other Western countries, China recognised that alliance relations were unreliable and would cause troubles. Hence, since the 10th National Congress of the CPC in 1982, China's foreign policy evolved into an independent and peaceful diplomacy.

Since the 1990s, the development of Sino-Russian relations has once again demonstrated that, under the dramatic evolution of the international situation, a mature and stable new-type relationship can also be established between two hostile big powers. China and Russia started to resolve the border issues left over by history and enhanced strategic mutual trust. In July 2001, the two sides signed the *Treaty of Good Neighborliness, Friendship and Cooperation* and set the new relations between the two countries featuring "three no": non-alliances, non-confrontation and not pointing at any third party. Therefore, unlike the ideological alliance relationship pointing at third parties in Cold War, the Sino-Russian relations in the twenty-fist century are based on the new understanding of their own national interests. After the signing of the treaty, President Jiang Zemin spoke at Moscow University, talking about "new-type state relations" three times, and adding "complete equality, mutually beneficial cooperation, good neighborliness and friendship" on the basis of "three no".[1] Therefore, from the perspective of China, "equality" and "mutual benefit" have been part of China's diplomatic principles since the 1950s. Chinese people's persistence in these principles and concepts has stood the test of quite a few major events, and it has become part of China's diplomatic culture.

On March 23, 2013, when speaking at the Moscow Institute of International Relations, Xi Jinping proposed the concept of "new-type international relations". When proposing this idea, he "Facing with profound changes in international situation and objective requirements of all countries in the world to help each other, all countries should jointly promote the establishment of a new-type international relations centered on cooperation and win–win results. We will uphold world peace and promote common development".[2] At the time, the definition of this concept just included "win–win cooperation" and there was no "mutual respect, fairness, and justice", even though these words appeared in the same speech.

In November 2014, at the Central Conference on Foreign Affairs, Xi Jinping emphasised that "we need to promote the establishment of new-type international relations centering on win–win cooperation, adhere to an open strategy of mutual benefit and win–win results and reflect the concept of win–win cooperation in politics, economy, security, culture and other aspects of cooperation in foreign affairs".[3] Since then, building a new-type international relationship centring on win–win cooperation has become an important guiding ideology for China's diplomacy.

In September 2015, when President Xi Jinping attended series of summits celebrating the 70th anniversary of the founding of the United Nations in New York, he proposed in the United Nations forum that "we need to inherit and carry forward the themes and principles of the UN Charter by building new-type international relations centering on cooperation and win–win results and a community with a shared future".[4] In September 2016, Xi Jinping pointed out during the 35th collective study of the 18th Central Political Bureau of the Communist Party of China that China "resolutely upholds the international order with the themes and principles of the UN Charter as the core ... to promote reforms in global governance concerning unfair and unreasonable arrangements".[5] In his speech, Xi Jinping constantly emphasised that some of the new ideas put forward by China have been widely welcomed by the international community. In the coming period of time, we should continue to elaborate on ideas of China to the international community. However, we must adopt a cooperative rather than a confrontational approach. We must adhere to the principle of achieving shared growth through discussion and collaboration, continue to seek maximum common interests and guide all parties to reach consensus. From this time on, "fair" and "reasonable" together with other words began to appear in the statements of new-type international relations.

In January 2017, at the UN headquarters in Geneva, Xi Jinping pointed out: "major countries must respect each other's core interests and major concerns, manage and control contradictions and differences, and strive to build new relationships featuring non-confrontation, mutual respect, and win–win cooperation".[6] On November 10, Xi Jinping stressed at the APEC CEO Summit in Da Nang, Vietnam that China "will attach great importance to a more balanced approach to uphold principles and pursue interests, actively develop global partnerships, expand the convergence of interests with other countries, and promote the building of new-type international relations featuring mutual respect, fairness and justice, and win–win cooperation".[7] This was Xi Jinping's first visit abroad after the 19th National Congress. It was also the first time that he elaborated to the US President Mr Trump on China's diplomatic concept of a new journey for 2050 on a multilateral occasion.

The main content of the new-type international relations

From the proposal of "new-type international relations" at the beginning of 2013 to the speech at the UN Headquarters in Geneva, the core phrase of "new-type international relations" remained "win–win cooperation". Therefore, the statements on "new-type international relations" before 2017 basically started from "win–win cooperation".

First, taking cooperation as the main mode of international relations is in the interest of most countries in the world, and it also reflects the trend of international relations since the end of the Cold War. In the history of international relations, war was once one of the main drivers for the formation of nation states, and it was also the origin of the realism theory in the history of international relations in the West. However, after the Second World War, the number of wars between major powers has substantially reduced. Since the end of the Cold War, human society has not yet witnessed a war between major powers. Therefore, in the theoretical circle of the West, liberal institutionalism and constructivism arose. The world events captured by these theories were in stark contrast with the concerns of realism, and more emphasis was placed on cooperation and the initiative of the state.

The development of technology in the late 1990s greatly changed traditional thinking, and the understanding of the world has changed considerably. On the one hand, due to technological progress, the division of labour progressed very rapidly. All parties got increased interests through cooperation; at the same time, negative factors in globalisation could also be amplified by technological factors such as terrorism, food security, major infections, climate change and some other non-traditional security issues. Objectively, these issues cannot be solved by a single country.

Judging from China's own history, the orientation of China's foreign policy has also largely shifted from confrontation in the early days of the cold war to cooperation. It can be said that the "new-type international relations" with cooperation as the core is a product of China's reform and opening up, and is a new perception China got in the process of integrating into the international community through deep participation in the international division of labour. Therefore, China's emphasis and understanding of cooperation is not entirely a product of the Western theory, but stems from China's practice and interaction with various countries.

Second, using "win–win" as another core word for "new-type international relations" is a reflection of China's positive views on the drive for globalisation and international cooperation. China advocates that in international relations, we should respect social systems and development paths chosen independently by various countries, attach great importance to a more balanced approach to uphold principles and pursue interests, and take account of the interests of all parties while safeguarding our own interests. We must seek for our own development while promoting common development. We are committed to achieving win–win and common beneficial outcomes.

A win–win situation is the value that common development pursuit for. In September 2015, when attending the General Debate of the 70th Session of the United Nations General

Assembly, Xi Jinping pointed out: "Common development is true development, and sustainable development is good development. To achieve this goal, we must uphold the spirit of openness by advocating mutual help and mutual benefits".[8] The question of "common development" raised by Xi Jinping is actually a major issue that has not been solved in human history. Many scholars in world economy believe that human society has entered the stage of modern economic growth since 1820 with the West being the leader. However, for a long time, the number of people living in developed countries hardly exceeded 20% of the total human population. Therefore, although capitalist system has led to rapid expansion of wealth, the distribution of wealth is very uneven. Today, developed countries have also fallen into the trap of polarisation, which is one of the major reasons for the new round of anti-globalisation. In January 2017, Xi Jinping gave a speech at the World Economic Forum in Davos and he believed that there were three major problems in world economy: the chronically bad performance of world economy, the gap between rich and poor and the gap between North and South. Unequal income distribution and unbalanced development in different regions are considered by Xi Jinping as "the biggest challenges facing the world today and important causes of social turmoil in some countries".[9]

Emphasising development issues is a feature of China's foreign relations. In the Western theory of international relations, no one has ever put development at such a high status as China does. This point is clear in the academic classifications of Western academic institutions because development issues have long been marginalised in international research community. However, there is a different story in China. As early as the mid-1980s, Deng Xiaoping proposed that peace and development were the world's themes. In this regard, Xi Jinping's view of taking common development and win–win outcome as the core of new-type international relations shows the logic of China's opening up and the value treasured by political elites from all period of Chinese history.

Third, at the end of 2016, Chinese government significantly increased the expression of "mutual respect" and "fairness and justice" in the statements on "new-type international relations". Chinese leaders have always attached importance to mutual respect between countries, along with sovereignty, equality and other rights. As early as 1954, the Five Principles of Peaceful Coexistence proposed by China and India included "mutual respect for sovereignty and territorial integrity, mutual non-aggression, non-interference in each other's internal affairs, equality, mutual benefit, and peaceful coexistence". Even though China has become a globally watched major country, Chinese leaders still advocate these principles. In January 2017, when Xi Jinping addressed the UN headquarters in Geneva, he re-emphasised that "big countries should treat small countries equally and shall not engage in arrogance and hegemony".[10]

In October 2017, the report to the 19th National Congress of the CPC said "We insist that all countries, regardless of size, power and wealth, are equal, support the United Nations in playing an active role and support developing countries in improving their representation and weight of words in international affairs".[11] Therefore, "mutual respect" and "fairness and justice" in the "new-type international relations" offers different kinds of definitions to the identification of China as a major country. Even being a country with strong comprehensive national strength and international influence in 2050, China will not forget developing countries.

The practical significance of the new-type international relations

Major-country diplomacy with Chinese characteristics is one of the eight components of the socialist ideologies with Chinese characteristics in the new era proposed in the 19th National

Congress of the CPC. The new-type international relations and the community with a shared future mark the two pillars of China's major-country diplomacy with Chinese characteristics. We can see that China views the building of new-type international relations as an important part of China's socialist practice and theoretical system.

The innovative feature of the international section in the report to the 19th National Congress of the CPC also shows that the CPC and the Chinese government are changing their world views. What is particularly worth emphasising is that the purpose of the CPC is universal: not only for the welfare of the Chinese people, but also for the cause of human progress. This has greatly expanded the sense of mission of the Chinese communists, demonstrating a rare idealistic sentiment. It is also the core of the community with a shared future for mankind. Regarding the government's targets, the overall goals of the new-type of international relations are to enhance mutual respect fairness, just, and win–win cooperation.

Notes

1 Jiang Zemin: *To Create a Better Future for China-Russia Relations Together—The Speech to Celebrates from all Groups of Russia at Moscow University*, Communique of State Council, 2001, 26, pp. 4–7.
2 Xi Jinping: *The Governance of China*, Beijing: Foreign Language Press, 2014, p. 271.
3 Xi Jinping: *The Governance of China II*, Beijing: Foreign Language Press, 2017, p. 443.
4 Xi Jinping: *The Governance of China II*, Beijing: Foreign Language Press, 2017, p. 522.
5 Xi Jinping: *The Governance of China II*, Beijing: Foreign Language Press, 2017, p. 448.
6 Xi Jinping: *The Governance of China II*, Beijing: Foreign Language Press, 2017, p. 541.
7 Xi Jinping: *Seizing the Opportunity of a Global Economy in Transition and Accelerating Development of the Asia–Pacific—Keynote Address at the APEC CEO Summit*, Xinhua News Agency, 10 November 2017, www.xinhuanet.com/politics/leaders/2017-11/10/c_1121938333.htm
8 Xi Jinping: *The Governance of China II*, Beijing: Foreign Language Press, 2017, p. 524.
9 Xi Jinping: *The Governance of China II*, Beijing: Foreign Language Press, 2017, p. 480.
10 Xi Jinping: *The Governance of China II*, Beijing: Foreign Language Press, 2017, p. 541.
11 Xi Jinping: *Secure a Decisive Victory in Building a Moderately Prosperous Society in All Respects and Strive for the Great Success of Socialism with Chinese Characteristics for a New Era—the Report to the 19th National Congress of the CPC*, the Assistant Book for Learning the Report to the 19th National Congress of the CPC, People's Press, October 2017, p. 59.

44
NEW-TYPE MAJOR-COUNTRY RELATIONS

Zhong Feiteng

New-type major-country relationship remains the key to understanding China's foreign policy. Although the frequency of this term has dropped significantly of late, it does not mean that the Chinese government has given it up. To a large extent, the intentions, connotations and goals of the new-style major-country relations have been integrated into "new-type international relations". Some countries call for the return of major power competition and the increased risk of the Thucydides trap. In this context, it is necessary to re-evaluate the efforts made by the Chinese government.

Forming the concept of a new-type major-country relations

Since the 1990s, the rise of China first appeared in discussions of economists and diplomats, but has received little attention from historians. The Chinese government is increasingly aware that in order to defeat the "China threat theory", it is necessary to introduce ourselves in our own words, leading the formation of the promotion of "new-type major-country relations" and "new-type international relations". In international relations, many discourses put forward by political leaders of major countries have led the development of international relations. For example, the revival of geopolitics in the 1970s was related to the decline of American hegemony and people like Nixon, Kissinger and others.

During the second round of China–US Strategic and Economic Dialogue in May 2010, State Councilor Dai Bingguo proposed that China and the United States should "create the new-type major-country relations on the basis of mutual respect, harmonious coexistence, and win–win cooperation between countries with different social systems, cultural traditions, and stages of development in the era of globalization". In February 2012, when Xi Jinping visited the United States, he proposed that China and the United States should work hard to build a new-type major-country relationship in the twenty-first century. Three months later, the fourth round of the China–US Strategic and Economic Dialogue was held in Beijing. President Hu Jintao delivered a speech entitled "Promoting the Development of New-type Major-country relationship of Mutual Benefits and Win–win Cooperation" and stated that China and the United States should "embarked a path of new-type major-country relationship based on mutual respect and win–win cooperation".[1]

In November 2012, the report of the 18th National Congress of the CPC clearly stated: "We will improve and develop relations with developed countries, broaden areas of cooperation, properly handle differences, and promote the establishment of long-term stable and healthy new-type major-country relationship".[2] Since then, new-type major-country relationships has become an important part of China's diplomatic strategy and has also attracted wide attention from international public opinion. The academic circles of China and the United States have conducted heated discussions around the connotation, implementation and target of the new-type major-country relationship.

In June 2013, when meeting with US President Barack Obama, Xi Jinping proposed the "new-type major-country relationship based on mutual respect, win–win cooperation, non-conflict and non-confrontation". In the key points of public speeches, Xi Jinping mentioned "new-type major-country relationship" five times.[3] Since then, this statement has become a formal expression concerning the new-type major-country relationship and has been widely used by many scholars and government agencies. In July 2014, Xi Jinping attended the joint opening ceremony of the sixth round of China–US Strategic and Economic Dialogue and the fifth round of China–US High-Level Consultations on People to People Exchange in Beijing, and delivered a speech entitled "Strive to build a new-type major-country relationship between China and the United States". Xi Jinping proposed: "The establishment of a new-type major-country relationship is a major strategic decision made by both sides based on the historical experiences and the national conditions of the two countries as well as the international situation". It is in line with the fundamental interests of the peoples of the two countries, and also reflects the determination of both sides to replace the traditional norm of confrontation with a new mode of relations between major countries.[4] In November 2014, during a meeting with President Obama in Beijing, Xi Jinping proposed to further promote the building of the new-type major-country relationship between China and the USA and the relating new-type military relations in six important aspects.

In September 2015, when Xi Jinping visited the United States and gave a speech in Seattle, Washington, he once again mentioned that China must persist in building the new-type major-country relationship, correctly judged each other's strategic intentions, unswervingly promoted cooperation and win–win outcomes, properly managed and controlled disagreements and deepened the friendship between two peoples to create a better future for Sino-US relations together. After meeting with Obama in Washington, both Xi Jinping and Obama said that they must continue to build a new-type major-country relationship between China and the US on the basis of mutual respect and win–win cooperation.

In June 2016, the eighth round of China–US Strategic and Economic Dialogue and the seventh round of China–US High-Level Consultations on People to People Exchange were held in Beijing. Xi Jinping addressed the meeting and recalled the meeting with President Obama three years ago. They reached high-level consensus on building the new-type major-country relationship between China and the USA. Xi Jinping said: "As the world's largest developing country and the largest developed country, as well as the two largest economies, China and the United States should work for the fundamental interests of peoples of the two countries and be brave enough to shoulder the burden of building the new-type major-country relationship between China and the US".[5]

The main content of the new-type major-country relationship

Three points highlight the new-type major-country relationship: non-confrontation, non-conflict; mutual respect; and win–win cooperation. Reviewing the developmental process, mutual respect and win–win cooperation have been clearly put forward during Hu Jintao's presidency. Non-conflict and non-confrontation were strengthened by Xi Jinping. What's more, this is also the main reason for the United States to accept this concept.

The areas of progress in cooperation between China and the United States can show the difficulties in shaping the new-type major-country relationship. On November 12, 2014, President Xi Jinping and President Obama met in Beijing, restressing the joint efforts to build the new-type major-country relationship between China and the USA. At the meeting, China and the United States made great progress in areas such as military cooperation, climate change, bilateral investment agreements, and information technology. However, big differences in South China Sea, human rights, cyber security and monetary policy remained. For a long period of time, the USA's influence on Asia–Pacific security and economy is still second to none, and the Asia–Pacific region cannot fully escape the control of the US market and the US authority. In March 2015, during the China Development Forum 2015, former Secretary of State Henry Kissinger believed that the new-type major-country relationship between China and the US proposed by Xi Jinping referred to the major-country relationship between potential competitors. At present, the task of both parties was to continuously enrich the content of this concept.[6]

Judging from the countries involved, although academic discussions focus on the bilateral relations between China and the United States, the Chinese government also includes Russia and Europe at least. In the first volume of Xi Jinping's *The Governance of China*, three speeches have been selected in the twelfth part *New-type Major-country Relationship* including: *Suiting the Trend of the Time and Promoting World Peace and Development* in March 2013, Moscow, *Forging the New-type Major-country relationship between China and the US* in June 2013 and *Building a Bridge of Friendship in Eurasian Continent* in April 2014.

In April 2014, the Chinese government issued *China's Policy Paper on the EU: Deepen the China–EU Comprehensive Strategic Partnership for Mutual Benefit and Win–win Cooperation* which was the second document concerning EU policies since the first one issued in October 2003. The document says that:

> the EU is China's important strategic partner for peaceful development and the multi-polarization in the world. It is an important partner for China to realize the New Four Modernizations and the Two Centenary Goals. Strengthening and developing China–Europe relations is an important task for China to establish long-term, stable, and healthy new-type major-country relationship and remains a priority for China's foreign policy.[7]

On June 28, 2015, Ivanov, former Secretary of National Security Council and former Foreign Minister of Russia, delivered a speech at the 4th World Peace Forum said that China and Russia had established an unprecedented new-type major-country relationship and the two countries focused on complementarities in politics, economic, humanitarian cooperation rather than check and balance under the framework of the new-type major-country relationship. He stressed that neither country sought dominance in bilateral relations by imposing one's will to the other. Instead, both sides tried to find a balance based on equality to get mutual benefit and win–win outcomes which differed with any major-country relationship in history.[8]

Realistic and theoretical significance of the new-type major-country relationship

Since the 18th National Congress of the CPC, the "new-type major-country relationship" has become the focus of both home and abroad. Most Western documents concerning this topic hold a policy-oriented rather than theory-oriented approach. Some Western commentators believe that China's "new-type major-country relationship" is another version of the "G2" which was rejected by China 5 years ago, and there is a risk that the new-type major-country relationship with the USA will damage the status of other major countries. Some American scholars are not optimistic about the new-type major-country relationship. What's more, they are strongly skeptical of the "new-type military relations" proposed by the Chinese military leaders during a visit to the USA in August 2013. For example, Joseph Nye emphasised that historical analogy should not restrict the understanding of China's new-type major-country relationship and China's challenge to the US world dominance was not comparable to Germany's challenge to the UK back in the nineteenth century because China still lagged far behind the USA in the per-capita sense. He also pointed that China's policies basically matched with its economic development, and its focus lay in the Asia–Pacific region rather than the world. Robert Zoellick emphasised that China and the United States needed to find new strategic focuses similar to the accession to the WTO.

One of the major historical and theoretical backgrounds of building the new-type major-country relationship between China and the USA is the fear of the so-called "Thucydides trap". In September 2015, President Xi Jinping pointed out in a speech in Washington State, USA: "There is no Thucydides trap in the world, only continuous strategic misjudgments between major countries may create a trap".[9] In November 2017, Graham Ellison, a Harvard professor who was the creator of the phrase "Thucydides trap", deliberately emphasised during a testimony to the US Senate that General Secretary Xi Jinping had mentioned the Thucydides trap in the 19th National Congress of the CPC. In his new book *Doomed to a World War: Can China and the United States Escape the Thucydides Trap?* Ellison uses many cases to elaborate the collisions caused by rising powers in the history. Among the 16 cases, only 4 avoid wars in the end, namely, Portugal and Spain in the late fifteenth century, Britain and the United States in the early twentieth century, the United States and the Soviet Union in the Cold War era and interdependent British–French ally and Germany in the 1990s. Obviously, peace among major countries increased significantly in the twentieth century. In addition to these 16 cases, Ellison also provided 14 cases for further research in the future. The preliminary conclusions seem to be that cases before the twentieth century are more likely to turn to war, and the cases after the twentieth century are less likely to turn to war. The study on this subject by the Western academic community is still in progress, providing a broad room for Chinese scholars and policy makers to explore.

In the discourse system of the West, the rise of major countries is basically a negative concept. After the global financial crisis in 2008, the Western world thought the key to the relationship between arising China and the international community lies in whether China can overcome the Thucydides trap. They summarise the far-reaching significance of China's rise with the significant historical events in Western civilisation and ideological tags which means that the discourse on the rise of China has turned from academia to general international opinion. The rise of China is already a historical fact. The West doubts whether such a rise is beneficial to the current turbulent international system. Therefore, the building of a new-type major-country relationship also shows the responsibility of China as a rising power.

Notes

1 Hu Jintao: *Selected Works of Hu Jintao* (third volume). Beijing: People's Press, 2016, pp. 583–586.
2 Hu Jintao: *Selected Works of Hu Jintao* (third volume). Beijing: People's Press, 2016, p. 652.
3 Xi Jinping: *The Governance of China*, Beijing: Foreign Language Press, 2014, pp. 279–281.

4 Xi Jinping, "Making Efforts for a New Model of Major-Country Relationship Between China and the US—Remarks at the Joint Opening Ceremony of the Sixth Round of the China–US Strategic and the Fifth Round of the China–US High-level Consultation on People-to People Exchange," *People's Daily*, July 10, 2014.
5 Xi Jinping, "Making Unremitting Efforts for a New Model of Major-Country Relationship Between China and the US—Remarks at the Joint Opening Ceremony of the Eighth Round of the China–US Strategic and the Seventh Round of the China–US High-level Consultation on People-to People Exchange," Xinhua News Agency, June 6, 2016, www.xinhuanet.com/world/2016-06/06/c_1118997076.htm
6 "The Importance of Cooperation should be Fully Recognized in Building New Model Major-Country Relationship between China and the US," Xinhuanet, March 21, 2015, http://news.xinhuanet.com/world/2015-03/21/c_1114718130.htm
7 "Deepening the China–EU Comprehensive Strategic Partnership for Mutual Benefit—China's Policy Document to the EU (full-text)," Xinhua News Agency, April 2, 2014, www.gov.cn/xinwen/2014-04/02/content_2651490.htm
8 "Former Foreign Minister of Russia: The Four Features in the New Model Partnership between China and Russia," China News, June 28, 2015, www.chinanews.com/gj/2015/06-28/7370842.shtml
9 "Ten Reasons for China and the US to Leapfrog the Thucydides Trap," Xinhuanet, September 27, 2015, www.xinhuanet.com/world/2015-09/27/c_1116689742.htm

45
THE COMMUNITY WITH A SHARED FUTURE FOR MANKIND

Li Zhifei

Elaboration and formation of the concept

The 18th National Congress of the Communist Party of China, held in November 2012, put forward the original form of the community with a shared future for mankind. The report of the congress states: "Human lives in the same global village and lives in the same time and space where history and reality meet. Humanity has been more and more interwoven with each other to become a community of a shared destiny".[1]

In late March 2013, Chinese President Xi Jinping first proposed the concept of the community with a shared future for mankind when he first visited Russia. In his speech at the Institute of International Relations in Moscow, he explained: "In this world, countries have become more interconnected and interdependent than ever before. Humankind lives in the same global village and lives in the same time and space where history and reality meet. Humanity has been more and more interwoven with each other to become a community with a shared future for mankind.[2] After that, President Xi Jinping further elaborated on the concept of the community with a shared future for mankind on many important diplomatic occasions.

On March 28, 2015, President Xi Jinping emphasised in the keynote speech at the annual meeting of the Boao Forum for Asia that "the community with a shared future for mankind requires that all countries should respect each other and treat each other as equals. That means we must adhere to win–win cooperation and common development, insist on achieving common, comprehensive, collaborative and sustainable security, adhere to inclusiveness and mutual learning among different civilizations".[3] On September 28, 2015, at the commemorative meeting of the 70th anniversary of the United Nations, President Xi Jinping delivered a speech entitled "Building a New Partnership for Win–win Cooperation and Building the Community with a Shared Future for Mankind Together". This was the first time that China's head of state had proposed and elaborated in detail the concept and core ideas of the community with a shared future for mankind. President Xi Jinping said: "In today's world, all countries are interdependent. We must inherit and carry forward the purposes and principles of the UN Charter, build new-type international relations centering on win–win cooperation, and build a community with a shared future for mankind". In order to realise the great goal of building a community with a shared future for mankind, President Jinping emphasised:

We must establish a partnership on the basis of equal footing, mutual consultation and mutual understanding. We must create a security pattern of fairness, justice, common development and shared outcomes. We must shape a future of openness, innovation, inclusiveness and reciprocity. We must promote harmonious and inclusive exchanges among different civilizations and build an ecological system that respects nature and green development.[4]

After the speech at the General Assembly of the UN, the idea of the community with a shared future for mankind has further developed. On January 19, 2017, President Xi Jinping, who attended the World Economic Forum at the UN headquarters in Geneva, delivered an important speech titled "Building a Community with a shared future for mankind Together", emphasising that "building a community with a shared future for mankind and achieving shared benefits" is the Chinese way to solve global challenges. As for the specific steps to take, President Xi proposed five ideas of global governance, and he believed that the international community should make efforts from partnerships, security arrangements, economic development, civilisation exchanges and ecological construction.[5] President Xi Jinping's speech marks the further improvement of the ideological system of the community with a shared future for mankind, taking it as the subject of the time by combining theory and practices.

In the report to the 19th National Congress of the CPC, President Xi Jinping emphasised that "China champions the development of a community with a shared future for mankind, and has encouraged the evolution of the global governance system. With this we have seen a further rise in China's international influence, ability to inspire, and power to shape; and China has made great new contributions to global peace and development".[6] As for the connotation, President Xi proposed that we need "to build a community with a shared future for mankind, to build an open, inclusive, clean, and beautiful world that enjoys lasting peace, universal security, and common prosperity".[7] "The building of a community with a shared future for mankind" has become a key to understand the core and content of the theory of socialism with Chinese characteristics in the new era.

In October 2017, after the deliberation of the 19th National Congress of the CPC, it was unanimously agreed that the concept of "building a community with a shared future for mankind" should be included in the Party Constitution as an important part of Xi Jinping's socialist ideology with Chinese characteristics, making it the guiding principle of the socialist construction with Chinese characteristics.

Main content

The thought of a community with a shared future for mankind is a major theoretical and practical innovation to Marxism and Chinese diplomatic thoughts made by the Central Committee of the CPC with comrade Xi Jinping as the core. It mainly includes five aspects.

First, the community with a shared future is a political community of sovereign equality and peaceful companion. President Xi Jinping once emphasised that:

> sovereign equality has been the most important principle in regulating relations between countries for hundreds of years. It is also the primary principle that the United Nations and all agencies and organiszations must follow. Sovereign equality means that countries, regardless of size, strength and wealth, enjoy sovereignty and dignity that should be respected by others. Their internal affairs should not be interfered, and they all have the rights to choose the social system and the road of development.

> In the new era, we must uphold the principle of sovereign equality and promote equity in rights, opportunities and rules.[8]

In the process of building a community with a shared future for mankind, "we must adhere to dialogues and consultations to build a world of lasting peace; adhere to common efforts and shared outcomes for a world with common security".[9] We should respect each other, discuss issues equally, resolutely reject Cold War mentality and power politics, and take a new approach to develop state-to-state relations of communication instead of confrontation, and of partnership instead of alliance.[10] Therefore, the idea of community of shared future for mankind advocated by China is a political community of sovereign equality and peace.

Second, the community with a shared future for mankind is a community of security featuring justice, fairness, common efforts and shared outcomes. In the process of global governance, conflicts and controversies remain in the world. Hegemony and power politics represented by the United States, and non-traditional security issues such as ecological security, terrorism, food security and cyber-security still challenge world security. Therefore, in the process of building a community with a shared future for mankind, we must "commit to settling disputes through dialogue and resolving differences through discussion, coordinate responses to traditional and non-traditional threats, and oppose terrorism in all its forms",[11] uphold "win–win cooperation to build a world with common prosperity"[12] and promote the building of the community with a shared security.

Third, the community with a shared future for mankind is an economic community that upholds inclusiveness, openness, and reciprocity and win–win outcomes. Economic globalisation has already been an irreversible trend. In the process of globalisation, "we must establish the sense of community with a shared future for mankind, promote all-round economic interconnectivity with all countries, improve global economic and financial governance, and reduce inequality and imbalance in global development to enable all people in all countries to enjoy the benefits of world economic growth in a fair manner".[13] In the process, "we must help each other, facilitate the liberalization of trade and investment, and make economic globalization more open, inclusive, reciprocal, balanced and common beneficial".[14]

Fourth, the community with shared future of mankind is a community of civilisations, advocating harmony while respecting differences and upholding mutual learning. The history of human civilisation is the history of the diversification and development of civilisations. With the development of globalisation, the theory of the "Clash of Civilisations" is gradually being favoured. It is believed that cultural differences make it difficult to avoid conflicts among countries. Some western countries attempt to promote the so-called "universal values" to interfere in others' internal affairs and even manipulate world issues. However, the concept of community with shared civilisations advocated by China recognises diversity among different civilisations in the world and advocates "respecting the diversity of world civilizations, advocating communication, mutual learning and coexistence instead of isolation, confrontation and supremacy among different civilizations".[15] "Adhering to exchanges and mutual understanding, we can build an open and inclusive world."[16]

Fifth, the community with a shared future of mankind is a green, low-carbon and environmental friendly community. The global eco-environmental crisis is the primary challenge to the community with a shared future for mankind. All countries must work together under the framework of the community with a shared future of mankind. President Xi Jinping once emphasised that "people and nature belong to the same community of life, and humans must respect, follow and protect nature",[17] and in the process of building a community with a shared future for mankind, we should "advocate green and low carbon development and build a clean and beautiful world. Following the concept of seeking integrity between human and nature by following the rules of nature, we seek a path of sustainable development. By advocating a green, low-carbon, cyclical, sustainable production and lifestyle and advancing the 2030 sustainable development agenda, we continuously broaden the path of healthy development featuring the combination of advanced production, wealthy lives and good ecosystems".[18] "We insist on an environmental friendly approach by coping with climate change together to better protect the planet we live on."[19] A good outcome of eco-environmental protection is the realisation of sustainable development of the community with a shared future.

Theoretical and practical significance of the concept

Since the Party's 18th National Congress, China's development has taken a new historical starting point. Socialism with Chinese characteristics has entered a new era. The Chinese nation has ushered in a bright future for the Great Rejuvenation. The Party Central Committee with President Xi Jinping as the core, standing at the height of the development of human history, has expanded and deepened the idea of the community with a shared future for mankind proposed during the Party's 18th National Congress and formed an ideological system of the concept with scientific integrity, rich content and far-reaching meanings. The idea of the community with a shared future for mankind is an innovative Chinese plan for "the definition to and the ways towards a future world".

First, the idea of the community with a shared future for mankind offers the Chinese programme and wisdom to the reform of the global governing system. The current global governing system was formed after the Second World War under the leadership of the developed countries. The changes in international power pattern and the rising global challenges highlight the existing problems in global governance. The three major problems of reducing "the deficits of global governance", promoting democracy in global governance and filling blanks in inadequate development are rising. Some major countries are losing the enthusiasm and motivation to deal with them, while many small countries lack the ability to respond. The idea of a community with a shared future for mankind proposed by China advocates win–win cooperation, shared responsibility and interests, inclusiveness and sustainable development to achieve fairness and justice in global governance and promote democracy in international orders.[20] The implementation of the idea can balance the pursuit of national interests with the interests of other countries. It can solve the problem of imbalance between responsibility and interest, meet the development demands of different countries and promote the solution of problems in global governance.

Second, the idea of a community with a shared future for mankind offers Chinese plans and wisdom to world peace. The world is still not peaceful; therefore, maintaining international peace is still a top priority for all countries in the world. As a responsible regional power, China proposed the idea of a community with a shared future for mankind, offering Chinese plans and wisdom for maintaining and building peace of the world. As the largest developing country in the world, China has maintained long-term domestic stability and prosperity, pursued the principle of peaceful consultation and equal dialogue with the outside world, participated extensively in regional cooperation and global affairs, and strived to build new-type international relations featuring non-conflict, non-confrontation, mutual respect and win–win cooperation. China also promotes new international cooperation in the deep sea, Polar Regions, outer space and cyberspace. Meanwhile, China has actively supported the solution to global terrorism and refugee crisis, promoted climate change and ecological security governance by consultation and joint efforts with other countries to forge a world of lasting peace and common security.

Third, the idea of a community with a shared future for mankind offers Chinese plans and wisdom to the democratic development of the international order. China has always adhered to the concept of development based on mutual cooperation and common development and promoted democracy in world order. In terms of economy, "we should strengthen coordination and improve governance so as to ensure sound growth of economic globalization and make it open, inclusive, balanced and beneficial to all. We should both make the cake bigger and share it fairly to ensure justice and equity. We should uphold WTO rules, support an open, transparent, inclusive and nondiscriminatory multilateral trading regime and build an open world economy".[21] In terms of politics, China advocates equal consultations and dialogues in resolving conflicts between nations. Terrorism, ecological governance, climate change and other non-traditional security issues should be solved through cooperation. The function of coordination practiced by multilateral organisations such as the United Nations in international affairs should be respected. With regard to culture, we respect diversity of civilisations and cultures, promote equal exchanges and mutual learning among different civilisations and tolerate different models of development in the world.

Fourth, the idea of a community with a shared future for mankind offers Chinese plans and wisdom to global ecological harmony. "Human and nature belong to the same community of life. Humankind must respect, follow and respect nature." China has already listed "green" as the basic content of the "Five Development Ideas" in Chinese domestic plans and treated it as a fundamental guideline for economic and social development. While promoting domestic eco-environmental security, China also contributes to global environmental governance by promoting the establishment of a fair and equitable international law system of environment.

Building a community with a shared future for mankind is the Chinese way to build an ecological law system, offering Chinese plans and wisdom to global governance and human development. This is the foundation and core of the theoretical system of the global eco-environmental governance, reflecting China's commitment to global sustainable development as a responsible major country.[22]

Notes

1 Hu Jintao, "The Report to the 18th National Congress of the CPC," Xinhuanet, http://news.xinhuanet.com/18cpcnc/2012-11/17/c_113711665.htm
2 Xi Jinping, "The Speech at the Moscow State Institute of International Relations (full-text)," Chinese Government website, www.gov.cn/ldhd/2013-03/24/content_2360829.htm
3 Xi Jinping, "The Keynote Speech at the Annual Meeting of Boao Forum for Asia (full-text)," Xinhuanet, http://news.xinhuanet.com/politics/2015-03/29/c_127632707.htm
4 "Building New Partnership of Win–win Cooperation and Forging a Community with Shared Future for Mankind," People.com, http://politics.people.com.cn/n/2015/0929/c1024-27644905.html
5 Xi Jinping, "The Speech at the Headquarter of the UN in Geneva (full-text)," Xinhuanet, http://news.xinhuanet.com/world/2017-01/19/c_1120340081.htm
6 "Secure a Decisive Victory in Building a Moderately Prosperous Society in All Respects and Strive for the Great Success of Socialism with Chinese Characteristics for a New Era—the Report to the 19th National Congress of the CPC," Chinese Government website, www.gov.cn/zhuanti/2017-10/27/content_5234876.htm
7 Ibid.
8 Xi Jinping, "The Speech at the Headquarter of the UN in Geneva (full-text)," Xinhuanet, http://news.xinhuanet.com/world/2017-01/19/c_1120340081.htm
9 Ibid.
10 "Secure a Decisive Victory in Building a Moderately Prosperous Society in All Respects and Strive for the Great Success of Socialism with Chinese Characteristics for a New Era—the Report to the 19thNational Congress of the CPC," Chinese Government website, www.gov.cn/zhuanti/2017-10/27/content_5234876.htm

11 Ibid.
12 "Building New Partnership of Win–win Cooperation and Forging a Community with Shared Future for Mankind," People.com, http://politics.people.com.cn/n/2015/0929/c1024-27644905.html
13 Xi Jinping, "Remarks at the G20 Summit 2016," Xinhuanet, http://news.xinhuanet.com/world/2015-12/01/c_1117309579.htm
14 "Secure a Decisive Victory in Building a Moderately Prosperous Society in All Respects and Strive for the Great Success of Socialism with Chinese Characteristics for a New Era—the Report to the 19th National Congress of the CPC," Chinese Government website, www.gov.cn/zhuanti/2017-10/27/content_5234876.htm
15 Xi Jinping, "Remarks at the G20 Summit 2016," Xinhuanet, http://news.xinhuanet.com/world/2015-12/01/c_1117309579.htm
16 "Secure a Decisive Victory in Building a Moderately Prosperous Society in All Respects and Strive for the Great Success of Socialism with Chinese Characteristics for a New Era—the Report to the 19thNational Congress of the CPC," Chinese Government website, www.gov.cn/zhuanti/2017-10/27/content_5234876.htm
17 "Ecological Environment and the Community with Shared Future," Xinhuanet, http://news.xinhuanet.com/globe/2017-11/01/c_136717143.htm
18 Xi Jinping, "The Speech at the Headquarter of the UN in Geneva (full-text)," Xinhuanet, http://news.xinhuanet.com/world/2017-01/19/c_1120340081.htm
19 "Secure a Decisive Victory in Building a Moderately Prosperous Society in All Respects and Strive for the Great Success of Socialism with Chinese Characteristics for a New Era—the Report to the 19th National Congress of the CPC," Chinese Government website, www.gov.cn/zhuanti/2017-10/27/content_5234876.htm
20 Li Xiangyang: "The Community with Shared Future Guides the Direction to the Reform of Global Governance", *People's Daily*, 8 March 2017.
21 Xi Jinping, "The Speech at the Headquarter of the UN in Geneva (full-text)," Xinhuanet, http://news.xinhuanet.com/world/2017-01/19/c_1120340081.htm
22 Huang Hui, "The Legal Guarantee of Ecology to the Building of the Community with Shared Future," *Chinese Social Sciences Today*, January 9, 2018.

46
TWO CENTENARY GOALS

Yang Danzhi

Proposal and definition

Since the founding of the PRC, it has been an important experience for the CPC to govern the country by proposing corresponding strategic objectives to lead the development of socialism in accordance with international and domestic situations and development conditions of the country. The proposal of the Two Centenary Goals undoubtedly confirms this assertion.

In October 1987, the 13th National Congress of the Communist Party of China proposed an overall strategic plan for China's economic construction in three steps. The first step is to double the GNP from 1981 to 1990 compared with that of 1980 to solve the problem of food and clothing for the people. This was basically achieved at the end of the 1980s. The second step is to double the GNP from 1991 to the end of the twentieth century, lifting people's lives to a moderately prosperous level. The third step is to basically achieve modernisation with per-capita GNP of moderately developed countries and relatively wealthy lives for the people.[1]

Since then, on the basis of solving the problem of food and clothing for the people and achieving moderately prosperous lives for the people in a general perspective, the 15th National Congress of the CPC proposed Two Centenary Goals.

The 15th National Congress of the CPC was held in Beijing from September 12 to 18, 1997. In the report to the 15th National Congress, the two centenary goals were firstly proposed. The first Centenary Goal is to finish building a moderately prosperous society in all respects by the time the Communist Party of China celebrates its centenary in 2021. The second Centenary Goal is to turn China into a modern socialist country that is prosperous, strong, democratic, culturally advanced and harmonious by the time the People's Republic of China celebrates its centenary in 2049.[2]

The report to the 18th National Congress of the CPC held in 2012 drew a blueprint for building a moderately prosperous society in all respects and accelerating socialist modernisation. It once again reiterated that we need to finish building a moderately prosperous society in all respects by the time the Communist Party of China celebrates its centenary in 2021, and to turn China into a modern socialist country that is prosperous, strong, democratic, culturally advanced and harmonious by the time the People's Republic of China celebrates its centenary in 2049. It also called on the Chinese people to march towards the Two Centenary Goals. "Two Centenary Goals" have since become fixed keywords and the common goals for people of all ethnic groups in the country.[3]

In public speeches and articles written by President Xi Jinping since the 18th National Congress of the CPC, "Two Centenary Goals" have appeared more than 100 times, which fully shows that the new generation of leadership attaches great importance to this idea. For the CPC, "Two Centenary Goals" have become not only the goals, but also the call of the time to lead China forward to realise the Chinese Dream.

On November 29, 2012, President Xi Jinping first elaborated the concept of the Chinese Dream when he visited the Revival Road exhibition in National Museum.

Xi Jinping pointed out, "In order to realize the Chinese Dream, we set the Two Centenary Goals".[4]

The core goal of the Chinese Dream can actually be summarised as the Two Centenary Goals: to gradually realise the Great Rejuvenation of the Chinese Nation by the time the Communist Party of China celebrates its centenary in 2021 and the People's Republic of China celebrates its centenary in 2049. By that time, the country will be prosperous, the nation will be strong and the people will live happy lives. The path of socialism with Chinese characteristics, the theoretical system of socialism with Chinese characteristics, together with national spirits and Chinese strength forms the practical approaches to the goals. Efforts should be taken in five aspects: politics, economy, culture, society and environment.

In the report to the 19th National Congress of the CPC held in October 2017, the timetable and roadmap for socialist modernisation were clearly drawn. On the foundation of a moderately prosperous society and the first Centenary Goal achieved by 2020, we will use another 15 years of hard work to see that socialist modernisation is basically realised. From 2035 to the middle of the twenty-first century, on the foundation of the socialist modernisation that has been realised, we will work hard for another 15 years and develop China into a great modern socialist country that is prosperous, strong, democratic, culturally advanced, harmonious and beautiful.[5]

So far, the Two Centenary Goals have been shared by people of all ethnic groups in the country and have been clearly and completely defined.

The theoretical and practical significance of the Two Centenary Goals

The idea of the Two Centenary Goals attributes to the collective wisdom of the Communist Party of China. It has great theoretical and practical significance.

First, the idea of the Two Centenary Goals is a strategic arrangement created by the CPC on the basis of the vision of the new historical position and the trend of the time to build a socialist modernised country. The Two Centenary Goals not only inherit the "three-step" strategic goals but also deepen and advance the "three-step" goals in new conditions. The Two Centenary Goals have made the goals of the Chinese Dream and the Great Rejuvenation of the Chinese nation more specific, and the efforts to achieve the goals have become even clearer.

The biggest issue in China today is to realise the Two Centenary Goals and the Chinese Dream. The most urgent task is to build a moderately prosperous society in all aspects by 2020.[6]

The interval between the 19th and the 20th National Congress of the CPC is the historical intersection of the Two Centenary Goals which are with great significance to the progress of China's socialist modernisation. In these 5 years, an on-time realisation of the building of a moderately prosperous society in all aspects and the first Centenary Goal will be an important milestone for China's socialist modernisation, marking success in this important developing period connecting the two stages of socialist modernisation. Starting the new journey of building a socialist, modernised country in all aspects, heading for the second Centenary Goal and deepening the Three Step Strategy of China's modernisation provide a higher starting point for us to make efforts to build a wealthy, strong, democratic, civilised, harmonious and beautiful socialist modern China.[7]

The interval years provide opportunity as well as challenges.

The realisation of the first Centenary Goal will surely lay a solid material foundation for the second. A smooth transition between the two goals will provide a favourable strategic situation for the realisation of the second Centenary Goal focusing on building a wealthy, strong, democratic, civilised, harmonious and beautiful socialist modernised country.

At the same time, in the period of historical interval between the Two Centenary Goals, business advances and develops together with new situations and problems. We will face more risks and challenges and shoulder more arduous tasks. From the perspective of domestic development, the problem of unbalanced, uncoordinated and unsustainable development remains outstanding. Judging from the external environment, the deep impact of the international financial crisis still persists. The global economic and trade growth is weak, protectionism has risen, geopolitical relations have undergone complex changes and traditional and non-traditional security threats are intertwined. Elements of instability and uncertainty are rising.[8]

To realise the great goal of the Chinese Dream, we must deepen comprehensive reforms to leapfrog the "middle-income trap". We need to vigorously advance the building of a harmonious world to leapfrog the "Thucydides trap" and earnestly strengthen the building of the ruling party to leapfrog the "Tacitus trap".[9] In this sense, the idea of the Two Centenary Goals is based on the meticulous examination and analysis of China's national conditions and the international situation.

Second, the proposal of the Two Centenary Goals has set the goal and direction for the CPC, the core leading all aspects of socialist building with Chinese characteristics in the new era, and the people of all ethnic groups in the country. It will enhance the connection between the CPC and people of all ethnic groups in the country and the leadership of the CPC to people of all ethnic groups in the country.

Over the past 40 years of reform and opening up, great achievements have been made in building socialism with Chinese characteristics. How to make further progress is a major and critical issue facing the whole party and the people of the country.

Xi Jinping pointed out in his important speech on July 26, 2017 that building a moderately prosperous society in all aspects must be approved by the people and withstand the test of history.[10] People's approval undoubtedly "embodies the people-centered development ideology and is the fundamental standard for building a moderately prosperous society in all aspects".[11] Xi Jinping also emphasised that:

> the original aspiration and the mission of Chinese Communists is to seek happiness for the Chinese people and rejuvenation for the Chinese nation. This original aspiration is what inspires Chinese Communists to advance. In our Party, every party member must make close connection with the people and share the same future with them. We must make our efforts to make the people live better lives. We must keep on striving toward the great goal of national rejuvenation.

At present, in the discourse system of the Communist Party of China today, there are two "Greats": one is the "Great Cause", the Great Cause of Chinese socialism with Chinese characteristics under the leadership of the CPC and the Great Cause of the Rejuvenation of the Chinese nation. The other is the "Great Project" of Party Building. The two "Greats" are dialectical and unified. The "Great Cause" cannot be separated from the "Great Project" and the "Great Project" must focus on and serve the "Great Cause".[12]

In the process of achieving the Two Centenary Goals and the Chinese Dream, the leadership and party building of the CPC are indispensable. For the CPC, the Two Centenary Goals will help it to know clearly about its missions and responsibilities. It also helps the CPC to prepare for danger in times of peace, get rid of the emotion of irritation and arrogance and work hard in a frugal style.

Third, the Two Centenary Goals echo internationally. Since the idea's formal proposal, President Xi Jinping has repeatedly referred to it in his visits abroad. He elaborated the Chinese goals in detail and has aroused widespread resonance in the world.

On March 23, 2014, during the 3rd Nuclear Security Summit in Netherlands, President Xi Jinping published an essay of his signature entitled *Opening the Doors of Europe to Create Prosperity Together* in the Dutch newspaper *New Rotterdam Business*. The article stated: "At present, China is moving toward the Two Centenary Goals, while the EU is also advancing 'Europe 2020' strategy. A stronger and wealthier country, a more impartial and fairer society and better lives for people are the common aspirations for both Chinese and European people. We are willing to work with all European countries to deepen mutual benefit and win–win cooperation, share opportunities, and create prosperity together".[13]

In many oversea visits, combined with local conditions, Xi Jinping always emphasised synergy between China and foreign countries in national development strategy, stressing that China would work with other countries in the world to ensure people of all countries live better lives.

Looking to the future, China will start a new journey to build a modern socialist country and realise the second Centenary Goal. Therefore, China needs to be more proactive in global governance, following the principles of world peace and development and contributeing China's wisdom and plan to world peace, global growth and the international order.[14] In this sense, the interests of the Chinese people and the peoples of the world are the same. Therefore, China's efforts towards the Two Centenary Goals will inevitably gain more and more understanding and support from peoples across the world.

Notes

1 "Marching Along the Path of Socialism with Chinese Characteristics—the Report to the 13th National Congress of the CPC," www.xjbz.gov.cn/ddh/communist/newfiles/m1060.html
2 Jiang Zemin, "Upholding the Great Banner of Deng Xiaoping Theory and Leading the Course of Socialism with Chinese Characteristics to the 21st century—the Report to the 15th National Congress of the CPC," http://cpc.people.com.cn/GB/64162/64168/64568/65445/4526285.html
3 Hu Jintao, "Unremittingly Marching Along the Path of Socialism with Chinese Characteristics and Making efforts towards the Building of the Moderately Prosperous Society in All Aspects—the Report to the 18th National Congress of the CPC," http://cpc.people.com.cn/n/2012/1118/c64094-19612151.html
4 "The Two Centenary Goals lead the Direction of the Time," Key words of Xi Jining's Governance of China 3, www.xinhuanet.com/politics/2016-01/18/c_128640419.htm
5 The Commentator of the Xinhua News Agency, "Deeply Understand the New Goal of Two Steps," www.xinhuanet.com/politics/19cpcnc/2017-10/21/c_129724346.htm
6 Li Junru, "One of the Researches on Strict Party Building; the Key role of the CPC in Dealing with all Problems in China," *Journal of the Party School of Tianjin*, 2016, 5, p. 4.
7 Huang Taiyan, "Grasping the Historical Interval between the Two Centenary Goals," *QiuShi*, 2017, 24, p. 43.
8 "How to Understand the Historical Interval between the Two Centenary Goals," www.81.cn/jfjbmap/content/2017-11/22/content_192485.htm
9 Zhang Yong, "Three Traps to Leapfrog in Realizing the Two Centenary Goal," *Theory Monthly*, 2015, 2, pp. 28–30.
10 "Fully Understand the Great Significance of the Speech on 26 July by President Xi Jinping," *Qiu Shi*, http://theory.people.com.cn/n1/2017/0815/c40531-29472572.html
11 Chu Xinyu, "The Requirements of the Two Centenary Goals, ", *Qiu Shi*, 2017, 19, p. 14.

12 Li Junru, "One of the Researches on Strict Party Building; the Key role of the CPC in Dealing with all Problems in China," *Journal of the Party School of Tianjin*, 2016, 5, p. 5.
13 The essay of Xi Jinping's signature in the Dutch newspaper *New Rotterdam Business*, www.xinhuanet.com/world/2014-03/24/c_119921282.htm
14 Chu Xinyu, "The Requirements of the Two Centenary Goals," *Qiu Shi*, 2017, 19, p. 14.

47
WIN–WIN COOPERATION

Yang Danzhi

"Win–win cooperation" usually means that the two or more parties involved in a transaction or task can get common benefit by taking a reciprocal approach.

In recent years, China's new generation of leadership with Xi Jinping as its core has repeatedly expounded win–win cooperation on major international occasions. In the practice of China's foreign relations, the concept of win–win cooperation has also been fully reflected.

The proposal of win–win cooperation

On March 23, 2013, President Xi Jinping delivered an important speech entitled *Conforming to the Trend of the Times and Promoting Peaceful Development of the World* at the Moscow Institute of International Relations during his visit to Russia. For the first time, the new-type international relations centred on cooperation and mutual benefit was proposed. Xi Jinping pointed out: "In this world, peace, development, and win–win cooperation have become the trend of the times. The old colonial system collapsed, and the group confrontation during the Cold War no longer exists. No country or a group of countries can dominate the world affairs alone". He also pointed out that:

> in today's world, countries are more interconnected and interdependent, and human beings live in the same global village. Living in the same time and space where history and reality meet, we are interconnected with each other. In face of profound changes in international situation, countries in the same boat of destiny should jointly promote the establishment of new international relations with win–win cooperation as the core. People of all countries should work together to safeguard world peace and promote common development.[1]

Xi Jinping emphasised that further multi-polarisation, economic globalisation, cultural diversity and social IT application of today's world can facilitate humanity to get peace and development by the approach of win–win cooperation. He also solemnly declared that China will unswervingly follow the path of peaceful development and commit itself to promoting open, cooperative and win–win development. At the same time, he called on all countries to take the path of peaceful development.

In November 2014, Xi Jinping's speech at the Central Conference on Foreign Affairs said that "In 21st century, we should not insist on the Cold War mentality and zero-sum game. Instead, we need to keep up with the pace of the times and promote cooperation. So, we need to build new-type national relations centered on win–win cooperation by respecting the concept in political, economic, secure, cultural and other aspects". Xi Jinping's speech at the Moscow Institute of International Relations in March 2013 and the speech at the Asia Info Summit in Shanghai on May 21, 2014 both mentioned that "we cannot keep the Cold War mentality and zero-sum game in the 21st century but to keep up with the times".[2]

In September 2015, President Xi Jinping attended series of summits on the 70th anniversary of the founding of the United Nations and delivered an important speech at the United Nations Headquarters in New York on September 26, entitled "Towards Win–win Partnership for Sustainable Development". On September 28, 2015, Xi Jinping clearly pointed out during the General Debate of the 70th UN General Assembly: "In today's world, countries are interdependent and interconnected. We must inherit and carry forward the purposes and principles of the UN Charter and build a new international relationship with win–win cooperation as the core to build a community with a shared future".[3]

In addition, during his visits to Europe, Africa, Latin America, and on major international multilateral occasions such as the Asia Info Conference, Xi Jinping have explained the concept of win–win cooperation. Constructing a new type of international relations centred on win–win cooperation has undoubtedly become an important guiding ideology for China's diplomacy in the new era.

China advocates the idea of building new-type international relations with win–win cooperation as the core. It adheres to the fine tradition of Chinese civilisation and the consistent policy of PRC's diplomacy. It is also in line with the UN Charter on sovereign equality, peaceful settlement of international disputes and international cooperation. The purpose and principle, in line with the development trend of the current era, is the transcendence and innovation of the traditional international relations theory, and is of profound theoretical connotation and great practical guiding significance.

The connotation of win–win cooperation

The concept of win–win cooperation has rich connotations, mainly reflecting in the following five aspects.

The first is to view common interests as an important basis for handling international relations. In today's world, countries are interconnected, interdependent and their interests are further interwoven. The practical needs and political will to create a peaceful and stable environment and seek common development and prosperity are also growing. Building new-type international relations with win–win cooperation as the core calls for a holistic rather than a fragmented perspective on international relations. It also advocates that countries should promote common interests of humanity while protecting their own national interests. Countries should respect each other and treat each other as equals on the basis of seeking common ground while reserving differences, and constantly consolidate and expand common interests. They also need to emphasise the expansion of common interests instead of harming others.

Second, cooperation is the main way to handle international relations. The new international relations with win–win cooperation as the core advocates shared destiny, shared opportunity and shared challenges showing the only correct choice for countries to get along with each other. It advocates that countries can effectively cope with the increasing global challenges and work together to solve global challenges like world development and human progress through continuous expansion of mutually beneficial cooperation and dialogue instead of confrontation.

The third is to make win–win outcome the basic principle for handling international relations. As a Chinese saying goes, "A single flower does not make spring; One hundred flowers in full blossom bring spring to the garden". China advocates respecting the social systems and development paths independently chosen by countries, attaching a balanced approach between friendship and interests and safeguarding their own interests while taking into account the interests of all parties. China will seek its own development and promote common development and strive to achieve win–win outcomes instead of zero-sum game.

Fourth, the concept is of distinctive Chinese characteristics and universal world significance. In traditional Chinese culture, we can find the source of ideas for today's win–win cooperation. For example, Confucias says "Benevolence and Love" (*The Analects of Confucius* 12:22), "The World for Common Good", "Love should not be given only to one's own parents and sons but to that of others" (*Book of Rites*). Laozi said "Virtue should be spread across the world" (*Tao Te Ching*, chapter 53). Zhuangzi said "People should fight for common good instead of the interests of his own" (*Zhuangzi Grand Master*). The traditional Chinese vision of the world shows a clear idea about the relationship between people and the world, advocating that people should benefit themselves by benefiting others instead of caring only for others without their own interests concerned.[4] Zhao Tingyang, a contemporary Chinese political philosopher, believes that the philosophy of the traditional Chinese concept of world (*tianxia*) is to think about problems with the entire world as background or coordinates. Many problems are global and need to be solved in a holistic approach. There must be a concept of the world to accommodate the understanding and practice of the community of a shared future.[5]

With strength increasing, the international environment China is in and the international situation China has to face have undergone tremendous changes. "Now we have entered or are close to the center of the world stage. We have to communicate with all kinds of countries in the world and develop relations with countries of different civilizations. Peaceful co-existence is not enough now. We must also hold high the banner of win–win cooperation."[6]

As a developing country with a rapid growth rate, China needs to make greater contributions to international peace and development as a responsible major country by offering the Chinese spirit, the Chinese concept and the China plan to guide all countries to push their domestic as well as international governance and cooperation to the same direction of peace and development. Only then can the value of peaceful, open and inclusive development be realised.

The fifth is to transcend the law of the jungle in the theory of Western international relations. The old concepts such as zero-sum game and Cold War mentality are outdated. Unilateralism can no longer protect the security of its own, and a "beggar-thy-neighbour" approach and alliance confrontation will definitely hit the wall. Winner-take-all should not be taken as granted.

On the whole, the concept of win–win cooperation emphasises peaceful and harmonious coexistence among countries with different social systems, development paths and cultural traditions. It conforms to the general aspirations of the international community and provides a more just and rational direction for the promotion of the international order. The new ideas not only indicate the correct path for the development of international relations under the new situation, but also inject strong momentum into the international community by expanding exchanges and cooperation and avoiding conflicts. The ultimate goal of win–win cooperation is to build a community with a shared future.

The practical significance of win–win cooperation

China is not only an active proponent of win–win cooperation, but also a positive practitioner. Its efforts mainly reflect in the following aspects.

First, we are actively committed to promoting international cooperation. Over the past 60 years, China has actively participated in international development cooperation. It has provided nearly 400 billion yuan in aid to 166 countries and international organisationsand dispatched more than 600,000 workers. More than 700 Chinese have sacrificed their lives to the development of other countries. China will also set up a South–South Cooperation Assistance Fund to provide US$2 billion in the first phase to support developing countries in implementing the development agenda after 2015. China will continue to increase investment in the least developed countries and strive to reach US$12 billion by 2030. China will waive the inter-governmental interest-free loan obligations that have not repaid up to the end of 2015 for the least developed countries, land-locked developing countries and small island developing countries. China will set up an International Development Research Centre to work with other countries to study and exchange development theories and development practices that suit their own national conditions. China is proposing to explore the construction of a global energy network that will meet global electricity demand in a clean and green way.[7]

The second is to promote a new pattern of inclusive development in economy. China's full participation in discussions and cooperation on issues such as sustainable development within the UN framework has actively promoted the development of the 2030 Agenda for Sustainable Development. China also promote participants in the G20 summit in Hangzhou to put the development issue at the forefront of the global macro policy framework for the first time which efficiently promote the world economy to achieve strong, sustainable, balanced and inclusive growth. China also took the opportunity of the G20 Hangzhou Summit to contribute to the development of an innovative, dynamic, coordinated and inclusive world economy by guiding members of the G20 to deepen reform, promote innovation and strengthen coordination.

The third is to gradually step out a new path of state-to-state exchanges. China adheres to the principle of "dialogue without confrontation, partnership and non-alliance" and has established different forms of partnership with more than 80 countries and regions or regional organisations forming a global network of partnerships. China conscientiously implements the peripheral diplomatic concept of amity, sincerity, mutual benefit and inclusiveness, and works with regional countries to build a community with a shared future in Asia. Cooperation at all levels and in all fields is fully carried out and interest in integration is deepening. China actively takes a balanced approach between friendship and interests, and focuses on strengthening solidarity and cooperation with all developing countries in Asia, Africa, Latin America and other regions.

In recent years, under the guidance of the concept of win–win cooperation, China's relations with African, Arab and Latin American countries have witnessed not only further consolidation but also all-round expansion. China–Africa relations, China–Arab relations and China–Latin America relations have become models of win–win cooperation.[8]

The fourth is to implement the overall national security concept in security. President Xi Jinping pointed out at the first meeting of the National Security Committee: "To implement the overall national security concept, we must attach importance to both external security and internal security. Domestically speaking, we want development, reform, stability and peace. Externally speaking, we want cooperation, win–win outcomes and a harmonious world".[9] China advocates a common, integrated, cooperative and sustainable security concept by putting forward the "Three Principles for Solving Hot Issues", playing an important role in solving hot issues such as the Iranian nuclear issue, Syrian issue and the Korean Peninsula nuclear issue. China advocates the "two-track thinking" regarding the South China Sea issue, resolutely safeguards the country's territorial sovereignty and maritime rights and interests and is firmly committed to maintaining peace and stability in the South China Sea together with regional countries. China is also actively participating in international anti-terrorism cooperation and in-depth participation in UN peacekeeping operations. It is the country with the largest number of peacekeepers among the five permanent members of the Security Council, and its contribution to peacekeeping funds has risen to the second place in the world. For seven consecutive years, Chinese warships have carried out escort missions in the Gulf of Aden and the Somali waters, and have escorted more than 6000 Chinese and foreign ships. In addition, China is also actively promoting cyber-security, coping with climate change, providing more and more public goods for maintaining world peace and security and fully demonstrating the responsibility of a responsible major country.[10]

The fifth is to create a new atmosphere of exchanges and mutual understanding between different civilisations in culture. China actively advocates mutual respect between different civilisations and promotes mutual exchanges and understandings among different civilisations. China has always respected the diversity of civilisations and the social systems and development paths that countries have chosen independently by replacing confrontation with mutual learning between civilisations. China promotes mutual learning between nations, cultures and religions. China proposes to seek common ground while reserving differences, to achieve common development, to build new type of international relations of win–win cooperation, to promote exchanges between people of different countries, cultures and historical backgrounds, to enhance mutual understanding and to build a community with a shared future.

Sixth is to actively promote the implementation of the Belt and Road Initiative, which has brought China closer to the countries along the Belt and Road and promoted sustainable growth of the world economy and brought benefits to peoples of the countries concerned. Although the Belt and Road Initiative is initiated by China, the dividends and opportunities created are shared by the world. China actively promoted the construction of interconnection and intercommunication, promoted the comprehensive development of major win–win cooperation projects under the framework of the Belt and Road and has achieved important early harvests. China vigorously deepens international capacity cooperation and initially forms an international capacity cooperation layout covering Asia, Africa, Europe and the United States. By doing so, China makes its own development achievements benefit more regions.

Notes

1 Xi Jinping, "Conforming to the Trend of the Times and Promoting Peaceful Development of the World," the speech at the Moscow Institute of International Relations, www.fmprc.gov.cn/web/ziliao_674904/zyjh_674906/t1024371.shtml
2 Ibid.
3 Xi Jinping, "Working Together to Forge a New Partnership of Win–win Cooperation and Create a Community of Shared Future for Mankind," statement at the General Debate of the 70th Session of the UN General Assembly, New York, September 28, 2015.
4 Ni Peimin, "The Philosophical Ideology of Community of Shared future and Win–Win Cooperation," *Philosophical Analysis*, 2017, 2.8.1, p. 104.
5 Zhao Tingyang, "The System of the World: Empire and World Norms," *World Philosophy*, 2003, 5.
6 "Win–win Cooperation is the Core of the Diplomatic Ideology of President Xi Jinping," http://world.huanqiu.com/hot/2015-12/8294606.html
7 Xi Jinping, "The Speech at the South–South Cooperation Roundtable on Promoting South–South Cooperation in the New Era,£ www.fmprc.gov.cn/web/ziliao_674904/zyjh_674906/t1300907.shtml

8 Wu Sike, "Chinese Wisdom Lead the Building of New-type International Relations with Win–Win Cooperation as Its Core," *Public Diplomacy*, 2017, 2, pp. 5–6.
9 Xi Jinping, "The Speech at the First Meeting of the National Security Committee," *People Daily*, April 16, 2014, http://cpc.people.com.cn/shipin/n/2014/0416/c243284-24905277.html
10 Wang Yi, "Building new-type international relations with win–win cooperation as its core—the Chinese answer to the future of international relations in 21st century," www.qstheory.cn/zhuanqu/zywz/2016-06/20/c_1119071966.htm

48
REGIONAL COMPREHENSIVE ECONOMIC PARTNERSHIP

Liu Junsheng

In the context of the current wave of anti-globalisation and trade protectionism, the Regional Comprehensive Economic Partnership (RCEP), which aims to establish a free trade zone and promote regional economic integration, has become a focus. As a giant free trade zone, once the RCEP is reached, it will bring great vitality to global trade liberalisation and will also promote economic growth in the Asia–Pacific region in the medium and long term.

Overview of RCEP: proposals, contents and guiding principles

The RCEP is a regionally integrated economic cooperation mechanism led and promoted by ASEAN. Its concept and draft were originally proposed at the 18th ASEAN Economic Ministers Meeting held in Naypyidaw, Myanmar on February 26, 2011. The 19th ASEAN Leaders Meeting in November formally approved the draft to create RCEP and adopted the ASEAN Regional Comprehensive Economic Partnership Framework Document.

Under the pressure of the high-standard TPP and the continuous expansion of its membership, RCEP has accelerated the pace of formation. At the end of August 2012, the ASEAN "10+6" Economic Ministers Meeting reached a substantial consensus and adopted the "RCEP Negotiation Guiding Principles and Objectives". The 10 ASEAN countries together with China, Japan, South Korea, Australia, New Zealand and India, which have signed free trade agreements with ASEAN, plan to start negotiations in 2013 and conclude negotiations in 2015 with the goal of achieving a modern, comprehensive, high-quality, mutually beneficial Regional Free Trade Agreement (RCEP).

Stimulated by the high standards of TPP, RCEP has the characteristics of "wider coverage and higher standard" compared with other the free trade zones in this domain. However, unlike TPP, a "North–North Cooperation" model, RCEP has also included development issues not covered by TPP in the negotiations on the basis of the five "10+1" FTA common issues. Compared with the TPP's "next-generation FTA model", RCEP is basically involved in issues other than disputes such as environment, government procurement, financial services and labour. Some of them are "beyond-WTO" issues, which is a big step forward compared with other FTAs in this region. In terms of standards, RCEP lagged behind by TPP, mainly reflected in the scope of tariff reduction, the period of protection, the scope of sensitive products, the form of service industry list and the implementation of issues.

In order to facilitate the negotiation, ASEAN also proposed guiding principles for the RCEP negotiations, including: ensuring consistency with the WTO, improving on the basis of the existing 10+1FTAs, improving trade, investment facilitation and transparency to improve participation in global and regional supply chain, taking appropriate flexibility to negotiate the least developed ASEAN countries, continuing to maintain the effectiveness of the existing FTA, adhering to open regionalism, focusing on development cooperation and capacity building and comprehensively and uniformly promoting negotiations in areas such as goods, services and investment, etc.

The scale, economic benefits and impact of RCEP

The RCEP has a total of 16 members, covering a population of 3.4 billion, a GDP volume of nearly US$20 trillion, and a total trade volume of about $10 trillion, accounting for 48%, 28% and 28% of the world's total, respectively (Table 48.1). In terms of scale, once the RCEP is reached, it will not only surpass the "10+3" and the China–Japan–Korea Free Trade Zone, which have been discussed in recent years, but will also surpass the more developed North American Free Trade Area and the European Union to become the world's largest free trade zone. In terms of economic development potential, RCEP includes India, China and Indonesia, which are among the world's most populous countries. They also have the most dynamic and potential economies and increasing GDP portions in the world. Moreover, RCEP is also the free trade zone with the greatest developmental differences. The per-capita GDP ranges from less than $1000 to more than $50,000, making the industrial structures of members more complementary.

According to a study by Peter A. Petri and others, once the giant FTAs such as RCEP and TPP are reached, they will bring huge economic benefits to Asia and the world. Among them, the economic benefits of RCEP are higher than TPP, the former and the latter will account for 0.6% and 0.4% of world GDP, respectively. Similarly, in the Asian Development Outlook 2013 released in April 2013, "In 2025, the establishment of RCEP will generate 640 billion US dollars of income, equivalent to 0.6% of the global GDP, showing great development potential".

As the first giant free trade zone in the Asia–Pacific region, the establishment of RCEP will have a huge impact on the region and the world.

Table 48.1 Comparison between regional cooperation frameworks (unit: trillion US dollars,%)

Frameworks	GDP (percentage)		Population (billions, percentage)		Trade volume (percentage)
	2011	2015	2011	2015	2011
RCEP	19.9 (28)	26.2 (32)	3.4 (48)	3.5 (48)	10.1 (28)
TPP	20.7 (29)	24.4 (30)	0.66 (9.4)	0.68 (9.4)	7.8 (21)
ASEAN	2.1 (3.1)	3.1 (3.8)	0.60 (8.7)	0.64 (8.8)	2.4 (6.5)
APT	16.5 (23)	21.8 (26)	2.1 (31)	2.2 (30)	6.8 (24)
CJK FTAP	14.3 (20)	18.7 (23)	1.5 (22)	1.5 (21)	6.4 (17)
APEC	38.8 (56)	48.5 (59)	2.7 (40)	2.8 (39)	17.6 (48)
NAFTA	17.9 (26)	21.1 (25)	0.46 (6.6)	0.47 (6.5)	5.4 (15)
EU	17.6 (25)	17.5 (21)	0.50 (7.2)	0.50 (7.0)	12.3 (33)

Recourses: Sanchita Basu Das, RCEP and TPP: Comparisons and Concerns, ISEAS Perspective, No. 02, 2013.

From the regional level: first, it will greatly improve the negative impact of the "noodle bowl effect" in the region, further open the market among members and improve resource allocation. Second, it will promote the integration process in East Asia and Asia–Pacific, and Northeast Asia and the South East Asian economies will be linked. And the Northeast Asian countries that are lack of regional identity will be included in the framework of the free trade zone. Third, with the principle of "comprehensive, high-quality, mutually beneficial", RCEP will be a model for high-standard FTA, enabling the Asia–Pacific region to participate in the making of "next-generation" trade rules with a bigger voice in global economic governance. Fourth, it will advance the upgrading of production networks in the Asia–Pacific region and the economic development environment in the region. Fifth, it will promote inclusive economic growth, and the development cooperation of RCEP together with the capacity building can be called the "East Asian version of the development round".

From the world level: first, it marks the rise of the giant FTA, which represents the new trend of FTA development after the global financial crisis in 2008. Second, it conforms to the trend of the eastward shift of the world economic centre, which is beneficial to the Indo-Pacific region rising as a pole in the world economic landscape. Third, it will inject new impetus to economic globalisation and regionalisation that are at a low point under the tide of anti-globalisation.

RCEP negotiation process and results

As of February 2018, the RCEP Summit had issued two statements, held several ministerial meetings and conducted 21 rounds of negotiations. On the whole, RCEP negotiations have entered the sprint stage. Although there are still differences in some areas, substantive advancement and preliminary consensuses have been made in most areas.

In negotiation, as great differences remain in the field of goods and services trade, the negotiation process was slow although the schedule was very intensive. The negotiations were not completed as expected in 2015. In the November 2015 East Asia Summit, a statement said the RCEP had made breakthrough and all teams should accelerate their efforts to conclude negotiations in 2016. In the US Presidential Election campaign, there was a dispute over the TPP, and Japan made it clear that if the TPP fails, it will shift to RCEP. After Trump announced his withdrawal from the TPP, both Australia and New Zealand expressed their desire for RCEP's early establishment. From the perspective of the negotiation process, there were 10 rounds of negotiations from 2013 to 2015, 6 rounds of negotiations in 2016 and 5 rounds of negotiations in 2017.

At present, RCEP has completed negotiations on economic and technical cooperation and SME chapters. The three key areas of goods, services and investment have been substantially promoted, and the parties have reached consensus on initial bidding models for goods trade, rules of origin, customs procedures and trade facilitation, market access and concession models, checklist forms, etc. New issues such as e-commerce are progressing rapidly. However, there are still differences in services and trade sectors such as investment, intellectual property and communications and finance.

Technical difficulties in RCEP integration

As the first giant free trade zone with East Asian countries as its main participants, RCEP has experienced nearly 5 years of negotiations. Although they have achieved initial results, the negotiations face many challenges and difficulties, undergoing twice delays, increasing subjects which make the number of the negotiating groups grow from 3 to 15.

According to the ASEAN Regional Comprehensive Economic Partnership Framework Document and the RCEP Negotiation Guiding Principles and Objectives, RCEP is to integrate five existing "10+1" FTAs centred on ASEAN and finally form a regional multilateral "modern, comprehensive, high quality, mutually beneficial" FTA.

As for the standard, the ASEAN–Australian and New Zealand FTA is in a leading position both in terms of negotiation and liberalisation. According to the guiding principle of "modern, comprehensive, high-quality, mutually beneficial" and the high standards of TPP, RCEP has a great possibility to integrate on the basis of the ASEAN–Australian and New Zealand FTA. However, there are significant differences in social and economic development among RCEP members. For example, the GDP of the most developed country, Japan, is 42 times bigger than that of Myanmar, the least developed country (2013). This not only leads to different positions of the negotiation, but also causes the huge differences between the 5 FTAs in the issue structure and the level of liberalisation, which leads to difficulties in integration through negotiation.

In terms of trade in goods, the ASEAN–Australian and New Zealand FTA has the highest level of liberalisation (95.7%), while the ASEAN–India FTA, the most critical one, has the lowest (79.6%). The other four have similar liberation rates above 90%. In this way, the integration of the ASEAN–India FTA with other FTAs is difficult.

In terms of rules of origin, there are obvious differences in the rules of origin among the 5 FTAs in ASEAN. Some adopt the regional value content (RVC) standard, some adopt the criteria of tax items change (CTC) standard and some adopt both.

In terms of service trade, RCEP requires a substantial non-restriction and non-discrimination policy just like the General Agreement on Trade and Service (GATS) of WTO. At the same time, obligations of the "10+1" FTA must be followed. Among the five "10+1" FTAs, ASEAN has signed the "Service Trade Agreement" with China and South Korea. A similar agreement was signed with India but was not announced. Regarding Australia, New Zealand and Japan the agreements were integrated in package agreements. In terms of specific commitments, huge differences remain in horizontal commitments and sector-specific commitments.

In terms of investment, except for the ASEAN–India FTA, the other four "10+1" all have investment terms with huge differences in national treatment, most favoured nation (MFN) status, performance requirements and transparency. Therefore, a higher uniform standard in investment will inevitably face difficulties.

In addition, differences in sensitive products and implementation stages remain to be solved.

Anti-globalisation and trade protectionism, together with the Comprehensive and Progress Trans-Pacific Partnership (CPTPP) bring increasing uncertainties to the RCEP negotiations. Although substantial breakthroughs have been achieved and some problems have entered sprinting stages after 21 rounds of negotiations, there are more sensitive and difficult issues to be solved. Therefore, it is not realistic to expect a nearly conclusion of the negotiations. The RCEP negotiations will test the political will and wisdom of all parties.

49
THE APPROACH OF UPHOLDING JUSTICE WHILE PURSUING SHARED INTERESTS

Yang Danzhi

Proposal

From March 24 to 30, 2013, during President Xi Jinping's visit to Tanzania, South Africa and the Republic of Congo, he first proposed the approach of upholding justice while pursuing shared interests.

In October 2013, PRC's first neighbouring diplomatic work conference was held. At the meeting, Xi Jinping stressed "it is necessary to cooperate with neighboring countries under the principle of mutual benefit by weaving a closer network of common interests, and further integrating different interests, so that neighboring countries can benefit from China's development and China can benefit from their development also". Xi Jinping also pointed out "it is necessary to find common ground and intersections of interests of China and neighboring countries, adhere to the approach of upholding justice while pursuing shared interests by attaching great importance to principles, friendship and justice and providing more assistance to developing countries".[1]

Since then, Xi Jinping has often referred to "the approach of upholding justice while pursuing shared interests" on many diplomatic and domestic occasions. He stressed that "we must adopt the approach of upholding justice while pursuing shared interests, and always be a reliable friend and sincere partner to developing countries ... We must take a right approach to justice and interests by putting justice before interests ... We must adopt the approach of upholding justice while pursuing shared interests by upholding credit, righteousness, justice and morality". In Xi Jinping's public speeches and signed articles, "the approach of upholding justice while pursuing shared interests" appeared more than 40 times.

On April 8, 2014, Xi Jinping met with Namibian Prime Minister Geingob in Beijing and said, "China holds the approach of upholding justice while pursuing shared interests in cooperation with Africa by giving advices on how to make money and attract foreign investment. So as to improve African countries' ability to grow, benefit African peoples, get mutual benefit, and realize their dream of development and rejuvenation".[2]

From November 28 to 29, 2014, the Central Conference on Foreign Affairs was held in Beijing. Xi Jinping delivered an important speech at the meeting. He clearly stated that the proposal and implementation of the approach of upholding justice while pursuing shared interests is one of the remarkable achievements of central government's foreign affairs since the 18th National Congress of the Communist Party of China. He pointed out that "we must adopt the approach of upholding justice while pursuing shared interests by upholding credit, righteousness, justice and morality. And we must uphold this approach to do a better job in foreign assistance and bring justice and interests together".[3]

On December 4, 2015, at the opening ceremony of the Johannesburg Summit of the China–Africa Cooperation Forum, President Xi Jinping further elaborated on China's "sincerity, practical results, affinity and good faith" and" the approach of upholding justice while pursuing shared interests".[4]

On July 17, 2016, Chinese President Xi Jinping gave a phone call to the 27th Summit of the African Union in Kigali, the capital of Rwanda, to warmly congratulate African countries and people on the successful convening of the conference. In the message, Xi Jinping emphasised that China attaches great importance to the development of China–Africa relations and will continue to uphold the true principles of sincerity, practical results, affinity and good faith and the approach of upholding justice while pursuing shared interests, comprehensively promote the implementation of China–Africa "Ten Cooperation Plans" and promote comprehensive strategic cooperation between China and Africa. The partnership has continuously advanced to a new level and will benefit the people of both sides.

In recent years, "the approach of upholding justice while pursuing shared interests" has appeared many times in President Xi Jinping's speeches on many major occasions at home and abroad, fully demonstrating that the new generation of leadership with Xi Jinping as the core attaches great importance to this concept.

The connotation of the approach of upholding justice while pursuing shared interests

Justice mainly refers to morality and responsibility. Chinese traditional culture always attaches great importance to morality and responsibility.

In ancient China, Confucius emphasised that "justice is the supreme principle to Gentleman". Mozi proposed that "justice can bring interests". Mencius advocated that "life is what I want, and justice is also what I want. If the two cannot be both got, I would like to sacrifice my life to get justice".

Regarding the "vision of justice and interests", President Xi Jinping made an important statement. He pointed out that:

> righteousness reflects our philosophy, the idea of communists and socialist countries. Some people in this world are living good lives, while other people are suffering, and that is not good. Real happiness is common happiness shared by all. We hope that the whole world will develop together with accelerating development in developing countries. We will uphold win–win outcomes by getting mutual benefit instead of winner-take-all principle. We are obliged to poor countries and will give help as much as we can, so we sometimes even need to attach more importance to justice.

Xi Jinping emphasised that justice means that we need to uphold righteousness, treat others as equals, oppose hegemonism and power politics and never concentrate on one's own interests at the expense of other's interests or regional peace and stability. Economic interests mean win–win outcomes and common development. The interests of those neighbouring and developing countries that have long been friends to China should be more considered. We cannot harm others' interests for our own benefit.

The old saying goes, "Glory will come if you value justice, and shame will come if you value interest". The Chinese nation is consistently holding the moral norms of treasuring justice. The traditional and contemporary visions of justice and interests all highlight justice and the balance between justice and interest. Justice priority does not exclude lawful and core interests.

In July 2014, Xi Jinping pointed out in a speech at Seoul National University in South Korea: "At present, economic globalization and regional integration are developing rapidly. Different countries and regions have interconnected, and their futures are bonded together. So, we must abandon the outdated zero-sum mentality and winner-take-all principle when dealing with international relations". Xi Jinping's speech expounds the inevitability and necessity of China's adherence to "the approach of upholding justice while pursuing shared interests".

Adhering to the theoretical and practical significance of the approach of upholding justice while pursuing shared interests

First of all, the approach of upholding justice while pursuing shared interests proposed by President Xi Jinping shows the strategic plan of the Party's new central leadership to the future international status and the function of China. This concept shows that China is an important force for safeguarding world peace, and it reflects China's determination to adhere to the path of peaceful development and its willingness to break the historical fate of the tragedy of war between great powers. Meanwhile, taking priority to justice also shows China's commitment to the international society, fully reflecting the style of a major country.

Adhering to the approach of upholding justice while pursuing shared interests shows that China will never be a "free rider" in the international system. Thinking about world peace and development, China will participate in international affairs more actively and will unswervingly promote peace and development, drive common development, maintain a multilateral trade system and contribute to global economic governance to advance human progression.[5]

In modern times, under the leadership of Western countries, some western concepts were taken as unchanged rules, such as "interests have supreme status" or "there are no eternal friends but eternal interests". Therefore, countries fight for their own interests by forming alliances.

In reality, China has consistently practised the approach of upholding justice while pursuing shared interests for decades. In the 1960s and 1970s, China sent tens of thousands of construction and technical personnel to the African continent to help build the Tanzania–Zambia Railway. Many of them sacrificed their lives. Half a century ago, China began to send medical teams abroad. So far, 23,000 medical personnel have been sent to 66 countries and regions in Asia, Africa and Latin America. They have given treatment to 270 million locals, receiving common praise in host countries.

Since the reform and opening up, with stronger comprehensive national strength, China has been more actively involved in foreign aid and international responsibility than ever. When the Asian financial crisis raged in 1997, China overcame difficulties and did not devalue RMB, providing valuable support for countries and regions concerned to overcome the crisis. When Somali pirates smashed in 2008, China sent ships to participate in peacekeeping operations. Until now, 19 patches of escorting fleets have escorted more than 5800 international ships in the Gulf of Aden.[6]

China has also exempted the debt of the least developed countries, announced the establishment of the 20 billion yuan "China Climate Change South–South Cooperation Fund" and provided US$60 billion to support the "Ten Cooperation Plans". These highlight China's responsibilities in international affairs.

On December 4, 2015, at the opening ceremony of the Johannesburg Summit of the China–Africa Cooperation Forum, President Xi Jinping further elaborated on China's "sincerity, practical results, affinity and good faith" and "the approach of upholding justice while pursuing shared interests". He said that China should join hands with African friends to further win–win cooperation and common development, and to promote a China–Africa new strategic partnership to a comprehensive strategic partnership. To this end, he also proposed five "pillars" that need to further strengthen and consolidate. First, political equality and mutual trust. Second, economic win–win cooperation. Third, exchange of mutual understanding between civilisations. Fourth, mutual help in security. Fifth, unity and cooperation in international affairs. The five "pillars" are guiding principles in the development of relations between China and African or even all countries in a new era.

Second, President Xi Jinping's important thinking of the approach of upholding justice while pursuing shared interests in diplomatic works further enrich the core values of Chinese foreign affairs. It not only guides the diplomatic works in new era, but also enriches the common value of humanity.[7]

Since the reform and opening up in the 1970s, China's national strength has been significantly improved, but countries of the world are concerned about the heading of China's development. In particular, neighbouring countries are worried that China will ignore the vital interests of them and transfer excess capacity to their land. They are afraid that China will take advantage of their imperfect law system and urgent needs for foreign investment and technology to grab their energy and resources. They also worry that China will neglect and ignore environmental and ecological protection in the development process, or fail to comply with relevant international conventions and corresponding international obligations. Some Western countries and non-governmental organisations even label China with "new colonialism".

The proposal and practice of the approach of upholding justice while pursuing shared interests undoubtedly declare to the world that China's own development is closely integrated with the development of the world. As the world's second largest economy, China will not evade or shirk its international responsibilities, and will not achieve its own development at the expense of the interests of other countries and that of the international community. The development pursued by China is a sustainable development. The development goals cannot be achieved by resources overuse, environment pollution and the cost of people's health. China's own stability, prosperity, democracy and progress alone are major contribution to world peace and development, and China will unswervingly move in this direction.

As Chinese Foreign Minister, Wang Yi said that the approach of upholding justice while pursuing shared interests was fully embodied the concept of a socialist country with Chinese characteristics and was a banner of Chinese diplomacy in the new era. Comrade Xi Jinping's important thinking on the approach of upholding justice while pursuing shared interests in diplomatic work reflects the inherent requirements of socialism with Chinese characteristics. Socialism with Chinese characteristics is the socialism that advocates peace. Peaceful development is an inevitable choice for socialism with Chinese characteristics. Under the new situation, adhering to the approach of upholding justice while pursuing shared interests is to uphold the unity of patriotism and internationalism, the integration of the interests of the Chinese people and the common interests of the people of all countries. Only through active interaction and win–win cooperation with the world can China forge ahead.[8]

The approach of upholding justice while pursuing shared interests is a transcendence of Western realism diplomacy. It helps to optimise, purify and sublimate contemporary international relations, and is conducive to consolidating and deepening the unity and cooperation between China and other countries.[9] The proposal and practice of the concept is undoubtedly a full expression of China's soft power in the new era, which is in line with the interests of the people of the world, and will also be widely recognised and supported by the international community.

Notes

1 Xi Jinping, "The Speech at the Symposium on Peripheral Diplomatic Work," http://politics.people.com.cn/n/2013/1025/c1024-23332318-2.html
2 Xi Jinping, "The Speech at the Meeting with Namibian Prime Minister Geingob," www.xinhuanet.com/politics/2014-04-08/c_1110144220.htm
3 Xi Jinping, "The Speech at the Central Conference on Foreign Affairs," www.xinhuanet.com/politics/2014-11/29/c_1113457723.htm
4 Xi Jinping, "The Speech at the Opening Ceremony of the Johannesburg Summit of the China–Africa Cooperation Forum," www.xinhuanet.com/world/2015-12/04/c_1117363197.htm
5 Wang Yi, "Upholding the approach of upholding justice while pursuing shared interests to be a responsible major country—the spirit of President Xi Jinping's important speech on foreign affairs," http://opinion.people.com.cn/n/2013/0910/c1003-22862978.html
6 Ibid.
7 Ibid.
8 Ibid.
9 "Xi Jinping's vision of justice and interests in diplomatic works," http://news.china.com/focus/xjpcfsg/11178989/20160619/22898640_all.html

50
AMITY, SINCERITY, MUTUAL BENEFIT AND INCLUSIVENESS

Li Zhifei

Elaboration and formation of the concept

In October 2013, the neighbourhood diplomacy work conference was held in Beijing. At the meeting, President Xi Jinping emphasised that China is committed to pursuing partnership with its neighbours and neighbourhood diplomacy of amity, sincerity, mutual benefit and inclusiveness and fostering a harmonious, secure and prosperous neighbourhood.[1] Since then, amity, sincerity, mutual benefit and inclusiveness have become an important concept of peripheral diplomacy in the new era.

President Xi Jinping repeatedly emphasised the need to uphold the peripheral diplomatic concept of amity, sincerity, mutual benefit and inclusiveness when he talked about Belt and Road Initiative, expressing the highest value of Chinese diplomacy. At AsiaInfo Summit in May 2014, President Xi Jinping made a speech entitled "Actively Establishing An Asian Security Vision to Forge A New Situation of Security Cooperation". He mentioned that "China is committed to pursuing partnership with its neighbors and a neighboring diplomacy of amity, sincerity, mutual-benefit and inclusiveness and fostering a harmonious, secure and prosperous neighborhood".[2]

In August 2014, President Xi Jinping referred to his visit to Mongolia as a "family member visit". On September 17, 2014, President Xi Jinping delivered a speech entitled "Working Together to Pursue the Dream of National Rejuvenation" during a state visit to India. In the speech, he stressed that "the Chinese nation has always paid great attention to the relationship with neighbors. It is China's consistent diplomatic philosophy. China regards periphery as the foundation for development and prosperity. We have proposed amity, sincerity, mutual benefit, and inclusiveness to live with our neighbors wholeheartedly, and promote common development and cooperation".[3] In April 2015, when President Xi Jinping gave a speech in the Pakistani parliament, he once again pointed out that "we will follow the principle of amity, sincerity, mutual benefit, and inclusiveness and deepen mutually beneficial cooperation with neighboring countries and strive to make our own development better to benefit neighboring countries".[4]

In October 2017, President Xi Jinping pointed out in the report to the 19th National Congress of the Communist Party of China that China should "follow the principle of amity, sincerity, mutual benefit, and inclusiveness and deepen mutually beneficial cooperation with neighboring countries".[5] The practice of this concept becomes an important part of implementing peaceful development path and the building of a community with a shared future. It has also become the core concept of China's neighbouring foreign works.

The main content

Amity, sincerity, mutual benefit and inclusiveness are integrated as one. Although they have different profiles, they cannot be separated. The concept highlights China's efforts to build a collective identity and a community with a shared future in neighbouring areas, promotes balance among sovereignty, development and responsibility in improving regional governance and shaping neighbouring order, and also shows the major country responsibility and style of China.

Amity

As a Chinese saying goes, "The essence of international exchanges lies in the amity between two peoples". Amity refers to a sense of identity and affinity created by geographical closeness and cultural relevance of neighbouring countries. Those ties, both geographical and emotional, should be consolidated. The "amity" that China advocates is to treat neighbours as relatives. This is China's new concept. The "amity" elaborated by Xi Jinping at the neighbouring diplomatic work conference is that China firmly commits to good-neighbourliness by promoting mutual help, equality, emotional ties and frequent visits. China will do more good things, so that neighbouring countries will be more friendly, closer, more identifiable and more supportive to China with enhanced affinity, appeal and influence. Amity in neighbouring diplomacy is based on geographical proximity, cultural affinity and the identification of the same community. China is willing to be an active contributor of public goods to promote the building of a community with a shared future.

Sincerity

"Sincerity " mainly means to be sincere and creditable, and to treat people with sincerity and honesty. "Sincerity" emphasises that we need to treat neighbouring countries sincerely to get more friends and partners. This shows that China pays more attention to sincerity and strategic transparency in peripheral diplomatic relations. In economic development, it stresses complementarities, mutual and win–win benefit, shared interest and the establishment of strategic mutual trust. Sincerity means justice and creditability. In diplomatic policies, it means to treat others honestly with acknowledgement of differences and contradictions, clarification of the bottom line and respect of other countries' feelings and reasonable interests. Disorder and jungle law still prevail in today's world, and China will never bully small countries and will not tolerate troubles made by the small countries.[6]

Mutual benefit mainly concerns interests and common development. "Mutual benefit" mainly means that it is necessary to cooperate with neighbouring countries under the principle of mutual benefit by weaving a closer network of common interests and further integrating different interests, so that neighbouring countries can benefit from China's development and China can benefit from their development also. Most of China's neighbouring countries are developing countries and rising economies. As the most dynamic economy in the world, China advocates "mutual benefit" by cooperating with neighbouring countries so that they can fully share the dividends of China's economic development to get common development. This fully shows China's responsibility as a responsible major country.

Inclusiveness

China has always advocated for countries to respect each other's social systems, development models and civilisations by promoting exchange and cooperation between different social systems, ethnical groups, religions and cultures to minimise the risk of war. "Inclusiveness" promotes inclusive thinking. Asia–Pacific is big enough for common development, and we must promote regional cooperation with a more open mind and a more positive attitude. Beside theoretical and ideological inclusiveness, an inclusive approach must be taken in the implementation of every specific policy to take every party's needs into consideration, so that shared interests and integrated systems can be achieved.

The theoretical and practical significance

Surrounding areas are vital to the development and prosperity of China. The thinking of amity, sincerity, mutual benefit and inclusiveness, an important inheritance and positive innovation of China's peripheral diplomatic ideology, is the conceptual framework of China's new leadership on neighbouring diplomacy. It also highlights the top priority of neighbouring diplomacy in the transformation of China's diplomatic strategy.

First, the concept of amity, sincerity, mutual benefit and inclusiveness is an innovative development of the surrounding diplomatic concept and is of great significance for China's neighbouring diplomacy. Since its founding more than 60 years ago, PRC has always upheld the independent diplomacy of peace, good-neighbourliness and mutual benefit and win–win outcomes in neighbouring diplomacy. However, the concept of "mutual benefit and win–win outcomes" is often interpreted by the outside world as an interest-driven policy. After the continuous enhancement of China's comprehensive national strength and the continuous improvement of international influence, the "China threat" theory has gained many supporters in neighbouring regions. Many neighbouring countries will inevitably doubt and even fear that China will contain their development, so a great sense of wariness against China is rising. At the same time, the US proposed the "Pivot to Asia" strategy. The two reasons jointly cause the imbalanced phenomenon of relying on China to develop economy while relying on the US to provide security.

Nowadays, putting the concept of amity, sincerity, mutual benefit and inclusiveness at the core of neighbouring diplomacy is an important thinking by the Central Committee of the Communist Party of China (CCCPC) with President Xi Jinping as the core on the future of neighbouring diplomacy. It is a summary and innovation to the 60-year-old good-neighbourliness diplomacy, showing the old tradition of treasuring good neighbours in Chinese culture. By lifting neighbouring relations to emotional ties and combining feelings with interests, China is shaping a community with shared interests, obligations and future to achieve innovative development in neighbouring diplomacy. As an old Chinese saying goes, good neighbours are well-wishers for each other and nothing is more valuable than good neighbours. This enlightens Chinese new leadership to adjust China's neighbouring diplomacy by combining historical experiences and current situations. The diplomatic concept of amity, sincerity, mutual benefit and inclusiveness shows that China will never seek hegemonism and containment, crushing the old mentality that hegemonism is the only way for great power, reflecting China's sincerity to neighbouring countries and showing China's willingness to build a community with a shared future with neighbouring countries. The implementation of the concept will certainly benefit political mutual trust, economic cooperation and people-to-people exchange between China and neighbouring countries. All these will promote the building of good-neighbourly relations and stable and peaceful neighbouring security environment to better serve the peaceful development of the nation.

Second, the concept of amity, sincerity, mutual benefit and inclusiveness is the basic concept for Belt and Road Initiative to promote cooperation and reshape the order in neighbouring regions. It shows China's view of mutual respect, mutual help, common development and common prosperity with neighbouring countries and China's vision of international norms featuring democracy, equality, cooperation and win–win outcomes. The Belt and Road Initiative implemented by China is the top-level design for surrounding diplomacy, connecting domestic and international layout of the Chinese diplomacy, and also showing Chinese resolve to peaceful development. By synergising strategies of China and other countries, China shares success and dividends of its own economic development with countries along the Belt and Road to promote economic development, people's living and the prosperity of these countries. The Belt and Road Initiative, following the concept of amity, sincerity, mutual benefit and inclusiveness, shows new models of regional cooperation.

The Belt and Road Initiative covers many countries with different political and economic systems, cultures, languages and customs in different regions of the world. The implementation of the Belt and Road Initiative shows the concept of amity, sincerity, mutual benefit and inclusiveness and win–win cooperation. In the process, cooperation in agriculture, chemical industry, energy, transportation, communication, finance, science and technology is carried out regardless of huge differences to realise interconnectivity and common development and prosperity of China and countries concerned. First of all, the concept of "amity" and "sincerity" is reflected in the sincere willingness to cooperate with Asia–Pacific and European countries to achieve common development and share the dividend of China's development in the process of building a community with a shared future. As President Xi Jinping mentioned in his keynote speech at the 2017 World Economic Forum in Davos, "The world will be better and people will live a better life only if we join hands to share responsibility and cope with difficulties together to build a community with a shared future".[7]

Mutual benefit is reflected in the cooperation ideology of the path of common development that is built and shared by all in Belt and Road Initiative. Over the last 3 years since the implementation of the Belt and Road Initiative, more than 100 countries and international organisations have reacted and more than 40 of them have signed cooperation agreements with China. The circle of friends is expanding. Chinese companies have invested more than $50 billion in countries along the Belt and Road, and a series of major projects have been launched, driving local economy with a huge number of new jobs. It can be said that the Belt and Road Initiative comes from China, but the results benefit the world.[8]

Inclusiveness is shown as China, a responsible major country, embraces differences in political systems of countries, and diminishes some historical and practical problems that have existed for a long time, such as the disputes over the islands and reefs of the South China Sea to create, a favourable political and security environment for cooperation. China also calls for peaceful communication in political areas and cooperation in economic aspect to get regional prosperity and the settlement of non-traditional security issues along the Belt and Road.

The Belt and Road Initiative is a sustainable development and cooperation framework under the banner of peace and development. It covers a large geographical area and has long-lasting influence. The combination of the concept of amity, sincerity, mutual benefit and inclusiveness and the Belt and Road Initiative will not only promote China's role in global governance and development, but will also advance common development and common welfare of China and the world.

Notes

1 Xi Jinping, "The Speech at the neighborhood diplomacy work conference," http://politics.people.com.cn/n/2013/1025/c1024-23332318-2.html
2 Xi Jinping, "Keynote speech at the fourth Asiainfo Summit," www.chinanews.com/gn/2014/05-21/6196012.shtml
3 Xi Jinping, "The speech at Indian World Affair Committee—Join hands for national rejuvenation," website of central government, http://cpc.people.com.cn/n/2014/0919/c64094-25690823.html
4 Xi Jinping, "The speech in Pakistan Parliament," Xinhuanet, http://news.xinhuanet.com/world/2015-04/21/c_1115044392.htm
5 Xi Jinping, "Seizing the Opportunity of a Global Economy in Transition and Accelerating Development of the Asia-Pacific—Keynote Address at the APEC CEO Summit," Xinhua News Agency, November 10 2017, www.xinhuanet.com/politics/leaders/2017-11/10/c_1121938333.htm
6 He Yafei, "The principle of amity, sincerity, mutual benefit, and inclusiveness and the Belt and Road Initiative," http://news.163.com/16/0118/16/BDKIIK7100014AEE.html
7 Xi Jinping, "The keynote speech at the opening ceremony of the 2017 World Economic Forum," Xinhuanet, www.xinhuanet.com/2017-01/18/c_1120331545.htm
8 Ibid.

51
SINCERITY, PRACTICAL RESULTS, AFFINITY AND GOOD FAITH

Yang Danzhi

Proposal of the principle

On March 25, 2013, Chinese President Xi Jinping delivered an important speech entitled "Always Be Reliable Friends and Sincere Partners" at the Nyerere International Conference Centre in Tanzania, which comprehensively expounded China–Africa relations and China's policy towards Africa. In his speech, President Xi Jinping clearly stated for the first time the principle of sincerity, practical results, affinity and good faith in China's policy towards Africa.

The first is to treat African friends with sincerity. Xi Jinping pointed out:

> We have always regarded the development of solidarity and cooperation with African countries as an important basis for China's foreign policy. This will never change with China's own development and international status. China insists that all countries, big or small, strong or weak, rich or poor, are all equal. China will hold justice and fight any bullying actions towards small, weak or poor countries. China opposes interference to other countries internal affairs, strengthens mutual support in core interests and vital issues of both sides, and supports the just cause of African countries on international and regional occasions to make greater contribution to peace and security of Africa.

Regarding the development of Africa, he pointed out:

> China will continue to firmly support African countries in exploring development paths suited to their national conditions, strengthen exchanges of experience with African countries in governing the country, and draw wisdom from each other's civilization and development practices to promote common prosperity.

In addition, China believes that "all African countries belong to a big family with a shared future and common interests". China "sincerely wishes and firmly supports Africa's efforts on the road of unity and self-improvement, and pushes the cause of peace and development in Africa to a new level". The Chinese side also believes that "Africa belongs to African people. Any country that wants to develop relations with Africa should respect Africa's dignity and autonomy".

The second is to carry out practical results in the cooperation with Africa. "China is committed to synergizing its own development, people's interests, and development opportunity with that of the African's. China has always supported and helped African friends while pursuing its own development." In recent years, China has enhanced its assistance and cooperation with Africa. Once promises are made, they will be fully implemented.

Practical results are reflected in financing, personnel training and assistance.

Xi Jinping pointed out: "China will continue to expand its investment and financial cooperation with Africa, and implement the commitment of another $20 billion loans to Africa within three years". China will make full use of the "African Transnational and Interregional Infrastructure Construction Partnership" to strengthen cooperation in agriculture, manufacturing and other sectors with African countries, and to help them make full use of their advantages in resources to boost independent and sustainable development.

The Chinese side will actively implement the "African Talent Programme". In the coming next three years, China will train 30,000 talents of various types for African countries, provide 18,000 scholarships for African students and strengthen cooperation in technology transfer and experience sharing with Africa.

The Chinese side also promised that "with economic strength and overall national strength rising, China will continue to provide due assistance to Africa's development without any political preconditions".

The third is to stick to affinity by strengthening the China–Africa friendship. Xi Jinping pointed out that the reason why the Chinese people and the African people have a natural affinity and can be intimate is that "we share the same vision through deep dialogue and practical action".

Xi Jinping attaches great importance to the mass foundation of China–Africa relations. He pointed out that the foundation and root of China–Africa relations lie in the two peoples. "We must pay more attention to people to people exchanges between China and Africa to enhance mutual understanding between Chinese and African peoples, so that to foster the social foundation of China–Africa friendship." At the same time, "China–Africa relations are a future-oriented cause which needs consecutive efforts of young men of several generations. The two sides should actively promote youth exchanges so that the Chinese–African friendship will be energetic".

The fourth is to insist on good faith when dealing with problems. Both China and Africa are in a process of rapid development, and mutual knowledge needs to be updated. "China is honest to the new problems and difficulties facing China–Africa relations and insists on a proper settlement on the basis of mutual respect and win–win cooperation. African countries will always be our best friends no matter how developed China will be."[1]

The proposal and practice of the principle of sincerity, practical results, affinity and good faith have further brought China–Africa relations closer. At present, Africans generally believe that today's China–Africa relations have entered an expressway of all-round development with frequent highlights in various sectors. The two sides established the China–Africa Cooperation Forum and built a comprehensive strategic partnership. China and Africa have continuously deepened cooperation in economic and trade engagement and people to people exchanges. The two sides have supported each other on issues involving the core interests and major concerns of each other and have written a new chapter for China–Africa relations.[2]

The basic connotation of the principle

The principle of sincerity, practical results, affinity and good faith is a conceptual framework of China's diplomatic work on Africa created by the new leadership with Xi Jinping as the core in new era. It is a review of the works of previous central leaderships. It has not only summarisation and inheritance, but also innovation and development.

Sincerity means that China treats African countries with sincerity. First, China cherishes the traditional friendly relations between China and Africa. Second, China respects sovereignty, dignity and core interests of African countries and does not interfere in the internal affairs of African countries. China insists that Africa belongs to Africans and Africans are free to choose their own way and model of developing. Africans can solve their own problems by themselves and China can contribute more to the peace and security of Africa. At the same time, China also firmly supports African countries to unite and strengthen them by supporting African Union playing an important role in regional affairs.

First, practical results are seen in China's practical assistance to Africa. China gives the Africans what they urgently need in capital, technology and human resources training without political preconditions. Second, practical results lie in China's credibility. China abides by its commitment to African countries. Once a commitment is made, China will overcome all difficulties and implement it.

Affinity refers to close ties between the two peoples. Transcending traditional political and geo-economic boundaries and geographically based ideology, the ties between the two peoples are based on trust and close relations grown from shared destiny and common interests.

Geographically, African countries are not close neighbours of China and do not share geographical proximity and cultural affinity with China. However, China and the African countries have a deep traditional friendship and good cooperative relations which have withstood the test of time and international changes. It is hailed as a model for relations among developing countries.

In this sense, African countries belong to China's "greater periphery" regions. The relations between the two are even closer than real neighbours. Through frequent interactions and mutual support, China and Africa can build a high-level mutual trust, and China's affinity, appeal and influence to the people of African countries will be further strengthened.[3]

Good faith means that China is honest to the new problems and difficulties facing China–Africa relations and insists on a proper settlement on the basis of mutual respect and win–win cooperation. China always and will continue to work with African countries to take practical measures to properly solve the problems in China–Africa economic and trade cooperation and to enable African countries to benefit more from cooperation. At the same time, the Chinese side also frankly pointed out that "we sincerely hope that African countries will provide corresponding conditions for Chinese enterprises and citizens to cooperate in Africa".

Theoretical value and practical significance

The proposal of the principle of sincerity, practical results, affinity and good faith has further enhanced China–Africa relations. "China will unswervingly support Africa's development and take African affairs as its own. Africa is also deeply impressed by China's desire to be friends with Africa, sincere and friendly attitude towards Africa, and the concept of win–win cooperation."[4]

The theoretical value and practical significance of practicing sincerity, practical results, affinity and good faith are mainly reflected in two aspects.

First, the principle of sincerity, practical results, affinity and good faith is of great significance for further consolidating the foundation of China–Africa relations and cooperation in new situations. The current development of China–Africa cooperation also faces many challenges. First, the impact of political transformation. In some African countries, political parties are rotating and government changes are frequent, so policies lack stability and continuity. Second, the business environment needs to be improved. African countries want foreign investment, but the laws and regulations to attract and protect foreign capital are not perfect and preferential policies and government services are not ready. Third, the bottleneck restricting development is outstanding. The supporting infrastructure is seriously lagging behind, and there is a shortage of skilled technicians, industrial workers, as well as money. Fourth, the security threats of terrorism, disease and social security are generally high. The fifth is the impact of the external economic environment. At present, the global economy continues to slump, and international commodity prices have fallen sharply, which has directly affects the export of African energy, mineral products as well as the enthusiasm of the international investors who want to invest in Africa. These have all seriously affected the development momentum of African countries.

As China's rise has accelerated, there have been discordant voices in China–Africa relations. First, some Western countries are worried that China will further engage in Africa, threatening their traditional influence in politics, economics and other sectors in Africa. Therefore, they have tried their best to smear China by taking all kinds of despicable means and calling China "neo-colonialist". They accuse China of only taking resources out of Africa regardless of local development and try to stir up troubles between China and Africa. As a result, some African countries have concerns and doubts about the strategic considerations behind China's efforts on developing relations with Africa. Second, African countries have misunderstood China's diplomatic strategy in the new era, arguing that China will invest more diplomatic and strategic resources in major countries and neighbouring countries; therefore, Africa's position in China's strategic considerations is relatively declining or even neglected. Third, some Chinese companies have been increasingly criticised over environmental protection, industrial relations and other aspects in the process of investing in Africa. The behaviour of some Chinese enterprises in African countries ignores or even violates local laws by committing fraudulent acts, seriously damaging China's image in Africa.

In the new era, new ideas are needed to lead China–Africa relations. As President Xi Jinping said in his speech at the International Conference Centre in Nyerere, Tanzania, "China–Africa relations must maintain vitality and must advance and innovate with the times. Looking back into the past half century, in every critical moment, the two sides could all see the big picture of bilateral relations to find new convergence points and growth points for better China–Africa cooperation."

The proposal of the principle of sincerity, practical results, affinity and good faith is an active effort made by the Chinese side in this regard. It not only sets goals and directions for further promoting the development of China–Africa relations under the new situation, but also proposes concrete, pragmatic and operational measures and programmes on how to implement the targets. At the same time, it is also a powerful counterattack against the Western countries' slanders on China's foreign policy towards Africa. In addition, the principle of sincerity, practical results, affinity and good faith does not only apply to Africa, it can also be used as reference for China's relations with all developing countries.

Second, the principle of sincerity, practical results, affinity and good faith is interconnected with the principle of amity, sincerity, mutual benefit and inclusiveness. Both are the basic ideology of the Belt and Road Initiative. The implementation of the principle of sincerity, practical results, affinity and good faith will promote the implementation of the Belt and Road Initiative in Africa. Actively participating in the building of the Belt and Road is the need of Africa's own development. Africa has a vast land of 30.29 million square kilometres. It owns the world's 53 most important minerals and some rare strategic resources. The arable land area is nearly 800 million hectares, but only 27% of them have been developed. Africa has abundant labour resources. The total population exceeds 1.1 billion, and is expected to reach 2.5 billion in 2050, of which the youth population covers over 50%, and in some countries this number exceeds 65%. From the perspective of developmental stages, African countries are generally eager to achieve industrialisation and economic diversification, and have urgent need for foreign investment and technology transfer. In addition, the great success of China's reform and opening up, together with the successful experience and development models, can be a mirror for Africa's economic independence and independent sustainable development. Africa's trend of "looking east" has formed.

African countries hope to enhance infrastructure, diversify their economic development and break the current backward economic development model. China has rich experiences in economic development and demands for capacity cooperation, which will help accelerate the industrialisation of Africa. The building of the Belt and Road, an important development initiative China has put forward to the world, has undoubtedly brought new opportunities to China–Africa cooperation. The relative development advantages of China's capital, technology, market, enterprise, talent and successful development experience will be closely integrated with Africa's abundant natural resources, huge demographic dividends and market potential. It is a win–win choice for China and Africa.

Notes

1 Xi Jinping, "Always Be Reliable Friends and Sincere Partner" at the Nyerere International Conference Centre in Tanzania, http://theory.people.com.cn/n/2013/0326/c136457-20914243.html
2 "The great charm of the principle of sincerity, practical results, affinity and good faith," Xinhuanet, www.xinhuanet.com/world/2017-03/25/c_1120692965.htm
3 Party's paper, "The Chinese wisdom in the neighboring diplomacy featuring affinity, honesty, mutual benefit and inclusiveness," www.the paper.cn/newsDetail_forward_1464944_1
4 "The great charm of the principle of sincerity, practical results, affinity and good faith," Xinhuanet, www.xinhuanet.com/world/2017-03/25/c_1120692965.htm

PART VIII

Core concepts

52
BRIDGE DEVELOPMENT STRATEGIES

Xu Xiujun

The concept

In March 2013, President Xi Jinping proposed the concept of "bridging development strategies" during his visit to Russia. Whilst in Russia, Xi Jinping delivered a speech entitled *Follow the Trend of the Times and Promote Peace and Development in the World*, in which he pointed out that China and Russia shall "bridge the development strategies of our respective countries and regions in an effort to create still more converging interests and growth areas in bilateral cooperation".[1] Following that, efforts on bridging development strategies have been widely applied in the realm of bilateral and multilateral relations. The concept of "bridging development strategies" refers to docking connection points and common grounds of development strategies formulated by realities of each country and region, with a purpose of enabling complementarities and common development, and finally achieving shared objectives.

After entering the twenty-first century, China made the timely decision of conducting strategic dialogues with major countries and regions in the world, and progressively initiated such discussions with major powers and blocs of power, such as the United States, Japan, Germany, Russia, India, France, Briton, Australia, Brazil, Republic of Korea, Indonesia, the European Union and the African Union. As the foundation of strategy bridging, strategic dialogues stress exchanging strategical views between dialogue partners, with the aim of improving strategic trust between dialogue partners, boosting cooperation, resolving disputes properly and increasing mutual interests, benefiting the two sides and the whole humanity. The wide-ranging strategic topics, encompassing the global situation, China's trend and bilateral, multilateral and international relations, consist of frank exchanges of strategies and views over issues of overall significance, strategic importance and farsightedness, such as the future of humanity, global order and global governance. They delve into fundamental discussions of understanding the changing world and each other's development, adjusting ideas, concepts, guidelines, policies and behaviours and bolstering trust and collaborations, so as to build a new-type major power relationship, promote a community of shared interests and future for mankind and safeguard the planet.[2]

Following the proposal of the Belt and Road Initiative, China has set greater store by development when engaging in strategic cooperation with other countries and regions, and expedited development strategy bridging with the rest of the world. During his visits, which began in 2013, to Russia, Mongolia, Tajikistan, Sri Lanka, India, Australia, New Zealand, Fiji, Pakistan, Belarus, the United Kingdom, Vietnam, Singapore, Zimbabwe, Saudi Arabia, Egypt, Iran, the Czech Republic, Serbia, Poland, Uzbekistan, Cambodia, Ecuador, Peru, Chile, Finland, Kazakhstan, Germany and Laos, President Xi Jinping stressed the need to strengthen bridging development strategies. He proposed intensified efforts to bridge development strategies in international conferences and critical diplomatic occasions including the Boao Forum for Asia, BRICS Leaders' Meeting, APEC CEO Summit, APEC Leaders' Informal Meeting, Shanghai Cooperation Organisation Heads of State Council, China–Arab Cooperation Forum, Asia–Africa Leaders' Meeting, Poverty Alleviation Development of high-level forums, China–Central and Eastern European leaders' meetings and the "Belt and Road" Forum for International Cooperation. In doing so, bridging development strategies has become a core component in promoting the Belt and Road Initiative and an important approach to deal with foreign relations.

Significance of bridging development strategies in the global era

Following the proposal of the Belt and Road Initiative, China strongly advocates coordinating development strategies with the world and fosters international cooperation under the Belt and Road framework into a new driver for globalisation.

For one thing, bridging development strategies theoretically reflect the innate requirement of globalisation. The deepening of globalisation is first reflected by the greater openness of the world and more inclusive cooperation between nations. Bridging development strategies conforms to this trend and upholds the opening-up philosophy to link the world and to build a new global economic system featuring openness. Bridge development strategies shall be based on but not be limited to the scope of the Ancient Silk Road. In comparison with the inward and enclosed modes of cooperation, such policy coordination proposed by China is an outward regional or cross-regional mode. Such bridging will not target any individual country or form any type of economic blocs, so any country that aspires and aims for development can engage in mutually beneficial cooperation through strategy coordination, with its probable outreach to all parts of the world. By upholding the principle of widening consultation, joint contribution and shared benefits, bridging development strategies can maximise the integration of strengths of all countries and resources of all types while sharing the outcomes of globalisation.

For another, the content of bridging development strategies lays a solid foundation for advancing globalisation. Each country's resources differ in strengths and highly complement each other, and there are huge potential and demands for mutual dependency. The relative backwardness in the building of interconnectivity, whether in software or hardware, however, gives rise to the lack of infrastructure and prerequisites for deepening globalisation. By bridging development strategies, all parties concerned can find the common grounds and points of complementarities, and thus plan cooperation programmes in underpinned areas. As collaborations in critical areas continue to intensify and cooperation planning continues to be pushed forward, transnational and transregional interconnectivity networks, which ceaselessly extend to the other parts of the world, are established in relevant countries, providing inexhaustible fundamental support for a new round of globalisation.

Also, bridging development strategies injects new impetus to practically spearheading globalisation under unique circumstances. From an individual perspective, bridging development strategies is a successful practice on account of China's Reform and Opening-up. Over the course of 40-year reform and opening-up, China ushered into a path of conforming to the national reality, putting people first, reform and innovation and seeking common development amidst opening up, and leapfrogged to the second seat in global economic strengths. Development in China afforded the world rich experiences and opportunities. Under new circumstances, China, guided by the philosophy of innovation, coordination, green development, openness and shared interests, will continuously stimulate growth drivers and market vitality, actively cultivate an investment environment that is loose and orderly and build the architecture of openness for common development, adding new drivers to economic globalisation. As China strengthens bridging development strategies under the Belt and Road framework, Chinese enterprises increase investment to countries along the Belt and Road, which offers huge amounts of opportunities to these countries in economic development and employment and subsequently turn them into new drivers for globalisation.

Finally, the outcomes of the bridging relieve the adverse effects of globalisation. Against the backdrop of economic globalisation, all countries have increasingly become an interdependent community of shared interests. Due to the unfair distribution of interests, however, some participants of globalisation have been impaired. Because of this, all forms of protectionism were on the rise, bringing in the biggest obstacle to globalisation. The purpose of bridging development strategies is to promote mutually beneficial cooperation, with the initial objective of achieving common prosperity of all participating nations. Mutually beneficial collaboration refers to seeking convergence of interests and expanding common ground in cooperation by taking into account each party's interests and concerns. It is the cooperation where the wisdom and creativity of each stakeholder are embodied, strengths and potential of each are fully unleashed. To steer each county and region into the track of mutual benefits, win–win and common prosperity is the guarantee for sustainable development for globalisation and where the meaning of deepening globalisation lies.

In short, bridging development strategies provide solutions against the negative impact of economic globalisation in new circumstances from the source. At present, the world economy is confronted with issues of lackluster growth momentum, imbalanced development, unequal development opportunities and uneven distribution of development benefits. Reforming global economic governance system has become more salient. The underlying deficiency in modes of economic growth, cooperation, governance and development is the fundamental issue confronting the current world economy. In light of this, China proposed the principle featuring innovation as the driver, coordination, keeping up with the trend of the time, fairness and inclusiveness, and committed to establishing a dynamic growth model, a mutually beneficial cooperation model, a fair and equitable governance model and a balanced and universal development model. To strengthen bridging development strategies, it is imperative to find priorities for addressing the challenges facing each party and tackling issues at global scales, actively contributing Chinese wisdom and exhibiting China's responsibility as a significant power in leading economic globalisation.

Models and practices for development strategies bridging

To intensify strategy bridging and policy communication is a safeguard for the pursuit of the Belt and Road Initiative. Since the unveiling of the Initiative, some countries have promulgated individual regional cooperation plans and national development plans to line up with it. It is seen that synergy and linkage for policies are rising and correspondent plans for bridging have been issued. Rich in connotation, bridging development strategies embodies the principle of achieving shared growth through discussion and collaboration and acts on boosting mutually beneficial cooperation. It follows the trend of the current world and meets the aspirations of countries and mankind for development.

In its practices for bridging development strategies, China has formed diverse, flexible and efficient modes of linkage, which are summed up as the following

One on one bridging. Such as a bilateral strategic linkage between China and an individual country. It is the basis for bridging development strategies under the Belt and Road framework.

One on multiple bridging. Such as the strategic bridging between China and one international institution or one type of states. It is China's innovation for developing foreign relations and bolstering international cooperation, as it inspires synergy between states of similar nature and increases cooperation efficiency.

Multiple on multiple bridging. This refers to strategic coordination between international institutions with Chinese participation and other counterparts or one type of states. Such a model is committed to the principle of global partnership and community of shared future for mankind. It maximises common interests and shares development outcomes.

At the bilateral and regional levels, China has bridged the Belt and Road Initiative with other development strategies, such as Turkey's "Intermediate Corridor" plan, Kazakhstan's "Bright Road" new economic policy, Tajikistan's "2030 National Development Strategy", Saudi Arabia's "2030 Vision Strategy", Mongolia's "Development Road" Initiatives, China–Vietnam "Two Corridors and One Circle" Plan, Cambodia's "Four-Corner Strategy", Thailand's "Eastern Economic Corridor" Plan, Laos "'Land-locked Country' Turning to 'Bilateral' Priority Development Policy", UK Infrastructure Upgrade Investment Plan and "Northern England" development plan, the "Opening to Hungary" policy, the Eurasian Economic Union, the overall planning of the ASEAN Interconnection and the "Amber Way" through North and South Europe. In doing so, the Belt and Road Initiative finds footholds in the Asian, European and African Continents, and complementarities and converging interests are guaranteed. At the global level, the Chinese government signed Belt and Road cooperation documents with nearly 20 international organisations.[3] The Chinese government has also signed the intergovernmental memorandum of understanding on "Belt and Road" cooperation with Mongolia, Pakistan, Nepal, East Timor, Singapore, Myanmar, Malaysia, Lebanon and 13 Central and Eastern European countries. Cooperation programmes and projects under the Belt and Road Initiative between China and the government departments of relevant states are also being carried out in an orderly manner.

Philosophies and actions of the "International Institution Plus Model" where China has been participating can also be regarded as a new form of practice for linking development strategies. For instance, in the BRICS cooperation institution, China proposed the BRICS Plus cooperation model. In September 2017, the "Emerging Market Countries and Dialogues for Development" held during the BRICS Leaders' Xiamen Meeting broke through the geographical restrictions of previous dialogues and expanded the BRICS partnership to a broader range. The BRICS Plus trailed the blaze for establishing the BRICS institution and promoted the New South–South Cooperation Model. It will achieve new progress and breakthroughs during the Xiamen Meeting. By implementing the BRICS Plus Cooperation Model, the member countries made headway in extensive cooperation and bridging development strategies with the vast number of developing countries.

In addition to the *Vision and Actions on Jointly Building Silk Road Economic Belt and 21st Century Maritime Silk Road* published in March 2015, the Chinese authorities released *Building the Belt and Road: Concept, Practice and China's Contribution* and policy papers on areas covering energy cooperation, agricultural cooperation, green development and maritime cooperation. These illustrate the policy planning and design to participants of the Belt and Road and lay the foundation for policy communication and strategy coordination.[4]

Notes

1 Xi Jinping, "Follow the Trend of the Times and Promote Peace and Development in the World," *People's Daily*, March 24, 2013.
2 Dai Bingguo: "A Few Thoughts on Strategic Dialogues," *People's Daily*, June 17, 2016.
3 Including the United Nations Development Program, the United Nations Industrial Development Organisation, the United Nations Human Settlements Programme, the United Nations Children's Fund, the United Nations Population Fund, the United Nations Conference on Trade and Development, the United Nations Economic Commission for Europe, the United Nations Alliance for Civilisations, the World Health Organisation, the World Intellectual Property Organisation, Interpol, World Economic Forum, International Road Transport Alliance, International Trade Centre, International Telecommunication Union, International Civil Aviation Organisation, International Development Law Organisation, World Meteorological Organisation, International Maritime Organisation, etc.
4 Including the *Vision and Actions on Promoting Energy Cooperation in the Silk Road Economic Belt and the 21st Century Maritime Silk Road* jointly issued by the National Development and Reform Commission and the National Energy Administration, the *Vision and Actions on the "Belt and Road" Agricultural Cooperation* jointly issued by the Ministry of Agriculture, the National Development and Reform Commission, the Ministry of Commerce and the Ministry of Foreign Affairs, *Guiding Opinions on Promoting the Building of the Green Belt and Road Initiative* jointly issued by the Ministry of Environmental Protection, the Ministry of Foreign Affairs, National Development and Reform Commission and the Ministry of Commerce and the *Vision for Maritime Cooperation under the Belt and Road Initiative* jointly issued by the National Development and Reform Commission and the State Oceanic Administration.

53
ASIAN INFRASTRUCTURE INVESTMENT BANK

Xu Xiujun

Background for establishing the Asian Infrastructure Investment Bank

With a vast landscape, huge population and broad markets, Asia is the region having the most robust economic vitality and growth potential. For the majority of Asian nations, the underdeveloped infrastructure such as railway, highway, bridges, ports, airports and communications severely slows down socioeconomic development. However, the primary cause of such underdevelopment is severely insufficient infrastructure investment. The sobering reality is that the gap for such investment demand is large and the funding provided by the multilateral organisations is limited. Given that the request for funding is vast, the term for implementation is long and revenue is uncertain about infrastructure investment, investment scale from the private sector is relatively small. In line with the above, the excessive deposits of some Asian countries have not been fully utilised, so the funding advantage is not fully leveraged.

As Asia's most significant and the world's largest developing economy, China is superior in capital and technology, but it also has the same demand. Furthermore, China has formed a whole industrial chain in equipment manufacturing for infrastructure and spearheaded in engineering sectors such as highway, bridges, tunnels and railway. However, China is still confronted with the salient issue of unbalanced, uncoordinated and unsustainable development, relatively huge gaps between urban and rural growth, regional development and people's income and severely backward infrastructure building in some regions, as well as comparatively numerous resource and environmental constraints. The resolution partly lies in the shift in economic development approaches and adjustment in economic structure and partly in increased investment in these sectors.

To achieve that, China has begun planning to set up an intermediary financial system in Asia underpinned by the appropriate and efficient use of capital to satisfy investment needs, so as to address issues of the insufficient fund for infrastructure and difficulty in financing. From October 2 to 8, 2013, during his visit to Indonesia, Chinese President Xi Jinping held talks with Indonesian President Susilo in Jakarta and proposed the establishment of an Asian Infrastructure Investment Bank initiative to promote the process of connectivity and economic integration in the region, and to offer funding to infrastructure development in developing countries in the area. From October 9 to 15, 2013, during his visits to Brunei, Thailand and Vietnam, Premier Li Keqiang once again proposed to the South East Asian countries to prepare for the establishment of the Asian Infrastructure Investment Bank (AIIB).

The proposed AIIB that underpins financing to the Belt and Road Initiative leverages the spurring role in the regional socioeconomic development and supplements multilateral development organisations. First, the AIIB creates a platform that guides deposits in countries with the high-saving rate in Asia to infrastructure building, and that intensifies cooperation between public and private sectors. By achieving active alignment and allocation of capital in and out of the Asian region, it covers the fiscal gap in Asian infrastructure building, thereby providing sustainable driving force to economic integration in the area. Second, the AIIB can sweep major obstacles in Asian infrastructural connectivity by formulating long-term development rules and leveraging diverse investment and financing measures. By offering concessional loans to enterprises and infrastructural organisations in each country, it helps lower their operating costs and reduce financing difficulty to a certain extent. Finally, AIIB can address the limits of investment focus, lack of fund, and deficiency in social programmes and poverty alleviation in Asia from the World Bank and the Asian Development Bank. It offers robust financial support to Asia's socioeconomic progress by allocating funds and directing them to the infrastructural building. Besides, AIIB can foster an environment in which multilateral development organisations in Asia compete with one another to bolster the efficiency in operation and quality in investment and financing. Moreover, AIIB can capitalise on the strengths of China in the infrastructural building to promote the development of Asian connectivity network led by China, sharing China's experiences and outcomes in development.

Preparations in progress for AIIB

After President Xi Jinping's visit to South-East Asia in 2013, during which he proposed launching the AIIB initiative, many countries have responded positively and the preparation for the establishment of the AIIB has started. To identify the preliminary structure and preparatory plan for the AIIB, five multilateral consultation conferences and one ministerial-level working dinner have been convened among prospective founding members. Through both bilateral and multilateral consultations, the founding of the AIIB received positive responses and extensive participation from many countries in and outside Asia.

On September 27, 2014, the Fifth Multilateral Consultation Meeting for the Preparation of the Asian Investment Bank was held in Beijing, during which representatives from Bangladesh, Brunei, Cambodia, India, Kazakhstan, Kuwait, Laos, Malaysia, Mongolia, Myanmar, Nepal, Oman, Pakistan, the Philippines, Qatar, Singapore, Sri Lanka, Thailand, Uzbekistan and Vietnam that intended to be founding members of the AIIB reached a final consensus on the final draft of the *Memorandum of Understanding on Establishing the Asian Infrastructure Investment Bank*. On October 24, 2014, the 21 countries formally signed the *Memorandum of Understanding on Establishing the Asian Infrastructure Investment Bank* for establishing the AIIB. Since then, the founding of the AIIB has been institutionalised, the multilateral interim secretariat was set up and representative meetings have been held.

On April 15, 2015, prospective founding members reached a total of 57, covering all 5 continents. Among them, 34 were in Asia, namely, Bangladesh, Brunei, Cambodia, China, India, Indonesia, Jordan, Kazakhstan, Kuwait, Laos, Malaysia, Maldives, Mongolia, Myanmar, Nepal, Oman, Pakistan, Philippines, Qatar, Saudi Arabia, Singapore, South Korea, Sri Lanka, Tajikistan, Thailand, Turkey, Uzbekistan, Vietnam, Kyrgyzstan, Israel, Georgia, UAE, Azerbaijan and Iran; 18 in Europe, namely, Austria, Denmark, France, Germany, Italy, Luxembourg, the Netherlands, Spain, Switzerland, United Kingdom, Sweden, Finland, Norway, Iceland, Russia, Portugal, Poland and Malta; 2 in Oceania, namely, New Zealand and Australia; 2 in Africa, namely, Egypt and South Africa; and 1 in the Americas, namely, Brazil.

On June 29, 2015, the signing ceremony of the Articles of Agreement of the Asian Infrastructure Investment Bank was held in Beijing. Heads of treasury or authorised representatives from the 57 prospective founding members participated in the ceremony, whereas 50 countries that have received domestic approval signed the agreement and the other founding members yet to pass internal adoption witnessed the signing.[1] On December 25, 2015, as 17 prospective founding member states having a total shareholding of 50.1% approved the AIIB Agreement and submitted an instrument of ratification, the AIIB was formally established. On January 16, 2016, the AIIB was inaugurated in Beijing. China's Minister of Finance, Lou Jiwei, was elected as the chairman of the first board of the AIIB and Jin Liqun was chosen as the first president of the AIIB. The next day, the AIIB held a ribbon-cutting ceremony and officially opened its headquarters in Beijing.

After the founding of the AIIB, some countries have applied for and received approvals. Having gone through four expansions, the approved members have grown to 84 in total. With the members growing, the AIIB has increased its influence in Asia and the world at large and has become a paradigm of cooperation between different regions in the world and between countries with different development levels.

Governance structure

The Board of Governors is the highest decision-making body of the AIIB, with all powers being vested in it. Apart from assimilating new members and determining the conditions for new members to join, increasing or decreasing the bank's authorised share capital, suspending membership, electing bank directors, suspending or discharging the position of the governor, determining the allocation and distribution of the bank's reserve funds and net income, revising the "AIIB Agreement", terminating banking operations and allocating bank assets, the Board of Governors may delegate some or all of its powers to the board of directors, and the board of directors reserves all powers for the implementation of decision making. The Board of Governors consists of one Governor and one Alternate Governor appointed by each member country. The Alternate Governor is entitled to vote only in the absence of the Governor.

The Board of Directors is the executive body of the AIIB, responsible for the direction of the Bank's general operations. The Board of Directors can exercise powers vested by the AIIB Agreement and all powers delegated to it by the Board of Governors, with the following: preparations for the Board of Governors; drawing up the bank's policies and delegating powers to the governor in accordance to banking policies and financial policies with a minimum of 3/4 of the total voting rights of members; normalising the supervision of bank management and business operations activities, and establishing a supervisory mechanism for this purpose by following the principle of transparency, openness, independence and accountability; approving banking strategies, annual plans and budgets; setting up special committees as appropriate; and submitting the audited accounts for each financial year, which will be approved by the Board of Governors. The Board of Directors of the AIIB shall consist of 12 members. Nine directors shall be elected from within the jurisdiction and three from outside the jurisdiction. The directors shall not be members of the Board of Governors. The chairman of the board of directors is concurrently headed by the governor.

The AIIB is headed by a governor who is responsible for chairing the Board of Directors and conducting daily banking operations under the guidance of the Board of Directors. The governor is the bank's legal representative and top management personnel. The governor is elected by the Board of Governors for a term of 5 years and can be re-elected once. The Board of Governors may decide to suspend or terminate the position of the governor through statutory procedures. The Governor shall be a national of a Member State within the jurisdiction and may not serve as a member, deputy director, director or deputy director during his term of office. The governor acts as the chair of the Board of Directors and has no voting power. He only has a deciding vote when the number of positive and negative votes is equal. The governor may attend the board meeting, but he has no voting rights. The governor may recommend to the Board of Directors the candidates for the appointment of deputy governors. The Board of Directors completes the assignment of deputy governors by the procedures of openness, transparency and merit, and decides the term of office, powers of exercise and duties in the management of the bank.

Note

1 The 50 countries that signed the agreement were: Australia, Austria, Azerbaijan, Bangladesh, Brazil, Cambodia, Brunei, China, Egypt, Finland, France, Georgia, Germany, Iceland, India, Indonesia, Iran, Italy, Israel, Jordan, Kazakhstan, South Korea, Kyrgyzstan, Laos, Luxembourg, Maldives, Malta, Mongolia, Myanmar, Nepal, the Netherlands, New Zealand, Norway, Oman, Pakistan, Portugal, Qatar, Russia, Saudi Arabia, Singapore, Spain, Sri Lanka, Sweden, Switzerland, Tajikistan, Turkey, United Arab Emirates, United Kingdom, Uzbekistan and Vietnam. The Philippines, Denmark, Kuwait, Malaysia, Poland, South Africa and Thailand did not sign the agreement on the same day.

54
SILK ROAD FUND

Xu Xiujun

Founding and positioning of the Silk Road Fund

Since the Belt and Road Initiative was proposed, the National Development and Reform Commission, the Ministry of Finance and the People's Bank of China have researched establishing the Belt and Road investment and financing mechanism. On November 4, 2014, at the eighth meeting of the leading group of financial leaders of the Central Committee of the Communist Party of China, Xi Jinping, head of the Central Financial and Economic Leadership Group, pointed out that the establishment of the Silk Road Fund is to use China's financial strength to directly support the Belt and Road Initiative, that attention should be paid to international practices and that lessons should be drawn from the long-term theoretical and practical experience accumulated by existing multilateral financial institutions. To ensure the success of the first batch of businesses, strict rules and regulations should be formulated and implemented, and transparency and inclusiveness should be bolstered. The relationship between the Asian Infrastructure Investment Bank and the Silk Road Fund and other global and regional multilateral development banks is complementary rather than substitutionary and will operate under the current international economic and financial order.[1]

On November 8, 2014, President Xi Jinping announced at the Dialogue Meeting of Host Partners for "Strengthening the Internet Partnership" held in Beijing that China will invest US$40 billion to establish the Silk Road Fund to offer financial support to connectivity programmes, such as infrastructural building, resource development, industrial cooperation and financial cooperation, in countries along the Belt and Road. It was pointed out that the Silk Road Fund is open, that subfunds can be established based on regions, industries, or types of projects and that investors inside and outside the Asian region are welcome to participate actively.[2] Such practice received the applaud and support from Bangladeshi President Hamid, Cambodian Prime Minister Hun Sen, Lao President Zhu Mari, Mongolian President Elbegdorj, President Burma Wu Dengsheng, Pakistani Prime Minister Sharif and Tajik President Rakhmon, Executive Secretary of UNESCAP Akhtar, SCO Secretary-General Metsutsev and leaders of international organisations.[3] On November 9, Chairman Xi Jinping once again announced this important step at the opening ceremony of the APEC CEO Summit in 2014.[4] He also gave a keynote speech titled "Seeking Long-term Development and Building Asia–Pacific Dreams". Silk Road Fund Co., Ltd was established in Beijing on November 29, 2014, with joint investment worthy of RMB 61.525 billion or US$10 billion from the State Administration of Foreign Exchange, China Investment Corporation, China Development Bank and Export–Import Bank of China, which formally launched the Silk Road Fund. On January 6, 2015, the Silk Road Fund held its first meeting of the first session of the Board of Directors; on February 6, the first session of the first session of the Board of Supervisors was held; on February 16, the Silk Road Fund was inaugurated. The Silk Road Fund thus entered the normal operating track.

Upholding the principle of marketisation, internationalisation and professionalisation, the medium- to long-term investment and development fund established by the Silk Road Fund underscores seeking investment opportunities and providing corresponding services for investment and financing in the course of Belt and Road development. Committed to the philosophy of openness, inclusiveness, mutual benefits and shared interests, the Silk Road Fund underpins providing financing support to economic cooperation under the Belt and Road framework and connectivity building both bilaterally and multilaterally. By engaging enterprises and financial institutions both home and abroad, it presses ahead with common development and prosperity in countries and regions along the Belt and Road. With the positioning as a development and investment fund in the medium and long term, the Silk Road Fund leverages diverse investment and financing approaches while relies mainly on equity. It underlines promoting the Belt and Road Initiative and programmes of infrastructure building, resource development, productivity cooperation and financial cooperation with related countries and regions, so as to ensure financial sustainability in the medium and long term and proper investment returns.[5] The Silk Road Fund plays a critical role in the following three aspects: first, advocating and promoting the Belt and Road spirit; second, actively supporting concepts of green development, environmental conservation and sustainable development; third, choreographing genuine cooperation between Chinese enterprises and financial institutions and their overseas counterparts to amplify effects of international cooperation.[6]

Business scope and governance structure

Underscoring the Belt and Road Initiative, the Silk Road Fund invests in areas such as infrastructure, resource development, capacity cooperation and financial cooperation. In the area of infrastructure, the Silk Road Fund is committed to promoting connectivity between infrastructural facilities and emphasising the alignment between plans for facility building and systems for technological standards, so as to establish a holistic and multi-tiered network of connectivity. As for resource development, the Silk Road Fund sets great store by collaborating on exploring and developing conventional energy resources, and advances multi-level interaction in the realm of clean energy and recycling energy, so as to forge broad cooperation. Regarding capacity cooperation, the Silk Road Fund is dedicated to bridging advantageous production capacity with overseas demands and facilitating Chinese equipment, technologies, criteria and services to go global to push forward local socioeconomic development. Regarding financial cooperation, the Silk Road Fund works on improving the framework for financing and investment cooperation, innovating models for financial cooperation, strengthening cooperation with international financial institutions and jointly building a financial cooperation platform featuring openness, diversity and win–win.

This Fund underpins infrastructure and connectivity, with priorities to invest in programmes from the Belt and Road Major Programme Reserve. The investment scope of the Silk Road Fund includes equity investment, debt investment, fund investment and asset trusteeship management, and foreign commissioned investment. Equity investment is the main form of investment, which encompasses equity investment in green space and brownfield projects, mergers and acquisitions (M&A) equity investment, initial public offering (IPO) and pre-IPO investment and priority Stock investment. Debt investment is divided into loans, bond investments (including subordinated debts, convertible bonds) and mezzanine investments. The Silk Road Fund may set up subfunds that engage in independent investment, initiate joint investment funds with international financial, domestic and foreign institutions, and may also invest in other funds.

The Silk Road Fund actively advocates an idea of mission, innovation, excellence and win–win, and commits to elaborating core business values and spirit featuring Silk Road Fund characteristics, which generate business cohesion and creativity. The mission is to service the Belt and Road and promote connectivity for the current era, to dedicate to economic cooperation under the Belt and Road framework and provision of financial support to connectivity. Innovation means to adopt a multiple commercial and investment tools to pursue new target markets and business realms, so as to proactively explore a path of sustainability that suits the innate features. Excellence refers to upholding best practices and code of conduct, staying firm to the orientation of marketisation, internationalisation and professionalisation and being committed to building world-class professional investment agencies. Win–win is interpreted as promoting equal cooperation with partners for win–win results and seeking common development and prosperity in pursuing the Belt and Road Initiative.

Underlined with the principle of marketisation, internationalisation and professionalisation, the Silk Road Fund engages in investment business by either providing services in the form of equity, creditor's right, fund and loans, or by establishing joint-investment funds with international development organisations and financial institutions in and outside China to conduct asset trust management and commissioned investment. Pursuant to the Companies Law of People's Republic of China, the Silk Road Fund sets up a board of directors, a board of supervisors and a management team to introduce various professional talents in a market-oriented manner, and establishes a scientific, normative and highly efficient corporate governance structure that matches the company's development. The capital scale of the Silk Road Fund is US$40 billion, which is pooled by foreign exchange reserves, China Investment Co., Ltd, China Import–Export Bank and National Development Bank, with the initial capital hitting US$10 billion. Of this amount, US$6.5 billion were from foreign exchange reserves through Buttonwood Investment Holding Company Ltd, its investment platform; US$1.5 billion each from China Investment Company through Seres Investment Company and China Import–Export Bank, respectively; and US$500 million from China Development Bank through China Development Capital Company.

According to the *Articles of Association*, the Board of Directors is the highest decision-making body of the Silk Road Fund. The board of directors consists of 11 directors, including one representative each from Ministry of Foreign Affairs of China, National Development and Reform Commission of China, Ministry of Finance of China, Ministry of Commerce of the People's Republic of China, People's Bank of China, State Administration of Foreign Exchange of China, China Investment Corporation, China Development Bank and China Export–Import Bank, one company executive director and one employee representative director. The confirmed list of Board of Directors will be submitted to the State Council for filing. The Board of Directors sets up one Chairman, nominated by over half of shareholders and appointed by the Board of Directors. The Chairman is the legal representative of the company. The Silk Road Fund sets up a Board of Supervisors that consists of six members, including one shareholder representative supervisor and one employee representative supervisor. The Board of Supervisors sets up one Chairman, elected by over half of all supervisors. The number of employee supervisors shall not be less than one-third of all supervisors. The highest position of senior management is present, who is nominated by over half of the shareholders and hired by the Board of Directors. The Silk Road Fund launches Investment Council, a decision-making body for investment. Under the leadership of the senior management, the Council is responsible for reviewing and making decisions for the company's investment business, with main responsibilities as reviewing the company's asset allocation and investment strategies, proposed investment matters, investment exit matters and other investment matters.

Operation principles and status quo

Following international standards and guidelines, the Silk Road Fund conforms to the laws and regulations of China and countries and regions with investment projects, underpins ecological conservation and sustainable development and assumes associated social responsibilities. The Silk Road Fund gives priorities to the connectivity of policies, infrastructure, trade, capital and people under the Belt and Road framework, and joins partners in building an open and collaborative platform for a better future.

Under the underlying philosophy of becoming a medium- to long-term investment and development fund for boosted socioeconomic development in countries and regions along the Belt and Road and bolstered multilateral and bilateral connectivity, the Fund's investment and operation adhere to the following four principles. One, the principle of bridging. The Silk Road Fund underlines supporting connectivity demands under the Belt and Road framework, and bridges with development strategies and plans of invested countries and regions. The Fund seeks investment opportunities in the course of Belt and Road development, and offers correspondent investment and financing pathways, promoting common development and prosperity for China and countries and regions along the Belt and Road. Two, the principle of mutual benefits. Following a market-oriented guideline, the Silk Road Fund invests in beneficial programmes for appropriate medium- to long-term returns and safeguards benefits of shareholders. The Silk Road Fund is neither a wealth fund nor an assistance fund. It invests in beneficial programmes for appropriate medium- to long-term investment returns. Three, the principle of cooperation. The Silk Road Fund secures internationally accepted market rules, abides by laws and regulations of China and the invested countries and regions, underlines ecological conservation and sustainable development and pursues mutually beneficial cooperation and complementarities with other financial institutions and enterprises. In this sense, the Silk Road Fund is not to substitute other counterparts but rather to complement with each other and achieve mutual benefits. Four, the principle of openness. Over the course of the Silk Road Fund operation, prospective investors are welcome to join or form cooperation on the level of subfunds. All types of organisations can effectively leverage each other's strengths through collaboration and contribute to the development and prosperity of the region and the world at large.[7]

Of the four tenets of the principle of bridging, mutual benefits, cooperation and openness, bridging is the core. The connotations of bridging, in essence, are complementarities and mutual benefits, which are manifested in four dimensions. The first is bridging strategies and plans. Under the Belt and Road framework, the Silk Road Fund directs its investment to facilitate bridging development strategies of each country and region. As each participating party shares understanding, balances interests and jointly solves problems, interaction and strategy harmonisation will be achieved by a shared consensus. The second is bridging capital with industries. Such bridging is manifested in bolstering capacities for competitive enterprises in transnational operation management, original innovation and resource allocation, and boosting upgrading of enterprises towards the higher end of the value chain, so as to realise the goal of using financial means to support real economy, economic structural adjustment and the Belt and Road Initiative. The third is bridging industrial chains. The Belt and Road Initiative is a process of adjusting resources and production capacity, of recreating the industrial chain and of leading related enterprises along the industrial chain, directly or indirectly, to go global. Under the Belt and Road framework, the Silk Road Fund will assist emperies to merge into the industrial chain of going global, to align with or contribute to international standards and to improve core technologies and operation and management, so that their leadership position will be strengthened. The fourth is bridging risks with benefits. This is the foundation of success for programme operation, the Belt and Road Initiative and common development. The project evaluation and due diligence of the Silk Road Fund strive to be as comprehensive, detailed and objective as possible. The investment plan takes into full consideration the risk mitigation and compensation mechanism. The infrastructure and public-service projects aim to ensure the government guarantee of the host country and correspondingly insist on an equal and reasonable return on investment in line with the level of risk.[8]

In the realm of investment management, the Silk Road Fund has launched a relatively standard and full-flow investment decision-making system, which covers all aspects of the front, middle and back offices, such as project selection, reserve, pre-qualification, project establishment, decision-making and post-investment management. Regarding project selection, the Silk Road Fund underscores cooperation with industrial capital and conducts joint investment in projects by giving priority to projects that drive connectivity and international production capacity cooperation. As a financial investor, the Silk Road Fund does not generally seek shareholding rights of the invested enterprises. Regarding project reserve, the Silk Road Fund proactively expands projects sources and seeks investment opportunities through investment object volunteering, the recommendation of other organisations, and automated tracking of the Silk Road Fund. A project reserve base is already in place.

Since its founding, the Silk Road Funs has signed a series of cooperation agreements and MOUs in less than 3 years, with considerable progress in every aspect of work. Since April 20, 2015, the Silk Road Fund signed an MOU with Three Gorges Group and Pakistan Private Power and Infrastructure Committee and started the first single foreign investment. As of December 2017, Silk Road Fund has signed 17 projects and promised to invest US$7 billion, with the total investment involved in the projects supported reached more than US$80 billion.[9] The investment covers Russia, Mongolia, Central Asia, South Asia, South East Asia, West Asia, North Africa and Europe and other areas of infrastructure, resource development, industrial cooperation and financial cooperation. Also, the Silk Road Fund invested US$2 billion to establish the Sino-Kazakhstan Capacity Cooperation Fund.

On May 14, 2017, President Xi Jinping announced at the opening ceremony of the Belt and Road International Forum that China will increase financial support to the Belt and Road Initiative by adding another RMB 100 billion to the Silk Road Fund. The expanded pool of capital will bolster the ability of the Silk Road Fund for providing multi-currency to the Belt and Road Initiative and sustainable financial support. At present, the Silk Road Fund is experimenting with how to use dollars and renminbi to provide better financing and investment services to programmes in countries along the Belt and Road.

Notes

1 "Accelerate the Building of the Silk Road Economic Belt and the 21st Century Maritime Silk Road," *People's Daily*, first edition, November 7, 2014.
2 Xi Jinping, "Connect to Lead Partnership—Dialogue on Strengthening Connectivity Partnership," *People's Daily*, 2nd edition, November 9, 2014.

3 "Joint Press Release on Dialogue on Strengthening Connectivity Partnership," *People's Daily*, 2nd edition, November 9, 2014.
4 Xi Jinping, "Seizing the Opportunity of a Global Economy in Transition and Accelerating Development of the Asia–Pacific," *People's Daily*, 2nd edition, November 10, 2014.
5 Refer to the website of the Silk Road Fund Co., Ltd, www.silkroadfund.com.cn.
6 Wei Gejun, Zhang Chi, "Fostering New Architecture of Belt and Road Cooperation for Investment and Financing—Interviewing Jin Qi, Chair of the Silk Road Fund," *China Finance*, 9th edition in 2017.
7 Jin Qi, "The Original Aspiration for Establishing the Silk Road Fund is to Facilitate Enterprises to Go Global," *China Enterprise News*, 18th edition, April 14, 2015.
8 Jin Qi, "How Would the Silk Road Fund Assist the Belt and Road Initiative?" *Yi Cai Daily*, December 31, 2015.
9 He Jia, "17 Signed Projects Over USD 80 Billion by Silk Road Fund," *21st Century Business Herald*, December 9, 2017.

55
NEW DEVELOPMENT BANK

Xu Xiujun

Background for founding the New Development Bank

The proposal for establishing the New Development Bank originated from a report by Joseph Stiglitz, noble laureate of economics, and Nicholas Stern, a professor at London School of Economics. In this report, they analyse the figures from international organisations and conclude that emerging economies have relatively large demands for investment and a large amount of mobile idle cash. In the *World Energy Outlook 2010* issued by the International Energy Agency, it is pointed out that as far as the energy sector is concerned, US$33 trillion worth of investment is required in the next 25 years, of which 64% comes from emerging and developing economies.[1] To properly and effectively utilise capital from the emerging countries and meet their incremental investment demands, Stiglitz mentions that a financial brokerage system should be established for the emerging and developing economies. The most feasible plan, amongst them all, is to set up a South–South development bank lead by emerging economies to meet the investment needs. The proposal by Stiglitz is based on a backdrop that multilateral development organisations have a certain degree of influence on infrastructural financing, but as for the increasing demands for emerging economies, the impact is rather limited.

By Stiglitz's report, India called for 4 other BRICS countries to jointly establish a new development bank led by the 5 countries. At the early stage of India's proposal, the proposed name of the bank was BRICS-led South–South Development Bank. To facilitate discussion and study by other BRICS countries for founding the New Development Bank, India offered initial planning for the objectives, financial sources, business activities, capital structure and progress arrangement of the bank.

Such an avocation was swiftly responded to by the other 4 countries. On March 19, 2012, during the BRICS Finance Ministers' Meeting, representatives of the countries reached consensus on establishing the Working Group of the New Development Bank and in March 2012, during the fourth BRICS summit, the BRICS leaders planned the objectives and goals of the New Development Bank and instructed the 5 finance ministers to review the possibility and feasibility of the initiative. In March 2013, the Fifth BRICS Leaders Meeting delivered the "Durban Declaration", and the leaders of the 5 nations formally agreed to establish a new development bank. This signified that the cooperation of the BRICS countries had entered a substantive stage, marking the fact that leaders of the BRICS countries had transferred from the previous macro-level consultations on the world and BRICS countries to full cooperation of economic and financial pragmatism.

Positioning of the New Development Bank

At present, the major multilateral development agencies in the world include the World Bank, the European Bank for Reconstruction and Development, the European Investment Bank, the Asian Development Bank, the Inter-American Development Bank, the African Development Bank and the Andean Development Group. From the angle of the purposes and functions of existing multilateral development institutions, there are four perspectives. One, reduce poverty and promote development. The multilateral institutions established after the Second World War, including the World Bank, the Asian Development Bank and the African Development Bank, can be regarded as following the conventional goal of development banks. Two, promote development in backward social realms. The European Investment Bank, the Inter-American Development Bank and the European Investment Bank all have this function. They mainly serve small and medium-sized enterprises and micro-enterprises. Three, advance sustainable development. The goal is to tackle climate change, protect the environment and ensure sustainable development. The European Investment Bank is one with such a purpose, as are other multilateral counterparts. Four, boost regional development and integration. The European Bank for Reconstruction and Development primarily serves the transformation of Eastern European countries, while the Andean Development Group serves the integration of the local region. Specifically, the World Bank's main function is poverty reduction and development; the European Bank for Reconstruction and Development aims to serve the transition of Central and Eastern European countries; the European Investment Bank is mainly to offer support to SMEs, development in underdeveloped regions, climate change tackling, environmental protection and sustainable development, knowledge economy, pan-European transport energy and communications network building; the Asian Development Bank is mainly based on poverty reduction and development in Asia; the Pan American Development Bank is mainly to serve SME development, private-sector development (especially micro-enterprises); the African Development Bank focuses on poverty reduction, technology and financial assistance; and the Andean Development Group aims to promote regional integration.

The positioning of the New Development Bank was agreed on during the fourth meeting in 2012 by BRICS leaders and was further clarified during the fifth meeting in 2013. In the Delhi Declaration and the Durban Declaration, the leaders of the 5 countries clearly pointed out that the new development bank aims to raise funds for infrastructure and sustainable development projects in the BRICS countries, other emerging markets and developing countries, and complement existing multilateral and regional financial institutions in the field of global growth and development. It can thus be seen that the purpose of the New Development Bank is to serve the BRICS countries, other emerging markets and developing countries. Its main functions include two aspects: promoting infrastructure construction and sustainable development.

To this end, the New Development Bank as a cross-regional financial institution with development financing as the core business must face the BRICS countries and support other developing countries. At the same time, it must also become a bridge for developing and developed countries. In the post-financial crisis era, the world is confronted with a dilemma of underinvestment. The bank not only provides development financing to emerging and developing countries but actively promotes investment from emerging economies to developed countries. This benefits development of emerging economies and stimulates recovery of developed economies. Also, as a newly founded multilateral development organisation, the New Development Bank shall draw on the lessons and experiences of its existing counterparts to set up operation mechanisms featuring simplifying the organisational structure, efficient decision making and flexible response. It shall innovate in investment modes and foster a financial development mode where policy banks and commercial banks merge, and direct financing and indirect financing integrate, so as to make contributions to global development financing.

Operation

After the opening, the New Development Bank adhered to the establishment of the purpose and functions of the establishment and based on the two underscores of infrastructure and sustainable development to provide support for related projects in the BRICS countries. In 2016, the various businesses of the New Development Bank officially started, and investment and financing operations were on track. In less than 2 years after the opening, the New Development Bank achieved a major headway in its banking business thanks to its independent policy, project and investment decision-making framework. Its loan projects were successively carried out and their impact began to appear.

Regarding investment, the New Development Bank approved some loan projects upholding the concept of sustainable development and an efficient operating mode. As of September 2017, the New Development Bank has accumulatively approved 11 loan projects, with a total amount of nearly US$3 billion and presence in almost all the member states. Among them, China approved 4 loan projects with a total of US$879 million, accounting for 29.4% of the total; approved 3 Indian loan projects, totalling US$1.07 billion, accounting for 35.8% of the total loans; ratified Russia's 2 loan projects, totalling US$560 million, accounting for 18.7% of the total loans; approved 1 loan project for Brazil, reaching US$300 million, accounting for 10.0% of the total loans; and approved 1 loan project for South Africa, hitting US$1.8 billion, accounting for 6% of the total.

Among the 11 approved loan projects, the majority lend support to wind energy, solar energy, hydropower and other renewable energy utilisation as well as road, environment, legal and other hardware and software infrastructure building. Currently, the BRICS countries have become a potent force in driving energy development. According to data from the International Renewable Energy Agency, in 2016, BRICS countries accounted for 39.4% of the global installed capacity of renewable energy power generation, of which China accounted for two-thirds of the total installed capacity of renewable energy in the BRICS, and Brazil and India around 5%, respectively. At the completion of these projects, the accumulated renewable power generation will reach 1500 megawatts, and reduced CO_2 emissions will reach over 4.3 million tons. The implementation of the 11 loan projects in less than 2 years is accredited to the streamlined structure and efficient business operations of the New Development Bank. This is beyond the reach of its counterparts.

In regard to financing, the New Development Bank, following the innovation-driven guidelines, issued local currency bond among the BRICS countries. As is shown in its next 5-year strategy, the New Development Bank formulated an RMB 10 billion bond issuance plan in accordance to the demands for the loan projects with preparations in 2016 and 2017 and possible loan support. In July 2016, the New Development Bank issued the first green financial bond with an amount of RMB 3 billion and a 5-year duration. This was the first appearance of the New Development Bank in the capital market, and it set a precedent for the approval of multilateral development banks to issue RMB green financial bonds in the Chinese interbank bond market. At present, the New Development Bank is planning issuance of new RMB bond.

Prospect of the New Development Bank

During 2 years of operation, the Bank has finished preparations for the initial stage of the bank. On the basis of current experiences for building, through development plan formulation, the New Development Bank has exhibited a broad prospect. In June 2017, the Board of Directors of the New Development Bank approved *General Strategy of New Development Bank 2017–2021* (hereinafter referred to as "the General Strategy"), which identifies how the Bank should fulfil due obligations to allocate resources to support infrastructure and sustainable development projects in BRICS countries, other emerging economies and developing countries and supplement existing multilateral and regional financial agencies in spurring global growth and development.

Regarding fundraising, the New Development Bank will gradually complete takeover of the principal and expand the international market. With the growing principals from the member states, the fund of the Bank grows larger. The current principal of the New Development Bank is merely US$2.2 billion. However, by 2022, the takeover will reach US$10 billion. In line with its capital demands and market situation, the Bank executes the identified bond issuance with an amount of RMB 10 billion. The New Development Bank will take into consideration of issuing INR bond, and seeks issuance opportunities in Brazil and Russia.

The New Development Bank will increase the number and scale of loan projects for investment. Between 2017 and 2018, the reserved programmes of the Bank have accumulated to 23, reaching US$6 billion, and 5 are in China, with a total scale of US$1.7 billion. According to the General Strategy, the approved project number will be between 50 and 75 by 2021. By excluding the possibility of increasing members and the amount of principal, in 2021, the approved minimum loan amount will hit US$10 billion and the maximum US$15 billion; the accumulated minimum loan amount will hit US$32 billion, while the maximum US$44.5 billion; and the accumulated loan payment will be between US$5.85 billion and US$14.6 billion (see Table 55.1).

In the area of management, the New Development Bank will adjust to new trends and create new operation models. The Bank is dedicated to achieving swift, flexible and efficient operation through more appropriate project evaluation, execution and supervision. At the moment, it has been applying a risk-based approach for project approval and supervision, in which pre-examination is more vigorously enforced in complex and high-risk projects and more streamlined procedures are adopted for low-risk ones. Given that the Bank will enlarge the ranks of professionals, key performance indicator (KPI) and incentive measures will be oriented by risk evaluation, loan payment and project outcomes, but not by approving projects. The simplified organisational structure of the Bank will lower management costs and improve decision-making efficiency. In the process of loan applications, the New Development Bank will further increase the efficiency of project evaluation and approval and shorten the span from application to approval to less than 6 months.

Considering the membership, the New Development Bank will add new members, aiming to attract support and participation from more emerging economies for building the Bank. At present, the Bank is developing entry criteria for new members and the membership enlargement scheme. In order not to restrict operation capabilities and decision-making progress

Table 55.1 Loan Schemes of New Development Bank for 2017–2021. Unit: million US$

	Scenario 1				Scenario 2			
	Approved loan (year)	Approved loan (accumulated)	Loan payment (year)	Loan payment (accumulated)	Approved loan (year)	Approved loan (accumulated)	Loan payment (year)	Loan payment (accumulated)
2016	1500	1500	0	0	1500	1500	0	0
2017	2500	3000	700	700	3000	4500	750	750
2018	3000	8000	1350	2050	5000	9500	1550	2300
2019	6000	14,000	2600	4650	8000	17,500	3150	5450
2020	8000	22,000	4100	8750	12,000	29,500	5350	10,800
2021	10,000	32,000	5850	14,600	15,000	44,500	8100	18,900

Note: Figures of 2016 are actual values.

Source: New Development Bank

and promote the Bank's development, the membership expansion is incremental. Under the General Strategy, the Bank will attract countries of varied sizes and development levels while maintaining geographic diversity. This manifests that the New Development Bank will open up to all countries including emerging and developing countries. In doing so, the Bank will become a global multilateral financial agency with a focus on development and membership from across the whole world.

Note

1 International Energy Agency, World Energy Outlook 2010.

56
CHINA–ASEAN COOPERATION FUND

Xu Xiujun

Founding of the China–ASEAN Cooperation Fund

In January 2007, at the 11th China–ASEAN Summit, China stated that it is willing to actively consider building a number of economic and trade cooperation zones with advanced infrastructure, complete industrial chains, high levels of linkages, driving force and regional influence in the ASEAN countries on the basis of mutual benefit and reciprocity, so as to achieve mutual benefit and common development with ASEAN countries at a higher level.[1] In the 11th China–ASEAN Summit hosted in November 2007, China advocated strengthening connectivity in highways, railways, waterways, aviation and information communications to meet the growing need for bilateral trade cooperation, which was widely responded by ASEAN leaders.[2]

Under the backdrop fast expanding China–ASEAN economic cooperation and ever-growing need for infrastructure building in ASEAN countries, China proactively expedited developing transport, power supply and communications regionally and subregionally, and gradually clarified an effective approach in realising internet application and connectivity of infrastructure. In April 2009, Premier Wen Jiabao announced at the Bo'ao Forum for Asia that China had decided to establish China–ASEAN Cooperation Fund (hereinafter referred to as "CAF") with a volume of US$10 billion to support regional infrastructure building.[3] In October 2009, Premier Wen Jiabao declared at the 12th China–ASEAN Summit that the initial US$1 billion fund-raising had come to a close and investment could begin before 2010, while China decided to increase the concessional loan to US$6.7 billion among the US$15 billion total, so as to bolster China's support to infrastructure building in the ASEAN countries.[4] As the China–ASEAN Free Trade Area is in full swing, demand for infrastructure connectivity increases and CAF has accelerated preparations. On January 7, 2010, under the witness of Chinese and ASEAN state leaders, the main sponsors, namely, China Export–Import Bank, China Investment Corporation, Bank of China, International Finance Corporation and China Communications Construction Group, formally signed the Memorandum of Understanding on the initiation of the Fund. On March 29, China Exim Bank, the main sponsor of CAF, signed a set of investment documents with financial institutions and enterprises from both home and abroad, marking the formal establishment and operation of CAF and fund management institutions.

Investment and operation

Initiated by China Import–Export Bank and approved by the State Council, CAF is a private equity fund registered outside China, facilitating financing for economic cooperation between Chinese and ASEAN enterprises. The mission of CAF is to invest in the infrastructure sector of ASEAN and elevate values of the invested companies through economic cooperation between China and ASEAN countries, so as to reap the most beneficial returns for CAF investors. Leveraging international and professional management and operation, CAF aims at integration in three aspects: integration between business success and economic sustainability, between government strategy guidance and market operation and between elements of China and ASEAN and CAF. In this respect, CAF is targeted at ASEAN member countries (Vietnam, Laos, Cambodia, Thailand, Myanmar, Malaysia, Singapore, Indonesia, Philippines and Brunei) and offers cross-regional funding support to ASEAN and other areas.[5]

CAF conforms to the following principles in investment: (1) underpinning investment models for asset value-adding, with a general choice of equity and class equity investment; (2) pursuing potential in asset value-adding; (3) forming a balanced and diverse asset portfolio, which may include both new and mature projects and investments at both the project level and company level; (4) increasing asset values through asset nurturing, management and financing techniques; and (5) optimising exit time to maximise project revenues. Therefore, CAF investments range from Greenfield projects under construction or to be constructed to brownfield projects undergoing either operation nurturing, growth or maturity. The single investment amount of CAF ranges from US$50 million to US$150 million. Committing to achieving common investment with other strategic investors while maintaining minority shareholder status, CAF does not pursue company shareholder rights, with less than 50% shares held and non-participation of project management. In selecting investment objects, CAF follows 5-faceted criteria: (1) sound business performance and trustworthiness; (2) a proven and sustainable business model; (3) the potential for adding value and predictable profitability; (4) stable and accountable cash flow; and (5) tested excellence and stable management teams. For each potential investment project, professional teams from CAF will perform full due diligence, covering areas of attractiveness and growth potential of industries, financial performance and competitiveness, capacity for sustainable development, environmental contributions by the enterprise and projects and social responsibility. On such a basis, CAF will form a strategic partnership with enterprises to assist them and their projects in executing effective business models and provide them with value-adding services.

The targeted industries by CAF are infrastructure, energy and natural resources. CAF prefers infrastructure assets that generate long-term stable cash flows. The related areas are transportation and logistics, such as highway, bridges, railway, inter-city railway, ports and airports; power, such as power plants, power grid and power transmission; renewable energy, such as wind power, hydropower, solar power, biomass energy and geothermal energy; public utilities, such as sewage treatment, urban water supply, heat supply and natural gas; communications, such as telecommunications tower, communication cable; pipeline and storage for petroleum and natural gas; and public facilities, such as schools, hospitals, medical and health facilities. When investing in natural resources, the timing of the market is critical to guarantee maximum returns. Natural resource projects include the mining, processing, and smelting of black and non-ferrous metals, precious metals, thermal coal, coking coal and other mineral resources such as rare earth and potash, and developing and processing of crude oil, upstream and downstream industries, (liquefied) natural gas, coal-bed methane and forest resources including woods, rubber and palm oil. CAF, however, does not favour early resource detection and exploitation projects.

In regard to the environment and social responsibility, CAF is dedicated to promoting the social and environmental development of the invested regions and improving quality of life. When evaluating and selecting investment opportunities, CAF takes into consideration the impact of enterprise value orientation and business norms on society and the environment. Apart from conforming to laws and regulations of the invested regions, CAF takes efforts to promote best practices of industries on social responsibility. CAF applies the highest standard in the social and environmental management system to normalise its social responsibilities. On top of regulations on society and environment, CAF follows multiple policies on anti-corruption and anti-money laundry. CAF has established a set of a comprehensive management system for the environment and social responsibilities that permeates the whole process of selection and evaluation for potential projects by the investment team. At the beginning of the trade, CAF goes through a detailed evaluation to ensure that the project's dominant values and business practices are in line with those of CAF. In the subsequent due diligence stage, CAF reviews the company's performance in environmental and social responsibilities based on its criteria for environmental and social responsibilities. Over the course of the investment, CAF will provide full support to investment portfolio companies in the realm of environmental and social responsibilities.

Operation progress of CAF

Since the founding of CAF, a group of projects has been carried out to link Chinese financial and industrial resources with ASEAN's socioeconomic development, which advanced connectivity among infrastructure in ASEAN and docking between hardware and software of Chinese industries and ASEAN member states, realising the dual objectives of business success and best social effects. Viewing its actual operation, CAF first round has invested in 10 projects in 8 ASEAN countries, covering areas of ports, shipping, communications, mining, energy, construction materials and medical services, which boosted industrial integration between China and ASEAN states and economic building of project resident countries.[6] For instance, the largest biomass energy company and the Laem Chabang Port, both in Thailand.

The second phase of CAF is concurrently under preparation and project reserves are carried out in an orderly fashion. In 2016, CAF Second Phase (limited partnership) was set up, with a total amount of US$1 billion and a duration of 9–10 years. With investment regions still being the ASEAN states, it invests in industries of production capacity cooperation, such as industrial parks, power, mechanics, construction materials, iron and steel and chemical engineering; of connectivity and infrastructure, such as ports, airports, power grid and communications backbone network; of resources and agriculture, such as high-end economic crops, deep processing of agricultural products and resource development; and of consumption, such as logistics, communications, medical treatment, tourism and emerging business models. The second phase of CAF absorbed funding from new investors. For instance, China Gezhouba Group Overseas Investment Co., Ltd invested US$150 million; China Road and Bridge Engineering Co., Ltd, a subsidiary of China Communications Construction Co., Ltd, invested US$100 million, of which around US$100 was invested by general partners, and the remaining funds were used to subscribe for shares of limited partners.

Notes

1 Wen Jiabao, "Jointly Write A New Chapter for China–ASEAN Relationship—at the 10th China–ASEAN Summit," *People's Daily*, third edition, January 5, 2007.

2 Wen Jiabao, "Expanding Mutually Beneficial Cooperation—at the 11th China–ASEAN Summit," *People's Daily*, third edition, November 21, 2007.
3 On April 18, 2009, Premier Wen Jiabao delivered a keynote speech entitled *Strengthen Confidence for Mutually Beneficial Cooperation* at the opening ceremony. Speech at the Opening of 2009 Bo'ao Forum for Asia; Wen Jiabao, "Strengthen Confidence for Mutually Beneficial Cooperation the Opening of 2009 Bo'ao Forum for Asia," *People's Daily*, first edition, April 19, 2009.
4 Li Teng, "Wen Jiabao at 12th China–ASEAN Summit," *Guangming Daily*, first edition, October 25, 2009.
5 See www.China–ASEAN-fund.com for further reference.
6 Zhang Min, *CAF First 10 Projects in 8 ASEAN States*. Retrieved February 28, 2018 from: www.asean-china-center.org/2015-12/31/c_134966557.htm

57
PRODUCTION CAPACITY COOPERATION

Xu Xiujun

Initiation, connotations and meaning

From the angle of connotation, production capacity cooperation is the fabrics of foreign economic cooperation of China, but for it to be a model of this activity began after the proposal of the Belt and Road Initiative. Capacity cooperation has thus become an important approach to promote the Belt and Road Initiative.

In terms of bilateral relations, China first discussed with Kazakhstan on the issues related to it. On December 14, 2014, Chinese Premier Li Keqiang met in Kazakhstan's capital Astana with Kazakhstan's President NursultanNazarbayev and Prime Minister Masimov and agreed to strengthen mutually beneficial cooperation, especially in the realm of capacity cooperation between Kazakhstan and China, with a subsequent framework agreement being formalised. The two sides believe that China has adequate and high-level equipment production capacity, and it is cost-effective to build Kazakhstan's large-scale infrastructure projects such as iron and steel, cement, plate glass production and thermal power, and to develop cooperation in deep processing of agricultural products. It is conducive to fostering new economic growth points, coping with downward pressure on the economy, promoting the upgrading of resource industries, boosting the process of Kazakhstan's industrialisation, promoting China's equipment to go global, and achieving mutual benefits and common development of both China and Kazakhstan.[1]

In regard to decision-making by the leadership, China began as early as December 2014 to incorporate capacity cooperation as one of the priorities in top leadership meetings. On December 24, 2014, Premier Li Keqiang of the State Council of China presided over the State Council's executive meeting and deployed major financial support enterprises to "go global" efforts to promote steady growth, structural adjustment and promotion of major issues. The meeting concluded that to coordinate the overall domestic and international situation, increase financial support for enterprises to "go global" is an important measure for stabilising growth and restructuring. It can promote China's advantages and excessive production capacity to go abroad, promote cooperation between Chinese and foreign production capacity, expand the development space, improve Chinese products, especially the international competitiveness of equipment, boost the optimisation and upgrading of the structure of foreign trade, and promote the development of the manufacturing and financial services industry to the high-end level.[2]

Consider policy making; China promulgated documents on international capacity in May 2015. On May 13, 2015, the State Council issued *Guiding Opinions on Promoting Cooperation on International Capacity and Equipment Manufacturing*, in which the underlying philosophies, general principles, objectives and policy measures on such cooperation are identified. This was the first government document of China guiding such cooperation, which bears significance in guiding international capacity cooperation at present and in the near future. Under such guidance, capacity cooperation entered a track of fast development.

Yet the definition of capacity cooperation was not clarified. In the early stage of this concept, international capacity cooperation was interpreted as an important way of resolving overcapacity of raw materials. The basis for such an idea are as follows: for one thing, as China entered a new normal stage of medium to high-speed economic growth, the excess capacity in this stage can hardly be dissolved by domestic demand; and on the other, as resource endowment and economic development differ between countries, the excess capacity in one country might not be excessive for another, or rather be in dire shortage.[3] Later on, the understanding of capacity cooperation became more general and practical. For example, some scholars have pointed out that international capacity cooperation is a joint approach to allocate supply and demand of production capacity between prospective countries and regions through cross-national or cross-regional means. It can be operated through product output and industrial transfer, and it is an output of both products and capital.[4] Other scholars quoted the State Council documentand held the belief that international capacity cooperation is China's approach to follow the trend of economic globalisation. Taking into consideration characteristics of the new normal domestic economy and matching China's strengths in industry and capital and foreign demands, such cooperation is market-oriented and implemented by enterprises. It encourages Chinese businesses individually, or by collaborating with foreign counterparts, to carry out overseas business operations in various forms, including project contracting and investing and building factories.[5] Viewing the connotation of capacity cooperation, some researchers find that the manufacturing sector is the entry point of capacity cooperation between China and countries along the Belt and Road based on the prerequisite that manufacturing is the primary driver for bolstering the international competitiveness of Chinese industries.[6] For the investment projects of capacity cooperation, China mainly deals with the difference between the overcapacity and the host country's demand. It is, therefore, possible to invest in industries that are in line with the comparative advantage of the host country, but at present, the host country does not have developed industries.[7]

Major objectives and implementation approaches for capacity cooperation

According to *Guiding Opinions on Promoting International Capacity and Equipment Manufacturing Cooperation* promulgated by the State Council, the main objectives for China are to promote such cooperation is to categorise developing countries with high alignment in equipment and capacity of China, strong intent for cooperation, sound cooperation conditions and foundation as key nations, to proactively extend such cooperation to markets in developed countries, to begin with pilots and successively expand. Industries such as iron and steel, non-ferrous metals, building materials, railways, electricity, chemicals, textiles, automobiles, communications, construction machinery, aerospace, marine and marine engineering are identified as key, and implementation will be carried out in an orderly fashion. To be more specific, they include the development of international cooperation in advanced production capacity in the building materials industry, the acceleration of the "going global" of railways, the expansion of rail transit equipment in the international market, the development and implementation of overseas power projects, the promotion of overseas investment in key chemical fields and the promotion of international cooperation in light industry and textile industry, expediting the development of independent brand cars to the international market, improving the international competitiveness of the information and communication industry, promoting the construction of global business networks by manufacturing companies such as construction machinery, promoting the export of aerospace equipment and opening up high-end markets for shipping and marine engineering equipment.

Focusing on the major tasks of international production capacity and equipment manufacturing cooperation, the Chinese government has gradually implemented the following four approaches. The first is to bolster capability of enterprises for going global, with specific measures as leveraging the leading role of enterprises as main market players, expanding models of foreign cooperation, innovating models for business operations, elevating capacity for outbound operations and regulating enterprise outbound operation activities; the second is to enhance government guidance and promotion, with specific measures as strengthening coordination, improving mechanisms for foreign cooperation, reforming systems for managing foreign cooperation, providing sound services for foreign affairs, establishing comprehensive information service platforms and leveraging the role of subnational governments; the third is to increase policy support, with specific measures such as improving policies for financial and taxation support, enlarging sources of financing and funding, increasing sources for equity investment and improving export credit and insurance; and the fourth is to intensify service guarantee and risk control, with specific measures such as fastening up international promotion of Chinese standards, elevating the role of industrial associations and intermediary agencies, building up the ranks of talents, working well on interpreting policies, and strengthening risk prevention and security.

Progress on capacity cooperation

China–Kazakhstan capacity cooperation spearheaded the landscape of Chinese capacity cooperation with foreign counterparts. In December 2014, Xu Shaoshi, Minister of the National Development and Reform Commission of China, and Aishishek Shev, Minister of Investment and Development of Kazakhstan, held the first dialogue of Sino-Kazakhstan capacity cooperation in Beijing to jointly promote and deepen the cooperation on production capacity and investment of the two countries. It was the first dialogue mechanism on capacity cooperation between Chinese and foreign government departments. The two sides signed the Meeting Minutes after negotiations, which preliminarily identified 16 projects for early harvest and 63 lists of prospective projects, covering sectors such as iron and steel, cement, plate glass, energy, power, mining and chemical engineering.[8] China international capacity cooperation reaped the first outcomes. On August 31, 2015, witnessed by President Xi Jinping and Kazakhstan President Nursultan Nazarbayev, the National Development and Reform Commission of China and the Ministry of Investment and Development of Kazakhstan signed *Framework Agreement on Strengthening Capacity and Investment Cooperation between the Government of PRC and the Government of Republic of Kazakhstan*. It was the first framework agreement on capacity cooperation between China and foreign government authority. On December 14, 2015, governments of China and Kazakhstan issued a joint communiqué and pointed out that the Sino-Kazakhstan capacity cooperation had created a new model for practical cooperation between the two countries, which is conducive to enriching the connotation of cooperation, and deepening the integration of interests, facilitating the process of industrialisation, and would help the two countries to better cope with the current complex situation in the international economy. Meanwhile, they agreed to continue adhering to the principle of enterprises as main players, market operations, and government promotion and to further promote Sino-Kazakhstan capacity cooperation and vigorously open up third-party markets.[9] In the meantime, China picked up the pace in signing agreements on capacity cooperation with other countries. As of September 2017, China had signed such agreement with 37 countries, including Kazakhstan, Egypt, Ethiopia and Brazil, began cooperation with regional organisations such as ASEAN, the Africa Union, the European Union and CELAC (the Community of Latin American and Caribbean States; Spanish: Comunidad de Estados Latinoamericanos y Caribeños, CELAC; Portuguese: Comunidade de Estados Latino-Americanos e Caribenhos), carried out institutionalised capacity cooperation and proactively promoted third-party cooperation in specific areas with specific countries.

Over a long-term practice, Chinese businesses now engage with countries along the Belt and Road in ever diversifying ways, from equipment supply on the outset to excogitation–purchase (EP), excogitation–purchase–construction (EPC), build–operate–transfer (BOT), build–operate–own (BOO), public–private partnership (PPP), mergers and acquisitions (M&A) and financing and leasing. Outbound economic and trade zones have concurrently become essential platforms for such cooperation under the Belt and Road Initiative, enabling direct docking between China and the demands for capacity cooperation in host countries. At the 2016 year end, Chinese enterprises had established 77 overseas economic and trade cooperation zones, covering 36 countries, with an accumulated investment volume of US$24.19 billion, 1522 resident enterprises and a total output of US$70.28 billion. The rapid development of outbound economic and trade cooperation led to the transfer of part of capacity in advantageous industries textiles, clothing, light industry, home appliances, building materials, automobile parts and non-ferrous metal to the world, which realised mutual benefits between host countries.

Over recent years, China has been proactively promoting the Belt and Road Initiative by steadfastly carrying out international capacity cooperation and improving the work system for going global, which expedited active participation of Chinese enterprises in economic globalisation. According to statistics from the Ministry of Commerce, as of the end of 2016, 24,400 domestic investors in China set up 37,200 foreign direct investment enterprises, covering 190 countries and regions across the globe and the total assets of overseas companies amounted to US$5 trillion. In 2016, net foreign direct investment from China hit US$196.15 billion, which was the highest in history and ranked second in the world with an increase of 34.7% over the previous year. The accumulated net foreign direct investment was US$1357.39 billion. In 2016, direct foreign investment from China covered 18 industrial categories of the national economy, among which the manufacturing sector raised the second seat for the first time. In 2016, the net foreign investment in manufacturing industry was US$29.05 billion, an increase of 45.3% over the previous year, accounting for 14.8% of the total volume of traffic in the year. It mainly went to sectors of automobile manufacturing, computer/communication and other electronic equipment manufacturing, special equipment manufacturing, and chemical raw materials and chemical products manufacturing, pharmaceutical manufacturing, rubber and plastic products, textiles, leather/fur/feathers and their products, footwear, railways/ships/aerospace and other transport equipment manufacturing and food manufacturing. Among them, US$14.25 billion flew to equipment manufacturing, up by 41.4% over the previous year, accounting for 49.1% of the total investment volume in the manufacturing sector.[10]

Notes

1 Wu Lejun, Huang Wendi, "China and Kazakhstan reach consensus on production capacity cooperation," *People's Daily*, second edition, December 17, 2014.

2 Li Keqiang, "Chair State Council Executive Meeting," *People's Daily*, 1st edition, December 25, 2014.
3 Wang Benli, Zhang Hailiang, and Zeng Kun, "International Capacity Cooperation: New Approach to Resolve Overcapacity," *China Industry Review*, 11th edition in 2015.
4 Guo Chaoxian, Deng Xueying and Pi Siming, "Status Quo, Issues and Resolutions of Belt and Road Capacity Cooperation," *China Development Observation*, 6th edition in 2016.
5 Yuan Limei, Zhu Gusheng, "Driving Factors and Strategies for International Capacity Cooperation in China," *Enterprise Economy*, p. 173 of 5th edition in 2016.
6 Zhao Donglin, Deng Baichuan, "International Capacity Cooperation Under The Belt and Road Initiative—Evidence Analysis Based on Industrial International Competitiveness," *International Trade Issues*, 10th edition in 2016.
7 Zhong Feiteng, "Analyzing International Political Economics of the Belt and Road International Capacity Cooperation," *Shandong Social Sciences*, p. 43, 8th edition in 2015.
8 Yang Chuan, Mei Miaolu, "First China–Kazakhstan Capacity Cooperation Dialogue in Beijing," *China Economic Herald*, A01 Section, December 27, 2014.
9 "Joint Communique between Governments of the People's Republic of China and Republic of Kazakhstan," *People's Daily*, section 3, December 15, 2015.
10 Ministry of Commerce, National Bureau of Statistics, and State Administration of Foreign Exchange, *Statistical Bulletin of China's Outward Foreign Direct Investment 2016*, September 2017.

58
CROSS-BORDER INDUSTRIAL PARKS

Xu Xiujun

Overseas business cooperation zones and their development

With the proposal of the Belt and Road Initiative, a group of landmark cooperation projects was carried out, constantly pressing ahead with real outcomes in the Belt and Road Initiative. Covering areas such as infrastructural building, industrial cooperation, economic cooperation and people-to-people exchanges, they have become important carriers to drive the Belt and Road Initiative and international capacity cooperation. Because of the effects on leading and influencing socioeconomic development in host countries and regions, overseas business cooperation zones and major engineering projects have become a platform and a mark for Chinese businesses to go global.

Overseas business cooperation zones are industrial parks established, under the guidance of governments of China and corresponding countries, by Chinese enterprises in these countries with the enterprises' investment or by both Chinese and host countries' enterprises as industrial parks with comprehensive infrastructure, identified leading industries and sound public service functions. By attracting enterprises from China, the host country, and other countries to reside and seek investment and development, they promote bilateral and multilateral investment cooperation and economic activities for local economic growth.

The founding of these zones began in 2006. Its usual process is as follows. The Ministry of Commerce initiates agreements with authorities whose country maintain political stability and sound relations with China, identify domestically approved enterprises to be building and managing entities, and such enterprises seal deals with foreign governments to establish business cooperation zones outside China. The business promotion will be implemented by these enterprises to attract business from both home and abroad to be residents, and form industrial clusters, such is equivalent to having Chinese enterprises engage in foreign direct investment and cooperation, either by fostering clusters or by collective participation.

Having practised for over 10 years, overseas business cooperation zones in China developed rapidly and became increasingly essential carriers for business cooperation and platforms for Chinese businesses that have gone global. Such zones have become a vital mode and approach for Chinese enterprises to engage in the socioeconomic development of host countries highly and holistically promote international capacity cooperation. Over recent years, overseas business cooperation zones have been developing fast, boosting the integration of the Belt and Road

Initiative into long-term development plans of major countries and regions. Currently, overseas business cooperation zones can be categorised into types of processing manufacturing, resource utilisation, agricultural industry, business and logistics and research and development, with obvious gravitational effects.

According to data from the Chinese Ministry of Commerce, as of the end of 2016, Chinese enterprises had built 77 foreign business cooperation zones, covering 36 countries around the world, with a total investment of US$24.19 billion, attracting 1522 enterprises to enter the parks and creating gross output value of US$70.28 billion. They generated US$2.67 billion taxes and fees and created 212,000 jobs for the local areas, playing a positive role in promoting industrial upgrading of and bilateral business relations with the host countries. Over the year 2016, new investment to 77 cooperation zones totalled US$5.45 billion, taking up 22.5% of the accumulated total. Resident enterprises stood at 413, which created values of US$38.75 billion and paid US$570 million taxes to the host countries.

In countries along the Belt and Road, remarkable outcomes were achieved in developing such zones. As most countries along the Belt and Road are in the early stage of industrialisation, they pose great market potential and have strong intent to attract foreign investment. As of 2016, 56 overseas business cooperation zones were distributed in 20 Belt and Road participating countries, accounting for 72.7% of the total number of these zones; cumulative investment amounted to US$18.55 billion, accounting for 76.6% of the total investment; 1082 enterprises settled in, occupying 71.1% of the total number of companies; output value of US$50.69 billion was generated, accounting for 72.1% of the total; US$1.07 billion taxes and fees were paid to the local authorities, accounting for 40.1% of the total; and 177,000 jobs were created, accounting for 83.5% of the total.

They not only pushed forward industrial upgrading in the host countries but made contributions to their socioeconomic development. They also boosted bilateral political and economic relations, as well as people-to-people exchanges and friendship. Establishing cooperation zones drives industrial progress and development of host countries, especially development and upgrading in key sectors, such as light textile, home appliance, iron and steel, building materials, chemical engineering, automobiles, machinery and mineral products. Through the development of these zones, countries engaged understand development philosophies and models for China's opening to the world, which has become a necessary approach to draw on Chinese Experiences and the Chinese Management Model, becoming increasingly recognised and welcomed in these countries. Moreover, cooperation zones actively fulfil social responsibility and participate in welfare activities, donating a total of over US$10 million to host countries, which were widely applauded.

Status quo of major overseas business cooperation zones

The China–Belarus Industrial Park is located in the Minsk Region of Belarus, the Eurasian hub of the "Silk Road Economic Belt". The third phase of development and construction planning covers a total area of 91.5 square kilometres. It is the largest overseas business trade cooperation zone invested by Chinese businesses. As of September 2017, resident businesses were from China, Austria, Lithuania, the United States and Belarus, involving warehousing and logistics, R&D, machinery manufacturing and electronic technology. The resident companies from China are China Merchants Logistics Group, ZTE, Huawei, Zoomlion and Weichai Holdings.

The Ethiopia Oriental Industrial Zone is located in Dukkam, adjacent to the capital city Addis Ababa. In November 2007, the Oriental Industrial Zone won the bid for the Overseas Business Cooperation Zone of the Ministry of Commerce of China. In April 2015, it was formally confirmed by both the Ministry of Finance and the Ministry of Commerce. The Ethiopian government lists the Industrial Zone as part of Sustainable Development and Poverty Reduction Programme (SDPRP) and a priority programme in its industrial development plan. The Chinese investor for the Industrial Zone is Jiangsu Yongyuan Investment Limited. The planned land area is 5 square kilometres. The Industrial Zone has become a beacon for Chinese enterprises to invest in Africa and for demonstrating Ethiopian industrial development. It provides a new development platform for Chinese SMEs to go global in groups. A number of resident companies are engaged in cement production, shoe-making, automotive assembly, rolling of steel products and textile and garment industries.[1]

The China–Egypt TEDA Suez Economic and Trade Cooperation Zone is located in the north-west economic zone of Egypt's Suez Bay, adjacent to the Suez Canal and the second batch of state-level overseas economic and trade cooperation zones approved by the Chinese government. Founded in 2008, the Suez Economic and Trade Cooperation Zone covers a land area of 10 square kilometres. As of 2016, infrastructure facilities with a cumulative value of US$44 million have been inaugurated, which provide access to roads, water and electricity, laying a solid foundation for resident companies to develop and produce.[2]

Lying on the East Coast of Thailand, the Thai–Chinese Rayong Industrial Zone was developed jointly by Holley Group from China and Amata Group from Thailand and was recognised by the Chinese government as one of the first Overseas Business Cooperation Zones. The construction and development of the Industrial Zone began in March 2006. The total planned area is 12 square kilometres, covering general industrial areas, bonded areas, logistics and warehousing areas and commercial and living areas. It mainly attracts competitive enterprises in auto parts, machinery, building materials, household appliances and electronics. As of the end of 2017, the Thai–Chinese Rayong Industrial Zone had completed construction of more than 5 square kilometres and 100 companies have invested in the Zone, stimulating China's investment in Thailand to exceed US$2.9 billion. It accumulatively achieved an industrial value of over US$10 billion, created nearly 30,000 jobs and housed more than 2000 Chinese employees, becoming an important platform for China–ASEAN capacity cooperation. In 2017, 12 new companies settled in; land sales grew by 170% year-on-year, operation revenues grew by 62% year-on-year.[3]

The Cambodian Sihanoukville Special Economic Zone (SSEZ) is a state-level economic and trade cooperation zone under the leadership of Hongdou Group and jointly developed by the Chinese and Cambodian enterprises in Sihanoukville, Cambodia. It is the first cooperation zone to sign a bilateral government agreement and form bilateral coordination mechanism and a landmark project of both the "Belt and Road" Initiative and the Lancang–Mekong Cooperation. As of the end of 2017, SSEZ has completed the first-phase development of 5 square kilometres, attracting a total of 20,000 resident companies and creating nearly 20,000 local jobs. Supported by SSEZ, per-capita GDP of Sihanoukville in 2017 hit US$2010, ranking first in Cambodia.[4]

Experiences in developing overseas business cooperation zones

Over 10+ years of development, Chinese overseas business cooperation zones have achieved outstanding results, become important channels for Chinese businesses to go global and contributed to the socioeconomic development of host countries. As seen from those with sound progress, the success lies in the following 5 aspects.

First, an in-depth understanding of host countries' foreign investment policies, laws, regulations, customs and norms, market status, consumption characteristics and industrial competitiveness. To invest abroad is to use other's resources and technologies to develop the cooperation zone itself. Therefore, it is imperative to know the ideas and interests of the other party, understand the attitude and requests of its people and government for Chinese investors, be clear of its legal environment, and study its industries, market status quo and development trend. Investing companies should know their comparative advantages in which industries and they should be able to appeal to local governments and consumers. All these are fundamental to the success of an investment. Understanding the law and regulations, in particular, is important because some countries are vigilant to large-scale mergers and acquisitions, so they usually opt for anti-monopoly legislation to limit M&A activities, whereas building factories with foreign capital is well-accepted and is offered with favourable policies.

Second, selecting appropriate countries and locations for establishing cooperation zones. In cooperating on economy and trade abroad, it is imperative to choose the proper nations for trial and pilot and focus on finding the right regional locations. The selection of places shall align with the need for external resources and market utilisation by a company's core business development. If the priority is utilising external resources, then the location should be where the resource acquisition costs are the lowest and most easily accessible; and if the priority is to use external market, then the location is where the products and services of the resident company are most popular and the cost of market entry is the lowest. As a general rule, the priority location is major cities with convenient transport, advanced telecommunications, flexible information, business opportunities and easy access to facilities.

Third, choosing the right partner. At present, overseas cooperation zones mainly pool funds with local governments, but also with local enterprises. Resident companies face greater difficulties when setting up wholly owned factories or purchasing whole shares, but fewer difficulties when pooling funds or buying some shares (including holdings). If a joint venture is adopted, it is necessary to perform a feasibility study and carefully select a suitable partner besides local governments to avoid falling into a joint venture trap.

Fourth, employing professional service institutions that are familiar with international finance, law and accounting, as well as capable professionals. They act as trusted agencies and agents for related businesses. There are professional institutions and professionals at home and abroad that can be employed by resident companies in the cooperation zone. The key is to conduct an in-depth investigation of the qualifications, abilities and creditworthiness of the entrusted agency and agent before commissioning to avoid hiring the wrong employers (institutions) and consequences of deception. Cooperation zones shall also set great store by fostering talents and establish systems for talent selection and employment.

Fifth, raising the awareness of risk prevention and control. To establish cooperation zones, given that their operations are affected and restricted by various host country factors, apart from conducting in-depth investigation and research before investment, one should formulate preventative measures against possible risks. Risks that might be encountered for cooperation zones are those involving politics and operating environment. They drive from local government authorities, businesses, financial institutions and local people, as well as partners. Methods for risk prevention are multiple, and the most important one is to apply investment insurance and guarantee so as to transfer some of the risks to other agencies.

Notes

1 Refer to the website of The Ethiopia Oriental Industrial Zone, www.e-eiz.com/indax.html.
2 Refer to the Suez Economic and Trade Cooperation Zone website, www.setc-zone.com.
3 Refer to the Thai–Chinese Rayong Industrial Zone website, www.sinothaizone.com.
4 Refer to the Sihanoukville Special Economic Zone website, www.ssez.com.

59
FREE TRADE AREA IN CHINA

Tian Feng

The concept of a Free Trade Area

To better elaborate on the connotation of Free Trade Area (FTA), on May 19, 2008, the Ministry of Commerce of China and General Administration of Customs jointly issued a *Letter on Regulating the Expression of Free Trade Area* under the explanations of the World Trade Organisation. The definition of Free Trade Area in the letter is two or more sovereign states or separate customs regions which have signed an agreement to further open their markets to each other on the basis of the most-favoured-nation treatment of the WTO, phased out tariffs and non-tariff barriers for most goods and improved market access for services and investment conditions, thus forming specific areas for realising trade and investment liberalisation.[1] The letter also explained that the scope covered by the "free trade zone" "is the entire territory of the customs that signed all the members of the free trade agreement, not one of them". However, with China signing a free trade agreement, China's customs territory does not include Hong Kong, Macau and Taiwan.

FTA and FTZ (Free Trade Zone) are different in nature.[2] The latter refers to a small area of a certain country or region that implements preferential taxation and special regulatory policies, similar to the "free zone" explained by the Customs Cooperation Council (formerly known as the World Customs Organisation). According to the interpretation of the "Kyoto Convention" concluded by the organisation in 1973: a free zone is a part of the territory of a Contracting Party. Any goods entering this part are normally considered off-season in terms of import duties and taxes and are exempted from the customs supervision measures. Other titles are adopted by some countries, such as free port or free warehouse. China's special economic zones, bonded zones, export processing zones, bonded ports, economic and technological development zones and other special economic, functional zones all share certain characteristics of the "FTZ". The China (Shanghai) Free Trade Zone, China (Guangdong) Free Trade Zone, China (Tianjin) Free Trade Zone, China (Fujian) Free Trade Zone, China (Liaoning) Free Trade Zone, China (Zhejiang) Freedom Trade Testing Zone, China (Henan) Free Trade Zone, China (Hubei) Free Trade Zone, China (Chongqing) Free Trade Zone, China (Sichuan) Free Trade Zone and China (Shaanxi) Free Trade Zone are, strictly speaking, more higher-level free trade zones.

Basic connotations of FTA

On December 6, 2015, the State Council promulgated *Opinions on Accelerating the Implementation of the Free Trade Area Strategy* (hereinafter referred to as Opinions), in which 8 requests and measures were stated to expedite building FTAs at a higher level.[3] The FTA covers the following main areas. The first is the goods trade. To reduce tariffs and non-tariff barriers with free trade partners and open goods trading market mutually. The second is the service trade. Service sectors such as finance, education, culture and medicine are opened in an orderly manner and restrict foreign capital entry in areas of nursing care for the infant and elderly, building design, accounting and auditing, business and logistics and e-commerce. On the basis of consensus with the free trade partners, the negative-list negotiation mode will be gradually promoted. The third is optimising the investment environment and facilitating trade and investment. Investment market opening and reform of foreign capital management systems will be promoted, and two-way investment entry between China and free trade partners will be substantially improved. We will steadily promote the pilot projects for convertibility of RMB capital projects, strengthen monetary cooperation with free trade partners and facilitate trade and investment. The fourth is new topics such as intellectual property rights and environmental protection. It is imperative to advance negotiations on new issues such as IP protection, environmental protection, e-commerce, competition policies and government purchase. The fifth is trade facilitation. Management of origin of production is strengthened, and the system of autonomous declaration of the origin of the approved exporter will be applied in a broader scale. We will reform management systems of customs supervision and examination and quarantine, strengthen cooperation in areas such as security checks, and gradually ensure that international trade affairs will be processed in a single window. The sixth is regulations and systems cooperation. Information on regulatory systems of free trade partners will be exchanged, proper integration of regulatory systems, procedures, approaches and standards will be enhanced, trade costs will be reduced and trade efficiency will be raised. The seventh is the facilitation of mobility of natural persons. More convenience will be offered to overseas investment personnel for exit and entry. The eighth is economic and technological cooperation. Topics on economic and technical cooperation such as industrial cooperation, development cooperation and the global value chain should be taken into proper consideration.

Progress in FTA development in China

China sets great store by FTA building, and uses it as a lever for bolstering openness and establishing a community of shared future for mankind.

In the 17th NPC report delivered in 2007, it clearly stated to carry out FTA strategy and enhance bilateral and multilateral economic and trade cooperation.[4] To elevate FTA development to the height of national policies will enable FTAs to be new approaches and ways of promoting reform and development. Some researchers in China then concluded that FTAs had become a vital measure to foster cooperation and competition between major powers and to accelerate changes in the global economic and political landscape. FTA has surpassed the domain of economy, but borne significance in diplomacy and politics. It closely links he economic interests of member states via concessional trade and investment terms. The convergence of interests in return enhances political and diplomatic relations between member states, forming a community of shared interests. Such a trend will push competition between nations to evolve into a contest between interest groups. The thrusting development in FTAs has a profound impact on global economic and political architecture. Against the backdrop where all nations, in particular, the major powers, are catching up on the FTA development, any inaction or backward development of FTAs will lead to suppressed development space and disadvantageous position in the ever-intensifying international competition.[5]

In the report of the 18th NPC published in 2012, it stressed that "we need to coordinate bilateral, multilateral, regional and sub-regional openness and cooperation, accelerate the implementation of FTA strategies, and advance connectivity with neighboring countries".[6]

In 2013, it was proposed during the 3rd Plenary Session of the 18th CPC Central Committee to "expedite the implementation of FTA strategies based on neighboring countries, and form a global FTA network of higher standards".

On December 5, 2014, the CPC Political Bureau organised the 19th workshop on accelerating the development of FTAs. When chairing the study, Secretary-General Xi Jinping emphasised to "press ahead openness at a higher level and expedite the implementation of the FTA strategy and the set-up of new systems of open economy".[7]

On December 6, 2015, the State Council of China promulgated *Opinions on Expediting the Implementation of the Free Trade Area Agreement* (Guo Fa [2015] No. 69). The document laid out the objectives and purposes of FTAs. In the short term, the focus is to elevate the level of liberalisation for existing FTAs, actively establish FTAs with neighbouring countries and regions of China, and ensure that trade volumes with free trade partners reach or exceed the level of most developed countries and emerging economies. "In the medium to long-term, the focus is to form a network that incorporatesneighboring countries and regions, countries along the Belt and Road, and major powers in the five Continents, so as to enable China to achieve liberalization and facilitation for foreign trade and two-way investment".[8] The document also planned for prioritising FTA building, with the overarching demand of forming 3 layers, namely, neighbouring countries, countries along the Belt and Road and the whole world.

> The first is to accelerate establishing FTAs in neighboring countries. We should strive to set up FTAs with all neighboringcountries and regions, continuously deepen economic and trade relations, and foster a huge market of mutually beneficial cooperation with neighbors. The second is to promote FTAs along the Belt and Road. By combining FTA development in neighbors and the promotion of international capacity cooperation, we actively negotiate building FTAs with countries along the Belt and Road, so as to form a Belt and Road market and make the Belt and Road a road of smoothness, trade, and openness. The third is to gradually form a global network of FTAs. We seek to establish FTAs with the majority of emerging economies, developing powers, major regional economic groups and some developed countries, and foster markets for BRICS countries, emerging economies, and developing countries.[9]

The 19th NPC report issued in 2017 reiterated that "China will adhere to the fundamental national policy of opening up for development, and actively promote international cooperation under the Belt and Road Initiative". China supports multilateral trading regimes, establishing FTAs, and promoting an open world economy.[10] China sets greater store by planning FTA building for the world and humanity, establishing a multilateral trading regime and promoting an open world economy.

According to data from China FTA service net,[11] as of February 2018, China had signed 16 FTA agreements, involving 24 nations and regions and free trade partners from Asia, Latin America, Oceania and Europe. These 16 agreements include free trade agreements between China and the Maldives, Georgia, Australia's Falia, South Korea, Switzerland, Iceland, Costa Rica, Peru, Singapore, New Zealand, Chile, Pakistan, and ASEAN, *Closer Economic Partnership*

Agreement (CEPA) between China's Mainland and Hong Kong and Macaw, 10+1 Agreement between China and ASEAN and the upgraded FTA between China and Chile. There are 11 FTAs undergoing negotiations: *Regional Comprehensive Economic Partnership Agreement Relations* (RCEP), China–GCC Free Trade Zone, China—Japan—South Korea FTA, China–Sri Lanka Free Trade Area, China–Israel Free Trade Area, China–Norway Free Trade Area, China second-phase negotiations on the Pakistan Free Trade Agreement, negotiations on the upgrade of the China–Singapore Free Trade Agreement, negotiations on the upgrade of the China–New Zealand Free Trade Agreement, the China–Mauritian Free Trade Zone and the China–Moldova Free Trade Zone. There are 10 FTAs under discussion: China–Colombia FTA, China–Fiji FTA, China–Nepal FTA, China–Papua New Guinea FTA, China–Canada FTA, China–Bangladesh FTA, China–Mongolia FTA, China–Panama FTA, China–Palestinian FTA and China–Peru FTA Joint Study Upgrades.

Notes

1 "The International Affairs Department of Ministry of Commerce," refer to www.mofcom.gov.cn/aarticle/b/e/200805/20080505531434.html,2008-05-14= for the full text of the letter.
2 Refer to http://fta.mofcom.gov.cn/article//zhengwugk/200809/566_1.html, September 18, 2008 for basic know-how of FTA.
3 "Report Interpretation: Elevate FTA Development to Strategic Height," *People's Net*, http://finance.people.com.cn/GB/1045/6655386.html
4 "Report on the 17th CPC National People's Congress by Hu Jintao (Full Text)," CPC People.Com, http://cpc.people.com.cn/GB/104019/104099/6429414.html
5 Report Interpretation: *Elevate FTA Development to Strategic Height*, *People's Net*, http://finance.people.com.cn/GB/1045/6655386.html
6 "Report by President Hu Jintao at the 18th CPC NPC," xinhua.com, www.xinhuanet.com/18cpcnc/2012-11/17/c_113711665.htm
7 Xi Jinping, "On Expediting the implementation of the FTA Strategy and the Establishment of New Systems of Open Economy," Xinhua.com, www.xinhuanet.com/politics/2014-12/06/c_1113546075.htm, December 6, 2014.
8 "Opinions on Expediting the Implementation of the Free Trade Area Agreement," gov.cn, www.gov.cn/gongbao/content/2016/content_2979709.htm
9 "Interpretation of Opinions on Expediting the Implementation of the Free Trade Area Agreement by officials from the Ministry of Commerce, website of the Ministry of Commerce," www.mofcom.gov.cn/article/i/jyjl/k/201601/20160101235344.shtml
10 "Report by Xi Jinping at the 19th CPC NPC," people.com, http://cpc.people.com.cn/n1/2017/1028/c64094-29613660.html
11 China FTA service net, http://fta.mofcom.gov.cn/

60
FREE TRADE PORTS

Zhang Zhongyuan

A free trade port refers to a port area that is located outside the borders of the country or territory and a customs jurisdiction, allowing the free movement of goods and funds from abroad. It exempts duty for all or a majority of goods coming in and out of the port and provides business activities of free storage, demonstration, disassembly, renovation, repackages, sorting out, processing and manufacturing.

International practices and experiences for building free trade ports (FTPs)

FTPs enjoy corresponding free trade policy systems and a high degree of openness. In FTPs, ordinary goods are not restricted by an import quota or other import permits; the tax regime is simple with low tax rates, and the free flow of people, goods, funds and information is enabled. They apply absolute equal treatments in investment policies, with little regulation in a majority of investment projects. In financial services, they adopt free exchange systems so that local and foreign capital can freely flow in and out, which remarkably facilitates financing for businesses. For instance, as an outward free port, Hong Kong has been upholding free trade policies, and the Hong Kong government is committed to fostering a favourable business environment by establishing the Business Facilitation Advisory Committee, whose objective is to improve local systems of regulation and management and to provide platforms for effective cross-department and cross-sector communications. The minimum level of licence control to import and export of goods is applied. A number of measures are employed to reduce the burden such control imposes on the industry, and the flow of goods, services, funds, information and personnel is relatively free. All goods apart from alcohol, tobacco and cigarettes, hydrocarbon oil and methanol enjoy zero tariffs in the import and export of goods. Foreign capital can have 100% holding, and wealth is freely remitted. Hong Kong's tax revenue is also low and simple. There are only three types of direct taxes, profits tax, salaries tax and property tax, and a tax allowance system is established.

Dubai is a world-famous commercial metropolitan area in the Middle East. After more than 30 years of development, Dubai Port has become the largest FTP in the Middle East. As a centre of trade, shipping, finance, logistics and technology for the United Arab Emirates (UAE) and even the Gulf region, Dubai exerts international influence through its free trade area. In

1985, the Dubai government established the Jebel Ali Free Trade Port, the first of its kind in the UAE. It has now become a large-scale special area integrating logistics, warehousing, import and export trade, production and processing. The Dubai government grants a number of preferential policies to resident enterprises, allowing foreign capital to set up wholly owned businesses in the area. Foreign investors in the region can control 100% holding, and the UAE company law does not restrict the foreign investment to more than 49%, with a 50-year exemption of taxes. Enterprises can repatriate their profits and capital abroad at any time, without any restrictions on financial and currency regulations. Goods can enter and leave the port freely. Customs supervise the inspection of goods in the area at any time; goods are not subject to import tariffs and value-added tax on storage, trade, processing and manufacturing in the area; all companies and enterprises in the area importing the required machines, equipment, parts and necessities are all exempted from customs duties; and workers in free zones are exempted from personal income tax.

Second, FTPs require a relatively high-level of socioeconomic development and governance. FTPs are more than just special areas with favourable policies; they require corresponding market openness and soft service measures. For instance, in order to meet the growing demand for information processing in FTAs, Singapore introduced a digital data interchange system trade network as early as 1989, so as to promote trade facilitation with digitalisation. It established e-windows and e-platforms such as impartial and secure trading platforms to offer services to FTA development, through which a document that used to be submitted multiple times to different departments needs to be submitted only once. Singapore has also set up high-tech "soft infrastructure" including Wi-Fi and broadband access, smart grid, digital applications and financial networks, as well as hard infrastructure encompassing roads, runways and storage. Its wholesome business ecosystem covers aspects of financial services, foreign exchange, insurance, legal arbitration and professionals, linking all stakeholders in Singapore, South East Asia and the world. Singapore has entrusted the management of the FTP to more efficient businesses. As the financial cost in Singapore is relatively low, a majority of trade companies have launched their financial and asset custodian centres in this country.

The Rotterdam Port of the Netherlands has complete supporting facilities. The terminals, stockyards, warehouses, roads, environmental protection facilities and support and security systems are perfect. Its port administration authority organises the development of land, terminals, channels and other facilities of the port area. It administers planning and construction of a logistics round area near the cargo terminal and intermodal facilities, which will bring into play the functions of port logistics and provide integrated services. The management of the Port of Rotterdam is also continuously innovating in the management system. The Rotterdam Port Authority has changed from the previous port management function to the logistics chain management function. The port logistics centre in Hong Kong has special transportation links with the terminals to provide the necessary equipment for logistics operations. It leverages the most advanced information technology and provides value-added services and customs on-site office services. Relying on the rapid development of the port industry, the Port of Rotterdam constructs ports and industrial parks. As the largest container terminal in Europe, Rotterdam Port has formed a complete collection and transportation system for railways, highways, and waterways, and the port also accelerates the construction of information ports. The operation methods are highly modernised. For example, a standardised service system for electronic data interchange (EDI) has been established. The cargo handling process is also completely controlled by computers to implement efficient and convenient shipping transportation management.

China's exploration on building free trade ports

Establishing free trade pilot areas

Since 2013, China has established 11 free trade pilot areas in Shanghai, Guangdong, Fujian, Tianjin and other regions. The main objective for establishing FTAs is to explore a new path and new model for China's opening up, and deepen the improvement of the trade supervision system focusing on trade facilitation, the investment management system with negative list management as the core, the financial innovation system with the goal of capital account convertibility and the opening of the financial services industry, and a supervisory system for dealing with and following up matters with the transformation of government functions as the core. FTAs should form an institutional innovation system that is linked to international trade and investment regulations, accelerate the transformation of government functions and administrative systems, promote the transformation of economic growth patterns and optimise the economic structure, and bring into play the technological innovation and advanced manufacturing of the free trade zone. FTAs should promote the use of radiation in key function-bearing areas such as finance and trade, and promote the development of openness, promote reform, promote innovation and build a free trade park with high openness, convenient trade and investment, free currency exchange, efficient and convenient supervision and a regulated legal environment, so as to form compliable and applicable experiences to serve the development of the whole country.

Establishing Hainan Free Trade Pilot Zone and free trade ports

In October 2017, China proposed to experiment building free trade ports in which greater freedom will be granted to their policies than those of existing FTAs and greater market access will be ensured. FTPs adopt international standards to ensure the free flow of goods, human resources, capital and investment and receive support from new rules and regulations, in this way, they are regarded as upgraded free trade pilot zones. On April 13, 2018, President Xi Jinping announced at the 30th Anniversary for Hainan Economic Special Zone that Hainan Free Trade Pilot Zone and Free Trade Port with Chinese Characteristics would be established. On April 14, the State Council issued *Guiding Opinions on Supporting Hainan to Comprehensively Deepen Reform and Opening Up*. These new measures for reform and opening up in Hainan signify a more comprehensive opening up at a higher level. These new measures of "early action and trial" will turn Hainan into a paradigm region for a new round of deepened opening up in China.

Significance for establishing Hainan Free Trade Pilot Zone and free trade ports

First, establishing free trade pilot zones and FTPs in Hainan is an important systemic attempt for China to explore deepening reform and opening up in an all-around way. China's opening to the outside world has entered a new phase, and the building of free trade pilot zones has accumulated, replicated and promoted a large number of reform experiences. On the basis of the "pre-accession national treatment + negative list" model for free trade pilot zones, new space needs to be further explored and opened. As China needs to continue expanding foreign trade and openness, FTAs and FTPs play critical roles in this course. Exploring FTP building will push for a new round of high-level opening up, especially in sectors of finance and service, and enable resource optimisation and allocation at a higher degree. The establishment of Hainan Free Trade Ports will further explore the acceleration of transformation of government functions, innovation of business and investment management models and deepened reform of Chinese service industry, with the aim of forming policies and systems for FTPs. Once it is achieved, the relevant experiences will fully dock the Chinese economy and generate "system dividends" at a larger scale.

Second, establishing Hainan Free Trade Ports benefits China's exploration of new rules for international trade, and assists in bridging new rules for international trade and investment. In the current context of competition in international trade and intensifying trade conflicts, formulating service, trade and investment agreements with higher standards has become core content for a new round of international trade negotiations and rule-making. As FTPs apply more special and loosened policies, more space for investment and development will be brought about. Hainan FTPs offer more open and convenient trade and investment access through system innovation, shore up weak links in service trading and investment agreements, become more aligned with new international standards and rules and strive for greater openness at higher criteria. In doing so, FTA negotiations at higher standards that benefit China and other countries and regions will be implemented, and FTAs at different levels will be developed, and new approaches to avoid trade barriers, participate in international labour division and formulate of international rules will be explored, creating external sound conditions for bolstering economic development and overall national strength.

Third, as vital carriers for opening up the service industry, Hainan Free Trade Pilot Zone and the FTP facilitates transforming and upgrading structure for the Chinese economy and foreign trade. The upgraded reform and opening-up in China is no longer the conventional one featuring cheap resources and human resources and the offer of fiscal and taxation benefits, but one that features open markets, improved services, stress on fairness and optimisation of resource allocation and commiting to newer and greater achievements. Centring on exploring the establishment of Free Trade Port with Chinese characteristics, the industrial positioning of Hainan is rather clear: underpinning tourism, modern service industry and high-tech industry instead of transit trade, processing and manufacturing. In accordance with the plan, by 2020, the Free Trade Pilot Zone makes major headway in development, with remarkable improvement in international openness; by 2025, the system for the FTP is preliminarily established, with business environment reaching state level; and by 2035, the system and operation model for the FTP becomes more mature, occupying top spots in a global business environment. Under the strong promotion of the national policy, Hainan will attract high-end industries such as ecology, science and technology, trade, business services and tourism. With the introduction of relevant support policies, Hainan's industries will usher in new opportunities for development and promote the Chinese service industry, which bears great significance to promoting the Chinese service industry and economic restructuring.

61
BILATERAL AND MULTILATERAL COOPERATION DIALOGUE MECHANISM FOR MACROECONOMIC POLICIES

Feng Weijiang

The Bilateral and Multilateral Cooperation Dialogue Mechanism for Macroeconomic Policies is an arrangement for international cooperation for dialogues, negotiations or policy coordination on macroeconomic issues under bilateral or multilateral occasions. It is generally organised by government bodies for macroeconomic management. Based on the levels of the chair or participant, the dialogue can be categorised as the level of heads-of-state, deputy premier, minister, deputy minister, director-general or deputy director general. Among them, the level at or above deputy premier stresses on discussions of strategic, overall and long-term issues in bilateral or multilateral relations. Based on the area of topics, the dialogue can be divided into policy dialogues in areas including finance, structural reform and economic development strategy.

The dialogue mechanism is a vital carrier for policy communication in jointly carrying out the Belt and Road Initiative. The Joint Communiqué of the Leaders Roundtable of the Belt and Road Forum for International Cooperation clearly states regarding cooperation measures that practical actions will be taken, including in-depth discussions on macroeconomic issues, improving existing multilateral and bilateral cooperation dialogue mechanisms and providing strong policy support to projects of pragmatic cooperation and large scales.[1]

Dialogue mechanisms on multilateral economic policies

Chain participates the following major dialogue mechanisms on multilateral economic policies: Macroeconomic Policy Dialogue under the G20 Mechanism, Macroeconomic Policy Dialogue under the BRICS Cooperation Mechanism, Macroeconomic Policy Dialogue under the APEC Mechanism, ASEAN+China, Japan and South Korea (10+3) Macroeconomic Policy Dialogue under the Cooperation Mechanism, Macroeconomic Policy Dialogue under the China–Japan–Korea Cooperation Mechanism, Macroeconomic Policy Dialogue under the ASEM Mechanism, Macroeconomic Policy Dialogue under the Shanghai Cooperation Organisation Mechanism, and 1+6 Round Table Dialogue.

The Macroeconomic Policy Dialogue under the G20 mechanism is mainly based on the G20 Finance Ministers and Central Bank Governors Meeting Mechanism. In response to the outbreak of the 1997 Asian Financial Crisis, 7 major industrial nations that form the G7, namely, the USA, United Kingdom, France, Germany, Japan and Italy, began to note that to resolve global economic and financial issues needs the participation of emerging economies. On September 25, 1999, finance ministers of the G7 states announced in Washington that G20 is established. The 1st G20 Finance Ministers and Central Bank Governors Meeting was held in Berlin, Germany, in December 1999. On top of G7 members, participants included China, South Korea, India, Indonesia, Saudi Arabia, Turkey, Russia, Brazil, Argentina, Mexico and South Africa as emerging economies, as well as Australia and the European Union. The President of the International Monetary Fund and the President of the World Bank attended the meeting as special guests. As an informal dialogue mechanism, the G20 hosts one finance ministers and central bank governors meeting per year, with a rotating mechanism for chair countries. Since the outbreak of the 2008 International Financial Crisis, such a mechanism was elevated to the leaders' summit. In September 2009, the Pittsburgh Summit determined the G20 as the main platform for global economic cooperation. The macroeconomic policy dialogue under the G20 mechanism began with the financial crisis. Its issues were initially focused on coordinating countries' macroeconomic policies for responding to crises, including jointly adopting financial assistance and economic stimulus measures, strengthening financial supervision and supporting developing countries in response to crises. As the world economy is still recovering, the G20 has shifted its focus to long-term governance for international economics, including boosting the robust, sustainable and balanced growth of the world economy, promoting reform of IMF and monetary systems, formulating and implementing standards and criteria for financial regulations, increasing infrastructure investment, and strengthening international taxation cooperation.

The Macroeconomic Policy Dialogue under the BRICS Cooperation Mechanism is mainly based on the BRICS Finance Ministers and Central Bank Governors Meeting Mechanism. To confront the impact of the 2008 Global Financial Crisis, China, India, Brazil and Russia hosted the first finance ministers and central bank governors meeting in Brazil in November, delving into topics of the global economic situation, issues related to G20 and financial and fiscal cooperation between the four countries. In 2011, South Africa joined the leaders meeting mechanism at a formal member, extending the BRIC to the BRICS mechanism. In February 2011, South Africa participated the BRICS Finance Ministers and Central Bank Governors Meeting as a formal member. The key topics for the dialogue and consultation on macroeconomic policies of the BRICS countries include the promotion of new development banks' progress, the promotion of the local currency bond market of the BRICS countries, public–private partnership (PPP), financial supervision and market integration, currency cooperation, tax coordination and countermeasures, the development of money laundering and counter-terrorism financial cooperation, as well as the improvement of the BRICS contingent reserve arrangement (CRA).

The Macroeconomic Policy Dialogue under the APEC mechanism is mainly based on the APEC Finance Ministers and Central Bank Governors Meeting Mechanism. APEC is the most influential official forum on economic cooperation in the Asia–Pacific Region. According to the decision of the first APEC leaders' informal meeting held in Seattle, USA, in November 1993, the finance ministers of APEC economies shall hold annual meetings since 1994 to engage in consultations and exchange of opinions on regional macroeconomic and financial issues. From March 18 to 19, 1994, the first APEC Finance Ministers Meeting was held in Honolulu, USA. As of 2017, APEC economies have hosted 24 finance ministers' meetings.

The Macroeconomic Policy Dialogue under the ASEAN+China, Japan and South Korea (10+3) mechanism are mainly based on the 10+3 Finance Ministers and Central Bank Governors Meeting Mechanism. The Asian financial crisis in 1997 prompted East Asian countries to recognise the necessity and urgency of strengthening regional financial cooperation. In April 1999, the first 10+3 finance ministers meeting was held in Manila, the Philippines. From May 2012 on, the 10+3 finance ministers meeting was changed to the 10+3 Finance Ministers and Central Bank Governors Meeting. The pinpointed areas by the dialogue mechanism are establishing regional multilateral financial aid mechanism, strengthening regional capability for economic monitoring and promoting Asia bond market development.

Macroeconomic Policy Dialogue under the China–Japan–Korea Cooperation Mechanism is mainly based on the finance ministers mechanism, jurisdiction multiple levels of platforms such as finance ministries and central banks deputies, director generals and symposiums. Finance ministers of the three states meet annually (usually back-to-back with the 10+3 finance ministers meeting). Deputies for finance and central banks and director generals for international affairs of the 3 nations hold informal meetings on an irregular basis, discussing major topics on the economic situation and regional fiscal and financial arrangement. The main objective of China–Japan–ROK finance ministers meeting is to exchange opinions on the regional macroeconomic situation and coordinate stances between the 3 states on issues such as Chiang Mai Initiative Multilateralisation, ASEAN+3 Macroeconomic Research Office (AMRO) and Asian Bond Market Development Initiative.

Macroeconomic Policy Dialogue under the ASEM Mechanism is primarily based on the ASEM finance ministers' meeting. The first ASEM finance ministers' meeting was held in Thailand in September 1997. As of 2017, 12 ASEM finance ministers' meetings have been hosted, with the most recent one being held in Ulaanbaatar, Mongolia, 2016. The ASEM finance ministers meeting is to primarily implement decisions made by ASEM on financial and fiscal issues, promote economic and financial cooperation between Asia and Europe through dialogue and consultation and press ahead with regional integration and global financial stability.

Macroeconomic Policy Dialogue under the Shanghai Cooperation Organisation Mechanism is mainly based on the Shanghai Cooperation Organisation Ministers and Central Bank Governors Meeting Mechanism. In December 2009, to jointly counter global economic and financial crisis, member states of the Shanghai Cooperation Organisation held the first finance ministers and central bank governors meeting in Almaty, Kazakhstan, exchanging ideas on intensifying fiscal and financial cooperation between member states and jointly mitigating the impact of financial crisis. The Shanghai Cooperation Organisation Ministers and Central Bank Governors Meeting underpins issues including the macroeconomic situation in a global or regional perspective, coordination between fiscal and monetary policies, local currency settlement between member states and establishing Shanghai Cooperation Organisation Bank and the corresponding particular account.

Initiated by China, the 1+6 Round Table Dialogue was held between China's Prime Minister and heads of the World Bank, the International Monetary Fund, the World Trade Organisation, the International Labour Organisation, the Organisation for Economic Cooperation and Development, and the head of the Financial Stability Council, regarding the macroeconomic situation, economic globalisation, structural reform, innovation, trade and investment, employment, financial supervision, sustainable development and global economic governance. The first two meetings were held in July 2016 and September 2017.

Dialogue mechanisms on bilateral economic policies

China participates in the following major dialogue mechanisms on bilateral economic policies: China–US Comprehensive Economic Dialogue, Sino-British Economic and Financial Dialogue, China–France High-Level Economic and Financial Dialogue, Sino-German High-Level Financial Dialogue, China–Canada Economic and Financial Strategic Dialogue, China–Russia Finance Ministers Dialogue, Sino-Japanese Finance Ministers Dialogue, China–EU Financial Dialogue, China–India Financial Dialogue and Economic and Financial Subcommittee Dialogue under the China–Brazil High-Level Coordination and Cooperation Committee.

China–US Comprehensive Economic Dialogue is a significant channel for coordinating macroeconomic policies between China and the USA. The predecessor of this dialogue is China–US Strategic and Economic Dialogue, initiated in December 2006. In April 2009, a consensus was reached between China and US leaders during a meeting in London on establishing the China–US Strategic and Economic Dialogue Mechanism on the basis China–US Strategic and Economic Dialogue. In April 2017, President Xi Jinping and President Donald Trump met in Mar-a-Lago Resort, Florida and the 2 sides announced to establish 4 dialogue mechanisms, including diplomatic security dialogue and comprehensive economic dialogue. In the high-level talks between China and the USA, a Deputy Premier is usually designated as the special representative for the Chinese president, and the US Treasury Secretary the special representative for the US president, with both being responsible for conducting dialogues on the economy.

The China–UK Economic and Financial Dialogue is the main channel for coordinating bilateral macroeconomic policies. In January 2008, the then Chinese Premier Wen Jiabao and his UK counterpart Gordon Brown jointly announced to initiate economic and financial dialogues at the deputy premier level. The China–UK Economic and Financial Dialogue is an effective platform for discussing strategic, profound and long-term issues that affect economic relations between the 2 countries.

The Sino-French High-Level Economic and Financial Dialogue Mechanism was established at the time of the French President's visit to China in April 2013 when the two heads of state announced the establishment of a dialogue mechanism at the deputy premier level. Such an arrangement is dedicated to conducting dialogues on strategic, profound and long-term issues arising from the economic and fiscal realms of the 2 countries, and promoting the development of new comprehensive strategic partnership and economic cooperation between China and France.

The Sino-German High-Level Financial Dialogue was a bilateral high-level financial dialogue that was announced in a joint statement during the visit of President Xi Jinping to Germany in March 2014. The Sino-German High-Level Fiscal and Financial Dialogue is a new platform for promoting and deepening the fiscal and financial cooperation between China and Germany. It focuses on the strategic, overall, and major long-term issues of the two countries in the financial sector, and communicates such problems as macroeconomic situation and policies, financial supervision and cooperation and international economic policy coordination.

The China–Canada Economic and Financial Strategic Dialogue was a bilateral dialogue agreed on by the Canadian Prime Minister and the Chinese leaders during the APEC Leaders' Informal Meeting in November 2014.

The Sino-Russian Finance Ministers' Dialogue was a dialogue mechanism announced by the 2 sides during the visit of Russian President Putin in March 2006. This is a ministerial dialogue, held once a year and alternately in the two countries. Issues covered in the dialogue include economic situation and financial and fiscal policies in China and Russia and international fiscal and monetary cooperation.

The Sino-Japanese Finance Ministers' Dialogue is an important bilateral mechanism established by the Ministry of Finance of China and Japan in March 2006 to exchange views on issues such as fiscal and economic policies, and regional and global economic development.

The China–EU Macroeconomic Policy Dialogue and China–EU Finance Dialogue are the two major mechanisms for macroeconomic policy coordination between China and the EU. The two sides exchanged views on their respective macroeconomic situations, policy orientations and structural reforms and measures, and exchanged in-depth views on the implementation of the China–EU leaders' consensus and the promotion of the "Belt and Road" initiative in connection with the "European Investment Plan". The China–EU Finance Dialogue is a consultation mechanism established by the Chinese Ministry of Finance and the European Commission to implement the consensus between China and the EU leaders on the implementation of China–EU macroeconomic policies and dialogues in the financial sector. The dialogue is, in principle, at the deputy ministerial level.

The ChinaiIndia Financial Dialogue Mechanism was established on the basis of the *Memorandum of Understanding between the Government of People's Republic of China and the Government of the Republic of India on Initiating the China–India Financial Dialogue Mechanism* signed by Chinese Premier Wen Jiabao during the visit to India in April 2005. The dialogue aims at promoting communication and substantive cooperation between the 2 sides in the fiscal and financial field through communication and talks.

The predecessor of the Economic and Financial Subcommittee Dialogue under the China–Brazil High-Level Coordination and Cooperation Committee is the China–Brazil Financial Dialogue Mechanism established pursuant to the *Memorandum of Understanding between the Ministry of Finance of the People's Republic of China and the Ministry of Finance of the Federal Republic of Brazil on Launching the China–Brazil Financial Dialogue Mechanism* signed in March 2006.

Note

1 "Joint Communiqué of the Leaders Roundtable of the Belt and Road Forum for International Cooperation," *People's Daily*, May 16, 2017.

62
NEW INDUSTRIAL INNOVATION COOPERATION

Tian Feng

The concept of new industrial innovation cooperation

In contrast to conventional industries, new industries refer to new industrial departments emerging from the application of new technologies. The connotations of new and conventional industries are changing.[1] The new industries encompass industries that are formed with the industrialisation of new technologies and conventional ones upgraded by new technologies. An article in the *Economist* published in April 2012 pointed out that the first industrial revolution enabled machines to replace workshops of manual labour; the second industrial revolution initiated the era of scaled production; and the current third revolution is pivoted on digital manufacturing, which will make the personalised and decentralised output a universal trend. At the heart of this industrial revolution is the rapid progress of information technology, with the drivers from innovative development in the fields of smart manufacturing, new materials, new energy and biotechnology.[2]

Correlations between new industrial development and scientific innovation

The development of new industries depends on the drive for scientific innovation. The prerequisite of the industrial revolution is a technological revolution, so once the latter is in place, the former is bound to occur. The new generation of information technology innovation will open up emerging industries such as smart terminals, big data, cloud computing and high-end chips; breakthroughs in scientific and technological innovations in deep seas, deep space and polar regions will trigger new developments in modern marine industries, modern aerospace industries and polar industries; the intensive innovation of life sciences and biotechnology will lead to the formation of industries of life and health, eco-agriculture and biopharmaceuticals at large scales; and the new expansion of low-carbon technologies will lead to the emergence of new industries such as green industries, new energy industries and environmental protection industries.[3]

New industrial innovation refers to pushing forward innovation through a series of activities such as technology development, introduction, localisation, production and industrialisation, and ultimately achieves the goal of improving industrial competitiveness, economic growth and green development. Innovation in a more general sense includes not only conventional technological advances, but reform of organisation and management capabilities, development of new products and innovation of information and knowledge capital.[4] With the increasing integration of science and technology, the form of technological innovation has become increasingly complex. A single enterprise's independent innovation has been unable to meet the needs of scientific research, technology development, product development and manufacturing in the innovation value chain. It requires the participation of each link of the innovation value chain to play a corresponding role. New industrial innovation requires the cooperation of innovation participants.

New content and new characteristics of new industrial innovation

First, disruptive innovations and industrial restructuring are emerging, and business models and industrial organisation modes have undergone thorough changes.[5] Over an extended period of time, a product life cycle usually undergoes an evolution from growth to maturity and the overall development trajectory is relatively stable. The rapid development of the information age, however, has broken the relative stability of product life cycles. Relying on new models and new industrial formats, the industrial development pathway can be altered over a short period, and the whole industry can be reshuffled worldwide. Take an example of the smartphone epitomised by Apple. It nearly took over traditional mobile phone manufacturers overnight. After launching new products, Apple relied on the business models of "Hardware+Software" and "End+Service" and led the wave of revolution in the smartphone industry worldwide. A number of disruptive innovations have continued across the world, which will bring fundamental changes in industrial organisation models.

Second, ever-deepening integrated development in industries. On the one hand, there is a new field of manufacturing and application service integration. As demands change, competition intensifies and technologies advance, service is playing an increasing role in the manufacturing value chain, and many manufacturing enterprises have even started to focus on research and development and marketing, becoming providers of integrated solutions. For instance, in the early 1990s, IBM began shifting towards service and transitioning towards high-value businesses. It eventually turned from being a hardware manufacturer to the world's largest IT service provider and product support service company, with over 80% revenue coming from services. In the field of satellite navigation, many Chinese enterprises rely on the Beidou System to foster new areas incorporating navigation technologies, manufacturing and application services and have preliminarily formed industrial chains covering core chips, the application ends, system integration and operation services. On the other hand, industries from different realms mutually permeate and integrate. Thus, new models and brand new service formats have been fostered on the basis of existing industrial foundations. With the fast development of the Internet Plus Mode, Big Data and Cloud Computing, the internet has widely permeated into fields of finance, education, business, medical care, transportation and tourism. Nearly all conventional industries have been changed by the internet. A significant number of internet enterprises have extended to integrated online–offline services by leveraging customer data resources, expanding to more areas rapidly.

Third, the industrial chain diverts vertically, following a development orientation of smart applications and network applications.[6] To adapt to totally new production models, the networked and virtualised organisation approach has become a trend within each industry and among all sectors. On the one hand, the production organisation is virtualised. Amidst the new industrial revolution, the rapid development of new generation information technologies has realised the process of turning matters into information, so that production organisation is edging towards virtualisation and digitalisation. On the other hand, industrial organisation is more networked. Traditional production processes occur internally in enterprises, with the latter purchasing raw materials and intermediate products externally, eventually making products that meet the demands of the market. With the burgeoning modulation of product design, research and development, and production and speedy development of outsourcing, modulation, as a new industrial organisation approach, is widely popular. Network technologies have changed the relations between large enterprises and small, medium and micro-enterprises from competitive coordination to networked coexistence, in which they are frequent participants of the platform network. Under the joint drive by leading enterprises and their followers, new technologies and outcomes are transferring rapidly. Thus emerging industries are growing strong. The network technology has also brought together production links of each nation, forming a global value chain system which is based on smart networks through new business models such as e-business platforms.

Fourth, intelligent manufacturing embedded with digital, networked and intelligent technologies will increasingly become mainstream. With information and manufacturing technologies being integrated, large-scale customisation is on a steady rise. The intelligent manufacturing, represented by 3D printing and new generation robots, has become a hotspot industry worldwide, with its application and improvements leading the frontier of manufacturing over a long period in the future. The former scaled and standardised production models might be discarded. The 3D printing technology creates products through direct layer-addition, thus greatly simplifying the manufacturing process and better satisfying the personalised demands of the consumer. Consumers, in this way, are no longer mere recipients of products, and they can participate in the design process first hand, becoming part of the "R&D to production" process.

Fifth, emerging countries are starting off not far behind from the developed countries. Therefore, it is possible to narrow the technology gap between them. To respond to the long-term economic downturn since the 2008 financial crisis, both developed and developing countries have inaugurated their respective rejuvenation plans. The developed ones formulated the Manufacturing Regression Strategy and Low Carbon Transformation Strategy, whereas the developing ones proposed to develop strategic emerging industries. In the embryo stage of the new industrial revolution, emerging countries and their developed counterparts are at the adjacent starting lines, at which emerging countries share same industrial innovation status and cooperation opportunities with the developed ones. Developing countries are also able to acquire similar capabilities in new technological and industrial models and narrow technical gaps.

Pathways for new industrial innovation and cooperation

During the 12th 5-year period from 2011 to 2015, strategic emerging industries in China had been mushrooming, including energy-saving and environmental protection, new-generation information technologies, life science, high-end equipment manufacturing, new energy, new materials and new-energy automobiles. The 13th 5-year period from 2016 to 2020 is a critical period, during which a new round of global technological revolution and industrial change will turn from gathering strength to emerging swiftly. It is also a period of strategic opportunities for China to achieve deciding victory in building a moderately prosperous society in all aspects and great outcomes from strategic emerging industries.[7] To tackle issues of insufficient global innovation resources and inefficient international innovation cooperation, China shall underscore international innovation cooperation, in-depth integration between sectors, the proactive introduction of global innovation resources, establishing international cooperation platforms, fostering global innovation network and integration into the global industrial chain, thus extending a new pathway for developing strategic emerging industries.[8]

First, introducing global resources for innovation cooperation. Allocating global innovation resources, new industries can import the world's innovation factors such as technologies, capital and professionals, and bolster supply quality and volume of elements for strategic emerging industries, introducing advanced technologies and shifting the enclosed innovation to open innovation. With the opportunities afforded by the Belt and Road Initiative, international capacity cooperation will press ahead, and technology import and collaborative research and development will be encouraged. Or by introducing and assimilating advanced technologies, China can create original innovations. As for the capital introduction, we shall leverage the spillover effect of R&D institutes funded by foreign capital to encourage transnational companies, world famous laboratories and other high-level R&D institutes to establish their R&D centres. In addition to the above-mentioned factors, we can also attract professionals.

Second, establishing new platforms for international cooperation to fuel innovation cooperation. Pinpointing aspects of institutional guarantee, industrial zone development and public services, the government will build platforms and carriers to stimulate new industries to intensify international cooperation. We should establish international cooperation mechanisms, provide an institutional guarantee at the national level and sign cooperation agreements of different categories, so as to secure and promote international cooperation for strategic emerging industries. We should establish industrial parks for international cooperation. In building overseas industrial zones, we should give priority to developed countries and countries along the Belt and Road, create international cooperation zones for featured industries of both sides by taking into consideration the development status of industries and the real demands from both sides, and guide competitive enterprises to establish cooperation zones overseas. In building domestic industrial parks, we should emphasise models of innovation cooperation, adopt models such as dual industrial parks in two countries, enhance industrial park building under bilateral or regional cooperation framework including FTAs, and bolster open cooperation capacity in key areas. We should strengthen public service platform building and establish public service platforms for international technological result transfer and incubation, professional training, information service, and research and development for universal vital technologies, so as to bolster capability and level of public services.

Third, developing global innovation development network to serve innovation cooperation for new industries. The formation of a global innovation development network will facilitate efficiently allocate global innovation resources and meet the need for the innovative development of emerging industries. (1) Service institutions for global innovation network need to be further developed, and platforms for international economic and technological exchanges and cooperation of varied kinds need to be established. We should increase the service capability of overseas agencies and improve their guiding and service abilities for developing strategic emerging industries internationally. We should leverage existing cooperation mechanisms including G20 and Summer Davos to conduct new exchanges on the economy. By fully leveraging the role of relevant industry associations and chambers of commerce, we will greatly advance international exchanges and cooperation for global economics and technologies. (2) Establishing efficiently coordinating global cooperation networks. We should guide social capital towards founding a number of transnational investment funds for strategic emerging industries, organise a number of cities to connect international cooperation for strategic emerging industries, establish a number of international cooperation and innovation centres, develop a number of competitive international intermediary service agencies, set up a number of overseas R&D centres and form global R&D systems. In doing so, an international network will be formed in which governments, enterprises, investment agencies, R&D agencies, legal institutions and intermediary agencies efficiently coordinate with one another. (3) Participating international technological cooperation schemes. At present, each discipline is mutually converging and permeating, and a number of major scientific research programmes or schemes are becoming more and more global. Research in the areas of energy saving and environmental protection, health, aerospace and marine technologies requires the participation of scientists from all countries.

Fourth, integrating into the global industrial chain to bolster innovation and cooperation for new industries. Holistic and in-depth integration can be achieved by engaging in one or a few aspects of the global industrial chain. For instance, at the national strategic level, we should strengthen the top design and coordinated consideration, promote global landscape for industrial chains, underpin important areas such as high-end equipment, new generation information technology, new energy and carry out diversified strategies for different countries. Targeting construction priorities, promotion approaches and implementation pathways of critical countries and regions, we can push forward resource optimisation and allocation along the industrial chain. For another example, supporting the industrial chain to go global. Carrying out innovative international capacity cooperation with strategic emerging industries supported by enterprises, industry associations, chambers of commerce and governmental departments, we provide the world with products covering the whole industrial chain and the entire life cycle, so that high-quality assets, technologies and management experiences acquired through going global can be leveraged for domestic scenarios and foster comprehensive competitive advantage. Moreover, promoting high-level enterprise cooperation. We can encourage leading enterprises in the fields of high-end equipment, new-generation information technology and bio-industries to engage in higher-level cooperation with famous international companies to acquire advanced corporate governance, operation management and technological innovation experiences from these companies. In doing so, they can constantly improve their international competitiveness, jointly expand international markets with the international famous companies and jointly participate and lead the global architecture of the industrial chain, achieving complementarities and win–win development.

Notes

1 Zhou Shulian, Pei Shupin, "On the Relations between Emerging and Conventional Industries," *Economic Study*, 1984, eighth edition, pp. 35–41.
2 Li Feng, "Strategic Choices for Global New Industrial Revolutions and Chinese Industrial Upgrading," *Journal of Shanghai Economic Management College*, 2016, fifth edition, pp. 31–36.
3 Huang Xiaofeng, Wang Tinghui, "Create New Landscape for Regional Innovation and New Engine for Economic Development," Xinhua Net, www.xinhuanet.com/comments/2016-06/13/c_1119029355.htm,2016-06-13.
4 Liu Shiguo, Wu Haiying, Ma Tao, et al., "Promote Industrial Upgrading Using Global Value Chain," *International Economic Review*, 2015, first edition, pp. 5–6, 64–84.
5 Li Feng, "Strategic Choices for Global New Industrial Revolutions and Chinese Industrial Upgrading," *Journal of Shanghai Economic Management College*, 2016, fifth edition, pp. 31–36.
6 Huang Xianhai, Chu Zhujun, "Pathway Selection for China's Industrial Upgrading under the Context of New Industrial Revolution," *International Economic Review*, 2015, first edition, pp. 112–120.
7 "Guidelines on Strategic Emerging Industry During the 13th Five-Year Plan Period (2016–2020)," gov.cn. Retrieved December 19, 2016 from: www.gov.cn/zhengce/content/2016-12/19/content_5150090.htm
8 "Advance Strategic Emerging Industries, Unleash Development and Extend New Pathway for Cooperation," Official Website of National Reform and Development Commission, http://gjss.ndrc.gov.cn/gjsgz/201703/t20170316_841130.html

63
PROMOTING THE INTERNATIONAL INFRASTRUCTURE NETWORK

Tian Feng

The concept for the international infrastructure network

Currently, there is no unified and universally accepted definition for the international infrastructure network. The meaning of infrastructure is broad. *The World Development Report 1994* by the World Bank divided infrastructure into economic infrastructure and social infrastructure. The former refers to permanent engineering architecture, equipment and facilities and services they provide for commercial production and residents, including 3 categories: public utility, public engineering and another transportation department. To be more specific, it covers facilities for power, gas, telecommunications, environmental sanitation, systems for collecting and processing sewage and solid waste, dams, water conservancy, highways, railways, city transport, seaports, water transport and airports. Service generally refers to the commercial service industry, and facilities for education, R&D, culture and sports.

Infrastructural connectivity is a concept first raised by China. It was first proposed as a priority measure to implement the Belt and Road Initiative, becoming a global initiative in the end.

> We should work with relevant countries to expedite infrastructure connectivity and build the Silk Road Economic Belt and the 21st Century Maritime Silk Road. We should link major intercontinental cooperation initiatives such as the Sino-EU cooperation and the Silk Road Economic Belt, and enhance infrastructure connectivity with the objective of fostering an Asia–Europe market. We should be committed to mutual benefits and common development, bridge development strategies, intensify infrastructure connectivity, promote practical cooperation in areas including industry, agriculture and human resources, foster cooperation highlights in green energy, ecological conservation, and e-commerce, and convert Asian-African economic complementarities to development drivers. We should leverage the influence and drive of infrastructure connectivity, assist developing countries and SMEs to be deeply involved in the global value chain, and promote further openness, exchanges, and integration of the global economy.[1]

On September 3, 2016, Chinese President Xi Jinping initiated a proposal for global infrastructure connectivity at the opening of G20 Business Summit, which called for overall coordination and cooperation for enhancing infrastructure connectivity programmes, accelerating the process for global infrastructure connectivity and solidifying infrastructure interactions.[2]

The international infrastructure network brings about strong economic drive. Infrastructure connectivity is vital for global trade and economic growth. It proactively expands infrastructure investment and affords access to breakthroughs for both short- and long-term economic development. As regional economic integration develops and intensifies, the need for cross-regional infrastructure connectivity increases.

In conclusion, it is believed that an international infrastructure network is a special form of infrastructure network, as it refers to that on the basis of respecting national sovereignty and security concerns of corresponding countries, bridging planning and technical standard systems for infrastructure of related countries to jointly promote the construction of international access, gradually forming an infrastructure network that connects each continent and subcontinental regions. At present, there are three main types of infrastructure: transportation, energy and communications.

Categorisation of the connotation for the international infrastructure network

Currently, based on the breadth and service scope of connectivity, infrastructure can be divided into international and domestic infrastructure networks.

The international one covers transportation, energy and communications. These three types are given priority in the Belt and Road Initiative in China. On March 28, 2015, the National Reform and Development Commission, the Ministry of Foreign Affairs and the Ministry of Commerce jointly formulated the *Vision and Action for Promoting the Silk Road Economic Belt and the 21st Century Maritime Silk Road*, which made a clear definition for infrastructure connectivity.[3]

The first is transportation infrastructure, which encompasses land, sea and air. Regarding highways, emphasis should be given to crucial access, key links and critical projects, with priorities in linking missing highway segments, making bottleneck highways accessible, supplementing facilities for highway security, protection and traffic control and bolstering benchmarking of highway accessibility. In terms of waterways, it is imperative to promote infrastructure for ports, link access of highways and waterways, advance cooperation between ports, add new sea routes and rotations and enhance cooperation for maritime logistics information applications. For the airways, it is important to hasten aviation infrastructure capability.

The second is energy infrastructure connectivity, including the development of oil, gas and electricity access. This is needed to jointly safeguard pipeline security for oil and gas, promote transregional power generation and transmission, and proactively conduct upgrading and improving regional power grid.

The third is communications infrastructure, which requires the joint development of cross-regional fibre and other trunk communication networks. It is needed to bolster capability for international communications connectivity and accessibility for the information Silk Road. We shall expedite the progress of two-way cross-border fibre, plan and construct submarine optical cable, improve aerospace (satellite) information channels and enlarge information exchanges and cooperation.

Development of the international infrastructure network

Along with the development of regional economy worldwide and global economic integration, interconnectivity infrastructure network programmes between countries in different regions have become a critical orientation for the current international infrastructure cooperation. In comparison with programmes within a region, cross-regional infrastructure programmes offer a more remarkable economic driving force. Human resources, finance, goods and information will reach balance and flow in a larger area, which allows each region to leverage its advantages to the most considerable extent, bringing new opportunities for connection between each country.

With proactive advocating by China since 2013, the international infrastructure network has been playing a critical role in promoting world economic cooperation and development. For example, the China–ASEAN FTA has given priority to interconnectivity development in the bilateral cooperation; the APEC 21st Leaders' Summit identified it as one of the three key topics; and the European Union proposed the Europe Infrastructure Connectivity Plan, South Africa initiated the Transnational Railway Corridor Plan and China issued the Belt and Road Initiative. In 2016, China, for the first time, introduced the issue of connectivity under the G20 framework, which enabled the G20 finance ministers and central bank governors to jointly approve the Global Infrastructure Connectivity Alliance Initiative. This alliance supports programmes of infrastructure connectivity at both the regional and global level, encourages information sharing of related projects and policies, increases docking between different initiatives and investment plans and facilitates resolving bottleneck issues hindering global connectivity, cross-region infrastructure development and connectivity between the hardware and the software, offering impetus to sustainable and balanced economic growth. The alliance is another grand global public product proposed by China after the Belt and Road Initiative and AIIB.[4]

The international infrastructure network plays a positive role and is strongly needed, but it faces many issues and challenges. First, financing. On the one hand, there is a capital gap as large as one trillion dollars each year, and on the other, a large sum of social capital has difficulty entering the field of infrastructure due to a lack of relevant policy environment and channels. Second, the imbalanced development between regions and difficulty in docking. As institutional building in some countries is relatively backward, the connection between transport infrastructure plan, policies and standards is not smooth, the level of connectivity is relatively low and there exist issues of insufficient infrastructure and inefficient operation. Third, many regions' infrastructure programmes, whether in aspects of the economy, society or environment, fail to meet the new requirements posed by other countries for infrastructure sustainability in socio-economic development.

China not only excels in offering constructive initiatives, but values more on the action. It has been continuously participating and supporting cooperation for global infrastructure programmes. Since the hosting of the First International Infrastructure Summit in 2010, China has carried out a number of infrastructure cooperation programmes in highways, railways, ports, bridges, electricity and telecommunications. By offering concessional loans, special loans, special cooperation funds and other measures, Chinese financial agencies have provided financing facilitation and support to international infrastructure cooperation. The Chinese government proactively establishes a platform and fosters the environment for multilateral and bilateral infrastructure cooperation, and has signed a great number of agreements, MOUs and accords for multilateral and bilateral cooperation. AIIB, BRICS New Development Bank, the World Bank and other multilateral development agencies have proactively established a financial cooperation network in which each agency has its underpinning, all agencies supplement each other and each agency acts at certain levels, advancing the resolution of financing difficulties in international infrastructure programmes. From the Belt and Road Initiative to AIIB, and then to the Global Infrastructure Connectivity Alliance, they all epitomise China's efforts under the framework of global infrastructure connectivity.

China has achieved outcomes in pursuing international infrastructure network in the current stage. In the field of transportation infrastructure, as of the end of 2017, China has put in place the world's most extensive highway network spanning 25,000 kilometres. It will reach 38,000 kilometres by 2025.[5] Relying on the New Eurasian Overland Bridge and the Siberian Land Bridge, China has formed 3 central European railways in the west, middle and east. It covers 46 regular trains between China and Europe and 24 new inter-city rails in China, reaching 24 cities in 11 European countries and accumulating 3200 regular trains. Through 73 highway and waterway ports, China has opened 356 international cargo transport routes, with shipping services reaching all countries along the Belt and Road. It has opened non-stop flights to 43 countries along the Belt and Road, with 4200 flights taking off each week.[6] In the field of energy infrastructure, crude oil pipelines crossing China and Myanmar, China and Kazakhstan and China and Russia are under operation, and natural gas pipelines in central Asia and between China and Myanmar have been completed. The strategic pipeline network for energy supply linking 3 directions is basically in place.[7] In the field of communications infrastructure, Beijing, Shanghai, Guangzhou, Kunming, Nanning, Urumchi, Fuzhou and Ha'erbin have been approved for establishing the first group of gateway administrations for international communications business, which will link China with high-capacity fibre in South East Asia, Central Asia and South Asia, with the international voice and data communications network between China and neighbouring countries taking the initial shape. All in all, the connectivity cooperation between China and countries along the Belt and Road has been extending from South East Asia to South Asia, West Asia, Central Asia, Mongolia and Russia, forming an all-round and multilevel interconnectivity landscape.

Notes

1 "Important Speech by Xi Jinping on the Work of Neighboring Diplomacy," October 24–25, 2013, http://zt.ccln.gov.cn/xxxjp/xddct/66267-all.shtml
2 "B20 Summit: Initiating Infrastructure Connectivity Alliance and Building Global Growth Chain of Mutual Benefits," *The Paper*, www.thepaper.cn/newsDetail_forward_1523718
3 *Vision and Action for Promoting the Silk Road Economic Belt and the 21st Century Maritime Silk Road*, website of Ministry of Commerce. Retrieved March 30, 2015 from: http://zhs.mofcom.gov.cn/article/xxfb/201503/20150300926644.shtml
4 "Global Infrastructure Connectivity Alliance Initiative," *China Leaders Study Net*, http://zt.ccln.gov.cn/xxxjp/xddct/66267-all.shtml
5 "China Highway Reaching 25,000 Kilometers," Sina.cn. Retrieved January 2, 2018 from: http://tech.sina.com.cn/roll/2018-01-02/doc-ifyqcsft9203654.shtml
6 "Unleashing the Vital Links for Flight," *Economics Daily*. Retrieved April 27, 2017 from http://paper.ce.cn/jjrb/html/2017-04/27/content_332068.htm
7 Fan Zuojun, He Huan, "Pinpointing Strategy for Infrastructure Connectivity in Countries Along the Belt and Road," *World Economy and Politics*, 2016, sixth edition, pp. 130—142.

64
STANDARD SETTING AND INSTITUTIONAL BUILDING FOR INTERNATIONAL INFRASTRUCTURE

Tian Feng

The concept

The standards and institutions for international infrastructure can be understood as those for establishing international infrastructure network, divided into a narrow sense and broad sense of connotation.

In the narrow sense, they refer to systems of standards, with the purpose of removing difference in infrastructure implementation standards and technological barriers, which reduce operating cost and improve operation efficiency, are universally defined through friendly negotiations with corresponding countries or by transnationals and are accepted by all stakeholders, adopting unified technical standards, operation rules, operation mechanisms, specified with set documents and applied bilaterally or multilaterally. They incorporate both technical standards for securing successful bridging of international infrastructure and a series of rules for enabling effective linking and efficient utilisation of international infrastructure. As a matter of fact, they represent the process of infrastructure standards and institutions going global and internationalisation of practical applications.

In the broad sense, they refer to standards and institutions formulated and applied by ISO, the International Electrotechnical Commission (IEC), the International Telecommunications Union (ITU) and those formulated by other organisations (including the International Atomic Energy Agency (IAEA), the International Union of Railways (UIC), UNESCO, WHO and the World Intellectual Property Organisation (WIPO)) with the identification and circulation by ISO and acceptance by the public. The latter interpretation is, in fact, a process of recognition by international organisations. It undergoes the following procedures: first, the member states initiate a standards proposal, which is approved by the committee with the setup of a working group; second, the working group formulates a working draft (WD) and submits it to the committee for review; third, the approved WD then becomes a committee draft (CD); fourth, the approved CD becomes a drafted international standard (DIS); fifth, the approved DIS becomes a finalised DIS (FDIS); and sixth, it is submitted to the ISO Committee for approval, and being published as a final intentional standard.

There are differences and continuity in international infrastructure standards and institutions. The first difference is that the footing is different. Broadly speaking, they are rooted in the international standardisation organisations, with the main objective of formulating universally applicable international standards. Yet, it is not a critical issue as to the country of origin for the model standards. In a narrow sense, they are rooted in the nationalstandards and institutions, with the purpose of letting them go global so that the domestic ones will be the model for other countries and the world at large to draw on. The second difference is the way of realisation. The broad approach is in strict accordance with operating procedures of international standardisation. The narrow path is to act with local realities, which is to formulate different rules under the difference of targeted countries and in standard strategies (for example, direct conversion, mutual recognition of standards, or joint formulation). The link between the 2 approaches is that the broad standards and institutions can be the most significant pathway for the narrow one. When the national standards and institutions become international models, then they will be more easily accepted by targeted nations. Another link is that the narrow rules and institutions are a critical stage for growing the broad ones. If the domestic ones are taken and applied by more countries, then there is a drive for them to become broader international ones.

At the moment, the international one covers transportation, energy and communications. The international standards and institutions also hinge on the 3 aspects, as is seen in "establishing coordination institutions for unified whole process transportation, promoting effective docking between international customs clearance, reloading, and multimodal transportation, so as to gradually form transportation rules that incorporate other regulations and achieve international transportation facilitation".[1] For transportation infrastructure, there are standard systems for railways, highways, waterways and civil aviation. For energy infrastructure, it includes standard bridging for oil and gas pipelines in countries along the Belt and Road, and international standardisation cooperation in electricity, power grid and new energy. For communications infrastructure, there are standards for information connectivity between cities, digital television standards, large-screen systems and laser projection and video-on-demand theatres.[2]

Pathway for forming international infrastructure standards and institutions

There have been standards of vast difference and barriers in institutions over China's promotion of transport infrastructure connectivity in carrying out the Belt and Road Initiative. The greater limit is found in the differing rail gauges, as there are the following 3: standard gauge of 1453 mm, such as in China; narrow gauge of 1000 mm, such as in Vietnam, Myanmar and Malaysia; and wide gauge of 1520 mm, mainly found in the former Soviet Union states, such as Kazakhstan, Kyrgyzstan and Uzbekistan. Under such a circumstance, goods transport needs to change rails while crossing regions with different gauges, which increases the costs and time of transport. In addition, the technical signs such as those for transport and road markings are vastly different between China and central Asian countries, which gives rise to severe technical barriers and ultimately reduces efficiency and interest of infrastructure connectivity.[3]

International infrastructure standards and institutions are formed by a process. Despite deep technical foundations and rich experiences in railways, airports, ports and other infrastructure and relatively higher-quality projects following domestic criteria, one nation cannot enforce other countries to adopt the same criteria. Such domestic criteria need to be elevated to the international level, or these standards and institutions need to be implemented via a set of stages and a number of ways after negotiations between 2 state governments on an equal footing or negotiations with transnationals following a market approach. There are primarily 6 approaches. First, upgrade the main content of a nation's standards and institutions into the international one so as to legitimately promote them across the world. Second, initiate mutual recognition of standards for infrastructure connectivity between nations, or formulate mutually and multilaterally recognised standards with partner countries. To resolve issues like disunification of highway transport supervision standards, it is possible to find reasonable solutions through two-way communication and consultations, set up standardised logistics facilities and operation procedures, formulate rules for taxation and compensation in standardised and unified transport and storage and establish fair and efficient mechanisms for emergency and dispute resolution. Third, promote direct adoption or converted adoption of national standards in targeted countries or regions. Fourth, assist or participate in the formulation and amendment of standard policies and specific standards of other countries, and enable them to be adopted in multiple countries in one region or even to become international standards. Fifth, for overseas projects, national standards should be prioritised according to mutual agreements or contracts. Sixth, following national realities, nations should equally adopt or modify standards from advanced countries or international standards.

Outcomes of standard setting and institutional building for international infrastructure

China actively calls for a global infrastructure connectivity alliance and promotes the formulation of international infrastructure standards and institutions. On October 20, 2015, China issued an Action Plan for Harmonisation of Standards Along the Belt and Road (2015–2017), which laid out the steps for infrastructure standards to become international. It mentioned that in infrastructure areas such as power and railways, international standards should be jointly formulated; meanwhile, in areas of infrastructure connectivity and energy resource cooperation, 500 urgently needed items of Chinese national and sectoral standards should be translated into foreign languages to promote the transmission of Chinese standards. From then until 2017, China and countries along the Belt and Road conducted bilateral and multilateral practical cooperation and connectivity, achieving remarkable outcomes.[4] First, infrastructure standards going global to assist cooperation in international capacity and equipment manufacturing. Registration and authorisation of 83 items of Chinese standards in Turkmenistan were achieved, helping the China National Petroleum Corporation to save 15% of the investment in the South Yolotan gas field project undertaken in Turkmenistan; and the Addis Ababa to Djibouti railway, or the Yage Railway, undertaken by both China Railway Construction and China Railway Construction applied Chinese standards. It is the first modern railway built overseas that uses all Chinese equipment.

Second, extending standardised cooperation to countries along the Belt and Road to boost connectivity. Standardised cooperation agreements were signed between China and 21 countries along the Belt and Road; 62 items of standards were mutually recognised with the UK and 11 with France and two-way standardised cooperation channels were established with the EU, ASEAN, central Asia, Mongolia and Russia in the economic corridor and the Bay Area. In cooperation with overseas projects and areas of strength, China has engaged in standardisation cooperation in China–France railways, Sino-UK graphene, Sino-Russian oil, gas and civil aircraft, and set up the "China–Russia Civil Aviation Standards Task Force" to form a China–Russia civil aircraft exchange standard and jointly develop standards. In areas such as railways and electric vehicles, it is seen that international standards were jointly promoted, 3 international standards for railways with France have been established, a Sino-German electric vehicle standardisation working group was launched, and 3 DC charging technologies in China have been included into international standards. In 2017, China and Russia, Belarus, Serbia, Mongolia, Cambodia, Malaysia, Kazakhstan, Ethiopia, Greece, Switzerland, Turkey and the Philippines jointly signed the Joint Initiative on Boosting Standard Cooperation to Promote the Belt and Road Initiative, which put forward deepening standardisation cooperation and the commitment to unifying standards for countries along the Belt and Road. The Joint Initiative was listed in the deliverables of the 2017 Belt and Road International Cooperation Summit, which showed that a consensus had been reached on the role of standardisation for supporting the Belt and Road Initiative, promoting connectivity at the fundamental and strategic level, and further boosting compatibility of standard systems.[5]

Third, strengthening comparison and research on standardisation. China has organised the railway industry to research the "High-Speed Railway Standard System Study" and "Pan-European High-Speed Railway System Interconnection and Interoperability Technical Standards" and other studies, and put forward the priorities of the high-speed railway standard revision. In terms of commercial logistics pallet RFID tags and international freight forwarding contracts, it has formulated 10 Central Asian Regional Economic Cooperation Federation of Carrier and Forwarder Associations (CFCFA) standards. In 2016, it conducted 17 translations of English and Russian standards in the field of international freight forwarder standardisation.

On December 26, 2017, China formulated an Action Plan for Harmonisation of Standards Along the Belt and Road (2018–2020) by implementing the Action Plan for Harmonisation of Standards Along the Belt and Road (2015–2017) and promoting overall requirement and critical tasks for pursuing the Belt and Road Initiative at a new stage. It puts forward deepening cooperation in infrastructure standardisation and supporting infrastructure connectivity network building.[6]

It is certain that Chinese infrastructure standards and institutions are not limited to countries along the Belt and Road, as Chinese high-speed railway standards are becoming "international standards". From 2012 on, China Railway has begun work on the complement of Chinese Electric Multiple Unit (EMU) Standards in China. China has a vast territory, complex terrain and varied climate, and the standards that have been tested by extreme cold, smog, catkins and sandstorm in China have gradually surpassed the European or Japanese counterparts and have been adopted by a growing number of countries. For example, the African Inner Mongolia Railway is a Chinese-standard gauged railway built by China for Kenya. Similarly, in the field of digital television, the Chinese Digital Television Standard has followed the International Telecommunication Union International Standard to be applied in 14 countries in the world, serving nearly 2 billion people. As of May 2016, China has seen 189 items of standard proposals become ISO international standards, especially in fields of high-speed railway, nuclear power, communications and automobiles, China has made a leapfrog from following behind to spearheading in the international standard setting. The ever-increasing influence means greater global responsibility. As an ISO permanent member state, China plays an increasingly critical role in the international standard environment, promoting global economic cooperation and connectivity. On September 14, 2016, the 39th ISO Meeting published the Beijing Declaration, with the theme of fostering global connectivity.

Notes

1 *Vision and Action for Promoting the Silk Road Economic Belt and the 21st Century Maritime Silk Road*, website of Ministry of Commerce. Retrieved March 30, 2015 from: http://zhs.mofcom.gov.cn/article/xxfb/201503/20150300926644.shtml
2 "Action Plan for Standards Bridging to Jointly Pursue the Belt and Road Initiative (2018–2020)," website of National Standardization Administration Commission. Retrieved January 19, 2018 from: www.sac.gov.cn/zt/ydyl/bzhyw/201801/t20180119_341413.htm

3 Cao Jia, "Infrastructure Building and Cooperation Progress for the Silk Road Economic Belt," *Jing Jishi*, 2015, sixth edition, pp. 32–34.
4 "Outcomes in Harmonizing Standards along the Belt and Road," China Quality Net, www.cqn.com.cn/zgzlb/content/2017-05/16/content_4296824.htm,2017-05-16.
5 "China Sign Belt and Road Standardization Joint Initiative with 12 Countries," *China Quality Net*. Retrieved May 8, 2017 from: http://epaper.cqn.com.cn/html/2017-05/18/content_87229.htm?div=-1
6 "Action Plan for Harmonization of Standards Along the Belt and Road (2018–2020)," website of National Standardization Administration Commission. Retrieved January 19, 2018 from: www.sac.gov.cn/zt/ydyl/bzhyw/201801/t20180119_341413.htm

65

GLOBAL VALUE CHAIN DEVELOPMENT AND SUPPLY CHAIN

Tian Feng

The concept

Global value chain refers to the effective linking and integration of activities dispersed in various value links around the world through the network organisation of global enterprises in order to better meet the requirements of consumers or users to maximise value in economic globalisation, i.e. using a certain governance mechanism to institutionalise the various value-added activities such as design, product development, manufacturing, marketing, delivery, consumption, after-sales service and recycling located in various countries, and to realise the value of all participants according to certain principles. In recent years, global value chain plays an ever-apparent dominant role in global economy. With the advent of a new round of technological and industrial revolution, the conventional value chain is confronted with the need for change, so a new global value chain is in process. Xi Jinping has mentioned on a number of occasions the need to collectively forge a new global value chain to realise mutual beneficial development among all countries.[1]

A supply chain is a network chain structure built by upstream and downstream companies to deliver products and services to end users during production and distribution. Such a network chain structure is a complete structure which plans, organises, coordinates and controls the flow of goods, logistics, information and capital using information technology. As the economy becomes globalised, the upstream and downstream related to the supply chain are not separated by regions. In this sense, a supply chain starts with the market resource allocation and procedures. Supply chain management is a close-knit chain of production procedures covering the purchase of raw materials and parts, transportation, processing, distribution and delivery, which achieves systematic optimisation of the whole supply chain and active information exchange between each link through operation activities of planning, control and coordination armed with modern information technology, realising lowest costs and best services. The essence of integrated supply chain logistics management is to realise informatisation. Through informatisation, fast and efficient delivery and integration of the whole production process are achieved, so that transaction costs are significantly lowered.[2]

The global value chain is the micro-foundation for the global value chain, so upgrading the value chain will undoubtedly affect the adjustment of the supply chain. As the global supply chain is an important guarantee for the smooth operation of the global value chain, in return, changes in the value chain will affect the supply chain. The integration of the global value chain by transnationals aims at combining the flow of goods, logistics, information and capital along the supply chain so as to manage supply chain relations and increase the supply chain efficiency. Over recent years, the supply chain has constantly been innovating and deepening integration along the supply chain. The capacity of control for the whole supply chain has been bolstered via approaches such as financing, M&A and direct investment, which allocated high-quality resources dispersed in different enterprises so as to enable multiple links along the supply chain to coordinate, reduce repetitions and waste and achieve larger added values.

Characteristics of global value chain development and supply chain

There are new trends and characteristics for global value chain development. In this process, the supply chain will make corresponding adjustments. Overall, there 7 features for global value chain development.

First, the global value chain changes from a manufacturing value chain to a string of innovations. Cross-border transfer and cooperation in technological innovations has become a significant development trend in the current economic globalisation, which further boosted the in-depth extension from a global value chain based on original manufacturing value chain to a global innovation chain. The nature of such an extension is to allow enterprises to search for appropriate knowledge resources on a worldwide scale, focus on the right of resource utilisation and form a highly open network innovation model for values.[3]

Second, data have become critical resources in global value chain allocation. Data amidst the new industrial revolution to enterprises and investors are closer in nature what land to the agrarian age. The internet giants such as Google, Facebook and Amazon have enormous stored data resources and have accelerated the process of turning them into assets. These data assets will determine the strategic choices of related enterprises in the future and the development of business models. To a certain extent, these enterprises, by leveraging strengths in data assets, have diverted or overtaken the power of control of conventional giant enterprise on the global value chain, which shifted the significance of different links in the global value chain and the speed of value adding.[4]

Third, the global value chain has seen reverse innovation among transnationals. With the rapid rise of emerging and developing economies and the gradual eastward transition of the global economic centre, the global consumer market is readjusting the landscape. As market demand for emerging and developing economies continually expands, transnationals adjust the global value chain layout to approach this new market. More R&D and innovation activities are placed in emerging market economies, which offers the foundation to distribute innovation products to the global market including developed countries, hence the reverse innovation.

Fourth, the global value chain expands from manufacturing to the service industry. As international production becomes increasingly fragmented and segmented, service industry plays an ever prominent role in the global value chain, which makes service an important adhesive for linking different links and stages of production to coordinate operation and manage headquarters. Service itself (such as R&D, design and marketing) has increasingly become a critical value-adding link in the value chain. Service has become a key component of the global value chain, which is both the embodiment and result of the global and fragmented development of the service industry.

Fifth, the global value chain has entered the remolding stage of "high-end reflux and low-end transfer". After the financial crisis, all countries have laid out several development strategies which set great store by technological innovation to pull economic development, such as the "advanced manufacturing" development strategy by the US, "Industry 4.0 Strategy" by Germany, "high-value manufacturing" strategy by Britain and "new industry France" strategy by France. The new industrial revolution and technological revolution will ultimately lead to changes in the fabric of the global industrial chain and supply chain. The reshaping and adjustment of technological and industrial revolutions include both changes in the global value chain itself (including the overall movement of the traditional "smile curve", the "silent curve" and "sadness curve" in line with the "smile curve", as well as the status of different countries in the global industrial chain and the so-called "manufacturing reflux" by advanced countries) and supply chain adjustment for cost "depression effect" in seeking the labour force.

Sixth, some industries tend to share work. Some enterprises that control the most cutting-edge technologies focus more on the internalisation of R&D so that the links that generate the highest values are firmly maintained within the enterprises. Internet companies constantly permeate to the upper stream and join the league of competition in new smart hardware equipment and service-oriented manufacturing. These enterprises fully leverage customer information collection at the lower stream and customer preferences, so as to bring to the market a new generation of integrated products featuring "experience first and simplified principles". The strategy activities of the value chain self-extension bring about the vertical integration for industries. Therefore, unlike the deepening of the division of labour between industrial enterprises in the international division of work in the 1990s and the first decade of the twenty-first century and the network-based global integrated division of labour supported by large-scale outsourcing, a new round of industrial division of labour has emerged, with the signs of a cloud model. Against the backdrop of the new industrial revolution, emerging countries relying on comparative advantages in manufacturing and export scales will further diminish the strength, resulting in the enlarged gap with developed nations in cutting-edge fields.

Seventh, the in-depth evolution of the global value chain exponentially boost the fostering of new global economic rules. As the global value chain continues to develop, especially the further development of manufacturing based value chain towards a global innovation chain, there is bound to be a higher requirement for an institutional guarantee for the latter. To be more specific, there is a higher demand for a country's economic policies and market environment about the degree of the rule of law, institutional quality, IP protection, production element market, environmental standard, a labour standard, fair competition and the transparency of business environment.

Development orientation of global value chain development and supply chain

Global value chain development plays a critical role in boosting global economic growth. The global value chain benefits each country in leveraging their own resource advantages, participating in the global industrial labour division, promoting trade and investment and bolstering their own economic development. This is in line with the objectives of the Belt and Road Initiative. Over the past 20 years, the wave of economic globalisation has catalysed deepened development of the global value chain as a major change, and 80% of global trade has been achieved through the value chain led by transnationals. The formation of the international labour division system induces not only profound changes in the worldwide supply chain, industrial chain and chain of goods, but also in international trade, cross-border investment and global economy and trade at large.

Economic globalisation bonds the countries much tighter, which forms a landscape featuring reciprocal link and interdependency. Peace, development, cooperation and common interests are the aspirations shared by people across the world. To lead economic globalisation under this trajectory, one needs to fully utilise the global value chain as a tool and an approach. Targeting the weaknesses of the global value chain, Chinese president Xi Jinping put forward the need to jointly forge a new global value chain. This Chinese solution clears the path for a new form of globalisation featuring openness, inclusiveness, balance and shared interests, contributing the Chinese wisdom to ushering in a new global age.[5]

Forming an inclusive and coordinative global value chain conforms to the objective need of vertical development of the economic development and the currently more specific evolution of international labour division. Some researchers hold that the pragmatic cooperation in global value chain under the G20 framework can be conducted in the following five aspects.[6] First, lowering the goods tariffs barrier. Against the backdrop of deepened development of the global value chain, the cross-border flow of intermediary goods is predominant in global trade. As one product crosses borders several times before being consumed, the impact of trade barriers on product costs has been magnified. Lowering international trade barriers across the board under the multilateral mechanism facilitates the development and deepening of the global value chain. Second, improving trade facilitation. Under the context of the global value chain, effective trade facilitation measures benefit lowering trade costs, reducing delays and uncertainties and bolstering a country's engagement capacity for the global value chain. For one country to participate in the global value chain, it needs not only to improve trade facilitation capacity but better the infrastructure in the entire region, so as to raise logistics efficiency, unblock supply chain barriers in the region and bolster regional connectivity. Third, expand the opening of the service market. Strengthening service trade and increasing shares of service trade are important means to increase shares of added value in per-unit export, and obtaining the key service links has become a critical approach in managing the global value chain. Fourth, promoting regional economic cooperation. Attracting more developing economies to participate in the regional economic cooperation can strengthen the bond of the regional value chain and bolster the appeal and influence of that region for the global value chain. Fifth, increasing interactions along the global value chain. Interactions between SMEs in developing countries and transnationals in developed countries need to be intensified. By improving coordination and supplement between domestic and foreign enterprises, the coordinating effect between local enterprises and transnationals along the value chain can be capitalised. In-depth engagement in international industrial labour division and coordination has become an effective approach for a myriad of developing economies to be embedded in the global value chain.

For China to deepen cooperation in the global value chain and align it with the pursuit of the Belt and Road Initiative, it is beneficial for global economic and trade governance to focus on the path of development, openness and inclusiveness.[7]

Notes

1 Xi Jinping, "Word Entry| Global Value Chain," China Leaders' Study Net, http://zt.ccln.gov.cn/xxxjp/xddct/66267-all.shtml
2 Ding Junfa, "Belt and Road and Global Supply Chain," *Globalization*, 2016, seventh edition, pp. 22–31.
3 Zhang Erzhen, Dai Xiang, "New Trend in Global Value Chain Development and Countermeasures for China to Transition Foreign Trade Development," *China National Conditions and Strength*, 2016, eighth edition, pp. 25–28.
4 Yang Danhui, "New Trend in Global Value Chain Labor Division in the Age of Big Data and New Hardware," Ministry of Commerce website. Retrieved February 25, 2016 from: http://gvc.mofcom.gov.cn/gvc/article/xsjl/201602/2121_1.html

5 Xi Jinping, "Word Entry| Global Value Chain," China Leaders' Study Net, http://zt.ccln.gov.cn/xxxjp/xddct/66267-all.shtml
6 Li Guanghui, "G20 Need Practical Cooperation along Global Value Chain," Ministry of Commerce website. Retrieved August 12, 2016 from: http://gvc.mofcom.gov.cn/gvc/article/xsjl/201608/2425_1.html
7 Shen Danyang, "Realizing Opportunities and Challenges to Actively Integrate into Global Value Chain," Xinhua Net. Retrieved March 27, 2016 from: www.xinhuanet.com/politics/2016-03/27/c_128837664.htm

66
PROMOTING RENEWABLE ENERGY AND ENERGY EFFICIENCY COOPERATION

Wang Yongzhong

Basic connotation for renewable energy

Renewable energy is energy from renewable resources. From the perspective of the human time scale, these renewable resources can be naturally supplemented without human intervention and are inexhaustible. Such power is contrary to non-renewable energy, and it encompasses solar energy, hydro energy, wind energy, biomass energy, wave energy, tidal energy, ocean temperature difference energy, geothermal energy and the like. The renewable energy is usually applied in four major areas: power generation, heating and cooling of air and water, transportation and energy services in villages, or areas away from the power grid.

The advantages of renewable energy are as follows. Wide geographical distribution, which can significantly shorten the energy transmission distance and alleviate energy supply security concerns; renewable energy is clean energy, so the environmental and health benefits are significant; renewable energy is sustainable and inexhaustible and renewable energy enhances energy efficiency.

Development status of renewable energy

In order to tackle issues of energy security, ecological conservation and climate change, all countries set great store by developing renewable energy, taking measures such as offering government subsidy, facilitating power grid combination and increasing R&D investment to encourage its development. Expediting the development and exploitation of renewable energy has become shared consensus and action for the international community. At present, the scale of global development and utilisation of renewable energy proliferates. As the cost drops, it has become a vital pathway for countries including China to advance energy transitioning and tackle climate change.

Currently, global renewable energy development demonstrates three characteristics.

First, developing renewable energy has become a strategic choice for global energy transformation and the realisation of climate change objectives. The trajectory for global energy transitioning begins with the change from a fossil fuel energy system to a low carbon energy system and finally to a sustainable energy system that mainly consists of renewable energy. The signatory states for the UN Paris Agreement have nearly all set up development objectives for renewable energy.

Second, renewable energy has become essential substituent energy. In recent years, countries in Europe and America annually install over 60% new power engines using renewable energy. In 2016 globally, new power installation capacity using renewable energy hit 165 gigawatts, accounting for nearly two-thirds of the total, of which photovoltaic power installations grew by 74 gigawatts, surpassing that of coal-fired installations for the first time. By the IEA estimation, from 2017 to 2022, renewable energy installed capacity will grow by 43% globally, with the installation capacity exceeding 920 gigawatts in 2022.[1] This development shows that a structural change is happening in the global power system building. For European countries such as Germany, in particular, renewable energy has become the mainstream energy.

Finally, renewable energy has become increasingly more economical. Along with the technological advancement and increased application scale for renewable energy, the cost for power generation using renewable sources has dropped significantly. Prices for wind power equipment and photovoltaic components have lowered by approximately 20% and 60%, respectively. The long-term purchase price of wind power in the United States and the new energy price in Germany are on a par with that of traditional energy. The subsidy intensity of renewable energy power generation has continued to decline, and the economic competitiveness has been significantly enhanced. In 2016, the bidding price for photovoltaic electricity has been as low as USD 3 cents per kWh. According to IEA estimation, from 2017 to 2022, the cost for photovoltaic power generation, wind power and maritime power will drop by 25%, 15%, and 33%, respectively.[2]

To mitigate the pressing issue of air pollution, reduce dependence on crude oil importation and secure national energy supply, the Chinese government actively promotes the development of renewable energy industries through fiscal subsidy and facilitating grid connection. Under the 13th 5-Year Plan on Renewable Energy Development, the objective for China's renewable energy development is to reach the shares of renewable energy consumption on one-time energy consumption at 15% by 2020 and 20% by 2030. Renewable energy has become the current important alternative energy in China. As the technologies quickly progress and their development and leverage expand constantly, the technology and equipment level for renewable energy in China elevates significantly, which pushes China towards power in renewable energy technologies, occupying a leading position in global renewable energy development. According to IEA statistics and estimation, the share of China's new photovoltaic installations hit 50% of the global total, and the share of China new renewable energy installations from 2017 and 2020 combined will reach 40% of the global total.[3]

In 2017, China's renewable energy generation capacity was 1.7 trillion kWh, accounting for 26.4% of total power generation, including 1194.50 billion kWh of hydropower, 305.7 billion kWh of wind power, 118.12 billion kWh of photovoltaic power generation and 79.4 billion kW of biomass power generation, with increases of 1.7%, 26.3%, 78.6% and 22.7%, respectively. As of the end of 2017, China's renewable energy power generation capacity reached 650 million kilowatts, accounting for 36.6% of all power installed capacity, including 341 million kilowatts of hydropower installed capacity, 164 million kilowatts of wind power installed capacity, 130 million kilowatts of photovoltaic power generation and 14.88 million kilowatts of biomass power generation, up by 2.7%, 10.5%, 68.7% and 22.6%, respectively.[4] Yet, renewable energy in China still faces obvious systemic and institutional constraints. The current power operation mechanism does not meet the needs of large-scale development of renewable energy; there are technical obstacles to large-scale grid connection of renewable energy power generation that led to abandonment of water, wind and photovoltaic energy; and renewable energy has a high dependence on financial subsidies.

Cooperation in renewable energy and energy efficiency

Cooperation in renewable energy and energy efficiency is a crucial approach to pursue the Belt and Road Initiative, which is urgently needed and possesses broad development potential. The reasons are as follows. First, many countries along the Belt and Road are relatively backward in socio-economic development. They are heavily reliant on fossil fuel energy, with highly polluted environment, backward energy technologies, low energy-use efficiency, low capacity in clean energy development and a strong intent to develop renewable energy and increase energy efficiency. Second, many countries along the Belt and Road are endowed with abundant oil and gas resources and renewable resources, but they are not yet fully developed, and the advantages in resources cannot be turned into economic strengths. Third, some countries that lack conventional fossil fuels have a strong need to reduce their reliance on external energy sources and safeguard domestic energy supply security through developing renewable resources and bolstering energy efficiency.

In the vision and action plan for promoting the Belt and Road Initiative publicised by China, they put forward that "we should increase cooperation in the exploration and development of coal, oil, gas, metal minerals, and other conventional energy sources; advance cooperation in hydropower, nuclear power, wind power, solar power and other clean, renewable energy sources; and promote cooperation in the processing and conversion of energy and resources at or near places where they are exploited, so as to create an integrated industrial chain of energy and resource cooperation" and "we should push forward cooperation in emerging industries. In accordance with the principles of mutual complementarities and mutual benefit, we should promote in-depth cooperation with other countries along the Belt and Road in new-generation information technology, biotechnology, new energy technology, new materials and other emerging industries, and establish entrepreneurial and investment cooperation mechanisms".[5] At the same time, the Joint Communiqué of the Leaders Roundtable of the Belt and Road Forum for International Cooperation advocates to "promote cooperation in the field of renewable energy and energy efficiency". The 2030 Agenda for Sustainable Development also stressed the need to "enhance international cooperation, promote the acquisition of clean energy research and technologies, including renewable resources and energy efficiency, as well as advanced and cleaner fossil fuel technologies, and increase investment in energy infrastructure and clean energy technologies".

In order to solidly promote the pragmatic cooperation between China and countries along the Belt and Road in the energy field, National Development and Reform Commission and State Energy Administration jointly issued the Vision and Proposed Actions Outlined on Jointly Building Silk Road Economic Belt and 21st Century Maritime Silk Road, which stresses to uphold the principle of green development, "actively promotes the development and utilization of clean energy, strictly control pollutants and greenhouse gas emissions, improve energy efficiency, promote green and efficient development of energy in all countries". It also regards "implementing the 2030 Agenda for Sustainable Development and the Paris Agreement on Climate Change, pressing ahead modern energy services that are affordable, reliable and sustainable to people across all countries, promoting investment, development and utilization of clean energy, and proactively conducting international cooperation in the field of energy" as a key area of cooperation. To ensure the smooth progress in renewable energy cooperation under the Belt and Road Initiative, the Chinese government announced two actions. First, to "continue to strengthen cooperation with international energy agencies such as the International Energy Agency, the Organization of Petroleum Exporting Countries, the International Energy Forum, the International Renewable Energy Agency, the Energy Charter, and the World Energy Council". Second, to "actively implement the China–ASEAN Clean Energy Capacity Building Programme and promote the China–Arab Clean Energy Centee and the China–Central and

Eastern Europe Energy Project Dialogue and Cooperation Centre. Continue to play the constructive role of the International Energy Change Forum and the East Asia Summit Clean Energy Forum".[6]

In the field of international energy efficiency cooperation, G20 published the G20 Energy Efficiency Action Plan and the G20 Energy Efficiency Leading Programme in 2014 and 2016, respectively, and both are the most influential and representative documents. The G20 states unanimously that enhancing energy cooperation results in improved economic activities, bolstered productivity, protected energy security and increased environmental efficacy. Consuming 80% of world's energy, the G20 states play a vital role in balancing energy supply and demand through continuously bolstering their energy efficiency.

The G20 Energy Efficiency Action Plan laid out a feasible plan for member states to flexibly enhance voluntary energy efficiency cooperation. The action plan identifies 6 key areas of focus, namely, transportation tools (especially heavy trucks), internet connection facilities, energy efficiency financing, architecture, energy management and power generation. The member states can choose to participate in cooperation projects that conform to national priorities and share knowledge, experiences and resources.

The G20 Energy Efficiency Leading Programme puts forward a long-term cooperation framework that is holistic, flexible and abundant in resources for the member states to voluntarily cooperate to bolster energy efficiency. On the prerequisite of voluntary cooperation, the G20 member states can uphold the principle of mutual benefit, innovation, inclusiveness and sharing and further enhance bilateral and multilateral international energy efficiency cooperation. Under the leading programme, the G20 member states will engage in 11 key areas of cooperation, namely, transportation tools (especially heavy trucks), internet connection facilities, energy efficiency financing, architecture, energy management, power generation and ultra-high energy efficiency equipment, best energy-saving technology and best practice, regional energy systems, energy efficiency knowledge sharing framework, end-device energy consumption data and energy-efficiency measurement.

Notes

1 International Energy Agency, "Renewables 2017: Analysis and Forecasts to 2022," Executive Summary, *Market Report Series*, 2017.
2 National Development and Reform Commission, *13th Five-Year Plan on Renewable Energy Development* (Public Edition), December 2016.
3 International Energy Agency, "Renewables 2017: Analysis and Forecasts to 2022," Executive Summary, *Market Report Series*, 2017.
4 Ding Yiting, "Renewable Power Hit 1.7 Trillion KWH by 2017," *People's Daily*, Retrieved January 26, 2018 from www.xinhuanet.com/power/2018-01/26/c_1122321547.htm.
5 National Development and Reform Commission, Ministry of Foreign Affairs and Ministry of Commerce: *Vision and Proposed Actions Outlined on Jointly Building Silk Road Economic Belt and 21st-Century Maritime Silk Road*, March 2015.
6 Ibid.

67
TACKLE CLIMATE CHANGE

Tian Huifang

Elaboration and formation of concept

The scientific basis for addressing climate change comes mainly from the multi-volume climate change assessment report issued by the Intergovernmental Panel on Climate Change (IPCC), an international organisation that assesses climate change established in 1988. So far, IPCC has successively published 5 assessment reports on climate change. The fifth assessment report in 2014 pointed out that global climate warming will continue in the future, and the average surface temperature of the Earth by the end of the twenty-first century will rise by 0.3–4.8°C on the 1985–2005 basis. The report also evaluates the existing credibility of the main conclusions of extreme climate events and analyses the root causes of disaster risks from the perspective of "extreme climate events + vulnerability + exposure", and integrates risk management into climate change actions of each country. The overall framework provides an important scientific basis.

In comparison with other global environmental issues, climate change is complex and unique. It is more than a purely natural phenomenon, but rather an issue with a socioeconomic nature. From the global perspective, once the global temperature rises, the climate becomes a public good which is mandatory for each country to consume, hence the notion of "mandatory public good". From the domestic perspective, climate change imposes adverse external effect, which is embodied by external sluggish economy and consumption. Nearly all activities by market participants cause emissions of greenhouse gas, including those in the energy, industrial and transport sectors as well as land use. As the consequences of the activities cannot be reflected by the market in time and not even in the current generation, there is a market failure. Besides, climate changes impose a generational impact, so if the actions against climate change are not initiated now, future generations might not enjoy the living environment they deserve, which is quite unfair. Therefore, managing climate change has moral significance. As there is a lack of governance models that surpass national sovereignty in the current international community, the unique feature of climate issue determines that to tackle global climate change, it is imperative to establish formal international cooperation mechanisms and rules to address it on the international level, so as to set emission targets, identify emission liabilities and set up regulation mechanisms.

The content for tackling climate change globally is not only reflected in the convention and documents of Paris Agreement under its framework but in transforming our world: the 2030 Agenda for Sustainable Development that was signed by 193 countries in 2015. To reduce carbon emission and follow the path of green, low-carbon and sustainable development is the most effective approach to thoroughly eradicate climate warming recognised by the international community.

Main content for addressing climate change

The convention has laid out the institutional arrangement for the international community to control the concentration of greenhouse gas in the atmosphere in the coming decades. It is the first international cooperation framework for the world to formally, authoritatively and comprehensively tackle climate change. It consists of a foreword and 26 items, which laid out several core components to address climate change: general principle, mitigation and adaptation, technology and funding, transparency and due diligence.

(1) General principle

The convention noted that the international community shall follow 5 general principles in the course of addressing climate change. The first is the principle of "common but differentiated responsibilities, fairness and respective capabilities", which is the important component of the international climate governance mechanism. It aims to set different emission reduction obligations and obligations for developed and developing countries. Thus, the international mechanism reflects the institutional characteristics of fairness and rationality. The second is the "special principle", that is, the response to climate change must consider and respect the national conditions and needs of special developing countries. The third is the "precautionary principle", that is, to establish a warning and emergency response mechanism for possible climate risks to prevent risks. The fourth is the principle of "sustainable development" that balances both climate change and economic development, considering the intergenerational impact, economic and socially sustainable development. Fifth, the "international cooperation principle" that promotes the coordination of climate change and international economic and trade relations.

(2) Emission arrangement

There are two general measures against global warming induced by greenhouse gas emissions. First, climate mitigation is through either reducing future greenhouse gas (GHG) emissions or increasing GHG absorption to lower emissions of GHG to the atmosphere, therefore curb the tendency for global warming. Second, climate adaptation, in other words, bolstering capabilities to respond to negative impacts of climate change. For mitigation measures, they consist of slashing GHG sources and increasing GHG absorption sinks/banks. The corresponding international policies are interpreted as three mechanisms in the Kyoto Protocol: mechanisms of joint implementation, emissions trading and clean development. The main objectives of the Paris Accords are as follows. (1) The developed countries should conscientiously fulfil commitments in the second commitment period of the Kyoto Protocol to maximise the mitigation efforts. (2) The developed countries shall fulfil commitments on providing funds, technologies and capabilities for related developing countries to tackle climate change and pragmatically develop feasible roadmaps. (3) Strengthening high-level engagement between 2016 and 2020 and nominating two high-level advocates every 2 years to promote reduction actions. Moreover, experience-sharing should be intensified and collaborative actions for climate change should be promoted. (4) Establishing higher-level cooperation networks, including setting up a non-state actor climate action portal and platform building, encouraging the participation of civil society, mobilising the enthusiasm of the private sector, attracting the participation of financial institutions and strengthening cooperation and action efforts at the city level and other subnational levels. In doing so, global mitigation actions will be promoted across the board. (5) Fully leveraging the role of the market mechanism, including formulating forceful climate policies between signatory parties and leveraging the role of carbon pricing and carbon market.

(3) The mechanism for funding and technologies

The eleventh item of the convention puts forward the need to establish a funding mechanism to promote technological transfer. It regulates that developed countries can fulfil funding commitment through diverse bilateral, regional and multilateral channels. There is no specific mandate on the sources, channels and types of funding and technologies; therefore, it is a vague commitment. The Paris Agreement, however, clearly explains the mechanism for funding and technologies. Regarding funding, developed countries are required to formulate an operational fund roadmap to fulfil their commitment to providing 100 billion yuan of funds per year to developing countries until 2020, whereas the volume of financial assistance after 2025 should be no less than US$100 billion per year. Through the operation of the Green Climate Fund and other public funds, the resources of the multi-party, including the private sector, multilateral development agencies and other bilateral or multilateral channels, can be fully mobilised. In regard to technology, the Paris Agreement has decided that the enforced technological mechanism is led by the technical executive committee and the technological climate centre and network, which expedite research and development of beneficial technologies and their demonstration and promotion, intensify assessment of new technology needs and transfer of technologies, create beneficial environment for technological research and development as well as transfer and eradicate development barriers.

(4) The mechanism for performance verification

This mechanism emphasises regular reporting on reduction commitments of each country, guarantees the transparency of information and data and updates regular reviews on progress. Since the measurable, reportable and verifiable (MRV) system was identified under the convention framework, it has been undergoing modification and improvement, with standards approaching unification. The Paris Agreement has set up an initiative for transparency capability building, which mandates that the national independent contribution target can only be exceeded but not postponed, and target review must be held every 5 years. It has also proposed to strengthen the national institutional building for transparency and enhance training and assistance to improve transparency gradually.

Major progress and trends in global efforts against climate change

The 45th UN General Assembly held in 1990 officially initiated the progress to tackle climate change in the international community. In 1992, 194 contracting states publicly signed the United Nations Framework Convention on Climate Change (hereinafter referred to as the Convention) at the United Nations Conference on Environment and Development, which came into force in 1994. This convention identified the internationally recognised principles for low-carbon development, and it is the most fundamental law for the international community to respond to climate change. In December 1997, the Third Conference of the Parties (COP3) of the Convention signed the Kyoto Protocol, including 28 articles and 2 annexes, which came into force in 2005. The protocol is the first mandatory agreement of quantitive arrangement laid out by the international community to tackle climate change. With the rapid increase of the overall strength and emissions of developing countries, developed countries have begun to vigorously call for new global emission reduction arrangements. Contracting parties have negotiated in the second commitment period of the Protocol (2013–2020) and for an international agreement that involves more countries. The international agreement was negotiated, and the Paris Agreement was adopted at the end of 2015. The agreement clearly stated that it is necessary to strengthen the global response to the threat of climate change, in addition to the goal of controlling the average temperature increase of global greenhouse gases by 2°C. The 1.5°C target is also included to minimise the long-term risks and impacts of climate change. The 1.5°C target was listed in the highest political agenda for global climate actions for the first time. Clinging on how to effectively promote the Paris Agreement and constantly improve the execution of each country, the current effort for climate change has manifested the following trends.

First, the climate agenda is increasingly integrated with the agenda for development, growth, trade and investment and finance. To achieve the national independent contribution target and to transition for low-carbon and green development, all countries have to intensify and adjust growth strategies and increase investment suitable for climate change by leveraging important opportunities of low-carbon development. Financing strategies should also be readjusted and strengthened. The system for green financing should be established to meet the need for low-carbon development capital.

Second, investment in sustainable infrastructure will be key to realising sustainable development goals and economic growth as well as climate targets under the convention. Investment in sustainable infrastructure can avoid fuelling high-carbon investment and leave space for creating ambitious reduction goals for policymakers so as to make it possible for the world economy to be rid of carbon by 2050. Such investment can also mitigate the impacts of global trade downturn, create jobs for countries and help them better respond to impacts by future climate change. As part of the sustainable infrastructure financing, the corresponding systemic financial risk-disclosure will advance the readjustment of global capital strategies, so as to create more climate-resilient global financial systems.

Third, the financing model for climate change will gradually unfold. The plan by developed countries to enlarge funding after 2020 on the basis of US$100 billion has been prolonged to 2025. With the US announcement of withdrawal from the Paris Agreement, relying on public climate fund to narrow the climate financing gap will be increasingly difficult. By the end of 2016, green financing made the debut in the UN climate management agenda to resolve insufficient climate financing. During the COP23 held in Bonn at the end of 2017, investment by commerce and industrial sectors in climate change became a key issue. Green financing began taking a more remarkable role. Over the past 10 years, some countries and financial institutions have taken steps to accelerate green transitioning in financial institutions and the market. Voluntary standards, such as the Equator Principles, enhance environmental risk management in many financial institutions. More than 20 global security exchanges have formulated the ESG Information Disclosure Guidebook for listed companies and created a number of green indexes. More and more institutions such as Bank of England and ICBC have started the practice of evaluating climate impacts on finance and new environmental stress tests for environmental policy change. Germany, the USA and the UK have developed procedures for green financing interest subsidy and security, as well as green investment banks supported by governments. The UK, in particular, has established a green development bank to invest heavily in green projects and attract private capital to participate. Since 2012, China has successively enacted a series of policies to stimulate green finance.

Fourth, non-sovereign state actors represented by multinational city networks become increasingly significant in the governance system. Cities play an increasingly important role in economic development, technological innovation and human progress, and they are a significant force in resolving climate issues. The transnational city network is a classical model where cities participate in climate management. The main features of this model are that on the basis of voluntary participate and equal-footed consultation, inter-city governance network and exchange platforms are formed to jointly promote best practices and share innovative low-carbon technologies and approaches, so as to reduce GHG emissions in cities and fully leverage the proactivity of cities in climate management and their political influence. In recent years, city alliances have been essential participants in arranging international climate management agenda, promoters of climate management norms, executors of climate cooperation programmes, and best platforms for sharing practices of low global carbon and sustainable development. There 2 ways for transnational city networks to participate in international climate management: First, establishing an international organisational structure. Member cities shall pledge action commitments and accept alliance supervision. The alliances provide the member cities with platforms for exchanges and study, allow information-sharing between member cities and promote transmission of climate technologies, actively innovating approaches for managing climate. Second, participating in external governance, including lobbying, advocating and filing reports, which exerts influence on the government and multilateral progress to gain more government support and project funding. It also gathers people, materials and information together via the internet, and motivates the dissemination of norms and technologies for low-carbon development at the city level.

68
SUSTAINABLE DEVELOPMENT

Tian Huifang

Elaboration and formation of sustainable development as concept

Sustainable development is a much-focused concept by government, scholars and industries. Scholars in different fields have described and explained it through different angles. Biologists generally believe that sustainable development is to strengthen production and regeneration capabilities of the ecology and environment. Sociologists hold that it means to increase the living quality of humanity without surpassing the limits of the ecological system. Economists, from the perspective of cost-effectiveness, think that the objective of sustainable development is to continuously bolster social well-being on the basis of protecting the environment. In 1987, the World Commission on Environment and Development presented a widely accepted authoritative definition of sustainable development in its report to the United Nations, *Our Common Future*: sustainable development is a development that meets the needs of the present without compromising the ability of future generations to meet their own needs. This definition was more systemically defined in the first comprehensive human sustainable development plan, Agenda 21, which was published at the 1992 United Nations Conference on Environment and Development and the Rio Summit on Earth (Rio+20). Agenda 21 divides sustainable development into four dimensions; namely, social and economic dimensions, conservation and management of resources for development, strengthening the role of major groups and means of implementation. Each dimensionis further divided into four levels; namely, the primary systems of sustainable development (economy and society, resources and environment, public and community, means and capabilities), fundamental aspects, plan areas and action initiatives. Agenda 21 also fully respects the differences among countries, especially the differences in responsibilities and obligations between developed and developing countries, and has developed more than 2500 action plans in 78 programme areas, including poverty alleviation, protection of diversity in the atmosphere, oceans and life, promotion of sustainable agriculture and change in ways of consumption and production to avoid excessive waste of resources. It has become a programmatic document guiding the international community to achieve sustainable development.

In 1972, American economist Donella Meadows published *The Limits to Growth*, a famous book that elaborated potential environmental stress posed by population growth from the angle of the population and the environment. Later, the United Nations held the first world conference on the human environment, which is the first large-scale environmental conference in human society, with over 10,000 delegates from 113 countries attending the conference. It announced The Declaration of the United Nations Conference on the Human Environment, which includes 37 common views and 26 universal principles and 109 action plans on protecting the global environment. This conference marked the beginning for humans to officially confront environmental issues and challenges and propelled the founding of the United Nations Environment Programme, signifying the formal initiation of cooperation in globally sustainable development actions. In March 1983, the United Nations established the World Commission on Environment and Development (WCED), which is responsible for formulating long-term environmental counter-measures and conducting research on approaches and pathways for the international society to adequately address environmental issues. It published *Our Common Future*, a famous report that elaborated on 3 aspects (common concerns, common challenges and common endeavours), which, for the first time, elevated environmental protection to the height of sustainable development for humanity.

Practices and connotation evolution of sustainable development

In 1992, the United Nations hosted the most important conference on environment and development in the history of the United Nations in Rio de Janeiro, Brazil, the famous Rio+20, where 183 national delegations and 70 international organisations reached a global plan on sustainable development that incorporates economic growth, social development and environmental protection, i.e. the aforesaid Agenda 21. It provides a blueprint for governments, UN organisations, development agencies, NGOs and independent groups to take steps to achieve sustainable development. To fully support the implementation of Agenda 21 across the board, the United Nations Committee on Sustainable Development (CSD) was approved by the General Assembly in December 1992, which is dedicated to ensuring effective implementation of follow-up actions from set out by the United Nations Conference on Environment and Development (UNCED), or the Earth Summit. Consisting of 53 members, CSD is an important committee under the UN Economic and Social Council. It is responsible for reviewing the implementation progress of Agenda 21 and the Rio Declaration on Environment and Development. It also provides policy guidance for following up the Johannesburg Plan of Implementation at the local, national, regional and international levels.

The 1994 Global Conference on the Sustainable Development of Small Island Developing States adopted the Barbados Programme of Action on the Sustainable Development of Small Island Developing States, which sets out specific actions and measures for the sustainable development of Small Island Developing States. The 1997 Special Session of the United Nations General Assembly (Special Session on the Fifth Anniversary of the Earth Summit) adopted the Programme for the Further Implementation of Agenda 21, which sets out the work Programme of the Commission on Sustainable Development from 1998 to 2002. The 2002 World Summit on Sustainable Development (Johannesburg, South Africa) assessed the obstacles encountered and achievements made in progress since the 1992 Earth Summit.

Upon entering the new millennium, the ecological foundations for human beings became ever more fragile, and the UN Millennium Development Goals were consequently introduced. In 2000, the Millennium Summit took place in New York, which passed the Millennium Declaration and set out a series of quantitative goals for eradicating poverty. The Millennium Development Goals (MDGs) contain 8 sections in the overall objectives that cover 4 areas of the economy, society, environment and international cooperation, with the overarching goal of eradicating extreme poverty and hunger and preventing diseases. The deadline for the Millennium Declaration was 2015.

In 2002, UN Secretary-General launched the Millennium Project. In 2005, an independent advisory body led by Professor Jeffrey Sachs submitted its final proposal to the Secretary-General for a comprehensive report, *Investing in Development: A Practical Plan for Achieving the Millennium Development*. In September 2005, the heads of state and government of the UN member states gathered again to capitalise this rare opportunity to make confident decisions in areas of development, security, human rights and UN reform, which was warmly received by organisations of all levels, including the civil group. In the unusual event for MDGs, Secretary-General Ban Kim-moon introduced to UN member states in his report that "everyone is entitled to a life of dignity". In the outcome document approved by the member states, world leaders reaffirmed their commitment to achieving the Millennium Development Goals and agreed to hold a high-level summit in September 2015 to adopt a new set of goals for achieving them. On September 23, 2013, the Secretary-General held a high-level forum in order to take further actions to promote and expedite achieving MDGs and solidify subsequent outcomes. It goes without saying that MDGs are the most vital global development goals in the history of the United Nations. Over 20 years of development and evolution, global sustainable governance has fostered 3 pillars of economic growth, social advancement and environmental protection and a comprehensive development framework with the heart of eradicating poverty, protecting nature, transforming unsustainable production and consumption modes. The international society has achieved positive progress in areas such as promoting economic development, eradicating hunger and poverty and improving well-being. All countries have integrated MDGs into their respective long-term development strategies, carried out diverse forms of international cooperation and intensified publicity and training on the concept of sustainable development.

Unfortunately, however, the world development has not truly followed the trajectory of sustainability. According to appropriate evaluations by UN, in the economic and social dimension, there are still issues of the high ratio of the population under extreme poverty, colossal development gaps between nations, gender inequality and refugees, despite remarkable progress made in sustainable development. The environmental dimension is even more severe, which is evidenced by little improvement in 24 out of the 90 total objectives, including climate change, desertification and drought and degeneration in 8 goals. Despite positive progress in environmental management in some regions, the overall global environment has been degenerating, and areas with environmental issues became more imbalanced.

From MDGs to SDGs: a new round of reform for global sustainable development

As 2015 set the deadline for the Millennium Development Agenda and MDGs, UN organisations began the work on developing a global development agenda after that year since 2010.

In 2012, the international community for sustainable development returned to Rio for another high-level Rio+20 at a large scale. The summit invited attendees from governments, the private sector, NGOs and other stakeholders to assess the progress in global sustainable development. It centred on 3 topics of discussion: (1) evaluating current commitments and the gap in implementation; (2) renewed commitments for sustainable development; and (3) identifying emerging global challenges. The discussions also focused on how green economy can propel sustainable development globally, eradicating poverty and building a complete development framework as well as relevant reforms. One major context for this summit is the 2008 global financial crisis. All countries were seeking new growth points to be rid of the crisis. Green economy, therefore, entered the arena for human history and the Green New Deal representing industrial and economic structural transformation was born. The Rio+20 Summit subsequently passed *The Future We Want*. The major objective of *The Future We Want* is to set out globally sustainable development goals after 2015. During the summit, the UN put forward the orientation and standards for a new round of governance and reform for global sustainable development, including establishing inclusive development framework that incorporates different sovereign nations, non-state actors, social groups and individuals; founding stable capital flows to support sustainable development; improving administrative efficiency; bolstering implementation capability; establishing dynamic methods and indexes that reflect changes in natural and social systems; and forming mechanisms for forceful accountability and measures securing transparency. In September 2015, the 2030 Agenda for Sustainable Development was unanimously approved by world leaders in the historic UN heads of states meeting. On January 1, 2016, 17 sustainable development goals (SDGs) set out in the 2030 Agenda for Sustainable Development officially took effect. In the 15 following years, with the unveiling of new targets that are universally applicable to all individuals, all countries will gather strength to end poverty in all forms, fight inequality and tackle climate change while ensuring that no one is left behind.

Sustainable development goals, also called global targets, are based on the success of MDGs, with the aim of further eradicating all forms of poverty. These new goals are unique in that they call for all countries to take action, promote global prosperity and protect the Earth. The new agenda also realised that poverty eradication must go hand-in-hand with strategies that stimulate growth, and social demands, including education, health, social protection and employment, be met in tandem with tackling climate change and protecting the environment. The new sustainable development agenda has listed environmental, social and economic goals as 3 equally critical overarching goals, and 17 SDGs. As global carbon dioxide emissions have increased by more than 50% since 1990, and the progress of climate change action in the old MDGs is not satisfactory, the 2030 Sustainable Development Agenda lists the Climate Change Goals (SDG13) separately, with the aim of US$100 billion being raised annually to meet the needs of developing countries, mitigate climate-related disasters and enhance the resilience and adaptability of vulnerable areas such as land-locked countries and island countries, from 2020 onwards. The Addis Ababa Action Agenda, presented at the Third International Conference on Financing for Development, provides specific policies and actions for the implementation of sustainable goals. It can be said that many of the environmental goals of the UN 2030 SDGs also point the way for global environmental governance for the next 15 years.

69
TRADE AND INVESTMENT FACILITATION

Feng Weijiang

Trade and investment facilitation is a series of actions to simplify international trade and investment procedures through comprehensive and coordinated implementation in accordance with internationally accepted norms, standards and practices, eliminate barriers to international trade investment, reduce transaction costs in international trade activities and capital flows and ensure efficiency, transparency and predictability in trade and investment procedures. To be more specific, trade and investment facilitation can be further divided into trade facilitation and investment facilitation. The World Trade Organisation (WTO) was the first organisation to put trade facilitation in the work agenda during the 1996 Singapore ministerial-level meeting, whereas investment facilitation becoming an independent topic of discussion first appeared in the Investment Facilitation Action Plan (IFAP) published by APEC in 2008.

Definition of trade and investment facilitation

Different international organisations and agencies have given their own definition of trade facilitation. WTO holds that it is a simplification, modernisation and harmonisation of the import and export process.[1] The import and export, or international trade, a process defined by WTO includes all activities, practices and procedures in collecting, displaying, exchanging and processing data and information required for transferring goods in international trade.[2] The World Bank believes that trade facilitation involves a series of complex customs and post-customs measures such as loosening customs restrictions and liberalising foreign currency markets. In a broad sense, it also incorporates general measures from reforming institutions and supervision to improving customs and ports efficiency.[3] The World Bank underscores promoting trade facilitation in areas such as infrastructure investment, customs modernisation, transit environment and document simplification, automation and digital data exchange, ports efficiency, supervision and competition for logistics and transport services, multimodal transport and transport security.[4] The Organisation for Economic Cooperation and Development (OECD) upholds that trade facilitation is streamlining and simplifying the international trade process.[5] The United Nations Conference on Trade and Development (UNCTAD) regards trade facilitation as building a transparent, consistent and predictable border trade environment by following simplified and standard customs processes, document requirements, goods and transit operations as well as arrangements of trade and transport conventions. Broadly speaking, any measure that simplifies the trade process and consequently reduces transaction time and cost can be categorised into the realm of trade facilitation. Viewed more specifically, UNCTAD holds that measures for trade facilitation should cover: (1) applying standardised and digital information of trade and transaction procedures and documents; (2) improving goods transport services, legal frameworks, transport and communications infrastructure and adopting modern information technology tools; and (3) establishing consultation mechanisms such as trade facilitation organisations for governments, service suppliers, traders and other players so as to timely discuss and share trade information.[6] The World Customs Organisation regards trade facilitation as avoiding unnecessary trade restrictions, which is achieved by improving regulation quality via modern technologies and approaches in an internationally coordinated manner.[7] APEC interprets trade facilitation as the simplification and rationalisation of administrative procedures in customs that cause delay, blockage or increase cross-border goods transportation. In other words, it is the reduction of red tape for importers and exporters on the border to help goods be delivered more efficiently and cost-effectively.[8]

There are different definitions for investment facilitation from each organisation. APEC defines it as a set of actions by governments to attract foreign investment. These actions take effect in each phase of the investment cycle to maximise the effectiveness and efficiency of management. Investment facilitation measures cover a wide spectrum of fields, with the ultimate goal of gaining maximum benefits by enabling the effective flow of investment. The most important principle of trade facilitation is transparency, simplicity and predictability.[9] UNCTAD takes investment facilitation as a set of policies and actions that dedicate to facilitating the launching and expansion of investment in host countries and the operation of daily businesses. The key to investment facilitation is removing investment barriers, for instance, increasing transparency and investors' access to information, finishing administrative procedures faster, or improving stability and predictability of policies and business environment.[10] OECD deems investment facilitation as a way of making investors launch new investment or expand existing investment easier. In this regard, it is a key factor to achieve such facilitation that one government department authorises one-stop service to lower costs related to procedures of acquiring investment permit. At the heart of investment facilitation is narrowing the gap in inconsistent or inaccurate information in current policies.[11]

Trade and investment facilitation both emphasise on making trade and investment policy environment more transparent, stable and predictable and reducing transaction costs through streamlining procedures and formalities. In actual research and policy practice, the two types of facilitation are combined as trade and investment facilitation.

Measurement of trade and investment facilitation

The index system for measuring the degree of trade facilitation is represented by the Enabling Trade Index (ETI) from the Global Enabling Trade Report published at the World Economic Forum (WEF). The report published in 2016 gives evaluations in 7 areas (domestic market access, foreign market access, efficiency and transparency in border control, accessibility and quality of transport infrastructure, accessibility and quality of transport services, accessibility and utilisation of information and communications technologies, and business operation environment) in 4 categories: market access, border control, infrastructure and business operation environment. Among them, market access, divided into domestic and foreign market access, measures the level of protection for one country's market and exporters in target countries. Domestic market access primarily evaluates the level and complex procedures of tariff protection in one country's trading policies, which incorporates 6 indexes, for instance, trade-weighted average tariff level, proportion of imported duty-free goods and the complexity of the tariff system that is expressed by the range of tariff change, the ratio of tariff peaks and specific tariffs and the number of tariff categories. Foreign market access mainly assesses the tariff barriers the exporter confronts in the target market, which includes 2 indexes, offered the average tariff level in the host country and margin of preference gained in target market through bilateral and regional trade agreements or trade preference. The effectiveness and transparency in border control evaluates the efficiency, transparency and cost related to import of goods, which encompasses a total of 13 indicators, such as assessment of scope, quality and comprehensive level of critical services provided by customs and related agencies, assessment of customs clearance time, cost and number of documents required, assessment of predictability and transparency of border process time and assessment of corruption in customs clearance. The availability and quality of transport infrastructure, mainly measuring the availability and quality of interstate highways, aviation, railways and port infrastructure, as well as the interconnection of air and sea routes, has 7 indicators. The accessibility and quality of transport services cover six indexes, namely, number and capability of transport and logistics businesses, and ease, cost, timeliness and mail efficiency in transport. The accessibility and utilisation of information and communications technologies, incorporating the use of mobile phones and the internet by domestic individuals, businesses and governments, the quality of internet access and the potential to fully leverage the internet, has 7 indicators. The business environment, having a total of 16 indexes, assesses the level of property rights protection in one country, the quality and impartiality of public institutions, the efficiency of contract enforcement, financial availability, openness (including openness to foreign funds and labour) and personal safety degree expressed by incidence of crime and the number of terrorist activities.[12]

The most representative index system for measuring the ease of doing business is the Doing Business Index in *Doing Business* formulated by the World Bank since 2003. Doing Business divides corporate investment operations into 11 first-level indicators, namely, start-ups, construction permits, access to electricity, registration of property, access to credit, protection of minority investors, taxation, cross-border trade, execution of contracts, bankruptcy and labour market supervision, and about 4 secondary indicators, forming a relatively complete investment facilitation evaluation system.

Implementation of trade and investment facilitation

Trade and investment facilitation is carried out at the national, regional and global levels. First, with the consideration of bolstering the competitiveness of domestic goods, countries might adopt measures for facilitating trade and investment independently or with a partnering nation, such as expanding market entry, improving border control, improving infrastructure and connectivity level, developing ICT and implementing more transparent and predictable trade and investment policies. For example, Singapore established the world's first Single Window for Trade in 1989. Having incorporated functions of 35 border organisations, it significantly improved customs clearance efficiency and lowered the cost of clearance.

Second, as there is increasing emphasis on trade and investment facilitation in economic cooperation at the regional level, regional trade arrangement has more broadly inscribed terms on such facilitation. The trade and investment facilitation for a regional trade started from slashing of related costs and transparency in clearance procedures initially, to measures of reducing trade documents and streamlining border organisations, and later encompassed content of more complex measures behind the borders. APEC is one of the regional cooperation organisations advocating investment and trade facilitation. It has long set the objectives for regional trade facilitation, such as a single window, verified operator and establishing digital procedures, implementing 2 rounds of schemes and proposing the action plan for investment facilitation.

Finally, under the multilateral institutions, some international organisations have been committed to promoting trade and investment facilitation at the global level. OECD has established, pursuant to trade policies under WTO negotiations, trade facilitation index consisting of 16 indicators, and offered input for prioritised trade facilitation measures in line with different development stages of each country. The World Bank and United Nations Conference on Trade and Development (UNCTAD) had reinforced studies on trade facilitation over recent years and offered trade facilitation measures from their own perspectives for general reference. In February 2017, Rwanda, Oman, Chad and Jordan, all WTO members, submitted the approval document for the Trade Facilitation Agreement to the WTO. The number of members who have ratified the Trade Facilitation Agreement had thus reached 112, which exceeded the legal threshold of two-thirds of the total number of WTO members required for the entry into force of the agreement. Therefore, the agreement officially came into effect and was implemented by members ratifying the treaty. In April 2017, China led the developing countries such as Brazil, Argentina and Nigeria to form the Friends of Investment Facilitation for Development to jointly promote the discussion of this topic in the WTO.

The Europe–Asia partnership following the principle of equality, openness and transparency was an economic cooperation initiative proposed by Russia, supported by China and participated in by countries in Europe and Asia as well as regional organisations. The Joint Communiqué of the Leaders Roundtable of the Belt and Road Forum for International Cooperation published on May 15, 2017 identified the Europe–Asia partnership following the principle of equality, openness and transparency as one of the cooperation frameworks and initiatives at the international, regional and national levels that are communicated and coordinated by BRI to bring cooperation opportunities for interconnected and sustainable development.

Notes

1 WTO, "Trade facilitation," www.wto.org/english/tratop_e/tradfa_e/tradfa_e.htm
2 WTO, "Trade facilitation," http://gtad.wto.org/trta_subcategory.aspx?cat=33121
3 World Bank, "Trade Facilitation," http://go.worldbank.org/QWGE7JNJG0
4 World Bank, "Trade Facilitation in the World Bank," http://siteresources.worldbank.org/INTRANETTRADE/Resources/Topics/Trade_Facilitation_Brochure_July_2005.pdf
5 OECD, "Trade facilitation," www.oecd.org/tad/facilitation/
6 UNCTAD, "Trade facilitation handbook, Part I national facilitation bodies: lessons from experience," http://unctad.org/en/Docs/sdtetlb20051_en.pdf
7 WCO, "What is Securing and Facilitating Legitimate Global Trade?" www.wcoomd.org/en/topics/facilitation/overview/customs-procedures-and-facilitation.aspx
8 APEC, "APEC's Second Trade Facilitation Action Plan," APEC paper 207-SE-05. 2007.
9 APEC, "APEC Investment Facilitation Action Plan (IFAP),". 2008/MRT/R/004. May 31, 2008.
10 UNCTAD, "Investment Facilitation: A Review of Policy Practices. February 2017," http://investmentpolicyhub.unctad.org/Upload/Documents/Investment-Facilitation_Review%20Note%203%20feb.pdf
11 OECD, "Draft chapter: Investment promotion and facilitation," 2014, www.oecd.org/daf/inv/investment-policy/PFI-update-investment-promotion-and-facilitation.pdf
12 For relevant content, refer to WEF, "The Global Enabling Trade Report 2016," 2016, http://wef.ch/getr16

70

PEOPLE-TO-PEOPLE EXCHANGES AND COOPERATION

Xiao He

People-to-people exchanges guided by understanding between people

People-to-people exchanges and cooperation have always been a major theme in China's foreign exchanges, and this also holds true for BRI. As a matter of fact, although BRI underscores the "hard" characteristics of infrastructure building and economic development, it does not neglect the "soft" exchanges and cooperation between humans. On the contrary, it has been identified as a main component and long-term foundation of BRI since the proposal of the initiative, and has been distilled into the concept of "understanding between people" that is a vital part of the interconnected development and a pillar of deepened cooperation for forming a community of shared future for mankind under the BRI. In September 2013, President Xi Jinping of China formally put forward the Silk Road Economic Belt and the concept of Five Types of Connectivity during his visit to Kazakhstan. He laid special emphasis on "Friendship between peoples is the key to good relations between states. To pursue productive cooperation in the above-mentioned areas, we need the support of our peoples. We should encourage more friendly exchanges between our peoples to enhance mutual understanding and traditional friendship, and build strong public support and a solid foundation for regional cooperation".[1] This statement laid the ground for the role and positioning of people-to-people exchanges in BRI and identified that understanding between people is the long-term foundation for policy coordination, infrastructure connectivity, unimpeded trade and financial integration. Such positioning highly affirms the significance of people-to-people exchanges and cooperation.

In October 2013, President Xi Jinping delivered a speech on working together to build a 21st Century Maritime Silk Road at the People's Representative Council of Indonesia, in which he gave more detailed explanations on the content and approaches for forging understanding between people. He stressed that "a tall tree grows from a small seedling; and the building of a nine-story tower starts with the first shovel of earth", and to ensure that the tree of friendship evergreen, the soil of social support for bilateral relations should be fertile—"increased interactions have nurtured a deeper bond between us and made our people feel ever-closer to each other". For that purpose, friendly exchanges between youth, think tanks, political councils, NGOs and social groups should be enhanced, and intelligence should be provided to bilateral relationship development apart from increased understanding and friendship, so that culture, education, health and medical programmes will be developed.[2] In the interconnected dialogue conference by the end of 2014, President Xi Jinping further elaborated the Five Types of Connectivity and pointed out that interconnectivity is more than merely building bridges and roads and connecting flat lines and single lines, but rather integration between infrastructure, regulations and personal exchanges.[3] Therefore, people-to-people exchanges and cooperation, guided by understanding between people, is ultimately promoting a two-way exchange between people of different countries and forming a people-to-people connection in parallel with the physical and regulatory connection. The exchange carriers are individuals and civic groups, in a narrow sense. In a broad sense, they refer to all social groups excluding administrative departments but including councils and political parties. Such an exchange is concentrated in "soft" areas such as tourism, culture, education, science and technology and healthcare.

As to how to forge understanding between people, President Xi Jinping has continuously summarised and put forward some fundamental guidelines and principles. First, understanding between people needs to forge a soft power of strengthening emotional exchanges and communication between people's hearts to coordinate with the hard power of politics, economy and security cooperation. Therefore, it is imperative to conduct two-way communication and interactions by treating each other as equals and should not regard understanding between people as enticing others with interests. Just as President Xi has stated: "Friendships built on benefits and power cannot last, and only friendships built on sincerity can last long".[4] Besides, one should be aware that although people-to-people exchanges seem simple, they are more difficult than building bridges and roads, travelling for business and sightseeing and carrying out government cooperation. Achieving truly mutual respect, mutual exchanges and mutual understanding between different societies is not an overnight job. Regarding people-to-people exchanges and cooperation, therefore, President Xi often restates that "the close ties between our peoples must be nurtured through constant efforts".[5] In the course of promoting understanding between people, it should be mindful that people-to-people programmes are long-term and strenuous, so there should be no haste.

Progress and outcomes

People-to-people exchanges and cooperation guided by understanding between people are threefold: first, exchanges at the citizen level, which both includes self-funded international travel and national programmes of student and technical personnel exchanges; second, exchanges at the professional organisational level, which is primarily about forming a network of mutual assistance in related fields to strengthen exchanges and cooperation in professional fields; and the third is establishing bilateral or multilateral cultural exchange mechanisms between national governments, or formulating schemes for the cultural industry and trade development that promote social exchanges between countries. At present, people-to-people exchanges and cooperation under the BRI have achieved fruitful outcomes, which strongly boosted pragmatic cooperation in the spectrum of politics and economy between China and BRI participating countries.

At the citizen level, the total arrivals from China to the BRI cooperating countries have been rising rapidly over recent years. The figures for 2017 were 2.7 times those in 2015. At present, the volume of tourism between BRI participating countries has accounted for over 70% of the world total, two-way tourism arrivals between China and BRI participating countries have exceeded 25 million persons. During the 13th 5-year period, China is estimated to send 150 million tourists to BRI-participating countries, which will generate a tourism consumption pull of over US$200 billion and in return attract 85 million visitors and generate nearly US$110 billion tourism consumption.[6] Apart from cross-border tourism, the Silk Road overseas study programme has been in full swing. Despite the existing overseas study programmes, the Chinese government has set up the Silk Road Scholarship, which recruits 10,000 new students annually. By the end of 2016, 200,000 students from BRI participating countries were studying in China. From 2012 onwards, China has sent a total of 350,000 students to BRI participating countries for study, with 75,000 students in 2016 alone. Besides, in the area of professionals' exchange, China has fostered exchange programmes such as the "Silk Road Cultural Tour", the "Silk Road Cultural Envoy" and the "Young Sinologist Training Programme", which will enable 30,000 personnel to participate in the annual cultural exchanges in 2020.[7]

At the organisational level, cooperation among education institutions was deepened with the rapid growth of personnel mobility. Since 2013, China has signed mutual recognition agreements for diploma and degrees with 46 countries and regions. As of the end of 2016, 2539 universities have paired up with Chinese counterparts in cooperative education, of which, four institutions and 98 programmes were set up in 14 BRI participating countries in collaboration with China.[8] Despite cooperative education, the Confucius Institute programme is an important approach for international people-to-people exchanges and cooperation in the field of education. By the end of 2016, 512 Confucius Institutes and 1073 Confucius Classes had been founded in 140 countries, which enabled full coverage in BRI participating countries. In regard to functions, Confucius Institutes introduce various kinds of exchange programmes such as sinologists' visit to China and foreign Chinese teachers visit China, on top of language education.[9] Besides education institutions cooperation, think-tank collaborations are equally important components of people-to-people exchanges under the BRI. Currently, the Belt and Road international symposium, the Belt and Road think-tank cooperation alliance and other high-end academic exchange platforms and cooperation mechanisms are improving. Chinese institutions of higher learning and research institutes have established over 300 Belt and Road research platforms and over 50 foreign think tanks have participated in research for the BRI. As the Belt and Road International Think-tank Cooperation Alliance are constantly growing, exchanges and cooperation among think tanks are deepening. In addition, China is actively promoting the establishment of cooperation networks for special agencies in arts, such as the "Silk Road International Theatre Alliance", the "Silk Road International Library Alliance", the "Silk Road International Museum Alliance", the "Silk Road International Art Gallery Alliance" and the "Silk Road International Arts Festival Alliance", which was widely noted in the international arena.[10]

At the governmental level, China sets great store by adding content on people-to-people exchanges and cooperation to intergovernmental cooperation frameworks. In the intergovernmental MOU on BRI jointly signed by BRI participating countries, China stressed strengthening cooperation in this area a number of times. As of the end of 2016, China has signed a total of 318 intergovernmental cooperation agreements on cultural exchanges and cooperation, mutually established 11 cultural centres in accordance with these agreements and hosted a variety of formal exchange activities such as education exchange years and cultural tourism years.[11] In 2017, in order to comb through existing people-to-people exchanges and cooperation programmes, the Ministry of Culture formulated the Action Plan on Developing Belt and Road Culture (2016–2020), which puts forward establishing the Belt and Road international exchange mechanisms and domestic cooperation mechanisms, improving Belt and Road cultural exchange and cooperation platforms, founding cultural centres for BRI participating countries, forming overall plans for Belt and Road cultural exchange and cooperation platforms and prioritising fostering cultural exchange marks including the Silk Road Cultural Envoys.[12] Moreover, with the joint promotion by the central and subnational governments, China expedited the building of Belt and Road Sister-City Clusters. As of May 2017, China had bonded with 245 provincial and state-level governments of relevant countries through 491 sister-city relations. The linear connection started from point-to-point links greatly pulled the multi-level exchanges among different societies, boosting mutual understanding between peoples.[13]

As for people-to-people exchanges and cooperation under the BRI, President Xi has laid out the role think tanks can play on some occasions. Regarding its breadth, President Xi Jinping calls for BRI participating countries to establish exchange platforms in areas of education, science and technology, culture, sports, tourism, health and archaeology and to jointly launch a Belt and Road network for think-tank cooperation. Regarding its depth, President Xi Jinping demands that think tanks should achieve real results in guiding public opinions and publicising progress made in BRI, and enhance academic research, theoretical support and discourse system building under the BRI. This clearly stated that think tanks should have special focus and advantages in promoting BRI. Research institutes including think tanks should leverage the role of gathering public opinions, exchanging public ideas and forging closer ties with the people in cooperation links of assessment in the early stage, planning in the medium stage and publicity in the late stage, so as to contribute to the promotion of BRI and building a community of shared future for mankind.

People-to-people exchanges and cooperation at the individual, organisational and governmental levels have effectively promoted social exchanges and understanding among BRI participating countries, which vigorously supported pragmatic cooperation in fields of politics and economy.

Notes

1 Xi Jinping, "Carry Forward the People-to-People Friendship for A Better Future—Speech at Nazarbayev University," Xinhua Net, September 7, 2013, www.xinhuanet.com/politics/2013-09/08/c_117273079_2.htm.
2 Xi Jinping, "Work Together to Build China–ASEAN Community of Shared Future—Speech at the People's Representative Council of Indonesia," Xinhua Net, October 3, 2013, www.xinhuanet.com/world/2013-10/03/c_117591652.htm.
3 Xi Jinping, "Connect to Lead Partnership—Dialogue on Strengthening Connectivity Partnership," *People's Daily*, 2nd edition, November 9, 2014.
4 Xi Jinping, "Co-Creating A Future of China-ROK Cooperation to Reinvigorate Asian Prosperity—Speech at Seoul National University," *People's Daily*, 2nd edition, July 5, 2014.
5 Xi Jinping, "Work Together for a Bright Future of China-Arab Relations—Speech at Arab League Headquarters," Xinhua News Agency, January 21, 2016.
6 Chinese Tourism Industry, "Belt and Road Tourism at Right Time," People.com, May 20, 2017. http://travel.people.com.cn/n1/2017/0520/c41570-29288338.html; "China Attract 85 million BRI Country Visitors During 13th Five-Year," CGTN, September 14, 2017, http://news.china.com/news100/11038989/20170914/31393273.html
7 "People-To-People Ties Reap Harvest with BRI Participating Countries," Xinmin Evening News, May 11, 2017.
8 Chen Wanling, "The BRICS Pathway for Belt and Road Cultural Exchanges," *Asia Pacific Economy*, p. 53, 3rd edition of 2017.
9 Zhao Mairu, "Research on People-To-People Exchange Base under BRI," *Journal of Nanjing University of Science and Technology (Social Sciences)*, p. 26, 3rd edition of 2017.
10 "People-To-People Ties Reap Harvest with BRI Participating Countries," Xinmin Evening News, May 11, 2017.
11 Han Yeting, "Culture as Media to Boost Exchange and Cooperation—New Progress in Belt and Road People-To-People Exchange and Cooperation," *Guangming Daily*, April 14, 2017.
12 "Action Plan on Belt and Road Cultural Development (2016–2020)," Ministry of Culture, Xinhua Net, January 6, 2017, www.xinhuanet.com/culture/2017-01/06/c_1120256880.htm
13 He Yafei, "BRI to Promote Cultural Exchanges," *FT China*, September 14, 2017, www.ftchinese.com/story/001074288.

71
EXCHANGES AND MUTUAL LEARNING AMONG CIVILISATIONS

Xue Li

Concept interpretation and formation

The concept is that all civilisations have strengths, so different civilisations should draw on others' advantages through exchanges (including dialogues) so as to secure world peace and achieve shared prosperity. This is the diplomatic philosophy and practice that has been strenuously promoted by the Chinese leadership over the past few years.

In a speech at UNESCO headquarter on March 28, 2014, President Xi Jinping expressed that "civilizations have become richer and more colorful with exchanges and mutual learning. Such exchanges and mutual learning form an important drive for human progress and global peace and development".[1] This was the first time Chinese leaders promoted exchanges and mutual learning among civilisations on an essential international occasion after the proposal of the BRI.

On June 28, 2014, at a meeting marking the 60th Anniversary of the Initiation of the Five Principles of Peaceful Coexistence, Xi Jinping stressed that "Diversity of civilizations is a defining feature of the human society. In today's world, there are 7 billion people of more than 2,500 ethnic groups who live in over 200 countries and regions and speak more than 5,000 languages. Different nations and civilizations are rich in diversity and have their own distinct features. No one is superior or inferior to others". Therefore, "we should respect the diversity of civilizations and promote exchanges, dialogue, peaceful and harmonious coexistence among different civilizations and should not seek supremacy or denigrate other civilizations and nations".[2]

In the Vision and proposed actions outlined on jointly building Silk Road Economic Belt and 21st Century Maritime Silk Road published on March 28, 2015, it mentions "enhance people-to-people and cultural exchanges, and mutual learning among the peoples of the relevant countries" in the Background and "encourage different civilizations to learn from each other and flourish together; and promote mutual understanding, peace and friendship among people of all countries" in the Frameworks. In the final section on Embracing a Better Future Together, it stated that the Belt and Road cooperation features mutual respect and trust, mutual benefit and win–win cooperation and mutual learning between civilisations.

In the keynote speech at Boao Forum on March 29, 2015, Xin Jinping underscored that "we need to ensure inclusiveness and mutual learning among civilizations" and "There need to be more exchange and dialogue among civilizations and development models, so that each could draw on the strength of the other and all could thrive and prosper by way of mutual learning and common development. Let us promote inter-civilization exchanges to build bridges of friendship for our people, drive human development and safeguard the peace of the world", and called for convening a conference of dialogue among Asian civilisations.[3]

On April 28, 2016, in the speech by Xi Jinping at the Opening Ceremony of the Fifth Meeting of The CICA Ministers of Foreign Affairs, he mentioned promoting exchanges and mutual learning among civilisations.[4]

On April 29, 2016, the Political Bureau of the CPC Central Committee conducted the 31st joint study on the historic Silk Road and the Maritime Silk Road in history, emphasising people-to-people exchanges and cultural programmes as the proper meaning of the BRI. It is the vision to incorporate cultural exchanges and dialogue among civilisations into the BRI and seek cultural development and mutual learning among civilisations.[5]

On January 18, 2017, Xi Jinping mentioned in his address at UN Geneva Headquarters that "diversity among human civilizations is the fundamental characteristic of the world, and the source for human progress" and "different civilizations should draw on from each other for common development so as to make exchanges and mutual learning among civilizations a drive for social progress of mankind and a bond for securing world peace".[6]

In May 2017, Xi Jinping advocated at the opening ceremony of the Belt and Road International Cooperation Forum when delivering remarks that in pursuing the Belt and Road Initiative, we should ensure that when it comes to different civilisations, exchange will replace estrangement, mutual learning will replace clashes and coexistence will replace a sense of superiority. This will boost mutual understanding, mutual respect and mutual trust between countries.[7]

In September 2017, Xi Jinping made the suggestion at the opening of BRICS Business Forum 2017 that "we should fully leverage the role of people-to-people and cultural exchange … we should hold more events like cultural festivals, movie festivals and sports games that are popular among the people … so that the BRICS story will be told everywhere, and the exchanges and friendship of the peoples of our five countries will become an inexhaustible source of strength driving BRICS cooperation".[8]

In the 19th NPC Report delivered on October 18, 2917, Xi Jinping stressed that a great number of steps should be taken for building a community of shared future for mankind, one of which is to "boost cross-cultural exchanges characterized by harmony within diversity, inclusiveness, and mutual learning".[9]

Main content and progress

The main content (1) refers to communication between different cultures and complementarities among one another; (2) emphasises cross-cultural exchanges, but as a majority of country-to-country exchanges arise from exchanges among civilisations, cross-cultural exchange and mutual learning are usually achieved through people-to-people exchanges; (3) Asia is a multicultural region and key area for implementing BRI. As a dialogue among civilisations is an important approach to enable cross-cultural exchanges and mutual learning, it should therefore be given special emphasis. (4) The Chinese government takes cross-cultural exchanges and mutual learning as a key approach to pursue BRI; therefore, several measures are carried out under the BRI framework, in which bilateral exchanges take hold, and multilateral and regional exchange mechanisms play a supporting role. In regard to content, there are primarily cultural exchanges, academic exchanges, professional exchange and cooperation, media cooperation, youth and women exchanges and volunteer services.[10]

The Chinese government has achieved fruitful results in promoting people-to-people exchanges.

The current people-to-people cooperation programmes, of all types, including the cultural year, the tourism year, the arts year, the film and TV bridge, seminars and think-tank dialogues under the Silk Road framework have forged closer ties between people through frequent exchanges.[11] As of May 2016, of the over 60 BRI participating countries, Mongolia, Russia, Egypt, Sri Lanka, Laos, Thailand, Nepal, Singapore and Pakistan have established Chinese cultural centres. Launching cultural centres of BRI participating countries in China has been listed on the development agenda.[12]

A transnational archeological dig is a typical example for exchanges among civilisation. Since China began to open up, over a dozen archeological teams from a dozen countries came to China to collaborate in over 70 projects. Seizing the momentum of the BRI, Chinese archeologists have travelled across borders for archeological cooperation. From 2012 to 2016, Chinese and Uzbek archaeologists conducted 4 joint excavations on the site of the Mingtape in the Ferghana Basin, and had a preliminary understanding of the age, nature and evolution of the site, achieving a series of notable gains. The joint archaeological excavation fully exemplifies techniques, thinking and philosophy of Chinese field excavation, increasing exchanges and mutual trust between scholars between China and Uzbek and displaying the significant influence of archaeology on protecting and studying Central Asian cultural heritage.[13]

China also proposes a conference of dialogue among Asian civilisations. At the opening of Boao Forum for Asia Annual Conference 2015, President Xi Jinping mentioned that "today, Asia has proudly maintained its distinct diversity and still nurtures all the civilizations, ethnic groups, and religions in this big Asian family". Therefore, "China proposes that a conference of dialogue among Asian civilizations be held to provide a platform upon which to enhance interactions among the youth, people's groups, local communities and the media and to form a network of think-tank cooperation, so as to add to Asian people's rich cultural life and contribute to more vibrant regional cooperation and development".

During the Boao Forum for Asia Annual Conference 2016 held in March, the Information Office of State Council hosted the Dialogue for Asian Civilisations in which Jiang Jianguo, director of the Information Office of State Council of China; former Prime Minister of Afghanistan, Aziz; Assistant Director-General of UNESCO, Noda; Iranian Ambassador to UNESCO, Professor Jalali; Nobel Prize winner, Mo Yan; Dean of Peking University National Development Institute, Lin Yifu; Director of the East Asian Institute of the National University of Singapore, Zheng Yongnian; and Dean of the Chinese Academy of Fudan University, Zhang Weiwei, had a dialogue. Jiang Jingguo stated at the event that China would promote dialogues among Asian civilisations.[14] In September 2016, Asia Pacific Youth Dialogue took place in Chengdu, China, which was taken into an active part of Dialogue for Asian Civilisations.[15]

On April 28, 2016, Xi Jinping attended the opening of the fifth meeting of the ministers of foreign affairs of the conference on interaction and confidence-building measures in Asia and recalled Dialogue for Asian Civilisations. He held that:

> we need to scale up exchanges and communication and turn the diversity of Asia into an impetus for more exchanges and cooperation, and facilitate inclusiveness, mutual learning and common development of different civilizations, to make a joint contribution to maintaining regional peace and stability. We can together explore channels and platforms, such as an Asia Civilization Dialogue Conference to pool wisdom and strength and solidify the foundation for comprehensive regional security governance.[16]

China co-sponsored with Greece to launch the "Ancient Civilisation Forum", which promotes the connection between countries with long civilisations and seeks wisdom and nutrition from different civilisations to meet the challenges confronting humanity. The first ministerial meeting was held in Greece in April 2017. Ministers and high-level officials from China, Greece, Egypt, Iran, Iraq, Italy, India, Mexico, Peru, Bolivia and other countries attended the meeting, and the Athens Declaration on the Establishment of the Ancient Civilisations Forum was announced.[17]

China participated and supported several dialogues for civilisations and exchange events. For instance: Soong Ching Ling Foundation organised a group of Chinese experts and scholars to attend the Dialogue of Civilisations—Rhodes Forum organised by Russia, India and Greece.[18]

Significance of cross-cultural exchanges and mutual learning

Mencius once said: "It is the law of nature that nothing is alike". Thus, there are diverse civilisations in mankind. Given that each civilisation has unique strengths, there is a value attached in exchanges and mutual learning among cultures. The Ancient Silk Road criss-crosses different river basins, civilisations and religions: Nile Valley, Tigris and Euphrates Rivers, Indus and Ganges, Yellow and Yangtze Rivers, Egyptian civilisation, Babylonian civilisation, Indian civilisation, Chinese civilisation, Buddhism, Christianity and Islamic religious settlements. Therefore, different civilisations, religions and races seek common ground while maintaining differences openly and inclusively, and jointly compose a poem of mutual respect and paint a scroll of common development.[19]

The relationship between nations relies on the affinity between their peoples, which depends on understanding between people. The cross-cultural exchange is a valuable approach to bring about understanding between people. It facilitates seeking wisdom and gaining nourishment from civilisations of different countries, providing intelligent support and solace of hearts for people. The long-term difference among civilisations, however, has long been the source of many conflicts in the Eurasian land. During the Cold War period, tensions between ideologies overshadowed tensions between nations as the root cause of conflicts in the land.

However, as the Cold War came to an end, ideological differences were no longer the primary cause of tensions among big powers. A group of people represented by Huntington believes that "civilisation" will replace "ideology" as the leading cause of conflict between countries. The contradiction between big powers will mainly be manifested between Western civilisation and non-Western civilisation (mainly Islamic civilisation and Chinese civilisation). Such a view was widely influential, but did not become a global consensus. Views on emphasising the possibility and necessity of coexistence between civilisations and advocating cross-cultural exchanges and dialogue are more broadly supported. For instance, the UN designated the year 2001 as Year for Dialogue among Civilisations and published the Declaration of Dialogue among Civilisations.

The Chinese government and scholars also hold reservations for the idea of clash among civilisations. Chinese scholars admit that there are differences among civilisations, but they can avoid conflicts and resolve differences through dialogues. Therefore, they advocate that nations should promote cross-cultural exchanges and mutual learning to achieve common progress among civiliaations.[20] An undeniable fact is that despite a great number of disasters in humanity caused by clashes among civiliaations, mankind still advances on the whole, and the time for conflicts among civilisations has been less than that of cooperation and exchanges.

After putting forward the BRI, the Chinese government, on the one hand, has continuously been stressing exchanges, dialogue and mutual learning among civilisations on occasions of foreign exchanges; and on the other hand, it has been promoting people-to-people exchanges in real practice through bilateral, multilateral and regional means. Although China is not the first country to advocate exchanges and mutual learning among civilisations, the Chinese government has taken it as a critical approach to build a community of shared future for mankind and a priority area for pursuing BRI. Taking a multi-pronged approach, it has promulgated a series of specific policies and provided human resources, finance and materials to carry it out, so that exchanges and mutual learning among civilisations has been elevated to a new height. This is another underlined cooperation area beside economic cooperation, which is bestowed with responsibilities of forging understanding between people, mitigate conflicts, complimenting each civilisation and driving common prosperity.

Notes

1 "Full Text: Speech by H.E. Xi Jinping President of the People's Republic of China At UNESCO Headquarters," Xinhua net. Retrieved March 5, 2018 from www.xinhuanet.com/world/2014-03/28/c_119982831_2.htm
2 "Full Text: Speech by Xi Jinping President At Meeting Marking the 60th Anniversary Of the Initiation of the Five Principles of Peaceful Coexistence," People.com. Retrieved March 5, 2018 from http://politics.people.com.cn/n/2014/0628/c1024-25213331.html
3 "Full Text: Keynote Speech by H.E. Xi Jinping President of the People's Republic of China At the Boao Forum for Asia Annual Conference 2015," Xinhua net. Retrieved March 5, 2018 from www.xinhuanet.com/politics/2015-03/29/c_127632707.htm
4 "Full Text: Speech By Xi Jinping At the Opening Ceremony of the Fifth Meeting of The CICA Ministers of Foreign Affairs," Xinhua net. Retrieved March 5, 2018 from www.xinhuanet.com/2016-04/28/c_1118761158.htm
5 Xie Jinying, "Make BRI a Platform of Dialogue Among Civilizations," Xinhua net. Retrieved March 5, 2018 from www.xinhuanet.com/comments/2016-05/04/c_1118795453.htm
6 "Full Text: Speech by President Xi Jinping At UN Geneva Headquarters," Xinhua net. Retrieved March 6, 2018 from www.xinhuanet.com/world/2017-01/19/c_1120340081.htm
7 "Full text of President Xi's Speech at Opening of Belt and Road forum," Xinhua net. Retrieved March 5, 2018 from www.xinhuanet.com/politics/2017-05/14/c_1120969677.htm
8 "Full text of President Xi's speech at opening ceremony of BRICS Business Forum", People's net. Retrieved March 5, 2018 from http://world.people.com.cn/n1/2017/0903/c1002-29511835.html
9 Xi Jinping, "Secure a Decisive Victory in Building a Moderately Prosperous Society in All Respects and Strive for the Great Success of Socialism with Chinese Characteristics for a New Era—Delivered at the 19th National Congress of the Communist Party of China," Beijing, People's Press, 2017, p. 25.
10 National Development and Reform Commission, Ministry of Foreign Affairs, Ministry of Commerce, *Vision and Proposed Actions Outlined on Jointly Building Silk Road Economic Belt and 21st-Century Maritime Silk Road*, March 28, 2015.
11 "Full text of President Xi's Speech At Opening of Belt and Road Forum," Xinhua net. Retrieved March 5, 2018 from www.xinhuanet.com/politics/2017-05/14/c_1120969677.htm
12 Xie Jinying, "Make BRI a Platform of Dialogue Among Civilizations," Xinhua net. Retrieved March 5, 2018 from www.xinhuanet.com/comments/2016-05/04/c_1118795453.htm
13 Jiang Xiao, "Chinese Archaeologists in China–Uzbek Joint Team," Xinhua net. Retrieved March 8, 2018 from www.xinhuanet.com/2016-06/22/c_1119094692.htm
14 "Dialogue for Asian Civilizations: A Clarion Call for Dialogue for Asian Civilizations," Chinese Government website. Retrieved March 8, 2018 from www.gov.cn/xinwen/2016-03/26/content_5058502.htm
15 "Asia Pacific Youth Dialogue Open for 46 Nations Youth Elite in Chengdu," People.com. Retrieved March 5, 2018 from http://world.people.com.cn/n1/2016/0921/c1002-28730823.html
16 "Full Text: Speech By Xi Jinping At the Opening Ceremony of the Fifth Meeting of The CICA Ministers of Foreign Affairs," Xinhua net. Retrieved March 8, 2018 from www.xinhuanet.com/2016-04/28/c_1118761158.htm
17 "Wang Yi Attend First Ministerial Meeting on Ancient Civilizations Forum," Ministry of Foreign Affairs website. Retrieved March 8, 2018 from www.fmprc.gov.cn/web/wjbzhd/t1456264.shtml
18 Liu Xu, "Dialogue of Civilizations—13th World Public Forum Held in Greece," China News. Retrieved March 8, 2018 from www.chinanews.com/gj/2015/10-09/7561136.shtml

19 Commentator at Guangming Daily Agency, "Promoting Exchanges, Mutual Learning and Co-existence of Civilizations—Six Arguments on Studying Principles of President Xi Jinping Speech at Opening of Belt and Road Forum for International Cooperation," *Guangming Daily*, May 20, 2017.
20 Song Jian, "Dialogue Among Civilizations: Common Aspirations of the World," People.com. Retrieved March 6, 2018 from www.people.com.cn/GB/guoji/24/20010921/566147.html

PART IX

Belt and Road Forum for International Cooperation

72
BELT AND ROAD FORUM FOR INTERNATIONAL COOPERATION

Ding Gong

Background and major objectives

Since the proposal of the Belt and Road Initiative (BRI) by President Xi Jinping in autumn 2013, China has been harmonising development strategies with BRI participating countries, with steady progress in related cooperation programmes and achievements exceeding expectations. Over the course of more than 4 years, the pursuit of the Belt and Road Initiative grew from scratch and formed a well-knit network, with the participation of over 100 countries and international organisations, 40 cooperation agreements and MOUs being signed, over US$3 trillion trade volume being achieved, and an accumulated investment amount of over US$50 billion to countries along the Belt and Road. In doing so, the broad consensus for international cooperation has been reached and profound effects have been generated. The United Nations General Assembly, Security Council, UNESCAP, APEC, ASEM, the Greater Mekong Sub-Regional Cooperation, as well as a number of international organisations and multilateral agencies have inscribed or represented some connotations of the Belt and Road Initiative in their respective decisions or documents. Steady progress has been made in establishing the economic corridors, the interconnectivity network has gradually come into shape and trade and investment have grown remarkably. Key cooperation programmes have made steady headway, yielding early harvests. The founding of AIIB and the Silk Road Fund have laid solid foundations for financial cooperation. It is seen that over the 3 since the Belt and Road Initiative was put forward, fruitful outcomes have been achieved in cooperation programmes, with the influence sweeping across the globe, making BRI the most popular international public product thus far and the most promising international cooperation platform at present. The Belt and Road Initiative was proposed by China, but its outcomes benefit the whole world.

Considering that the BRI is at a critical stage of full-fledged promotion, the Chinese government believes it is necessary to host a summit to plan for the future by summing up past experiences. In January 2017, at the Davos World Economic Forum, President Xi Jinping announced to the world that China would host the first Belt and Road Forum for International Cooperation in May 2017, Beijing, with the aim of seeking cooperation programmes through building cooperation platforms and sharing cooperation benefits, finding solutions for current global and regional economic issues and injecting new impetus to dynamic development, so the BRI will better improve the well-being of people of all nations.[1] On March 5, 2017, Prime

Minister Li Keqiang stated in the *Report on the Work of the Government delivered at the Fifth Session of the 12th National People' Congress* that China will host the Belt and Road Forum for International Cooperation and choreograph a new chapter of cooperation.[2] On March 8, 2017, Wang Yi, Minister for foreign affairs, expressed at the "two sessions" press conference that the forum consists of the roundtable summit with state leaders, and a more inclusive high-level meeting, as well as 6 parallel sessions on the 5 types of connectivity and think-tank exchanges.[3]

Main content

From May 14 to 15, 2017, 1500 representatives from 130 countries and 70 international organisations, including 29 heads of state and government, gathered in Beijing for the First Belt and Road Forum for International Cooperation hosted by China. Nearly 4000 journalists from all countries reported this grand event. According to the agenda, the forum consists mainly of the opening ceremony, the roundtable summit and the high-level meeting and related parallel sessions. On the morning of May 14, 2017, President Xi Jinping delivered a keynote speech at the opening, followed by the Belt and Road International High-level Plenary Meeting for International Cooperation; in the afternoon, 6 parallel sessions were held. Thousands of guests from home and abroad focused on the "five types of connectivity" and think-tank exchanges for insights. A series of agreements were signed and a number of consensuses were reached. During May 15, 2017, President Xi Jinping hosted the Leaders Roundtable Summit, including 2 phases of thematic meetings and working lunches, and introduced the significant outcomes of the Forum at a subsequent press conference.[4]

First, the opening ceremony and high-level meetings. On May 14, 2017, President Xi Jinping attended the opening of the Belt and Road Forum for International Cooperation and delivered a keynote speech entitled *Work Together to Build the Silk Road Economic Belt and The 21st Century Maritime Silk Road*. Subsequently, Russian President Vladimir Putin, Turkish President Erdogan and UN Secretary-General Guterres also delivered speeches at the opening.

After the opening ceremony, Zhang Gaoli, member of the Standing Committee of the Political Bureau of the CPC Central Committee and Vice Premier of the State Council, attended the high-level plenary meeting and delivered a speech on the Five types of connectivity. At the high-level plenary meeting, Chilean President Bachelet, Czech President Zeman, Ethiopian Prime Minister Haier Mariam, Greek Prime Minister Tsipras, Pakistani Prime Minister Sharif, British Prime Minister's Special Envoy, Chancellor of the Exchequer Hammond, French President's representative, Chairman of the Senate Foreign Affairs Committee, former Prime Minister Raffarin, German Federal Government and Prime Minister, Economic and Energy Minister Chipris, 71st Session of the UN General Assembly President Thomson, World Bank President Kim Min Jong, International Monetary Fund President Lagarde, World Trade Organization Director-General Azevedo, and World Economic Forum President Schwab delivered a speech subsequently.[5]

Second, thematic sessions on the 5 types of connectivity and think-tank exchanges. The session on "policy coordination" is hosted by National Development and Reform Commission and Development Research Centre of the State Council, with the theme of "Innovating Mechanisms for Common Development". The participating parties comprehensively expounded the profound connotation and far-reaching significance of policy communication and development strategy coordination, shared the practical experiences of bilateral and multilateral policy coordination and development strategy bridging, and signed 32 bilateral and multilateral cooperation documents and enterprise cooperation projects, involving 18 countries and 8 international organisations.

The thematic session on infrastructure connectivity was jointly hosted by National Development and Reform Commission and Ministry of Transport, with the theme of "connectivity for prosperity". Participants conducted extensive and in-depth exchanges on strengthening the Belt and Road infrastructure interconnection and comprehensive cooperation, harmonising planning and technical standards, promoting the construction of international backbone channels, expanding early harvest results, and promoting economic prosperity along the line and regional economic cooperation.

The session on unimpeded trade was hosted by the Ministry of Commerce, with the theme of "Unimpeded trade for effective Belt and Road economic cooperation". The meeting issued the MOU on Belt and Road Trade Connectivity. The MOU participants unanimously held that it is necessary to promote Belt and Road trade connectivity for more dynamic, more inclusive and more sustainable economic globalisation. According to the MOU, China will begin hosting China Import Expo in 2018.

The session on financial connectivity was hosted by both the Ministry of Finance and People's Bank, with the theme of "building diverse investment and financing system to promote BRI". During the meeting, the Ministry of Finance and finance departments of relevant countries signed the Belt and Road Financing Guideline. It also signed a MOU under the BRI framework with AIIB, BRICS New Development Bank and the World Bank to strengthen financial cooperation. People's Bank signed a MOU on building a China–IMF capacity building centre with IMF and signed an MOU with the Central Bank of the Czech Republic.

The session on people-to-people connectivity was hosted by International Department of Central Committee of CPC, with the theme of "building a people-to-people bridge for prosperity and development". The meeting invited representatives from BRI participating countries to tell the real experiences of engaging in the pursuit of BRI and demonstrated the results of exchanges and cooperation between China and other relevant international organisations in the fields of culture, education, science and technology, tourism, health and journalism. It announced the launching of *Action Plan of China's Social Organisation for Stronger People-to-People Connectivity along the Belt and Road (2017–20)*, China NGO Network for International Exchanges and the International Think-Tank Cooperation Programme on Enhancing People-to-People Connectivity along the Belt and Road.

The session on think-tank exchanges was hosted by Publicity Department of Central Committee of CPC and organised by China Centre for International Economic Exchanges, with the theme of "jointly building a Silk Road of Intelligence". There was a turnout of 200 participants from 40 countries, including heads of well-known think tanks, former statesmen and scholars. The event focused on 3 topics (BRI's role in boosting strong, balanced, inclusive and sustainable development of world economy, a Silk Road that is open, inclusive and mutually reinforcing and an international cooperation blueprint for Belt and Road innovative development) and achieved a number of results, such as think-tank consensus, a joint research report and a Belt and Road Research Institute. Liu Qichen, member of the Political Bureau of the CPC Central Committee, secretary of the Central Secretariat and Minister of the Publicity Department attended the thematic session and delivered a keynote speech entitled "Work Together to Build a Silk Road of Intelligence". He expected that think tanks from both home and abroad would strengthen exchanges and cooperation and establish a think-tank alliance and cooperation network so as to jointly build a silk road of intelligence.[6]

Third, Roundtable Summit. On May 15, leaders of 30 states and heads of UN, World Bank and IMF attended the roundtable summit, which was themed with "enhancing international cooperation and pursuing BRI to achieve mutual benefits and common development" and consisted of the first-phase meetings on coordinating development strategies, promoting connectivity and fostering people-to-people exchanges, a work luncheon and the second-phase meetings. President Xi Jinping presided over the event and delivered speeches at both the opening and closing. A joint communiqué was approved following the meeting. All parties unanimously agreed on the significance of BRI and expected to elevate the cooperation to a higher level, with a larger scope and deeper meaning. They agreed to intensify coordination for macroeconomic policies to foster a sound international environment and hoped to practically implement development strategy bridging, so as to strive for a landscape where all countries integrate for common development and shared interests. All parties have agreed on giving priority to connectivity in Belt and Road cooperation, which includes improving infrastructure connectivity and "soft connectivity" in policies, regulations and standards, so as to fully leverage the influence of connectivity on the real economy and create an architecture of financial connectivity and cooperation in a stable yet diverse fashion. They have unanimously held that economic cooperation and people-to-people exchanges should be equally emphasised when pursuing the BRI. Such a course should be oriented by improving the well-being of people and services for sustainable development.[7]

Effects and responses

This forum established a platform for sharing lessons and exchanging results among nations, in which all participants can engage in in-depth discussions and broad exchanges of views to further strengthen interactions and cooperation. Attending state leaders and heads of international organisations highly acclaimed the BRI and the forum, and they looked forward to jointly promoting the BRI for common prosperity. In summary, this Belt and Road Forum for International Cooperation has the following highlights.

First, broad coverage and great openness. One striking feature of this forum is the multi-party participation and strong representation. Heads of states and governments from 29 countries turned out at the forum; 1500 representatives from more than 130 countries and 70 international organisations joined the events, achieving a media coverage of major areas of all 5 continents, making a real inclusive event without any blind spots.

Second, strong efficacy and fruitful outcomes. This forum is the highest-level international event that has ever taken place under the BRI framework. It is also a unique multi-party diplomatic event initiated and hosted by China at the highest level and the largest scale since 1949, as well as the most crucial home diplomacy activity in 2017. Through this platform, China has conducted full-scale policy coordination with participating countries and international organisations, signed several dozen cooperation documents and identified priority areas and pathways shortly. On top of dialogues and exchanges, the forum has signed bilateral agreements for project cooperation and organised press interviews and press conference for pragmatic cooperation. During the forum, 270 cooperation documents in 76 types and 5 categories were formulated among participating nations. China injected another RMB 100 billion to the Silk Road Fund and encouraged financial institutions to conduct RMB overseas fund business, with an estimated volume of RMB 300 billion.[8]

Third, thoughtful arrangement and preparations. The success of the forum is accredited to the strong leadership of Xi Jinping at the core and also the shared efforts of each government department and subnational jurisdiction. All relevant departments and Beijing authorities made significant contributions to the preparation. Participants also lent tremendous support and cooperative efforts. As the host city of the forum, Beijing, in particular, invested heavily and prepared meticulously in meeting arrangements, venue construction and personnel allocation, achieving positive effects and receiving wide acclaim from media of all nations. For those most concerned air quality issue, the Beijing municipal government drew on full reference from the Olympic Indexes and applied harsh measures on limiting pollutant emissions and restricting factory operation for atmospheric control, making every effort to meet air quality standards. Moreover, the Chinese hosts organised special arts and musical shows on the Silk Road, which epitomise the historic bond between traditional Chinese culture and the Ancient Silk Road, but also the exchanges and integration among local cultures of BRI participating countries.

Notes

1 "Full text of President Xi Jinping's Keynot Speech at the Opening of World Economic Forum 2017," Xinhua.Net, www.xinhuanet.com/2017-01/18/c_1120331545.htm.
2 "B&R Forum on Countdown 20 State Leaders Confirm to Attend," China Government website, www.yidaiyilu.gov.cn/xwzx/gnxw/9621.htm.
3 "Foreign Minister Wang Yi Meets the Press," Xinhua.Net, www.xinhuanet.com/politics/2014lh/foreign-minister/.
4 "Belt and Road Forum for International Cooperation," website of MOF, www.beltandroadforum.org/.
5 "Zhang Gaoli Attend B&R Forum Plenary Meeting for Speech," Belt and Road Forum.org, www.beltandroadforum.org/n100/2017/0514/c24-347.html.
6 "Liu Qichen Attend B&R Forum Thinktank Thematic Session," Belt and Road Forum.org, www.beltandroadforum.org/n100/2017/0514/c24-345.html.
7 "Xi Jinping Chair B&R Forum Roundtable Summit," Belt and Road Forum.org, www.beltandroadforum.org/n100/2017/0515/c24-418.html.
8 "Yang Jiechi Meet Press on B&R Forum," website of Belt and Road Forum, www.mfa.gov.cn/web/zyxw/t1462847.shtml.

73
THEMATIC SESSION ON CONNECTIVITY OF DEVELOPMENT POLICIES AND STRATEGIES

Ding Gong

The forum made special arrangement for a Thematic Session on Connectivity of Development Policies and Strategies, aiming to underline the important bearing and unique advantages on pooling strengths and wisdom for pursuing BRI.

Main content

On the afternoon of May 14, 2017, during the Thematic Session on Connectivity of Development Policies and Strategies, Belt and Road Forum for International Cooperation, guests in attendance held a number of bilateral and multilateral talks and meetings and signed 32 bilateral and multilateral cooperation documents and business cooperation programmes, involving 18 countries and 8 international organisations. This thematic session was hosted by National Development and Reform Commission and Development Research Centre of the State Council. With the theme of innovating mechanisms for common development, it is dedicated to deepening understanding on BRI, improving mutual trust, reaching consensus, promoting the connection of policies and plans of nations and fostering impetus for BRI development. During the session, 360 guests from 70 countries and over 40 international organisations participated in the discussions, and 31 foreign ministers and heads of international organisations, subnational governments, political parties, businesses and think tanks delivered remarks.

Concordantly, guests delved into discussions on the content, meaning and practice of policy and strategy connectivity, and exchanged views on market player demands, subnational governments' roles and think-tank support. Opinions and feasible suggestions were put forward as well. The keynote speech session was hosted by Li Wei, Director General of the Development Research Centre of the State Council. Zhang Xiaogang, President of the International Organisation for Standardisation, and Melinde, President of the Centre for International Trade and Sustainable Development, presided over the 2 discussions.[1] He Lifeng, Director-General of the National Development and Reform Commission, UN Secretary-General Guterres and Swiss Federal President Roy Had each delivered a keynote speech. The French President's representative, the Chairman of the Senate Foreign Affairs, Defence and Armed Forces Committee and former Prime Minister Raffarin also spoke at the meeting. Long Guoqiang, Deputy Director-General of the Development Research Centre of the State Council, concluded the meeting.

Li Wei, Director-General of the Development Research Centre of the State Council, expressed that a cuurent pressing and arduous task is to further policy coordination and engage in broad and in-depth discussions on building a platform to pool strengths, smoothen exchange channels and achieve effective strategy coordination, so as to formulate effective policy mechanisms and actions plans and make the Belt and Road a road of peace, prosperity, openness, innovation and civility.

He Lifeng, Director-General of National Development and Reform Commission, pointed out in his keynote speech that policy coordination is the foundation for pragmatic cooperation across the board and an important guarantee for jointly promoting BRI. Pursuing BRI is a Chinese solution for resolving challenges and conundrum in international politics and economy, showing Chinese wisdom that draws on past experiences and meets future development. As is shown in practice, sound bilateral and multilateral policy coordination need to strengthen connectivity at 4 levels. First, in connecting development strategies, maximum converging interests should be sought at the macro-level to align with common action orientations. Second, in connecting development plans, the vision identified by the development strategy should be specified into timetables and roadmaps so that cooperation objectives will be achieved in different stages. Third, in connecting mechanisms and platforms, executing bodies of nations should be conclusively linked to establishing channels and mechanisms for uninterrupted communication, exchanges and consultations, so as to resolve issues and difficulties arising from implementing plans and carrying out programmes in a timely manner. Fourth, in connecting specific projects, common development should be achieved through collaborations in fields of infrastructure, trade and economy, finance and people-to-people ties. He Lifeng stressed that guided by the Silk Road Spirit of peace, cooperation, openness, inclusiveness, mutual learning and reciprocity, China, together with the international community, will stay committed to the principle of achieving shared interests through consultations and common development and promote infrastructure connectivity, unimpeded trade, financial integration and understanding between people on the basis of policy coordination.[2]

UN Secretary-General Antonio Guterres said that the Belt and Road Forum for International Cooperation fully reflects the ambitions and consensus of all parties. Through this forum, all participating countries can find a more suitable cooperation area in the common pursuit of BRI. Guterres pointed out that pursuing the BRI is conducive to implementing the 2030 Sustainable Development Agenda, introducing green technologies and green investment to BRI participating countries and boosting exchanges in fields of national economy, society and people-to-people exchanges.[3]

Guterres emphasised that the Belt and Road is a key platform for sharing global best practices, promoting the fair and equitable development of UN member states. He also encouraged relevant countries, guided by the principle of achieving shared interests through consultations and common development, to proactively participate in the promotion of BRI by establishing mechanisms and platforms for cooperation, innovating collaborating approaches and conducting broad and pragmatic collaborations so as to benefit people of all countries.

Doris Leuthard, President of the Swiss Federation, held that the BRI promotion bears significance to regional infrastructural connectivity, with the important foundations as shared technical standards, policies and regulations and strategic plans, and expressed that the Swiss are willing to strengthen coordination of development strategies and policies under the BRI framework to advance higher-level pragmatic bilateral cooperation.

Elaborating on the connotation, meaning and practice of policy and strategy coordination, as well as related requirements, actions and suggestions, Raffarin, representative of the French President, Chair of Foreign Affairs, Defenxe and Armed Forces Committee of the French

Senate and former Premier of France, pointed out in his address that France is dedicated to building a multi-polar world and supporting initiatives for world peace, prosperity and development, whereas BRI is an important carrier for realising the vision for policy coordination between Asia and Europe and infrastructure connectivity. Intensifying development policy and strategy coordination providea critical institutional guarantee to building a more open, stable and prosperous world.[4]

From the perspective of Sultan, Minister for National Affairs, UAE, efforts for policy coordination should not be temporary, but institutionalised and normalised. He expressed that the UAE has the intent to host the next conference for connectivity and to be the propeller and catalyst for prosperity and development of the BRI. Taware Agre, Uruguayan Minister of Agriculture, Animal Husbandry and Fisheries, said that Uruguay has a leading position in the fields of science, technology and agriculture and hopes to play an active role in pursuing the BRI. As a reliable and modernised agricultural provider, Uruguay is committed to solving issues of world peace, environmental change and natural asset protection, which are key to building a peaceful and secure world. This leads to the choice of participating in the BRI.

Li Yong, Director-General of the United Nations Industrial Development Organisation, believed that development is the core, and industry is a strong drive for development. BRI development should promote the development of green industry and the use of cleaner production technologies, thereby creating trade competitiveness, promote humanity and achieve Sustainable Development Goals. Zhang Jun, Deputy Director-General of Development and Research Centre of the State Council, stated in the speech that think tanks play a unique and critical role in policy and strategy coordination, so they can more effectively engage in the Belt and Road policy and strategy coordination. Especially in the early stage of coordination when national governments have not established institutionalised channels of exchanges, government-sponsored think tanks are an integral force to strengthen policy communication and strategy connectivity.

Long Guoqiang, Deputy Director-General of the Development and Research Centre at the State Council, concluded for the meeting that nations, organisations and business representatives share different focuses, which in turn highlights the significance for policy and strategy coordination in the pursuit of BRI. It is impossible to treat all focuses as priorities. Therefore, communication and coordination are needed to formulate a more effective roadmap. This thematic session in itself bears exemplary significance for policy and strategy coordination. The coordination discussed in the session is more of a government-led activity, yet it does not exclude private-sector participation, especially that of businesses. In fact, as the main players of BRI promotion are businesses, coordination among policies and strategies and platform building by the government should aim to better mobilise businesses in the BRI endeavour, and establish a sound business, investment and cooperation environments that are more efficient, transparent and conform to market laws.

By and large, all attending guests believed that intensifying such coordination guarantees BRI progress. Intergovernmental cooperation should be strengthened to proactively establish a macro-policy coordination mechanism that is multi-level and intergovernmental, intensifies convergence of interests and stimulates political mutual trust, which ultimately reaches a new consensus on cooperation. In turn, BRI participating countries can fully engage in exchanges on economic development strategies, guidelines and policies, joint formulation of regional cooperation plans and measures, consultations for resolving issues arising from cooperation, and provide decision-making references and policy support for pragmatic cooperation and large-scale programme implementation.

Effects and responses

The Thematic Session on Connectivity of Development Policies and Strategies took place against the backdrop of the world economic development, China's development, and BRI progress all being in the critical stage, which sends out positive signals to all stakeholders to jointly promote Belt and Road international cooperation and establish a community of shared future for mankind, bearing remarkable significance to China and the world at large. From the respective perspective of governments, international organisations, political parties, businesses and think tanks, the participating parties comprehensively expounded the profound connotation and far-reaching significance of policy communication and development strategy bridging, shared the practical experience of bilateral and multilateral policy and strategy coordination. Given the realities of each nation and local regions, ministers of the nations put forward the pressing need for stronger policy coordination under the BRI framework. Subnational governments and businesses shared their respective policy hindrances in the course of development and called for nations to reach more political mutual recognition under the BRI framework, promote harmonisation of regional and global policies and provide an institutional guarantee to regional development integration and economic globalisation. It is unanimously agreed that this session is distinctive in its prominent theme, rich connotation, broad participation and varied forms and that this session enhanced policy coordination, identified orientation and key tasks for policy coordination and intensified unification of recognitions for BRI development.

Notes

1 "Strengthen Policy Coordination for Common Development," website of National Development and Reform Commission, http://helifeng.ndrc.gov.cn/zyhd/201705/t20170515_847409.html
2 He Lifeng, "Strengthen Policy Coordination for Four-Pronged Approach," website of National Development and Reform Commission, http://helifeng.ndrc.gov.cn/zyhd/201705/t20170515_847388.html
3 "32 Agreements Signed at Policy Coordination Session of B&R Forum," Xinhua Net, www.xinhuanet.com/2017-05/14/c_1120970716.htm
4 "Thematic Session on Policy Coordination of B&R Forum Opens," *China Economic Times*, May 15 2017.

74
THEMATIC SESSION ON INFRASTRUCTURE CONNECTIVITY

Ding Gong

Connectivity in infrastructure is likened as "the joint" in the Belt and Road, which assists and enables flexible movements, bearing significance to social and economic development in BRI participating countries and the well-being of their peoples. Under such a context, the Belt and Road Forum has decided to identify the theme of this session as Connectivity for Prosperity.

Main content

On the afternoon of May 14, 2017, the Thematic Session on Infrastructure Connectivity of the Belt and Road Forum for International Cooperation was hosted in the National Convention Centre, with topics including infrastructure facility development, network linkage, technical standard harmonisation and facilitation of international operation. More than 200 ministers from 48 countries and 11 international organisations in the fields of transportation, energy and communications and business representatives attended the session. A total of 32 guests including Swiss Federal President Doris Leuthard, European Commission Vice-Chair Kathon, Serbian Deputy Prime Minister Zola L. Mikhailovich, Uzbekistan Deputy Prime Minister Azimov, ministers from Pakistan, Thailand, Malaysia and Russia and heads of international organisations, as well as Minister of Industry and Information Technology Miao Wei and Nur Bakri, Deputy Director-General of the National Development and Reform Commission and Director General of the National Energy Administration delivered speeches at the event. The meeting was co-sponsored by the Ministry of Transport and the National Development and Reform Commission. Minister for Transportation Li Xiaopeng made an opening speech and the concluding address. Hu Zucai, Deputy Director-General of the National Development and Reform Commission, and Dai Dongchang, Deputy Director-General of the Ministry of Transport, presided over the meeting.

In his speech, Minister Li Xiaopeng emphasised that infrastructure connectivity is the foundation of cooperation and development. Priority should be given to connectivity of the land, sea, air and internet, and the focus should be on key channels, cities, projects in linking overland highways, railway networks and maritime port networks, which bears strong guiding significance to accelerating infrastructure connectivity under the BRI framework. As the connectivity underlines linking infrastructure and people, by promoting common pursuit under consensus, sharing interests amid common pursuit and achieving reciprocity while sharing interests, China, with the commitment of mutual benefits and shared efforts, is willing to work with other countries in accelerating infrastructure connectivity and opening a new chapter of BRI promotion.[1]

The Russian Federation's Minister of Energy, Alexander Nowak, believed that the current global economy is facing challenges and that the people of the world should unite their capabilities to overcome difficulties. Russia has proposed the Great Eurasian Initiative, with the overarching task of linking China's BRI by emphasising railway and port building in Russia, accelerating new energy pipeline and power grid building and ultimately forming a Big Asian Energy Ring through cross-regional cooperation to contribute to the energy security of each nation.[2] The Vice-Chairman of the European Commission, Katynin, expressed that the Belt and Road Initiative will link China and Europe and will benefit countries and partners participating in the BRI. A bridge should be built between Asia and Europe for cooperation and consultations, instead of a high-wall separating each other. Matt Pottinger, the special assistant to the US President and senior director of Asian affairs at the White House National Security Council, said that high-quality infrastructure development would help promote economic connectivity. The USA is willing to use its experience in global infrastructure development to participate in the Belt and Road Initiative. Akhtar, Executive Secretary of the UN Economic and Social Commission for Asia and the Pacific, believes that the comprehensive development of infrastructure will help promote the convergence of the multimodal transportation, promote low-carbon energy conservation and information dissemination. She also suggests that the joint pursuit of BRI should surpass bilateral project constraints, enhance the formulation of bilateral policy structures and standards and strengthen cross-departmental cooperation.[3]

Miao Wei, Minister for Industry and Information Applications, delivered a keynote speech entitled "Strengthening Information and Communications Connectivity for Mutual Benefits and Common Development". He stated that China is currently proactively committed to intensifying infrastructure connectivity in communications with all countries. China has established 34 cross-border overland cables and a number of international marine cables in 12 BRI participating countries, directly linking Asia, Africa and Europe. China cooperated with international organisations such as the International Telecommunication Union and the United Nations Economic and Social Commission for Asia and the Pacific to promote multilateral cooperation initiatives such as the East African Information Highway and the Asia–Pacific Information Superhighway. China's information and communication enterprises have participated in the construction of information and communication infrastructure in more than 170 countries around the world. Miao Wei suggested that through improving policy coordination, innovating cooperation models and advancing multi-party cooperation, communications infrastructure connectivity can be jointly promoted to achieve mutual benefits and common development.[4]

In the field of energy infrastructure cooperation, Nur Becker, Deputy Director of the National Development and Reform Commission and Director of the National Energy Administration, responded to the general trend of energy transformation in the information age, deepened the Belt and Road energy cooperation and proposed three initiatives: first, strengthening policy coordination. Nations shall ante up exchanges and coordination among policies, plans, strategies and standards, explore possibilities of a Belt and Road energy cooperation club and jointly establish a green and low-carbon global energy governance system. Second, improving integration between energy and production. Nations shall seize the huge opportunity in a new round of technological revolution by strengthening research on energy, carrying out joint programmes on key technologies and core equipment, promoting pragmatic cooperation in major programmes, advanced standards and engineering services, so as to coordinate and improve capabilities for regional and global energy supply and security. Third, strengthening infrastructure connectivity. China intends to join the ranks of all nations to proactively press ahead with cross-border energy pipeline programs, and, in particular, to follow the trend of energy restructuring and revolution in energy technologies, build global energy networks, achieve green and low-carbon development and share energy development results.[5]

In the Thematic Session on Infrastructure Connectivity, stakeholders formulated efficacious cooperation intents and policy documents covering areas of transport, energy and communications, and formalised over 50 papers, including International Road Transport Agreements relating to international transport, energy development and information connectivity between the Government of the People's Republic of China and the Government of Uzbekistan, *Letter of Intent between China Civil Aviation Administration and International Civil Aviation Organisation* and *Letter of Intent on Strengthening Telecommunications and Information Network under the BRI* between Ministry of Industry and Information Technology and International Telecommunication Union. The former programme will help nurture ranks of shipping professionals and improve capacity building; the latter will enable in-depth cooperation in areas of improving aviation security in countries along the Belt and Road, improving safety and security surveillance in BRI participating countries and promoting liberalisation and facilitation of air transport in these countries. In addition, Miao Wei, Minister for Industry and Information Technology, exchanged views with Pichet Durongkaverote, Minister for Digital Economy and Society, on bolstering cooperation between China and Thailand on information and communications.

Effects and responses

During this session, guests of all sides delved into the topics of major objectives, focus areas, cooperation mechanisms and models of implementation of Belt and Road infrastructure connectivity, reaching broad consensus and providing a range of feasible ideas and suggestions to promoting BRI across the board. The final agreements were reached by participants as the following.

First, linking the past with the future. BRI enables participating countries to acquire greater development space and inject new impetus to interconnected development; therefore, cooperation should be bolstered among these countries. To achieve this objective, all parties agreed that they need to improve mutual trust and build greater consensus. On the occasion of the Thematic Session on Infrastructure Connectivity, it was agreed that, by upholding the principle of pursuing shared interests through consultations and common development, they should fully respect each other's interests and concerns, enhance understanding, build consensus and achieve win–win on cooperation mechanisms and models, laying the foundations for deepened cooperation. They agreed to identify priorities and strive for greater breakthroughs. Confronted with challenges of uneven connectivity in some key routes and disunification of technical standards of each country, they sought solutions through consultations, promoted key channels, links and projects, and gave priority to strengthening weak sections of routes, improving capacities and levels of connectivity. They held that it is needed to strengthen the harmonisation of operation and management of infrastructure facilities, promote unified coordination mechanisms and strive for infrastructure facilitation at a higher level. They also agreed on building platforms and promoting more pragmatic cooperation. The Thematic Session on Infrastructure Connectivity is a platform for pragmatic cooperation, during which more than 50 documents including MOUs on transport, energy and communications, cooperation roadmaps, letters of intent and specific programmes were signed. It catalysed the implementation of cooperation projects and promoted pragmatic cooperation in infrastructure connectivity for countries participating in BRI.[6]

Second, connectivity of physical facilities plays a pioneering role. As it is the key guarantee for the BRI visions, all stakeholders shall intensify pragmatic cooperation and jointly elevate it to a new height.[7] Infrastructure connectivity offers foundational support, an important guarantee to the BRI visions, playing a key pioneering role. To push forward such connectivity under the principle of achieving shared interests through consultations and common development, they will, on the one hand, stimulate dynamic linkage in transnational transport and international multi-modal linkages, enabling facilitation of international transport. On the other, it helps improve domestic and international passageway connection, smoothen holistic transport and logistics networks and promote sharing of BRI results for BRI participating countries. Therefore, it is beneficial to enhance mutual trust among BRI participating countries through connectivity in line with characteristics of infrastructure networks, accelerate the formation of connectivity networks featuring all-roundedness, multi-tiers and mixed models, promote regional mobility of factors, spearhead regional coordinated development, benefit countries and peoples participating in the BRI and reap early harvest of connectivity.

Third, unimpeded and unblocked linkage is key to infrastructure connectivity. They should, under the principle of achieving shared interests through consultations and common development, fully respect each stakeholder's interests and concerns and pool strengths in both the hardware and software, so as to achieve the effect of "1 plus 1 outweighing 2". In the area of transport infrastructure, Emphasis should be given to key access, key links and key projects, with priorities in linking missing highway segments, making bottleneck highways accessible, supplementing facilities for highway security, protection and traffic control and bolstering benchmarking of highway accessibility. It is imperative to promote infrastructure for pots, link access to highways and waterways, advance cooperation between ports, add new sea routes and rotations, and enhance cooperation for maritime logistics information applications. It is needed to establish platforms and mechanisms for overall civil aviation cooperation to bolster capacities of aviation bases. It is needed to strengthen energy infrastructure connectivity, jointly safeguard pipeline security for oil and gas, promote transregional power generation and transmission and proactively conduct upgrading and improving regional power grid. It is required to commonly develop of cross-regional fibre and other trunk communication networks, bolster capability for international communications connectivity and accessibility for the Information Silk Road. To sum up, while promoting the "hard connectivity" incorporating the land, sea, air and internet, a nation should also promote the "soft connectivity" so as to constantly improve infrastructure networks under the BRI.

Notes

1 "Infrastructure Connectivity Session Open, Minister for Transport Li Xiaopeng Speaks at Opening and Closing," website of Ministry of Transport, www.mot.gov.cn/buzhangwangye/lixiaopeng/zhongyaohuodonghejianghua/201705/t20170514_2203957.html.
2 "Thematic Session on Infrastructure Connectivity of B&R Forum Convened," China Central Government website, recorded at www.gov.cn/xinwen/2017-05/19/content_5195227.htm.
3 "Thematic Session on Infrastructure Connectivity Reach Three Consensus on Three Infrastructure Software and Hardware Connections," website of National Development and Reform Commission, http://jtyss.ndrc.gov.cn/gzdt/201705/t20170515_847376.html
4 "Miao Wei at B&R Forum," website of MIIT, www.miit.gov.cn/n1146290/n1146397/c5643548/content.html
5 Nur Becker, "Address at Thematic Session on Infrastructure Connectivity," website of China Energy Administration, www.nea.gov.cn/2017-05/17/c_136292234.htm
6 "Profile of Thematic Session on Infrastructure Connectivity of B&R Forum Convened," China Central Government website, recorded at www.gov.cn/xinwen/2017-05/10/content_5192398.htm.
7 "Promote Connectivity to Forge Development Ties—Interview with Minister for Transport Li Xiaopeng," *People's Daily*, May 13, 2017.

75
THEMATIC SESSION ON TRADE CONNECTIVITY

Ding Gong

The Belt and Road Initiative affords the world trade a huge development opportunity and broader developmental space. The keys to unimpeded trade under the BRI are removing investment and trade barriers through innovative trade models, fostering a sound business environment for regions and nations, coalescing investment and trade by reducing regional and cross-border trade costs, stimulating trade through investment, unleashing cooperation potential and making the pie of cooperation bigger. Considering the rise of protectionism and isolationism world-wide, negative effects are generated for the Belt and Road trade cooperation under such a context. Therefore, it bears significance to enable unimpeded trade under the BRI through in-depth discussions on this topic, pooling wisdom and building consensus.

Main content

On the afternoon of May 14, 2017, the Thematic Session on Trade Connectivity of the Belt and Road Forum for International Cooperation took place at the National Convention Centre in Beijing. This session is a parallel session under the 1+6 High-level Meeting of the Belt and Road Forum for International Cooperation, sponsored by the Ministry of Commerce and organised by the Ministry of Science and Technology, General Administration of Customs, State Administration of Taxation, General Administration of Quality Supervision, Inspection and Quarantine and CCPIT, with the theme of "unimpeded trade for common development and deepened BRI economic cooperation". The main leaders of the relevant departments of the Chinese government and guests from some countries and international organisations exchanged views on promoting trade facilitation, revitalising mutual investment, trade and sustainable development issues and watched the video short film "Shared Future". A 200-strong turnout covering representatives from over 60 countries (regions) and 10 international organisations showed up, of which representatives from 20 countries and 5 international organisations spoke at the meeting.[1]

A total of 9 guests, namely, Chris Pist, Deputy Prime Minister of Belgium and Minister of Foreign Trade Affairs of Employment, Economy and Consumer Industry, Yu Guangzhou, Director General of General Administration of China Customs, Bosnia and Herzegovina Deputy Prime Minister and Minister of Foreign Trade and Economic Cooperation Sharovich, Director General of China's State Administration of Taxation Wang Jun, Moldova Deputy

Prime Minister and Minister for Economy Octaviane Kalmyk, Zhi Shuping, Director of the General Administration of Quality Supervision, Inspection and Quarantine of China, First Deputy Prime Minister and Minister of Economic Development and Trade of Sweden Stepan Kubif, Director General of the World Trade Organisation Robert Azevedo and UN Under-Secretary-General, UN Secretary-General of UNCTAD, Musissa Kituyi, all delivered speeches. Zhong Shan, Minister for Commerce, delivered a keynote speech followed by the launching of Promoting Belt and Road Trade Connectivity with over 60 countries.

Minister Zhong Shan stated that to boost unimpeded trade under the BRI; China would import US$2 trillion volume of goods from countries and regions along the Belt and Road and host China Import Expo starting from 2018. In the coming 5 years, China will provide training positions to 10,000 persons and send 50 senior trade and economic experts to BRI participating countries for professional and intelligence support and consultations.[2]

Director-General of the General Administration of Customs, Yu Guangzhou, made a keynote speech entitled "Deepening Customs Cooperation Mechanism to Promote Unimpeded Trade under BRI", in which he introduced China's efforts in large-scale customs clearance cooperation in "information exchange, supervision and mutual recognition, law enforcement and mutual assistance" with BRI participating countries, and proposed 5 suggestions for deepening cooperation: (1) deepening institutional cooperation and harmonisation—countries should intensify exchanges and coordination in aspects of management rules, law enforcement procedures, regulatory measures and reform practices; (2) deepening cooperation in regulation innovation—countries should explore mutual recognition of regulatory results, expand cooperation in AEO mutual recognition, promote applications of high-tech and equipment and implement accurate and intelligent regulation; (3) deepening cooperation in information-sharing—countries should promote the harmonisation of single window standards for international trade, implement standardised data swap and establish data sharing and exchange platforms in customs along the Belt and Road featuring efficiency, security and standardisation; (4) deepening cooperation in trade safety—countries should strengthen information exchange cooperation in customs along the Belt and Road, expand cooperation in joint law-enforcement and anti-terrorism and severely punish cross-border smuggling and law-violating activities; (5) deepening cooperation in capacity-building—countries, by upholding the principle of inclusive customs along the Belt and Road, should bolster the sharing of past experiences and wisdom, conduct mutual learning and improve capacities jointly.[3]

Pakistan's Minister for Commerce, Kuram Dasgir Khan, exchanged views on Pakistan's participation in the BRI at the session. He expressed that Pakistan has engaged in the pursuit of BRI and noted that the magnificent bridge and busy port in the short film are projects completed in Pakistan. The Belt and Road Initiative underscores the fundamental issue of development, which in turn cements peace.

Bosnian Deputy Prime Minister and Minister of Foreign Trade and Economic Cooperation Sharovich said that Bosnia and Herzegovina has a strong interest in participating in the BRI and hopes to strengthen cooperation with China in vigorously implementing the Bosnia and Herzegovina trade promotion plan. He stated that direct investment and fostering local supply chains are equally important, so Bosnia hopes to cover more areas of agriculture and high-tech in collaboration with China. At present, Bosnia is proactively participating in the BRI, yielding fruitful results, whereas the Steiner power plant in Bosnia with Chinese participation has been established, which is one of the early harvests in the BRI development.[4]

Zhi Shuping, Director General of the General Administration of Quality Supervision, Inspection and Quarantine, emphasised during his speech that as an internationally recognised national quality infrastructure, standards, measurement, certification and inspection are the common technical language of countries and a bridge for unimpeded trade. As the supervisory body for setting up fundamental quality and techniques, the administration, by conscientiously implementing the proposals of President Xi Jinping, proactively strengthened pragmatic cooperation with BRI participating countries, established cooperation mechanisms and platforms, promoted links between and pilots for quality and fundamental sciences, carried out pragmatic cooperation in trade facilitation and strengthened endemic and epidemic control and prevention, achieving initial results. For that purpose, the general administration intends to collaborate with BRI participating countries to proactively promote quality and basic techniques connectivity, ensure quality safety, break technological barriers and make international trade unimpeded.[5]

Musissa Kituyi, UN Under-Secretary-General, UN Secretary-General of UNCTAD, believes that from the perspective of developing countries, economic globalisation needs to bolster effective productivity and investment climate so as to enable trade integration. In this respect, China assisted improving trade standards, logistics chains and standard chains of developing countries, bolstering the production capacity of relevant countries to ensure no country is left behind, displaying real leadership. Stepan Kubif, Ukraine's First Deputy Prime Minister and Minister of Economic Development and Trade, said that China is an important strategic partner of Ukraine and the second largest trading partner. The Belt and Road Initiative provides an opportunity for Ukraine to diversify its trade. One of the 7 overseas centres of Huawei is in Ukraine, and the country welcomes investments from China that facilitate mutual benefits.

Wang Jun, director general of the State Administration of Taxation of China, said that BRI participating countries should improve the tax system and focus on eliminating tax barriers; they should strengthen bilateral cooperation and effectively reduce the tax burden; and they should deepen multilateral collaboration, jointly improve taxation capacity and further serve and advance the BRI. The taxation agreement is an international legal guarantee for levying taxes that promote fair and reciprocal transnational economic activities. He also suggests that nations should expedite processes of negotiation, signing and improvement of taxation agreements, streamline procedures of implementation, bolster execution, improve taxation conflict resolution mechanisms and effectively reduce taxation burdens for cross-border investors. In the progress of reinforcing capacities on levying and management and the level of taxpaying services, China received tremendous support from the international community, so it is willing to make greater contributions to help other countries in the field. China genuinely hopes to build a long-term mechanism for Belt and Road taxation cooperation with other countries, establish a meeting and communication platform for heads of taxation authorities in BRI participating countries, promote coordination for tax policies and to levy, so as to better leverage the role of taxation in global economic governance.[6]

Brigitte Chipris, German Federal Minister of Economy and Energy, spoke highly of the positive results of the pragmatic cooperation between Germany and China in the energy field in recent years. The minister hoped to further deepen cooperation in various fields of energy and to actively participate in global energy transformation.

Abiladi Dandapeng, Minister for Commerce of Thailand, said that 99% of the enterprises in Thailand are small and medium-sized enterprises. In this context, the BRI development is creating a better life for ordinary people. Steven Chopbo, Australian Minister of Trade, Tourism and Investment, said that China is the most valuable tourism market for Australia.

Australia is willing to cooperate with China to achieve a win–win situation through economic and trade collaboration, and the "Belt and Road" can provide such valuable opportunities. George Gaharia, Minister of Economics and Sustainable Development of Georgia, said that he represents Georgia as the first country having signed a free trade agreement to the meeting. The FTA is an important achievement for sustainable development. Ivan Scalfalotto, Deputy Minister for Economic Development of Italy, said that Italy is the ideal bridge for the Eurasian continent. Globalisation is a common destiny. No one can be left alone. We must join hands to promote global sustainable development.

Belarusian Minister of Economy Zinovsky said that Belarus is a useful ally and strategic partner. The China–Belarus Industrial Park has become a beacon on the Silk Road economic belt, hoping that more Chinese high-tech enterprises will come to Belarus. The establishment of the factory will bring advanced technology and management concepts to promote the economic development of Belarus and achieve mutual benefit and win–win results.

Finally, the session also announced the adoption of the Belt and Road Trade Connectivity Cooperation Initiative. The participants believe that in the context of the current lack of global economic growth, it is necessary to promote more dynamic, inclusive and sustainable economic globalisation while respecting the development goals of each country. Efforts should be made for trade and investment liberalisation and facilitation, resisting protectionism, boosting unimpeded trade cooperation under the BRI and achieving win–win cooperation.

Effects and responses

This session was hosted at the right time, as it deepened recognition of the pursuit of BRI and elevated understanding on political mutual trust and free trade cooperation. Guests engaged in topics of major objectives, key underscores, cooperation mechanisms and promotion approaches in unimpeded trade and offered a range of feasible thinking, methods and suggestions in Belt and Road unimpeded trade. The speakers put forward insights that it is best to resolve issues of investment and trade facilitation, cover more trade areas, optimise trade structures, explore new growth points and strike for trade balances, which were highly acclaimed by all attending guests and representatives. Roberto Azevedo, Director-General of the World Trade Organisation, expressed his appreciation for China's commitment to maintaining and advancing globalisation. He believed that China's commitment to multilateral trade regimes bears positive meanings for WTO members. Hosting the Thematic Session on Trade Connectivity is a major approach of China to promote economic globalisation and support multilateral trading regimes.

Notes

1 "Thematic Session on Trade Connectivity of B&R Forum Held in Beijing," website of Ministry of Commerce, http://zhongshan.mofcom.gov.cn/article/activities/201705/20170502574666.shtml
2 "Thematic Session on Trade Connectivity of B&R Forum Held in Beijing," website of Ministry of Commerce, http://zhongshan.mofcom.gov.cn/article/ldjianghua/201705/20170502574661.shtml
3 "Yu Guangzhou at Thematic Session on Trade Connectivity," website of General Administration of Customs, recorded at www.customs.gov.cn/customs/302249/302425/671563/index.html
4 "Proactively Promote Market Openness," *Economic Daily*, May 15, 2017.
5 "Zhi Shuping Stress Unimpeded Trade at Trade Connectivity Session of B&R Forum," website of General Administration of Quality Supervision, Inspection and Quarantine, www.aqsiq.gov.cn/ldzz/zsp/zyhd/201705/t20170515_488401.htm
6 "Three Measures to Strengthen Belt and Road Tax Cooperation," website of State Administration of Taxation of China, www.chinatax.gov.cn/n810219/n810724/c2611635/content.html

76
THEMATIC SESSION ON FINANCIAL CONNECTIVITY

Qu Caiyun

The sustainable and stable development of BRI relies on stable monetary security. The resolution of financing issues needs joint efforts from BRI participating countries, which requires the government participation and the full leverage of market strengths in mobilising multiple funding channels to engage in the BRI pursuit.

This session centres its discussions on building platforms for exchanging and mutual learning of financing practices for BRI development; building consensus on principles of financing among BRI participating countries, international organisations, financial institutions and think-tank enterprises; and fostering cooperation for government, financial institutions, enterprises and think tanks of BRI participating countries and jointly pushing forward establishing a diverse financing system that is long-term, stable, sustainable and risk controllable.

Main content

The Thematic Session on Financial Connectivity was jointly hosted by the Ministry of Finance and the People's Bank of China at the National Convention Centre on May 14, 2017, in Beijing. Over 260 representatives from governments, financial institutions, enterprises and think tanks of 50 countries and international organisations attended the session. With the theme of "establishing diverse financing system to boost BRI development", the session included the opening and 2-panel discussions.

Xiao Jie, Minister for Finance, delivered a keynote speech entitled "Establishing Sustainably Diverse Financing Mechanism for A Better Future of BRI". He pointed out that the bottlenecks in financing are an underlined challenge for achieving connectivity and capital connectivity is vital to support for BRI development. To promote capital connectivity more effectively, finance ministries in 27 countries including China, jointly verified the Belt and Road Financing Guideline. To overcome financing difficulties and pursue BRI more effectively, Xiao Jie set out the direction for BRI participants to work on. First, effectively leveraging the guiding and supporting role of government policies. Countries should promote strategy bridging with countries in the region to form regional infrastructure planning and financing arrangement and strengthen policy coordination in law, taxation, trade and investment, creating transparent, friendly and unbiased financing and environment. Second, fully leveraging the decisive role of market mechanisms in allocating resources. Countries should encourage financial investors that are policy-driven, development-oriented or commercial and related institutional investors to generate greater influence, permeate government and social capital cooperation, and foster a sound architecture where all finance from each party participates. Third, strengthening cooperation with multilateral development agencies. They should leverage each other's strengths to engage in multilateral financing flexibly. The World Bank, AIIB and 4 other international financial institutions will sign MOUs with China to intensify cooperation under the BRI. Fourth, with the commitment of controlling risks, countries should innovate financing models, channels, tools and services, develop and improve the equity financing market and local currency bond market, so as to benefit countries participating the BRI and promote sustainable and inclusive development.[1]

Zhou Xiaochuan, Governor of China People's Bank, put forward 4 pieces of advice for Belt and Road financial connectivity. First, using development financing to propel Belt and Road financial connectivity. It is proven from practice that development financing possesses a range of advantages, as it can link both the government and market while allocating resources from multi-parties, it can also provide medium- to long-term credit support to specific demanders. It is exemplary to commercial capital and offers support through market approaches. Second, promoting the networked landscape of commercial banks to offer better financial services to trade and investment. Third, strengthening connectivity of financial infrastructure, especially universal financial development represented by community banking and internet/telecommunications payment. Fourth, proactively leveraging the role of local currencies in BRI development. China has made some useful attempts in signing local currency swap agreements, direct currency transactions, RMB clearing banks and RMB cross-border payment systems (CIPS), and is willing to share the relevant experience with countries participating the BRI. Moreover, Zhou Xiaochuan expressed that China hopes to further develop capital markets such as stock and bond markets and expand the connectivity of equity and bond financing markets.[2]

World Bank President Jim Yong Kim expressed that the World Bank accumulated rich experiences cooperating with developing countries in areas of trade facilitation and infrastructure building and said: "We are keen and ready to provide any form of financial support for the BRI development". Developing countries, especially the poor ones, are confronted with many challenges in infrastructure development, so the World Bank will mobilise its funds and those from other sources to steadfastly support developing countries, including those participating the BRI, to cooperate and develop. "Let the poorest countries integrate into the world market system to benefit from it and share the dividend of economic globalization."[3]

The IMF Chair put forward 3 policy priority areas. First, attracting FDI to high-quality infrastructure programmes. Last year, the combined net investment volume to emerging economies and developing countries was less than 1% of the combined GDP. If these countries hope to stimulate an influx of FDI, they could opt for prudent macro-economic policies, greater trade transparency and improved business and regulation environment. Second, bolstering financial inclusiveness, especially in developing economies. Analysis by the IMF showed that when comparing economies with strong and relatively weak financial inclusiveness, the strong ones have a 2–3-percentage point advantage. Third, leveraging fin-tech. In big cities of China, such as Beijing and Hangzhou, people can lead a cashless life and finish payment through mobile applications such as Alipay and WeChat.[4]

Hu Huaibang, Chair of National Development Bank, stated that development financial institutions have distinct advantages and influences in the pursuit of BRI. They are dedicated to constantly supporting infrastructure programmes, basic industries and key projects and keeping close ties with government authorities and all social sectors, which is beneficial for coordinating related policies. Concordantly, developing financial institutions use medium- to long-term investment and financing as major approaches to match large-volume and medium- to long-term financing needs in major projects. Development financial institutions form a relationship of the division of functions and complementarities with policy, commercial and other types of financial institutions, jointly forming reciprocal ties for Belt and Road financial connectivity.[5]

New Development Bank President Kmart believes that the "Belt and Road" building needs to meet many challenges, one of which is how to de-risk. Another key risk lies in foreign exchange. As BRI programmes are generally long-term, it is not realistic to assess possibilities of tomorrow based on forex of today; therefore, priority should be given to local currency in investment and currency swap with other countries.[6]

Yu Liqun, President of AIIB, said that the AIIB must adhere to 3 principles when providing funds for the "Belt and Road" countries. First, financing projects must be feasible and operable. Second, projects must be environment-friendly. Third, projects must be received by target countries.

Jin Qi, Chair of the Silk Road Fund, stated that finance should serve the real economy, so the Silk Road Fund underscores providing financial services to infrastructure, energy, assets and industrial programmes to support the development of the real economy. In the pursuit of BRI, the primary task is to guarantee financial connectivity. This is the key.[7]

Attendees shared views on overcoming Belt and Road funding difficulties and establishing institutional financial networks for Belt and Road financial cooperation. They also put forward opinions and input for promoting financial connectivity. As BRI involves huge quantities of infrastructure and capacity cooperation and participating countries are at different developmental phases, along with vastly different national realities, the challenges for risk control are enormous. The Belt and Road financing requires highly sustainable financing, which underscores project success, profit earning and effective risk prevention. It also needs to attract varied types of capital to form a long-term, stable and sustainable financial support system.

Deliverables

The Thematic Session on Financial Connectivity effectively boosted exchange of views and cooperation in areas of establishing financing channels, strengthening financial institutional cooperation and increasing financial support, yielding several results.

The Silk Road Fund added another RMB 100 billion.

China encourages financial institutions to carry out RMB overseas funding business, with the initial volume totaling RMB 300 billion to support BRI.

The National Development and Reform Commission will launch a China–Russia Fund for cooperation, development and investment, with a total amount of RMB 100 billion and an initial phase of RMB 10 billion. It will promote development cooperation between the north-east of China and the far east of Russia.

Xiao Jie, China's Minister for Finance, and the finance ministers or the authorised finance representatives of 26 countries including Argentina, Belarus and the United Kingdom, signed the "Guidelines for the Belt and Road Financing". This is the first time that the parties have funded the Belt and Road guideline document on financial connectivity. Six multilateral development agencies, including the Ministry of Finance and the Asian Development Bank, the Asian Infrastructure Investment Bank, the European Bank for Reconstruction and Development, the European Investment Bank, the New Development Bank and the World Bank Group have signed the MOU on Strengthening Cooperation in Related Areas under BRI.

Ministry of Finance in China launches multilateral development and financing cooperation centre in collaboration with multilateral development banks.

Financial Connectivity

The China–Kazakhstan Capacity Cooperation Fund was put into practical operation and signed the *Framework Agreement for Supporting Chinese Telecom Enterprises to Participate in the "Digital Kazakhstan 2020" Planning*.

The Silk Road Fund and SCO Interbank Consortium signed a Memorandum of Understanding on Partnership Foundations. The Silk Road Fund signed a cooperation agreement with the Uzbekistan National Foreign Economic Bank.

China Development Bank set up a Belt and Road infrastructure special loan (100 billion yuan equivalent), a Belt and Road capacity cooperation special loan (100 billion yuan equivalent) and a Belt and Road financial cooperation special loan (50 billion yuan equivalent).

The Export–Import Bank of China has set up a special loan for the "Belt and Road" (100 billion yuan equivalent) and a special loan for the "Belt and Road" infrastructure (30 billion yuan equivalent).

China Development Bank and France National Investment Bank jointly invested in China–France SME Fund (Phase II) and signed the "Equity Subscription Agreement"; it signed the "Memorandum of Understanding on the Establishment of Sino-Italian Joint Investment Fund" with the Italian Deposit and Loan Company; and carried out financing, bond underwriting and other fields of pragmatic cooperation with Iranian Commercial Bank, Egypt Bank, Hungarian Development Bank, Philippine Capital Bank, Agricultural Bank of Turkey, Austrian International Bank, Cambodian Bank of China and Malaysian Malayan Bank.

The Export–Import Bank of China has signed the *Credit Line Framework Agreement* with the "Asian Export–Import Bank Forum" member institutions such as the Export–Import Bank of Malaysia and the Export–Import Bank of Thailand and has carried out pragmatic cooperation in areas of loan-to-loan and trade finance.

China Export Credit Insurance Corporation signed cooperation agreements with counterparts from Belarus, Serbia, Poland, Sri Lanka and Egypt, Ministry of Investment and International Cooperation of Egypt, the Ministry of Finance of Laos, Ministry of Finance of Cambodia, the Indonesian Investment Coordinating Committee, the Polish Investment and Trade Bureau, Kenya's Ministry of Finance, the Iranian Central Bank, Iranian Ministry of Finance and Economic Affairs and other relevant government departments and the Saudi Arabian Development Fund, the Turkish Industrial Bank, the Turkish Guarantee Bank, the United Bank of Pakistan and other relevant national financial institutions.

The People's Bank of China and the International Monetary Fund signed the MOU between the People's Bank of China and the International Monetary Fund on Establishing a China–IMF Joint Capacity Building Centre; and the People's Bank of China and the Czech National Bank signed the MOU between the People's Bank of China and the Czech National Bank.

The Export–Import Bank of China and the United Nations Industrial Development Organisation signed the Joint Statement on Promoting Cooperation on Sustainable Industrial Development in Countries Participating in the Belt and Road Initiative.

The Asian Financial Cooperation Association was formally established.

The Industrial and Commercial Bank of China and the major banks in Pakistan, Uzbekistan, Austria and other countries jointly launched the Belt and Road Bank Cooperation Action Plan and established the Belt and Road bank normalisation cooperation and exchange mechanism.

The Thematic Session on Financial Connectivity established the guiding principles for financial connectivity for the first time, which effectively promoted the exchanges and cooperation between the "Belt and Road" participants in building financing channels, strengthening financial institutions and increasing financial support. The Belt and Road Initiative has a significance in overcoming financial difficulties and building a long-term, stable, sustainable and risk-controlled diversified financing system.

Notes

1 "Minister Xiao Jie Spoke at Thematic Session on Financial Connectivity," website of Ministry of Finance. Retrieved January 25, 2018 from www.mof.gov.cn/zhengwuxinxi/caizhengxinwen/201705/t20170514_2600078.htm
2 "Zhou Xiaochuan Elaborate Four Ideas on B&R Financing," Xinhua Net. Retrieved January 25, 2018 from www.xinhuanet.com/money/2017-05/17/c_1120984974.htm
3 "Input by Guest to Session on Financial Connectivity: Establish Diverse Financing System," China Economic. Retrieved January 26, 2018 from www.ce.cn/xwzx/gnsz/gdxw/201705/15/t20170515_22802960.shtml
4 "IMF Chair Lagard: One Chopstick Breaks but A Bundle Stand," China Economic. Retrieved January 26, 2018 from http://m.ce.cn/bwzg/201705/15/t20170515_22803916.shtml
5 "Input by Guest to Session on Financial Connectivity: Establish Diverse Financing System," China Economic. Retrieved January 26, 2018 from www.ce.cn/xwzx/gnsz/gdxw/201705/15/t20170515_22802960.shtml
6 "Input by Guest to Session on Financial Connectivity: Establish Diverse Financing System," China Economic. Retrieved January 26, 2018 from www.ce.cn/xwzx/gnsz/gdxw/201705/15/t20170515_22802960.shtml
7 "Silk Road Fund Chair Jin Qi Say Positioning is Equity Investment," ifenghuang. Retrieved January 29, 2018 from https://item.btime.com/0133iq9h9ep9gqmg19daj3i6qgf

77
THEMATIC SESSION ON PEOPLE-TO-PEOPLE CONNECTIVITY

Qu Caiyun

Understanding between people is the social foundation for BRI promotion. The gist of the Thematic Session on People-to-People Connectivity is to gather participants of BRI, strengthen exchanges and communication, elevate people-to-people connectivity to a new stage and at a higher level, establish platforms and multi-tiered people-to-people cooperation mechanisms, usher in more cooperation channels, carry out deep people-to-people cooperation and make the people the beneficiaries and main players in the pursuit of BRI.

Main content

The Thematic Session on People-to-People Connectivity was sponsored by the International Department of the CPC Central Committee and organised by the Ministry of Education, the Ministry of Science and Technology, the Ministry of Culture, the National Health and Family Planning Commission, the National Tourism Administration, the Overseas Chinese Affairs Office of the State Council, the National Federation of Trade Unions, the Central Committee of the Communist Youth League, the All-China Women's Federation and the Chinese People's Association for Friendship with Foreign Countries, the China Disabled Persons' Federation and the China Red Cross Society and other departments at the Beijing National Convention Centre on the afternoon of May 14, 2017. A turnout of 400 representatives from governments, political parties, enterprises and social organisations of over 60 countries as well as from international organisations such as the UN attended the Thematic Session on People-to-People Connectivity. With the theme of building a bridge linking peoples' hearts for prosperity and development, the session is composed of the keynote speech, guest address, story sharing, result demonstration and a conclusion.

Song Tao, Minister of the International Department, delivered a keynote speech entitled "Building a Bridge Linking Peoples' Hearts to Pursue BRI". Song Tao pointed out that strengthening people-to-people ties will solidify social foundations for economic cooperation between nations, inject impetus to the reform and improvement global governance system, provide platforms for cultural exchanges and mutual learning, and create conditions for building a community of shared future for mankind. To effectively foster understanding between people, Song Tao put forward the philosophy of shared efforts, emotions, pragmatism and inclusiveness.

"Shared efforts" refer to coordination and cooperation between nations to intensify the awareness of shared responsibility, fulfil duties, increase implementation efficiency of people-to-people programmes, and promote the normalisation and institutionalisation of people-to-people connectivity. "Emotions" refer to activities that can spur emotional bonds between peoples, so that friendship will grow stronger and people will be closer. "Pragmatism" underscores universalism of people-to-people programmes, increasing the engagement and sense of fulfilment for people of BRI participating countries in different groups and social status. "Inclusiveness" refers to countries, by following the principle of inclusiveness and openness, should constantly improve multi-player cooperation models to engage with more countries, international organisations and social strengths. Upholding the principle of achieving shared interests through consultations and common development and implementing the philosophy of "shared efforts, emotions, pragmatism and inclusiveness", countries should enhance communication, exchanges and cooperation in the spirit of self-realisation to build a bridge linking peoples' hearts and achieve common development.[1]

Irina Bokova, Director-General of UNESCO, delivered a speech at the session and believed that the "Belt and Road" has played an important role in promoting the development and exchange of culture and education in countries pursuing the BRI, and said that the BRI is key to universal development, equality and tolerance.[2]

Dr Margaret Chan, Director-General of the World Health Organisation, delivered a speech and expressed "deep appreciation for the principles of achieving shared interests through consultations and common development. I firmly believe that the Memorandum of Understanding and the implementation plan will provide a good opportunity for China and WHO to strengthen cooperation. I expect to strengthen global and regional health and security through coordinated efforts, building a healthy Belt and Road".[3]

Mohamed Shabaz Sharif, Pakistan's Punjab Chief Minister, made a speech and stated: "While global trade negotiations are stagnating, China is seeking new trade routes and renovating old routes to support developing countries in restoring physical and human resources infrastructure. This is a civil partnership based on mutual respect and well-being".[4]

President Mijintsev of the Russian–Chinese Friendship Association delivered a speech, arguing that BRI as an economic development strategy has created conditions for the development of new cooperation between many countries and nations in the East and the West and has become a unified corridor for people-to-people exchanges and private diplomacy in areas along the Ancient Silk Road. Fostering understanding between people through dialogue is an important link and foundation for improving traditional friendship between people of all countries and a guarantee for the unimpeded and effective development of political and economic relations of each country.[5]

The heads of several international organisations and international non-governmental friendship organisations, and representatives of countries along the "Belt and Road" and overseas Chinese businesses elaborated on their views and opinions on the work of people-to-people ties under the BRI. Representatives from Myanmar, Uzbekistan, Sri Lanka, Greece, Tanzania, Pakistan and other countries participating in the BRI shared the personal experiences of participating in the "Belt and Road" development and the stories of Belt and Road people-to-people connectivity.

The session demonstrated the results of exchanges and cooperation between China and other relevant international organisations in the fields of culture, education, science and technology, tourism, health and journalism. It announced the launching of Chinese Social Organisations' Action Plan for Stronger People-to-People Connectivity along the Belt and Road (2017–2020), China NGO Network for International Exchanges and the International

Think-Tank Cooperation Programme on Enhancing People-to-People Connectivity along the Belt and Road.

Participants believed that the BRI development advocated by China is a key approach for improving the well-being of nations participating in the BRI and a bridge fostering people-to-people ties. They want to actively promote exchanges and cooperation for people of all countries and cement public opinions on BRI promotion.

Deliverables

The Thematic Session on People-To-People Connectivity reached some consensuses, initiated the Action Plan on Belt and Road Scientific and Innovative Cooperation and signed numerous agreements and MOUs, yielding fruitful outcomes.

The Chinese government will increase aid to developing countries participating in the BRI and the total amount in the next 3 years will reach RMB 60 billion.

It will provide RMB 2 billion emergency food aid to developing countries participating in the BRI. China adds another US$1 billion to South–South Cooperation Assistance Fund to initiate China–UN 2030 Sustainable Development Agenda Cooperation Initiative and support 100 Happy Family, 100 Poverty Assistance and 100 Rehab Medical Assistance programmes in countries participating in the BRI. China offers US$1 billion to related international organisations and jointly promote the implementation of international cooperation programmes benefitting BRI participating countries, including 100 refugee assistance programmes ranging from food and tents to portable houses. It sets up a refugee scholarship, offers educational opportunities to 500 youths and funds 100 refugee athletes to participate in international and regional sports events.

The Chinese Government and the Lebanese Government signed the *2017–2020 Implementation Plan for the Cultural Agreement between the Government of the People's Republic of China and the Government of the Republic of Lebanon*. The Chinese Government signed the *Agreement between the Government of the People's Republic of China and the Government of the Republic of Tunisia on the Establishment of Cultural Centres* with the Tunisian Government, and the *Agreement between the Government of the People's Republic of China and the Government of the Republic of Turkey on the Establishment of Cultural Centres* with the Turkish Government.

The Chinese Government and UNESCO signed the *Memorandum of Understanding on China–UNESCO Cooperation (2017–2020)*.

The Chinese government signed an intergovernmental tourism cooperation agreement with the Polish government.

The Chinese government initiated the launching of *Action Plan on Belt and Road Scientific and Innovative Cooperation*, implementing programmes on sci-tech and people-to-people exchanges, joint establishment of research labs, cooperation between science parks and technological transfer.

The Chinese Government has signed assistance agreements with the World Food Programme, United Nations International Organisation for Migration, UNICEF, UNHCR, World Health Organisation, International Committee of the Red Cross, United Nations Development Programme, United Nations Industrial Development Organisation, World Trade Organisation, International Civil Aviation Organisation, United Nations International organisations such as UNFPA, the United Nations Conference on Trade and Development, the International Trade Centre and UNESCO.

The Ministry of Education of China has signed cooperation documents with the education departments of Russia, Kazakhstan, Bosnia and Herzegovina, Estonia and Laos, signed a mutual recognition agreement of higher education qualifications and degree agreements with Cyprus, and established a music education alliance with countries participating in the BRI.

The Ministry of Science and Technology of China and the Mongolian Ministry of Education, Culture, Science and Sports signed a memorandum of understanding on the joint implementation of the Sino-Mongolian exchange programme for young scientists. The ministry signed a memorandum of understanding with the Mongolian Ministry of Education, Culture, Science and Sports on the establishment of a science park and innovative infrastructure development cooperation in Mongolia. In addition, the ministry signed a memorandum of understanding with the Hungarian National Research and Innovation and Innovation Agency on joint funding of Sino-Hungarian scientific cooperation projects.

The Ministry of Environmental Protection of China issued the Belt and Road Ecological Environmental Protection Cooperation Plan and established the Belt and Road eco-environmental big data service platform, and jointly announced with the United Nations Environment Programme the establishment of the "Belt and Road" green development international alliance.

The Chinese Ministry of Finance will establish the Belt and Road Financial and Economic Development Research Centre.

The National Health and Family Planning Commission of China has signed cooperation documents with the Ministries of Health of the Czech Republic and Norway, respectively.

China National Tourism Administration signed a tourism cooperation agreement with Uzbekistan National Tourism Development Committee, an MOU on tourism cooperation with the Chilean Ministry of Economy, Development and Tourism and an action plan for the MOU on tourism cooperation with the Cambodian Ministry of Tourism.

The State Administration of Press, Publication, Radio, Film and Television signed respective cooperation documents with the Turkish Radio and Television Supreme Council and the Saudi Arabian General Administration of Audiovisual Management. China Central Television and the mainstream media of the relevant countries established the "Belt and Road" news cooperation alliance.

The Information Office of the State Council of China signed respective MOUs on media exchanges and cooperation with the Cambodian Ministry of Information, the Brunei Prime Minister's Office, the UAE National Media Commission and the Palestinian Ministry of Public Information, and the Albanian Council of Ministers Media and Citizenship Relations.

The Information Office of the State Council of China signed respective MOUs on the cooperation plan for think-tank cooperation with the Ministry of Foreign Affairs and International Cooperation of Cambodia, the Institute of Policy and Strategy of the Ministry of Foreign Affairs and Trade of Brunei, the Ministry of Foreign Affairs of Israel and the Ministry of Foreign Affairs of Palestine and the Ministry of Foreign Affairs of Albania.

China National Development Bank will host Belt and Road bilateral and multilateral exchanges and workshops and establish Belt and Road Special Scholarship.

The China Association for the Promotion of International Organisations of China's Non-governmental Organisations and more than 80 Chinese non-governmental organisations launched the *Action Plan of China's Social Organisations on Promoting People-to-People Connectivity (2017–2020)*, the China Association for the Promotion of International Organisations and more than 150 Chinese and foreign civil organisations established a "cooperative network of civic organizations along the Silk Road". The Belt and Road Think-Tank Cooperation Alliance launched International Think-Tank Cooperation Programme for Enhancing Belt and Road People-to-People Connectivity.

The Development Research Centre of the State Council of China and the United Nations Industrial Development Organisation signed a memorandum of understanding on collaboratively pursuing the BRI. More than 50 international members and partners of the Silk Road

People-to-People Connectivity

International Think-Tank Network jointly issued the Beijing Joint Action Declaration of Silk Road International Think-Tank Network with China.

The China International Urban Development Alliance signed letters of intent for cooperation with the United Nations Human Settlements Programmr, the World Health Organisation, the World Cities and Local Government Organisations in the Asia–Pacific region, respectively.

The Thematic Session on People-to-People Connectivity effectively boosted multi-field and multi-level exchanges and cooperation between BRI participants in culture, education, science and technology, health and media. It bears significance for BRI participants in strengthening public engagement, ties, mutual trust and mutual learning among different civilisations.

Notes

1 Song Tao, "Building A Bridge Linking Peoples'Hearts—Keynote Speech at the Thematic Session on People-To-People Connectivity of the Belt and Road Forum," *Contemporary World*, p. 5 of 6th edition of 2017.
2 "Director-General of UNESCO Irina Bokova Deliver Speech," website of International Department of CPC Central Committee. Retrieved January 9, 2018 from www.idcpc.gov.cn/ztzl/hylt/zjmxxt/jbzc/201705/t20170512_89648.html
3 "Speech by Margaret Chan, Director-General of the World Health Organization," website of International Department of CPC Central Committee. Retrieved January 9, 2018 from www.idcpc.gov.cn/ztzl/hylt/zjmxxt/jbzc/201705/t20170512_89649.html
4 "Speech by Mohamed Shabaz Sharif, Pakistan's Punjab Chief Minister," website of International Department of CPC Central Committee. Retrieved January 9, 2018 from www.idcpc.gov.cn/ztzl/hylt/zjmxxt/jbzc/201705/t20170512_89652.html
5 "Speech by President Mijintsev of the Russian–Chinese Friendship Association," website of International Department of CPC Central Committee. Retrieved January 9, 2018 from www.idcpc.gov.cn/ztzl/hylt/zjmxxt/jbzc/201705/t20170512_89725.html

78
THEMATIC SESSION ON THINK-TANK EXCHANGES

Qu Caiyun

Background and purpose

Think tanks are the bridge linking the government with the public and linking policy research with knowledge transmission. Since the proposal of the BRI, the academic circles of both home and abroad have responded proactively and conducted broad and in-depth study. At present, think tanks and Belt and Road research institutes in China have exceeded 400 in number, over 50 prestigious think tanks outside China have joined Belt and Road research with a range of research results. Centring on pursuing the BRI, related research institutes were established, and think tanks from BRI participating countries have continuously intensified exchanges and cooperation, launching some critical research results. Chinese think tanks have published more than 400 books on the Belt and Road, and approximately 50 famous foreign think tanks have issued over 100 special reports on the Belt and Road. Think tanks have built a bridge for BRI in promoting communication, enhancing understanding and building consensus.

Think tanks will play more positive roles in BRI development. First, through joint research and transnational cooperative research, they create high-quality research results, provide consultations to governments and offer suggestions to strategy coordination between nations. Second, promoting ideological innovation. They shall intensify research innovation in international cooperation, investment and trade, project development and science and technology, so as to improve governance capability in countries participating in the BRI and enhance drive for sustainable development. Third, enhancing conceptual recognition, which is to impartially interpret the BRI and transmit authentic, realistic and holistic information. Fourth, strengthening dialogues and exchanges, which includes exchanges and mutual learning among nations and civilisations, deepen mutual understanding and recognition and establish platforms and carriers for information exchange, pooling wisdom and exchanging views.[1]

Think tanks are important components of Belt and Road international cooperation, which play special roles in promoting connectivity, in particular, people-to-people ties. Over 4 years, think tanks have played important roles in promoting the Belt and Road study, implementing the Belt and Road philosophy and coordinating the BRI with national development plans of corresponding countries. BRI development needs to draw on the vision and in-depth views of scholars from both Chinese and overseas think tanks. President Xi Jinping stated in the Belt and

Road Forum that "we shall leverage the role of think tanks and establish a think tank alliance and cooperation network".[2]

The Thematic Session on Think-Tank Connectivity underscores facilitating broad exchanges with think tank professionals from each country, sharing past practices, mutual learning, building consensus and establishing platforms for pooling wisdom; establishing new mechanisms and pathways for pursuing BRI and building bridges for cooperation and exchanges between the East and the West under the BRI; and turning the Belt and Road visions into realities and pursuing an "Intelligent Silk Road" of common development and prosperity.

Content

Hosted by the Publicity Department of CPC Central Committee and organised by the China International Economic Exchange Centre, the Thematic Session on Think-Tank Exchanges was held at the Beijing National Convention Centre on the afternoon of May 14, 2017. A turnout of 200 think-tank chiefs, former political leaders and scholars from over 40 countries and regions attended the session. With the theme of "Working Together to Build a Silk Road of Intelligence", the session consisted of guest speeches and panel discussions.

Liu Qichen, member of the Political Bureau of the CPC Central Committee, Secretary of the Central Secretariat and Minister of the Publicity Department, delivered a keynote speech entitled "Working Together to Build a Silk Road of Intelligence". He put forward 4 pieces of advice for establishing such a silk road. First, pursuing BRI should be included under the broad vision of building a community of shared future for mankind. They should combine the concept of community of shared future for mankind and the Silk Road Spirit, study conscientiously and elaborate on connotation, so as to make it a beacon guideline for the common pursuit of BRI of all countries and the anchor for stakeholders to pool strengths and collaborate. Second, planning BRI development in the grand arena of economic globalisation. By advocating of openness and sharing, the BRI promotion commits itself to the connectivity of policies, roads and rules, so as to combine the development of China with that of BRI participating countries and inject strong impetus to world economic development. Third, studying the BRI under the landscape of evolving international relations. The BRI affords us opportunities, promotes development and strives for reciprocity, which will strongly boost fairness and justice of international relations. Fourth, the BRI development should be assessed under the vision of mutual learning among human civilisations. To pursue the BRI, we need to promote common development under the context of exchanges and mutual learning for different civilisations, so as to make it a bridge of friendship among nations, a drive propelling social progress and a bond securing the world peace. In doing so, more high-end research results will be formulated, and intelligence support will be offered to benefit people of all countries.[3] He wishes to strengthen exchanges and cooperation among think tanks from both home and abroad, establish think-tank alliances and cooperation networks, create more high-end research results and jointly foster a Silk Road of Intelligence.

Zeng Peiyan, head of the China International Economic Exchanges, talked about how think tanks play a role in the promotion of BRI. He believes that think tanks should delve into the innate development rules of BRI, extract BRI cooperation and governance models and work towards providing intelligence support to BRI participating countries, leveraging the role of think tanks as a "secondary orbit" of the Belt and Road.[4]

Rudd, head of the American Asia Society's Policy Research Institute and former Australian Prime Minister, said that from a historical perspective he saw that the ancient Silk Road brought exchanges of trade and culture, not conflicts and wars; from the current perspective, he saw that the "Belt and Road" continues to promote the reform and development of the international order; from a future perspective, he has seen that the success of the "Belt and Road" can help hundreds of millions of people out of poverty, protect our planet and create global cooperation. This requires the wisdom of the world and our wisdom for mutual understanding and bridging differences.[5]

Attendees elaborated on 3 key topics: BRI in promoting strong, balanced, inclusive and sustainable development; the Silk Road featuring openness, inclusiveness and mutual learning; and a blueprint of innovation, development and international cooperation under the BRI. They underpinned the positive role BRI plays in expanding global demands, bolstering global supply and fostering new drives, its role in promoting global trade and investment mechanisms, as well as promoting global, inclusive development, creating conditions for youths and SMEs of all nations to participate international cooperation. They also discussed green Belt and Road development, strengthening think-tank exchanges and cooperation and leveraging the role think tanks play in BRI promotion, and press ahead with coordination between BRI and key development strategies and plans of related countries and regions, promoting healthy development of BRI and long-term cooperation and development mechanisms for pursuing BRI.

Participants held that the pursuit of BRI needs the engagement of think tanks and that building a Silk Road of Intelligence is a key subject in BRI development. Think tanks play the role of an explorer, who seeks out an effective way of combining BRI policies, cooperation models and approaches of common development and win–win and disseminate it. Think tanks can pool strengths, jointly develop new platforms, explore new pathways, foster new growth drivers and boost common prosperity in countries participating in the BRI. Think tanks can leverage advantages in talents and offer enterprises with policy consultation and intelligence support through research on risk evaluation.[6]

Deliverables

The session reached important consensus, formulated think-tank joint research reports and agreed on jointly establishing Belt and Road research institutes.

The "Consensus on Building A Colourful Silk Road", published by 16 think tanks including China International Economic Exchange Centre and Lee Kuan Yew Public Policy Institute of the National University of Singapore, put forward 6 points of consensus. One, think tanks should join hands to establish a colourful silk road and extend new space for BRI development. Two, think tanks should jointly establish a theoretical framework and systems for building a community of shared future for mankind and form a broad consensus on BRI. Three, think tanks should jointly promote communication and coordination for economic policies and bolster balance and inclusiveness of economic growth of BRI participating countries. Four, think tanks should jointly advance development strategy coordination among countries participating in BRI and launch mechanisms for think tanks to participate in the work on coordination. Five, think tanks should jointly explore new models for BRI development and offer beneficial references to global governance. Six, think tanks should launch long-term cooperation mechanisms for think tanks and establish bilateral and multilateral think tank exchange networks.

National Development and Reform Commission on behalf of the Chinese government and United Nations Development Programme (UNDP) signed the Action Plan on the Belt and Road Initiative, which underscores information exchanges, program cooperation, policy coordination, partnership building and capacity building.

UNDP and China International Economic Exchange Centre jointly issued the "Belt and Road Initiative—New Thinking in Evolutional Global Governance Propelling Sustainable Development".

The Research Institute of National Development Bank, China International Economic Exchange Centre and Silk Road Planning Research Centre jointly released the Report on BRI Trade and Investment Indexes, which offered in-depth research results through data-intensive analytical approaches to reveal development status of BRI in trade and investment.

The Thematic Session on Think-Tank Exchanges promoted exchanges and cooperation among think tanks in the BRI study. It bears significance for think tanks of each country in sharing past practices, pooling wisdom, discussion on BRI long-term cooperation mechanisms, bilateral and multilateral joint research on BRI development, establishing partnership networks of win–win and accruing feedback and inputs.

Notes

1 "Profile of Thematic Session on Infrastructure Connectivity of B&R Forum," China Central Government website. Retrieved January 16, 2018 from www.gov.cn/xinwen/2017-05/10/content_5192398.htmhtm#5
2 "Xi Jinping Opening Remarks at Belt and Road Forum," Xinhua Net. Retrieved January 16, 2018 from www.xinhuanet.com/world/2017-05/14/c_1120969677.htm
3 Liu Qibao, "Working Together for A Silk Road of Intelligence," State Council website. Retrieved January 19, 2018 from www.scio.gov.cn/ztk/dtzt/36048/36583/36584/Document/1552880/1552880.htm
4 Zeng Peiyan, "Pooling Wisdom for A Silk Road of Intelligence," State Council website. Retrieved January 19, 2018 from www.scio.gov.cn/ztk/dtzt/36048/36583/36584/Document/1552880/1552849.htm
5 Kevin Rudd, "Viewing BRI from Three Perspectives," State Council website. Retrieved January 20, 2018 from www.scio.gov.cn/ztk/dtzt/36048/36583/36584/Document/1552880/1552861.htm
6 "Thematic Session on Think Tank Exchanges Propose A Silk Road of Intelligence," website of Chinese Social Sciences. Retrieved January 23, 2018 from www.cssn.cn/zk/zk_jsxx/zk_zx/201705/t20170515_3518167.shtml

PART X

International action plans relevant to the Belt and Road Initiative

79
THE SUSTAINABLE DEVELOPMENT OF THE 2030 AGENDA WITH THE BELT AND ROAD INITIATIVE

Tian Huifang

Chinese plan for sustainable development

China has greatly contributed to the implementation of Millennium Development Goals of the United Nations. During the period of 2000–2015, the Chinese economy grew annually by 8% on average to eradicate the poverty of nearly 700 million Chinese people. China also actively participates in the South–South Cooperation and assists more than 120 developing countries in implementing the Millennium Development Goals. Because a huge need is caused by the growth of the Chinese economy, the Chinese trade connection is improved with regions such as Africa and Latin America, which plays an important impetus in the growth and poverty alleviation in these regions. Therefore, it can be said that Chinese achievement and experience are an important guarantee to overall realise the Millennium Development Goals of the United Nations.

Since the Sustainable Development of the 2030 Agenda (hereinafter referred to as "the 2030 Agenda") became effective on January 1, 2016, China still firmly supports and contributes to the sustainable development goals of the United Nations. However, 4 challenges exist in the implementation of the 2030 Agenda: (1) due to climate change, the energy sector should not only decarbonise but also cope with the urbanisation of more than 2 billion people; (2) due to the infrastructure need from large-scale immigration, humanitarian assistance occupies traditional development resources, and their relation should be coordinated; (3) due to the very vulnerable state, the international financial and tax system should be transformed; and (4) the international trade system should be transformed to better accommodate the 2030 Agenda, and be included into the social and environmental standards. Therefore, 17 sustainable objectives and 169 concrete objectives stipulated in the 2030 Agenda must be integrated by all countries concerned according to their actual conditions, which should be included in their medium- and long-term national development strategy, so as to establish a synergic and complementary relation between the international agenda and domestic strategy.

In April 2016, the "Position Paper on the Implementation of the 2030 Agenda of Sustainable Development" was first released by China to actively support the implementation of sustainable development goals. At the G20 Summit in 2016 (Hangzhou, China), the resources and politics were mobilised to implement the 2030 Agenda and the Paris Agreement; the means for boosting the implementation of sustainable development objective and climate objective were merged into various agendas of G20, like growth, trade, investment and finance; and a series of measures were specified, including dialogue, policy coordination and strengthening of deeper international cooperation. In September 2016, the "National Plan for the Implementation of the 2030 Agenda for Sustainable Development" was released by China: specifying the Chinese guidelines and general principles for boosting the implementation work; illustrating in detail the Chinese path for boosting the 2030 Agenda from 7 aspects, i.e. strategic alignment, system guarantee, social mobilisation, resources input, risk control, international cooperation and supervision assessment; and offering a concrete plan for implementing 17 sustainable development objectives and 169 concrete objectives. As the world's first country to formulate a detailed objective-oriented implementation plan with all fields covered, China converts the sustainable development objective to concrete tasks in such fields as economy, society and environment since China formulated National Outline for Innovation-driven Development Strategy; National Plan for Agricultural Sustainable Development (2015–2030); Outline for "Health China (2030)" Plan; and Chinese Strategy and Action Plan for Biological Diversity Protection (2011–2030).

The Chinese Plan is not only devoted to the sustainable development of China, but also points out that China will work hard to help other developing countries pioneer the global implementation, which offers a good example and model for accommodating the global and national specific development strategy. China strives to boost an international exchange and cooperation such as South–South Cooperation; and has established such institutions as the South–South Cooperation Aid Found; China–the United Nations' Peace and Development Fund; the Institute of South–South Cooperation and Development; and the Knowledge Centre for International Development. The Belt and Road Initiative proposed in 2013 aims to create a comprehensive trade and development network across the Asian–European–African continents, and jointly strives to realise the objective of global sustainable development.

Sustainable development concept in the Belt and Road Initiative

In 2015, just before the release of the 2030 Agenda, the "Vision and Action on Jointly Building the Silk Road Economic Belt and the 21st Century Maritime Silk Road" was issued by China. As specified in this document, China will spread the achievement of joint construction to wider areas; strengthen a dialogue across different civilisations while respecting the development road and mode selection of all countries concerned; seek a conjunction of interests and the "biggest common denominator" for cooperation; promote a common development and realise a common prosperity following the concept of "peace and cooperation, openness and inclusiveness, mutual learning and mutual referencing, mutual benefit and win–win". Therefore, a peaceful development is considered as official ideology in the Belt and Road Initiative, i.e. to promote the economic development via the infrastructure investment; and promote cooperation to minimise the conflict possibility. At the opening ceremony of "the Belt and Road Summit Forum for International Cooperation" in May 2017, Xi Jinping mentioned and quoted the following contents at his keynote speech: deficit in peace, development and governance poses a daunting challenge to mankind. The regions along the ancient Silk Road used to be a land of milk and honey. Yet today these places are associated with conflict, turbulence, crisis and challenge. In pursing the Belt and Road Initiative, we should focus on the fundamental issue of development, release the growth potential of various countries, achieve an economic integration and interconnected development and deliver benefits to all.

Even though they came from different backgrounds, the Belt and Road Initiative and the 2030 Agenda have many common values and characteristics. Both adopt sustainable development as an overall objective; aim to deepen the connection of infrastructure, trade, finance and policies among all countries/regions concerned, and especially the connection of people, which is the most important aspect; create an opportunity; increase a supply of global public products; and realise cooperation and win–win. Antonio Guterres, Secretary-General of the United Nations, once highly praised the role of the Belt and Road Initiative in boosting the 2030 Agenda regarding the current challenge of globalisation and free trade, as he said, an initiative for global close union will build a great confidence that there will be a better globalisation, that a free trade can benefit the whole world and that a global sustainable development will not leave any other country behind, while the Belt and Road Initiative exactly describes a "new vision" from China for the global development, which offers a new opportunity for the international community to cope with various global challenges of climate change, food security and water shortage.

Development bonus of the Belt and Road Initiative

In the 2030 Agenda, 3 pillars are proposed: economic growth, social inclusiveness and environmental sustainability. Under the Belt and Road Initiative, an extensive common benefit is guaranteed in various aspects for all countries along the Belt and Road: economic development, improving people's livelihood, coping with financial crisis and acceleration of transformation/upgrading. By mainly proposing the economic and humane cooperation, it combines the strategic plan and arrangement of China and different countries into a framework, representing an international economic cooperation framework of a larger scope and a higher level.[1]

(1) To promote poverty alleviation and growth. Compared with those in developed countries, the Belt and Road countries mostly have such problems as low-level and poor quality logistics/infrastructure. Above defects in infrastructure brings a high transportation cost, which will block market entry, cross-border trade and economic development to cause a risk for downside development in these countries. However, such risk can be reduced through the cooperation in infrastructure, regional trade and investment. During the period of 2014–2016, the GDP of Belt and Road countries grew by 4.2% on average as compared with a global average growth rate of 2.6%; in 2016, the GDP of these countries accounted for 68% of the global GDP increase, among which the Asian contribution was far more than 50% (including China). Through a better infrastructure and a wider regional connectivity, the Belt and Road countries can enjoy a greater opportunity for entering the global market to better utilise the comparative advantages and support long-term development. At the Belt and Road Forum for International Cooperation, participating countries agreed on a practical cooperation in boosting the infrastructure construction of road, railway, harbour, energy pipeline and telecommunication.

(2) To boost a green transformation. In Chinese green action of the Belt and Road Initiative, 4 main objectives are specified.

To promote an overseas sustainable development. In 2015, China invested up to US$400 billion in green industry; and up to 2020, China plans to release a renewable energy of at least US$360 billion within its territory. More and more Chinese renewable energy companies are investing abroad. Through the Belt and Road Initiative, China can boost and demonstrate a larger scale of green growth by providing other countries with cheap renewable energy equipments, and offer precious experiences and lessons by assisting other countries in implementing a renewable energy and reducing an emission.

To ensure the construction of infrastructure with climate toughness. The sustainable infrastructure investment can avoid locking an investment in high carbon; leave room for policy makers to define an ambitious objective of emission reduction in future; and make it possible to decarbonise the global economy by 2050. The sustainable infrastructure investment can also balance the influence of downturn global trade on all countries concerned; create an employment opportunity for all countries concerned; and help them better cope with the future influence of climate.

To boost an establishment of green financial system. In recent years, a series of measures has been formulated by China to reform its financial system, so as to establish an all-round green financial system. China is the only country to establish and perfect a green credit system in banking sectors. China has also established a national green development fund and provincial green fund to support the development of green enterprises. In 2016, the market size of the Chinese green bond accounted for 39% of the total global bond. With mature experience in policy-making and practising in the field of green finance development, China can help other developing countries realise a green financial system through the Belt and Road Initiative.

To ensure that the investment of overseas enterprises conforms to the global code of conduct for environment, society and governance (ESG). At present, the guidelines for environmental and social risk management of overseas investment have been issued by the Chinese government and industrial associations concerned. These voluntary guidelines will enable a close monitoring of Chinese overseas investment and the stakeholders in invested countries, and ensure that the enterprises sincerely treat the environmental and social risk during the investment.

(3) To reshape an economic and trade relation in this regions. Although it is still difficult to quantify the economic influence of the Belt and Road Initiative, the trade investment and construction activity are increasing. China and the participating countries of the Belt and Road Initiative also strive to boost the facilitation of trade and investment, improve a business environment and revitalise main international trade routes through the large-scale infrastructure projects with Information and Communication Technology (ICT) as one of the most important investment fields. In developed countries, developing countries and least developed countries, the internet popularisation rate is currently more than 80%, only 40% and 15%, respectively. Investment in ICT can play a very important role in business growth, and can also accelerate the sustainable development objective of the United Nations and narrow the digital gap between developed areas and developing areas. Through the Belt and Road Initiative, all countries concerned are cooperating jointly to win the joint projects of larger scale and more possibly raise the necessary funds. After the completion of the ICT infrastructure, a new impetus will be brought to the community development and a new market will be opened for business partners.

(4) To provide a stable and sustainable financial guarantee. China is a main participant in global development financing. In order to provide a development fund for the Belt and Road Initiative, 3 institutions are proposed by China: Asian Infrastructure Investment Bank (AIIB), New Development Bank (NDB) and Silk Road Foundation (SRF). In 2016, US$1.7 billion was loaned by AIIB for 9 development projects of Belt and Road. ADB also announced that by 2020, the total climate financing volume from ADB will be doubled from US$3 billion to US$6 billion to mainly support the renewable energy project, energy efficiency project, sustainable traffic project and smart city construction project, and at the same time it will focus on improving the adaptability to climate change, upgrading the infrastructures, developing the climate intelligent agricultures and improving the ability to withstand climate disaster of underdeveloped countries. An agreement for financing the Belt and Road projects has been signed by ADB and the Ministry of Finance of PRC.

Moreover, multilateral financing institutions such as AIIB, NDB and ADB also strive to improve the environmental standards for projects. During the current investment on infrastructure, these institutions attach a greater and greater importance to the renewable energy projects and green energy projects instead of traditional energy projects. AIIB has positioned itself as "lean, clean and green", intending to help all countries concerned realise their national commitment in the Paris Agreement under its environmental and social framework. Ever since it was formally open to business at the beginning of 2016, AIIB has aided 24 infrastructure projects, including 7 clean energy projects with a total value of US$1 billion. In the draft plan of energy in 2017, AIIB promised to loan the coal-fired power plants only under special situations. Up to now, AIIB has not yet approved a loan for any project involving coal.

As a whole, with the same concept and overall direction, the Belt and Road Initiative and the 2030 Agenda promote each other, jointly strive to boost the connectivity of the global infrastructure, carry out a wider regional cooperation and realise a global common, green and sustainable development. Based on the principle of "extensive negotiation, joint contribution and common benefit", China jointly boosts the Belt and Road construction with the international community. Therefore, the Belt and Road Initiative is not a geopolitical tool, but a tool for the global growth and prosperity. If the Belt and Road Initiative and the 2030 Agenda can be integrated successfully in the future, a new international multilateral cooperation platform is very likely to form, which will not only provide a strong impetus for the global sustainable development but also set a new model for the cooperation among all countries and regions.

Note

1 Lu Feng, Li Xin, et al., "Why is China? – Economic logics behind the B&R Initiative," *International Economic Review*, 2015, Issue 3.

80
ADDIS ABABA ACTION AGENDA WITH THE BELT AND ROAD INITIATIVE

Liu Wei

The Belt and Road Initiative mainly aims to boost global connectivity and sustainable development, and especially promote the powerful sustainable development of the global economy by continuously financing the infrastructure construction. The Addis Ababa Action Agenda (hereinafter referred to as "AAAA") is an important achievement of UN member states in jointly boosting the sustainable development, which provides a global framework for financing the sustainable development. With a common mission for boosting the global sustainable development, the Belt and Road Initiative and AAAA strengthen a strategic alignment and coordination, establish a closer international development partnership, boost the South–North Cooperation, South–South Cooperation and Triangular Cooperation, and provide a strong foundation for the global sustainable development agenda after 2015.

AAAA lays a global framework for development financing after 2015

On July 15, 2015, at the 3rd International Conference on Financing for Development of the United Nations held in Addis Ababa, capital of Ethiopia, the AAAA was reached by the member states to form a global framework for development financing after 2015. In the AAAA, a series of bold measures created for investment are included to thoroughly reform a global financial practice and solve economic, social and environmental challenges. It is a new milestone to strengthen the global cooperation partnership on environmental protection while promoting a generalised and inclusive economic prosperity and improving the people's happiness.[1]

The AAAA aims to eradicate poverty or starvation and realise sustainable development through promoting inclusive economic growth, protecting the environment and boosting social inclusiveness.[2] In order to realise such objectives, AAAA advocates all countries concerned to strengthen and revitalise the sustainable development partnership; establish an integral country financing framework; and dominate the sustainable development strategy under the consistency of international rules.

(1) To establish a framework for financing the international development and perfect a global development environment. In order to create a good international development environment, the following actions are advocated by AAAA for all countries concerned: strengthen a coordination; maintain a free open multilateral trade system; realise a multilateral trade system which is universal, rule-based, open, transparent, predictable, inclusive, non-discriminatory and fair;

and implement an active trade liberalisation.³ In the financial field, all countries concerned should perfect supervision over the financial market, maintain financial stability and establish a global financial safety network; boost the reform and perfection of global economic governance system; strengthen the dominant role of the United Nations in promoting a development; and reach a stronger, more consistent, more inclusive and representative international framework for promoting a sustainable development while respecting the authorisation of their organisations concerned.⁴ As claimed by Achim Steiner, Deputy Secretary-General of the United Nations and Executive Officer of the United Nations Environment Programme, an operable framework for the future financing system is set by AAAA, which will change the international economic layout and thus better serve mankind's needs and the future sustainable development.⁵

(2) To actively mobilise the domestic resources, and play a dominant role of local countries in boosting a sustainable development strategy. As restated in AAAA, a local country assumes fundamental responsibility for its own economic and social development, and is especially respected while observing the relevant international rules; a country autonomously formulates its national policies, makes its development strategy, tries to eradicate poverty and boosts sustainable development. At the International Conference for Development Financing, the autonomous role of developing countries is emphasised during the sustainable development, especially its core significance for sustainable development in formulating the public policies for domestic resources while considering its own autonomy and mobilising or effectively utilising domestic resources.⁶

(3) To boost an international cooperation in development and reinforce a global partnership in sustainable development. In order to remedy the insufficiency of all countries concerned in mobilising the domestic public resources, AAAA actively boosts an international public financing in various forms and reinforces an international cooperation in development. Official development assistance is promised by many developed countries at a proportion of 0.7%, and 0.15–0.20% especially for the developed countries, to its gross national income (GNI). Official development assistance is also promised by the European Union at the proportion of 0.7% to its GNI within the post-2015 Agenda deadline; 0.15–0.20% to its GNI for developed countries in the near term; and 0.20% to its GNI for developed countries within the post-2015 Agenda deadline. As also proposed in the Agenda, a triangular cooperation should be strengthened to coordinate the action of all countries concerned and improve the relevant experiences or special knowledge in development and cooperation. In the Agenda, the role of multilateral development banks and other international development banks is also highly stressed in the aspects of raising funds for sustainable development; providing a special skill; and continuing to utilise their donation and stable preferential or non-preferential development loan.

(4) To boost an innovation of financing mechanism, mobilise and utilise the resources of multiple stakeholders and expand a source channel for funds. In order to realise a sustainable development, a specific and more inclusive financing principle is proposed in AAAA. In order to extensively leverage the funds and continuously finance for the sustainable development of economic, social and environment fields, a series of measures are also specified in AAAA for reforming an investment and financing mechanism, including an elastic and excellent infrastructure investment plan into the sustainable development strategy; encouraging the investment-promoting institutes to better optimise the investment environment through project preparation and investment guidance; encouraging all countries concerned to reinforce a public–private partnership; and actively utilising the diversified financial tools (e.g. mixed financing). In order to coordinate and boost the role of multilateral development banks, national development banks, official development partners and private sectors in the financing for infrastructure construction, the Agenda also proposes that multilateral development banks should lead to establish a global infrastructure forum. In order to maximise a fund source and play the

financing function of financial products of different types, the Agenda proposes to combine and utilise different financing tools.

A diversified financing mechanism in the Belt and Road Initiative offers a solution for infrastructure financing

Continuous financing is the guarantee for a smooth implementation of the Belt and Road construction. With the characteristics of risk concentration and revenue scattering, infrastructure projects have been short of fund for a long time. As estimated by the Asian Development Bank (ADB), an investment of US$26 trillion will be needed for the infrastructure in Asia during the period of 2016–2030, i.e. an annual average of US$1.7 trillion.[7] As estimated by the Development Research Centre of the State Council of China, a total investment of at least US$10.6 trillion is required in infrastructure for the Belt and Road counties during the period of 2016–2020.[8] It is an important challenge for the Belt and Road construction to establish a set of financing mechanism for continuously financing the international infrastructure construction.

By fully absorbing the experience in Chinese infrastructure construction and boldly exploring in an innovative way, an investment and financing system suitable for infrastructure construction is gradually developed from the Belt and Road construction and a diversified investment and financing mechanism is formed under the Belt and Road Initiative. On May 14, 2017, at a parallel subject conference promoting a fund circulation to the high-level conference of the Belt and Road Forum for International Cooperation, the "Guiding principles for financing the Belt and Road construction" was jointly approved and released under the proposal and promotion of China by the Ministry of Finance of PRC and the ministries of finance of 26 other countries, such as Argentina and Belarus. By establishing a diversified investment and financing framework via mobilising the public/private sectors and matching the fund need and supply, this guiding principle provides a comprehensive protocol for breaking the bottleneck in financing to revitalise infrastructure construction and realise a sustainable development.

(1) To play the guiding role of local governments, and coordinate the entity of diversified investment and financing. The Belt and Road Initiative emphasises alignment with the development strategy of relevant countries and encourages local countries to formulate a development strategy or plan for infrastructure and provide a project financing, public service and policy guarantee for the Belt and Road construction by actively utilising their public fund. Local governments should actively guide a fund flow by aligning with a development strategy and plan and cooperating in a development financing field.[9] Meanwhile, relevant countries should continue to utilise the existing public fund channels of intergovernmental cooperation foundation and foreign assistance fund, and coordinate a fund flow from various commercial financial institutions such as policy financial institutions, export credit institutions, commercial banks, equity investing fund, insurance companies, lease companies and guarantee companies and long-term institutional investors of pension fund and sovereign wealth fund to be involved in infrastructure construction.

(2) To play a full role of development financing, and reinforce a public–private partnership. As represented by multilateral development banks and national development banks, the development financial institutions are advantageous in sustainable financing, institutional-specific technology and intelligent service. Under the Belt and Road Initiative, the development financial institutions are proposed for more financing support and technological assistance and encouraged to participate in the construction of cross-border infrastructure through various financing channels of loan, equity investment, guarantee and joint financing. Meanwhile, the development financial institutions should strengthen a cooperation/coordination with market

entity; encourage an entry of private capital; play a decisive role of market mechanism in allocating the financial resources; and realise a financing layout for joint participation between public sectors and private funds. For the Belt and Road construction, development financial institutions, national special foundations and official development assistances will actively play a catalytic role in development financing; the mode of public–private partnership (PPP) will be boosted; and the mechanism of return and risk sharing in cross-border construction will be optimised to attract the participation of more private funds.

(3) To combine the diversified financing tools and establish a multi-level investment and financing system. The Belt and Road construction projects have a diversified financing need, including loan, equity financing, bond financing, financial lease and assistance. Relevant countries are jointly establishing a multi-level financing system to finance the Belt and Road construction in a diversified way of loan, equity financing, bond financing and development assistance. Besides the ordinary loan of commercial banks and the concessional loan of development financial institutions, an equity investment becomes an important financing method, including private equity investment of shorter term; industrial funds and regional or national funds of medium and long term; and special Belt and Road funds. The Belt and Road bond financing includes governmental bonds issued by the relevant Belt and Road governmental organs in the Shanghai Stock Exchange and Shenzhen Stock Exchange; corporate bonds issued by the relevant Belt and Road enterprises and financial institutions in these 2 stock exchanges; and corporate bonds raised for the Belt and Road construction issued by the Chinese and foreign enterprises in these 2 stock exchanges. All countries concerned agree to boost the development of local currency bond market and expand the sources of medium- and long-term funding. A pilot work of Belt and Road bonds has been started in China. On March 2, 2018, the "Notice for launching the business pilot of Belt and Road bonds" was successively released by the Shanghai Stock Exchange and Shenzhen Stock Exchange. Three days later, a Belt and Road corporate bond was successfully issued by Hengyi Petrochemical Co., Ltd. The financing tools based on the Belt and Road bonds will provide a strong fund guarantee for the Belt and Road construction.[10]

(4) To specify the social responsibility of environment and reinforce a security guarantee of investment/financing. The Belt and Road financing attaches a great importance to protecting the social environment, improving the social responsibility of enterprises, and increasing the continuity of debts. By emphasising the continuity of debts, the sustainability of environment and the influence on local people's livelihood, the Belt and Road financing prevents the projects from causing or exacerbating the instability of local countries.[11] By introducing best practice in international financing, the Belt and Road financing mechanism has improved the security guarantee of investment/financing; effectively dispelled doubts of international community; and boosted the alignment with other arrangements of international development financing.

Notes

1 News from the United Nations, "Addis Ababa Action Agenda—an achievement document reached at the 3rd International Conference on Financing for Development of the United Nations in Addis Ababa." Retrieved May 1, 2018 from https://news.un.org/zh/story/2015/07/239302
2 United Nations, Addis Ababa Action Agenda of the Third International Conference on Financing for Development (Addis Ababa Action Agenda), Resolution adopted by the General Assembly on 27 July 2015 (A/RES/69/313), p. 2.
3 United Nations, Addis Ababa Action Agenda of the Third International Conference on Financing for Development (Addis Ababa Action Agenda), Resolution adopted by the General Assembly on 27 July 2015 (A/RES/69/313), p. 20.

4 United Nations, Addis Ababa Action Agenda of the Third International Conference on Financing for Development (Addis Ababa Action Agenda), Resolution adopted by the General Assembly on 27 July 2015 (A/RES/69/313), pp. 25–26; United Nations, Addis Ababa Action Agenda of the Third International Conference on Financing for Development (Addis Ababa Action Agenda), Resolution adopted by the General Assembly on 27 July 2015 (A/RES/69/313), p. 29.
5 Wang Yurang, "China initiates a boosting of innovative financing," *People's Daily*. July 19, 2015, p.3.
6 United Nations, Addis Ababa Action Agenda of the Third International Conference on Financing for Development (Addis Ababa Action Agenda), Resolution adopted by the General Assembly on 27 July 2015 (A/RES/69/313), p. 7.
7 Asian Development Bank, "Meeting Asia's infrastructure needs. Mandaluyong City," Philippines: Asian Development Bank, 2017. Retrieved March 1, 2018 from www.adb.org/sites/default/files/publication/227496/special-report-infrastructure.pdf
8 Zhang Liping (Research group of "Facility connectivity under the B&R Initiative", Development Research Center of the State Council), "Need and Chinese role in the investment and financing of the B&R infrastructure. Investigation report [No.17 (2017): (General No. 5092)],". February 15, 2017. Retrieved March 1, 2018 from www.drc.gov.cn/n/20170215/1-224-2892687.htm
9 Liu Wei, "Solution for infrastructure financing provided by the diversified financing mechanism under the B&R Initiative." Retrieved May 30, 2017 from www.china.org.cn
10 Wang Siwen, "Quota of the B&R bonds to be further enlarged," *Securities Daily*, March 7, 2018, Column B1.
11 Yao Zhizhong, "Breaking the bottleneck in the B&R construction," *Guangming Daily*, May 28, 2017, Column 07.

81

AFRICAN AGENDA 2063 WITH THE BELT AND ROAD INITIATIVE

Xiao He

Proposal and implementation

In May 2013, the 21st African Conference of Heads of State and Government was held in Addis Ababa, the capital city of Ethiopia. 2013 also marked the 50th Anniversary of the founding of the Organisation of African Unity, nowadays known as the African Union (AU). In order to celebrate the independence of African countries and the founding of the AU, accelerate the development of the African continent and strengthen cooperation among African countries, all attending heads of state and government discussed and determined a strategic framework document, i.e. the African Agenda 2063 (hereinafter referred to as "the Agenda"), which defines the transformation of the African economy and society over the next 50 years, and mainly including the African Aspirations for 2063. In the Agenda, the content of several long-term development plans are absorbed or combined: the Lagos Plan of Action; the Abuja Treaty; the Minimum Integration Programme; the Programme for Infrastructural Development in Africa (PIDA); the Comprehensive Africa Agricultural Development Programme (CAADP); and the New Partnership for Africa's Development (NEPAD).[1]

At subsequent AU conferences of heads of state and government, the framework and contents of the Agenda were continuously improved and implemented. In June 2015, at the 25th Conference of Heads of State and Government of AU in Johannesburg, the capital city of South Africa, the Draft First Ten-Year Implementation Plan was formulated for the Agenda. In January 2018, at the 30th Conference of Heads of State and Government of AU in Addis Ababa, the Single African Air Transportation Market as the first flagship project of the Agenda was started as a major decision on its implementation, when 23 AU member states announced to implement the project immediately. This action has strongly implemented the objective in the Agenda to remove an entry barrier for air transportation among African countries and realise the liberalisation of civil aviation.[2]

After the continuous improvement, the current agenda aims to establish a united, prosperous and peaceful Africa through the African people themselves, and become an active force at the international stage. The conceptual basis for the Agenda is mainly sourced from the Constitutive Act of the African Union; the African Union Vision; The 8 Priority Areas of AU 50th Anniversary Solemn Declaration; and African Aspirations for 2063. With the most direct correlation and the greatest influence, African Aspirations for 2063 mainly specifies 7 objectives: (1) a prosperous

Africa on the basis of inclusive growth and sustainable development; (2) an integral continent of political unity on the basis of pan-Africanism and African revitalisation; (3) Africa with good governance, democracy, respecting human rights, justice and the legal system; (4) a peaceful and safe Africa; (5) Africa with a profound cultural recognition, and a common historical heritage, view of values and code of ethics; (6) Africa will be developed through the impetus of the African people and their potential, especially women, youth and children; and (7) Africa will become a strong, united, perseverant and influential international actor and partner.[3]

At present, the following projects have been determined as priority areas: the AU Flagship Projects/Programmes; key fields in the plans of other countries/regions; intercontinental cooperation framework such as PIDA and CAADP; and AU conference resolutions like Silence the Guns by 2020. In the AU Flagship Projects/Programmes, various fields are covered from infrastructure construction, technological innovation, trade and finance to people-to-people exchange: unifying the AU electronic passport; single African air transportation market; pan-African high-speed railway network; African virtual and network universities; pan-African internet; intercontinental financial facilities; African outer space strategy; African strategy for daily necessities; intercontinental free trade zone, annual African forum; and Great Inga hydro-power station project.[4]

Alignment of the Belt and Road Initiative with the 2063 Agenda

China keeps a close and deep long-term partnership with African countries in trade, people exchange and economy. After the proposal of the Belt and Road Initiative, Africa naturally becomes an important partner under this framework. Both sides show a strong interest in aligning the Belt and Road Initiative with the Agenda. In May 2014, not long after the proposal of the Initiative, Premier Li Keqiang visited 4 African countries including Ethiopia and paid a visit to Addis Ababa, the headquarters of the AU. Premier Li Keqiang proposed the "4-6-1 items" of Sino-African cooperation framework in Addis Ababa, i.e. adhere to 4 principles of equal treatment, united and mutual trust, inclusive development and innovative cooperation; boost 6 cooperation programmes in industry, finance, poverty reduction, ecological and environmental protection, people-to-people exchange and peace/security; and perfect the important platform of Forum on Sino-African Cooperation to upgrade the cooperation between China and Africa. As especially emphasised by Premier Li Keqiang, China wishes to support Africa with finance, people and technology in the high-speed railway, road and regional aviation network.[5] These Chinese proposals share the important content of the AU flagship projects in the Agenda. Meanwhile, this visit unveiled the prologue for both sides to align the Belt and Road Initiative with the Agenda.

Half a year later in January 2015, a memorandum of understanding on 3 networks and 1 industrialidation of African traffic and infrastructure (high-speed railway, expressway, regional aviation network and infrastructure industrialisation) was jointly signed by Zhang Ming, a special envoy of the Chinese government and Deputy Minister of the Ministry of Foreign Affairs of PRC and Dlamini Zuma, chairman of the African Union Commission.

In December 2015, the Forum on Sino-African Cooperation was held in Johannesburg, the first time it had been held in an African country after it was founded in 2000.[6] At the 15th anniversary of this forum, such arrangement demonstrated China's focus on the development and cooperation of China and Africa after the Belt and Road Initiative was proposed, and also showed the emphasis on the entity of African countries in this cooperation. This forum was jointly presided over by Xi Jinping, Chairman of China and Jacob Zuma, President of South Africa, attended by 42 heads of state and government and 52 representatives of member states.

Two documents were signed: the Declaration of the Johannesburg Summit of the Forum on Sino-African Cooperation; and the Action Plan of the Johannesburg Summit of the Forum on Sino-African Cooperation (2016–2018). At the opening speech of the forum, Chairman Xi Jinping comprehensively elaborated to upgrade the new strategic partnership into an overall strategic partnership between China and Africa; and deeply align the framework and mode of the Belt and Road Initiative with the Agenda. Meanwhile, 10 cooperation plans were also proposed for the next 3 years: (1) an industrialisation cooperation plan, to build and upgrade a batch of industrial parks in Africa; establish a relevant competence centre; and train the technical staff; (2) an agricultural modernisation cooperation plan, to encourage Chinese agricultural enterprises to develop in Africa; transfer agricultural technologies; increase the income of local farmers; jointly establish an agricultural scientific research cooperation mechanism; and provide emergency food assistance to countries stricken by agricultural disaster; (3) an infrastructure cooperation plan, to support Chinese enterprises in actively participating in the planning, design, construction, operation and maintenance of African infrastructure; and cooperate to build 5 traffic universities; (4) a financial cooperation plan, to expand the bilateral business of RMB settlement and local currency swap business; and encourage Chinese financial institutions to open branch offices in Africa; (5) a green development cooperation plan, to support Africa in strengthening a green, low-carbon and sustainable development ability; (6) a trade and investment facilitation cooperation plan, to implement 50 trade-promoting assistance projects; and support Africa in improving the soft and hard conditions for trade and investment; (7) a poverty-reduction and people-benefiting cooperation plan, to increase the assistance to Africa; implement a poverty-reduction project with women and children as the main beneficiaries; exempt the relevant developed African countries from intergovernmental interest-free loan debt; (8) a public health cooperation plan, to support Africa in constructing a public health system; assist Africa with some medicines; and encourage Chinese pharmaceutical enterprises to produce locally in Africa; (9) a humanistic cooperation plan, to support the construction of 5 cultural centres; provide 2000 education quotas of academic credential/degree and 30,000 quotas of government scholarship; annually organise 200 African scholars to visit China and 500 African youth to go for further studies; assist to train journalists; and actively launch a bilateral direct flight and travel; and (10) a peace and security cooperation plan, to loan the AU US$60 million for weapons; support the AU in constructing and operating a standing army and crisis response force; support the United Nations' peacekeeping operation in Africa; and support African countries in constructing security competence. In addition, in order to implement these 10 cooperation plans, China will grant a total of US$60 billion of financial assistance and support: free assistance and interest-free loan of US$5 billion; concessional loan and export credit limit of US$35 billion; another S$5 billion to the Sino-African Development Fund and a special loan for the development of African small and medium-sized enterprises separately; and set-up of the first batch of the US$10 billion fund as the Sino-African Fund for Industrial Cooperation.[7]

Alignment achievement and influence of the Belt and Road Initiative with the Agenda

According to the incomplete statistics, since the 10 cooperation plans were proposed at the Johannesburg Summit, more than 250 economic and trade cooperation agreements valued over US$50 billion have been signed by both sides. Meanwhile, China has become the largest trade partner of Africa, with an investment/financing inventory of more than US$100 billion in Africa.[8] In 4 early model countries of China–Africa industrial cooperation of Kenya, Ethiopia, Tanzania and Congo, more than 10 projects have been approved by the China–Africa Fund for

Industrial Cooperation, with a total investment amount of more than US$1.07 billion. Various landmark flagship projects like the Addis Ababa–Djibouti Railway and the Mombasa–Nairobi Railway have been completed and put into operation. Up to 2018, more than 100 industrial parks have been completed, are under construction or at construction preparation by China in Africa, 40 of which have been put into operation. The Ethiopia Oriental Industrial Park, Suez Economic & Trade Cooperation Zone in Egypt and Nigeria Lekki Industrial Park have played a significant active role in realising an industrial transfer, improving local employment and improving the foreign exchange earning ability of African countries.[9]

The alignment of the Belt and Road Initiative and the Agenda is an economic cooperation on the fully equal basis. China not only highly respects the individual wishes and plans of the African countries, but also actively supports the development blueprint of African countries while observing the principle of "righteousness going before benefit" and "righteousness weighing over benefit". These Chinese actions greatly benefit African countries as follows: they really grasp the initiative of development; they boycott the Western developed countries against indiscreet criticism over or interference in their economic and social development; they provide a good environment and the necessary economic support for exploring and deepening their reform and opening-up; and they facilitate the formation of an independent and autonomous "African road".[10] As the Chinese economy develops continuously and the alignment is continuously deepened for the development proposal between China and Africa, the favour of the African people is increasingly won for the Chinese development mode to stress a national function of public management and a construction of national ability. During the construction of competent development-oriented nation and the realisation of the plan stipulated in the Agenda, China has become an important target for African countries to refer to and learn from.[11]

In February 2018, in order to meet the realistic need of rapid development in the China–Africa cooperation relation, the Forum on China–Africa Cooperation to be held in Beijing, China in September 2018 was jointly announced by Wang Yi, Foreign Minister of China and Moussa Faki Mahamat, President of the African Union Commission paying a visit to China to be upgraded to the Beijing Summit of the China–Africa Cooperation. As especially specified by Minister Wang Yi, the Belt and Road Initiative would be further aligned with the Agenda to better combine African development with Chinese development, Eurasian continent revitalisation and such trends as regional integration and economic globalisation.[12]

Notes

1 African Union, "About Agenda 2063," https://au.int/en/agenda2063/about
2 Cooperation and Exchange Office of the Mission of the People's Republic of China to the Africa Union. Formal initiation of Single African Air Transportation Market. January 30, 2018. http://africanunion.mofcom.gov.cn/article/jmxw/201801/20180102706410.shtml
3 Africa Union, "About Agenda 2063," https://au.int/en/agenda2063/about
4 Ibid.
5 "Premier Li Keqiang proposes 4-6-1 cooperation framework to create an upgraded version of China–African cooperation," China News Network, May 6, 2014. www.chinanews.com/gn/2014/05-06/6135600.shtml
6 Shu Yunguo, "The B&R Initiative and African Aspirations for 2063: new opportunity for China–African development cooperation," *Contemporary World*, December 2015, p. 5.
7 Xi Jinping, "Speech at the opening ceremony of Johannesburg Summit of the Forum on China–Africa Cooperation: starting a new era of cooperation double-win and common development between China and Africa," Xinhua Network, December 4, 2015, www.xinhuanet.com/world/2015-12/04/c_1117363197.htm

8 He Wenping, "China–African relationship at a golden stage and mature stage," *People's Daily* (overseas edition), February 10, 2018, Column 1.
9 Zhang Zhuomin, "China–African cooperation in production capacity: possibly as new hot point in the future 5 years," *International Business Daily*, January 8, 2018.
10 Liu Qingjian, "Utilization of African Aspirations for 2063 and development aid: Chinese experience and EU's role," *Contemporary World*, 2015, 12, p. 21.
11 Njonga Michael Mulikita, "Constructing a competent development-oriented country in Arica: basic motion for realizing the African Aspirations for 2063," *African Studies*, 2015,Volume 1.
12 "Beijing Forum on China–Africa Cooperation (September) to plan a blueprint of China–African cooperation in a new era," Forum on China–Africa Cooperation, February 11, 2018, www.mfa.gov.cn/zflt/chn/zxxx/t1533993.htm

82
ANCIENT CIVILISATIONS FORUM WITH THE BELT AND ROAD INITIATIVE

Xiao He

Founding of the Forum

During the period of April 24–25, 2017, the 1st Ministerial Conference of Ancient Civilisations Forum (hereinafter referred to as "the Forum") was held in Athens, the capital city of Greece, which was jointly sponsored and organised by Greece and China. Representatives from 10 countries—Greece, China, Egypt, Iran, Iraq, Italy, India, Mexico, Peru and Bolivia—attended the Forum. In Greece, the Forum is also called "Great Civilizations 10".[1] Among 10 ten attending countries, 6 other than Mexico and India attached great importance to the Forum by assigning their officials at the level of minister or deputy minister to attend this conference: Wang Yi, Minister of Foreign Affairs of the People's Republic of China; Sameh Shukry, Minister of Foreign Affairs of Arabia Republic of Egypt; Nikos Kotzias, Minister of Foreign Affairs of the Hellenic Republic; Mohammad Javad Zarif, Minister of Foreign Affairs of the Islamic Republic of Iran; Ibrahim al-Jaafari, Minister of Foreign Affairs of the Republic of Iraq; Angelino Alfano, Minister of Foreign Affairs of the Republic of Italy; Del Solar, Minister of Culture of the Republic of Peru; and Guadalupe Palomeque, Deputy Minister of the Plurinational State of Bolivia. The 1st Ministerial Conference of the Forum was jointly presided over by Minister Nikos Kotzias and Minister Wang Yi.

At this conference, Athens Declaration on the Establishment of the Ancient Civilisations Forum was passed (hereinafter referred to as "this declaration"). As specified in this declaration, the abundant and diversified cultural heritages in great ancient civilisations always play a decisive role in the proceedings of human development, and all countries concerned are obliged to protect their cultural heritage by themselves or through international cooperation with the United Nations Educational, Scientific and Cultural Organisation (UNESCO), and other special sectors of the United Nations or programmes. In this declaration, the following actions are emphasised: strengthen the protection of cultural relics, archeological vestiges and cultural heritage; attack the smuggling of cultural relics; stop terrorism against cultural heritage; stress the civilisation and culture as a soft strength; promote mutual understanding, acceptance and magnanimity among different cultures and nationalities through the interaction and exchange of civilisation; and meet the challenge of international community in cultural, social, economic and political fields. In the organisational structure of this forum, 8 countries were announced as the official initiating countries of the Ancient Civilisations Forum—Bolivia, China, Egypt,

Greece, Iran, Iraq, Italy and Peru. With an open identity, the member states of this forum will rotate as the rotating presiding country of its annual ministerial conference, and strengthen cooperation with relevant international institutions such as UNESCO. The ministerial conference of this forum of 2018 will be held in Bolivia. Peru and Iraq also wish to undertake the ministerial conference in 2020 and 2021, respectively.[2]

Greece and China are both the initialling countries of this forum. However, Greece is its earliest and most active advocator; and this forum is initiated by Greece as one of multilateral cultural diplomatic proposals according to its geographic position and cultural resources. Besides this forum, two conferences were initiated and presided over by Nikos Kotzias, the current Minister of Greece: the International Conference on Religious and Cultural Pluralism and Peaceful Coexistence in the Middle East (abbreviated as the "International Religion Conference") in Athens in October 2015, and the Conference for Security and Stability in the East Mediterranean (abbreviated as the "Rhodes Island Conference") in Rhodes Island in September 2016. These two conferences aim to promote exchange, coexistence and cooperation among different civilisation communities by fully utilising the geographic position of Greece as the converging place of different civilisations and its profound historic culture; and fully play the influence of Greece in cultural diplomacy. At present, the 2 conferences have been held, respectively, twice in Greece. At the 2nd Rhodes Island Conference, there were 15 countries from the East Mediterranean and the Middle East, with representatives from the League of Arab States and the Gulf Cooperation Council.[3] Through these mechanisms of multilateral cultural diplomacy, Greece has also won greater regional influence.

The concept and founding of this forum are also boosted by Minister Nikos Kotzias. At the beginning of 2015, Greece started to consider and prepare to establish the international cultural exchange mechanism with Athens as the centre, which was actively favoured by Italy and Egypt. Subsequently, such establishment was responded successively by Mexico, China and India. China especially expressed its support to boost the initiative. After obtaining the support of these 5 countries, at the 1st International Religion Conference held in Athens, Minister Nikos Kotzias officially proposed to launch a secretariat for international civilisation exchange, which planned to invite 10 countries with longest history.[4] Finally, this proposal developed into a cooperation framework of the Ancient Civilisations Forum. Subsequently, Iraq, Iran, Bolivia and Peru were invited as its founding member states.

Birth of the Ancient Civilisations Forum by the Belt and Road Initiative

As a founding member state and co-initialling country of this forum, China plays an important role in founding and operating such a new mechanism of international cultural and civilisation exchange. China and Greece closely cooperate under the framework of this forum to realise: an important action to boost both sides in deepening a bilateral cooperation from the surface to the centre, and from the outside to the inside under the Belt and Road framework; an important step to boost the people interlinking in these two countries; a precious achievement through the persistent and deep economic and trade cooperation of both sides under the Belt and Road framework for many years, especially after the outbreak of the Western financial crisis and Greek debt crisis; and a significant role of China-proposed connectivity in enhancing an intercountry relations.

On the one hand, this declaration emphasises the Greeks' Olympic Games and peaceful spirits; boosts the Belt and Road Initiative for international cooperation; and affirms the important role of the Belt and Road Initiative in promoting a dialogue of intercivilisation and realising people interlinking. This standpoint embodies a mutual response, mutual support and mutual referring between Eastern and Western spiritual cultures. At the keynote speech, Minister Wang Yi praised that this forum initialled by Greece, with Greece playing an active role under the international situation of increasing uncertainty; pointed out that the spirit of this forum for treating a cultural and civilisation exchange is of the same origin as that of Silk Road, promoting peace, cooperation, openness, inclusiveness, mutual learning, mutual referencing, mutual benefit and win–win. This forum can also provide precious support and cultural assistance for the Belt and Road construction. Moreover, Minister Wang Yi especially elaborated how to combine the historic identity of ancient civilisations with the people interlinking proposed by the Belt and Road Initiative: (1) "as an ancient civilization, we should realize more deeply than other countries that each civilization is not discriminated in high or low level and superiority or inferiority, but all are worth respecting/cherishing"; (2) "as a globally-representative original ancient civilization, we should more actively advocate a dialogue and interaction among civilizations; oppose a conflict and rejection of civilization; strive to transcend a difference and discrimination in social system and ideology; and enhance the mutual understanding and trust among the people of all countries concerned".[5]

On the other hand, as the co-initialling countries and co-organisers, China and Greece held the Ancient Civilisations Forum. It shows that the 2 countries not only have similar opinions on civilisation, culture and peaceful coexistence, but also their bilateral trust in politics and culture have reached a certain level. Such a high level of cooperation and trust is absolutely not inherent or a matter of course, but an achievement through the persistent all-round cooperation between China and Greece. After the outbreak of the financial crisis in 2008, China obviously increased investment in European countries with Greece included, especially in their large-scale infrastructure so as to better combine Chinese funds and technologies with the intrinsic advantages of a local country. Especially, as a predominant project, the Piraeus Port project of Greece is smoothly implemented despite some twists and turns.

In July 2016, several days after the Piraeus Port project was approved by the Hellenic Parliament, Alexis Tsipras, Premier of Greece, went to Beijing to start his visit to China. He successively met with Li Keqiang, Premier of China and Xi Jinping, Chairman of China. During their meeting, Chairman Xi Jinping expressed that: (1) Piraeus Port should be built to be the largest container transshipment harbour in the Mediterranean Sea, a bridgehead of sea–land combined transportation and an important pivot of the Belt and Road cooperation; (2) by fully utilising common ground as ancient civilisations, both countries should strengthen a mutual referencing to take humanistic exchange as a bridge and tie for communication between people of both countries. As specified by Premier Alexis Tsipras, Greece will cooperate in aligning the Greek's development strategy with China's Belt and Road Initiative, and play a pivotal role in connecting the east with the west in the fields of energy and transportation[6] during the economic and social revitalisation, and emphasise cooperation in cultural and technological fields. This visit also became a milestone in determining that China and Greece will carry out an overall cooperation under the Belt and Road framework.[7] This forum is exactly a major achievement and a new starting point for both sides to continuously deepen bilateral connectivity, especially the people interlinking through such route.

Great potential prospect for aligning with the Belt and Road Initiative

At the eve of the Belt and Road Summit Forum for International Cooperation, the 1st Ministerial Conference of Ancient Civilisations Forum was held in 2017. Therefore, the 2 meetings coordinated with and complemented each other. Minister Nikos Kotzias, a main impeller of this forum, metaphored the Belt and Road Summit Forum for International

Cooperation and this forum as 2 sides of the same coin: the Belt and Road Initiative will build a continuous and feasible cooperation network in various fields, including infrastructure, traffic and energy so as to guarantee a general spillover effect for connectivity and mutual dependence; this forum will consolidate a common cultural basis and characteristics of all countries concerned to trigger a wish for further cooperation. As "twin engines" of this forum, both countries should facilitate more cooperation through the interaction between this forum and the Belt and Road Summit Forum for International Cooperation.[8] In other words, as one of the objectives, this forum consolidates and enriches the connectivity under the Belt and Road framework through cultural exchange.

This forum was also presided over by Minister Wang Yi. On May 13, Premier Alexis Tsipras came to Beijing and attended the Belt and Road Summit Forum for International Cooperation. At this visit and meeting, Chairman Xi Jinping raised that as important representatives of the Eastern and Western civilisations, both countries should fully utilise the advantages of profound culture; continuously exploit the potential for humanistic cooperation between the 2 countries; and boost the exchange and dialogue of different civilisations by making full use of this forum as a new platform. As a breakthrough point, Piraeus Port will be built to be an important container transshipment port in the Mediterranean Sea; a bridgehead of sea–land combined transportation; an international logistic allocation centre; and an important pivotal role in the China–Europe Land–Sea Express Route and the Belt and Road construction. As responded by Premier Alexis Tsipras, Greece will, with great pleasure, participate in the cooperation of the Belt and Road construction; under the new situation, both sides as ancient civilisations should boost extensive and pragmatic cooperation in the economic, investment, financial, energy, agricultural and new technological fields.[9] At this visit, both sides agreed to reaffirm an active relation of mutual promotion and mutual support between civilisation communication and pragmatic cooperation; and consolidate a consensus of cooperation between 2 countries and between both initiatives. In the future, Greece will continue to become an important communication bridge between China and the European Union, and act as an exchange hub among different civilisations to participate in the Belt and Road Initiative and promote its continuous deepening. Therefore, a strategic alignment between this forum and the Belt and Road Initiative will certainly create an enormous potential and strong vitality.

Notes

1 GC-10, " New initiative of the Hellenic Ministry of Foreign Affairs," Hellenic Chinese Centre for Entrepreneurship, www.chinese-center.gr/gc-10-new-initiative-ministry-foreign-affairs/.
2 Athens Declaration for Establishing the Ancient Civilisations Forum. Ministry of Foreign Affairs of PRC. April 28, 2017. www.fmprc.gov.cn/web/ziliao_674904/1179_674909/t1457692.shtml.
3 Second Conference for Security and Stability (Rhodes, 22–23 May 2017). Hellenic Republic Ministry of Foreign Affairs, 21 May 2017, www.mfa.gr/en/current-affairs/news-announcements/second-conference-for-security-and-stability-rhodes-22-23-may-2017.html; "Second International Conference on 'Religious and Cultural Pluralism and Peaceful Coexistence in the Middle East' (Athens, 30–31 October 2017)," Hellenic Republic Ministry of Foreign Affairs, 27 October 2017, www.mfa.gr/en/current-affairs/statements-speeches/second-international-conference-on-religious-and-cultural-pluralism-and-peaceful-coexistence-in-the-middle-east-athens-30-31-october-2017.html.
4 "New initiative of the Ministry of Foreign Affairs," *Independent Balkan News Agency*, October 25, 2015, www.balkaneu.com/initiative-ministry-foreign-affairs/
5 Wang Yi, "Speech at the 1st Ancient Civilizations Forum: revitalizing the ancient civilization and jointly constructing a community of shared future for mankind," Ministry of Foreign Affairs of PRC. May 2, 2017. http://gjjls.seac.gov.cn/art/2017/5/2/art_8277_280053.html

6 "Chairman Xi Jinping meeting Alexis Tsipras (premier of Greece)," Xinhua Network. July 5, 2016. www.xinhuanet.com/politics/2016-07/05/c_1119169554.htm
7 "Piraeus Port is just a starting: as the dragon head of Greece–Chinese cooperation is raised, the whole body will rise accordingly," Chinese Embassy in Greece. July 4, 2016. www.fmprc.gov.cn/ce/cegr/chn/ztlm1/qplszlfwzg/t1377193.htm
8 "Special interview of Nikos Kotzias (foreign minister of Greece)," Huanqiu Network. April 23, 2017. http://world.huanqiu.com/hot/2017-04/10526413.html
9 "Chairman Xi Jinping meeting Alexis Tsipras (premier of Greece)," *People's Daily*. May 14, 2017, Column 2.

83
CONNECTIVITY BLUEPRINT OF ASIA–PACIFIC ECONOMIC COOPERATION WITH THE BELT AND ROAD INITIATIVE

Liu Wei

Proposal

In October 2013, at the 21st APEC Economic Leaders' Meeting held in Bali, Indonesia, 3 topics were discussed: Bogor goal, connectivity and sustainable and fair growth. Then, connectivity formally entered the agenda of APEC, and became a breakthrough point for boosting the Asia–Pacific regional cooperation. At this conference, 3 connectivity pillars of hardware, software and people exchange were proposed to realise the objective of a seamless overall connectivity and integrity of Asia–Pacific region. Moreover, 2 achievement documents were passed: APEC Connectivity Framework and APEC Multi-Year Plan on Infrastructure Development and Investment. In September and October 2013, the cooperation initiative to construct the New Silk Road Economic Belt and the 21st Century Maritime Silk Road was proposed by Xi Jinping, Chairman of China in Kazakhstan and Indonesia, respectively. The Belt and Road Initiative mainly aims to promote the construction and connectivity of infrastructure, and realise a linking and synergic development.

In November 2014, China served as the host country of APEC conference to further boost a connectivity agenda. At the 22nd APEC Economic Leaders' Meeting held in Beijing, China, 1 of 3 key topics was to strengthen an overall connectivity and infrastructure construction. By expanding and deepening two achievement documents passed at the APEC in Indonesia, the Connectivity Blueprint of Asia–Pacific Economic Cooperation (hereinafter referred to as "this blueprint") was approved at APEC in Beijing. In this blueprint, an action plan in 3 fields of hardware connectivity, software connectivity and people exchange was proposed to realise the seamless connectivity of the Asia–Pacific region by 2025.[1] As mentioned in this blueprint, despite much progress in promoting the connectivity, APEC still faced great challenges. In terms of hardware connectivity, the Asia–Pacific region is yet unbalanced in the popularisation and quality of infrastructure and ICT facilities. In terms of software connectivity, due to management limits and the ability gap, the existing regulations are as yet insufficient to promote connectivity. In terms of people-to-people connectivity, a joint effort should be made to reduce the barrier of people exchange/flow and promote a smooth flow of persons.

Therefore, the "Vision of connectivity in 2025" is proposed by APEC with the following objectives: accomplish the initiatives and indices jointly determined by all countries concerned by 2025; strengthen the connectivity of hardware, software and people exchange; and realise a long-term objective of seamless overall connection and merging of Asia–Pacific. In the new action plan, directional guidance is specified for the next action in strengthening the connectivity of hardware, software and people exchange.[2] In terms of hardware, the APEC member states will improve the investment environment; strengthen the financing of APEC economies in the infrastructure fields of energy, ICT and traffic transportation through the public–private partnership (PPP) and other channels; and help the region break a fund bottleneck in connectivity construction. During the process, the member states will strengthen the operation of good practice; and actively boost the financial minister mechanism and APEC PPP expert consulting group for knowledge sharing and ability construction. In terms of software, the APEC member states will take joint actions to solve major problems in the fields of trade facilitation, structure and regulation reform; traffic and logistic facilitation to realise a modernisation of customs and border management organs; establish a single-window system in each economy by 2020; promote the mutual applicability and paperless trade in each single-window system; strengthen the alignment and cooperation of regulations by sharing best practice, regulations and case study; and continue to boost the implementation of relevant plans like APEC Multi-Year Project on Business Facilitation. In terms of people exchange, the APEC member states will be devoted to facilitate a cross-border flow of people and an exchange of innovative concepts; promise to continue to expand the quantity and function of APEC Business Travel Card holders; boost the cooperation in cross-border education; relax the restriction of travel visas; simplify the procedure of customs clearance; strengthen the cultural exchange activity of APEC; boost the cross-border exchange of technology and innovation; and establish the professional qualification standard for traffic and logistic industry. Finally, this blueprint proposed to accelerate the connectivity implementation through boosting an ability construction, enhancing the cooperation with private sectors and strengthening such means as supervision, assessment and review.

Implementation status

In November 2015, at the 23rd APEC Economic Leaders' Meeting held in Manila, Philippines, the relevant documents and assessment mechanisms were passed through the discussion of all countries concerned to implement the "APEC Connectivity Blueprint (2015–2025)" and specify the development direction of regional connectivity for the next 10 years in the Asia–Pacific region. The APEC member states actively take a collective or autonomous action to implement this blueprint.

(1) APEC has made active progress in implementing the initiative for facilitation of doing business. As a new grand objective issued by member states in the "Action plan for business-doing facilitation (2016–2018)", the facilitation degree of doing business will be improved by 10% before 2018 in 5 existing priority fields of pioneering, grant of building permit, cross-border trade, credit obtaining and contract performance. On the basis of this objective, all countries concerned formulate a concrete implementation protocol for this action plan, perform relevant formalities and join the WTO Trade Facilitation Agreement to reduce the cost of cross-border trade.

In order to improve the efficiency of customs clearance and reduce the trade cost, China advocates under the framework of APEC to establish the Asia–Pacific Model E-port Network (APMEN), which aims to realise a data connectivity and interavailability among supply chain systems. APMEN has been regarded by the APEC Commission on Trade and Investment as a core component in the APEC framework of trade facilitation, and has become an important programme to boost the trade connectivity under the APEC framework. After running for 3 years,

APMEN has gradually transited from the stage of preliminary establishment to the stage of substantial cooperation and has been well recognised by APEC leaders.[3] The operation centre of APMEN is located in Shanghai, China. At present, APMEN has been joined with 14 electronic ports or harbours in 10 economies of APEC member states like China and Vietnam. In the future, the construction of APMEN will boost the connectivity and interavailability of data among supply chain systems; provide a high-quality and high-efficiency information and technological service for ports in the Asia–Pacific region; and realise a transparency of supply chain information and an integration of port information platform and single-window platform in the Asia–Pacific region. By constructing an electronic port network, the APEC member states will further implement the WTO Trade Facilitation Agreement and the Action Plan for Supply-Chain Connectivity Framework—a proposal framework for the second stage from 2017 to 2020. In addition, the APEC member economies are encouraged to initiate the construction projects of new ability related to the implementation of the above agreement and the proposal framework, including APEC Supply Chain Union; and APEC Cooperation Network of Green Supply Chain.

(2) APEC actively boosts a fund circulation and standard consistency between the member states to leverage a regional trade and dredge an investment channel. In order to further explore the financing channel for the development and cooperation in the Asia–Pacific region and break the financing bottleneck in the infrastructure construction, APEC actively develops the PPP mode; extensively mobilises the private capital to participate in the infrastructure construction; fosters the capital market; explores a long-term infrastructure investment; improves the quality of investment opportunity; and strengthens an inclusive infrastructure construction during the urban development and regional connectivity. In order to reduce the obstruction of different standards for regional trade and investment, APEC actively boosts the standard consistency in the region, especially in ICT and emerging technological fields, the digital economy and its relevant trade and investment activities, and a peer review mechanism and ability construction in the construction and investment of infrastructure.

(3) APEC actively boosts a people flow in the Asia–Pacific region. APEC actively boosts a sustainable tourism industry, promotes a facilitation of cross-border travel and actively plays the role of tourism industry in the economic development of remote areas. In the Declaration of the 25th APEC Economic Leaders' Meeting, the APEC member states promised to receive 800 million tourists in the Asia–Pacific region before 2025; actively authorise distribution of the APEC Business Travel Card; and promote facilitation of visa granting and customs clearance for business travellers. Moreover, an important field for APEC is to boost the people flow through cross-border education and scientific research cooperation. As a vision plan in the education field, the "APEC Education Strategy 2016–2030" jointly formulated by the APEC member states actively boosts the cooperation in education field; actively releases the measures for facilitating and rewarding the studying abroad in the region; strives to realise annually 1 million people for cross-border exchange in the Asia–Pacific region before 2020; and greatly improves the level and scope of scientific research cooperation in the region. The Australian Council for Educational Research (ACER) studied the collaboration among research persons from 21 APEC economies, and found that during the period of 2011–2015, more than 680,000 publications (9%) were finished through a coordination and cooperation by APEC researchers, and the proportion of joint publication among APEC economies increased greatly at an overall growth rate of 24%.[4]

Strategic alignment between this blueprint and the Belt and Road Initiative

Connectivity is an important topic for APEC and the Belt and Road Initiative. Many Asia–Pacific economies are both APEC member states and important participating countries of the

Belt and Road Initiative. With a member overlapping and complementary cooperation field, the Belt and Road Initiative and the APEC connectivity agenda lay a solid foundation for their strategic alignment. The participating countries of both APEC and the Belt and Road Initiative all express to actively boost the coordination and alignment of connectivity proposal in various fields and strive to improve the cooperation level of connectivity.

APEC actively boosts the subregional connectivity and interinitiative coordination through the forum and working groups; actively initiates and implements the "Action plan for the coordination between the member economies of APEC and the Global Infrastructure Hub"; and implements the coordination between different initiatives as alignment and cooperation among different infrastructure connectivity projects in this region. Under the APEC framework, the APEC member states put efforts in constructing a cross-border traffic transportation system, establishing the Asia–Pacific Model E-port Network, implementing the "APEC framework for the facilitation of cross-border electronic commerce", perfecting the policy environment of electronic commerce; and establishing the APEC cooperation network of green supply chain, which mutually complements and assists the measures of the Belt and Road countries for trade facilitation and supply chain connectivity.

All participants of the Belt and Road construction actively boost the alignment and coordination between different connectivity initiatives and development strategies, and strive to realise an integral sustainable development framework. In the Joint Communiqué of Leaders' Roundtable of the Belt and Road Forum for International Cooperation, the heads of states concerned emphasise that a communication/coordination between the international, regional and national cooperation frameworks and initiatives can bring about a cooperation opportunity in boosting the connectivity and sustainable development. It is proposed to strengthen an international cooperation between the Belt and Road Initiative and various development strategies and establish a closer partnership. Five long-term approaches in the Belt and Road Initiative, i.e. policy coordination, infrastructure connectivity, unimpeded trade, financial integration and understanding between people, coincide with 3 pillar fields in the action plan of this blueprint, i.e. hardware connectivity, software connectivity and people exchange. Therefore, both initiatives complement and promote each other and jointly boost an integration and sustainable development of regional economy in the Asia–Pacific region. The Belt and Road construction greatly improves the cooperation level between China and Asia–Pacific countries in various fields, and actively supports the APEC member states in realising the objective of connectivity and sustainable development. Both initiatives are not only highly consistent in the objective and realisation route of connectivity, but also highly integrated in reshaping the agenda of regional cooperation and sustainable development, so as to provide a new impetus for the cooperation and common development in the Asia–Pacific region.

Notes

1 Ming Yuan, "Implementing the connectivity blueprint, and activating the Asia–Pacific economy," *Guangming Daily*, November 11, 2017, column 06.
2 See APEC Connectivity Blueprint (2015–2025). *China Youth Daily*, November 12, 2014, column 07.
3 Ministry of Commerce of PRC, "Third public–private dialogue on the Asia–Pacific Model E-port Network," Central Government Portal. Retrieved March 1, 2018 from www.gov.cn/xinwen/2017-05/19/content_5195344.htm
4 Ali Radloff, "Mapping Researcher Mobility: Measuring research collaboration among APEC economies," Asia–Pacific Economic Cooperation (APEC), Singapore, 2017.

84

ASEAN COMMUNITY VISION 2025 WITH THE BELT AND ROAD INITIATIVE

Xue Li and Liu Tianyi

Conceptual description and subject contents

The ASEAN Community Vision 2025 (hereinafter referred to as "this vision") is an important document for promoting an integration of ASEAN. As an economic cooperation deepens increasingly among ASEAN countries, especially after the outbreak of the Asian economic crisis from 1997 to 1998, ASEAN realises that regional stability and development can only be guaranteed through strengthening the cooperation in political, economic, security, social and cultural fields and establishing various mechanisms for coping with external impact. Therefore, the ASEAN Community was established, which is similar to the European Union. In September 1997, the ASEAN Vision 2020 was issued by ASEAN, which draws a blueprint for the future development of ASEAN, proposes a concept of ASEAN Community and announces that ASEAN is devoted to establishing a world-oriented community with characteristics of peace, progress and prosperity and full of developing vitality. In October 2003, at the 9th ASEAN Summit, the Declaration of ASEAN Concord II was passed, which proposed to establish an ASEAN Community in 2020. In the ASEAN Community, there are 3 pillars to boost the cooperation in the fields of regional political security, economic development and socioculture: ASEAN Security Community (ASC); ASEAN Economic Community (AEC); and ASEAN Socio-Cultural Community (ASCC).[1] In January 2007, at the 12th ASEAN Summit, the "Cebu Declaration on the Acceleration of the establishment of an ASEAN Community by 2015" was passed to set the founding date of ASEAN Community in advance to 2015. In February 2009, at the 14th ASEAN Summit, two blueprints were passed, i.e. Blueprint for ASEAN Political Security Community; and Blueprint for ASEAN Socio-Cultural Community. It was decided at the meeting to combine the above two blueprints with the "Blueprint for ASEAN Economic Community" signed at the 13th ASEAN Summit into "Route map for constructing the ASEAN Community (2009–2015)". In November 2015, at the 27th ASEAN Summit, the "Kuala Lumpur Declaration on ASEAN 2025: Forging Ahead Together" and ASEAN Community Vision 2025 were passed to set a direction for the development of ASEAN Community in the next 10 years. On December 31, 2015, the ASEAN Community was formally established.

This vision is a bold, progressive and prospective document. It aims to maintain an impetus for regional integration in ASEAN, and further promote and strengthen the construction of ASEAN Community. In the ASEAN Community, there are 3 pillars: ASC focuses on mutual political trust and regional security; AEC stresses economic development and regional cooperation; and ASCC emphasises social progress and humanistic exchange. These 3 communities are mutually dependent and promote each other.

ASEAN wishes to establish a uniform, inclusive and flexible political security community by 2025, so as to improve the cooperation level of ASEAN in political and security fields, and ensure that ASEAN countries coexist peacefully and are in a just, democratic and harmonious environment with other countries. ASC mainly has three objectives: (1) to establish a community with a shared value and rule and on the basis of system: ASEAN people observe the basic principles, norms and values of ASEAN and also accept magnanimous and mean values; ASEAN ensures a human right and fundamental freedom for people, and creates a fair, democratic, harmonious and equal environment in the principle of democracy, rule by law and rule by goodness; ASEAN fully respects the different religions, cultures and languages of people of all countries concerned, and maintains common values in the spirit of pursuing a common ground while reserving differences; (2) to undertake joint responsibility for general security and establish a cohesive, peaceful and vigorous area. ASEAN keeps a good cohesion and response in treating a challenge in regional peace and security and plays a key role in shaping a regional structure of continuous development; (3) to establish a dynamic and outward area in the world of increasing integration and mutual dependence: ASEAN strengthens its uniformity, cohesiveness and centrality, and maintains its impetus in shaping a regional structure of continuous development under the mechanism of ASEAN dominance. ASEAN will deepen its contact with other countries or regions, and make its collective contribution to the global peace, security and stability.[2]

ASEAN wishes to establish a highly integral, competitive, innovative, dynamic and vigorous economic community before 2025. ASEAN will merge into a tide of world economy in the form of more flexible, inclusive and people-oriented economic community. AEC has 4 main objectives: (1) to establish a single market and production base. ASEAN wishes to boost an agenda of single market by strengthening the goods trade commitment and effectively solving the non-tariff barrier, promote a deep merging of service trade inside ASEAN, and strengthen a free flow of seamless investment, skilled labour, businessmen and capital; (2) to establish a competitive regional economy. ASEAN wishes to establish a competitive, innovative and vigorous community for promoting a strong growth of production force through knowledge innovation, green technology and digital technology, while ASEAN should strengthen an economic governance, supervision and transparency inside ASEAN and formulate an effective mechanism for dispute settlement; (3) to promote a balanced development of regional economy. ASEAN wishes to establish a flexible, inclusive and people-oriented community to promote a fair development and inclusive growth of economy. ASEAN will further promote a balanced development of regional economy through supporting the development of small and medium-sized enterprises; strengthening the participation of enterprises and stakeholders; promoting the cooperation in subregional development projects; providing more economic opportunities; and supporting an eradication of poverty; (4) to merge into global economic system. ASEAN wishes to become globalised to take more systematic and continuous measures for external economic relation. ASEAN also wishes to become united in order to have more rights to speak at the global economic stage; play a greater role in solving international economic problems; strengthen its participation in the global value chain; actively merge into the global economic system; and keep a concerted relation with the external economy.[3]

ASEAN wishes to establish a people-oriented sociocultural community with a sense of social responsibility before 2025 so as to make such achievements as realising a union, stability and consistency between ASEAN people and countries; erecting a common identity; establishing a society of common care, happiness sharing, inclusiveness and harmony; and strengthening and improving a life/welfare of local people.[4] ASCC has 6 main objectives: human development; social welfare and social guarantee; social justice and civil right; ensuring sustainable environmental development; common identity of ASEAN; and narrowing of development gap.[5]

Alignment with the Belt and Road Initiative

With many common points, the ASEAN Community and the Belt and Road Initiative can realise a strategic alignment to a certain extent. As a core idea of the Belt and Road Initiative, the concept of "openness, inclusiveness, cooperation and win–win" was not only first initiated by China but also shared by all countries concerned, so as to realise a vision of common development.[6] As an original intention, this vision promotes economic development, social stability and cultural exchange in ASEAN, which simultaneously can ensure regional peace and stability, promote a balanced development of economy and strengthen a harmonious exchange of culture during this process. Therefore, the Belt and Road Initiative advocates a mutual political trust, economic merging and cultural inclusiveness to build a responsibility community, interest community and destiny community; and 3 pillars of the ASEAN Community, i.e. ASC, AEC and ASCC, cover political security mutual trust, regional economic merging and sociocultural exchange, respectively. As a whole, they have many similarities, so as to align gradually and achieve an economic effect of advantage complementation, cooperation and win–win.

This vision is mainly aligned with the Belt and Road Initiative in economic terms. (1) ASEAN is competent to play an important role in the Belt and Road Initiative, and is also a priority direction in the construction of the 21st Century Maritime Silk Road. (2) AEC coincides with the Belt and Road Initiative in terms of objectives: ASEAN wishes to establish a flexible, innovative, inclusive and highly integral economic community before 2025, so as to achieve a free flow of goods, service, investment, capital and skilled labour, promote a balanced development of regional economy and actively merge into the world economic system. The Belt and Road Initiative aims to promote an orderly and free flow of economic elements, a high-efficiency allocation of resources and a deep merging of market, boost a coordination of economic policies among the Belt and Road countries, launch a regional cooperation of larger scope, higher level and deeper layer, and jointly build an open, inclusive, balanced and generally beneficial regional economic cooperation framework,[7] realise a mutual benefit of all countries concerned, and merge the Chinese economy into the world economic system. Therefore, their objectives and planning are greatly connected. (3) AEC and the Belt and Road Initiative are mutually aligned in key cooperation points. This vision aims to realise the connectivity of ASEAN, i.e. infrastructure connectivity, institutional connectivity and non-governmental connectivity. The Belt and Road cooperation mainly emphasises a policy coordination, infrastructure connectivity, unimpeded trade, financial integration and understanding between people. Therefore, they are very similar. (4) AEC and the Belt and Road Initiative both preferentially develop infrastructure construction. Infrastructure construction is always the priority field for the Belt and Road construction. As an important strategic action of AEC implementation, the "Master Plan on ASEAN Connectivity" first proposes the regional infrastructure connectivity plan, including the construction and improvement of such infrastructure as traffic transportation, telecommunication network and energy security, which mainly constructs various infrastructure projects in ASEAN such as the road network, the Trans-Asian Railway, the inland river transportation network, the sea and air transportation network, the comprehensive transportation corridor, telecommunication and energy to expand the cooperation of infrastructure investment and financing and popularise the PPP mode.[8] Because most ASEAN countries are relatively lagging behind in infrastructure construction and obviously insufficient in such infrastructures as sea, land and air transportation facilities, power supply and auxiliary industries, ASEAN can cooperate with China in the infrastructure construction under the Belt and Road Initiative.

This vision can be aligned with the Belt and Road Initiative at 2 levels. At the national level, China can strengthen a policy communication with any of the ASEAN countries and launch the production capacity cooperation or project investment. The Belt and Road Initiative can be deeply aligned with the development plan of ASEAN countries such as the Global Maritime Fulcrum strategy from Indonesia; transforming from a land-locked to land-linked country strategy from Laos; the Rectangular Strategy from Cambodia; the Ambition 2040 Strategy from the Philippines; and the One-circle and Two-corridor Strategy from Vietnam, which can continuously optimise the top-level design and plan of pragmatic cooperation between China and ASEAN countries in various fields.[9] China provides the ASEAN countries with funds, equipment and technology so as to meet the needs for investment and technology in the South East Asian region while reducing excessive production capacity in China, and complementing the Chinese advantages in production capacity with the ASEAN advantages in labour and resources. At the regional level, this vision can cooperate and complement with the Belt and Road Initiative: to strengthen the construction of China–ASEAN Free Trade Area; reinforce the cooperation between China and ASEAN in the above-mentioned fields of capital flow, technological innovation, connectivity and infrastructure construction; to fully play the role of the cooperation mechanism of China–ASEAN (10+1) and China–ASEAN Expo; to establish an all-round, multi-level and composite connectivity network between China and ASEAN; and to realise a diversified, autonomous, balanced and sustainable development of ASEAN countries.

Notes

1 Wang Qin, "ASEAN entering the era of community: current situation and prospect," *Journal of Xiamen University* (a quarterly for studies in arts & social sciences), 2016, 5, p. 80.
2 ASEAN 2025, "Forging Ahead Together," Association of South East Asian Nations, November 24, 2015. Retrieved February 25, 2018 from www.asean.org/wp-content/uploads/2015/12/ASEAN-2025-Forging-Ahead-Together-final.pdf
3 Ibid.
4 Wang Qin, "ASEAN entering the era of community: current situation and prospect," *Journal of Xiamen University* (a quarterly for studies in arts & social sciences), 2016, 5, p. 84.
5 ASEAN 2025, "Forging Ahead Together," Association of South East Asian Nations, November 24, 2015. Retrieved February 27, 2018 from www.asean.org/wp-content/uploads/2015/12/ASEAN-2025-Forging-Ahead-Together-final.pdf
6 Xu Bu (Chinese ambassador in ASEAN. Article in the *Jakarta Post* (Indonesia)). Accommodation between the B&R Initiative and ASEAN Community Vision (2025). Ministry of Foreign Affairs of PRC. Retrieved February 25, 2018 from www.fmprc.gov.cn/web/dszlsjt_673036/t1460913.shtml
7 "Vision and Action on Boosting the Joint Construction of Silk Road Economic Belt and 21st-century Maritime Silk Road," Ministry of Commerce of PRC. Retrieved February 25, 2018 from http://zhs.mofcom.gov.cn/article/xxfb/201503/20150300926644.shtml
8 "Master Plan on ASEAN Connectivity 2025," Association of South East Asian Nations, January 25, 2018. Retrieved February 27, 2018 from http://asean.org/?static_post=master-plan-asean-connectivity-2025-2
9 Xu Bu (Chinese ambassador in ASEAN. Article in the *Jakarta Post* (Indonesia)). Accommodation between the B&R Initiative and ASEAN Community Vision (2025). Ministry of Foreign Affairs of PRC. Retrieved February 25, 2018 from www.fmprc.gov.cn/web/dszlsjt_673036/t1460913.shtml

85
ASIA–EUROPE MEETING AND ITS CONNECTIVITY WORKING GROUP WITH THE BELT AND ROAD INITIATIVE

Liu Wei

Origin and development

With the end of the Cold War and the increasing trend of the world political multi-polarisation and global economic integration, Asia and Europe wish to establish a dialogue mechanism, reinforce the regional contact and pursue a common development. In July 1994, the "Towards a New Asia Strategy" was formulated by the European Union, which proposes a more extensive dialogue with Asia and regards the overall reinforcement of Asia–Europe relation and economic and trade cooperation as one of key contents for European all-round diplomacy and foreign economic and trade strategy. In October 1994, during the visit to France, Goh Chok Tong, Premier of Singapore proposed to hold the Asia–Europe Meeting (ASEM), which was responded extensively and actively. In January 1996, the 1st Asia–Europe Cultural Forum was held in Venice, Italy. In March 1996, the 1st ASEM was held in Bangkok, Thailand. At this meeting, 4 aspects were discussed by heads from 10 Asian countries and 15 European countries: to promote Asia–Europe political dialogue; to strengthen Asia–Europe economic cooperation; to promote an exchange and cooperation in other fields such as technology, culture and environmental protection; and subsequent action for ASEM. After a consensus was reached, the "Chairman's Statement of the 1st Asia–Europe Meeting" was released, which symbolised an the official start of ASEM.[1] Under the Asia–Europe Cooperation Framework, all countries concerned will strengthen political dialogue, economic cooperation and sociocultural exchange between Asia and Europe to enhance mutual understanding and trust, and boost the establishment of a new comprehensive Asia–Europe partnership.

According to the Chairman's Statement of the 1st Asia–Europe Meeting, ASEM has the following objectives: to establish a new and comprehensive partnership between the Asian and European continents to promote the growth; to strengthen the bilateral dialogue, understanding and cooperation; to create a favourable condition for economic and social development; and to keep world peace and stability. The following consensus has been reached by the ASEM member states for the main principles: to launch a dialogue on the basis of equal partnership, mutual respect and mutual benefit; to promote the formation of basic rights, an obligation of observing international laws and non-interference in the internal affairs in other countries; to keep the process of opening-up, and add a member state only after the consensus of governmental heads from the existing member states; to keep an informal but no institutional proceeding; to promote dialogue and cooperation among Asia–Europe governments, and to promote dialogue, communication and cooperation among industrial and commercial departments and between people in the 2 continents; and to emphasise and boost political dialogue, economic cooperation and cooperation in other fields.

ASEM has formed a non-institutional and multi-level cooperation mechanism. Besides the summit, ASEM also includes foreign ministers' conferences, senior officials' conferences and other ministers' conferences. The daily work of ASEM is communicated and coordinated through its senior officials' conference. The summit of ASEM is responsible to determine the guiding principles and development direction of ASEM, which is alternated in Asia and Europe and has been held 11 times. In October 2018, the 12th ASEM Summit will be sponsored by the European Union in Brussels, Belgium. The foreign ministers' conference of ASEM is responsible for policy planning and overall coordination of ASEM's activities, which alternates with its summit every 2 years and has been held 13 times. The senior officials' conference of ASEM is often periodically alternated in Asia and Europe for 2–3 times a year before its senior officials' conference and its foreign ministers' conference. Its aim is to coordinate and manage the activities in various fields of ASEM, and prepare in advance the summit and foreign ministers' conference of ASEM, including reviewing new initiatives and consulting documents, and preliminarily exchanging the viewpoints on international or regional problems of common concern. The coordinator mechanism of ASEM is responsible for daily coordination and is composed of 4 members from Asia and Europe with 2 members from each continent. At the periodical meeting, the coordinators report the status in their areas, summarise the standpoints of all countries concerned and coordinate accordingly. The European coordinators are assumed by the European Union and its rotating presiding country; and for the ASEAN, Northeast Asia and South Asia each assigns one coordinator. The other ministers' conference of ASEM in economic, fiscal, cultural, customs, technological, environmental, education, traffic and agricultural fields is responsible for implementing the decision of its summit in various fields, formulating the cooperation plan and launching relevant activities. ASEM also has the business forum and the people's forum, which actively boosts exchange between industrial and commercial circles and unofficial organisations, and reflects the viewpoints at social and market level. In 1997, ASEM established the sole standing sector, the Asia–Europe Foundation (ASEF), which accepts donations from ASEM member states to boost the Asia–Europe exchange of academy, culture and people and promote an unofficial mutual understanding.

On the basis of boosting an economic and trade cooperation, ASEM established a comprehensive partnership between Asia and Europe. In order to boost a bilateral trade and investment activity between Asia and Europe, ASEM actively boosts their trade facilitation and investment liberalisation. In 1997, the ASEM Investment Promotion Action Plan (IPAP) was formulated by ASEM, which improves the investment environment in the member states and promotes a two-way investment flow between Asia and Europe through 2 pillars of investment promotion and exchange on investment policies and regulations. Subsequently in 1998, the ASEM Trade Facilitation Action Plan (TFAP) was passed by ASEM to guide the cooperation of member states in fields of customs procedures, standard consistency, governmental procurement, animal and plant quarantine, intellectual property right, businessman flow and market entry of distribution industry, which reduces the trade cost between the 2 continents and promotes trade development. Furthermore, various documents were released by ASEM such as the Work Objective of the ASEM Trade Facilitation Action Plan (2002–2004), which reinforces the Asia–Europe economic and trade cooperation and boosts a regional and multilateral dialogue of trade policies in Asia–European countries.

New starting point of ASEM: connectivity and pragmatic cooperation

In October 2014, at the 10th ASEM Summit held in Milan, Italy, Li Keqiang, Premier of China, proposed to take joint boosting of Asia–Europe connectivity and trade and investment liberalisation as 1 of 3 key fields to deepen the Asia–Europe cooperation. He also proposed to hold an ASEM Industry Dialogue on Connectivity. In 2015, at the ASEM Industry Dialogue on Connectivity held in Chongqing, China, all countries concerned showed a firm resolution to promote Asia–Europe connectivity and draw a basic outline of an ASEM Connectivity Initiative. By focusing on the topic of "Advancing Asia–Europe connectivity through innovation", the "Chongqing initiative of ASEM industry dialogue on connectivity" was reached by the representatives of industrial, commercial, governmental and academic circles from the ASEM member states. As supported and encouraged by all countries concerned, the ASEM member states improve the hardware and software level of their infrastructure, and constructed a highly efficient, competitive and comprehensive infrastructure network.

On July 15, 2016, the 11th ASEM Summit held in Ulaanbaatar, Mongolia became a turning point of revitalisation for ASEM. The meeting also marked the 20th anniversary of ASEM. It undertook a heavy responsibility for revitalisation and future expansion of ASEM. China played an active leading role in determining the development direction and agenda of ASEM. With a theme of "20 years of ASEM: Partnership for the Future through Connectivity", this summit summarised the experience of ASEM in the past 20 years and blueprinted its third 10-year development plan. As restated by all attendants, ASEM will continue to adhere to the cornerstone of Asia–Europe partnership stipulated in the Asia–Europe Cooperation Framework, in the informal political dialogue and the cooperation proposal in economic, social and humanistic fields and guide the third 10-year development of ASEM by strengthening partnership, focusing on pragmatic cooperation, promoting all-round connectivity and boosting informality, network relation and flexibility. In the Chairman's statement of the 11th ASEM Summit, the heads of all countries concerned agreed to establish a connectivity working group to implement relevant work.

In the Chairman's statement of the 11th ASEM Summit and the Ulaanbaatar Declaration of the ASEM 3rd Ten-Year Development Plan, the connectivity was formally included into the mainstream cooperation framework of ASEM. Three pillars of Asia–Europe partnership in fields of political dialogue, economic and financial cooperation and sociocultural exchange have been included in the relevant activities of ASEM such as politics, economy, digitalisation, technology, socioculture and people exchange.

ASEM is revitalised in a way that the member states agree that Asia–Europe connectivity is the future key direction and policy priority of ASEM, and the mechanism of ASEM is transformed to boost a pragmatic cooperation in various fields and boost all countries concerned to transform the consensus to the concrete action. First, member states focus on the cooperation fields of common attention and ensure a continuity of cooperation proposal. Second, they further improve the working methods and internal coordination to maintain an informality of ASEM while improving its efficiency. In order to ensure a more effective institutional memory, heads of all countries concerned emphasised to resume and periodically hold the ASEM Economic Ministers' Conference (which has been suspended for 13 years), support the Asia–Europe Foundation to play a greater role in improving the visibility of ASEM and support to align the activities of Asia–Europe Foundation with the priority cooperation fields of ASEM, and encourage all stakeholders to participate in the proceedings of ASEM. Third, ASEM encourages the inclusion of common people, especially youth, and industrial and commercial circles into pragmatic cooperation fields, and boost the common people to be involved more in the activities of ASEM. Finally, ASEM will pay closer attention to improving the ability construction of developing members of ASEM.

Prospect and challenge of aligning ASEM with the Belt and Road Initiative

The connectivity is regarded by ASEM as an important direction of boosting the Asia–Europe comprehensive partnership, which coincides with the 5 long-term approaches in the Belt and Road Initiative, i.e. policy coordination, infrastructure connectivity, unimpeded trade, financial integration and people-to-people field. The ASEM Connectivity Initiative and the Belt and Road Initiative are also highly consistent in the main covered areas. All member states of both initiatives wish to strengthen communication and coordination of policies, boost alignment among different initiatives and jointly advance regional cooperation. The ASEM Connectivity Initiative will be boosted in concert with the Master Plan on ASEAN Connectivity; Connecting Europe Facility Plan; Digital Agenda for Europe; Trans-European Transport Networks; Europe–Asia traffic connection projects dominated by the United Nations Economic Commission for Europe and the United Nations Economic and Social Commission for Asia and the Pacific, Silk Road Economic Belt, and the 21st Century Maritime Silk Road Initiative and the Belt and Road Initiative to jointly promote the connectivity and common development of Asia–Europe.

Starting with pragmatic projects, the Belt and Road Initiative boosts 5 concepts in the policy, trade, infrastructure, finance and people-to-people fields so as to provide a practical path for ASEM to implement cooperation consensus. Through early achievement in the Asia–European area, the Belt and Road construction can also provide a new and strong impetus for deepening the Asia–Europe cooperation. ASEM is mutually complemented with the Belt and Road Initiative and each encourages the other to jointly promote the peaceful and continuous development in the region. First, ASEM's consensus on the intrinsic contents, working scope and schedule of connectivity coincides with the vision and action of the Belt and Road Initiative. Asia–Europe connectivity covers all transportation modes, policies and regulations, infrastructures, finance, trade, investment, digital information, energy, education and research, human resources and humanistic and tourism. Second, the ministerial conference and the connectivity working group of ASEM will become an important carrier to align ASEM with the Belt and Road Initiative. According to the Ulaanbaatar Declaration of ASEM 3rd Ten-Year Development Plan, the ministerial conferences of ASEM boost an overall dominance of connectivity, and the connectivity working group of ASEM concretely implements the relevant work. In 2018, the working group's conference will be held 3 times to discuss and pass the achievement documents of the working group. Third, with a priority for constructing the Asia–Europe traffic system, ASEM and the Belt and Road Initiative enjoy great potential for cooperation in the planning and construction of large-scale traffic projects. ASEM proposed to formulate the strategic plan for developing and strengthening the corridor and route of Asia–Europe transportation, improve the connectivity of Asia–Europe traffic transportation through comprehensive combined transportation, intermodal transportation system and infrastructure, effectively utilise digital connectivity and enhance the social and economic connection between Asia and Europe. Finally, ASEM coordinates with the Belt and Road Initiative in unifying the standards and rules of connectivity, including standards, sustainability, economic feasibility and relevant international laws and norms.

For the alignment with the Belt and Road construction, ASEM also faces some challenges. On the one hand, a complete cooperation framework or uniform attitude is not available by the whole of Europe for the Belt and Road Initiative. As wished by Germany and the European Union, the European Union cooperates as a whole with China for the Belt and Road Initiative, balances the "16+1" mechanism between China and Central and Eastern European Countries through Asia–Europe connectivity, establishes multilateral standards and rules and continues to dominate the proceedings of Asia–Europe cooperation. However, the Central and Eastern European countries wish to continuously strengthen economic and trade cooperation with China through the "16+1" mechanism between China and Central and Eastern European Countries. Therefore, it becomes more difficult for the member states to reach a consensus on the operation layer in boosting Asia–Europe connectivity and realising the alignment of ASEM with the Belt and Road Initiative. On the other hand, after the outbreak of the Ukraine crisis, the geopolitical relations between Russia and Western European countries has become tense. The Eurasia Economic Union is mutually repelled with the regional integration with the European Union as the centre. The space of strategic choosing is also limited for relevant countries, which puts the boosting of Asia–Europe cooperation and the regional economic integration into a certain unfavourable light. Finally, terrorism, refugee problems and European populism are also important challenges for ASEM and the Belt and Road Initiative to jointly boost Asia–Europe connectivity.

Note

1 Ten Asian countries: Malaysia, Philippines, Indonesia, Thailand, Brunei, Singapore, Vietnam, China, Japan and South Korea. Fifteen European countries: UK, France, Germany, Italy, Spain, Portugal, Finland, the Netherlands, Belgium, Luxembourg, Sweden, Austria, Ireland, Denmark and Greece.

86
COOPERATION BETWEEN CHINA AND CENTRAL AND EASTERN EUROPEAN COUNTRIES WITH THE BELT AND ROAD INITIATIVE

Tian Feng

Concept

As defined in the "16+1 cooperation" framework set by the Ministry of Foreign Affairs of PRC in 2012, the Central and Eastern European (CEE) countries herein include: 4 Visegrad Group countries, i.e. Poland, Hungary, the Czech Republic and Slovakia; Eastern and Southern European countries of Romania, Bulgaria, Slovenia, Croatia, Serbia, Macedonia, Bosnia–Herzegovina, Montenegro and Albania; and 3 Baltic Sea countries, i.e. Estonia, Latvia and Lithuania.[1] Cooperation between China and Central and Eastern European Countries means China's cooperation with the above 16 countries. In 2012, China and 16 CEE countries jointly established a new cooperation platform, i.e. Cooperation between China and Central and Eastern European Countries (hereinafter referred to as "the 16+1 cooperation plan"). After the joint efforts of all countries concerned for 5 years, a leaders' meeting mechanism and a cooperation platform in various fields of policy coordination, economy and trade, culture, education, agriculture, traffic, tourism, technology, health, think tank, locality and youth have been established under the "16+1 cooperation" plan framework, which has made a substantial achievement and been extensively welcomed by the people from China and CEE countries.[2]

As an important region along the Belt and Road, the CEE region plays an important role in boosting the Belt and Road construction. The cooperation between China and CEE countries promotes a benign interaction and overall balanced development of the Belt and Road Initiative in the CEE region.[3] In synchronicity with the overall situation of China–Europe cooperation, the "16+1 cooperation" plan is devoted to establishing a new partnership of openness, inclusiveness, mutual benefit and win–win, creating a new route for cooperation between China and European countries, realising the win–win among China, CEE countries and the European Union, and setting a new mode of pragmatic cooperation among the countries across different regions and different systems. CEE is a forerunner and practitioner of the Belt and Road

Initiative, so the cooperation between China and CEE countries will become an important process in the Belt and Road construction, an antecedent practice in creating a community of shared future for mankind, and an effective action for China's practising the right approach to justice and interests.

The Belt and Road Initiative also creates many important opportunities for the cooperation between China and CEE countries.[4] It arouses a strong desire of CEE countries for common development. The Belt and Road Initiative not only assists the CEE countries in pursuing new growth impetus, but also promotes the complementation of economic structure between China and CEE countries. The connectivity projects boost the alignment of cooperation and development between China and CEE countries, explore a potential of regional market, promote investment and consumption, create demand and employment, match the benefit claim between both sides and boost the benign economic and trade development of both sides. It erects a cooperation platform of mutual benefit between China and CEE countries. With the implementation of the Belt and Road Initiative, China strengthens the interaction and exchange with the Belt and Road countries, including CEE countries, releases various preferential policies and measures, and establishes several cooperation platforms of mutual benefit such as the "16+1 cooperation" plan. It creates a good environment for Chinese enterprises to invest in local countries and promote their development. Under the boosting of the Belt and Road Initiative, the "Going Globally" strategy is continuously boosted by Chinese enterprises, and the business opportunity in CEE is greatly improved in fields such as investment, merger and acquisition, listing and project bidding. The common benefit and mutual need are improved for both sides, while the economic and trade relation becomes closer.

With the continuous boosting of the Belt and Road construction, a pragmatic cooperation develops rapidly between China and CEE countries. In 2017, some representative achievements of the past 5 years were analysed and summarised into a list of achievements by the Ministry of Foreign Affairs of PRC with a total of 233 concrete achievements in 5 categories: policy communication, connectivity, economy and trade, finance and humanistics.[5] There are 28 achievements concerning building the policy communication platform, and 40 achievements concerning improving the connectivity level, 52 achievements concerning boosting the pragmatic cooperation of economy and trade, 28 achievements concerning perfecting the cooperation framework of finance and 75 achievements concerning tightening the people-to-people exchange.

Achievements for the cooperation between China and CEE countries and the Belt and Road construction

Since the cooperation mechanism between China and CEE countries was established in 2012, numerous cooperation projects in the Belt and Road construction have been produced to strongly promote the economic and trade, and financial cooperation between both sides and the Belt and Road construction as well.

(1) Numerous policy cooperation frameworks are achieved around the Belt and Road Initiative, and the cooperation becomes mature. In November 2015, the "Medium-term plan for cooperation between China and Central and Eastern European countries" was jointly formulated by 17 countries, which specifies the working direction and focal point over the period of 2015–2020, further releases potential for cooperation, and boosts the improvement of quality and efficiency of the "16+1 cooperation" plan. The plan mentioned to welcome and support an establishment of China–Europe connectivity platform. Meanwhile, the "16+1 cooperation" plan will fully seize the important opportunity brought by the Belt and Road

construction to continuously expand its cooperation space and make more contributions to the Belt and Road construction.[6] In May 2017, heads of some CEE countries were present at the Belt and Road Forum for International Cooperation in Beijing China and all 16 CEE countries were included in the Belt and Road framework. On July 14, 2017, at the 2nd Dialogue of Political Parties between China and Central and Eastern European Countries in Bucharest, the capital city of Romania, a total of more than 600 persons were present, including representatives of 35 political parties, local governments and entrepreneurs from 16 CEE countries and the delegation from China. It marked that an exchange platform of political parties is institutionalised under the "16+1 cooperation" plan framework. In November 2017, the "Budapest Outline for the Cooperation between China and Central and Eastern European countries" was jointly released by China and 16 CEE countries, which emphasises to continue a joint discussion, construction and sharing of the Belt and Road; and boost the alignment of the Belt and Road Initiative with major initiatives like an Investment Plan for Europe and national development plans of all countries concerned while relying on the "16+1 cooperation" plan. Therefore, the cooperation between China and CEE counties has developed from a "window period" to a "mature period".

(2) A development direction of friendly communication in the policies of CEE countries towards China provides a guarantee for the implementation of Belt and Road projects. On one hand, more and more CEE countries regard China as a strategic partner, upgrade the cooperation and release such governmental documents as outline or policies towards China. In 2016, China established a strategic partnership with the Czech Republic and a comprehensive strategic partnership with Poland and Serbia, respectively. On May 13, 2017, the partnership between China and Hungary was upgraded into a comprehensive strategic partnership. China has established a strategic partnership of different degrees with 4 CEE countries. In April 2017, the "Development Outline for the Economic Relation between Slovakia and China (2017–2020)" was released by the Slovakian Parliament, which specifies utilising a better and being-reinforced political relation between both sides for economic purposes by the following measures: to increase the number of Slovakian diplomats in China, attract Chinese investors and tourists to start a "Home of Slovakia" in China and attempt to formulate a plan for constructing the Slovakian infrastructure through Chinese capital. On the other hand, the CEE countries generally accept the development mode of China. At present, the CEE countries are increasingly dissatisfied with the values of diplomacy coerced by great European powers like Germany. However, pragmatic cooperation with China is increasingly welcomed by the CEE countries due to no political pressure being exerted or any precondition on the placement of Syrian or Libyan refugees. As mentioned by Marek Hrubec, Director of the Global Research Centre, Czech Academy of Sciences, the "16+1 cooperation" plan during the development has successfully attracted the close attention of politicians, media, social scientists and common people.

(3) It has made fruitful achievement in economic, trade and financial cooperation. The economic and trade cooperation between China and CEE countries has expanded in scale and also deepened. According to the statistical data of the Chamber of Commerce of PRC, since the "16+1 cooperation" plan was launched in 2012, the import and export volume between China and 16 CEE countries increased by 13% from US$52.1 billion in 2012 to US$58.7 billion in 2016, and the proportion among the import and export volume between China and Europe increased from 7.1% to 9.8% over the corresponding period. Meanwhile, Chinese enterprises are increasingly enthusiastic for investment in CEE countries. According to the incomplete statistics, Chinese enterprises invested more than US$8 billion in the CEE region in 2016, and 16 CEE countries invested more than US$1.2 billion in China in the fields of machine manufacturing, automobile spare parts, chemicals, finance and environmental protection. As shown

by the data of General Administration of Customs of PRC, the bilateral trade volume between China and 16 CEE countries increased at a year-on-year rate of more than 15% in 2017. Poland is China's largest trade partner among the CEE countries. In 2017, the China–Poland trade volume reached US$21.35 billion at a growth rate of 20%. The cooperation expanded in scale and also deepened. The China Investment Forum which has been held in the Czech Republic for several years has become an important platform for deepening economic and trade cooperation between China and the CEE countries. The economic and trade cooperation between China and the CEE countries has not only strongly boosted the economic development of relevant countries, but also provided an effective channel for Chinese equipment, technologies, standards and service to go global.

Financial cooperation has also deepened. The Coordinated Investment and Financing Cooperation Framework between China and Central and Eastern European Countries began to be implemented. On November 27, 2017, the China–CEE Banking Union was formally established, which is co-sponsored by China Development Bank and the financial institutions of the CEE countries. All 14 members are government-holding policy/development financial institutions and state-owned commercial banks in China and CEE countries. In November 2016, the Commercial Industrial Bank of China led to establishment of the Sino-CEEC Financial Holding Company and the China–CEE Foundation. The China Development Bank provided a development financial cooperation loan equivalent to 2 billion EUR, and in the China–Central and Eastern Europe Investment Cooperation Fund, the second phase of US$1 billion was set up and put into operation. Such financial cooperation strongly boosts the infrastructure construction in CEE countries and infrastructure connectivity in the Belt and Road countries. In CEE countries, China mainly invests in such fields as infrastructure construction, and also greatly improves investment of merger and acquisition and green land. By 2017, the preferential project loan from the Chinese special loan of US$10 billion had been used up, which was mainly provided for the construction of infrastructure, hydropower and expressway. The Belgrade bridge over the Danube is completed and open to traffic; the Stanari Thermal Power Plant (Bosnia–Herzegovina) is combined with the grid for power generation; and major projects of infrastructure connectivity are stably boosted (e.g. the Hungary–Serbia Railway and the China–Europe Land–Sea Express Route). Such projects have not only improved the local employment level but also promoted local economic development, and the Chinese influence in these regions is also improved.

(4) It enriches an activity of humanistic exchange. Enthusiasm and level of the "16+1 cooperation" plan has been improved from various angles and at various levels by important humanistic exchange activities such as the China–CEE Media Exchange Year, the China–CEE Cultural Cooperation Forum and the China–CEE Education Policy Dialogue held in 2017. However, during the overall boosting of humanistic exchange, the activity quantity and input are still unbalanced for the exchange between China and other countries.

In the tide of the Belt and Road construction, China and CEE countries are striding forward on the way of joint discussion, joint construction and sharing, putting efforts to practise the concept of community of shared future for mankind, and plot a beautiful future of mutual benefit, win–win and common prosperity.[7]

Direction for the cooperation of China with CEE countries and the Belt and Road construction

In the future, the Belt and Road Initiative and cooperation between China and the CEE countries will mainly work to perfect a general plan design and the multi-level policy communication, fully consider and stress the difference of CEE countries, promote long-term cooperation through the objective of mutual benefit, mutual trust and win–win and gradually boost cooperation through the model of key projects: (1) to continue to implement the programmes under the Belt and Road framework such as the route maps specified in the "Medium-term Plan for Cooperation between China and Central and Eastern European countries" and the "Budapest Outline for the Cooperation between China and Central and Eastern European countries", boost the construction of major connectivity projects and economic and trade cooperation parks, create a new cooperation platform of production capacity, promote the growth of both trade and investment, strengthen the cooperation in investment and financing, expand the cooperation in fields of tourism, technology, education, service and agriculture and improve a level of humanistic and social exchange; (2) to boost implementation of Belt and Road connectivity projects: the Asian Infrastructure Investment Bank and the Silk Road Foundation will strengthen the support of infrastructure connectivity projects in CEE countries to improve the financial supporting ability for key projects in CEE countries and support the alignment of CEE railways, roads and ports with the Eurasian Land Bridge and encourage the China Railway Express to serve the CEE countries along the Belt and Road; (3) to balance trade cooperation: China will pay closer attention to boosting cooperation with the CEE's non-EU countries. These countries have a comparatively lower level of economic development and limited ability of fiscal support, but have no policy restriction from the European Union on trade, investment and finance, so a larger space, a greater opportunity and an easier achievement can be expected for cooperation between China and these countries; (4) to boost cooperation with CEE countries by strengthening China–Europe cooperation. Based on strengthening the cooperation with the CEE EU countries, more Chinese enterprises will invest and do business in the CEE countries, and make great efforts in the negotiation of China–Europe Investment Agreement and China–Europe Free Trade Area.

Notes

1 "Inherent need of Chinese policies by the Central and Eastern European Countries: cooperation at a mature stage," *The Paper Network*. Retrieved February 8, 2018 from www.thepaper.cn/baidu.jsp?contid=1989625
2 "List of five-year cooperation achievements between China and the Central and Eastern European Countries," Ministry of Foreign Affairs of PRC. Retrieved November 28, 2017 from www.mfa.gov.cn/web/zyxw/t1514537.shtml
3 "Cooperation between China and the Central and Eastern European Countries: assisting the B&R construction," Xinhua Network. Retrieved February 23, 2018 from www.xinhuanet.com/silkroad/2018-02/23/c_129814889.htm
4 Wu Zhicheng, "The B&R Initiative and Cooperation between China and Central and Eastern European Countries," *Journal of United Front Science*, 2017, 6, pp. 107–112.
5 "List of five-year cooperation achievements between China and the Central and Eastern European Countries," Ministry of Foreign Affairs of PRC. Retrieved November 28, 2017 from www.mfa.gov.cn/web/zyxw/t1514537.shtml
6 "Medium-term Plan for Cooperation between China and Central and Eastern European Countries," Ministry of Foreign Affairs of PRC. Retrieved November 24, 2015 from www.fmprc.gov.cn/web/zyxw/t1317976.shtml
7 "The B&R Initiative assisting China and Central and Eastern European Countries to jointly construct a community of shared future for mankind," Central Government Portal. Retrieved November 27, 2017 from www.gov.cn/xinwen/2017-11/27/content_5242500.htm

87

CHINA–EUROPE LAND–SEA EXPRESS ROUTE WITH THE BELT AND ROAD INITIATIVE

Xue Li

Conceptual description and formation process of the China–Europe Land–Sea Express Route

The China–Europe Land–Sea Express Route (hereinafter referred to as "this express route") is a new channel of goods trade between China and Europe. It is composed of 2 routes, i.e. a land transportation route and a marine transportation route. In its land transportation route, which is a railway line, there are Budapest of Hungary and Piraeus Port of Greece, respectively, at the two ends, with Serbia and Macedonia in the middle. In its marine transportation route, there are Piraeus Port and Chinese coastal ports, respectively, at the two ends, sequentially through the Mediterranean Sea, the Red Sea, the Persian Gulf, the Indian Ocean, the Malacca Strait (or via a detour of either Sunda Strait or Lombok Strait), the South China Sea, the East China Sea and the Yellow Sea.

In November 2013, at the 2nd Meeting of Heads of Government of China and Central and Eastern European Countries in Romania, Li Keqiang, Premier of China, agreed with the premiers of Hungary and Serbia to jointly renovate and upgrade the Hungary–Serbia Railway, i.e. a railway line between Budapest and Belgrade, to increase its running speed from 40 km/h to 200 km/h.

In June 2014, during a visit to Greece, Premier Li Keqiang and Antonis Samaras, Premier of Greece, jointly visited the Piraeus Port, which is a container wharf operated by China COSCO Shipping Group. After its extension, the handling capacity of this port will be greatly improved so as to far exceed the need of the Greek market of over 10 million population. Therefore, both sides explored a possible channel and mode for deepening the port cooperation between the 2 countries.

In December 2014, during a visit to Serbia, Premier Li Keqiang agreed with Serbia, Hungary and Macedonia to jointly build this express route. Therefore, the Hungary–Serbia Railway will be extended southwards to Piraeus Port: goods are directly transported via freight train by way of Greece, Macedonia, Serbia and Hungary to the European hinterland; the handling capacity of Piraeus Port is fully utilised while a section of voyage is saved other than loading/unloading at a Western European port.

In November 2015, at the 4th Meeting of Heads of Government of China and Central and Eastern European Countries in Suzhou, China, some cooperation documents on the

Hungary–Serbia Railway project were jointly signed by China, Hungary and Serbia, and the Export–Import Bank of China was determined as its main financing bank after the discussion.

Relation between the China–Europe Land–Sea Express Route and the Belt and Road Initiative

As specified by Xi Jinping, Chairman of China, at the Belt and Road Forum for International Cooperation, the Belt and Road construction mainly orients on the Asian–European–African continent, and is also open to all friends; and the international partners of the Belt and Road construction can come from Asia, Europe, Africa or America.[1] This statement coincides with the "Vision and action on jointly boosting the Belt and Road construction": jointly construct the Belt and Road; and strive for a connectivity of Asian–European–African continents and adjacent seas.[2] Therefore, Eurasia is certainly the key area of the Belt and Road construction. Moreover, the Belt and Road Initiative mainly targets the countries around China and the developing countries, but not developed countries, mainly because China can enjoy a comparative advantage and show a responsibility of great power in these countries to display China's wisdom and China's plans.

According to the "Vision and action on jointly boosting the Belt and Road construction and the 21st Century Maritime Silk Road" issued in March 2015, 2 routes are specified for the Belt and Road construction: the Silk Road Economic Belt includes 3 main lines, i.e. from China to Europe (the Baltic Sea) via Central Asia and Russia; from China to the Persian Gulf and the Mediterranean Sea via Central Asia and West Asia; and from China to South East Asia, South Asia and the Indian Ocean; and the 21st Century Maritime Silk Road includes 2 main lines, i.e. from Chinese coastal ports to the Indian Ocean across the South China Sea, and further to Europe; from Chinese coastal ports to the South Pacific across the South China Sea.[3] Therefore, a total of 8t lines are listed by the Chinese government. In the 21st Century Maritime Silk Road (the marine Silk Road), there are 2 lines: from Chinese coastal areas, across the South China Sea, the Malacca Strait and the Indian Ocean and ending at East Africa, West Asia and Europe; from Chinese coastal areas, through the South China Sea, across Indonesia and ending at the South Pacific. In the Silk Road Economic Belt, or the land Silk Road, there are 6 lines: the China–Mongolia–Russian Economic Corridor; the New Eurasian Land Bridge; the China–Central Asia–West Asian Economic Corridor; the China–Indo China Peninsula Economic Corridor; the China–Pakistan Economic Corridor; and the Bangladesh–China–India–Myanmar Economic Corridor.[4]

As seen from above, this express route neither belongs to 1 of the above 6 economic corridors, nor completely coincides with 2 lines of the marine Silk Road. In fact, this express route can be regarded as a combination of the marine Silk Road and the land Silk Road, or more accurately as a combination of the western line of the marine Silk Road and the New Eurasian Land Bridge. During the boosting of the Belt and Road construction, China plans this express route by further refining the marine Silk Road and the land Silk Road according to the characteristics of 16 Central and Eastern European (CEE) countries. Among 16 CEE countries, Warsaw, Poland, Lodz, Poland and Dobra, Slovakia are terminal cities of China Railway Express participating in the construction of New Eurasian Land Bridge.[5]

This express route is a project of the Belt and Road Construction customised by China for 4 Balkan countries, so as to showcase their location advantage, remedy their shortage in scale and drive their economic development. Moreover, this express route arouses great enthusiasm of 4 Balkan countries (especially Serbia and Macedonia). In other words, the land part of this express route well embodies the following requirements of "Vision and action on jointly boosting the Belt and Road construction and the 21st Century Maritime Silk Road": to adhere to the principle of joint discussion, joint construction and sharing; and actively boost a mutual alignment in the development strategy of the Belt and Road countries.[6]

Significance of this express route

Europe is the largest trade partner of China. Geographically, Budapest is located in the central position of Europe, and Piraeus Port is an important external contact portal of the southern Europe. This express route erects a convenient trade channel between China and CEE countries. The goods can be rapidly transported between China and European central areas. After the completion of this express route, the sea shipping time of goods between China and Europe will be reduced by 7–11 days.

In order to reinforce mutual cooperation, the "Cooperation between China and Central and Eastern European Countries" (the 16+1 cooperation plan) was started by China and CEE countries from 2011. A series of progress has been achieved in the recent several years: to formulate the "Medium-term plan for cooperation between China and central and eastern European countries"; to establish more than 20 institutional exchange platforms; to plan such major projects as the Hungary–Serbia Railway, the China–Europe Land–Sea Express Route and Cooperation among the Port Areas in Adriatic Area, the Baltic Sea and the Black Sea; and to release more than 200 concrete measures to realise a rapid growth in fields of investment, trade and tourism.[7] It is also the joint wish of the 4 Balkan countries to construct the land line of this express route.

This express route opens up a new connectivity channel of China–Europe economic and trade cooperation. By strengthening foreign trade cooperation and especially opening up a convenient transportation route of goods between China and Europe under an overall downturn trend of world economy, the relevant countries will enjoy a great development opportunity. It has a very practical meaning for these countries to realise mutual benefit, win–win and common development. Across Greece, Macedonia, Serbia and Hungary, this express route will directly radiate to more than 32 million people, producing a huge radiation effect of economic areas and bringing the prospect of great benefits for China–Europe trade, goods transportation and people exchange.

At an opportunity in constructing this express route, China takes an action of "one export and one import": export the China-made products and China-innovated products to Europe and open up a new market; implement an active strategy of import promotion and strengthen the import of items such as technologies, products, service and daily necessities closely related to daily life. Multiple gains are obtained through this action: to promote the upgrading of China–Europe trade cooperation; to boost a structural adjustment of Chinese industries; to improve a level of opening-up and cooperation; and to substantially benefit the people of all countries concerned.

If this express route proves to be successful, China will gain a new experience in the innovative implementation of Belt and Road Initiative, so as to promote an implementation of Belt and Road Initiative in such developing countries as Africa and Latin America. Therefore, this express route is deemed as a flagship project of China–Europe cooperation under the Belt and Road Initiative.

Notes

1 Xi Jinping, "Speech at the opening ceremony of B&R Forum for International Cooperation: jointly boosting the B&R construction," Xinhua Network. Retrieved February 26, 2017 from http://news.xinhuanet.com/politics/2017-05/14/c_1120969677.htm

2 National Development and Reform Commission of PRC, Ministry of Foreign Affairs of PRC and Ministry of Commerce of PRC, "Vision and Action on Boosting the Joint Construction of Silk Road Economic Belt and 21st Century Maritime Silk Road," March 28, 2015.
3 Authorised for publication. "Vision and Action on Boosting the Joint Construction of Silk Road Economic Belt and 21st-century Maritime Silk Road," Xinhua Network. Retrieved February 27, 2018 from www.xinhuanet.com/world/2015-03/28/c_1114793986.htm
4 Ibid.
5 Liu Weidong et al., *Research on the B&R Strategy*. Beijing, Commercial Press, 2017 edition, pp. 98–100.
6 National Development and Reform Commission of PRC, Ministry of Foreign Affairs of PRC and Ministry of Commerce of PRC, "Vision and Action on Boosting the Joint Construction of Silk Road Economic Belt and 21st Century Maritime Silk Road," March 28, 2015.
7 "Origin of the 16+1 cooperation: as said by the premier of China and Hungary," Central Government Portal. Retrieved February 28, 2018 from www.gov.cn/xinwen/2017-11/28/content_5242918.htm

88
MIDDLE CORRIDOR INITIATIVE WITH THE BELT AND ROAD INITIATIVE

Xue Li

Conceptual description and formation process of the Middle Corridor Initiative

The Middle Corridor Initiative (hereinafter referred to as "this plan") is also called the Middle Corridor Project, and it is a development plan proposed by the Turkish government to build a transportation network connecting Turkey and China: from Turkey, by way of Georgia, Azerbaijan, the Caspian Sea, Turkmenistan, Kazakhstan, Uzbekistan, Afghanistan and Pakistan, and finally to China.[1]

Historically, Turkey was an important node in the Silk Road, and even Constantinople (now called "Istanbul") was the destination of the Silk Road in the powerful and prosperous period of the Ottoman Empire. Currently, many clothes brands, restaurants, colleges and Turkish roads are named after the Silk Road, and the Silk Road has become an important resource for Turkey to show its sense of national pride. Many Turkish people like to say that Turkey and China lie at the starting point and destination in the Silk Road, respectively. Therefore, matters related to the Silk Road are well accepted by Turkey. After he assumed power in 2002, Recep Tayyip Erdogan, Chairman of Justice and Development Party, adjusted the diplomatic focus of invariable westward orientation, emphasised the eastern countries more and intentionally exploited the resources of the Ancient Silk Road.

In 2009, during a visit to China, Abdullah Gul, the President of Turkey, said to Hu Jintao, Chairman of China, that the Ancient Silk Road should be revitalised through the common effort of both governments.[2]

In 2011, during a visit to Turkey, Xi Jinping, the Vice-Chairman of China, discussed with the government heads of Turkey to attempt to revitalise the Silk Road. In 2012, during a visit to China, Erdogan again discussed with the government heads of China how to revitalise the Ancient Silk Road.

In July 2015, Erdogan visited China. Li Keqiang, Premier of China, expressed the wishes of China: to align the Belt and Road Initiative of China with the Middle Corridor Initiative of Turkey; to strengthen cooperation in infrastructure construction such as the railway and such industries as new energy, light industry and telecommunication; to boost a balanced growth of bilateral trade; to expand cooperation in the emerging fields of aviation, aerospace and finance; to help Turkey facilitate and support Chinese enterprises to invest in Turkey; to help both sides coordinate cooperation in the fields of politics, economy, trade and humanistics by utilising the mechanism of vice-premier intergovernmental cooperation commission. President Erdogan expressed the wishes of Turkey: to greatly develop a relationship with China; to welcome China to expand investment and cooperation in fields of Turkey such as infrastructure construction, energy, ICT, finance, aviation and project contracts; to become a production or logistic base of Chinese enterprises; and to join hands with China to launch cooperation in the third-party market, mainly in the countries involved in this plan.[3]

In October 2015, at the G20 Summit in Antalya, Turkey, China and Turkey jointly signed the "Memorandum of understanding on aligning the Belt and Road Initiative with the Middle Corridor Initiative" to provide a guideline for relevant cooperation fields of both sides.[4]

In November 2016, during a visit to Ankara, Wang Yi, Foreign Minister of China, and Mevlut Cavusoglu, Foreign Minister of Turkey, reached a consensus: to deepen the alignment between the Belt and Road Initiative and this plan; to innovate a concept and mode of cooperation; to boost large-scale cooperation projects such as the East–West High-Speed Railway; to strive for early harvest and realise a common development.[5]

In May 2017, at the Belt and Road Forum for International Cooperation, President Erdogan clearly expressed to include this plan as an important component of the Belt and Road Initiative.

Relation of the Middle Corridor Initiative with the Belt and Road Initiative

China can construct a land transportation channel to Europe via the the China–Central Asia–West Asian Economic Corridor, the China–Pakistan Economic Corridor and the Bangladesh–China–India–Myanmar Economic Corridor, but not via Russia. However, in the Bangladesh–China–India–Myanmar Economic Corridor and its transportation channel, the future becomes unpredictable due to slow progress from India. The China–Pakistan Economic Corridor is a flagship project of the Belt and Road Initiative. Many projects are being rapidly boosted such as Karot Hydropower station and Gwadar Port. The Karakoram Highway of upgrading renovation has been mostly completed, and the main road which passes through from the south to the north of Pakistan is being upgraded. The China–Pakistan Trans-Karakoram Railway has also been by Pakistan. Once it is completed, people will be able to use the existing railway lines of Pakistan to reach Zahedan, Iran to be connected to the Iran railway at Fahraj, Iran via ferry and then travel westwards to be connected to the Turkish railway, and finally to be connected to the railway network of Europe. In the China–Central Asia–West Asian Economic Corridor, the China–Kyrghizstan–Uzbekistan Railway goes westwards through Turkmenistan to be connected to the railway network of Iran, and then further to Turkey, and this option is shorter than the route across Pakistan.

Turkey has planned to upgrade the railway between Kars in the east and Edime in the west to a high-speed railway,[6] among which the Istanbul–Ankara section, 533 km long, was opened to the public in 2014 with a running speed 250 km/h. In Edime, the existing railways have been connected with Bulgaria, and will be connected with the East Europe–Mediterranean Corridor in the future, 1 of 9 transportation corridors to be preferentially developed by the European Union. In Kars, the existing railways have been connected with Baku, Azerbaijan and Tabriz, Iran, but the existing railways in Iran are dead-ends at the Mashhad–Turkmenistan and Fahraj–Zahedan sections.

Therefore, this plan proposed by Iran intends to respond to the Belt and Road Initiative, especially the China–Central Asia–West Asian Economic Corridor and the China–Pakistan Economic Corridor. This plan will boost the construction of these corridors, and thus wins recognition and support from China. Subsequently, both countries should explore the protocol for aligning this plan with the Belt and Road Initiative, such as how to gain support from relevant countries.

Significance, favourable conditions and challenge of the Middle Corridor Initiative

This plan greatly benefits China: to add a strong partnership country in constructing the China–Central Asia–West Asian Economic Corridor and the middle and southern route of New Eurasian Land Bridge; to further show the vitality of the Belt and Road Initiative, and to be beneficial to implement the China–Pakistan Economic Corridor and the Belt and Road Initiative in Iran. And as Turkey, with the highest gross economic volume in West Asia and an increasing influence in the Muslim world, actively responds to the Belt and Road Initiative, doubts about China will be reduced and enthusiasm for participating in the Belt and Road construction will be improved in the countries of Central Asia, South Asia and Transcaucasia, especially Kyrghizstan, Turkmenistan and Azerbaijan.

Moreover, this plan is significant for Turkey in various aspects.

(1) It can reinforce the relationship with China. After the proposal of the Belt and Road Initiative, Chinese enterprises will obviously increase investment in Turkey, and Chinese high-techn enterprises as represented by telecommunication, nuclear power, high-speed railway and new energy are all settled in Turkey, indicating that the investment environment in Turkey is attractive.[7] Considering that the Belt and Road construction often involves large-scale infrastructure projects, China attaches great importance to their attitude while selecting the cooperation countries. There are very few such countries as Turkey to propose the alignment with the Belt and Road Initiative in a developing country. Therefore, China will not only cooperate with Turkey in boosting the construction of Middle Corridor, but also probably increase investment in Turkey. For example, during the upgrading and renovation of the railway from the east to the west of Turkey, Chinese companies participated in the Phase II renovation project of the Istanbul–Karachi section, and the 158-km long railway was completed to high quality in 2014, which lays a sound foundation for further cooperation between both countries.

(2) It can help to build Turkey into a traffic hub between Asia and Europe. The 2000-km long Kars–Edime Railway crosses the whole territory of Turkey. After its upgrading renovation into a high-speed railway, transportation between the east and the west of Turkey will be greatly improved. After its westward adjoining with the European high-speed railway system and eastward connection with the Chinese transportation channel, Turkey will establish a position as a traffic hub between Asia and Europe. Because the Eastern Europe–Mediterranean Corridor proposed by the European Union is situated in the west of Turkey, Turkey can urge the European Union to connect this corridor with Turkey. Therefore, it is well justified for Turkey to respond to the Belt and Road Initiative through an action in the east of Turkey. After all, as long as several dead-end roads are completed, Turkey has a direct railway to China.

(3) It can improve the international position of Turkey and boost its national revitalisation. While assuming the post as president, Recep Erdogan continued to adhere to the policy of "Integration into Europe" at the beginning. However, during subsequent years, setbacks were repeatedly encountered. By realising that the European Union is a club of Christianity but not an union of civilisation, President Erdogan modified his diplomatic policies, and started to adhere to a New Osmanlism: to advocate an ethnical and religious equality; to improve the influence of Turkey in the Muslim world under the premise that western countries are not abandoned; to boost the coalition of Turkic countries; to take various measures to reinforce the politics, economy and culture of the Turkic Union, including the member states of Turkey,

Kazakhstan, Kyrghizstan, Uzbekistan, Turkmenistan and Azerbaijan; and to reinforce relations with East Asian countries.

A stable and strong support from governments is necessary for the success of large-scale infrastructure construction, especially for cooperation projects in a developing country, e.g. the Middle Corridor; and China–Central Asia–West Asian Economic Corridor. At present, the political situation is stable in Turkey, which is favourable for the construction of these corridors.

Despite many favourable factors and a great prospect, the alignment between this plan and the Belt and Road Initiative should overcome some challenges for its execution.

(1) Difficulty in the route design. The shortest route of the Middle Corridor is as follows: from Kars, Turkey to Baku, Azerbaijan via Armeniad; across the Caspian Sea to Turkmenbasy, Turkmenistan; eastwards along the railways of Turkmenistan; and finally to China via Uzbekistan and Kyrghizstan. However, due to disputes among the coastal countries, the Caspian Sea is seriously limited in its utilisation, e.g. the development of oil and gas resources, sea oil and gas pipeline and shipping. Despite being the best choice, the construction of a sea bridge is unlikely to be implemented in the foreseeable future.

(2) Impedance from the relationship between the USA and Iran by rerouting Iran to Turkmenistan or Pakistan. Donald Trump, President of the USA, obviously reverted the Iran policies of Barack Hussein Obama, former President of the USA, to make the toughness the main tone of US policies to Iran. Although President Erdogan does not coordinate with the USA as before, it is difficult for Turkey as an ally of the North Atlantic Treaty Organisation to develop a relationship with Iran on a grand scale by completely ignoring the viewpoints of the USA. Moreover, the schedule has not yet been set for implementing the China–Kyrghizstan–Uzbekistan Railway and the Trans-Karakoram Railway.

(3) Limited funding of Turkey for the construction of the Middle Corridor. Since Erdogan assumed power in 2003, Turkey has shaken off serious inflation to enter a stage of rapid economic development. In 2016, the GDP of Turkey reached US$856.7 billion[8]; Turkey became the 17th largest economy in the world and the 1st largest economy among the West Asian countries. However, Turkey has very limited funds for overseas investment for the following reasons: numerous funds are needed for domestic investment; low personal saving rate; and a serious deficit in the current account.[9] Therefore, Turkey can mainly provide political support for the construction of the Middle Corridor.

(4) Security problems in Turkey influence the implementation of this plan. In order to retaliate against the action of the Turkish government, the Partiya Karkern Kurdistan frequently launches terrorist attacks, whose influence has spread from the south and the south-east of Turkey to such key cities as Ankara[10] and Istanbul.[11] Therefore, the number of tourists to Turkey drops greatly, which will inevitably influence the investment and construction in Turkey, especially in eastern areas.

Notes

1 Zheng Qingting, "The president of Turkey wishes the Middle Corridor to become an important component of the B&R," *21st Century Business Herald*, May 15, 2017.
2 Li Zhenhuan, "Rudimentary formation of Turkish block of the B&R," *Guangming Daily*, April 19, 2015.
3 Tan Jingjing, "Li Keqiang meeting President Erdogan of Turkey," Xinhua Network. Retrieved March 2, 2018 from www.xinhuanet.com/world/2015-07/29/c_1116082658.htm
4 "Spotlight: China, Turkey working toward modern Silk Road," Xinhua Network. Retrieved March 2, 2018 from www.xinhuanet.com/english/2016-11/28/c_135864545.htm
5 Shi Chun, Zou Le, "China and Turkey deeply accommodating the B&R Initiative with Middle Corridor Plan," State Council Information Office of PRC. Retrieved March 2, 2018 from www.scio.gov.cn/ztk/wh/slxy/31200/Document/1519441/1519441.htm

6 "Spotlight: China, Turkey working toward modern Silk Road," Xinhua Network. Retrieved March 4, 2018 from www.xinhuanet.com/english/2016-11/28/c_135864545.htm
7 Wu Yu, "The B&R Initiative as division line for Chinese enterprises investing in Turkey," Xinhua Network. Retrieved March 4, 2018 from www.sh.xinhuanet.com/2017-10/23/c_136699694.htm
8 In 2016, the GDP of Turkey increased by 2.9%. Ministry of Commerce of PRC. Retrieved March 5, 2018 from www.mofcom.gov.cn/article/i/jyjl/j/201704/20170402553307.shtml
9 "Overview: Turkey vigorously invests in the infrastructure construction to drive an economic growth," Huanqiu Network. Retrieved March 5, 2018 from http://world.huanqiu.com/hot/2016-06/9080851.html
10 "Claiming of an organization related to the Partiya Karkeren Kurdistan for terrorist attack to Ankara City," China News Network. Retrieved March 5, 2018 from www.chinanews.com/gj/2016/03-17/7801391.shtml
11 "Increasingly severe situation of anti-terrorism in Turkey," People's Network. Retrieved March 5, 2018 from http://world.people.com.cn/n1/2016/1213/c1002-28946935.html

89
CHINA–EU CONNECTIVITY PLATFORM (JUNCKER PLAN) WITH THE BELT AND ROAD INITIATIVE

Liu Wei and Wei Siying

Response of the European Union to the Belt and Road Initiative

Since the proposal of the Belt and Road Initiative, the European Union as an integral whole and another 28 member states have not been specified as Belt and Road countries although the terminal of the Belt and Road is set as Europe.[1]

However, the China–CEE connectivity projects are first included by the Central and Eastern European (CEE) countries into the Belt and Road framework. In June 2014, at the China–CEE Ministerial Conference on Promoting Trade and Economic Cooperation, the "Joint document of China–CEE Ministerial Conference on Promoting Trade and Economic Cooperation" was jointly released by the heads of all countries concerned, which proposes that all countries concerned should continue to adhere to the principle of "mutual respect, equality, mutual benefit and advantage complementation"; by seizing the opportunity in boosting the Silk Road Economic Belt and the 21st Century Maritime Silk Road, EU member states should, according to their own laws and regulations and the relevant laws and regulations of the European Union, further strengthen the economic and trade dialogue, improve the level of economic and trade cooperation, expand the new cooperation field and promote a common development and prosperity.[2]

Subsequently, some Western European countries began to contact China about the Belt and Road Initiative. In June 2014, during a visit by Li Keqiang, Premier of China, Greece wished as follows: to become a portal and hub for Chinese products to enter Europe; to strengthen marine cooperation with China; to jointly boost the construction of the 21st Century Maritime Silk Road; and to boost a continuous new achievement in Greece–China cooperation and Europe–China cooperation.[3] In March 2014, Xi Jinping, Chairman of China, visited the headquarters of the European Union, and the "Joint statement on deepening the China–EU comprehensive strategic partnership for mutual benefit and win–win" was jointly released, which expressed that both sides should jointly exploit the accommodation points between the Silk Road Economic Belt Initiative and the policies of the European Union, and explore a joint proposal for starting a cooperation among the Silk Road Economic Belt.[4] In March 2015, in the "Vision and actions on jointly building the Silk Road Economic Belt and the 21st Century Maritime Silk Road" from China, the Belt and Road Initiative was formally confirmed to strive for a connectivity in the Asian–European–African continents and adjacent sea. Although Europe is the destination of the Belt and Road Initiative, China progressively decides to include the European Union into the Belt and Road framework.

Even though China and Europe have reached a preliminary intention to strengthen cooperation under the Belt and Road framework, the European Union and Western European countries overall still take a wait-and-see attitude for the Belt and Road Initiative; and a definite aligning point has not been found by China and the EU. In March 2014, Chairman Xi Jinping visited Duisburg, Germany. Then, the Chinese embassy in Germany and Think-Tank Foundation from Berlin jointly organised a series of relevant activities on the Belt and Road Initiative to discuss various contents of Belt and Road Initiative such as concept, scope and depth. However, no substantial cooperation plan has been reached by both sides.[5] With the boosting of Belt and Road construction, the European Union and some of the main Western European countries are at a complex state of mind. In the viewpoint of the European Union, the Belt and Road Initiative is both an opportunity and a challenge for Europe: (1) the Belt and Road Initiative will promote an infrastructure connectivity and trade and investment growth to benefit the growth of regional economy; (2) the Belt and Road Initiative will jeopardise consistency of internal standards and rules in Europe.[6]

Strategic alignment between the Investment Plan for Europe of the EU and the Belt and Road Initiative

At the end of November 2014, the Investment Plan for Europe (also called "The Juncker Plan", hereinafter referred to as "this plan") was released by the European Union, which became a turning point in the alignment between the European Union and the Belt and Road. At the new European Commission, a promotion of growth, employment and investment was specified in this plan, including 3 main parts: (1) to establish the European Fund for Strategic Investments (EFSI) with a total volume of 21 billion EUR in order to drive an industrial, governmental and private investment of at least 315 billion EUR during the period 2015–2017. The EFSI is the core pillar for the Juncker Plan; (2) to jointly establish a trustworthy project platform through coordination between EFSI and the relevant assistance plans of the European Union to attract an investment of private sectors in the most necessary fields and meet the need of real economy; (3) to formulate a route map for attracting more investment; improve the business environment and financing conditions; and remove the barrier of industrial, financial and non-financial investment.

This plan is proposed by the European Commission, and it intends to lever private investment through the fund and public resources of the European Union; attract an investment of funds in real economy of the European Union; promote employment, economic growth and investment in the European Union; encourage investment in fields of strategic infrastructure, digital, energy and industrial centre, traffic infrastructure, education, research, employment promotion and sustainable environment; and actively support the investment in small and medium-sized enterprises, which may face market invalidation. Moreover, various concrete measures and action protocols such as energy alliance, capital market alliance, a digital unified market strategy and circular economy plan are boosted by the European Union to remove a real barrier and improve an investment environment.[7]

This plan aligns with the Belt and Road Initiative at a highly strategic level in the following aspects.

(1) They pay close attention to the same priority areas and are complementary in experiences and advantages. Among the agenda of the investment plan of the European Commission, the Trans-European Transport Network involves the construction of transportation corridors inside the European Union such as roads, rail, ports, airports and inland water transportation; and a unified European traffic transportation system to be completed by 2030 is a key field of their alignment. In addition, the European Union actively boosts connection of European energy infrastructure, including: inter-regional cross-country power network, especially supply network and nuclear power project; and the key fields of their alignment also include various projects of information communication infrastructure (broadband, cloud computation and big data), digital economy, electronic commerce, information technological infrastructure, smart city and internet of things.

(2) They both have a great need for financing attraction and risk sharing. Due to the largest challenge of insufficient investment fund, this plan hopes to lever extensive private capital through a public fund to increase investment, create jobs and improve competitive power. Europe takes an attitude of opening and welcoming for third-party funds, especially the Belt and Road financing. The Belt and Road construction also hopes to attract the participation of European multilateral development banks and commercial financial institutions, so as to realise joint financing and risk-sharing. Both sides enjoy an extensive cooperation space in the fields of developing a public–private partnership, promoting investment of small and medium-sized enterprises and boosting sustainable development financing.

(3) They mutually promote creation of the business environment, reduction of the investment barrier and boosting of the laws and regulations regarding comprehensive, complete and standard coordination.[8] As an important agenda, this plan aims to improve the business environment and financing conditions and remove various investment barriers; and the Belt and Road construction proposes a policy communication, fund circulation and facility connection to create a market environment of more freedom, opening-up and connectivity. The influence of the European Union in various fields of system mechanism, laws and regulations and concept guiding can be actively utilised to create an open and inclusive market rule for the Belt and Road construction.

The highly strategic matching between the Belt and Road Initiative and this plan also lays the foundation for strategic alignment between China and Europe. At the end of June 2015, at the 17th EU–China Summit, the heads of China and the European Union made the following resolutions: to align the Belt and Road Initiative with this plan; to establish the China and Europe Mutual Investment Fund; to establish the China–EU Connectivity Platform (hereinafter referred to as "this platform"); and to reach a comprehensive China–Europe Investment Treaty as soon as possible. At this summit, various concrete aligning measures were also specified: to establish a joint working group; to refine the aligning method; to strengthen cooperation in this platform; and to establish a transparent portal of European investment projects.[9] On September 28, 2015, at the 5th China–EU High-Level Economic and Trade Dialogue, three consensus items were reached. (1) As the first non-EU country of such announcement, China invests in the EU Investment Plan (whose total initial investment amount is estimated at 315 billion EUR). (2) A Joint Working Group is established to boost an overall cooperation in investment fields between both sides, which is composed of experts from institutions of the National Development and Reform Commission of PRC; the European Commission; the Silk Road Foundation of China; and the European Investment Bank. (3) Both sides mainly explore a mode and framework for establishing the Sino-European Cooperation Fund.[10] The "Memorandum of understanding on the China–EU Connectivity Platform" was also signed by both sides to strengthen the coordination and cooperation between the Belt and Road Initiative and this platform. This platform will promote the cooperation of both sides in fields of infrastructure, equipment, technologies and standards; create various business opportunities; and promote the employment, growth and development of both sides. This platform relies on cooperation with the European Investment Bank.[11] This dialogue launches a good commencement for strategic alignment between the Belt and Road Initiative and this plan.

China–EU Connectivity Platform: multilateral effort in the international cooperation of the Belt and Road Initiative

In September 2015, at the 5th China–EU High-level Economic and Trade Dialogue, China and the European Union jointly announced to establish this platform upon the proposal of the European Union, indicating that a formal mechanism is established for the alignment between this plan and the Belt and Road Initiative. After the establishment of this platform, 2 chairman conferences and 1 working group conference have been held. On June 29, 2016, at the 1st Chairman Conference of the China–EU Connectivity Platform, the working group reported its early work progress and the future cooperation suggestion of this platform, and submitted a work mechanism and a priority action list of demonstrative projects to the chairman of both sides for review.[12] On November 24–25, 2016, according to the requirements of the minutes on the 1st Chairman Conference of the China–EU Connectivity Platform, the 1st Conference of Expert Panel on the Investment and Financing Cooperation of the China–EU Connectivity Platform was held: both sides fully exchanged their own financing policies, mode and potential cooperation mechanism; mainly discussed the priority action list of demonstrative projects of this platform; introduced relevant conditions such as project overview, current progress and financing mode in detail; and explored the financing supporting policies and future cooperation opportunity.[13] On June 1, 2017, the 2nd Chairman Conference of the China–EU Connectivity Platform was held in Brussels, Belgium to cover the following contents: to listen to the working report of both sides in fields of the project list, policies and regulations, technical specifications and project investment and financing; and to reach a consensus on strengthening the alignment of strategies and policies; boosting the implementation of demonstrative projects; and deepening cooperation in China Railway Express; green low-carbon traffic, customs clearance facilitation, standards and technical specifications.[14] This platform will effectively boost the alignment between the Belt and Road Initiative and this plan, especially on the policy alignment and standard coordination between the Belt and Road construction and Trans-European Transport Networks, improve the transparency of market environment and realise a substantial cooperation of projects.

On the one hand, the European Union shows an effort in boosting the China–Europe multilateral cooperation under the Belt and Road framework by proposing an establishment of this platform. The EU hopes to attract Chinese funds to the EFSI in order to strengthen the connectivity cooperation in infrastructure, rules and standards. The EU hopes to include the project cooperation between China and European countries, especially EU member states, in the fields of infrastructure, traffic, transportation and telecommunication in the framework of this plan to boost the multilateral route for China–Europe cooperation under the Belt and Road framework; and play the influence of the EU in the European economy, system and norms so as to ensure that the EU has a controlling power in the participation of the Belt and Road construction. On the other hand, the EU is worried about the unity of the European Union being influenced by the bilateral cooperation and subregional cooperation such as the 16+1 cooperation plan between China and EU member states; China may adopt standards inconsistent with those of the EU for the Belt and Road projects by bypassing the EU to weaken the uniform market rules in the EU.[15] The EU boosts the coordination under the multilateral platform as represented by this platform, intending to coordinate China in following the European rules and standards of investment for the Belt and Road projects; establish a common framework through this platform; determine the strategies, plans and policies of cooperation; and specify the legal issues on rules and principles for joint projects.

Notes

1. Zhang Ji, Cheng Zhimin, "China–European accommodation under the B&R Initiative: double-layer visual angle of EU," *World Economics and Politics*, 2015, 11, p. 37.
2. Common documents of the China–CEE Ministerial Conference on Promoting a Trade and Economic Cooperation. June 9, 2014. Retrieved March 1, 2018 from www.mofcom.gov.cn/article/ae/ai/201406/20140600616162.shtml
3. "Li Keqiang at joint attendance and speech with Premier Samaras of Greece," People's Network. Retrieved March 1, 2018 from http://politics.people.com.cn/n/2014/0621/c1024-25179666.html
4. "Joint declaration for deepening a comprehensive strategic China–European partnership of mutual benefit and double-win," Central Government Portal. Retrieved March 1, 2018 from www.gov.cn/xinwen/2014-03/31/content_2650712.htm
5. Jan Gaspers, "Germany and the Belt and Road Initiative: Tackling Geopolitical Implications through Multilateral Frameworks," in Frans-Paul van der Putten et al., editors, *Europe and China's New Silk Roads, A Report by the European Think-tank Network on China (ETNC)*. December 2016, p. 26.
6. Michal Makock, "The EU Level: Belt and Road Initiative Slowly Coming to Terms with the EU Rules-based Approach," in Frans-Paul van der Putten et al., editors, *Europe and China's New Silk Roads, A Report by the European Think-tank Network on China (ETNC)*. December 2016, p. 67.
7. Thibault Heuzé, "The European Investment Plan: Main Features and Possible Synergies with OBOR Initiative," EU–China Public Lectures, Delegation of the European Union to China, Chengdu, 2016.
8. Dragan, "Suggestions of policies for promoting an accommodation between the B&R Initiative and the Investment Plan for Europe," *Chinese Journal of European Studies*, 2015, 6, p. 39.
9. "Factsheet on 'EU–China Investment Cooperation'," EU–China High Level Economic Dialogue, Beijing, September 28, 2015, http://ec.europa.eu/priorities/jobs-growth-investment/plan/docs/factsheet-eu-china-investment-cooperation_en.pdf
10. Thibault Heuzé, "The European Investment Plan: Main Features and Possible Synergies with OBOR Initiative," EU–China Public Lectures, Delegation of the European Union to China, Chengdu, 2016.
11. Yan Lei, "China will accommodate with the Investment Plan for Europe," *Economic Information Daily*, September 29, 2015, column 004.
12. "Successful holding of 1st Chairman's Conference of China–EU Connectivity Platform," National Development and Reform Commission of PRC, Retrieved March 1, 2018 from www.ndrc.gov.cn/gzdt/201606/t20160630_809633.html
13. "1st Conference of the Investment and Financing Expert Panel of China–EU Connectivity Platform held in Beijing City," Central Government Portal. Retrieved March 3, 2018 from www.gov.cn/xinwen/2016-11/30/content_5140147.htm
14. "Hu Zucai (deputy head) attending the 2nd Chairman's Conference of China–EU Connectivity Platform," National Development and Reform Commission of PRC. Retrieved March 1, 2018 from www.ndrc.gov.cn/gzdt/201706/t20170608_850292.html
15. Michal Makock, "The EU Level: Belt and Road Initiative Slowly Coming to Terms with the EU Rules-based Approach," in Frans-Paul van der Putten et al., editors, *Europe and China's New Silk Roads, A Report by the European Think-tank Network on China (ETNC)*. December 2016, pp. 69–70.

90
EASTERN PARTNERSHIP WITH THE BELT AND ROAD INITIATIVE

Xiao He

Formation of the Eastern Partnership

The Eastern Partnership (EaP, hereinafter referred to as "this plan") is a part of the European Neighbourhood Policy (ENP) framework proposed by the European Union in 2004. ENP is a joint initiative framework jointly proposed by the European Union, EU member states and EU's eastern and southern neighbouring countries, aiming to improve the level of political coalition and economic integration between the European Union and the above countries. There are 16 target countries in the ENP, which are classified into 2 types: target countries of the Eastern Partnership and target countries of the Euro-Mediterranean Partnership. Among the Eastern Partnership, there are 6 ENP target countries: Armenia, Azerbaijan, Belarus, Georgia, Moldova and Ukraine. Different from the governance inside the European Union and the EU governance for EU-accession and potential candidate countries, the ENP emphasises a Europeanised renovation of target countries in political, economic and social fields, but the ENP's target countries are not intended for EU accession within a short time. Therefore, ENP essentially aims to realise an outward development of internal policies of the European Union under a premise that the scope of the European Union is not expanded, which is a neighbourhood Europeanisation.[1]

This plan is mainly supported by eastern and northern European countries wishing for an eastward movement of the European Union. In 2007, the concept of the Union for the Mediterranean was first proposed by Nicolas Sarkozy, President of France, which was generally supported by the EU member states advocating a southward movement of the EU. At the end of 2007, this plan was proposed by Poland, which was supported by Sweden. In May 2008, at the European Union Conference on Foreign Affairs and General Affairs, this plan was jointly initiated by Poland and Sweden. In June 2008, at the European Union Summit, this plan was passed in the same year, after the outbreak of the Georgia crisis and the Russia–Georgia War, the formation of this plan was boosted. In December 2008, a concrete policy framework for this plan was proposed by the European Commission, which was formally passed in March 2009. On May 7, 2009, at the 1st European Union Summit on the European Eastern Partnership, the "Declaration of European Eastern Partnership" was jointly signed by the governmental heads or representatives of 27 EU member states and 6 countries of this plan in Prague, which indicated that this plan was officially formed and launched.[2]

Since it was held in 2009 for the first time in Prague, Czech, the EU–Eastern Partnership Summit has been held 5 times, among which the Summit held in Riga, Latvia in 2015 was of the greatest influence. At the Summit, the "20 Deliverables for 2020 Proposal" was jointly proposed by all attendants to specify fields and projects of priority development in this plan by 2020 and 4 development objectives, i.e. stronger economy, stronger governance, stronger connectivity and stronger society. Among the concrete objectives, the most important objectives include: to upgrade the traffic infrastructure by constructing the Trans-European Railway Network (TEN-T Network); to strengthen the political ownership of high-efficiency energy; to provide more financial support for small and medium-sized enterprises; to reduce tariffs among partner countries; to increase trade opportunity among partner countries; to strengthen contact with grass-root citizen organisations; and to give more support to youth groups.[3] This proposal is a basic development guideline for cooperating under the framework of this plan in future years. In 2017, at the 5th EU–Eastern Partnership Summit in Brussels, this proposal was restated by Donald Franciszek Tusk, Chairman of the European Commission: in the future, the European Union and all countries concerned will mainly invest in fields of small and medium-sized enterprises, digital economy, traffic, energy and infrastructure. In addition, with a continuous challenge from the Ukraine crisis, the Summit also emphasised the need to support partner countries in maintaining their sovereignty, independence and territorial integrity and peacefully settle a dispute on the basis of relevant international laws. Moreover, actual actions were taken to further strengthen the relationship with Armenia; the "Comprehensive Partnership Strengthening Agreement" and an aviation agreement were signed; and the Trans-European Railway Network was extended to European eastern partner countries.[4]

The Belt and Road Initiative and Central and Eastern European countries under the framework of this plan

As shown in the key development fields of this plan specified at the 3rd EU–Eastern Partnership Summit in Riga, this plan and the Belt and Road Initiative obviously have joint benefits and match concepts. In fact, China actively promotes alignment between the Belt and Road Initiative and this plan from the level of the European Union and its member states, which also significantly influences the development and economic cooperation plan of CEE countries. As a whole, the Belt and Road Initiative mostly accommodates with the EU member states of this plan on the "20 Deliverables for 2020 Proposal" in the fields of investment in infrastructure, reduction of trade barrier and improvement of trade liberalisation degree.

(1) Infrastructure. As actively supported by the EU member states, especially the CEE countries as represented by Hungary, China enlarges the infrastructure investment in this area within the Belt and Road Initiative. The following measures are always taken by both sides: to actively discuss the alignment between the Belt and Road Initiative and the European Investment Fund; to establish the China–EU Connectivity Platform; to promote the construction of cross-border railways such as the Trans-European Railway Network to alleviate the imbalance of infrastructure investment and economic development between the east and west of Europe; and to reinforce the internal cohesiveness of the European Union and the vitality of this plan by strengthening internal connectivity in Europe.[5] In September 2015, at the 5th China–EU High-level Economic and Trade Dialogue, the European Commission stated that both sides aligned the Belt and Road Initiative with the Investment Plan for Europe, which was proposed at the end of 2014 by Jean-Claude Juncker, Chairman of the European Commission. Moreover, the "Memorandum of understanding on establishing the China–EU Connectivity Platform" was signed to promote a better alignment of both sides in the infrastructure construction,

investment plan and policies and regulations.[6] Among the member states, in April 2017, at the Visegrad Foreign Ministers' Conference in Warsaw, all attendees advocated the European Union to pay more attention to the development of this plan; and Peter Szijjarto, Foreign minister of Hungary emphasised vigorously promoting energy cooperation and transportation connection among CEE countries, which will also benefit the Belt and Road Initiative.[7] In October 2016, the China Railway Express from Yiwu, China to Riga, Latvia was opened, which greatly promotes the development of Eastern Europe as a key node of Eurasian logistics. In addition, the Hungary–Serbia Railway connecting Greece and Hungary is also under active preparation.

(2) Trade liberalisation. Under the Belt and Road framework, various measures are taken by China to boost the construction of port and land transportation, reduce the trade barrier and facilitate customs procedures, which have not only significantly promoted the trade between China and CEE countries but also improved the trade level between other EU member states and 16 CEE countries. According to the statistical data, the import trade volume of CEE areas from the European Union will increase by 0.99% if the procedures of their customs are simplified by 1%, and by 0.11% if the level of their land infrastructure is improved by 1%.[8] Up to 2016, the total trade volume between China and CEE countries reached US$58.64 billion, which accounted for 10.19% of the total trade volume between China and Europe and grew by 9.5%; on the contrary, in 2016, the total trade volume of China overall dropped by 6.8%, and by 3.3% to Europe, which was a clear contrast.[9] At present, Poland, the Czech Republic and Hungary have become the 3 most important trade partners of China in CEE areas, and the hub connecting the Belt and Road Initiative with this plan.

At present, through a multilateral mechanism, including the 16+1 cooperation plan, the Belt and Road Initiative has progressively aligned with the EU member states under the framework of this plan. In November 2017, the Budapest Guidelines was reached at the summit between China and central and eastern European countries held in Budapest, which clearly specified to more deeply coordinate the planning and boosting of the Belt and Road Initiative, 16+1 cooperation plan, China–EU Connectivity Platform and Eastern Partnership Plan.[10] Therefore, this indicates that in the future, China will also cooperate more with the EU member states under the framework of this plan.[11]

The Belt and Road Initiative with 6 eastern partner countries under the framework of this plan

Besides the EU member states, 6 non-EU eastern partner countries of this plan, i.e. Belarus, Ukraine, Moldova, Armenia, Azerbaijan and Georgia, launched economic cooperation and plan alignment with China under the Belt and Road framework, which has made a demonstratively early achievement in Belarus and other countries.

Among the 6 eastern partner countries, Belarus is the country which has the earliest alignment and the smoothest cooperation with the Belt and Road Initiative, and is also one of the countries whose cooperation has developed most rapidly worldwide under the Belt and Road framework. As early as January 2014, the "Cooperation agreement on jointly constructing the Silk Road" was jointly signed by the Ministry of Commerce of PRC and the Ministry of Economy of the Republic of Belarus. In May 2015, Alexander Grigoryevich Lukashenko, President of Belarus, clearly stated to completely support the Belt and Road assumption proposed by China and wished to become its important pillar of the initiative. Subsequently, the "On developing a bilateral relationship between Belarus and China" (President executive order No. 5) was released by Belarus to renew and coordinate Belarus's existing development plans from a starting point of participation in the Belt and Road Initiative. In September 2016, the "List of measures for jointly boosting the Belt and Road construction between Belarus and China" was formally launched by heads of China and Belarus.[12] Through these cooperation measures, Belarus has become a pivot country during the whole Belt and Road construction, and occupies a critical position in the Belt and Road Initiative. China–Belarus Great Stone Industrial Park at a critical stage of combined development and operation has become a demonstrative achievement for a successful alignment between the Belt and Road Initiative and Belarus's development strategy, and is regarded as a pearl in the Silk Road Economic Belt.

Ukraine is the first European country to announce its support for the Belt and Road Initiative. As early as December 2013, during a visit to China, Viktor Fedorovych Yanukovych, the Premier of Ukraine, signed a series of agreements with China on the implementation of the Belt and Road Initiative. Although serious domestic and foreign politics and military crises subsequently broke out in Ukraine, China has persisted in cooperating with Ukraine under the Belt and Road framework. Up to 2017, the cooperation has been expanded in trade, especially agricultural products, and various agreements have been reached on the infrastructure construction and investment with a total value of more than US$6 billion, including such large-scale landmark projects in Ukraine such as construction of the DSSC Wharf; channel dredging of Yuzhne Port (Odessa); and Metro Line 4 of Kyiv.[13] In January 2017, at a meeting in Davos, Switzerland, Xi Jinping, Chairman of China, and Peter Poroshenko, Premier of Ukraine, further confirmed that both sides will strengthen the cooperation of mutual benefit and win–win under the Belt and Road framework.

Three Transcaucasian countries and Moldova also show strong enthusiasm for participating in the Belt and Road Initiative, and Georgia especially takes a very active attitude. In June 2016, Giorgi Kvirikashvili, Premier of Georgia, wrote an article by himself to wish to play the role of location advantage for the Europe–Asia connection under the Belt and Road construction; and build Georgia into a central hub in Eurasia logistic transportation through the Chinese investment in infrastructure. In 2014, the "Associated Country Agreement" was signed between Georgia and the European Union. By actively utilising an advantage of trade environment granted by this agreement, Georgia vigorously developed the bilateral trade with China and attracted Chinese investment in manufacturing industry. Subsequently, the alignment of bilateral development was rapidly launched. In 2015, Georgia became the first Eastern European country to negotiate with China on a free trade agreement, and signed the "Memorandum of cooperation on strengthening a joint construction of the Silk Road Economic Belt".[14] Georgia attempts to realise rapid development by closely coordinating with the Belt and Road Initiative. In addition, Azerbaijan and Armenia hope that China will further play a role in the economic cooperation in the Transcaucasian area. For example, a preferential policy of "income tax reduced or exempted by 50% within 7 years" was released by Azerbaijan for China in the fields of agriculture and energy. The South–North Highway, its road artery in Armenia, was constructed by Sinohydro Corporation from China.[15] In December 2017, the "Memorandum of understanding on starting the negotiation on free trade agreement" was jointly signed by Moldova and China, which formally started the negotiation of free trade agreement between both sides. The above achievements of the countries concerned have been made by continuously deepening the development and alignment through the Belt and Road initiative.[16]

Notes

1 Ren Sang, "Shifting from section-based governance to network-based governance: analysis of governance of countries around the Eastern Europe," *Chinese Journal of European Studies*, 2015, 3, p. 50.
2 Xu Gang, "Evaluation of Eastern Partnership Plan of EU," *International Forum*, 2010, 5, p. 26.

3 Eastern Partnership. European Union External Action, https://eeas.europa.eu/headquarters/headquarters-homepage/419/eastern-partnership_en
4 Eastern Partnership summit, 24/11/2017. Council of European Union, www.consilium.europa.eu/en/meetings/international-summit/2017/11/24/
5 Zheng Dongchao, "Viewpoints of China–CEEC Think Tanks Network for the B&R Initiative," *China Investment*, 2017, 4, p. 56.
6 "European Commission welcoming an accommodation between the B&R Initiative and the Investment Plan for Europe," Xinhua Network. September 29, 2015. www.xinhuanet.com/world/2015-09/29/c_1116708073.htm
7 "Foreign ministers of Visegrad Group advocate the European Union to stress a development of Eastern Partnership Plan," Xinhua Network. April 13, 2017. www.xinhuanet.com/world/2017-04/13/c_1120803290.htm
8 Sun Yuqin, Su Xiaoli, "Comparison of export of China and European Union influenced by the trade facilitation among the Central and Eastern European Countries under the B&R Initiative," *Journal of Shanghai University of International Business and Economics*, 2018, 1, p. 34.
9 Luo Qiong, Zang Xueying, "Problems in the diversified cooperation between China and Central and Eastern European Countries under the B&R background," *Journal of International Economic Cooperation*, 2017, 9, p. 80.
10 "The Budapest Guidelines for Cooperation between China and Central and Eastern European Countries," Chinese embassy in USA. November 8, 2017. www.china-embassy.org/eng/zgyw/t1514534.htm
11 "Preliminary achievements in strategic accommodation with the B&R Initiative," *People's Daily* (overseas edition), April 17, 2017, column 1.
12 Zhao Huirong, "Belarus and the B&R Initiative," *Russian Central Asian & East European Market*, 2017, 4, pp. 48–49.
13 Zhang Hong, "Risks and their countermeasures in the B&R cooperation between China and Ukraine," *Peace and Development*, 2017, 4, pp. 112–115.
14 Premier of Georgia, "Role playing of regional superiority in Europe–Asian connection under the B&R construction," Xinhua Network. June 28, 2016. www.xinhuanet.com/world/2016-06/28/c_129096319.htm
15 "Geographical superiority of Transcaucasian countries along the B&R," People's Network. May 8, 2017, http://world.people.com.cn/n1/2017/0508/c1002-29260637.html
16 "Starting a free trade negotiation between China and Moldova on December 28, 2017," Belt and Road Portal, www.yidaiyilu.gov.cn/slxwzy/41571.htm

91
EURASIAN PARTNERSHIP PLAN BASED ON EQUAL, OPEN AND TRANSPARENT PRINCIPLES WITH THE BELT AND ROAD INITIATIVE

Feng Weijiang

On May 8, 2015, the "Joint statement for cooperating in the construction alignment between the Silk Road Economic Belt and the Eurasian Economic Union" was jointly released by China and Russia in Moscow, Russia, which is an important consensus. On June 17, 2016, at the "Plenary meeting of St Petersburg International Economic Forum", Vladimir Putin, President of Russia, appealed at his speech to establish the Greater Eurasian Partnership Plan (hereinafter referred to as "this plan"), which includes the Eurasian Economic Union (EEU), China, India, Pakistan, Iran, countries of the Independent Commonwealth States and other interested countries or international organisations. He proposed to enlarge the synergy within a flexible integrated and structural framework and effectively accomplish a series of production and economic tasks just through a common effort and mutual coordination under the current objective situation.

This appeal was actively responded by to China. On June 25, 2016, the "Joint statement of the People's Republic of China and the Russian Federation" was jointly signed by President Vladimir Putin during his visit to China and Xi Jinping, Chairman of China. The statement clearly specified that China and Russia proposed to build the Comprehensive Eurasian Partnership Plan on the basis of opening-up, transparency and mutual benefit. The EEU, Shanghai Organisation Cooperation and ASEA member states may be included into this plan and the deepening of regional integration proceeding will be boosted by implementing this plan. In order to implement this joint statement, the "Joint statement for formally initiating a negotiation on the Economic and Trade Cooperation Agreement between China and the Eurasian Economic Union" was signed between the Ministry of Commerce of PRC and the Eurasian Economic Commission, which formally initiated such negotiation. On July 4, 2017, at a witness of Chairman Xi Jinping and President Vladimir Putin, the "Joint statement for joint feasibility study on the Eurasian Economic Partnership Agreement" was signed in Moscow by Zhong Shan, Minister of the Ministry of Commerce of PRC, and Maxim Oreshkin, Minister of the Ministry of Economic Development of Russia, to launch a feasibility study on the Eurasian Economic Partnership Agreement. The signing of the statement shows the firm confidence of both countries to deepen cooperation of mutual benefit, boost a trade liberalisation and regional economic integration, and a common wish to explore a comprehensive, high-level arrangement of trade and investment liberalisation to be open to other economies in the future.

The cooperation scope of this plan is still continuously expanded. The heads of EEU member states will also negotiate with both India and Egypt, Iran and Singapore on the free trade zone. This plan is also open to Europe. As said by President Vladimir Putin, this plan is an open initiative, and coordination with the European Union would benefit both sides. In the future, this plan may involve countries and organisations in Europe and Asia, i.e. East Asia, South East Asia, South Asia and Central Asia.

Principles of the Eurasian Partnership Plan

This plan adheres to a principle of "equality, opening-up and transparency".

(1) Equality is a basic principle for handling an international relationship, especially international economic cooperation. With no discrimination in small or large territories, weak or strong powers and poor or rich economies, all partners in this plan are equal members and have an equal right to participate in economic cooperation in this plan. Any affair involving all countries concerned should be handled through joint discussion. All countries concerned should adhere to the concept of "friendly negotiation, joint construction and achievement sharing"; consider the benefit and concern of all countries concerned; reach a consensus as far as possible to ensure a equality, equal opportunity and equal rules quality for all countries concerned with economic cooperation in this plan.

(2) The opening up is a source impetus for international economic cooperation. As proven by the history of world economic development, the opening up brings progress, while isolation results in backwardness. By returning to the old route of "shifting one's troubles onto others", its own crisis and recession cannot be shaken off, and furthermore a common space of international economic cooperation and development will be narrowed, causing a lose–lose situation. In the principle of opening up, the Eurasia partnership is to adhere to a concept of "openness, inclusiveness, general benefit and win–win"; establish a Eurasia regional cooperation framework of equal negotiation, common participation and general benefit; revitalise an engine effect of trade and investment; strengthen an open and inclusive arrangement of trade and investment; maintain a multilateral trade system; but not make a fragmented, closed or exclusive arrangement.

(3) Transparency is an important guarantee for international economic cooperation. The fair, reasonable and transparent rule and system of economy, trade and investment can create a stable and predictable environment for doing business with transparent norms and which is favourable for opening up and development; promoting liberalisation and the facilitation of trade and investment, ensuring orderly flow of production essentials, high-efficiency allocation of resources and a deep merging of the market in each partner of this plan; and finally forming a large-scale open economic space across Eurasia.

Cooperation contents of the Eurasia partnership

Although a roadmap similar to the "Vision and action on jointly boosting the Belt and Road construction" has not been released by Russia for the Eurasia partnership, the following contents are included in this plan according to its official opinions and think-tank analysis.[1] (1) To reduce a non-tariff barrier, promote a facilitation of trade and investment, i.e. to simplify and normalise the regulations and procedures for investment, health, customs and intellectual property protection; and promote the simplification of mutual investment and developing industrial cooperation. (2) To strengthen cooperation in infrastructure construction with connectivity: as one of key infrastructure constructions in this plan, the Eurasia Corridor High-Speed Railway connects Berlin, Germany and Urumqi, China via Poland, Belarus, Russia and Kazakhstan to Berlin, Germany. On August 24, 2017, a pre-feasibility study report on the construction project of the Eurasia Corridor High-Speed Railway was discussed at the meeting of the Ministry of Transport of Russia. On this railway line, the section within Russian territory accounts for 44.3% of the whole length, with a designed running time of 9.5 hours, while the section from Brest, Belarus to Dostyk, Kazakhstan has a designed running time of 19.5 hours. The average running speed is designed at 250 km/h. The freight transportation is mainly executed through the section from China to Europe (7.9 million tons), and the annual passenger capacity will reach 36.9 million person-times by 2050. In addition, the Polar Silk Road (i.e. the northern route of the Arctic Ocean) is also boosted by Russia. As an integral and global project, the enlarged Eurasia partnership also includes the Turkmenistan–Afghanistan–Pakistan–India natural gas pipeline, the cross-Korean railway, the Greater Dooman River Initiative and the South East Asian Economic Corridor. (3) To cooperate in currency and finance: to promote an increase of local currency settlement in trade, direct investment and loan; to create a currency swap; to deepen cooperation in export credit, insurance, project and trade financing and bank card; and to strengthen cooperation among financial institutions of the Asian Infrastructure Investment Bank, the Silk Road Foundation and the SCO Consortium. (4) To jointly construct industrial parks and cross-border economic cooperation areas.[2]

Alignment of the Eurasia partnership with the Belt and Road Initiative

With the principle of equality, opening-up and transparency, this plan is very similar to the Belt and Road Initiative in aspects of objective, concept, key cooperation regions and field, which lays a cooperation foundation for their alignment.

(1) Objective. The joint construction of the Belt and Road initiative intends to promote an orderly free flow of economic essentials, a high-efficiency allocation of resources and a deep merging of the market; boost a coordination of economic policies among the Belt and Road countries; launch a regional cooperation of larger scope, higher level and deeper layer; and jointly establish a regional economic cooperation framework of openness, inclusiveness, balance and general benefit. The Belt and Road Initiative is a road of cooperation and win–win for promoting a common development and realising a common prosperity; and also a road of peace and friendship for enhancing understanding and trust and strengthening all-round exchange.[3] This plan strives to strengthen the stability of the Eurasian space to ensure prosperous and stable development. Therefore, both documents have the same objectives.

(2) Concept. Both the Eurasia Partnership and the Belt and Road Initiative implement the spirit of peace, cooperation, openness, inclusiveness, mutual learning, mutual referencing, mutual benefit, win–win, equality, transparency and mutual respect; strengthen the cooperation based on a joint discussion, joint construction and sharing while following the principles of rule by law and equal opportunity. In the "Joint Communiqué of Leaders' Round-Table of the Belt and Road Forum for International Cooperation", the confirmed principles of equal negotiation, mutual benefit, win–win, harmony, inclusiveness, market-based operation, balance and sustainability were accepted by the heads of many EEU countries including President Vladimir Putin.

(3) Cooperation regions. The Belt and Road Initiative preliminarily advocates a route across the Asian–European–African continent: with an active East Asian economic circle at one terminal and a developed European economic circle at the other terminal, while broad hinterland

countries in the middle. The Silk Road Economic Belt connects 3 main routes: from China to Europe (the Baltic Sea) via Central Asia and Russia; from China to the Persian Gulf and the Mediterranean Sea via Central Asia and West Asia; and from China to South East Asia, South Asia and the Indian Ocean. The 21st Century Maritime Silk Road opens 2 main routes: from Chinese coastal ports to the Indian Ocean and further to Europe across the South China Sea; and from Chinese coastal ports to the South Pacific Ocean across the South China Sea.[4] At the Belt and Road Forum for International Cooperation, it was specified to be rooted in the historic soil of the Silk Road; orient on the Asian–European–African continent; open up to all friends[5]; strengthen the Eurasian connectivity; and open up to other areas such as Africa and Latin America.[6] This plan cooperates with the key countries and areas which are almost the same as those in the Belt and Road Initiative, and also emphasises the opening up to other interested countries and organisations.

(4) Cooperation fields. Both documents advocate to liberalise and facilitate trade and investment; develop infrastructure construction and connectivity; strengthen cooperation in currency and finance, including settlement via local currency; strengthen the exchange of people; and boost the civilisation, mutual referencing, openness and inclusiveness.

In recent years, with a principle of equality, opening-up and transparency, a more solid foundation has been laid for the alignment between this plan and the Belt and Road Initiative through various consensuses and a series of joint statements reached by 2 or more sides, such as between China and Russia, between China and the Eurasian Economic Union and via the Belt and Road Forum for International Cooperation.

Notes

1 Li Ziguo, "Greater Eurasian Partnership Plan and the B&R Initiative," *Overseas Investment & Export Credits*, 2017, 5.
2 Andrey Denisov, "Accommodation of Eurasian Economic Union with the Silk Road Economic Belt: new direction for comprehensive coordinative Russia–Chinese strategic partnership," *China Investment*, 2015, 7.
3 National Development and Reform Commission of PRC, Ministry of Foreign Affairs of PRC, Ministry of Commerce of PRC, "Vision and Action on Boosting the Joint Construction of Silk Road Economic Belt and 21st-century Maritime Silk Road," March 2015. www.xinhuanet.com/world/2015-03/28/c_1114793986.htm
4 Ibid.
5 Xi Jinping, "Speech at the opening ceremony of B&R Forum for International Cooperation: joining hands to boost the B&R construction." May 14, 2017. www.xinhuanet.com/politics/2017-05/14/c_1120969677.htm
6 "Joint communiqué of the Round Table Summit of B&R Forum for International Cooperation." May 15, 2017. www.xinhuanet.com/world/2017-05/15/c_1120976819.htm

92
INITIATIVE FOR INTEGRATION OF THE REGIONAL INFRASTRUCTURE IN SOUTH AMERICA WITH THE BELT AND ROAD INITIATIVE

Xiao He

IIRSA and COSIPLAN

In 2000, the 1st Summit Meeting of South American Presidents was jointly held in Brasilia, Brazil by 13 South American countries: Argentina, Bolivia, Brazil, Chile, Colombia, Ecuador, Guyana, Paraguay, Peru, Surinam, Uruguay, Venezuela, etc. At this summit, the "Initiative for Integration of the Regional Infrastructure in South America" (IIRSA) was jointly proposed by heads of these countries to improve the modernisation level of regional transportation, energy and telecommunication facilities; improve the regional connectivity level under a premise that all countries concerned have equal sovereignty and rights with sustainable development; and improve the overall competitive power of South America. Then, this annual summit was gradually formalised and institutionalised. In December 2004, at the 3rd Summit Meeting of South American Presidents, the "Cuzco Statement" was released to announce an establishment of the South American Community of Nations (CSN). In 2008, the "Constitutive Treaty of UNASUR" was formulated in Brasilia, Brazil, by all attending countries under the proposal of Venezuela to establish the Union of South American Nations (UNASUR). Correspondingly, the IIRSA (Initiative for Integration of the Regional Infrastructure in South America) Initiative was also included into the governance framework of UNASUR. In January 2009, at the 3rd Council of UNASUR, the South American Infrastructure and Planning Council (COSIPLAN) was formally established as a ministerial commission. IIRSA was also included in the COSIPLAN to provide technological support for the regional connectivity plan of COSIPLAN.[1]

In the COSIPLAN, there are three categories of institutions: (1) 4 special working groups: telecommunication and railway integration, geographic information system and network, finance and guarantee; (2) a coordinating committee composed of representatives of all countries concerned; and (3) an IIRSA Technical Forum, with 8 executive technical groups for boosting integration proceedings in definite fields: transportation and logistics, aviation, port and shipping, railway, telecommunication, border, trade and finance. In addition, the Technical Coordinating Committee of IIRSA provides consulting support for relevant decisions, which is composed of representatives of financial institutions: the Inter-American Development Bank (IDB); the Corporation Andina de Fomento (CAF); the River Plate Basin Financial Development Fund (FONPLATA); and the Brazilian National Development Bank (BNDES).[2]

According to the statistical data in 2016, among the project complex of the South America infrastructure integration in the COSIPLAN, 89% of projects involved traffic transportation, which accounted for 71% of the total planned investment, and the remaining projects mainly involved energy. In 8 fields, the proportion of number of projects was listed as follows: road 44.2%, inland shipping 12.7% and railway 11.3%. In terms of amount of investment, the proportion of projects among the total investment amount was listed as follows: road 32.6%, energy 28.9% and railway 26.3%. Therefore, the construction of the road and railway network is the focus of IIRSA for boosting infrastructure integration. The road projects mainly concentrates on the MERCOSUR-Chile Hub and the Capricorn Hub, among which 60% of road projects have been started or completed, and only 10% of road projects are at the stage of early planning. At present, 39% of railway projects are still at the stage of early planning. Among all planned projects, the projects of the Andean Hub account for 3% and 38% in terms of quantity and amount of investment, respectively. In terms of amount of investment, the projects of the Capricorn Hub and the Parana Waterway account for 27% and 21% of all planned projects, respectively.[3]

Alignment of the Belt and Road Initiative with the IIRSA Initiative

The planning and implementation of the Belt and Road Initiative always attracts the close attention of many South American countries. In 2016, the Chilian ambassador to China stated as follows in public: Latin American and Caribbean States should be included into the Belt and Road Initiative; and especially the cross-border infrastructure of South America can be newly built, improved or restarted through the Chinese infrastructure investment, including the Cross-Andes International Railway which connects Chile with Argentina across the Andes.[4]

As a response, in July 2014, soon after the proposal of the Belt and Road Initiative, Xi Jinping, Chairman of China, visited Brazil, Argentina and Venezuela and attended the "Conference of Leaders of China, Latin American and Caribbean States" in Brasilia, Brazil. In the Brasilia joint statement of this conference, the significance of infrastructure was jointly emphasised by all attendees that infrastructure can promote trade and economic growth and social development; and it is especially important to construct and renovate the railways, roads, ports, airports and telecommunications. At the keynote speech of "Striving to construct a community of shared future for mankind for joining hands and progressing together", Chairman Xi Jinping promised that China would formally implement the China–Latin America infrastructure special loan of US$10 billion and the quota of the special loan will be increased to US$20 billion.[5] As specified by the heads of China, Brazil and Peru, 3 countries will not only provide funding support, but will also jointly produce a basic feasibility study on the construction of the Twin Ocean Railway, so as to realise a railway connection of Brazil with Peru and expand the construction of traffic infrastructure in South America.[6]

In January 2015, at the "1st Ministerial Meeting of the Forum of China and the Community of Latin American and Caribbean States" in Beijing, China, the "Cooperation plan of China, Latin American and Caribbean States (2015–2019)" was passed, which clearly specified encouraging powerful Chinese and Latin American enterprises to participate in the key projects for benefiting the integration of Latin America and the Caribbean, and improving the connectivity between China and member states of the Community of Latin American and Caribbean States; and supporting key cooperation projects between China and member states of the Community of Latin American and Caribbean States by fully utilising the China–Latin America Cooperation Foundation; China–Latin America infrastructure special loan; and Chinese concessional loan and other financial resources.[7] In the same year, during a visit to Brazil, Colombia and Chile, Li Keqiang, Premier of China proposed a series of production capacity cooperation plans, which included formally starting the basic feasibility study on the Twin Ocean Railway. As also stated by Dilma Rousseff, President of Brazil, at this meeting, Brazil will invite Chinese companies to participate in the project construction of the Twin Ocean Railway, which will become a convenient channel of shorter distance and lower cost from Brazil to Asia.[8]

Subsequently, China and South American countries continuously deepened the cooperation in infrastructure construction. In April 2015, Brazil joined the Asian Infrastructure Investment Bank as a founding member state. Then, some South American countries successively applied to join the Asian Infrastructure Investment Bank: Peru, Venezuela, Bolivia, Chile and Argentina. Under the support of China, many achievements have been made in connectivity construction of some South American countries. For example, China undertook the construction of several roads and several hydropower stations in Ecuador, including Coca Codo Sinclair Hydropower Station at the largest scale.[9] In 2017, through the active interaction of both sides, a new stage was finally reached for a strategic alignment of the Belt and Road Initiative with South American countries and the IIRSA Initiative. On May 10, 2017, at the eve of the Belt and Road Forum for International Cooperation, the "Joint Belt and Road construction: concept, practice and Chinese contribution" was released by China to adjust the positioning of Belt and Road Initiative, which clearly stated to welcome the Latin American and Caribbean region to participate in the Belt and Road construction. China will be dedicated to aligning the development strategies with Latin American and relevant Caribbean countries, and boost a pragmatic cooperation in various fields through the concept, principle and cooperation mode of joint Belt and Road construction.[10] Through such new positioning, the Belt and Road Initiative is changed to break the past regional restriction; respond to the active appeal of South American countries for participating in the Belt and Road Initiative; and encourage both sides to further launch the alignment of regional infrastructure integration under the Belt and Road framework. Through such a starting point, the alignment between the Belt and Road Initiative and the IIRSA Initiative is upgraded from the practical level to the formal level.

Prospect for South American countries to participate in the Belt and Road Initiative

After the scope of the Belt and Road cooperation is formally expanded and a formal alignment is implemented between the Belt and Road Initiative and the IIRSA Initiative, a new stage is rapidly entered for the cooperation of China with South American and Latin American countries. In May 2017, at the Belt and Road Forum for International Cooperation, China first reached a joint statement with Argentina, which was the first joint statement between China and South American countries for the Belt and Road Initiative. It confirmed that both sides will strengthen the alignment of development strategy under the Belt and Road framework, boost connectivity and linking development and continue to implement the existing key cooperation projects of hydropower, nuclear energy and railway.[11] In November 2017, the "Memorandum of understanding on constructing the Belt and Road and cooperating in the railway traffic system" was jointly signed by China and Panama as the first memorandum of understanding between China and Latin American countries for the Belt and Road construction. As also proposed by Panama for facility connectivity, Panama is to be built into a hub radiating to the Central America and Caribbean areas and a railway is to be constructed connecting Panama with Costa

Rica through the Chinese funds and technologies.[12] On December 19, 2017, Ecuador, Belarus, the Cook Islands and Vanuatu jointly joined the Asian Infrastructure Investment Bank, which enabled the number of South American countries who applied to join the Asian Infrastructure Investment Bank to rise to 6. In a word, an extremely great potential and prospect is enjoyed for China to cooperate with South American and Latin American countries in the construction of regional infrastructure integration.

Because the construction of roads and railways is the key investment field of IIRSA, the greatest prospect and the most profound influence will undoubtedly be enjoyed for China to cooperate with South American countries in the construction of railway integration in the future. At present, a general railway construction plan has been determined by the Executive Technical Group of Railway Integration (COSIPLAN) under the IIRSA framework: 3 east–west horizontal routes—from Valparaiso Port, Chile to Buenos Aires, Argentina; from Antofagasta, Chile to Paranagua Port, Brazil; and Peru–Bolivia–Brazil Twin Ocean Railway. In 2015, Chile stated to welcome Chinese enterprises for participating in the construction of tunnel project at the Chile–Argentina section of the Twin Ocean Railway; and one vertical route from Buenos Aires, Argentina to Santa Cruz, Bolivia. In addition, 2 important railway routes in South American areas have been jointly explored by China, Brazil and Peru many times: 1 horizontal route of the Twin Ocean Railway from Kampos, Brazil to Puerto Bayovar Port, Peru; and 1 vertical route from Rio Grande State, Brazil to Belem, Brazil. In a word, an integrated railway network of 4 horizontal routes and 2 vertical routes will be built in South America.[13]

Notes

1 History: South American Infrastructure and Planning Council of UNASUR, www.iirsa.org/Page/Detail?menuItemId=121
2 Organization: South American Infrastructure and Planning Council of UNASUR, www.iirsa.org/admin_iirsa_web/Uploads/Pages/files/organigrama%20web%20ingles.PNG
3 "Transportation Projects Top the COSIPLAN Portfolio," Inter-American Development Bank, http://conexionintal.iadb.org/2016/04/07/las-obras-en-transporte-encabezan-la-cartera-del-COSIPLAN/?lang=en
4 "Chile wishing an expansion of the B&R," China Investment, www.chinainvestment.com.cn/type_hgzc_tzsj/6268.html
5 Xi Jinping, "Keynote address at the Conference of Leaders of China, Latin American and Caribbean States: striving to construct a community of shared future for mankind for joining hands and progressing together," Xinhua Network, July 18, 2014. www.xinhuanet.com/world/2014-07/18/c_1111688827.htm
6 "Declaration of Chin–Brazil–Peru for cooperation in the Twin Ocean Railway," Central Government Portal. July 18, 2014. www.gov.cn/xinwen/2014-07/18/content_2719749.htm
7 "Cooperation Plan of China, Latin American and Caribbean States (2015–2019)," People's Network. January 10, 2015, http://world.people.com.cn/n/2015/0110/c157278-26360355.html
8 "China–Brazil Cooperation projects, closely relevant to everyone," People's Network. May 20, 2015, http://politics.people.com.cn/n/2015/0520/c1001-27031855.html
9 Xie Wenze, "Accommodation with the B&R Initiative, and boosting a construction of fate community of between China and Latin America," China Social Science Network, December 27, 2017, http://ex.cssn.cn/skyskl/skyskl_jczx/201712/t20171227_3795709.shtml
10 "Joint construction of the B&R: concept, practice and Chinese contribution," Xinhua Network. May 2017, www.xinhuanet.com/politics/2017-05/10/c_1120951928.htm
11 "Joint declaration of China and Argentina," China Network. May 18, 2017, www.china.com.cn/news/2017-05/18/content_40842903.htm
12 "Memorandum of understanding for joint boosting the construction of Silk Road Economic Belt and 21st-century Maritime Silk Road (signed by China and Panama)," Belt and Road Portal. November 25, 2017, www.yidaiyilu.gov.cn/xwzx/gnxw/35763.htm
13 Xie Wenze, "Railway cooperation between China and South America under the B&R view," *Pacific Journal*, 2016, 10, pp. 54–55.

93
THE MASTER PLAN ON ASEAN CONNECTIVITY 2025 WITH THE BELT AND ROAD INITIATIVE

Xue Li and Liu Tianyi

Conceptual description and main contents

On September 7, 2016, at the 27th ASEAN Summit, the Master Plan on ASEAN Connectivity 2025 (hereinafter referred to as "this plan") was passed. This plan will become a part of "Kuala Lumpur Declaration of ASEAN 2025: forging ahead together", and also the subsequent document in the Master Plan on ASEAN Connectivity 2010. As an overall objective, this plan aims to establish an merged, linked and integrated ASEAN and improve the competitiveness, inclusiveness and cohesiveness of ASEAN. A connectivity of ASEAN is also a fundamental means to boost the formation of the SEAN Community of political security and mutual trust, regional economic merging and sociocultural exchange. In this plan, 3 pillars are set: infrastructure connectivity, such as transportation, information, energy and telecommunication technology; institutional connectivity, such as the liberalisation of trade, investment and service; and people-to-people connectivity, such as education, culture and tourism. Moreover, 5 priority strategic fields are specified: sustainable infrastructure, digital innovation, seamless logistics, excellent supervision and people flow.

(1) As an important content of ASEAN connectivity construction, the strategy of sustainable infrastructure has 3 main objectives: to increase the public and private investment on infrastructure in each ASEAN member state when necessary; to coordinate the existing resources to support the whole life cycle of ASEAN infrastructure and significantly improve ASEAN's ability of infrastructure construction; to exchange the experience in the mode of smart urbanisation among the ASEAN member states and accelerate a more extensive popularisation of this mode in ASEAN so as to promote a growth of society and economy and improve the quality of life of the common people. Three proposals are also raised: to set a cyclical rotary list of ASEAN infrastructure projects and sources of funding; to establish an ASEAN platform to measure and improve the production force of infrastructure; and to formulate a sustainable urbanisation strategy for each city of ASEAN.

(2) ASEAN strives to realise a strategy of seamless logistics through 2 main objectives: to reduce the cost of supply chain among ASEAN member states and establish a mechanism for supporting cooperation among logistic companies in ASEAN member states to remove the

bottleneck of supply disjoining in key areas; and to improve the speed and reliability of supply chain among the ASEAN member states and strengthen a sharing of logistic experience and measures among ASEAN member states. Two proposals are also raised: to improve the competitive power of ASEAN by improving the smoothness of trade route and logistics in ASEAN; and to improve the efficiency of the supply chain in ASEAN by improving the bottleneck problem of transportation obstruction in key areas.

(3) The strategy of excellent supervision has 2 main objectives: to make the key departments of ASEAN member states reach a consensus and mutual acceptance on the standard coordination and technical specifications of products; and to reduce the trade distortion among ASEAN member states caused by non-tariff measures. Two proposals are also raised: to reach consensus on product standards, mutual acceptance and technical specifications of priority products for ASEAN connectivity construction; and to improve transparency and strengthen supervision during the ASEAN connectivity construction to reduce the trade distortion caused by non-tariff measures.

(4) In the strategy of people flow, 4 proposals are raised: to facilitate access to travel information and promote tourism development in ASEAN; to facilitate visa handling among ASEAN member states; to formulate a common training protocol for professional qualification and issue a uniform qualification certificate according to the national situation of ASEAN member states; and to support the exchange of cross-country higher education among ASEAN member states.[1]

Alignment of the Master Plan on ASEAN Connectivity 2025 with the Belt and Road Initiative

As specified in this plan, there are 3 pillars of infrastructure connectivity, institutional connectivity and people-to-people connectivity and 5 priority strategic fields of sustainable infrastructure, digital innovation, seamless logistics, excellent supervision and people flow. These pillars and strategic fields directly correspond to the 5 long-term approaches specified in the Belt and Road Initiative, i.e. policy coordination, infrastructure connectivity, unimpeded trade, financial integration and understanding between people.

(1) Policy coordination. The Belt and Road Initiative can align with individual strategies of ASEAN member states, and deeply align with their own development plans, i.e. the Marine Fulcrum strategy from Indonesia; the strategy of changing from land-locked country to land-linked country from Laos; the rectangular strategy from Cambodia; the ambition 2040 strategy from the Philippines; and the 1-circle and 2-corridor strategy from Vietnam to continuously optimiae a top-level design and plan for pragmatic cooperation in various fields. China and ASEAN countries[2] can strengthen intergovernmental cooperation; actively establish multi-level intergovernmental communication and exchange mechanism for macroscopic policies; deepen the benefit merging; promote mutual political trust; reach a new consensus on cooperation; fully exchange and align on the strategies and counter-measures of economic development; jointly formulate plans and measures for boosting regional cooperation; solve problems in cooperation through negotiation; and jointly provide policy support for pragmatic cooperation and large-scale project implementation.

(2) Infrastructure connectivity. ASEAN can align with China in connectivity and infrastructure construction. The infrastructure construction is an important component of ASEAN connectivity, and also a priority field of the Belt and Road Initiative. At the 8th ASEAN–China Strategic Seminar on Connectivity, Elizabeth Buensuceso, rotating Chairperson of the ASEAN Connectivity Coordination Committee, expressed that ASEAN would like to boost cooperation in aligning this plan with the Belt and Road Initiative and welcomes multilateral

financial institutions such as the Asian Infrastructure Investment Bank to actively participate in the infrastructure construction of ASEAN.[3] China and ASEAN can cooperate in fields of traffic transportation, telecommunication network and energy security, including the projects of the ASEAN road network, the Trans-Asian Railway, the inland river transportation network, the seaway, the air transportation network, a comprehensive transportation corridor, telecommunication and energy infrastructure.

(3) Unimpeded trade and financial integration. ASEAN can have more cooperation with China in commerce and trade. With continuous improvement of economic strength, China has become the most important trade partner for many countries and regions. In 2010, the China–ASEAN Free Trade Zone was established, which was then upgraded and developed. At present, many Chinese entrepreneurs have made huge investments in the traffic, residence and building fields of ASEAN. With strong economic strength, Chinese people with foreign nationality and overseas Chinese people in South East Asia have become an important bridge for China and ASEAN to establish a connectivity relationship. China and ASEAN should further expand the field of trade; optimise the structure of trade; exploit a new growth point of trade; promote a balance of trade; organically combine the investment with trade; drive the development of trade through investment[4]; accelerate investment facilitation; and remove the barrier to investment. At present, Chinese internet hi-tech enterprises of Alibaba Group, Huawei Technologies Co., Ltd and Zhongxing Telecommunication Equipment Corporation are actively investing in ASEAN countries such as Indonesia and cooperating with local enterprises, which can promote employment growth; establish and perfect the supply chain, industrial chain and value chain of ASEAN enterprises in ASEAN areas; and improve the position of ASEAN countries in the global industrial layout.[5]

(4) Understanding between people. ASEAN and China should continuously strengthen the people exchange, which has reached annual 30 million person-times. China has become the largest source country of tourists to Thailand, Vietnam, Indonesia and Cambodia and the second largest to Singapore. The tourist exchange of both sides not only deepens mutual understanding, but also brings about economic benefits.[6] In order to lay a solid foundation among the common people for deepening bilateral and multilateral cooperation, China and the ASEAN countries should extensively launch the activities of cultural exchange, academic communication, talent exchange and cooperation, media cooperation, youth and women communication and volunteering services.

Notes

1 "Master Plan on ASEAN Connectivity 2025," Association of South East Asian Nations, January 25, 2018. Retrieved February 27, 2018 from http://asean.org/?static_post=master-plan-asean-connectivity-2025-2
2 Xu Bu (Chinese ambassador in ASEAN. Article in the *Jakarta Post* (Indonesia)), "Accommodation between the B&R Initiative and ASEAN Community Vision (2025)," Ministry of Foreign Affairs of PRC. Retrieved February 25, 2018 from www.fmprc.gov.cn/web/dszlsjt_673036/t1460913.shtml
3 "Representatives of ASEAN wishing to boost an accommodation between the ASEAN Connectivity Plan and the B&R Initiative," Xinhua Network. Retrieved February 25, 2018 from http://news.xinhuanet.com/2017-07/14/c_1121322257.htm
4 Issuance of "Vision and Action on Boosting the Joint Construction of Silk Road Economic Belt and 21st-century Maritime Silk Road". Ministry of Commerce of PRC. Retrieved February 27, 2018 from http://zhs.mofcom.gov.cn/article/xxfb/201503/20150300926644.shtml
5 Xu Bu (Chinese ambassador in ASEAN. Article in the *Jakarta Post* (Indonesia)), "Accommodation between the B&R Initiative and ASEAN Community Vision (2025)," Ministry of Foreign Affairs of PRC. Retrieved February 25, 2018 from www.fmprc.gov.cn/web/dszlsjt_673036/t1460913.shtml
6 Ibid.

94
THE PARIS AGREEMENT WITH THE BELT AND ROAD INITIATIVE

Tian Huifang

Since the Belt and Road Initiative was released in 2013, there has always been a worry about its potential influence on climate change. The coal-fired power plant with China's participation attracted special attention. Up to the end of 2016, China has participated in 240 such plants, including 106 plants being planned or under the construction stage in 25 Belt and Road countries. Because the objective of the Paris Agreement (hereinafter referred to as "this agreement") can only be realised by greatly reducing global emissions, there is still an important problem: are the ambitious projects of the Belt and Road Initiative the start of a new green development mode or just a promoter of incontinent growth? A clear answer is given in the Belt and Road Initiative.

Challenge of climate for the Belt and Road countries with the Paris Agreement

At the end of 2015, this agreement was signed, which shows a great victory of international community against climate crisis. Moreover, it creates a brand new mode of international climate governance, which gives full understanding and support for the development need of developing countries and strengthens global action for coping with climate change. Through an inclusive and dynamic mode of doing what the strength allows and only making a progress but not a recession, flexibility and seriousness is combined in global coping with climate change problems, and the forces and resources of various global countries and levels are more easily mobilised to jointly cope with a global climate crisis and avoid system upheaval, so that the climate action can persist for a long time and a future direction is specified for international climate governance. As stipulated in this agreement, the average temperature rise caused by the global greenhouse gas is controlled at 2°C and even 1.5°C so as to minimise long-term risk and influence caused by climate change. In this agreement, by including all countries for global emission, the global need for the traditional energies of coal, oil and gas will undoubtedly drop continuously to influence their enthusiasm for investment in traditional energy.

According to the statistics of the National Centre for Climate Change Strategy and International Cooperation under the National Development and Reform Commission of PRC, the Belt and Road Initiative countries, with a population and GDP as 2/3 and 1/3 of the global level, respectively, not only provide 60%, 55% and 70% of the global petroleum, natural gas and coal resources, but also consume nearly 50% of the global primary energy, electric power and such primary production resources as steel and timber. Due to large populations, the average per-capita energy and electric power consumption of Belt and Road countries accounts for only 80% of the average world level, thus there is great potential to increase.[1] At present, the greenhouse gas emissions of Belt and Road countries including China accounts for more than 50% of total global emissions. As shown in the assessment of the Chinese Academy of Sciences on resource and environmental performance,[2] the unit GDP energy consumption of 38 Belt and Road countries accounts for more than 50% of the average world level, but their unit GDP consumption of steel products, cement, non-ferrous metal and water is more than twice the average world level. With carbon emissions at more than 60% of the global level, the Belt and Road countries have a high energy need, and will also be the main areas with an increase of greenhouse gas emissions in the future. As predicted by the International Energy Agency (IEA), in the future, the request for coal will rise greatly in the Belt and Road countries of India and South East Asian countries, and the need for petroleum may tend to increase in the Middle East and some other Asian countries. However, the Belt and Road countries are mostly extremely sensitive to climate-related activities due to the vulnerable ecological environment, including 6 of 10 global countries most vulnerable to climate change; low level infrastructure construction; dense population; rigorous natural conditions in some areas and lower ecological carrying capacity.

Relevant stipulations on overseas investment are not specified in this agreement, and all countries make their commitment on intended nationally determined contributions (NDCs) according to their national situations: their stipulated actions of emission reduction are only applicable to their domestic scope, but do not involve the clauses of overseas investment supervision. As legally stipulated in this agreement, host countries can expropriate and nationalise energy investment according to the obligations of emission reduction stipulated in this agreement. Under the framework of this agreement, climate responsibility formally becomes legally binding social responsibility. Due to such change, political and legal risk will undoubtedly increase for energy investment. In terms of investment entry, an investment need of the Belt and Road countries for traditional energy will be further reduced by the obligations of emission reduction stipulated in this agreement, and climate responsibility probably becomes a powerful barrier for host countries to block the entry of investors; an investment at a traditional mode after the entry may still be expropriated or nationalised by the host countries with the excuse of climate responsibility, so that the investing countries are in an unfavourable position.[3]

Green commitment of the Belt and Road Initiative

As the contents of the Belt and Road Initiative are continuously enriched and sublimated, the concept of green development is gradually merged into the Belt and Road construction. In March 2015, the "Vision and action on jointly boosting the Silk Road Economic Belt and the 21st Century Maritime Silk Road" was jointly released by Chinese departments of the National Development and Reform Commission of PRC, the Ministry of Foreign Affairs of PRC and the Ministry of Commerce of PRC to strengthen cooperation in energy infrastructure connectivity and extensive cooperation in the fields of coal, oil, gas and renewable energy; to emphasise the concept of ecological civilisation for investment and construction; and to strengthen cooperation in coping with climate change. In June 2016, at a speech in the Legislative Chamber of Supreme Assembly of Uzbekistan, Xi Jinping, Chairman of China, emphasised the need to deepen cooperation in environmental protection; to practice a concept of green development; to strengthen the protection of the ecological environment; and to jointly construct a green Silk Road. In the 13th Five-year National Plan for Ecological Protection, special chapters are set for boosting a green-based Belt and Road construction, and the general work on ecological protection along the Belt and Road is uniformly planned for the future 5 years. In May 2017, in the keynote speech at the opening ceremony of the Belt and Road Forum for International Cooperation, Xi Jinping further emphasised the need to practice the new concept of green development; to advocate a green, low-carbon, cyclable and sustainable mode of production and living; to strengthen cooperation in ecological protection; to construct an ecological civilisation; to jointly realise the objectives of sustainable development in 2030; to establish a big-data service platform for ecological protection; to establish the International Alliance of Green Belt and Road Development; and to help relevant countries cope with climate change.

In May 2017, in order to implement the relevant Chinese deployments for accelerating a Green Belt and Road construction, the "Guidelines for boosting the green Belt and Road construction" was jointly released by 4 Chinese ministries such as the Ministry of Environmental Protection of PRC to specify the future green objective of the Belt and Road construction: to build up a pragmatic and highly efficient cooperation and exchange system, a supporting and service platform and an industrial technological cooperation base for ecological protection within 3–5 years; to perfect a service guarantee system of ecological protection; and to boost the implementation of important ecological projects within another 5–10 years. As a programmatic document for China to boost the green Belt and Road construction, this guideline overall merges the Chinese concept of green development into concrete tasks and the measures of 5 long-term approaches, i.e. policy coordination, infrastructure connectivity, unimpeded trade, financial integration and understanding between people; it plots a clear road map for China to construct a green Silk Road; and it shows the firm resolution of China to boost green development and strengthen strategic alignment and policy communication on the ecological protection among the Belt and Road countries for a green, prosperous and friendly Belt and Road construction.

Green action and direction of the Belt and Road Initiative

As a large-scale project, the Belt and Road Initiative influences the climate change in a complex way. As realised by China, an unbearable loss will be induced if the Belt and Road Initiative is not climate-friendly. Therefore, the leaders of China promise to make the Belt and Road construction green-based; actively promote ecological progress in investment and trade; strengthen cooperation in protecting the ecological environment, protecting biological diversity and coping with climate change; and build the Silk Road into a environmentally friendly road. In September 2016, at the G20 Summit in Hangzhou, China, the concept of green finance was proposed, and China promised to become the largest issuer of green bonds. In 2015, at the UN Leaders' Summit, the South–South Cooperation Fund was proposed by Chairman Xi Jinping to improve the ability of global south countries for coping with the climate change. At present, China has helped developing countries in the Chinese way. In 2015, at the Paris Climate Conference, China promised to support other developing countries at a value of US$3.1 billion, i.e. 20.5 billion RMB, through the South–South Cooperation Fund, which provides funds for developing countries through different financial institutions such as the Green Climate Fund. In addition, the China Climate Fund will launch 10–100–1000 projects of South–South cooperation in climate change, i.e. 10 demonstrative projects of low carbon, 100 projects of climate mitigation and adaptation and 1000 quotas of trainees in the developing countries for coping with climate change. These actions of China conform very well to the objective of this agreement.

On May 12, 2017, in order to boost the further implementation of "Guidelines for boosting the green Belt and Road construction", the "Cooperation plan for the ecological protection along the Belt and Road route" was printed and distributed by the Ministry of Environmental Protection of PRC to further specify that cooperation in ecological protection is a fundamental requirement of green Belt and Road construction. In this plan, the planning objectives of the Belt and Road Initiative 2030 are also formulated: to boost a concept merging ecological civilisation and green development into Belt and Road construction to form a good cooperative situation in environmental protection with the Belt and Road countries by 2025; to jointly boost a realisation of the objectives of sustainable development 2030, and continue to deepen the cooperation in ecological protection and improve cooperation level overall by 2030.

In December 2017, in order to further specify the working direction of green Belt and Road construction in the next 3 years, the "Action plan of standard connectivity for the Belt and Road joint construction (2018–2020)" was printed and distributed by the office of "Leading Group for Boosting the Work of Belt and Road Construction" to strengthen the formulation of the green Belt and Road standard and deepen cooperation in standardising the energy-saving fields. In this action plan, the objectives in the next 3 years are also formulated: to accelerate study and formulation of evaluation standards for green products; to boost the establishment of a product standard system; to strengthen cooperation exchange on the standards, certification and acceptance of green products; to popularise green product standards; to boost international mutual acceptance of certification and labelling of green products; to reduce the barriers to green trade; to promote the development of green trade; to boost the standardisation construction of green infrastructure; to improve the green and low-carbonisation level during the operation, management and maintenance of infrastructure through the standards; to reinforce the quality guarantee of ecological environment; to boost coordination with energy-saving standards of key Belt and Road countries; to launch cooperation and study on the energy-saving standardisation in the fields of air-cooling, air-conditioning and lighting products; and to support the construction of green industry and ecological cooperation projects. In 2016, China became the largest investor in clean energy with an investment amount of US$78.3 billion. Through the huge investment, a batch of suppliers for clean energy products emerges. In 2016, among the world top 10 enterprises of solar energy assembly and wind turbine, there were 8 and 5 Chinese manufacturers, respectively.

In September 2017, the "Environmental Risk Management Initiative for China's Overseas Investment" was proposed for Chinese financial institutions and enterprises participating in overseas investment: to fully borrow the international experience; to understand the environmental regulations and standards and relevant environmental risks in the location of projects; to observe the highest environmental standards of the relevant industries as far as possible; to reinforce information disclosure of environment, society and governance (ESG); to follow the principle of responsible investment; and to merge the concept of ecological civilisation and green development into the whole process of investment decision and project implementation. In January 2017, the "Guidelines for environmental and social risk in overseas investment" was released by the China Banking Regulatory Commission, and a working group was assigned for inspecting the overseas investment of banks so as to ensure that the overseas investment meets the requirements of this guideline. Moreover, the "Regulations on the enterprises' overseas investment" is being drafted and the list of environmentally sensitive industries is formulated by the National Development and Reform Commission of PRC.

All current striving directions of China consist with anticipations of this agreement. As always verified by China in a unique firm way, the Belt and Road Initiative will facilitate but not destroy global efforts in coping with climate change.

Notes

1 Chai Qimin, Qi Yue, Fu Sha, "Boosting the B&R countries for joint construction of low-carbon community," *China Development Observation*, 2017, Z2.
2 Research Group of Sustainable Development Strategy, the Chinese Academy of Sciences, *China sustainable development report (2015): remolding the ecological environment governance system*. Science Press, 2015 edition.
3 Liang Xiaofei, "International energy cooperation under the B&R Initiative: from the angle of Paris Climate Change Accord," *Theory Monthly*, 2017, 5, pp. 161–164.

95

TRANS-EUROPEAN TRANSPORT NETWORKS WITH THE BELT AND ROAD INITIATIVE

Feng Weijiang

Trans-European Transport Networks (TEN-T, hereinafter referred to as "this plan") is a series of EU plans and policies for integrating the various traffic means of Europe, such as roads, railways, airports and canals, into a uniform traffic transportation network. By coordinating and improving the main traffic management systems of road, railway, inland river channel, airport and port, this plan aims to form an integral and intermodal long-distance and high-speed transportation network.

Formation process of TEN-T

This plan stems from the "European common market plan (1992)". In 1992, the Maastricht Treaty was issued, which lays a legal foundation for this plan in infrastructure construction of traffic, telecommunication and energy. In 1993, a white paper on "Economic growth, competitive power and employment" was issued by the European Union, which specified that investment should be strengthened in the cross-European traffic network, which was regarded as one of the important development topics for suppressing the economic recession during 1992–1993. In June 1994, at the Conference of the European Commission, a catalogue of 11 priority traffic transportation projects was first passed. Six months later, at the Conference of the European Commission in Essen, Germany, it was decided to newly build and extend the existing road networks and expand 11 planned projects to 14 projects. The European Commission would provide a subsidy of European Communities for this plan.[1]

In 1996, Resolution 1692/96/E and the "Development guidelines for pan-Europe traffic transportation network" were passed through the review of the European Commission. Then, according to this resolution, a plan was formulated by the European Parliament and the European Council that a catalogue of 14 priority traffic transportation projects was chosen to be the core to realise the policies of traffic infrastructure. In May 2001, the Resolution 1346/2001/EC was passed by the European Parliament and the European Council that a development objective for coastal ports, inland waterway ports and inter-modal transportation hubs was added, which was included into the framework system of this plan. In April 2004, the Resolution 884/2004/EC was passed by the European Parliament and the European Council that a regional adjustment on the basis of Resolution 1692/96/EC was made to adapt to the change in traffic volume caused by the eastward expansion of the European Union. Due to the gradual increase in the number of member states, 30 priority projects were further determined by the European Union. In November 2007, the European Union announced a construction fund of 5 billion EUR for these 30 priority projects, including a total investment amount of 3934 million EUR for high-speed railways. In 2009, in order to formulate the the "EU financial budget framework (2014–2020)" in a more reasonably way, the economic and social benefit of this plan was systematically summarised by the European Union. After the regional adjustment in 2004, a transportation corridor connecting the eastern and the western EU member states has been completed according to this plan, which accelerates east–west connectivity. It is considered to be one of the most important achievements in this plan within the past 10 years. Through the development for more than 20 years, the scale of EU's comprehensive traffic network is continuously expanded and its structure tends to become more reasonable, so as to effectively support the economic and social development of the EU member states.[2]

In January 2014, after approval from the European Parliament and the European Council, this plan started the next stage of its work: to plan the infrastructure construction projects in a form of space layout to be completed and renovated by 2050, i.e. road, railway, aviation, inland water transportation, shipping, port, airport and goods storage, loading and unloading; to mainly open up 9 core transportation corridors across the whole Europe; and to solve the problems in unbalanced development and incompatible technical standards of European traffic transportation infrastructure. It is estimated that by 2050, the European Union will construct 94 large-scale ports with railway and road connection; 38 large-scale airports with direct railway connection to big cities; upgrading of 15,000-km long railways to high-speed railways; and 35 cross-border projects[3] to reduce the bottleneck of traffic transportation. Because the new EU member states have more backward infrastructure conditions, the development of EU economies and these countries will be substantially restricted and obstructed if the current situation is maintained and extra policies and measures are not taken. In order to solve the above problems, the European Union specified to provide a special fund of 26 billion EUR to relevant traffic projects, possibly increasing the relevant investment to 500 billion EUR by 2020, and plans to accomplish a core traffic network by 2030.

On June 17, 2016, 195 traffic projects within the territory of the European Union were announced by the European Commission. These projects will be funded at 6.7 billion EUR from the Connecting Europe Facility Plan, and will additionally lever a public and private investment of 2.9 billion EUR to possibly create 100,000 jobs by 2030. Moreover, these 195 projects are mostly at the core position of this plan.

Contents of TEN-T

The ultimate objective of this plan is to narrow the gap; remove the bottleneck; eliminate the technical obstacle among the transportation networks of the EU member states; strengthen the cohesiveness of the European Union in social, economic and regional fields; and contribute to the establishment of a single European transportation system. This objective is realised by this plan through the following measures: construct a new physical infrastructure; adopt innovative digital technology, alternative fuel and general standard; upgrade amd modernise the existing infrastructures and platforms.[4] This plan is composed of 2 parts: a comprehensive network covering all European regions and an important connection with the most important nodes in this comprehensive network.

In this plan, each transportation mode has its own network, including a cross-European road network, a cross-European railway network (including a pan-Europe high-speed railway network and a pan-Europe ordinary railway network), a cross-European inland waterway network and inland river port, a cross-European harbour network; a marine expressway, a cross-European airport network, a cross-European intermodal transportation network, a cross-European shipping management and information network, a cross-European aviation management network and a cross-European positioning and navigation network (including Galileo positioning system).

In this plan, 30 priority projects are determined: the Berlin–Palermo railway axis, the Paris–Brussels–Cologne–Amsterdam–London high-speed railway axis, the southwestern European high-speed railway axis, the eastern European high-speed railway axis, the Betuwe railway line, the Lyon–Chop railway axis, the Igoumenitsa–Budapest expressway axis, the intermodal transportation axis between the Iberian Peninsula and other European countries, the Cork–Stranraer railway axis, the Milan–Malpensa airport, the Oresund Strait Bridge, the railway/road axis of the Northern European delta, the Ireland–Benelux road axis, the West Coast Main Line, the Galileo positioning system, the Sines–Paris freight railway axis, the European central axis, the Rhine River–Danube River inland waterway axis, the Iberian Peninsula high-speed railway axis, the Fehmarnsund Strait Bridge, the marine expressway, the Athens–Nuremberg/Dresden railway axis, the Gdansk–Vienna railway axis, the Lyon/Genoa–Rotterdam/Antwerpen railway axis, the Gdansk–Vienna expressway axis, the Ireland–European continent railway/road axis, the Rail Baltica axis, the EuroCap-Rail axis, the Ionian Sea–Adriatic Sea intermodal transportation axis and the Seine River–Scheldt River inland waterway axis.

In this plan, 9 transportation corridors (including 2 vertical, 3 horizontal and 4 diagonal routes) lay a foundation for infrastructure construction under the European core traffic network: Scandinavian–Mediterranean Corridor (Helsinki–Valletta), North Sea–Baltic Corridor (Helsinki–Antwerpen), North Sea–Mediterranean Corridor (Belfast–Paris), Baltic Sea–Adriatic Corridor (Gdynia–Koper/Trieste), Eastern Europe to Eastern Mediterranean Corridor (Hamburg–Patras/Igoumenitsa), Rhine River–Alps Corridor (Genoa–Zeebrugge), Atlantic Corridor (Algeciras–Mannheim/Strasbourg), Rhine River–Danube River Corridor (Strasbourg–Sulina) and Mediterranean Corridor (Algeciras–Ukraine border).

TEN-T with the Belt and Road Initiative

With the infrastructure connectivity as one of important contents, the Belt and Road Initiative has an inherently same objective as that of this plan. As proposed in the "Vision and action on jointly boosting the Silk Road Economic Belt and the 21st Century Maritime Silk Road", the infrastructure connectivity is the priority field of Belt and Road construction. On the basis of respecting the sovereignty of relevant countries and caring for their security, the Belt and Road countries should strengthen the alignment of planning and technical standard system in infrastructure construction; jointly boost the construction of international backbone channel; gradually form an infrastructure network connecting Asian subregions and connecting Asian, European and African continents; grasp the key channels, key nodes and key projects in traffic infrastructure; preferentially open up a disconnected road section; remove transport bottlenecks; match and perfect road security protective facilities and traffic management facilities and equipment; improve the connectivity of roads; boost the establishment of a uniform whole-course transportation coordination mechanism; promote an organic connection of international customs clearance, transshipment and intermodal transportation; gradually form a compatible and normalised transportation rule; realise the facilitation of international transportation; boost the construction of port infrastructure; build a smooth land–water transportation channel; boost the cooperative construction of ports; increase the number and run of marine routes; strengthen the cooperation in marine logistic informatisation; expand and establish the platform and mechanism of overall cooperation in civil aviation; and rapidly improve the level of aviation infrastructure. In the "Joint Communiqué of Leaders' Round-Table of the Belt and Road Forum for International Cooperation", it was proposed to boost a pragmatic cooperation in fields of road, railway, port, sea transportation, inland river transportation, aviation, energy pipeline, power, submarine cable, optical fiber, telecommunication and ICT; welcome the construction of multi-modal comprehensive corridors and international backbone channels such as a New Eurasian Land Bridge, Northern Sea Route and Middle Corridor; and gradually establish an international infrastructure network. For the purpose of "revitalising the investment in the European Union, promoting an economic growth and increasing employment", the Juncker Plan proposed by the European Union is also aligning with the Belt and Road Initiative, including the alignment of this plan with such projects as the China–Europe Land–Sea Express Route and the New Eurasian Land Bridge in traffic infrastructure.

At the 17th EU–China Summit, the China–EU Connectivity Platform was proposed for establishment so as to promote mutual communication and policy coordination between this plan and the Belt and Road Initiative. On June 22, 2016, the "Essentials of EU's new strategy toward China" was passed by the European Commission to specify the important direction of the EU's relationship with China in the future 5 years. As an important policy forum jointly established by both sides, the China–EU Connectivity Platform intends to synergise the EU's policies and projects with the Belt and Road Initiative and boost the cooperation in infrastructure, including financing, interoperability and logistics. As stated by Violeta Bulc, European Commissioner for Transport, the European need for effective traffic infrastructure outside the European Union will increase with continuous development of economic internationalisation; the importance of other long-distance infrastructure development plans such as the Belt and Road Initiative from China should not be neglected by Europe; and the China–EU Connectivity Platform aims to ensure that the Belt and Road Initiative can coexist harmoniously with the development of this plan.[5] In the "Joint Communiqué of Leaders' Round-Table of the Belt and Road Forum for International Cooperation", this plan has been listed as one of international, regional and country-level cooperation frameworks and initiatives to be mainly aligned with the Belt and Road Initiative.

Notes

1 Zhang Tianyue, Lin Xiaoyan, "Boosting role of transportation in the coordinative development of regional economy: take Trans-European Transport Networks as example," *Technology Economics*, 2011, 8.
2 Zhang Chen, "Reference and inspiration of EU's guiding policies for traffic transportation industry," *Transportation Enterprise Management*, 2015, 6.
3 "EU's planning of 9 corridor routes for Trans-European Transport Networks," China News Network. September 18, 2014. www.chinanews.com/gj/2014/09-18/6605727.shtml
4 European Commission, "About TEN-T." https://ec.europa.eu/transport/themes/infrastructure/about-ten-t_en
5 Zheng Qingting, "Special interview of Violeta Bulc (commissioner of Mobility and Transport Agency): accommodating the Trans-European Transport Networks with the B&R Initiative," *21st Century Business Herald*, July 4, 2016.

96
WESTERN BALKAN 6 CONNECTIVITY AGENDA WITH THE BELT AND ROAD INITIATIVE

Xiao He

Six Western Balkan countries and this agenda

In order to promote its member states in organising and coordinating the infrastructure construction, the Western Balkan 6 Summit was held by the South-East Europe Transport Observatory (SEETO). In addition, the Western Balkan Summit was at a larger scale. At these 2 summits, a series of connectivity agendas had been proposed by the Western Balkan, which was generally called the "Western Balkan 6 Connectivity Agenda" (hereinafter referred to as "this agenda"). "Six Western Balkan countries" means the Western Balkan countries without EU accession: Albania, Serbia, Montenegro, Bosnia–Herzegovina, Macedonia and Kosovo. The Steering Committee of SEETO is composed of representatives of these 6 countries. The enlarged Western Balkan Summit was also attended by EU member states in the Western Balkan area and other relevant countries, including Croatia and Slovenia inside the Western Balkan area; and Germany, Italy, Austria and France outside this area.

In June 2004, according to the "Memorandum of understanding for the development of the core regional transport network", SEETO was established by the European Union and non-EU Balkan countries as a special institution to boost the construction of regional traffic facilities. At that time, its member states included the current 6 Western Balkan countries and Croatia, which had no EU accession at that time. Its core tasks are to make early coordination and preparation for extending the Trans-European Transport Networks (TEN-T) to the Western Balkan area, including coordinating and improving the policies and technical standards of traffic transportation in all countries concerned; and formulating a protocol for integrating the traffic network in Western Balkan area with that of the European Union.[1] Under SEETO, there are several standing institutions: a steering committee; the railway and combined transportation working group established in 2006; the road security working group established in 2009; and a secretariat. As its supreme decision mechanism, the Annual Meeting of Ministers (AMM) is composed of transportation ministers from 6 Western Balkan countries and representatives of the European Commission, and is responsible for reviewing the extension and integration protocol of the transportation network submitted by the subordinate institutions of SEETO.[2]

As a "soft" exchange mechanism established later under the SEETO framework, the Western Balkan 6 Summit and Western Balkan Summit were established to strengthen cooperation in infrastructure fields between the European Union and 6 Western Balkan countries;

to offset the increasing influence of Russia in the Southeastern European area; and to prevent the Southeastern European countries from being at odds with the European Union due to the hopeless EU accession. After the outbreak of the Ukraine crisis, a series of preventive measures were taken by some EU member states as represented by Germany to prevent Russia from expanding its influence in the Western Balkan area. In August 2014, the Western Balkan Economic Forum was presided over by Angela Dorothea Merkel, Premier of Germany, in Berlin, Germany. This forum started the Berlin Process to overall support and promote the EU accession of the Western Balkan countries, and was a high-level Western Balkan conference held by the European Union after 11 years. This standpoint of Germany was also supported by the European Union.[3] In October 2014 and March 2015, under the boosting of the Berlin Process, a ministerial conference was held successively by the SEETO member states. In April 2015, at the Western Balkan 6 Summit in Brussels, Belgium, a joint statement was released by the heads of SEETO member states to support the Berlin Process and the Western Balkan Summit to be held in August 2015; to accelerate a reform of their own policies; and to boost an extension of standards and core transportation networks of the European Union to the Western Balkan area.[4]

In August 2015, the Western Balkan Conference was formally upgraded to the Western Balkan Summit, which had been held 3 times. At each summit, i.e. at Vienna in 2015, at Paris in 2016 and at Trieste in 2017, the Annual Connectivity Agenda was released. Up to 2017, 20 connectivity projects have been proposed by the European Union and Western Balkan countries under the framework of such agenda, including 5 energy projects and 15 projects of railway, bridge and wharf. An assistance of 1 billion EU was promised by the European Union in the form of a pre-accession instrument, which will drive infrastructure investment of 4 billion EUR by 2020. In this agenda (2017), the following measures were emphasised to establish a regional economic area: invest in traffic and energy; open the market; remove the barrier; realise transparency of administration measures; and strengthen communication of people, especially youth, between 6 Western Balkan countries and the European Union.[5] Essentially a part of the Berlin Process, this agenda aims to accelerate the EU accession of 6 Western Balkan countries and finally realise overall integration. Although this agenda makes an important breakthrough in expanding the existing core transportation networks of the European Union proposed by SEETO, its integration topic is expanding to the economic, trade and social fields.

Alignment with the Belt and Road Initiative

In this agenda, 8 countries are mainly involved: Albania, Serbia, Montenegro, Bosnia–Herzegovina, Macedonia, Kosovo, Croatia and Slovenia. In a broad sense, the Western Balkan countries are part of the Central and Eastern European (CEE) countries; but compared with other countries, most of these still keep a less political, economic, trade and social relation with China. Despite a generally active impression of China, they do not actually understand China and the Belt and Road Initiative. In addition, compared with other CEE countries, many Western Balkan countries have a smaller territory and economic volume, and therefore a smaller potential for economic cooperation. With a more perfect infrastructure construction, Croatia and Slovenia need less to participate in the Belt and Road Initiative; with a long-term war and upheaval, Serbia has a huge need for infrastructure.[6] Although there are many cooperation spaces in the infrastructure and energy investment between the Belt and Road Initiative and this agenda, the actual conditions of their alignment are greatly different due to this special structure.

In the Western Balkan area, Serbia is most active in the Belt and Road Initiative and makes the greatest achievements with China. As early as November 2013, at the Summit of Heads of

China and Central and Eastern European Countries, a consensus was reached by the premiers of China, Serbia and Hungary to jointly construct the Hungary–Serbia Railway, a modernised railway between Belgrade and Budapest. In addition, Serbia takes many active measures to boost China's participation in several infrastructure projects; to entrust Chinese enterprises; to construct many expressway, thermal power plant and canal projects; and to gain Chinese loans and financing for such projects as the Kostolac Power Plant (Phase B) and the Morava Canal.[7] In June 2015, the Hungary–Serbia Railway was formally included into the Belt and Road framework, and became a flagship project in step with the China–Europe Land–Sea Express Route. In November 2015, under the smooth alignment of cooperation, development and strategy, an intergovernmental memorandum of understanding was formally signed by both sides to jointly boost the Belt and Road construction, indicating that the China–Serbia cooperation had entered a new stage. In June 2016, at a state visit of Xi Jinping, Chairman of China to Serbia, the "Joint statement for establishing a comprehensive strategic partnership" was jointly signed by the heads of China and Serbia, which specified focusing on a key cooperation field; expanding a major cooperation project; preferentially cooperating in infrastructure construction as a mutual pragmatic cooperation; and strengthening the alignment of Serbia's national development strategies with the Belt and Road construction.[8] Through the current infrastructure construction under the Belt and Road framework as represented by the Hungary–Serbia Railway and the Serbia–Montenegro E763 Expressway, Serbia will greatly improve its position in the European transportation network, and very rapidly merge into the high-speed railway network and expressway network of Europe.[9] Therefore, Serbia is exactly a typical model of successful alignment between the Belt and Road Initiative and this agenda.

Macedonia also actively aligns this agenda with the Belt and Road Initiative. In 2013, soon after the proposal of Belt and Road Initiative, a contracting construction of 2 expressways, Macedonia's largest single contract of overseas bid award was entrusted by Macedonia National Road Company to Sinohydro Corporation: the Kicevo–Ohrid Expressway in No. 8 European corridor; and Miladinovci–Stip in the east–west European corridor.[10] In addition, the China–Europe Land–Sea Express Route planned as an extension of the Hungary–Serbia Railway will cross the south and the north of Macedonia. In 2014 and 2017, Macedonia imported from China 6 D-series EMU trains as the first entry of Chinese high-end whole vehicles into the European market and 4 electric locomotives to be used for the trans-European No. 10 railway across Macedonia.[11] In November 2017, at the Summit of Heads of China and Central and Eastern European Countries, Zoran Zaev, Premier of Macedonia, stated that the Belt and Road Initiative has brought about a great investment prospect for Macedonia; and Macedonia will further start such large-scale infrastructure investment projects as modernised renovation of pan-European No. 10 railway and renovation of nationwide road networks.[12]

Prospect of the Belt and Road for Southeastern Europe

Due to the influence of various internal and external environmental factors, other Western Balkan countries are slow in participating in the Belt and Road Initiative when compared with Serbia and Macedonia, but they still all welcome the Belt and Road Initiative, indicating that a broad prospect and great potential can be expected for a strategic alignment of the Belt and Road Initiative with Western Balkan countries and this agenda. In recent years, Albania has obviously accelerated participation in the Belt and Road Initiative. In 2017, at the Belt and Road Forum for International Cooperation, a memorandum of understanding on the Belt and Road construction was first signed by Albania and China. In December 2017, at the Summit of Heads of China and Central and Eastern European Countries, a memorandum of understanding was jointly signed by Albania and China on investment in customs, energy and infrastructure, and on cooperation in the development of the Skavica Hydropower Station.[13] In addition, rapid progress has been made in cooperation between Slovenia and China under the platform of the 16+1 cooperation plan. From the end of 2016, Chinese enterprises successively participate in various projects in Slovenia such as the development of Maribor Airport; and the civic lighting system and airport special transfer bus in Ljubljana and level of bilateral policy communication and trade has also obviously improved. In April 2017, during a visit to Slovenia, Zhang Gaoli, Vice Premier of the State Council of China, wished to intensify negotiations and the signing of an intergovernmental memorandum of understanding for boosting the Belt and Road construction.[14]

In Montenegro, Croatia and Bosnia–Herzegovina, the Belt and Road Initiative is gradually being understood by local governments, society and the common people, and the desire to is increasingly strengthened. In September 2017, the "Forum on globalisation and the Belt and Road Initiative" was held by the Montenegro Association of Economists and Managers, who had an extensive influence when the people of academic, industrial and commercial circles in several Western Balkan countries were invited to attend. As stated by Dusko Markovic, Premier of Montenegro, the Belt and Road Initiative offers a development opportunity for Montenegro to jointly develop with the Belt and Road countries and realise the objective and vision of Montenegro.[15] As wished by Croatia, China shifts the target of infrastructure investment to Croatia under the framework of China–Europe cooperation, such as defining a port of China–Europe Land–Sea Express Route in Rijeka, Croatia, or upgrading the Rijeka–Zagreb Railway.[16] In Bosnia–Herzegovina, the Belt and Road Initiative is publicised and popularised by the governments and unofficial organisations of both countries. In 2017, the Centre for Constructing and Promoting the Belt and Road was even established by Bosnia–Herzegovina. Through these measures, a solid foundation has been laid for a future deep cooperation between Bosnia–Herzegovina and China under the Belt and Road framework.

Notes

1 South East Europe Transport Observatory, "Welcome to SEETO," www.seetoint.org
2 South East Europe Transport Observatory, "About Us," www.seetoint.org/about
3 Wang Hongqi, "Germany's starting the Berlin Process of Balkan Peninsula to solve three key problems," Euro-Asian Social Development Research Institute, Development Research Centre of the State Council. May 27, 2016. www.easdri.org.cn/newsitem/277392684
4 European Commission, "Western Balkans 6 Summit: Building Networks, Connecting People," April 24, 2015, https://ec.europa.eu/commission/commissioners/2014–2019/hahn/blog/western-balkans-6-summit-building-networks-connecting-people_en
5 European Commission, "Connectivity Agenda: Co-financing of Investment Projects in the Western Balkans 2017," www.seetoint.org/seetodocuments/1626
6 Long Jing, "Opportunity and challenge of the B&R Initiative in the Central and Eastern European areas," *International Review*, 2016, 3, pp. 125–126.
7 "Basic conditions of Serbia and implementation conditions for the B&R Initiative," Ministry of Commerce of China. February 16, 2015. www.mofcom.gov.cn/article/i/dxfw/jlyd/201503/20150300910892.shtml
8 "Talks of Xi Jinping with President Nikolic of Serbia," Xinhua Network. June 16, 2016. www.xinhuanet.com/world/2016-06/18/c_1119068674.htm
9 "Serbia: jointing constructing the B&R, sharing the achievements of five linking items," *Guangming Daily*. December 21, 2017, 10th edition.
10 "China obtaining the Macedonia largest outward single-project contract: another achievement under the B&R Initiative," China Foreign Investment Network. February 7, 2016. www.fdi.gov.cn/1800000628_5_341_0_7.html

11 Wang Hongqi, "The B&R Initiative: analysis of opportunity and security risk for Macedonia," *New Vision*, September 6, 2017. www.dunjiaodu.com/top/2017-09-06/1772.html
12 Premier of Macedonia, "Great investment prospect of the B&R Initiative for Macedonia," Ministry of Commerce of PRC. November 28, 2017. www.mofcom.gov.cn/article/i/jyjl/m/201711/20171102676744.shtml
13 "China and Albania signed various cooperation documents," Office of Economic and Business Councilor, Chinese embassy in Albania. December 5, 2017. http://al.mofcom.gov.cn/article/jmxw/201712/20171202692265.shtml
14 "Zhang Gaoli visited Slovenia," Xinhua Network. April 15, 2017. http://news.xinhuanet.com/2017-04/15/c_1120817018.htm
15 Premier of Montenegro, "The B&R Initiative assists Montenegro in realizing the development prospect," Xinhua Network. September 14, 2017. www.xinhuanet.com/world/2017-09/14/c_1121659474.htm
16 Liu Zuokui, "Croatia wishing to seize the opportunity of the B&R Initiative," China Network. July 23, 2015, http://opinion.china.com.cn/opinion_80_134180.html

97
TRADE FACILITATION AGREEMENT OF WTO WITH THE BELT AND ROAD INITIATIVE

Feng Weijiang

The Trade Facilitation Agreement (TFA, hereinafter referred to as "this agreement") is the package agreements on goods trade reached through a multilateral trade negotiation of WTO, which is included in WTO rules among WTO legal systems after it becomes effective. This agreement is the first multilateral trade agreement reached during 23 years of the founding of WTO, and also the first achievement with legal binding force after the initiation of the Doha Round Negotiations. In February 2017, this agreement was approved by more than two-thirds of WTO members and then formally became effective. Its validation and overall implementation will promote cross-border trade flow and reduce trade cost. As shown by the research of WTO economists, this agreement can reduce the trade cost of all countries concerned by 14.3% on average and bring about the greatest benefit to developing and developed countries. In addition, this agreement may still reduce time of goods import and export by 1.5 and 2 days, respectively, at a decrease rate of 47% and 91% of that before its validation and overall implementation.[1] As unimpeded trade is one of the core contents of "Vision and action on jointly boosting the Belt and Road construction", the validation of this agreement will strongly boost the smooth implementation of the Belt and Road Initiative.

Issuance and validation of this agreement

In WTO and even its former General Agreement on Tariffs and Trade (GATT), the relevant clauses on trade facilitation can be found, for example in Articles 5, 7, 8, 9 and 10 of GATT about freedom of transit; customs valuation; fees and formalities of import and export; mark of origin; publication and implementation of trade regulations; and in Section 4 of Part III in the "Agreement on Trade-Related Aspects of Intellectual Property Rights", i.e. relevant special requirements of border measures. However, these clauses are not systematic or coordinative due to a scattering in several agreements, and some of them are quite abstract and not operable.

In December 1996, at the 1st WTO Ministerial Conference in Singapore, the optional issues for the new round of Negotiations, generally known as "Singapore Issues", were listed, e.g. trade facilitation and investment, competition policies and transparency of governmental procurement. In January 1997, the problem in trade facilitation was listed into the working schedule by the WTO Council for Trade in Goods. In 2003, at the 5th WTO Ministerial Conference in

Cancun, Mexico, a consensus was not reached on most problems, and trade facilitation in the Singapore Issue was included as the sole issue into Doha Round Negotiations.

In July 2004, the Doha Work Programme (July Package) was passed by the WTO General Council, and a negotiation was started on the basis of its Appendix D "Negotiation mode of trade facilitation". In December 2013, at the 9th WTO Ministerial Conference in Bali, Indonesia, a historic breakthrough was made in the negotiation of trade facilitation after the deadlock of Doha Round Negotiations. At this conference, the Bali Ministers' Declaration was published when the Bali Package Agreements were reached on various issues, including agriculture, cotton and trade facilitation. This agreement is one of Bali Package Agreements, and the first multilateral trade agreement reached after the founding of WTO.

As stipulated in the relevant clauses, the first deadline for validation procedures of this agreement was set at July 31, 2014, but this agreement was not passed on schedule due to the objection of some countries, such as India and Cuba. On November 27, 2014, this agreement was passed by the WTO General Council and was included into Appendix 1A of WTO Agreement. This agreement can formally become effective only after the approval of more than two-thirds of WTO members. In December 2014, Hong Kong became the first WTO member to access this agreement. On February 22, 2017, this agreement was approved by Rwanda, Oman, Chad and Jordan, and then it formally became effective because it was approved by a total of 112 WTO members, i.e. more than two-thirds of 164 WTO members. On February 9, 2018, Namibia submitted an acceptance letter of this agreement to WTO, which realised an approval of 131 WTO members.

The main content and implementation of this agreement

This agreement is divided into 3 parts with a total of 24 articles: Part I measures trade facilitation; Part II special and differential treatment for developing and developed WTO members; and Part III institutional arrangement and final provisions.

In Part I there are 12 articles, including cross-border goods flow, goods release and customs clearance. In this part, the relevant clauses in the "General Agreement on Tariffs and Trade (1994)" are clarified and improved, i.e. Articles 5, 8 and 10, and some contents are stipulated, such as procedure simplification and customs cooperation. The contents of each article are described as follows. Article 1: Publication and accessibility of information. It is stipulated that relevant information on the procedures of import, export and transit such as forms, documents, taxes, laws and regulations should be published in time by each member in a non-discriminatory and accessible way and should be published and updated in time via the internet. Each member should set a consultation point and notify the relevant information to the WTO Trade Facilitation Commission. Article 2: Chance for review of information before the validation and consultation. It is stipulated that traders should enjoy the chance to air their opinions on relevant laws and regulations and information and a periodical consultation is required among the border institutions, traders and other stakeholders. Article 3: Pre-adjudication. Relevant matters of goods tariff classification and mark of origin submitted by the applicant should be pre-adjudicated by the relevant authorities of each member and reasons should be given in case of non-adjudication. Article 4: Procedures of appeal or review. A right to lodge an administrative reconsideration and even a judicial review for relevant administrative decisions should be ensured by the legislative organs. In Article 5, other measures for strengthening fairness, non-discrimination and transparency are stipulated: procedures of quarantine, detention and inspection for animals and plants; principle of fairness, non-discrimination and transparency. Article 6: Disciplines on the expropriation of import and export or the relevant charges, fees on import, export and penalty. There are 3 types of disciplines: general disciplines, special disciplines and penalty disciplines. Article 7: Goods release and customs clearance. The customs procedures are stipulated in detail: handling of pre-arrival procedures; electronic payment; separation of goods release from the final determination of relevant items, i.e. tariff, internal tax, charges and fees; risk management; subsequent inspection; determination and publication of mean release time; trade facilitation measures for certified operators; and concrete stipulations on the customs clearance of fast goods and perishable goods. Article 8: Cooperation of border institutions. The following contents are stipulated: coordination among border institutions inside a member; cooperation of members with a common border in fields of working day and time; procedures and formalities; construction and sharing of common facilities; joint supervision; and establishment of one-stop border supervision station. Article 9 stipulates the movement of imported goods under the supervision and control of the customs. In Article 10, the following contents are stipulated: relevant formalities for import, export and transit; requirements for simplifying formalities and documents; settlement of problems caused by paper or electronic duplicates of documents; applicable international standards for the formalities of import, export and transit; the setting of a single window; requirements of pre-shipping inspection; settlement of problems in the agency and use of customs declaration; requirements of applicable common border procedures and uniform documents; stipulations on the goods of denied entry; and issues in temporary import approval of inbound- and outbound-processed goods. In Article 11, a freedom of transit is stipulated in detail. Article 12: Customs cooperation. This includes measures for promoting law-abiding cooperation; exchange and provision of information; and sharing of cooperation expenses.

In Part II, there are 10 articles, mainly involving the contents of special and differential treatment (SDT) for developing and developed members, including the deadline and ability of implementation. The agreement stipulates that developed members should perform the obligations to immediately implement all clauses of Part I after this agreement becomes effective. However, the developing and developed members can classify the implementation of its clauses into three classes, A, B and C, and determine the class of each relevant clause by themselves. The clauses of Class A mean the clauses to be implemented immediately after this agreement becomes effective (or those to be implemented by the developed members within one year after its validation); the clauses of Class B mean the clauses to be implemented after a certain transition period; and the clauses of Class C mean the clauses to be implemented after a certain transition period, and furthermore after the acceptance of assistance and possession of implementation ability. All transition periods and implementation requirements stipulated in this agreement are valid only after the developing and developed members possess the implementation ability.

In Article 13, the general provisions are stipulated on the special and differential treatment for developing and developed members: the implementation degree and deadline of its clauses should be relevant to the implementation ability of developing and developed members. In Article 14, 3 classes of A, B and C of clauses are introduced, and the developing and developed members are required to determine the class of each clause by themselves. Article 15 stipulates the notice and implementation of clauses of Class A. Article 16 stipulates the notice for the final implementation date of clauses of Class B and Class C. Article 17 stipulates an extension of the implementation date of Class B and Class C clauses. Article 18 stipulates an implementation of Class B and Class C clauses. Article 19 stipulates a conversion between the clauses of Class B and Class C. Article 20 stipulates a grace period for "Understanding on the rules and procedures governing a settlement of disputes". Article 21 stipulates the assistance provision for ability construction. Article 22 stipulates the assistance information submitted to the WTO Trade Facilitation Commission.

As stipulated in this agreement for the first time in the history of WTO, the obligations for the developing and developed countries to implement the relevant clauses are connected with their implementation ability. The special countries can be assisted or supported to enable them to gain the corresponding implementation ability. In order to assist the developing and developed countries in implementing this agreement, the Trade Facilitation Agreement Facility (TFAF) is established by the WTO members. In 2014, this agreement was passed by the WTO General Council and then TFAF was put into operation. The following assistance items are provided by TFAF: to assist the developing and developed members to apply for an assistance in evaluating their implementation ability of this agreement and their necessary assistance for the implementation of its special clauses; to maintain an information sharing platform to assist and determinate potential assistance granters; to formulate or collect the cases and training materials on guiding the implementation of this agreement; to match the assistance granters with assistance receiver; to provide an early work subsidy for the WTO members determined as potential assistance granters who cannot launch the corresponding assistance projects and are difficult to obtain a support of project proposal and early work from other channels; and to provide a project implementation subsidy for the implementation of this agreement when a fund cannot be obtained from other channels. The above assistances are only limited to "soft infrastructure", i.e. to realise a modernisation of customs laws through the consultation service, domestic seminar or specialist training.

According to the database of this agreement, up to February 23, 2018, the clauses of Class A, Class B and Class C had been announced by 107, 49 and 39 members, respectively. The overall implementation rate of this agreement reached 58.7%, including 100% in developed members, 56.4% in developing members and 1.7% in developed members.[2]

This agreement with the Belt and Road Initiative

The validation and implementation of this agreement plays a significant and boosting role in unimpeded trade under the Belt and Road framework. Unimpeded trade is one of the key cooperation fields of the Belt and Road Initiative, and an investment and trade cooperation is the key content of the Belt and Road construction. In the "Vision and action on jointly boosting the Silk Road Economic Belt and the 21st Century Maritime Silk Road", the following efforts are emphasised: to study and solve the problems in investment and trade facilitation; remove the barrier in investment and trade; and create a good environment for doing business in the regions and countries concerned. In the "Joint Communiqué of Leaders' Round-Table of the Belt and Road Forum for International Cooperation Agreement", this agreement is regarded as one of international-, regional- and country-level cooperation frameworks and initiatives for communication coordination with the Belt and Road Initiative. It specified to strengthen the information exchange such as the customs clearance procedure; to boost a mutual acceptance of supervision, a mutual assistance of law enforcement and a sharing of information; to strengthen the customs cooperation; to promote a trade facilitation through various methods of formality unifying and cost reduction; and to promote the cooperation in intellectual property protection. Through the implementation of the Belt and Road Initiative, the trade facilitation objective of this agreement can be boosted for realisation.

Notes

1 WTO, "Trade Facilitation Agreement marks first anniversary since entry into force," February 22, 2018. www.wto.org/english/news_e/news18_e/fac_22feb18_e.htm
2 Ibid.

© PART XI

International plans similar to the Belt and Road Initiative

PART XI

98
SILK ROAD TOURISM PROGRAMME (UNITED NATIONS)

Wei Siying

The Silk Road Tourism Programme (hereinafter referred to as "this programme") was initiated by the United Nations World Tourism Organisation (UNWTO). By fully mobilising the relevant resources, it aims to strengthen international cooperation and realise sustainable development of tourist industry in the Silk Road countries. Specifically, this programme has the following 3 main objectives: (1) to maximise the effect of tourism development in Silk Road countries so as to benefit them; (2) to stimulate investment to protect the natural/cultural heritage along the Silk Road; (3) to vigorously promote greater cooperation among the Silk Road countries/areas to realise seamless linking of the travel experience along the Silk Road and construct various high-quality tourism projects.

Overview

This programme was first proposed in 1993, at the 10th Plenary Meeting of UNWTO in Indonesia. As cultural exchange, trade and the tourist industry flourishes again along the Silk Road, the UNWTO determined to redesign the Ancient Silk Road as a tourism concept, and the Asian–European–African continent is connected again through a tourism programme of more than 12,000 km area. This programme is jointly boosted by the UNWTO and the United Nations Educational, Scientific and Cultural Organisation (UNESCO). By creating a tourism concept emphasising a cultural/natural heritage and travel diversity (land and marine route), 25 Silk Road countries are connected (e.g. Italy, Uzbekistan and Japan). This programme aims to create a new concept of tourism, i.e. to realise common benefit between local countries (e.g. construction ability, local empowerment and business network) and tourists (through a richer travel experience).

In 1994, at the 1st Silk Road International Conference (UNWTO) in Samarkand City (capital of Uzbekistan) with the representatives of 19 countries, the "Samarkand declaration for the tourism of the Silk Road" was passed, which indicated a formal initiation of this programme. This declaration specifies the following main spirits: maintain regional cooperation and stability; realise economic prosperity through sustainable development; establish a tourism brand of multi-party participation and high quality; and link culture with tourism to fully exploit the profound natural/cultural heritage of the Silk Road countries.

In 1999, at the Seminar on Tourism and Culture (UNWTO and UNESCO) in Khiva City (Uzbekistan), the "Khiva Declaration" was passed: emphasising the important role of culture in peace/prosperity protection and mutual understanding among different cultures; and appealing to the Central Asian countries to protect their natural/cultural heritage. This declaration is also supported by the European Commission.

In 2002, at the 4th Silk Road International Conference (UNWTO) in Bukhara City (Uzbekistan), the "Bukhara Declaration" was passed: emphasising again the significance of improving the sustainability of tourism; and listing the measures for stimulating cultural and ecological travel in the destination countries of this programme. In addition, a series of arrangements for relevant issues are made in this declaration, e.g. invite the destination countries of tourists and international interest parties to jointly invest in the tourist industry along the Silk Road; and establish the "Office of Silk Road Tourism Programme" in Samarkand City (Uzbekistan).

In 2009, against the background of the world economic crisis, the 18th Plenary Meeting of UNWTO was held in Astana (capital of Kazakhstan) and the "Astana Declaration" was passed: the member states of this programme further strengthened mutual merging; and the United Nations Development Programme (UNDP) and UNESCO further supported the activities of the Silk Road.

In 2010, the 5th Forum of Mayors of Tourism Cities along the Silk Road was held by UNWTO in Shiraz City (Iran) to pass the "Shiraz Declaration", which was attended by the representatives of 26 countries and 48 cities.

As a document of principle and guidance on the tourism concept of this programme, all the above declarations have the following common grounds: design and boost this programme; strengthen the relevant cooperation in this programme to contribute to regional stability and prosperity; connect the interested parties at all levels to build a tourism brand of high quality; and create a new tourism concept by enriching the natural/cultural meaning related to the Silk Road.[1]

On October 8–9, 2010, the 5th Silk Road International Conference (UNWTO) was held in Samarkand City (Uzbekistan) to cover the following issues: focus on development problems of the Silk Road countries; carry out this programme; and formulate the "Action Plan for the Silk Road Tourism Programme (1st edition)". As a cooperation framework for marketing/ability construction, this action plan has the following objectives: promote cooperation between the Silk Road countries and the sustainable development of their tourist industry; continuously construct various tourism projects of this programme; and boost the development of the Silk Road countries in a sustainable, responsible and world-competitive way. Therefore, the Working Group of the Silk Road Tourism Programme was established by UNWTO.

In the general action plan of this programme, the following objectives are specified. (1) Become a world famous brand of seamless travel experience; win extensive international support and marketing cooperation; assist the Silk Road countries in constructing high-quality infrastructure; and assure the smooth launch of cross-border travel. (2) Promote economic prosperity of the destination Silk Road countries; continuously stimulate investment; attract the Silk Road countries through considerable returns to emphasise and support the development of the tourist industry; and directly or indirectly create employment through the development of the tourist industry. (3) Closely cooperate among interested parties to realise mutual benefit and double-win; boost the Silk Road countries for strengthening mutual cooperation; establish a double-win partnership between public and private sectors; and increase the duration of stay of tourists to improve local revenue. (4) Improve cultural and environmental management through the development of the tourist industry; assist the Silk Road countries in establishing an advanced cultural management system; improve sustainability of development; protect the natural environment; and strengthen their tourism competitiveness through these measures. (5) Become a tool for maintaining peace and promoting cultural understanding; promote cultural diversification; intensify intercultural dialogue; realise cross-cultural cooperation; and become a critical force to strengthen social cohesiveness and realise enduring peace.[2]

Up to January 2016, this programme had 33 member states: Albania, Armenia, Azerbaijan, Bangladesh, Bulgaria, China, Croatia, North Korea, South Korea, Egypt, Georgia, Greece, Iran, Iraq, Israel, Italy, Indonesia, Japan, Kazakhstan, Kyrgyzstan, Mongolia, Pakistan, Romania, Russia, Saudi Arabia, San Marino, Spain, Syria, Tadzhikistan, Turkey, Turkmenistan, Ukraine and Uzbekistan.

Concrete measures

This programme mainly stresses the following 3 fields.[3]

(1) Marketing and popularisation. In terms of marketing for travel destinations, the Silk Road countries possess a firm foundation. As shown by the studies of UNWTO, recently, the Silk Road is one of travel routes most discussed online. The Silk Road countries should jointly market the brand of Silk Road in a cooperative way, which plays an important role in boosting the upgrade of the Silk Road brand image and the improvement of travel attractiveness.

Concrete measures: extensively contact the tourist industry, improve the influence of the Silk Road in various important international tourism expos (e.g. International Tourismus Boerse Berlin and World Travel Market London) and expand the Silk Road brand to other areas in the world; contribute more wisdom to this programme through data mining and potential study, strengthen tourism cooperation among the Silk Road countries through an effective popularisation strategy of the Silk Road brand, and improve the acceptance of tourists; establish a special website or marketing portal for introducing the destination of this programme and enrich the online materials of Silk Road tourism; formulate a marketing strategy according to the interests and expectations of the main source market of tourists; hold various international festivals of the Silk Road; and create a new marketing opportunity by strengthening cooperation with other relevant international theme travel routes, e.g. Maritime Silk Road (China), Spice Road (India), Amber Road (Poland) and Tea Road (China–Mongolia–Russia).

(2) Ability construction and destination management. With a rich natural/cultural heritage and tourist scene, the Silk Road countries are ideal sources of regional investment. However, these countries also face many challenges: they are greatly different in various aspects (e.g. cultural products, service level, hotels and language ability); travel information is not very concentrated; cultural heritage is at a poor management level; tangible/intangible heritage is at great threat; the local governments are at a low level of participation; and there is no travel comment in some areas. Therefore, this programme should be developed by managing the destination countries in a sustainable, uniform way.

Concrete measures: promote the participation of the tourist industry in the decision and development of this programme through the existing modes (e.g. the ministerial conference and working group conference of this programme); further promote the Silk Road countries in developing a tourist industry of local basis through various cross-country measures (e.g. the Silk Road heritage corridor programme of UNESCO and UNWTO); strengthen the training and development of relevant industries through online courses, manuals and workshops; boost a construction plan of special ability for heritage management/protection in tourist destination countries; vigorously develop an innovative tourism cultural product of high-quality experience and superior-quality service; cooperate with national investment institutions to attract more investments and thus upgrade the brand image of Silk Road tourism; improve understanding and acceptance of the international community for cultural heritage through the training plan of travel guidance; boost a public–private partnership (PPP) to input a greater vitality for the sustainable development of the Silk Road countries.

(3) Tourism facilitation. Although the Silk Road countries are currently a hub of business and tourism, the development of their tourist industry is restrained by some factors (e.g. out-of-date visa policies, low-efficiency cross-border formalities and diverse, complicated customs stipulations). Therefore, UNWTO actively cooperates with the member states of this programme, mainly boosting facilitation of visa formalities and strengthening intercountry connectivity, so as to realise the objective of the relevant countries (e.g. an increase in international tourists, economic development and employment improvement).

Concrete measures: strengthen relevant studies to make the Silk Road countries realise that the difficulty of granting visas is very significant for an increase in international tourists, economic development and employment improvement; continue to trace a reform of visa policies, improve the modernisation level and mutual benefit nature of visa-handling procedures, minimise the time necessary for visa handling and boost continuous progress in the "common visa" concept of this programme; keep close contact between the formulators of visa policies and the tourist industry, and improve the awareness of decision-makers for promoting tourism; develop the Silk Road travel route, and increase connectivity among the relevant destination countries; formulate a complete set of sign-making instructions for this programme to boost the Silk Road countries in producing signs of extensive favour, that are rich in information and uniform in style; strengthen connectivity and route development, and maintain a close partnership between airport, airline company and aviation administration; boost a barrier-free development of people intercourse among the Silk Road countries, and promote cross-border travel and individual tourists exchange.

Alignment with the Belt and Road Initiative and future development

Through an objective of promoting economic development of the Silk Road countries, this programme highly conforms to the Belt and Road Initiative with a broad cooperation space. As one of the member states of this programme, China has twice held the Plenary Meeting of UNWTO. As predicted in the "Action Plan for the Silk Road Tourism Program (2016–2017)", through the continuous implementation of this action plan, the number of international tourists to the Silk Road countries for various purposes (e.g. leisure and business) will reach 1.8 billion person-times by 2030 (i.e. 5 million person-times a day); and thus the Asia–Pacific area will become the outbound travel destination of fastest development during the period 2010–2030. Moreover, due to various factors (i.e. improvement of internet access; generalisation of smartphone; and scientific application caused by technological popularisation), the trend of international tourism will be further influenced and the Silk Road countries will be boosted for further developing the tourist industry.

On October 19–24, 2003, at the 15th Plenary Meeting of UNWTO in Beijing City (China) attended by the tourism ministers and representatives from more than 100 countries, the "Memorandum of understanding on the implementation protocol for self-paid group travel of Chinese citizens to Jordan" was jointly signed by He Guangzhang (head of China National Tourism Administration) and Tawil (head of Ministry of Tourism and Ancient Relics of Jordan), indicating that Jordan formally became a travel destination country for Chinese citizens. Up to the end of 2003, a total of 29 countries/areas had been approved by China as a destination of self-paid group travel for Chinese citizens.

Silk Road Tourism Programme

On September 11–16, 2017, the 22nd Plenary Meeting of UNWTO was held in Chengdu City (China), with important officials and relevant tourists from more than 130 countries. At this meeting, the "Chengdu initiative for cooperation in the Belt and Road tourism" was formed, which was actively responded by the representatives of various countries (e.g. Russia, Kazakhstan, Sri Lanka, Cambodia and Madagascar). As proposed in this initiative, several countries will be merged into the Belt and Road Initiative in various aspects (e.g. improve tourism facilitation; strengthen treatment ability of tourism risk; and launch joint popularisation of tourism), so as to further deepen a tourism exchange and cooperation among the Belt and Road countries.

Notes

1 United Nations World Tourism Organisation. http://silkroad.unwto.org/en/content/declarations. February, 2018.
2 United Nations World Tourism Organisation. http://silkroad.unwto.org/en/content/objectives. February, 2018.
3 UNWTO Silk Road Action Plan 2016/2017, p. 8. http://cf.cdn.unwto.org/sites/all/files/docpdf/sr2016web.pdf. February, 2018.

99
NEW SILK ROAD PLAN (USA)

Wei Siying

The New Silk Road Plan (hereinafter referred to as "this plan") is a cross-development of regional economy plan initiated by the USA for Afghanistan and other Central Asian countries to integrate the resources in this area for improving its development potential as a transit area between Europe and East Asia. In July 2011, this plan was formally proposed by Hillary Diane Rodham Clinton (secretary of United States Department of State): by relying on the advantage of Afghanistan in the geographical position connecting Central Asia and South Asia, reconstructing various infrastructures and strengthening the economic link between Afghanistan and neighbouring countries, Afghanistan is built into a traffic/trade hub in this area, thereby driving transformation of its domestic economy; after the withdrawal of US troops and the North Atlantic Treaty Organisation, Afghanistan can still realise sustainable development of its national economy and a steady transition of power; with Afghanistan as the centre, an economic circle connecting Central Asia and South Asia is created, and a strategic objective of "Energy going southwards and goods going northwards" is boosted for realisation.

Background conditions

In 1999, 2006 and 2011, one edition of this plan was separately proposed by the USA to reflect the American strategic concept for the Greater Asian area before, during and after the Afghanistan War, respectively.[1]

The concept of this plan was first proposed by Prof. Frederick Starr (head of Central Asia–Caucasus Institute, Johns Hopkins University): by relying on the historic and geographical advantage of Central Asia as a central zone of the Ancient Silk Road and its abundant natural resources, mutual promotion and common development is realised between Central Asia and South Asia. After the termination of the Cold War and the dissolution of the Soviet Union, this concept was accepted by the USA to help the recently independent Central Asian countries shake off the influence of Russia/Iran and realise diversified importing through the oil/gas resources in the Caspian Sea areas. In May 1999, the "Silk Road Strategy Act (1999)" was passed by the USA. However, due to the September 11 attacks and the USA launching the Afghanistan War, this strategic plan was then laid aside.

In 2005, the concept of the New Silk Road was proposed by Prof. Frederick Starr again: with Afghanistan as the centre, a cooperation between Central Asia and South Asia is boosted in various fields (e.g. politics, security, energy and traffic); a new geopolitic plate is established from the pro-USA countries, market economy orientation and secular political system; the Central Asia and West Asia rich in oil/gas resources are connected with India and South East Asia with rapid economic development; an advantage complementation is promoted among the countries concerned and among several major regions; and the economic/social development of regional countries (including: Afghanistan) is boosted to serve the American strategic benefit in this area. This concept was also called as "Greater Central Asia Plan". In a report of Prof. Frederick Starr ("Greater Central Asia partnership plan for Afghanistan and its neighbouring countries"), Afghanistan and 5 Central Asian countries are first regarded as integral (i.e. "Greater Central Asia"). Then, a department/institution structuring was adjusted by the United States Department of State: the affairs of 5 Central Asian countries and South Asia managed by the Bureau of European Affairs are combined to establish a new institution (i.e. the Bureau of South and Central Asian Affairs) for overall boosting the Greater Central Asia Strategy.

On May 4, 2006, the "Silk Road Strategy Act (2006)" was passed by the United States Senate: after the liberation from Taliban ruling and during the opening process of political/economic fields, Afghanistan may be merged into Central Asia again; because the stability, prosperity and democracy of Afghanistan is threatened by various global and regional factors (including terrorism, political/religious extremism and addictive drug production/smuggling), Afghanistan should certainly be recognised as one of the Central Asian countries but not isolated from them due to its geographical position and cultural/historic identity.

In May 2010, the report "Key for success of Afghanistan: the New Silk Road Strategy" was jointly released by the American Centre for Strategic and International Studies (CSIS) and the Central Asia–Caucasus Institute of Johns Hopkins University: by restoring the position of Afghanistan as a traffic/trade hub between Europe, the Middle East, South Asia and South East Asia, the American military achievements in Afghanistan can be consolidated, and the American focus is shifted from the military field to economic/social development.

In July 2011, at the 2nd USA–India Strategic Dialogue in India, a new edition of this plan was proposed by Secretary Hillary Diane Rodham Clinton: serve the American strategic action of troops withdrawal from Afghanistan to prevent a landsliding reverse of Afghanistan's security situation after the withdrawal of these troops; and safeguard a strategic benefit of USA in the Central and South Asian area. Same as in previous editions, the new edition of this plan aims to strengthen economic cooperation between Central Asian and South Asian countries with Afghanistan as a hub. At all following conferences, this plan is an important topic: Ministerial Conference of New Silk Road Plan (September 2011); Istanbul Conference on Afghanistan Issues (November 2011); Bonn Conference on Afghanistan Issues (December 2011); and NATO Summit (May 2012).

This plan is boosted by the USA mainly according to the following strategic considerations.

(1) Establish a regional energy market in Central Asia. For the USA, this plan means a series of joint investment projects and regional trade groups potentially causing economic growth/stability in Central Asia. In his state administration report (2014), the core of American strategy is specified by William Joseph Burns (deputy secretary of United States Department of State) to establish a regional energy market in Central Asia.

(2) Strengthen economic cooperation among Central Asia, Afghanistan and South Asia to promote steady development of the Afghan economy after the withdrawal of American troops and prevent a deterioration of its domestic security situation. In 2009, the relevant diplomatic policies started to be formulated by the USA to help Afghanistan establish an independent economy. As estimated by the World Bank, after 2014, it will be very difficult for Afghanistan to continue to maintain its current economic growth rate, and its economy will be at a risk of collapse. As wished for by the USA for the implementation of this plan, a trade channel

connecting Central Asia, Afghanistan and South Asia is opened up to provide Afghanistan with energy, create an employment opportunity and develop a product market.

(3) Strengthen the relationship with Pakistan. A need for energy is increased progressively by 1.6 billion people in India, Pakistan and other South Asian areas and a reserve of hydropower and natural gas in Kazakhstan and Turkmenistan is an ideal source of energy for South Asia. Therefore, the following contents were specified by Marc Grossman (special representative of the USA in Afghanistan and Pakistan during the period 2011–2012): at the next critical stage, investment and pioneering of private sectors is linked between Afghanistan and Pakistan; the fruits of Afghanistan and the cements of Pakistan are currently still restricted by a trade barrier; and this plan aims to promote an economic development and employment in Pakistan.

(4) Strengthen the strategic partnership with India. India will greatly benefit from the following contents of this plan: boost energy cooperation between Central Asia and South Asia (which is very attractive for India due to energy shortages); boost infrastructure construction with Afghanistan as a hub (which coincides with the Indian objective of Afghanistan revitalisation through ongoing huge investment); and boost regional cooperation and stability of the Afghan economy (which meets the interest of India).

Main contents

The contents of this plan are classified into 2 main types. In terms of software construction, the following contents are specified: trade liberalisation; reduction of trade barriers; perfection of management systems; simplification of transit procedures; acceleration of customs clearance; overcoming officialism; eradication of corruption/embezzlement; and improvement of the investment environment. In terms of hardware construction, infrastructure is built to connect Central Asia, Afghanistan and South Asia (e.g. railway, road, power network and oil/gas pipeline). Through the software and hardware construction, a transit free flow of goods, service and persons is accelerated between the Central Asia, South Asia and Afghanistan. During the concrete construction of this plan, 4 actions will concurrently be taken by the USA: construct a regional energy market; promote a facilitation of trade and transportation between Central Asia, Afghanistan and South Asia; improve customs procedures and border formalities; and strengthen the link between enterprises and between individuals.[2]

As defined by Secretary Hillary Diane Rodham Clinton, the New Silk Road is an economic and transportation network for reintegrating this area which has been split for a long time due to conflict and political isolation. Relevant measures can be classified into the following 4 aspects.[3]

(1) Regional energy market. With a rapid economic growth and more than 1.6 billion population, South Asia progressively increases the need for cheap, high-performance and reliable energy. Meanwhile, the Central Asian area is abundant in energy resources (including: petroleum, natural gas and hydropower). If some of these resources are introduced from the Central Asia via Afghanistan to the South Asia, a double-win situation will be created for both the suppliers and consumers of energy in this area. Therefore, a series of investment/aid projects are launched by the USA in this area: support the construction of CASA-1000 regional power network (including the various funds in March 2014: an investment of US$ 526 million via the World Bank; and a fund aid of US$ 15 million for CASA Secretariat); boost an energy/power transmission route, hydropower station and relevant reform in Afghanistan (investment amount: US$1.7 billion); support the construction of the power network in Pakistan, increase power generation of 1000 MW in Pakistan power plants, and provide power for more than 16 million people.

(2) Trade and transportation. In 2011, the "Almaty Consensus" was reached through the help of United States Agency for International Development (USAID), which is a regional

cooperation framework between Central Asian countries: reduce the trade barrier; develop exporting ability; and support Kazakhstan and Afghanistan in WTO accession. The following aids are provided by the USA: construct or renovate a road of more than 3000 km long in Afghanistan; provide a technological aid for the Afghanistan–Pakistan Transit Trade Agreement (APTTA, 2010); and support the Cross-Border Transportation Agreement (CBTA) between Kyrghizstan, Tadzhikistan and Afghanistan.

(3) Customs and border action. The following achievements have been made through the aid of the USA. From 2009, regional trade volume in Central Asia grew by 49%. From 2011, the cost of regional transit dropped by 15% on average. The customs procedures in 7 transit points of Afghanistan have been simplified to drive the fast development of trade; and the average time of customs clearance dropped from 8 days in 2009 to 3.5 hours in 2013 (with an annual saving of US$38 million).

(4) Intercourse of enterprises and people. A study subsidy is provided for several hundreds of Afghan students in Central Asia. The "Seminar on the Women's Economy in the Central Asia and Afghanistan" and the "Seminar on the Female Entrepreneurs in the South Asia" are sponsored to support several thousands of female entrepreneurs and enterprise proprietors. A trade transaction of more than US$15 million is produced at the trade delegations, meetings and conferences in Almaty City (Kazakhstan), Islamabad City (Pakistan), Kabul City (Afghanistan), Mazar-e-Sharif City (Afghanistan) and Ter Metz.

Current situation and prospect

As stated by Ambassador Richard Hoagland (the First Deputy Assistant Secretary of United States Department of State, responsible for affairs of South and Central Asia), this plan and the construction of Silk Road Economic Belt are interlinked/complement each other, and especially possess great prospects for cooperation in various fields of the Central Asian area (e.g. energy resources development and infrastructure connectivity); the USA and China should strengthen exchange/communication to explore their cooperation means in a third country and realise a situation of double-win. However, since Hillary Diane Rodham Clinton failed in the United States' presidential election in 2016, this plan has been laid aside and the role it will play in the future is as yet uncertain .

Due to the following factors in the South Asian and Central Asian countries, the American objectives are difficult to realise quickly (e.g. boost regional trade facilitation and strengthen regional connectivity): low overall level of economic development; sensitive complicated relationship; and low general acceptance of regional economic cooperation. Moreover, under the following conditions, this plan certainly cannot be boosted overall due to the lack of vigour and funds during the presidential period of Barack Hussein Obama or Donald Trump: unsteady situation of regional security; poor general fiscal conditions in the USA; and inward orientation of the American global strategy. Therefore, a narrowing of this plan will most meet the interest of the USA in this area. However, although this plan is stagnant after the power assumption by Donald Trump, the plan and control of Central Asia is not waived by the USA and some projects of this plan are still under the process of boosting.

Notes

1 Zhao Jianglin, "Strategic direction and implementation route: Comparison study on the B&R Initiative and New Silk Road Plan," *Journal of Strategy and Decision-making*. October 2015.
2 Ibid.
3 Congress of United States. https://2009–2017.state.gov/p/sca/ci/af/newsilkroad/index.htm. February 2018.

100
EURASIAN ECONOMIC UNION (RUSSIA)

Tian Guangqiang and Liu Wei

Formation process

The Eurasian Economic Union (EEU) is a regional organisation established under the dominance of Russia to boost integration procedures of regional economy. On May 29, 2014, based on the "Declaration for the integration of Eurasian economy" (November 18, 2011), the "Treaty on the Eurasian Economic Union" was jointly signed in Astana (capital of Kazakhstan) by Belarus, Kazakhstan and Russia to announce that the EEU was formally established on January 1, 2015. On January 2 and August 12, 2015, respectively, Armenia and Kyrgyzstan were approved as EEU member states. In April 2017, Moldova became the first observer state of EEU.

The EEU has become an important regional economic organisation. With a coverage of 182.7 million population and 20 million km^2, the EEU was at a different proportion of global value in corresponding fields: 3.2% (GDP in 2014, i.e. up to US$2.2 trillion); 2.2% (total industrial output in 2016); and 3.7% and 2.3% (export and /import volumes in 2014).[1]

A schedule has been made by the EEU for its economic integration: realise a free flow of internal goods, service, funds and labour by 2025; and establish an economic union similar to the European Union as the ultimate objective. Meanwhile, the EEU aims to actively boost economic cooperation with the countries and organisations outside this area: sign an agreement on the alignment cooperation with China; and sign the first free trade agreement with Vietnam.

Strategic alignment with the Belt and Road Initiative

(1) Policy communication. In 2014, the "Joint statement for the new stage of comprehensive strategic and coordinative partnership" was jointly signed by China and Russia: both sides seek feasible alignment between the Silk Road Economic Belt and the EEU.[2] On May 8, 2015, the "Joint statement for the alignment cooperation between the construction of Silk Road Economic Belt and Eurasian Economic Union" was jointly signed by China and Russia in Moscow (Russia): China supports Russia in actively boosting an integration proceeding under the EEU framework and will initiate an agreement negotiation with EEU on economic/trade cooperation; both sides strive through a joint consultation to align the construction of the Silk Road Economic Belt with that of EEU, so as to ensure a continuous stable growth of regional economy, strengthen an integration of regional economy and maintain

regional peace/development. According to the consensus reached by the heads of China and Russia, a cooperation coordination mechanism workshop at a level of deputy foreign minister was established for the alignment between the construction of the Silk Road Economic Belt and the EEU. Moreover, the "Joint statement for initiating the Economic and Trade Partners Agreement between China and Eurasian Economic Union" was signed by the Ministry of Commerce of PRC and the Eurasian Economic Commission to establish a free trade area.[3] On June 25, 2016, the "Joint statement for formally initiating a negotiation on the Economic and Trade Partners Agreement between China and Eurasian Economic Union" was signed by the Ministry of Commerce of PRC and the Eurasian Economic Commission. The Economic and Trade Partners Agreement between China and the EEU mainly focuses on specific fields (e.g. trade facilitation, industrial problems and customs cooperation).[4]

(2) Facilities connection. Infrastructure connectivity is an important component of alignment between the EEU and the Belt and Road Initiative. In February 2015, the China–Kazakhstan Logistic Special Railway Line (the first entity project of the Belt and Road Initiative) was formally opened to traffic. Then, Lianyungang Port (China) will become the sole port for the transit transportation of Kazakhstan's importing/exporting via China, and also improve connectivity between China and the EEU.[5] The Moscow–Kazan High-speed Railway is a section of the Moscow–Beijing High-speed Railway and the Silk Road connecting China with the European and Near Eastern markets: its design work plans to be completed within 2017; and its construction will be started in 2018.[6] The Western Europe–Western China International Expressway (8445-km long) starts from eastward Lianyungang Port (China) to westward Saint Petersburg City (Russia) and connects with European road networks via dozens of cities in China, Kazakhstan and Russia.

(3) Trade smoothening. With complementary trade, China and EEU enjoy a great potential for trade. In 2016, the import/export value between EEU and China reached US$78.56 billion. With a continuous increase in total investment amount from China, the EEU has become a key area of Chinese investment. The stock of Chinese direct investment in EEU countries has increased greatly: during the period 2008–2016, the cumulative amount of direct investment of Chinese enterprises in EEU countries grew by 138% to US$25.7 billion.[7] To cooperate in constructing the industrial parks is also an important content of economic cooperation between China and the EEU, e.g. China–Russia Silk Road High-Tech Industrial Park (in Xi Xian New Area (Shaanxi Province, China); and a high-tech industrial park (in Moscow, Russia). In 2015, China–Belarus Industrial Park began to be jointly constructed by China and Belarus; it is currently the industrial park of Chinese outward cooperation with the highest cooperation level, the largest covered land area and has the most favourable policy conditions; it has become a landmark project in constructing the Silk Road Economic Belt; and it will deepen a trade connectivity between China and EEU.[8]

(4) Fund circulation. China strengthens cooperation with the EEU in financial fields. A bilateral agreement on local currency swap was signed between China and the EEU member states, which will improve the intensity and depth of economic cooperation between China and the EEU. Meanwhile, China and the EEU countries actively cooperate in the multilateral financial institutions (e.g. the Asian Infrastructure Investment Bank; the BRICS Development Bank; and the SCO Interbank Consortium).

(5) People interlinking. A relationship between countries relies on contact between their people, which relies on an interlinking of minds. Various cultural activities related to the Silk Road are held by China and the EEU countries. During December 9–10, 2014, the 1st Silk Road International Cultural Forum was held in Astana (capital of Kazakhstan), with the theme of "jointly construct the 21st Century Silk Road Cultural Belt". During September 13–15,

2015, the 2nd Silk Road International Cultural Forum was held in Moscow, with a theme of "developing a partnership, and jointly consulting on cultural cooperation".[9] Various cultural activities are mutually held by China and the EEU countries (e.g. arts festival, cultural years, book fairs and film festivals). Up to December 31, 2017, 30 Confucius Institutes and 36 Confucius schools had been established in the EEU countries.[10] China has become the main destination for studying abroad for the EEU countries. On May 22, 2015, the University Alliance of the Silk Road was formally established under the proposal of Xi'an Jiaotong University (China). This alliance has been joined by many universities of EEU countries (e.g. Moscow Power Engineering Institute; Nazarbayev University; and Al-Farabi Kazakh National University).[11]

Conditions for alignment with the Belt and Road Initiative

Despite different natures of economic cooperation mode, the Silk Road Economic Belt and the EEU still possess a solid foundation in cooperation. In particular, by slowing down its internal deep integration to create a more extensive partnership in the Eurasian area, the EEU creates conditions for alignment with the Belt and Road Initiative.

(1) EEU expands integration of the regional economy in the Eurasian area, which coincides with the objective of the Belt and Road Initiative in boosting connectivity. In March 2016, the possibility and mechanism for establishing an economic continent partnership under the space of Shanghai Cooperation Organisation (SCO) was jointly discussed among the economic ministers of China, Russia, Kazakhstan, Kyrgyzstan and Tajikistan. In addition, Russia actively boosts the EEU to establish a free trade area with other countries. In May 2015, thee EEU signed the free trade agreement with Vietnam; and an agenda was started for negotiation on the free trade agreement with some other countries (e.g. India, Iran, Cambodia and Egypt). With expansion of the scope of cooperation, the EEU also enjoys a wider space for alignment with the Belt and Road Initiative.

(2) They emphasisze an overlapped key cooperation field. Importantly, the EEU aims to boost free flow of internal goods, capital, service and persons; and the Belt and Road Initiative aims to realise 5 long-term approaches. They enjoy a huge cooperation space in the coordination and concrete project implementation of market rules and industrial technological standards. In September 2015, at the Conference of the EEU Inter-Governmental Commission, the "Basic direction of industrial cooperation between the member states of Eurasian Economic Union" was released: the relevant projects listed herein in various fields (e.g. industry, traffic, energy, new high-technologies, agriculture and finance) are important fields of common concern.

(3) Strategic mutual trust between China and Russia lays a political foundation for alignment between the EEU and the Belt and Road Initiative. Through a strategic partnership and high mutual political trust of China with Russia and Central Asian countries, a political premise is provided to boost alignment between the construction of the Silk Road Economic Belt and the EEU.

(4) The SCO provides a platform for the alignment between the EEU and the Belt and Road Initiative. As a cooperation mechanism of mature development in the Eurasian area, the SCO strongly boosts the cooperation of its member states in various fields (e.g. customs, traffic transportation, energy, finance, electronic commerce, agriculture and telecommunication). The objective of SCO highly coincides with that of the EEU. All SCO member states are important countries in the Silk Road Economic Belt. With a special position, the SCO can provide an effective platform for an alignment between the Silk Road Economic Belt and the EEU.

Prospect and challenge in alignment with the Belt and Road Initiative

In May 2015, the "Joint statement for an alignment cooperation between the construction of the Silk Road Economic Belt and EEU" was signed, indicating that the alignment process between the Belt and Road Initiative and the EEU was formally begun. In this statement, China and Russia are required as follows to: align the construction of the Silk Road Economic Belt with the construction of the EEU; ensure continuous stable growth of the regional economy; strengthen integration of the regional economy; maintain regional peace and development; and open up a common economic space in the whole Eurasian continent. Moreover, the following fields are specified in this statement for strengthening alignment cooperation between the EEU and the Silk Road Economic Belt: strengthen connectivity in traffic infrastructure, logistics and multi-modal combined transportation; expand cooperation in investment/trade; realise trade facilitation; optimise trade structure; promote facilitation of mutual investment and cooperation in production capacity; promote financial cooperation, realise currency swap and settlement via local currency and deepen financing for projects and trade; and boost regional/global multilateral cooperation.

The Silk Road Economic Belt cannot only strengthen connectivity between Eurasian economies, but also expands the exporting of EEU member states through the huge scale of the Chinese market to drive economic development of all countries concerned. Alignment between the EEU and the Belt and Road Initiative is considered by EEU member states to be an important growth point in various aspects: revitalising their technological advantages; changing the negative influence of de-industrialisation; restoring the competitive power of their manufacturing industries; and revitalising their economy.[12] The cooperation of alignment between the Silk Road Economic Belt and the EEU is considered by China as an important impetus for connectivity in the Eurasian area. Therefore, a very great prospect will be enjoyed for the alignment between the Belt and Road Initiative and the EEU. In the future, various measures will be boosted by both sides to open up a common economic space in the Eurasian area: promoting the facilitation of regional trade; establishing the China–EEU Free Trade Area; constructing cross-border economic cooperation areas and industrial parks; strengthening connectivity in various fields (e.g. logistics, traffic infrastructure and multi-modal combined transportation); boosting alignment of industrial production capacity; strengthening financial cooperation; and boosting implementation of concrete cooperation projects. Although a good alignment condition is created by the strong impetus of cooperation between China and the EEU member states, the future cooperation of alignment between EEU and the Belt and Road Initiative will be challenged due to the EEU's problems and the special conditions of the Eurasian area. Especially, due to the following non-traditional security-threatening factors, cooperation in regional connectivity will be restricted: almost similar economic structure and very low market need inside the EEU; higher barrier of trade/investment between the EEU and non-EEU economies; continuous increase in the pressure of external competition on the EEU; and political upheaval, social instability, competition of great power and terrorism in the Central Asian area. Therefore, in order to cooperate in alignment between the EEU and the Belt and Road Initiative, long-term effort and persistence is required, and the impetus for cooperation should be continuously converged through the steady implementation of concrete projects.

Notes

1 The Eurasian Economic Union, "General Information." Retrieved January 2, 2018 from www.eaeunion.org/?lang=en#about-info
2 "Joint declaration of China and Russia for new stage of comprehensive strategic coordinative partnership," Xinhua Network. Retrieved January 3, 2018 from www.xinhuanet.com/world/2014-05/20/c_1110779577_3.htm

3 Head of Ministry of Commerce of China, "Final establishment of Free Trade Area between China and Eurasian Economic Union," Central Government Portal. Retrieved January 2, 2018 from www.gov.cn/xinwen/2015-05/10/content_2859756.htm
4 "Starting the negotiation of Economic and Trade Partners Agreement between China and Eurasian Economic Union," Ministry of Commerce of China. Retrieved January 3, 2018 from www.mofcom.gov.cn/article/i/jyjl/e/201607/20160701351179.shtml
5 "China–Kazakhstan Logistic Railway Special Line to be open to traffic," *People's Daily* (overseas edition), January 14, 2015, 2nd edition.
6 "Moscow–Kazan High-speed Railway to be started for construction in 2018 (Russian Railways Corporation)," Office of Economic and Commerce, Chinese consulate general in Khabarovsk. Retrieved January 3, 2018 from http://khabarovsk.mofcom.gov.cn/article/jmxw/201708/20170802628084.shtml
7 "Cumulative direct investment growth by 138% for Chinese enterprises in Eurasian Economic Union in the recent 8 years," Ministry of Commerce of PRC. Retrieved January 6, 2018 from http://fec.mofcom.gov.cn/article/ywzn/xgzx/guonei/201702/20170202516552.shtml
8 "China–Belarus Industrial Park as China largest overseas industrial park," *Shenzhen Special Zone Daily*. Retrieved January 6, 2018 from http://sztqb.sznews.com/html/2016-10/21/content_3642062.htm
9 Silk Road International Cultural Forum, www.scforum.org/china/
10 "About the institutes and schools of Confucius. Headquarter of Confucius institutes." Retrieved January 6, 2018 from www.hanban.edu.cn/confuciousinstitutes/node_10961.htm
11 University Alliance of the Silk Road, http://uasr.xjtu.edu.cn/sy1/sy.htm
12 Wang Weiran, Wang Jingliang, "Analysis of development prospect of Eurasian Economic Union," *Contemporary International Relations*, 2015, 8, p. 54.

101
QUALITY INFRASTRUCTURE PARTNERSHIP PLAN (JAPAN)

Liu Jingye

In 2015, the "Quality Infrastructure Partnership Plan" (hereinafter referred to as "this plan") was proposed by Shinzo Abe (chancellor of Japan): strengthen private finance; improve cooperation among Japan International Cooperation Agency (JICA), Asian Development Bank (ADB) and Japan Bank for International Cooperation (JBIC); realise an investment on high-quality infrastructure in Asian areas; and make the infrastructure benefit economy, society and environment. Since the Belt and Road Initiative was proposed in 2013, Japan has not officially stated its attitude of support for a long time. From the end of 2017, support for the Belt and Road Initiative started to be stated by Chancellor Shinzo Abe. With a huge cooperation space in the economic field, both opportunity and challenge are faced by China and Japan in realising an alignment between this plan and the Belt and Road Initiative.

Conceptual description and main contents

On May 21, 2015, at the dinner party of 21st International Conference on the Future of Asia, this plan was proposed by Chancellor Shinzo Abe: Japan will cooperate with other countries and international organisations in boosting an investment on high-quality infrastructure; Japan and ADB will jointly provide Asia with a fund of nearly US$110 billion in the next 5 years[1]; private finance is strengthened; and equal importance is emphasised for quality and quantity. A high-quality infrastructure has the following characteristics: economic efficiency, security, withstanding of natural disaster; environmental and social effect; and it is beneficial to the local society and economy.

This plan has 4 pillars, with the following concrete measures.

(1) Expand assistance by utilising the economic cooperation of Japan. Coordinate a loan, technological cooperation and large-scale assistance from Official Development Assistance (ODA); strengthen JICA investment in private sectors; increase the Japanese ODA loan to Asian infrastructure 25%; adopt a new mode of ODA to provide funding to developing countries and insure PPP projects of infrastructure construction; especially, accelerate the JICA loan and overseas investment/financing; shorten the time for handling relevant formalities in the governmental departments to ⩽1.5 years and ⩽2 years to apply the JICA loan for important and ordinary projects, respectively; and review by 3 central ministries/departments the application of private enterprises for overseas investment/financing via JICA in principle within 2 weeks after the application date.

(2) Strengthen cooperation between Japan and the ADB. Support the projects of ADB (e.g. strengthen its loaning ability); expand a proportion of the loan to private sectors; shorten the preparation time for projects; encourage a proposal for future fund growth of ADB; support private infrastructure construction projects (e.g. PPP) through a new cooperation mode between JICA and ADB; establish a new trust fund in the ADB by JICA at the end of 2015, which will provide an investment/financing of up to US$1.5 billion in the next 5 years; cooperate between ADB and JICA in formulating a long-term support plan to boost the construction of high-quality public infrastructure; launch technological cooperation with foreign governments; provide funding support; provide financing of US$10 billion by ADB and JICA for such construction in the next 5 years; and periodically hold high-level policy dialogues with Japan, ADB and JICA to smoothly implement this plan.

(3) Reinforce the function of JICA, and double the funding support for projects. Improve a support means for overseas infrastructure construction (e.g. grant or add the Grade II loans and purchase a bond); strengthen the fund-supporting ability for PPP infrastructure projects (e.g. higher-risk projects); invest in overseas telecommunication/broadcasting/postal industries and establish the Japan Information, Communication and Technology Fund (JICT); provide a fund support for overseas high-speed railway construction projects through the Japan Overseas Infrastructure Investment Corporation for Transport and Urban Development (JOIN, which was established in October 2014) and by relying on Japanese Shinkansen technology; and promote a traffic/urban development in other countries through JOIN.

(4) Popularise this plan, and make it an international standard. Propagate via the media successful practice in this plan; explore cooperation between the multilateral development banks (MDBs) and the ADB to invest in infrastructure construction projects; formulate the "Collection of cases on the investment in high-quality infrastructure", translate it into English and release it to all countries concerned and update its contents in time; provide a chance for directly experiencing the advanced technologies of Japan; hold a seminar for this plan together with international organisations (e.g. World Bank and ADB) and partner countries; stress the importance of this plan at international conferences (e.g. G20 and the United Nations conferences); and launch technological cooperation in this plan.[2]

In addition, during the implementation of this plan, 5 basic essentials of this were proposed by Japan: (1) effectively invest through various modes (e.g. PPP); (2) adapt to the need of social/economic development and development strategies in the developing countries/areas; (3) protect the social environment through high standards; (4) ensure quality of infrastructure construction (including: economical low cost, inclusivity, security, firmness, sustainability and facilitation); and (5) contribute to the local society/economy.[3] This plan is vigorously boosted by Japan in the Asian area. For New Delhi Metro (India), Japan emphasises the principle of security dominance and the friendship of natural environment. Through Japanese technology, Ulaanbaatar Sun Bridge (Mongolia) was completed to alleviate local traffic pressure. In the Vietnam–Japan Bridge Friendship project, Japanese technology is referred and traffic security is emphasised during the development. In addition, this plan is also popularised by Japan in international platforms (e.g. the G7 Group).

Current conditions and prospect of alignment with the Belt and Road Initiative

At the end of November 2017, a guideline on the cooperation of private enterprises between China and Japan was jointly formulated by 5 Japanese central departments: the Cabinet Public Relations Office; the Ministry of Foreign Affairs of Japan; the Ministry of Finance of Japan; the

Ministry of Economy, Trade and Industry of Japan; and the Ministry of Land, Infrastructure, Transport and Tourism of Japan. In this guideline, the allowable cooperation fields are specified for the enterprises participating in the Belt and Road construction: energy-saving and environmental protection (development and operation of solar power plant and wind power plant); industrial agglomeration (jointly develop industrial parks in eastern Thailand); and logistic construction (boost improvement of the relevant systems by making good use of the China–Europe railway network). As especially specified in this guideline, the development of ports, possibly for military purpose, cannot be supported. Moreover, a mutual cooperation mode began to be explored by the government-supported financial institutions. Meanwhile, Japan strives to persuade the irresolute Japanese enterprises to participate in the cooperation with China.[4]

The alignment cooperation between China and Japan under the Belt and Road framework has also gradually started. On the one hand, Japan pays close attention to cooperation between China and Japan, and encourages enterprises to participate in Belt and Road cooperation. On the other hand, Japan continues to restrain China in strategic aspects. In November 2017, Donald Trump (president of USA) visited Japan and the "Free open India–Pacific strategy" was announced by Japan, which showed the intention to restrain the emerging economy of China.

Future development direction

This plan is a cooperation plan of regional infrastructure connectivity proposed by Japan for Asian connectivity. Although concrete cooperation projects on their alignment have not recently been launched between China and Japan, this plan and the Belt and Road Initiative possess a certain potential alignment according to the development situation of regional economy and their development objectives, means and contents.

(1) In terms of geo-economic factors, a need for connectivity construction is reinforced by the development of economic merging in Asian area. As stipulated in the report "Meeting the Asian need for infrastructure construction" of the ADB, if a current trend of growth is maintained in the Asia–Pacific area, a total investment of more than US$22.6 trillion (i.e. US$1.5 trillion annually) will be needed for its infrastructure construction by 2030.[5] In many Asian countries, infrastructure conditions are more lagging. China and Japan possess stronger economic strength in the Asian area and have experience in infrastructure construction. Therefore, strengthening their cooperation will benefit a joint realisation of Asian connectivity, which conforms to the need and trend of economic development in the Asian area.

(2) Both initiatives have almost same the development objectives for regional prosperity and development. This plan emphasises equal importance in quality and quantity of infrastructure, and a social environment and economic effect of infrastructure construction. The Belt and Road Initiative stresses green development, i.e. the concept of a green Belt and Road. Therefore, with a certain similarity in the development contents/objectives, both initiatives are possible to cooperate in their alignment.

(3) Both initiatives enjoy realistic conditions for cooperation by mutually emphasising infrastructure connectivity and diversified means of financing. As one pillar of this plan, the cooperation with such institutions as international organisations is emphasised to jointly carry out investment in high-quality infrastructure. Under the Belt and Road framework, the Asian Infrastructure Investment Bank was established to provide a mechanism and organisational condition for concrete alignment between both initiatives.

However, due to competition between countries and between regional cooperation mechanisms, there are still some restriction factors for alignment between both initiatives. On the one hand, China and Japan compete for a dominant position in the Asia–Pacific cooperation mechanism. For historic and realistic reasons, both countries lack mutual political trust and always compete for dominance in regional cooperation, which results in Japan not actively responding to the Belt and Road Initiative. Therefore, it is a major challenge in their alignment how to settle conflict in dominance during the alignment of their regional cooperation plans. On the other hand, there are several regional cooperation mechanisms in the Asia–Pacific area, which reduces the possibility for their cooperation to a certain degree. For example, Japan always supports TPP, and still vigorously boosts its implementation even after the USA announced its intention to quit the TPP. Moreover, China and Japan have a certain gap in economic development, and have different standards/rules for regional economic cooperation. Therefore, they will face a certain challenge in the rules and details of alignment.

With a combination of opportunity and challenge, China and Japan should strengthen alignment from various aspects (e.g. high-level consensus; project cooperation and unofficial cooperation). (1) Form a cooperation consensus by aiming to promote regional prosperity and development: although China and Japan compete to a certain extent in regional cooperation, both initiatives aim to promote the development of regional economy; and therefore, under the common objective of promoting a regional development, a consensus should be expanded on the common benefit and development objective of both sides, so as to lay a solid foundation for their cooperation. (2) Promote the cooperation of both sides through the concrete projects: since 5 long-term approaches are specified in the contents of the Belt and Road construction, cooperation projects can first be initiated to promote a cooperation procedure before a cooperation framework is agreed between China and Japan. (3) Start with unofficial cooperation to strengthen unofficial economic contact between China and Japan: since the outbreak of the Diayu Island event in 2012, the China–Japan relationship has cooled to further influence the economic intercourse of both sides; as the unofficial behaviour is of a certain flexibility, the cooperation of both sides can be driven by unofficial economic exchange.

Notes

1 Announcement of "Partnership for Quality Infrastructure: Investment for Asia's Future." May 21, 2015. Retrieved February 7, 2018 from www.mofa.go.jp/mofaj/gaiko/oda/about/doukou/page18_000075.html
2 質の高いインフラパートナーシップ」. Ministry of Foreign Affairs of Japan. Retrieved February 7, 2018 from www.mofa.go.jp/mofaj/gaiko/oda/files/000112659.pdf
3 Collection of cases on the investment in high-quality infrastructure. Japan International Cooperation Agency, Ministry of Foreign Affairs of Japan, p. 6. Retrieved February 7, 2018 from www.mofa.go.jp/mofaj/gaiko/oda/files/000083884.pdf
4 中国に手を差し出す日本...「一帯一路」への参加を具体化」、the hankyoren. December 5, 2017. Retrieved February 7, 2018 from https://headlines.yahoo.co.jp/hl?a=20171205-00029156-hankyoreh-kr
5 Asian Development Bank, "Meeting Asia's Infrastructure Needs." Retrieved February 10, 2018 from www.adb.org/sites/default/files/publication/227496/special-report-infrastructure.pdf

102
PROJECT MAUSAM PLAN (INDIA)

Wu Zhaoli

Origin, contents and development

The Project Mausam Plan (hereinafter "this plan") is fully known as "Project Mausam: Maritime Routes and Cultural Landscapes". On June 20, 2014, at the 38th World Heritage Convention in Doha City (Qatar), this plan was announced by the Ministry of Culture of India. It is a cross-country initiative covering various essentials on the World Heritage List (e.g. natural and cultural heritages). As an Arabic word, *mausam* originally means the season suitable for safe navigation of ships. This climatological terminology cited in this plan means the special monsoon circulation in the North Indian Ocean formed by the influence of the tropical monsoon climate in South Asia. In the summer (May–September), a clockwise ocean gyre is formed under the influence of the south-western monsoon; in the winter (November–March), a counterclockwise ocean gyre is formed under the influence of the north-eastern monsoon. Based on the adaption to and the utilisation of the natural environment, a trade and humanistic exchange inside and across the Indian Ocean area was launched using monsoon circulation since ancient times.

The concept of this plan is proposed not only to yearn for a historic glory of trade transaction and humanistic exchange in the Indian Ocean area, but also to strive for responsibility/ mission of restoring the past glory. At that time, this plan was praised by the Director-General of the United Nations Educational, Scientific and Cultural Organisation (UNESCO) and attracted the interest of some countries both inside and outside this area. This plan involves several departments of India: leadership by the Ministry of Culture of India; implementation and coordination by the Indira Gandhi National Centre for Arts (IGNCA) in New Delhi City (India); and support by the Archaeological Survey of India (ASI) and the National Museum of India (NMI). Meanwhile, several subjects of this plan are mainly implemented through the various cultural conventions issued by UNESCO.

As a multi-disciplinary programme, this plan will rebuild the long-lost ties between countries in the Indian Ocean region and establish a new channel of cooperation/exchange channel. As a core essential of this plan, the cultural route and marine landscape not only link the different coastal areas of Indian Ocean, but also connect coastal centres with the hinterland; more importantly, the shared knowledge systems/thoughts are transmitted through these routes to influence the coastal centres and their surrounding broad areas. Therefore, this plan has two dimensions of strategic objective: (1) in macroscopic view, re-link and re-establish various contact channels among the Indian Ocean countries to consolidate their mutual understanding on the view and concern of culture/value; (2) in microscopic view, focally strengthen a cultural understanding among different races under the regional marine environment.

At the preliminary stage of boosting and implementation, this plan has 3 objectives: (1) boost a cross-country joint application as a World Heritage list for the marine traffic and cultural transmission route in the Indian Ocean; (2) establish a comprehensive database of marine cultural landscapes and routes and set the relevant online platform in UNESCO; and (3) coordinate the relation of various cultural conventions of UNESCO with the Convention Concerning the Protection of the World Cultural and Natural Heritage to remove a barrier for jointly applying this plan as a World Heritage list.[1] Therefore, at the preliminary stage, this plan completely focuses on cultural projects in the Indian Ocean area.

This plan has 3 development stages and is transformed from a single cultural project to a comprehensive national strategy covering various essentials (i.e. politics, economy, culture and security). At Stage 1 (before June 2014), the cultural research was mainly performed by unofficial think tanks. At Stage 2 (June 2014–September 2014), cultural research was performed by Indian governments instead to upgrade this plan to Indian national cultural strategy with the following objectives: boost a collective application of coastal countries of the Indian Ocean as a World Heritage list; revitalise the ancient sea route of the Indian Ocean and the cultural link among the countries around the Indian Ocean; and reinforce the core cultural position of India in the Indian Ocean area. At Stage 3 (after the special conference on this plan in September 2014), this plan began to be transformed from a single cultural strategy to a comprehensive national strategy covering various essentials (i.e. politics, economy, culture and security).[2]

On September 16, 2014, a special conference on this plan was held by the Ministry of External Affairs of India and the Ministry of Culture of India: this plan not only emphasises the cultural position of India, but should covers relevant solemn strategies.[3] Therefore, this special conference was regarded as a sign for this plan to transform from a cultural strategy of single function to a national strategic plan of comprehensive functions and diplomatic strategy. On November 17, 2014, a national conference "Indian Ocean area: Indian cultural landscapes and marine trade route" was held in Cochin City (India) by the Archaeological Survey of India and the Tourism of Department of Kerala to boost this plan for establishing a cross-cultural link and restoring the historic maritime culture and economic relationship. As stressed at a speech by the Secretary of the Ministry of Culture of India, various contents are included in this plan, i.e. productive labour, astronomy, navigation, ship manufacturing, port construction, coastal cultural landscapes, immigrant and immigrant community.[4]

In March 2015, the objective of this plan was reported by India to establish an Indian link with 39 countries closely related to the Indian Ocean, e.g. South Africa, Mauritius, Yemen, Bahrain, Egypt, Iraq, Pakistan, Bangladesh, Thailand, Cambodia, Philippines, Indonesia, Singapore, China and Sri Lanka.[5]

In March 2015, in order to boost this plan, Narendra Modi (Premier of India) visited 3 Indian Ocean countries (the Seychelles, Mauritius and Sri Lanka) to expand political, economic and military links with these countries, verifying that this plan has been successfully transformed from a single cultural project to a comprehensive strategic initiative.

The current situation and problems of the connection between "Monsoon Plan" and "the Belt and Road Initiative"

In September and October of 2013, a construction of the Silk Road Economic Belt and a reconstruction of the 21st Century Maritime Silk Road were successively proposed by China. In June

2014, this plan was proposed by India as a national cultural strategy, which was 8 months later than the proposal date of the Belt and Road Initiative. Due to some features (highly coincident geographical range, similar in essentials of connotation and common in implementation route and ultimate objective), this plan of expanded connotation and the Belt and Road Initiative do not naturally resist each other, but enjoy an opportunity for realising mutual alignment and even mutual merging.

During the boosting of the Belt and Road construction, China adheres to the concept of joint discussion, joint construction and double-win. In February 2014, at the 17th round of talks of special representatives on the problems of the China–India border, India was formally invited by China to participate in the construction of the 21st Century Maritime Silk Road.[6] Manmohan Singh (Premier of United Progressive Alliance (UPA)) said that India would actively participate in the construction of the Bangladesh–China–India–Myanmar Economic Corridor and the Silk Road Economic Belt.[7] Despite not being a coastal country of the Indian Ocean, China was preliminarily included into the framework of this plan, which aimed to establish cross-cultural, economy and trade links with 39 coastal countries of the Indian Ocean.[8]

However, such active situation for China at the preliminary stage of this plan was not continued. After the inauguration of Narendra Modis in May 2014 (Premier of India, National Democratic Alliance (NDA)), the previous active standpoint of the UPA for the Belt and Road Initiative was changed, and this plan was not directly linked with the Belt and Road Initiative during its implementation. Neither their alignment nor hedging were specified by Premier Narendra Modi for the following reasons: prevent the international community from apprehending this plan as a strategic hedging behaviour for the Belt and Road Initiative; and repel the direct participation of influential China to show the dominance right and discourse power of India during the implementation of this plan.

As generally recognised in the Indian strategic circle, the upgrading of this plan from a cultural strategy to a comprehensive strategy aims to cope with the negative influence of the Belt and Road Initiative and especially counter-attack the 21st Century Maritime Silk Road. However, in the viewpoints of Chinese scholars, China and India can avoid conflict, build consensus and develop cooperation through the alignment of concept, function and culture.[9] However, although China always strives to invite India to participate in the Belt and Road construction, the Indian standpoint for the Belt and Road Initiative is gradually transformed from ambiguous and wait-and-see way to a doubtful and opposed state.

Although India deeply doubts the Belt and Road Initiative, China always strives to align the mutual development strategies, and wishes to effectively align the Belt and Road Initiative with this plan. In April 2015, the Chinese ambassador in India specified the following Chinese viewpoints at a speech at the Indian Institute of Technology: pay close attention to Indian viewpoints and suggestions for the Belt and Road Initiative; further strengthen policy communication with India; align the Belt and Road Initiative with various Indian plans (e.g. the Spice Road and this plan); and form a cooperation of the greatest common divisor.[10]

In June 2016, at the Annual Conference of Nuclear Suppliers Group (NSG) in Seoul City (South Korea), the China–India contradiction was opened and surfaced because India regarded China as a reason for its failure in NSG accession. With an obvious rise of anti-China emotion in India, the recognition of the Indian strategic circle for China is overall reversed; and the Indian policy orientation for the Belt and Road Initiative is changed from ambiguous to clear (i.e. take an attitude of open opposition, competition and hedging; and do not attend the Belt and Road Forum for International Cooperation in Beijing City in May 2017). Among the policy standpoint for the Belt and Road Initiative, India adheres to an obvious attitude of hedging and competition: (1) criticise the Belt and Road Initiative as not open or transparent but threatening to the fiscal sustainability of relevant countries; (2) clearly oppose the China–Pakistan Economic Corridor with the excuse that a connectivity project should respect the integrity of sovereignty/territory and that this corridor crosses the Pakistan-controlled Kashmir area (a disputed area between India and Pakistan); and (3) delay the proceedings of the Bangladesh–China–India–Myanmar Economic Corridor, and do not respond to any Chinese suggestion for the construction of the China–Nepal–India Economic Corridor.

In order to compete and hedge with the Belt and Road Initiative, various cross-regional, regional and even subregional cooperation initiatives/plans are pertinently released by India. In the South Asian area, the Bangladesh–Bhutan–India–Nepal Subregional Cooperation Corridor is actively boosted by India to hedge the Chinese initiative of economic corridor for this area. Meanwhile, in the cross-regional fields, India reinforces cooperation with Japan and proposes the "Asia–Africa Growth Corridor". In May 2017, the vision plan of the Asia–Africa Growth Corridor was jointly proposed by India and Japan, which coincides with the 21st Century Maritime Silk Road in geographical range. The following contents is specified in this vision plan: cover the construction in 4 fields (development and cooperation of projects; high-quality infrastructure and institutional connectivity; ability construction and skills improvement; and unofficial partnership); stress the construction of infrastructure (especially the ability construction); and involve several infrastructure projects which are constructed by Japan and India in Africa, Iran, Sri Lanka and South East Asia.

In fact, by considering the following factors, China does not stress the participation of India but emphasises the alignment of mutual development strategies: Indian doubt for the Belt and Road Initiative; change of the Indian standpoint; and comfortability of other countries for participating in the Belt and Road construction. For example, China suggests to actively explore alignment between the Belt and Road Initiative and Indian strategies (e.g. Act East Policy); and the scholars of both countries are discussing the possibility of aligning this plan with the Belt and Road Initiative (especially the 21st Century Maritime Silk Road). However, the China–Pakistan Economic Corridor (as a flagship project of the Belt and Road Initiative) is clearly opposed by India, which as a diplomatic standpoint/tool of India has restrained India in selecting an overall policy for the Belt and Road Initiative.[11]

Notes

1 Zeng Xiangyu, Du Hong, "Connotation, influence and countermeasures of various marine cooperation initiatives," *South Asian Studies Quarterly*, 2016, 3, p. 17.
2 Chen Fei, "Study on the strategic accommodation between the B&R Initiative and Project Mausam Plan," *World Outlook*, 2015, 6, pp. 15–32.
3 Sachin Parashar, "Narendra Modi's Mausam manoeuvre to check China's maritime might," *The Times of India*, September 16, 2014. Retrieved January 8, 2018 from https://timesofindia.indiatimes.com/india/Narendra-Modis-Mausam-manoeuvre-to-check-Chinas-maritime-might/articleshow/42562085.cms
4 "Meet on Indian Ocean trade routes, sites begins," *The New Indian Express*. November 19, 2014. Retrieved December 9, 2017 from www.newindianexpress.com/cities/kochi/Meet-on-Indian-Ocean-Trade-Routes-Sites-Begins/2014/11/18/article2528470.ece
5 Rumani Saikia Phukan, "India's Tourism Sector: Achievements and the Road Ahead," *Maps of India*. May 31, 2015. Retrieved January 5, 2018 from www.mapsofindia.com/my-india/government/indias-tourism-sector-achievments-and-the-road-ahead
6 Vijay Sakhuja, "The Maritime Silk Route and the Chinese Charm Offensive," In Aparupa Bhattacherjee, editor, *The Maritime Great Game: India, China, US & the Indian Ocean*. IPCS Special Focus, p. 6. Retrieved from www.ipcs.org/pdf_file/issue/SR150-IPCSSpecialFocus-MaritimeGreatGame.pdf
7 "Premier Singh of India met Yang Jiechi," Chinese Embassy in India. February 11, 2014. Retrieved January 2, 2018 from www.fmprc.gov.cn/ce/cein/chn/zywl/t1127457.htm

8 Rumani Saikia Phukan, "India's Tourism Sector: Achievements and the Road Ahead," *Maps of India*. May 31, 2015. Retrieved January 3, 2018 from www.mapsofindia.com/my-india/government/indias-tourism-sector-achievments-and-the-road-ahead
9 Chen Fei, "Study on the strategic accommodation between the B&R Initiative and Project Mausam Plan," *World Outlook*, 2015, 6, p. 27.
10 Le Yucheng, "Speech at the Seminar on the B&R Initiative in Jawaharlal Nehru University," Chinese Embassy in India. April 7, 2015. Retrieved January 5, 2018 from www.fmprc.gov.cn/ce/cein/chn/sgxw/t1252684.htm
11 Ye Hailin, "Studies on the issue by issue diplomacy strategy of Modi government for China: India's attitude to the B&R Initiative under this strategy," *Journal of Contemporary Asia–Pacific Studies*, 2017, 6, p. 44.

103
GLOBAL MARITIME AXIS STRATEGY (INDONESIA)

Liu Jingye

In October 2013, during a visit to Indonesia, the 21st Century Maritime Silk Road Initiative was proposed by Xi Jinping (chairman of China). In 2014, the Global Maritime Axis Strategy (hereinafter referred to as "this strategy") was proposed by Joko Widodo (President of Indonesia). Then, during the integration practice between this strategy and the Belt and Road Initiative, China and Indonesia cooperated in the following aspects: policy coordination, infrastructure connectivity, financial integration, unimpeded trade and understanding between people. In the future, both countries will continue to further strengthen cooperation through infrastructure, production capacity and unofficial exchange.

Conceptual description and main contents

In 2014, at the inaugural speech, President Joko Widodo stated: Indonesia strives to become a marine country again; the future of Indonesian civilisation relies on the oceans, sea areas, straits and bays. In November 2014, at the ASEAN Summit, President Joko Widodo again stated his administrative objective for building Indonesia into a global marine axis, and proposed 5 priority pivots for construction: revitalise a marine culture; protect and operate marine resources; develop marine traffic infrastructure; execute marine diplomacy; and improve marine defence ability.[1] Then, this strategy was in a rudimentary form.

Specifically, this strategy will promote economic development in 2 aspects. (1) Marine connectivity. As the essential of marine connectivity construction, Indonesia should strengthen traffic transportation between archipelagos and upgrade the construction of port infrastructure, which involves an island area of up to 6 million km². In the next 5 years, Indonesia plans to build 49 large-scale dams, 24 modernised ports, 15 airports and a 1000-km long expressway, with an estimated total investment amount of more than 700 trillion IDR (about US$55.4 billion). After the successful implementation of this plan, the logistic cost to Indonesia will decrease to about 19% of GDP.[2] (2) Development of marine business. The Masterplan Percepatan Pembangunan Perluasan Ekonomi Indonesia (MP3EI) will be vigorously implemented by mainly developing and utilising marine resources so as to guide the Indonesian economic development into a mode of sustainable development. The key contents are specified by Indonesia: 8 development fields (agriculture, mining, energy, industry, marine, tourism, telecommunication and strategic core areas); and 6 economic island corridors (Sumatra, Java, Kalimantan, Sulawesi, Bali and

Papua New Guinea).³ This strategy pays close attention to economic development and political reform in Indonesia. Moreover, this strategy is proposed on the basis of the Indonesian economic development situation. Due to a relative lagging of Indonesian infrastructure construction, Indonesian economic development is restrained by various factors (e.g. logistic transportation); and Indonesian development of domestic and outward economy is also restrained by its unbalanced economic structure. Therefore, this strategy aims to reform the unfavourable aspects of economic development, realise Indonesian economic prosperity and thus strengthen its regional and outward influence. However, some problems may be encountered during the projection of this strategy to diplomatic policies, e.g. emphasise a balance issue between marine culture and Indonesian Islamic culture in the outward association; and realise a coordination between Indonesian marine security and regional security/stability.

Conditions and progress in alignment with the Belt and Road Initiative

Indonesia is a country of mature alignment development with the Belt and Road Initiative. In October 2013, during a visit to Indonesia, Chairman Xi Jinping proposed the 21st Century Maritime Silk Road, and announced together with Susilo Bambang Yudhoyono (President of Indonesia) to upgrade the China–Indonesian relationship into a comprehensive strategic partnership. In geographic position, Indonesia is not only a pivotal country of the 21st Century Maritime Silk Road, but also the place of its first initiation. In terms of development stage, a precious opportunity is enjoyed for the China–Indonesian relationship. Exchange/cooperation between China and Indonesia is continuously boosted and the bilateral relation develops stably. Therefore, with the better conditions of alignment between this strategy and the Belt and Road Initiative, both countries have made certain achievements in high-level consensus, policy coordination and cooperation fields.

(1) The policy coordination realises a preliminarily effect. The Belt and Road Initiative is also welcomed by Indonesia. On February 2, 2017, Arrmanatha Nasir (spokesman of the Ministry of Foreign Affairs of Indonesia) said: in recent years, the direct investment of Chinese enterprises to Indonesia has been rapidly increased; Indonesia expects to strengthen a cooperation with China in infrastructure and energy fields; and Indonesia will align this strategy with the Belt and Road Initiative to be of more benefit to Indonesia.⁴ In May 2017, at the 1st Belt and Road Forum for International Cooperation, Chairman Xi Jinping stated: In October 2013, the 21st Century Maritime Silk Road was first proposed by him in Indonesia; this strategy was proposed by President Joko Widodo after assuming the post; in recent years, both countries have actively aligned both initiatives, deepened cooperation and made plentiful achievements, which adds a richer connotation for the bilateral relationship and opens a broader space for cooperation. At this meeting, President Joko Widodo stated: Indonesia thinks highly of the Belt and Road Initiative and praises China for this forum; the Belt and Road construction will bring about more opportunities for economic cooperation between Indonesia and China. Indonesia will further cooperate with China, deepen cooperation under the Belt and Road framework; improve the level of economy, trade and investment; discuss the construction of economic connectivity corridors; launch key projects in such fields as industry, agriculture, power, port and tourism; and deepen a humanistic exchange.⁵ In August 2017, at the 3rd conference of high-level economic dialogue between China and Indonesia, both countries stated: continue to deeply align the 21st Century Maritime Silk Road with this strategy; and jointly boost continuous deep development of economic/trade cooperation between China and Indonesia.⁶ On February 9, 2018, during a visit to China, Retno Marsudi (Foreign Minister of Indonesia)

said: the Indonesia–China relationship has developed rapidly, and plentiful achievements have been made; Indonesia will strengthen a high-level exchange visit with China, expand economic/trade cooperation, deepen humanistic exchange and boost the construction of the Jakarta–Bandung High-Speed Railway; and China is welcomed to actively participate in the construction of Indonesia's Triple North Comprehensive Economic Corridor. At this visit, Li Keqiang (Premier of China) said: China attaches great importance to the development of the relationship with Indonesia; China will keep a close high-level intercourse with Indonesia; China will better align the Belt and Road Initiative with the development strategies of Indonesia, boost more achievements in key cooperation fields (e.g. infrastructure) and thus bring about new impetus for development of the relationship between China and Indonesia.[7] Therefore, the high-level leaders of China and Indonesia have recognised the importance of cooperation alignment, and have made relevant efforts for boosting such alignment.

(2) Infrastructure connectivity is boosted continuously. On October 25, 2016, Bengkulu Thermal Power Plant began construction in Bengkulu City (Indonesia), whose investment was participated by Power Corporation Construction of China. This project had a total investment amount of about US$360 million, 75% of which was supported by the syndicated loan of Industrial and Commercial Bank of China and Export–Import Bank of China and 25% of which was raised from the funds of joint venture enterprises. This project plans to formally start a commercial operation from 2019 for 25 years. In January 2017, an initiation ceremony of pile foundation engineering of Java No. 7 Project was held in Serang City (Banten Province, Indonesia), indicating that this thermal power plant of largest single installed capacity in Indonesia formally started construction; and Chinese enterprises participated in its investment . On July 15, 2017, the Walini Tunnel (a project in the Jakarta–Bandung High-Speed Railway) began construction in Walini City (West Java Province, Indonesia), which was undertaken by China Railway Group Limited. With a total length of 142 km and the highest designed running speed of 350 km/h, the Jakarta–Bandung High-Speed Railway plans to be open for traffic after 3 years.

(3) Financial cooperation is strengthened continuously. In February 2017, the PIK subbranch of Jakarta Branch of the Bank of China was open for business: the Bank of China is the earliest Chinese enterprise to enter Indonesia. In March 2017, an unveiling ceremony was held for China Construction Bank (Indonesia) Corporation, indicating that China and Indonesia continuously deepen cooperation fields and improve the level of cooperation. On January 5, 2018, the "Agreement on establishing a representative office of Bank Indonesia in China" was signed by Zhou Xiaochuan (President of People's Bank of China) and Agus D.W. Martowardojo (President of Bank Indonesia). As the ninth representative office of foreign central banks in China, this representative office of Bank Indonesia in China will strengthen cooperation between the central banks of both countries, and promote further development of a bilateral relationship in finance, economy and trade.[8]

(4) The exchange of people is deepened continuously. In October 2017, the 1st Fair of Studying and Working in China was held in Jakarta City: this fair provides information on studying and working in China for the students and Chinese language learners in Indonesia and also offers a bridge for Indonesian students to study in China. In November 2017, a film "Mega Tsunami" was formally started for shooting in Jakarta City, which narrated the event of a Chinese rescue group participating in the rescue activity for the Indian Ocean Tsunami at the end of 2004. As the first film jointly produced by China and Indonesia, this film is the initiation project of film cooperation agreement and the key project of people-to-people cooperation between China and Indonesia.

Notes

1 Pandu Utama Manggala, "Rethinking Indonesia's global maritime axis," *The Jakarta Post*, March 22, 2015. Retrieved February 13, 2018 from www.thejakartapost.com/news/2015/03/22/rethinking-indonesia-s-global-maritime-axis.html
2 Ma Bo, "Study on the strategic integration between the Belt and Road Initiative and Indonesia's Global Maritime Axis Strategy," *World Outlook*, 2015, 6, p. 37.
3 Commercial Counsellor's Office of Chinese Embassy in Indonesia, "Indonesian new government continues to implement the MP3EI plan," September 11, 2014. Retrieved February 13, 2018 from http://id.mofcom.gov.cn/article/ziranziyuan/huiyuan/201409/20140900727570.shtml
4 "Indonesia expects a strategic integration between the Belt and Road Initiative and Indonesia's Global Maritime Axis Strategy," *People's Daily Online* (overseas edition), March 3, 2017. Retrieved February 13, 2018 from www.yidaiyilu.gov.cn/ghsl/hwksl/9109.htm
5 "Xi Jinping meets Indonesia's president: boost a comprehensive cooperation between both countries under the framework of the Belt and Road Initiative," Xinhua Net, May 14, 2017. Retrieved February 13, 2018 from www.yidaiyilu.gov.cn/xwzx/xgcdt/13403.htm
6 "Holding of third conference of high-level economic dialogue between China and Indonesia: deeply boost the Belt and Road construction," People's Daily Online, August 13, 2017. Retrieved February 13, 2018 from www.yidaiyilu.gov.cn/xwzx/gnxw/24492.htm
7 "Li Keqiang meets Retno Marsudi (foreign minister of Indonesia)," Chinese Governments Portal. Retrieved February 13, 2018 from www.yidaiyilu.gov.cn/xwzx/xgcdt/47836.htm
8 "Bank Indonesia establishes a representative office in China," *China Daily Online*, January 14, 2018. Retrieved February 13, 2018 from www.yidaiyilu.gov.cn/xwzx/gnxw/43906.htm

104
NORTHERN AUSTRALIA DEVELOPMENT PLAN (AUSTRALIA)

Pang Jiaxin

Overview

Northern Australia covers the area of Western Australia State and Queensland State north of the Tropic of Capricorn and that of the whole Northern Territory. Despite a vast land area (more than 3 million km²), Northern Australia has a population of only 1.3 million (i.e. about 5% of the total population in Australia) and the majority of its population is distributed in cities near the Australian coastline (e.g. Townsville, Cairns, Mackay and Kelvin). In addition, in Northern Australia, there are about 190,000 aborigines, who account for 30% of the total Aborigine population in Australia.

In Northern Australia, there are 3 main industries: mining, energy and agriculture. In terms of mining, Northern Australia possesses more than 70% of Australian-proved reserves of metallic ores (e.g. iron, lead, zinc and silver) and nearly all of the Australian ore reserves of magnetite, diamond and phosphorite. In terms of the energy industry, Australia is the world's second largest exporter of coal and the world's fourth largest producer of coal; 60% of Australian coal resources come from Northern Australia; the Northern Territory and Western Australia State abound in liquefied natural gas; and the state of Queensland is rich in coal-bed methane. In terms of agriculture, the gross output value of animal husbandry industry and planting industry in Northern Australia reached up to AU$5.2 billion in 2012. Under the driving effect of these 3 industries (especially mining and energy), the export industry has developed rapidly in Northern Australia. During the period 2012–2013, the port export value in Northern Australia reached AU$121 billion, which accounted for 55% of total export value in Australia.

In addition, Northern Australia plays a significant role in national defence and regional defence cooperation. Many Australian and American military bases are in Northern Australia; Australia inputs an annual defence expenditure of AU$1.5–2 billion in Northern Australia (including: up to AU$0.9 billion for military facilities).

In June 2015, the white paper "Our north, our future: a vision for developing North Australia" was issued by Australia to propose the "Northern Australia Development Plan" (hereinafter referred to as "this plan").[1] In October 2017, the phasic implementation report of Northern Australia Development Plan was released by Australia.[2] In this plan, the main contents are shown.

(1) Reduce the limitation of land use rights and improve the utilisation rate of water resources. Two knotty problems are faced in the development and utilisation of land in Northern Australia: (1) numerous crown lands are leased to operators for pastoral purposes; in principle, such land must not be used by the operators for other economic activities; the scope of land use rights can be expanded by operators only after the approval of governmental organs level by level; and the rights and interests of such land should be guaranteed in a degree far lower than that of private lands. (2) The right for aborigine land is shown in the form of native title, i.e. such land is collectively owned by the Aborigine community and not owned by any aborigine individual; the utilisation of aboriginal land for ensuring the rights/interests of aborigines will instead limit the individual right of land use and reduce the utilisation efficiency of land and the economic benefit of Aborigines. Therefore, various measures are attempted by Australia for pastoral land: reform the relevant management rules/regulations of pastoral land use; establish a safe and reliable exchange system of land use rights; and input AU$10.6 million for piloting diversified land use. For the Aborigine land, the following measures are taken by Australia: investigate the Aborigine land to study the mode of its exclusive use for commercial purposes; promote cooperation between Aborigines and outward investors through the propaganda of the Council of Australian Governments; and provide the residents and investors of Northern Australia with more business information to improve efficiency of production/investment.

As the main problems in water resources, the water conservancy infrastructure in Northern Australia is insufficient, old and outdated. Therefore, the National Water Infrastructure Development Fund was established by Australia to build relevant facilities. Meanwhile, the current situation and potential of water resources utilisation are assessed in the Northern Australian area, and a water resource exchange market will be established.

After the practice for 2 years, the diversification degree of land use has obviously improved in Northern Australia; 8 pilot areas for Aborigine land reforming have been established; and the commercial agreement with a total value of up to AU$284 million has been newly signed by the Aborigine enterprises. Fifteen investigations on the optimisation of water resources utilisation are underway, and all will be completed by 2019. AU$130 million has been input to the Fitzroy River Water Conservancy Project (Queensland City) by the National Water Infrastructure Development Fund, with AU$147 million remaining.

(2) Create an amicable investment environment. For a long time, superfluous approval formalities and complex rules/regulations have been faced at investment to Australia, and many unnecessary policy risks have been borne by investors. According to this plan, the following effects can be achieved when Australia creates an amicable investment environment for investors: promote free capital flow; high-efficiency integration of Northern Australian resources through funds and technologies of Asia–Pacific countries; spur on the economic development; and build Northern Australia into an Australian portal of trade and investment. Therefore, the following measures will be taken by Australia: hold a "Northern Australian Investment Forum" in 2015 and 2017 to provide investors with information on policies, industries and projects; improve economic connectivity with ASEAN and APEC countries; open an electronic tourist visa to China and India, introduce a visa of multiple rounds within 10 years, and pilot a visa application in Simplified Chinese; simplify the supervision procedures for the fishery industry and the aquatic products industry; and establish a special committee for discriminating ambiguous or inexecutable supervision regulations. In addition, the fund will be provided by Australia for various programmes: AU$2.5 million for incubating a commercial cooperation of Northern Australia with Indonesia, Papua New Guinea and East Timor;

AU$13.6 million for developing and operating the tourist industry of Northern Australia; AU$75 million for establishing a joint research centre for this plan, mainly on agriculture, food and tropical diseases; and a fiscal budget of AU$2 million for establishing an office for the simplification of market entry formalities in Darwin (Northern Territory, Australia) to improve administration efficiency.

At present, a series of Australian measures have made preliminary achievements. In 2015, the "Northern Australian Investment Forum" was attended by over 350 investors from more than 20 countries and some investment projects were ascertained. Nineteen projects of resources, energy and aquatic products are supported by the office for the simplification of market entry formalities. Australia has signed a free trade agreement with China, Japan, South Korea and ASEAN, which has increased Australian export volume to these countries year by year.

(3) Accelerate construction of infrastructure. In Northern Australia, most construction of infrastructure is driven by industrial capital (e.g. roads and ports for various resources and energy industries): the private capital is good at cost–benefit analysis and more efficient for single projects, but there is no regional general plan, and thus the area overall is difficult to develop rapidly. The following supports are specified in this plan: a financing loan of AU$5 billion (for infrastructure construction); priority support of AU$0.6 billion (for expressway construction projects in the northern area); a special fund of AU$0.1 billion (for constructing the transportation roads of beef products to upgrade and improve the supply chain of beef products); release of an auditing report on the infrastructure in northern area (launch a feasibility study on the construction of northern freight railway and provide the investors with information on feasible infrastructure projects); and AU$39.6 million for upgrading airport facilities and air transportation service in northern remote areas, and organising the investors for investigation on the protocol of improving the northern airway business.

Up to 2017, AU$0.7 billion has been planned by Australia to construct 38 expressways for perfecting the northern road traffic network, including: an investment of about AU$0.1 billion for 18 transportation road projects of beef products. AU$15 million has been appropriated by Australia and the fund will continue to be added to for upgrading the airports in remote areas, including: 22 completed projects and 25 projects under construction.

(4) Provide competent, plentiful labour. In Northern Australia, there is a sparse population and insufficient labour; the jobs are vary greatly in level of skill, causing a great gap in income. The following actions are taken by this plan: play the role of industrial skills foundation to provide the enterprise proprietors and workers with consultation and skills training service; expand the employment opportunity for Aborigines to facilitate them to work in road construction; support the Northern Territory in reforming the work qualification certification system, so that the labourers with a work qualification certificate from other areas can be accepted by the Northern Territory; and create more flexible employment policies for foreign immigrants in the areas of labour shortage, implement the "Designated Area Migration Agreement" (DAMA), and provide a work visa of 2 years for labourers of Pacific Islands countries.

(5) Improve the governance ability of governments. This plan can succeed only by coordinated cooperation of Australian governments at each level and by changing their poor governance method. The following proposals are raised in this plan: establish a strategic partner mechanism of Northern Australia (i.e. annual meeting mechanism among the chancellors and deputy chancellors of Australia and the chief administrators of the northern provinces); establish the Northern Australia Joint Commission and its standing committee in parliament, which annually reports the progress of northern development to parliament; move the Northern Australia Office to the northern area so as to manage the affairs of northern development; and reinforce

cooperation among the governmental departments at each level and improve the governance efficiency of governments.

Prospect of alignment with the Belt and Road Initiative

In November 2014, at a state visit to Australia, Chairman Xi Jinping stated that China will, at the invitation of Australia, actively participate in this plan. However, for various reasons, Australia has not yet participated in the Belt and Road Initiative.

(1) Infrastructure construction. With relatively poor cooperation in infrastructure construction, China has participated in very few infrastructure projects of this plan. In April 2015, John Holland Corporation (the third largest construction company in Australia, with the qualification for management and operation of railway infrastructure) was wholly acquired by CCCC International Holding (Hong Kong) Co., Ltd of China Communications Construction Corporation. In October 2015, Shandong Landbridge Group obtained 80% of shares in Darwin Port from Northern Territory Government through a lease agreement (with a lease term of 99 years). In January 2016, Pacific Hydro Corporation was acquired by State Power Corporation Investment Limited of China to become the second largest Australian wind power company, with an installed capacity of 0.43 MW and 4.14 MW for hydropower and wind power, respectively. China and Australia seldom cooperate in telecommunication infrastructure, and Australia is even reported to have obstructed Huawei Technologies Co. Ltd from laying the submarine optical cable from South Pacific Islands Countries to Australia.[3]

Although the fund has been appropriated by Australia for this plan, infrastructure construction is still short of funds and there is an insufficient labour in Northern Australia. Therefore, an opportunity is enjoyed for Chinese enterprises to participate in the construction of northern infrastructure through such modes as PPP and transfer–operate–transfer (TOT). However, due to the influence of the political environment in Australia, Chinese enterprises may find it difficult to win telecommunication infrastructure projects, but can strive for the construction of traffic and energy infrastructure.

(2) Agriculture. In Northern Australia, more than 50% of land is for agricultural purpose (including numerous pastoral lands) and the natural conditions are different from China. Therefore, the agriculture of both countries is very strongly complementary. On the one hand, Chinese enterprises can further develop trade of agricultural products with Northern Australia and enlarge investment in the agriculture of Northern Australia. On the other hand, the Chinese disadvantage in an undersupply of high-end agricultural products can be remedied by the Australian advanced agricultural production technology.

(3) Tourist industry. In Northern Australia, there are many beautiful natural scenes, including the famous Great Barrier Reef. Full development and utilisation of northern tourism resources is also proposed in this plan. The number of Chinese tourists to Australia increases year by year, which boosts the development of the Australian tourist industry. The investment of Chinese enterprises in the Australian tourist industry cannot only better serve Chinese tourists, but also promote understanding between peoples from both countries to a certain degree.

(4) Emerging industry. As one of the objectives, this plan aims to promote the development of diversified industries in Northern Australia. Some industrial parks have been established (e.g. technology, pharmaceuticals, biology and environmental protection). Chinese enterprises can learn from the advanced Australian experience in some industries, play their superiorities/ specialties in some fields (e.g. electronic commerce and mobile payment) and thus expand cooperation.

Notes

1 http://northernaustralia.gov.au/sites/prod.office-northern-australia.gov.au/files/files/NAWP-FullReport.pdf
2 http://northernaustralia.gov.au/sites/prod.office-northern-australia.gov.au/files/files/Our-North-Our-Future_2017-Implementation-Report_0.pdf
3 "Australia obstructs Chinese enterprise from laying a submarine optical cable," UK media. Netease News Online. http://news.163.com/17/1231/15/D70AJRB100018AOQ.html

105
AMBER RAILWAY FREIGHT CORRIDOR (POLAND)

Pang Jiaxin

Background

On March 1, 2016, the Amber Railway Freight Corridor (the No. 11 letter of construction intent) was signed by the transportation departments of Hungary, Poland, Slovakia and Slovenia (hereinafter "these 4 countries"), which was then submitted to the European Commission. On December 5, 2017, the "Memorandum of cooperation on the joint construction of Amber Railway Freight Corridor" was jointly signed by these 4 transportation departments, indicating a formal initiation of this corridor.[1]

This corridor is constructed for both historic factors and for realistic consideration.

Historically, just like the Silk Road, the Amber Road was an ancient trade channel for amber transportation, which links the south and north of the European continent to greatly promote commercial/trade intercourse in the European area. Subsequently, the Amber Road gradually spread eastwards to connect with the Silk Road in Poland and thus to Persia, India and China in Asia. In ancient times, the Amber Road and the Silk Road jointly constituted a major channel of connectivity/exchange between eastern and western civilisations. In 2013, the Belt and Road Initiative was proposed by Xi Jinping (Chairman of China), which inspired to a certain degree the resolution of Central and Eastern European countries to revitalise the Amber Road. With the name of amber, this corridor not only shows a historic symbol, but also realises the following objectives: revitalise the Amber Road; align the New Amber Road with the Belt and Road Initiative; and reconstruct a major channel of trade logistics for eastern–western connectivity.

The following realistic factors are considered. (1) With a continuous boosting of economic globalisation and regional integration, world economic growth and trade are profoundly adjusted to require a strengthening of regional cooperation and an arousal of development vitality. (2) After the financial crisis in 2008, the economy of Central and Eastern European countries grows slowly and is at a development stage of transition/transformation; the social reform and development enters an important period; and thus more advanced perfect infrastructure should be constructed to promote the steady development of the national economy and realise the prosperity of the regional economy. (3) These 4 countries lie in the intermediate zone of the Eurasian continent; there are fewer ports and huge demand for freight; and the efficiency of goods transportation needs to be improved. (4) The Belt and Road Initiative assists

European–Asian–African countries in infrastructure transformation/upgrading and boosts regional connectivity; this corridor can exactly align with the Belt and Road Initiative to dredge a European–Asian channel of trade logistics and promote common prosperity.

Main content

As part of the European railway freight network, this corridor is the first new railway freight corridor after the completion of the original European railway freight network. This corridor aims to promote transit railway freight, improve infrastructure service quality and perfect the European railway freight network. According to the memoranda signed by these 4 countries, this corridor will start to be constructed within 2 years (i.e. by January 31, 2019).[2] In order to ensure effective implementation of its construction, an executive committee is established under the organisation of these 4 countries, and the headquarters of the supervising implementation institution is set in Hungary.

This corridor will roughly run along the Ancient Amber Road between the Baltic Sea and the Mediterranean Sea, northwards from the north of Warsaw City (capital of Poland) and the Poland–Belarus border, and southwards to Koper Port (Slovenia) and the Hungary–Serbia border. This corridor mainly connects Koper Port (Slovenia) through the west of Hungary with the industrial centres of Poland and Slovakia, so as to realise connectivity among these 4 countries. In this corridor, the main nodes are shown: Koper–Ljubljana–Zalaegerszeg–Sopron/Csorna border (between Hungary and Serbia)–Kelebia–Budapest–Komarom–Leopoldov/Rajka–Bratislava–Zilina–Katowice/Krakow–Warsaw–Terespol border (between Poland and Belarus).[3] This corridor connects industrial centres and the multi-modal combined transportation ports of Hungary with Adriatic Sea coastal countries and Balkan countries, and extends to the Budapest–Clavier Railway aided by China, so that most goods can be transported from such areas as China and South East Asia to Koper Port (Slovenia) and Athens Port (Greece) and then to the European area via rail transportation.

As the core of this corridor, the GYSEV railway network mainly constructs or upgrades a comprehensive traffic infrastructure of sea–land–air multi-modal combined transportation from Sopron Port (Hungary) to Koper Port (Slovenia) and connecting main ports and the industrial areas of these 4 countries.[4] In the future, an extension of this corridor will be increased for other EU member states according to actual need, so as to strengthen actual benefit and promote trade/logistic connection.

This corridor has great strategic significance in the development of these 4 countries and even Europe. (1) This corridor constructs and upgrades the infrastructure in the neighbouring areas (e.g. power and traffic) to improve the regional investment environment and promote steady development of the economy. (2) This corridor provides a direct channel for freight in the east of the Alps to strengthen the transportation capacity of international southern–northern railway in the east of the Alps, realise a high efficiency of goods transportation and improve the position of GYSEV railway network in the southern–northern axis. (3) This corridor promotes connectivity among the Slovenian ports of the Adriatic Sea, the Hungarian inland ports of the Danube River and Slovakia to reinforce the freight capacity. (4) This corridor promotes the development of railway traffic in Serbia and may further improve railway transportation in Eastern Europe and the Eurasian Land Bridge. (5) As the junction point between the Amber Road and the Silk Road, Poland possesses a unique location advantage in alignment with the Belt and Road Initiative.[5] This corridor not only meets the traffic needs of these 4 countries and neighbouring areas, but also realises deeper connectivity of the Eurasian continent through alignment with the Belt and Road Initiative, promotes transformation of the regional development mode and thus increases the transportation capacity of this corridor.

Future development prospects

In June 2016, during a visit to Poland, Chairman Xi Jinping proposed: connect the Silk Road with this corridor; strengthen cooperation/exchange; realise alignment between the Belt and Road Initiative and European development strategies; and promote the connectivity of the Eurasian continent. The Belt and Road Initiative geographically stresses a linking of the Eurasian continent: by connecting several important European cities, this corridor is an important node for the Belt and Road to reach Europe and realise the 5 long-term approaches (i.e. policy coordination, infrastructure connectivity, unimpeded trade, financial integration and understanding between people). At present, China has established a good partnership with these 4 countries in various fields (e.g. infrastructure construction, energy, finance, manufacturing industry and automobile industry). In the future, strong cooperation and great development potential will be enjoyed for the alignment between the Belt and Road and this corridor.

(1) Strengthen strategic alignment and assist the construction of a global strategic partnership. In June 2015, the "Memorandum of intergovernmental understanding for the Belt and Road Initiative" was signed between China and Hungary; and Hungary became the first European country to sign a cooperation document on the Belt and Road Initiative with China and guide the cooperation of Central and Eastern Europe with China.[6] The Belt and Road Initiative remedies Hungary's insufficient funds for implementing the policy of "Opening up to the east", promotes improvement/development of Hungarian economic conditions and reinforces the economic/trade partnership between both countries. In November 2015, the "Memorandum of understanding on the Belt and Road construction" was signed by China, Poland and Slovakia. In June 2016, a comprehensive strategic partnership was formally established between China and Poland; Poland becomes a firm partner in the Belt and Road construction; both countries continuously expand cooperation, seek a point of benefit fitness and cooperate in some fields (e.g. manufacturing industry, agriculture, energy, online Silk Road, clean energy and innovation).[7] China and Slovakia also reached a consensus on cooperation under the Belt and Road Initiative, grasped the opportunity for cooperation and deepened economic/trade cooperation between both countries. China and Slovenia keep a good development situation under the Belt and Road framework and the 16+1 cooperation plan, deepening bilateral cooperation and have made many pragmatic achievements. China and these 4 countries continuously strengthen strategic cooperation, realise common development and bring about cooperation impetus for the alignment between the Belt and Road and this corridor.

(2) Promote connectivity infrastructure and create the connectivity of the Eurasian continent. As one of the main contents, the Belt and Road construction removes the closed state, promotes construction of nearby infrastructure and realises the connectivity of the Eurasian continent. This corridor aims to construct and upgrade the nearby infrastructure and construct a higher-efficiency network of sea–land–air aligned transit freight logistics. Both initiatives highly coincide in content and enjoy great potential cooperation/development. The Hungary–Serbia Railway jointly constructed by China and Hungary is the first access of a complete set of Chinese railway technologies/equipment to the European market, is an important component of the 16+1 cooperation framework and plays an important role in boosting railway cooperation between China and Europe.[8] The Hungary–Serbia Railway offers a very good mode for both initiatives to realise the integration of infrastructure construction, and is also a successful

attempt of China in some aspects (realise an extensive consultation, joint contribution and shared benefit with these 4 countries; connect the Silk Road with the Amber Road; and form a barrier-free network of trade/logistics in the Eurasian continent). In the future, the alignment of both initiatives will not only boost the smooth implementation of infrastructure projects, but also produce an effect of "One plus one is greater than two" and promote the prosperity of regional economy.

(3) Strengthen economic/trade cooperation and connect the economic circle of the Asia–Pacific and Europe. As Chinese all-round opening to the outward world enters a higher stage, China continuously deepens/expands economic/trade cooperation with the countries along the Amber Road under the Belt and Road framework, and has made a physical achievement. Except for the European Union, China becomes the largest trade partner of Hungary and Hungary also becomes the largest Chinese-invested country in the Central and Eastern European area. Under the currently continuous downturn and recession of the world economy, China–Hungary trade grows against the trend, which indicates the great potential of trade intercourse and symbolises and embodies a friendly relationship between both countries.[9] As the junction point between the Silk Road and the Amber Road, Poland is also an economic power in Central and Eastern Europe, has a more complete economic structure and thus enjoys a very large cooperation space with China. China also actively seeks for a point of benefit coincidence in cooperation with Poland, continuously improves the level of economic/trade cooperation with Poland, strengthens complementation of advantages and boosts friendly cooperation. China has become Slovenia's largest trade partner in Asia. In order to coordinate the vast Chinese market with Slovenian high-new technologies and sophisticated products and play an economic complementation, both countries have completed a series of economic/trade cooperation projects and continuously expand the cooperation channels. China actively develops a trade partnership with Slovakia. In May 2017, the "Outlines for economic relation development between Slovakia and China (2017–2020)" was submitted by Slovakia to strengthen bilateral cooperation and cooperate in some fields in the future (e.g. investment, trade, transportation, tourism and research innovation).[10] With a huge cooperation space in economics and trade, the alignment between both initiatives not only promotes a non-impedance of freight logistics, but also plays a linking effect to boost economic/trade cooperation of deeper level and wider fields among neighbouring countries and radiate the economic circle of Europe and Asia.

Notes

1 "Amber rail freight transport corridor established," Website of the Hungarian Government, December 7, 2017.
2 "Memorandum of Understanding between the Ministries Responsible for Transport of Poland, the Slovak Republic, Hungary and the Republic of Slovenia on the establishment of the Executive Board of the Amber Rail Freight Corridor." December 5, 2017. Retrieved February 7, 2018 from http://imss.dz-rs.si/imis/0e8a25578f80c2c3473a.pdf
3 "Amber Rail corridor established," Trade Trans website. December 28, 2017. Retrieved February 7, 2018 from www.tradetrans.com/content/amber-rail-corridor-established
4 Ibid.
5 "Poland is considered as Xi Jinping as a junction of the Silk Road and the Amber Road: expert interpretation of the Amber Road," Huanqiu Net, June 21, 2016. Retrieved February 9, 2018 from http://world.huanqiu.com/hot/2016-06/9066191.html
6 "The Belt and Road Initiative aligns with the 'Opening up to the east' policy; Hungary leads in the cooperation with China among the Central and Eastern European countries," *The Paper Online*, December 1, 2016. Retrieved February 9, 2018 from www.thepaper.cn/newsDetail_forward_1572276

7 "Poland is considered as Xi Jinping as a junction of the Silk Road and the Amber Road: expert interpretation of the Amber Road," Huanqiu Net, June 21, 2016. Retrieved February 9, 2018 from http://world.huanqiu.com/hot/2016-06/9066191.html
8 "The Belt and Road Initiative aligns with the 'Opening up to the east' policy; Hungary leads in the cooperation with China among the Central and Eastern European countries," *The Paper Online*, December 1, 2016. Retrieved February 9, 2018 from www.thepaper.cn/newsDetail_forward_1572276
9 Ibid.
10 Head of the Ministry of Economy of Slovak, "Slovak actively participates in the Belt and Road Initiative," Xinhua Net. May 13, 2017. Retrieved February 2018 from www.xinhuanet.com/2017-05/13/c_1120965221.htm

106
SUEZ CANAL ECONOMIC CORRIDOR (EGYPT)

Tian Guangqiang

On November 17, 1869, the Suez Canal was formally opened to navigation, with a length of about 169 km and 194 km including the approach channel. As a main international sea transportation channel connecting the European, Asian and African continents, the Suez Canal is globally reputed as "sea transportation shortcut between the east and the west" and "world throat-cutting seaway channel", and is praised by the Egyptian people as the main artery of Egyptian prosperity. By connecting the Mediterranean Sea and the Red Sea, the Suez Canal connects the Atlantic Ocean with the Indian Ocean and the Pacific Ocean, so as to greatly shorten the voyage between Europe and Asia. The Suez Canal is one of the world's most important international channels. In terms of annual ship passage quantity and involved countries/areas, the Suez Canal occupies first position in the global canals. The freight volume of the Suez Canal accounts for 20% and 80% in the global and Eurasian total marine freight volume, respectively; and 22% of global containers passes through the Suez Canal, which involves about 10% of global trade. The Suez Canal is also one of the world's most important petroleum transportation channels, and is known as the world's throat of petroleum transportation together with other places (e.g. Hormuz Strait, Malacca Strait and Panama Canal), which offers a navigation for 25% of oil tankers.[1] Therefore, the Suez Canal occupies a crucial position in the world's sea transportation trade.

With the rapid development of international trade, the old Suez Canal is insufficient to meet navigation need. On August 5, 2014, in order to improve its navigation capacity, Egypt decided to start the project of new Suez Canal (including the digging of a 35-km long new waterway and the expansion of a 37-km long old waterway) with the following main purposes: create a condition of dual navigation for existing course; allow the passage of larger ships; and improve the navigation efficiency of the Suez Canal. On August 6, 2015, the new Suez Canal was formally opened to navigation to realise the following goals: change the original one-way navigation to dual navigation; greatly increase the navigation capacity of the Suez Canal; and shorten the navigation waiting time from the current 22 hours to 11 hours. As estimated by Egypt, up to 2023, the daily average number of merchant passage ships will increase from a current 49 ships to 97 ships, and the annual revenue of the canal will increase from the current US$5.3 billion to US$13.2 billion.[2] Meanwhile, Egypt plans to construct the Suez Canal Economic Corridor (hereinafter referred to as "this corridor") along the Suez Canal in the future (including the construction of such infrastructure as roads, airports and ports). After the whole completion of this corridor, an annual revenue of up to US$100 billion will be created for Egypt, which accounts for about one-third of Egyptian GDP. Therefore, the new Suez Canal is known as the corner stone for restoring the national sense of pride and revitalising the national economy.

Egypt is an important loop of the ancient Land Silk Road and Marine Silk Road; and the Suez Canal connecting 2 seas and 3 continents is an important component of the 21st Century Maritime Silk Road. When the new Suez Canal is open to navigation, the Belt and Road construction is exactly started for boosting; and thus their alignment can be considered a result of timely opportunity, geographical advantage and human unity.

On December 22–25, 2014, Abdel Fattah Al Sisi (President of Egypt) paid a state visit to China, and both countries decided to upgrade the China–Egypt relationship into a comprehensive strategic partnership. Xi Jinping (Chairman of China) said: China will align the Belt and Road Initiative with Egyptian major development plans. President Sisi stated: the Belt and Road Initiative provides an important opportunity for Egyptian revitalisation; Egypt will actively participate in and support this initiative; Egypt will cooperate with China in developing various projects (e.g. this corridor and Suez Economic Cooperation Area) to create a better condition for attracting the investment of Chinese enterprises in Egypt.[3] In the "Joint statement for establishing a comprehensive strategic partnership" signed by both countries, Egypt emphasises: the Belt and Road Initiative is very significant, and meets the benefit of future cooperation between both countries; and both countries will jointly explore the cooperation mode under the Belt and Road framework.[4] On March 28, 2015, the "Vision and Action on Boosting the Joint Construction of Silk Road Economic Belt and 21st Century Maritime Silk Road" was jointly released by the National Development and Reform Commission of PRC, the Ministry of Foreign Affairs of PRC and the Ministry of Commerce of PRC: as a key direction, the 21st Century Maritime Silk Road starts from Chinese coastal ports across the South China Sea to the Indian Ocean and further to Europe.[5] The Suez Canal is an important throat-cutting channel in this route. On January 20, 2016, at a state visit to Egypt, Chairman Xi Jinping said to President Sisi: both countries should align their own development strategies with the Belt and Road Initiative and make Egypt a pivotal country along the Belt and Road through the major breakthrough points of infrastructure construction and production capacity cooperation; China will participate in the construction of various Egyptian projects (e.g. this corridor and a New Administrative Capital) and expand cooperation in various fields (e.g. trade, financing, aerospace and energy). President Sisi stated: Egypt will align its development plan with the Belt and Road Initiative, and boost cooperation in various fields under the framework of the Asian Infrastructure Investment Bank (e.g. infrastructure).[6] On January 21, 2016, the "Five-year implementation outline for strengthening a comprehensive strategic partnership" was released by China and Egypt: Egypt supports the Belt and Road Initiative; both countries will strengthen cooperation under the framework of this initiative; in particular, China supports Egypt in various Egyptian plans for economic recovery, including: major country-level projects (e.g. this corridor) and other important projects deemed as economically feasible by both countries.[7] The "Memorandum of understanding on jointly boosting the construction of Silk Road Economic Belt and 21st Century Maritime Silk Road" was also signed by China and Egypt. In May 2017, the Belt and Road Forum for International Cooperation was attended by a delegation of Egypt. On September 5, 2017, at a meeting with Chairman Xi Jinping in Xiamen City (China), President Sisi stated: Egypt will support the Belt and Road Initiative, align its development strategies with this initiative and enlarge a cooperation with China in various fields (e.g. investment and infrastructure).[8]

China has become Egypt's largest trade partner and import source. As Egypt realises strategic alignment with the Belt and Road Initiative, the unfavourable balance of trade between China and Egypt will be reduced to a certain degree and the trade between both countries will tend to be more balanced. In 2017, the bilateral goods import and export volume between China and Egypt reached US$10,866 million, which dropped by 4.05% over that in 2016: Chinese export volume to Egypt reached US$9535 million, a decrease of 11.52%; Chinese import volume from Egypt reached US$1331 million, an increase of 142.59%; and a favourable balance of trade was reached at US$8205 million between China and Egypt, a decrease of 19.78%.[9] Chinese direct investment to Egypt is increasing continuously. According to the statistical data of the Ministry of Commerce of PRC, by the end of 2016, Chinese direct investment to Egypt reached a flow of up to US$0.12 billion and a reserve of up to US$889 million, which provided direct employment for more than 10,000 people; a total of 1312 Chinese enterprises invested over US$0.6 billion in Egypt, which occupied the 21st position among the overseas investment countries in Egypt; and more than 140 Egyptian China-funded business institutions were filed in the Economic and Commercial Counsellor's Office of the Chinese embassy in Egypt to launch the economic/trade activity in Egypt.[10] As the infrastructure construction is vigorously boosted by Egypt, the number of Egyptian projects contracted by China will be increased rapidly. According to the statistical data of the Ministry of Commerce of PRC, by the end of 2016, Chinese enterprises newly signed 31 Egyptian contracting agreements valued at US$8022 million and accomplished a business volume of US$2281 million; China delegated 2119 workers of various types to Egypt, with 1546 workers remaining at the end of 2016.[11] In 2017, agreement on 2 projects was formally signed between China and Egypt: a suburban light railway in 10th Ramadan City (as the first electric light railway in Egypt) and a central business district in the New Administrative Capital of Egypt.[12] In order to boost economic cooperation, China and Egypt accelerate cooperation in the financial field. In December 2016, an agreement on bilateral local currency swap (at a scale of 18 billion RMB) was jointly signed by the central banks of China and Egypt. In the next 2 years, a loan and credit with a signed amount of more than US$5 billion has been provided to Egypt in various forms by Chinese financial institutions (e.g. China Development Bank, Export–Import Bank of China, Asian Infrastructure Investment Bank, Industrial and Commercial Bank of China and China Export & Credit Insurance Corporation).[13]

The Suez Canal is an important cooperation field between China and Egypt. It is an important navigation passage for Chinese overseas trade: 60% of Chinese trade to Europe is transported via the Suez Canal, which accounts for more than 10% of navigation ships in this canal[14]; and annually about over 1800 merchant ships of Chinese nationality pass through the Suez Canal, paying a toll of more than US$0.3 billion.[15] In 2008, the China–Egypt Suez Economic Cooperation Area was formally put into operation, which was the second batch of country-level overseas economic cooperation areas approved by the Chinese government and the key overseas economic cooperation area developed and constructed by gathering country-level resources. Up to the end of 2016, in the start-up zone of the Suez Economic Cooperation Area, there were a total of 70 enterprises, which attracted an investment with a cumulative signed value of nearly US$1 billion and provided more than 3000 jobs for local people. In September 2014, the extended zone (6 km^2) of the Suez Economic Cooperation Area was initiated by China and Egypt, which would be developed through 3 phases and a total investment amount of about US$0.23 billion. On November 30, 2015, China TEDA Investment Holding Co. received the land for Phase I project (2 km^2) from Egypt after signing the "Agreement on the hand-over of land of Phase I project of Suez Economic Cooperation Area". In January 2016, during a visit to Egypt, Chairman Xi Jinping and President Sisi jointly unveiled the initiation of the extended zone.[16] By the aid of the new Suez Canal, this corridor was proposed by Egypt with the following objectives: drive the development of various industries through the location advantage of the new Suez Canal (e.g. automobile assembly, high-new electronic technology, petroleum refinery/chemicals, aquaculture, ship manufacturing and light textile); and build Egypt into a world-class centre of economy, trade and logistics. As estimated by Egypt, after the completion of this corridor, an annual revenue of US$100 billion will be earned for Egypt and more than 1 million jobs will be created.[17] Egypt wishes Chinese enterprises to actively participate in the development of this corridor.

Notes

1 Su Qingyi, "Influence of new Suez Canal on the international economy and trade," *Maritime China*, 2015, 9, p. 20.
2 "Opening of new Suez Canal, with an anticipated significance for politics and economy," Xinhua Net. Retrieved March 1, 2018 from www.xinhuanet.com/mrdx/2015-08/08/c_134494343.htm
3 "China–Egypt relationship is upgraded into comprehensive strategic partnership," Xinhua Net. Retrieved March 1, 2018 from http://world.people.com.cn/n/2014/1224/c157278-26268908.html
4 "Joint statement for establishing a comprehensive strategic partnership," *People's Daily Online*. Retrieved March 1, 2018 from http://politics.people.com.cn/n/2014/1223/c70731-26262928.html
5 "Vision and Action on Boosting the Joint Construction of Silk Road Economic Belt and 21st Century Maritime Silk Road", Xinhua Net. Retrieved March 2, 2018 from www.xinhuanet.com/world/2015-03/28/c_1114793986.htm
6 "List of achievements of Xi Jinping's visit to Egypt," *People's Daily Online*. Retrieved March 2, 2018 from http://politics.people.com.cn/n1/2016/0124/c1001-28080021.html
7 "Five-year implementation outline for strengthening a comprehensive strategic partnership," Xinhua Net. Retrieved March 2, 2018 from www.xinhuanet.com/world/2016-01/22/c_1117855474.htm
8 "Xi Jinping meets Abdel Fattah Al Sisi (president of Egypt)," Xinhua Net. Retrieved March 2, 2018 from www.xinhuanet.com/world/2017-09/05/c_1121607635.htm
9 "By December 2017, Chinese export to and import from Egypt increased by 13.92% and 28.67%, respectively," Economic and Commercial Counselor's Office of Chinese embassy in Egypt. Retrieved March 3, 2018 from http://eg.mofcom.gov.cn/article/i/201801/20180102706840.shtml
10 *Guideline for the countries/regions of outward investment and cooperation: Egypt*. Ministry of Commerce of PRC, Edition 2017, p. 56.
11 *Guideline for the countries/regions of outward investment and cooperation: Egypt*. Ministry of Commerce of PRC, Edition 2017, p. 59.
12 "Overview of China–Egypt cooperation in 2017," Economic and Commercial Counselor's Office of Chinese embassy in Egypt. Retrieved March 3, 2018 from http://eg.mofcom.gov.cn/article/zxhz/201801/20180102702850.shtml
13 Ibid. (accessed on: March 3, 2018)
14 Yu Jiefei, "Significance of new Suez Canal," *Guangming Daily*, August 9, 2015, column 6.
15 *Guideline for the countries/regions of outward investment and cooperation: Egypt*. Ministry of Commerce of PRC, Edition 2017, p. 33.
16 *Guideline for the countries/regions of outward investment and cooperation: Egypt*. Ministry of Commerce of PRC, Edition 2017, p. 60.
17 Yu Jiefei, "Significance of new Suez Canal," *Guangming Daily*, August 9, 2015, column 6.

107
LAMU PORT–SOUTH SUDAN–ETHIOPIA TRANSPORTATION CORRIDOR (KENYA)

Pang Jiaxin

Overview

Lamu Port–South Sudan–Ethiopia Transport Corridor (LAPSSET or Lamu Corridor) is a part of Kenya's "Vision Strategy 2023". This corridor aims to realise long-term national development, develop Kenya into a middle-income emerging industrialised country by 2030 and provide security guarantee and high-quality life for the Kenyan people. This strategy has 3 objectives: political, economic and social; as an economic objective, it aims to realise an annual economic growth rate of more than 10% until 2030.[1] In March 2012, this corridor was initiated jointly by Kenya, Sudan and Ethiopia, so as to promote a development of regional economy and alleviate the traffic pressure of Mombasa–Uganda Transportation Corridor. As Kenya's largest infrastructure construction plan in "Vision Strategy 2023", this corridor aims to open up the Kenya second traffic transportation corridor, establish a multi-modal combined transportation channel, realise a seamless connection between Kenya, South Sudan and Ethiopia, and promote an economic development in the northern, eastern, north-eastern and coastal areas of Kenya.

This corridor is divided into 2 parts: an infrastructure corridor (including such projects as road, railway, pipeline and cable); and an economic corridor (mainly for attracting investment and industrial development). The projects of this corridor cover more than half of the Kenyan territory, and involve a total investment amount of more than US$25 billion. In 2015, this corridor was approved by the African Union as Presidential Infrastructure Championing Initiative (PICI) and Programme for Infrastructure Development in Africa (PIDA). In 2016, this corridor was evaluated in Washington (USA) as "Global infrastructure leadership project (2016)" and as the largest project on the African continent after the independence of African countries.[2] Lamu (Kenya) is the key node of this plan. By utilising the development of its ports and oil pipelines in Lamu as the main catalyst and by relying on the great business/employment opportunities from the construction of its special economic zones and vacation cities, Kenya will construct an aligned traffic network (road, railway and airway) and infrastructure (power and water conservancy) so as to create an important condition for its development/transformation and build it into an international metropolis. Therefore, this corridor is composed of key infrastructure projects and other infrastructure construction projects.[3] There are 7 key projects: Lamu Port; inter-regional railways of standard rail gauge, inter-regional expressways, oil pipelines, international airports, vacation cities and multi-functional large-scale dams. Other infrastructure construction projects mainly include: public facilities (including the urban auxiliary public facilities of optical cable, telecommunication system and sewage treatment plant; power infrastructure is preferentially constructed); and Lamu Oil Refinery Plant (for refining the petroleum products to Kenya and Ethiopia; with an estimated daily production capacity of 0.12 million barrels; plans to be completed by 2020).

This corridor is very significant for the sustainable development of the East African area. (1) This corridor benefits a social stability: the geographical range covered by this corridor is deemed as robber rampage and continuous social conflict, which is obviously reduced after the implementation of this corridor. (2) After the completion of this corridor, the following objectives are achieved: facilitate South Sudan in shaking off dependence on the ports and crude oil pipelines of Sudan, and reduce their bilateral conflict; increase an import/export channel for Ethiopia and accelerate economic development in the southern area of Ethiopia; and bring about considerable revenues of petroleum transportation/operation for Kenya. (3) Through the gradual perfection of infrastructure, many benefits are seen: create a great investment opportunity and promote stable economic development in East African countries; and stimulate the development of emerging industries along this corridor and form many vigorous emerging cities in Kenya (e.g. Lamu, Turkana and Meru). (4) Numerous sustainable posts are provided for local residents by the implementation of infrastructure projects; and Kenya provides a scholarship for poor but capable students, cultivates the technicians of fitting specialty and realises better employment for Kenyan people. (5) Many benefits are brought about by the construction of vacation cities and auxiliary traffic facilities (road, railway and airway): accelerate Kenya in opening up some new tourist scenes; greatly boost the development of Kenya's tourist industry; and assist the growth of service industry.

Alignment with the Belt and Road Initiative

This corridor aligns with the Belt and Road Initiative under the "4–6–1" framework of China–Africa cooperation: 4 principles (equality, pragmatism, sincerity and faithfulness); 6 projects (industry, finance, poverty reduction, ecological protection, humanistic exchange and peace and security); and 1 platform (Forum on China–Africa Cooperation). In January 2015, the "Memorandum for boosting the African construction of three networks and one industrialisation" was signed by China and the African Union to promote a construction of high-speed railways, expressways, airways and industrialisation infrastructure in Africa. In December 2015, at the Johannesburg Summit of Forum on China–Africa Cooperation, the "Forum on China–Africa Cooperation–Johannesburg Plan of Implementation" was released by China and the African Union: propose 10 cooperation plans (industrialisation, agricultural modernisation, infrastructure, finance, green development, trade/investment facilitation, poverty reduction and people benefit, public health, humanistic and peace and security); and provide a fund of US$60 billion to jointly construct a China–African community with a common future.[4] This corridor aims to solve the long-term problems of poor infrastructure in the East African area; and the infrastructure construction is just one important component of the Belt and Road construction. This corridor and the Belt and Road Initiative are aligned in the following aspects of benefit coincidence.

(1) Construction of traffic infrastructure. The construction of most infrastructure construction projects in Kenya has been undertaken by China at a great phasic achievement (including: railway, road, port, airport, oil pipeline, power and house construction). There are several representative projects. In November 2012, the Nairobi–Thika Expressway was opened to traffic (8 lanes, 50-km long): its construction was jointly undertaken by 3e Chinese

companies; it is Kenya's first modernised expressway and the model for driving the economic development of Kenya by roads; and it aims to promote better economic fusion/cooperation among all Kenyan areas and greatly improve the role of Kenya as regional economic hub.[5] In May 2017, the Mombasa–Nairobi Railway was formally opened to traffic (standard gauge, 480-km long, designed transportation capacity of 25 million tons, 33 stations): it was constructed by China Road & Bridge Corporation; it is the first new railway constructed in Kenya in the past 100 years; it connects Nairobi (capital of Kenya) with Mombasa Port (the largest port of East Africa); it is a modernised railway constructed through Chinese standards, Chinese technologies and Chinese equipment[6]; and it promotes the economic development of Kenya, provides great employment opportunities, facilitates the connection of the railway network in East Africa and boosts connectivity of the African continent. In addition, the construction of some Kenyan infrastructure projects is also undertaken by Chinese enterprises: the Nairobi–Malaba Railway; many berths in 3 ports (Nairobi Container Inland Port, Mombasa Port and Lamu Port). According to the statistical data, during the period of January–October 2017, 72 projects were signed by Chinese contracting enterprises in Kenya, with a total contract value of US$3.3 billion.[7] Such infrastructure creates great employment opportunities for Kenya, consolidates the role of Kenya as a logistic hub of East Africa and boosts the deep development of the Belt and Road cooperation.

(2) Investment/cooperation in production capacity. Since 2015, China has become Kenya's largest source of outward direct investment. According to the statistical data of the Economic and Commercial Counsellor's Office of Chinese embassy in Kenya, Kenya–China Economic and Trade Association had 85 member enterprises, most of which were central enterprises, local enterprises and larger private enterprises mainly in the fields of project contracting, commerce, trade and logistics.[8] As shown by the investigation report of the World Bank, China invested in 400 Kenyan enterprises; and China became the country with the largest investment amount in manufacturing industry of Kenya (i.e. 64% of all investments in Kenya), mainly in the fields of automobile spares/parts, food, consumer electronic products, agricultural processing, building materials and telecommunication appliances.[9] Kenya is greatly aided by China: develop infrastructure; accelerate construction of traffic network for connectivity among East African countries; establish economic zones; and improve the production force of Kenya through industrial transfer. In December 2017, the 1st China–Africa Cooperation Expo on Production Capacity and the China–Africa Cooperation Forum on Production Capacity were held in the Kenyatta International Conference Centre of Nairobi: exhibit the high-quality products and advanced technologies of China; strengthen an industrial connection; and boost a development of deep level and broad field in production capacity cooperation.[10]

(3) Strengthen financial cooperation. Financial support is key for the smooth implementation of the various projects in Kenya. In 2015, the "Cooperation agreement on the overall infrastructure development" was signed by Kenya and the Industrial and Commercial Bank of China to jointly support a renovation of Kenyan infrastructure and establish a new platform for production capacity cooperation: the Industrial and Commercial Bank of China provides Kenya with an investment/financing aligned service (e.g. financing and senior financial consulting) in various fields (e.g. infrastructure, power, telecommunication, power transmission/transformation and traffic).[11] In 2016, at the Forum on China–Africa Cooperation, more than 40 cooperation agreements between Chinese/African financial institutions and enterprises were signed by China and Africa, which had a total contract value of about US$18 billion.[12] In 2017, a financing agreement was signed: a loan of US$0.25 billion is provided by the Export–Import Bank of China for the Eastern and Southern African Trade and Development Bank to meet the need of various funds (e.g. China–Africa financing cooperation). In addition, a fund is provided by

the China–Africa Development Fund and the China–Africa Fund for Industrial Cooperation to support the African construction of 3 networks and 1 industrialisation.

(4) Boosting of energy cooperation. China has become an important force for investment and construction of Kenya's power and energy infrastructure to boost the development of construction of Kenya's energy infrastructure. In June 2015, a cooperation agreement on the construction of Lamu Power Plant (Kenya's largest thermal power plant) was signed by the Power Corporation Construction of China and Kenya: this plant greatly increases the power supply capability of the Kenyan power grid, improves the structure of power and promotes the complementary development of various energy forms (e.g. hydropower, thermal power, wind power and geothermal heat).[13] In September 2016, the Garissa Photovoltaic Power Plant (50 MW, Kenya) was formally initiated: this plant was jointly constructed by China and Kenya and it is the largest photovoltaic power plant combined to the grid in Kenya and East Africa and one of Africa's largest photovoltaic power plants.[14] In 2016, the Kipeto Wind Power Plant (Kenya) was jointly constructed by China and the USA to boost the development of clean energy in Africa. In May 2017, a cooperation agreement on the construction of the Lamu Coal-fired Power Plant (1050 MW, Kenya) was signed by the Power Corporation Construction of China: this plant is the largest power-generation facility in East Africa, Central Africa and South Africa (excluding the Republic of South Africa).[15]

(5) Promotion of understanding between people. Through the investment and construction of various projects, a good relationship has been established between Chinese and Kenyan people. In order to cultivate the talents of railway operation for Kenya, China is preparing to establish the "China–Africa Friendship Kenya Railway Institute" and helps Kenyan colleges to establish a major in railway engineering.[16] Meanwhile, China has aided the cultural fields of Kenya: set the China Global Television Network in Nairobi (a television station of broadcasting and telecommunication); established the Confucius Institutes; granted a scholarship for African students studying in China; and introduced the course of Chinese language into Kenya schools.[17]

Notes

1 LAPSSET Planning and Investment Framework. Retrieved January 18, 2018 from https://drive.google.com/file/d/0B7w3900K6lYnSVBTMW93OFN3RkU/view
2 Ibid.
3 LAPSSET Project Report 2016.
4 "China–Africa cooperation in production capacity under the Belt and Road Initiative," website of Forum on China–Africa Cooperation. Retrieved February 1, 2018 from www.fmprc.gov.cn/zflt/chn/zxxx/t1478626.htm
5 "Nairobi–Thika Expressway constructed by China was open to traffic: the first expressway in Kenya," *China Daily Online*. Retrieved February 1, 2018 from www.chinadaily.com.cn/hqgj/jryw/2012-11-10/content_7471425.html
6 "Mombasa–Nairobi Railway constructed by China was formally open to traffic: as an important project under the Belt and Road Initiative," Belt and Road Portal. Retrieved February 2, 2018 from www.yidaiyilu.gov.cn/xwzx/hwxw/14942.htm
7 "China becomes the Kenya largest source country of outward direct investment; the economic and trade cooperation between both countries was continuously deepened," Belt and Road Portal. Retrieved February 2, 2018 from www.yidaiyilu.gov.cn/xwzx/roll/43082.htm
8 "Our life is changed by the investment of Chinese enterprises," *People's Daily Online*. January 9, 2018. Retrieved February 2, 2018 from http://world.people.com.cn/n1/2018/0109/c1002-29752989.html
9 Ministry of Commerce of PRC, "Up to 400 Chinese enterprises invest in Kenya." April 6, 2016. Retrieved February 2, 2018 from www.mofcom.gov.cn/article/i/jyjl/k/201604/20160401290541.shtml
10 "China–Africa Cooperation Expo on Production Capacity was held in Kenya," *People's Daily Online*. December 15, 2017. Retrieved February 2, 2018 from http://world.people.com.cn/n1/2017/1215/c1002-29707956.html

11 "The Industrial and Commercial Bank of China signed the 'Cooperation agreement on the integral development of infrastructure' in Kenya," *China Daily Online*. July 21, 2015. Retrieved February 2, 2018 from http://caijing.chinadaily.com.cn/2015-07/21/content_21370152.htm
12 "Over 40 agreements on economic and trade cooperation were signed by China and Africa," *Economic Information Daily*. August 1, 2016. Retrieved February 2, 2018 from http://dz.jjckb.cn/www/pages/webpage2009/html/2016-08/01/content_21903.htm
13 "Power Corporation Construction of China signed the 'General contract on Lamu Power Plant (valued at 1 million USD)'," website of Power Corporation Construction of China. June 2015. Retrieved February 2, 2018 from www.spem.com.cn/news/news1041.html
14 "Largest photovoltaic power plant was started to be jointly constructed by China and Kenya," Huanqiu Net, September 30, 2016. Retrieved February 2, 2018 from http://world.huanqiu.com/hot/2016-09/9505115.html
15 "Power Corporation Construction of China signed the 'Cooperation agreement on Lamu Coal-fired Power Plant'," website of State-owned Assets Supervision and Administration Commission of the State Council. May 19, 2017. Retrieved February 2, 2018 from www.sasac.gov.cn/n103/n2549214/n2594106/n2596627/c2610945/content.html
16 Ibid.
17 "As stated in the foreign media, the Belt and Road Initiative assists the development of Kenya: China wins a respect through the efficiency," website of Forum on China-Africa Cooperation. June 12, 2017. Retrieved February 2, 2018 from www.fmprc.gov.cn/zflt/chn/zxxx/t1469376.htm

108
TWO-CORRIDOR AND ONE-RING PLAN (VIETNAM)

Liu Jingye

The two-corridor and one-ring plan (hereinafter referred to as "this plan") was proposed by Vietnam to promote an economic cooperation between China and Vietnam. In 2004, a consensus was reached on this plan by both countries. Subsequently, this plan made relevant achievements in the various field of cooperation (e.g. border trade facilitation, agriculture and medicine). Since the Belt and Road Initiative was proposed in 2015, both countries had cooperated in the alignment of both initiatives and had made preliminary achievements in various fields (e.g. policy coordination, unimpeded trade and infrastructure connectivity).

Conceptual description and main contents

This plan is a concrete achievement in the development of economic cooperation between both countries under the framework of China–ASEAN Cooperation and Lancang–Mekong Subregion Cooperation. On May 20, 2004, during a visit to China, Phan Van Khai (Premier of Vietnam) suggested Wen Jiabao (Premier of China) to jointly construct this plan. In October 2004, at a visit of Premier Wen Jiabao to Vietnam, the "China–Vietnam joint communiqué" was released by both countries to actively explore the feasibility for two corridors and one ring: Kunming–LaoCai–HaNoi–HaiPhong–QuangNinh Economic Corridor; Nanning–LangSon–HaNoi–HaiPhong–QuangNinh Economic Corridor; and Beibu Gulf Rim Economic Ring. Then, this plan entered the stage of governmental conceptual cooperation. In terms of geographical range, this plan covers 4 southern provinces of China (i.e. Yunnan Province, Guangxi Province, Guangdong Province and Hainan Province) and 5 areas of Vietnam (i.e. LaoCai City, LangSon City, QuangNinh Province, HaNoi City and HaiPhong City). In terms of long-term development, this plan can radiate to the surrounding countries of the Greater Mekong Subregion. In terms of cooperation characteristics, various goals are realised by this plan through construction infrastructure (e.g. railway, road and airway): strengthen cooperation between both countries in trade, investment and industry; realise a cross-country flow and optimised allocation of resources and production essentials; and form a regional international economic corridor.[1]

During the boosting process of this plan, the policies and infrastructure construction were adjusted correspondingly by Vietnam. On July 11, 2008, the "Resolution on approving the development plan of LangSon–HaNoi–HaiPhong–QuangNinh Economic Corridor (2020)" (Resolution 98/2008/QD-TTg) was released by Vietnam with the following general objectives: establish the Nanning–LangSon–HaNoi–HaiPhong–QuangNinh Economic Corridor with modern synchronous infrastructure; improve the competitive power of investment environment; benefit the border areas of both countries in developing the economy, trade and cooperation; create favourable conditions for cooperation between enterprises of both countries and third countries; build this corridor into a new growth point of economic/trade cooperation between both countries; play an important role of this corridor in China–ASEAN economic/trade cooperation[2]; form a trading facilitation mechanism in relevant ports; and establish a transit economic cooperation area. In March 2015, the "Development plan of LangSon–HaNoi–HoChiMinh–MocBai (near to 2020, prospective to 2030)" was released by Vietnam with the following anticipated objectives by 2020 (i.e. South–North Economic Corridor): contribute to GDP by up to US$200–220 billion (i.e. 70% of total GDP in Vietnam); attract 9–9.5 million foreign tourists and 40–41 million Vietnamese tourists with a tourism revenue of US$15–16 billion[3]; and provide a policy support for further implementation of this plan.

In addition, the development plan of Beibu Gulf Coastal Economic Ring was proposed by Vietnam to strengthen a construction of economic zones in Vietnam and provide favourable conditions for alignment with this plan. On March 2, 2009, the "Resolution on approving the development plan of Beibu Gulf Coastal Economic Ring (2020)" (Resolution 34/2009/QD-TTg) was released by Vietnam. This ring includes QuangNinh Province and HaiPhong City, covering a geographical area of 7418.8 km² and a population of nearly 2.9 million. The following objectives by 2020 are set for this ring: develop into a vigorous economic zone; integrate with 2 economic corridors between Vietnam–China and the southern coastal areas of China; create favourable conditions for Vietnam to effectively expand cooperation of trade/development with China and ASEAN; achieve about 6.5–7% of total GDP of Vietnam; and realise a per-capita GDP of up to US$3500–4000.[4] (1) Infrastructure construction. The construction of the expressway provides hardware support for the construction of this plan. In September 2014, the HaNoi–LaoCai Expressway was wholly open to traffic, which is the first expressway to connect with the Vietnam–China border; in December 2015, the HaNoi–HaiPhong Expressway was wholly open to traffic, which adds a new impetus for economic development in Northern Vietnam; and in 2014, the HaNoi–LangSon Expressway was commenced for construction, whose HaNoi–BacQiang section had been completed and which will be connected with the Nanning–Huunghi Expressway.

(2) Cooperation mechanism between China and Vietnam. The Conference of Economic Corridor Cooperation among Five Provinces/Cities (i.e. Yunnan Province of China; and LaoCai, HaNoi, HaiPhong and QuangNinh Provinces of Vietnam) is an important cooperation platform between both countries. This conference has been held 8 times since 2004. Certain achievements have been made by both countries in various cooperation fields (e.g. trade, investment, traffic transportation, tourism, cultural education, person training, agriculture and medicine). According to the statistical data of General Customs Administration of PRC in 2014, Vietnam surpassed Singapore as China's second-largest trade partner in the ASEAN area.[5] China–Vietnam trade always maintains stable growth. According to the data of General Statistics Office of Vietnam in 2017, the bilateral trade volume between China and Vietnam was estimated at US$93.8 billion; the unbalanced trade conditions were improved to a certain degree; and the growth amplitude of Vietnamese export to China was enlarged.[6]

(3) Connectivity. Both countries accelerate the development of connectivity. In terms of land traffic, 16 passenger transportation lines, 7 ports and 20 freight transportation lines have been put into operation: the Kunming–LaoCai–HaNoi–HaiPhong line, the Nanning–LangSon–HaNoi

line and the Shenzhen–LangSon–HaNoi line go deep into the hinterland of Vietnam, which is very significant for promoting trade between both countries (especially the logistic transportation between Guangxi Province (China) and Northern Vietnam).[7] On November 22, 2017, at the 8th Conference of Economic Corridor Cooperation among Five Provinces/Cities in HaiPhong City, an extensive consensus on strengthening various cooperation aspects (e.g. economic/trade investment and connectivity) was reached by these 5 provinces/cities after a deep exchange; and the minutes and 6 agreements on strengthening the cooperation in various fields (e.g. finance, tourism and logistics) were signed.[8]

Current conditions and progress of alignment with the Belt and Road Initiative

After the proposal of the Belt and Road Initiative, both countries not only transform from a high-level consensus to a policy coordination by providing a powerful policy support for alignment between this plan and the Belt and Road Initiative, but also practically boost project integration to realise their alignment.

(1) The high-level leaders of both countries exchange continuously, and their alignment is upgraded by both countries from the stage of preliminary concept to the stage of consensus. On September 18, 2015, at the opening ceremony of the 12th China–ASEAN Expo, Nguyen Xuan Phuc (Vice Premier of Vietnam) said: Vietnam welcomes and actively studies the participation in the relevant initiatives (including: the Belt and Road Initiative) proposed by China on the basis of mutual respect and mutual benefit to enhance a regional exchange and cooperation.[9] In 2015, Xi Jinping (Chairman of China) visited Vietnam, and both countries agreed as follows: to integrate the advantages of both countries; to intensify a negotiation on the cooperation under the framework of this plan and the Belt and Road Initiative; to coordinate/boost the production capacity cooperation in multiple fields; to strive to construct the major projects; to vigorously boost border/financial cooperation; and to boost balanced, sustainable development of bilateral trade.[10] In September 2016, during a visit to China, Premier Nguyen Xuan Phuc stated the following wishes of Vietnam: accept each other by jointly constructing the connectivity projects; strengthen a close relationship between both countries; and cooperate with China in integrating this plan with the 21st Century Maritime Silk Road.[11] In May 2017, at the Belt and Road Forum for International Cooperation, Tran Dai Quang (Chairman of Vietnam) was interviewed as follows: at present, Vietnam and China are boosting an effective alignment between this plan and the Belt and Road Initiative to realise various goals(expand a trade investment between both countries and between them and other countries; continuously expand a market; and attract more investments in infrastructure construction).[12] Then, both countries have reached a certain consensus on their alignment.

(2) Through the policy communication, both countries realise their alignment in terms of policies. In November 2017, Chairman Xi Jinping visited Vietnam, and the "Memorandum of cooperation in jointly boosting the construction of the Belt and Road Initiative and the Two-corridor and one-ring Plan" was signed by both countries: implement the signed cooperation documents on the joint construction of both initiatives; determine priority fields, key direction and projects of cooperation as soon as possible; boost the 5 long-term approaches between both countries (i.e. policy coordination, infrastructure connectivity, unimpeded trade, financial integration and understanding between people); and create favourable conditions for quality improvement and upgrading of comprehensive strategic cooperation.[13] On November 12, 2017, the "Memorandum of understanding for accelerating the negotiation proceeding in construction framework agreement on the China–Vietnam Cross-Border Economic Cooperation

Area" was formally signed in HaNoi by Zhong Shan (head of the Ministry of Commerce of PRC) and Tran Tuan Anh (head of Ministry of Industry and Trade of Vietnam).[14] On November 13, 2017, at a meeting with Nguyen Xuan Phuc (Premier of Vietnam), Li Keqiang (Premier of China) expressed the wishes for both countries: accelerate alignment of development strategies; accelerate alignment between both initiatives by jointly cooperating in 3 fields (i.e. marine, land and finance); promote the balance of bilateral trade between total trade volume improvement and inclusive/diversified development; and better realise a mutual benefit and double-win. Premier Nguyen Xuan Phuc also expressed the wishes of Vietnam: continue to meticulously cultivate a friendship between Vietnam and China; deepen a comprehensive strategic partnership; boost an alignment of development strategies; strengthen a cooperation in various fields (e.g. production capacity, traffic facilities, transit economic cooperation area, agriculture, finance and environmental protection); and boost bilateral economic/trade relation to a new level.[15]

(3) Both countries accelerate the implementation of their alignment in various aspects (e.g. infrastructure construction and economy/trade cooperation). At the end of 2018, the CatLinh–Hadong Light Railway was formally put into operation: this railway was constructed by China Railway Sixth Group Co., Ltd; it is the first Chinese light railway in Vietnam and the first light railway in Vietnam. In order to effectively alleviate the current power shortage in Southern Vietnam, Vinh Tan Phase I Power Plant was jointly constructed at an investment amount of up to US$1.8 billion by 3 companies: China Southern Power Grid Company Limited; China Power Development International Limited; and Vietnam Vinacomin Power Co. Ltd. On December 9, 2016, the China–Vietnam (Shenzhen–HaiPhong) Economic Cooperation Area commenced for construction, which becomes a new platform for boosting an alignment of their development strategies. In November 2017, the China Railway Express from Nanning (China) to HaNoi (capital of Vietnam) was open to traffic for the first time: this transit container direct transportation line opens a new channel for economic/trade cooperation between Guangxi Province (China) and Vietnam and improves the capacity of the transit logistic channel through various transportation advantages (e.g. large transportation capacity, security, high efficiency and substantial benefit).[16] According to the data of Foreign Investment Agency in the Ministry of Planning and Investment of Vietnam, up to December 20, 2017, the agreement value of Chinese investment in Vietnam reached US$2.17 billion, including: 284 newly invested projects, 83 investment-added projects and 817 projects of capital injection or share purchase.[17]

Notes

1 Liu Zhi, "Vietnam's Two-corridor and one-ring Plan under the background of economic globalization and regional integration," *Journal of Contemporary Asia–Pacific Studies*, 2006, 10, p. 28.
2 Li Bihua, "Vietnam's Two-corridor and one-ring Plan and China's Belt and Road Initiative," *Around Southeast Asia*, 2016, 5, p. 37.
3 "South–North Economic Corridor/Two-corridor and one-ring Plan of Vietnam," Belt and Road Portal. March 17, 2015. Retrieved February 10, 2018 from www.yidaiyilu.gov.cn/zchj/gjjj/1067.htm
4 Li Bihua, "Vietnam's Two-corridor and one-ring Plan and China's Belt and Road Initiative," *Around Southeast Asia*, 2016, 5, p. 38.
5 "Vietnam became the China second largest trade partner of ASEAN," General Administration of Customs of PRC. November 20, 2014. Retrieved February 10, 2018 from http://vn.mofcom.gov.cn/article/zxhz/tjsj/201411/20141100804400.shtml
6 "In 2017, China–Vietnam bilateral trade volume reached 93.8 billion USD," *China Daily Online*, January 18, 2018. Retrieved February 10, 2018 from www.chinadaily.com.cn/interface/toutiaonew/53002523/2018-01-18/cd_35530738.html
7 "Deputy Head of the Ministry of Transportation of Vietnam talked about the connectivity between China and Vietnam," website of Voice of Vietnam, 2013.

8 "Eighth Conference of Economic Corridor Cooperation among Five Provinces/Cities was held in HaiPhong City (Vietnam)," Foreign Affairs Office of Yunnan Provincial Government. November 27, 2017. Retrieved February 10, 2018 from www.yfao.gov.cn/zbdt/201711/t20171127_645942.html
9 Vice Premier of Vietnam, "Vietnam will actively participate in the Belt and Road construction," China News Service website, September 18, 2015. Retrieved February 10, 2018 from http://finance.ifeng.com/a/20150918/13981831_0.shtml
10 "List of achievements of Xi Jinping's visit to Vietnam and Singapore," Xinhua Net, November 8, 2015. Retrieved February 10, 2018 from www.xinhuanet.com/world/2015-11/08/c_1117074341.htm
11 "China–Vietnam Joint Communiqué (full text)," Xinhua News Agency, September 14, 2016. Retrieved February 10, 2018 from http://politics.people.com.cn/n1/2016/0914/c1001-28716858.html
12 Chen Daguang, "Boosting of Vietnam's Two-corridor and one-ring Plan and China's Belt and Road Initiative," China Economic Net, May 12, 2017. Retrieved February 10, 2018 from http://news.sina.com.cn/gov/2017-05-12/doc-ifyfeivp5623677.shtml
13 "China will join hands with Vietnam and Laos to jointly construct the Belt and Road," China News Net. Ministry of Foreign Affairs of PRC. November 15, 2017. Retrieved February 10, 2018 from www.yidaiyilu.gov.cn/xwzx/gnxw/34744.htm
14 "China and Vietnam signed a memorandum to accelerate the construction of China–Vietnam Cross-Border Economic Cooperation Area," Ministry of Commerce of PRC, November 14, 2017. Retrieved February 10, 2018 from www.yidaiyilu.gov.cn/xwzx/hwxw/34542.htm
15 "Li Keqiang met Nguyen Xuan Phuc (premier of Vietnam): accelerate an integration of policies of both countries through the joint cooperation in three fields," Xinhua Net, November 14, 2017. Retrieved February 10, 2018 from www.yidaiyilu.gov.cn/xwzx/xgcdt/34520.htm
16 "China Railway Express from Guangxi Province (China) to Vietnam was open to traffic for the first time, which upgrades the capability of transit logistic passage," *People's Daily Online*, November 29, 2017. Retrieved February 10, 2018 from www.yidaiyilu.gov.cn/xwzx/dfdt/37382.htm
17 "China accelerates the investment to Vietnam: added 284 investment projects in 2017," website of Ministry of Commerce of PRC, January 5, 2018. Retrieved February 10, 2018 from www.yidaiyilu.gov.cn/xwzx/hwxw/42720.htm

109
STEPPE ROAD PLAN (MONGOLIA)

Tian Guangqiang

Overview

After the Belt and Road Initiative was proposed by China in 2013, Mongolia gave an active response. In 2013, Mongolia proposed the construction of 5 connection channels for China–Mongolia–Russia (i.e. railway, road, petroleum, power and natural gas). In 2014, according to the geographical advantage between Europe and Asia, the Steppe Road Plan (hereinafter "this plan") was proposed by Mongolia to drive resource development through trade transportation and thus revitalise the Mongolian economy. On September 2, 2014, Resolution 282 was issued by Mongolia to formally initiate this plan. Then, a working group was established, which is composed of vice premiers and more than 10 ministerial heads of Mongolia (e.g. Ministry of Economic Development, Ministry of National Defence, Ministry of Environmental Development and Ministry of Foreign Affairs). In 2014, Resolution 34 was issued by the Parliament of Mongolia; as specified in its "Measures for guaranteeing a stable economic growth", the work and institutional construction necessary for this plan is determined by Resolution 282 of Mongolia.

This plan includes 5 projects, requiring a total investment amount of about US$50 billion: the China–Russia expressway (997 km); an electric railway (1100 km); expansion of the cross-Mongolia railway, natural gas pipeline and oil pipeline; and development of the Asia–European transit transportation via Mongolia. As predicted by Mongolia, this plan will bring about more investments, drive industrial upgrading and thus upgrade Mongolia's energy/ore industry to a new level. Through operation of the China–Russia transit transportation of natural gas and petroleum, a revenue of 200 billion MNT is estimated for Mongolia by 2020.[1]

Strategic alignment with the Belt and Road Initiative

Mongolia is an important original channel of the Ancient Silk Road. Therefore, the alignment between this plan and the Belt and Road Initiative will revitalise the traditional Silk Road and boost active development of Mongolia itself and the China–Mongolia–Russia Economic Corridor. As specified by Gao Shumao (the Chinese ambassador in Mongolia), the plan proposed by Mongolia according to its national conditions highly coincides with the Belt and Road Initiative; Mongolia is historically the key channel of Tea Road and Steppe Silk Road;

and boosting of their alignment is crucial for the development of Mongolia itself and the construction of the China–Mongolia–Russia Economic Corridor.[2] (1) Policy coordination. On August 22, 2014, at a state visit to Mongolia, Xi Jinping (Chairman of China) expressed the wishes of China at an important speech in the State Great Khural: "Keep a watch and help defend each other to jointly create a new development era of China–Mongolia relationship": strengthen cooperation with Mongolia under the framework of the Silk Road Economic Belt; and take an active open attitude to this plan proposed by Mongolia.[3] On September 11, 2014, at the 1st Summit of China, Russia and Mongolia in Dushanbe (capital of Tajikistan), a high coincidence in the development strategy of these 3 countries was jointly accepted by Xi Jinping (Chairman of China), Vladimir Putin (President of Russia) and Tsakhiagiin Elbegdorj (President of Mongolia). China proposed to jointly construct the Silk Road Economic Belt, which was actively responded by Russia and Mongolia. The following actions can be taken by China: align the Silk Road Economic Belt with the Cross-Eurasia Major Transportation Channel (Russia) and this plan (Mongolia); construct the China–Mongolia–Russia Economic Corridor; strengthen a connectivity construction (e.g. railway and road); boost a facilitation of customs clearance and transportation; promote a cooperation in transit transportation; study the construction of transit power transmission network among these 3 countries; and launch a pragmatic cooperation in various fields (e.g. tourism, think tank, media, environmental protection and disaster reduction/relief).[4] On March 28, 2015, the "Vision and Action on Boosting the Joint Construction of Silk Road Economic Belt and 21st Century Maritime Silk Road" was jointly released by the National Development and Reform Commission of PRC, the Ministry of Foreign Affairs of PRC and the Ministry of Commerce of PRC: the China–Mongolia–Russia Economic Corridor is positioned as international economic cooperation corridor for key construction.[5] On July 9, 2015, at the 2nd Summit of China, Russia and Mongolia in Ufa (Russia), an important consensus on the alignment of these 3 initiatives was jointly reached by Chairman Xi Jinping, President Vladimir Putin and President Tsakhiagiin Elbegdorj. Meanwhile, the "Medium-term route map for trilateral cooperation" was jointly released by these 3 countries: based on the alignment of these 3 initiatives, the "Outline for cooperation plan of China–Mongolia–Russia Economic Corridor" was formulated.[6] In July 2016, Li Keqiang (Premier of China) visited Mongolia, as the first visit to Mongolia by a Chinese premier in the recent 6 years and that by foreign leader after the formation of Mongolia's new government. At this visit, China and Mongolia signed more than 10 cooperation agreements and agreed to accelerate the boosting of alignment between this plan and the Belt and Road Initiative.

(2) Infrastructure connectivity. Mongolia is applying to the Asian Infrastructure Investment Bank for financing several railway projects (including to build a 550-km long railway connecting China and Europe). In October 2014, the State Great Khural approved the Chinese standard-gauge rail for the Tavan Tolgoi–GashuunSukhait Railway and the Hotte–Biqigetu Railway: GashuunSukhait borders on Ganqimaodou Port (China); and Biqigetu borders on Zhuengadabuqi Port (China).[7] During the period of April 9–10, 2015, a consultation conference on the cooperation in railway transportation among China, Russia and Mongolia was held in Ulaanbaatar (Mongolia) to express the following consensus of these 3 countries: cooperate in the transit railway transportation under the framework of these 3 initiatives; expand the transportation capacity of the existing railways and further develop them; study the possibility for establishing a trilateral transportation logistic joint venture; take the measures for balanced development; improve the transportation capacity at each section of the Ulam Uhde–Naushki–Suhe Bator–Dzamyn Ude–Erenhot–Jining Railway; overall cooperate and exchange mutual experience with education institutions on the development of railway transportation; cultivate, train, re-educate the talents/teachers; develop a research cooperation; formulate a joint action plan for developing cooperation in railway transportation

by making full use of the existing cooperation mechanism; and hold an annual conference on the problems of transit railway transportation.[8] In May 2015, the DzamynUde–Ulaanbaatar–Altanbulag Expressway was formally started for construction: this expressway is the first project under the strategic alignment between this plan and the Silk Road Economic Belt, and also the first expressway in Mongolia.[9] In June 2016, a consensus on constructing 8 double-track or electric railways was reached by these 3 countries under the framework of "Outline of construction plan for China–Mongolia–Russia Economic Corridor": a railway from Erdenet (Mongolia) northwards to Russia; a new railway in the eastern and western areas of Mongolia; southwards via China to the ports in the Far Eastern area of Russia; and a new Moscow–Beijing High-speed Railway.[10] In 2016, the "Construction and development plan for China Railway Express (2016–2020)" was released by China to construct the middle channel of China Railway Express: outbound via Erenhot Port (Inner Mongolia, China), by way of Mongolia, to the Trans-Siberian Railway (Russia) and further to European countries.[11]

(3) Unimpeded trade. China and Mongolia are greatly complementary in economic/trade cooperation. Mongolia is rich in natural resources (especially mineral resources), but has a poor industrial basis, which requires the import of numerous mechanical equipments and light industrial products; with a rapid economic development (especially industrial manufacturing), China not only provides Mongolia with numerous mechanical equipments and light industrial products, but also greatly demands Mongolia's mineral resources. Meanwhile, with a small population, Mongolia lacks human resources; China abounds in highly competent human resources. Therefore, both countries are strongly complementary in economy. China is Mongolia's largest partner country of trade and investment. In the past 20 years, the scale of China–Mongolia trade grew 50-fold, and China became Mongolia's largest partner country of trade and investment continuously for over 10 years. In 2015, Chinese trade to Mongolia accounted for 62% of Mongolia's total outward trade.[12] With the strategic alignment of this plan with the Silk Road Economic Belt and the continuous boosting of the China–Mongolia–Russia Economic Corridor, a great potential is enjoyed for economic/trade cooperation between both countries.

(4) Financial integration. Both countries actively cooperate in the financial field. In 2014, Mongolia became one of the first batch of founding member states of the Asian Infrastructure Investment Bank. On August 21, 2014, the "Joint declaration for establishing and developing a comprehensive strategic partnership" was signed by both countries: further consolidate financial cooperation; increase the scale of local currency swap; support trade settlement by local currency; and strengthen cooperation in various forms (e.g. commercial loan and project financing).[13] On November 11, 2015, the "Joint statement for deepening the development of comprehensive strategic partnership" was signed by both countries: under the framework of the Belt and Road Initiative, Mongolia cooperates with financial institutions (e.g. the Asian Infrastructure Investment Bank and the Silk Road Foundation) in financing the large infrastructure construction projects in Mongolia. Since 2014, China has provided Mongolia with numerous concessional loans. On October 23, 2015, the China–Mongolia transit RMB transaction centre was formally established by the Agricultural Bank of China in Huhhot (China), which greatly shortens the settlement time of China–Mongolia transit RMB funds from originally 2 hours to currently real time.[14] Meanwhile, both countries continuously boost the procedure of currency swap between RMB and MNT. In 2011, a bilateral local currency swap agreement of 5 billion RMB was signed by the People's Bank of China and the Bank of Mongolia, which was renewed in 2014 to expand a swap amount to 15 billion RMB and also renewed in 2017 with a valid period of 3 years (to be extended) to maintain a swap amount of 15 billion RMB (or 5.4 trillion MNT).

(5) Understanding between people. At present, China has established 3 Confucius Institutes and 5 Confucius schools in Mongolia. On May 2, 2014, the opening ceremony

of the China–Mongolia Cultural Education Foundation and the China–Mongolia Social Development Fund was held in Ulaanbaatar, which mainly helps and improves the cultural education level, economic development and social progress in Mongolia. Then, an agreement on strategic cooperation was signed by the Institute of Confucius in the National University of Mongolia with the Ulaanbaatar representative office of the Bank of China and the China–Mongolia Cultural Education Foundation: provide the Mongolian nationality students of good moral and excellent achievement with an annual scholarship for receiving an education in the Chinese language; and organise/sponsor a popularisation of Chinese language education in Mongolia.[15] On August 21, 2014, the "Joint declaration for establishing and developing a comprehensive strategic partnership" was signed by both countries: a mechanism of exchange visits and communication is negotiated on establishment for the teenagers of both countries; within 5 years after 2015, 100 Mongolian teenagers and 50 Chinese teenagers are annually invited for a visit to their counterpart, respectively; in the coming 5 years, China provides 1000 training quota for Mongolia, adds 1000 quota of Chinese governmental scholarship for Mongolian nationality students and invites about 250 representatives of Mongolian new media to visit China.[16] On October 25, 2014, the "Outline for medium and long-term development of strategic partnership" was signed by both countries to specify the following actions of China: in the coming 5 years, annually provide not less than 1000 quota of Chinese governmental scholarship through various channels to Mongolian nationality students (including: not less than 200 quota for undergraduates); support the teaching of the Chinese language in Mongolia, increase the appointment of voluntary teachers of the Chinese language to Mongolia, cooperate with Mongolia's colleges/universities in setting the course of teachers or preparatory courses of Chinese language, and support/help various aspects of teaching materials (e.g. provision and formulation); establish a mechanism of biennial exchange visit and communication for the delegation of teenagers of both countries; and mutually hold the activity of summer camp for students in primary/middle schools.[17] On November 11, 2015, both countries decided to study the establishment of a common committee of humanistic exchange, which boosts cooperation in humanistic fields and lays a solid foundation for friendly understanding between people. On October 3, 2016, the first translation and publication centre of Chinese-themed books was formally established by China Renmin University Press and Mongolian State University of Education with the following objectives at the commencement ceremony of China–Mongolia cultural cooperation in Ulaanbaatar: boost the publication and distribution of Chinese-themed books in Mongolia; promote the cooperation and trade of copyrights between both countries; establish and certify the aid projects of translating Chinese/Mongolian books; strengthen cooperation in press and publication between both countries; and establish the sole intergovernmental cooperation/exchange platform of press and publication between both countries.[18] On October 1, 2016, the Television Chinese Theatre was open for broadcasting and the Dubbing Centre for Chinese Films and TV Programmes in Khalkha–Mongolian Language was formally established, so as to recommend excellent Chinese films and TV programmes to Mongolian people.

Under the joint active boosting of both countries, the strategic alignment between this plan and the Belt and Road Initiative has overall progressed into a new stage of rapid development.

Notes

1 Commercial Counsellor's Office of Chinese Embassy in Mongolia, "Mongolia initiated the Steppe Road Plan to revitalize the economy," website of Ministry of Commerce of PRC. Retrieved February 10, 2018 from http://mn.mofcom.gov.cn/article/jmxw/201409/20140900746042.shtml

2 Qiu Haifeng, "The Belt and Road Initiative and the Steppe Road Plan," *People's Daily* (overseas edition), July 15, 2016, column 2.
3 "Xi Jinping's speech in the State Great Khural of Mongolia," Xinhua Net. Retrieved February 13, 2018 from www.xinhuanet.com/world/2014-08/22/c_1112195359.htm
4 "Joint construction of China–Mongolia–Russia Economic Corridor," website of Ministry of Commerce of PRC. Retrieved February 10, 2018 from www.mofcom.gov.cn/article/i/jyjl/j/201409/20140900728588.shtml
5 "Vision and Action on Boosting the Joint Construction of Silk Road Economic Belt and 21st Century Maritime Silk Road," Xinhua Net. Retrieved February 13, 2018 from www.xinhuanet.com/world/2015-03/28/c_1114793986.htm
6 "Medium-term route map for trilateral cooperation among China, Russia and Mongolia," Chinese Governments Portal. Retrieved February 15, 2018 from www.gov.cn/xinwen/2015-07/10/content_2894909.htm
7 "Chinese standard-gauge rail is approved for two sections of southern railway route of Mongolia," Huanqiu Net. Retrieved February 15, 2018 from http://world.huanqiu.com/article/2014-10/5179370.html
8 "Consultation conference on the cooperation in railway transportation among China, Russia and Mongolia was held in Mongolia," Chinese Governments Portal. Retrieved February 15, 2018 from www.gov.cn/xinwen/2015-04/14/content_2846109.htm
9 Du Shiwei, *Mongolia's Steppe Road and China–Mongolia–Russia Economic Corridor. Assessment of security situation around China* (2016) (chief editor: Zhang Jie). Social Sciences Academic Press, 2016, p. 115.
10 "China and Mongolia will implement the integration between the China's Belt and Road Initiative and Mongolia's Steppe Road Plan," Netease Net. Retrieved February 15, 2018 from http://news.163.com/16/0922/21/C1JKDU2R00014SEH.html
11 "Integration of Mongolia's Steppe Road Plan with the China's Belt and Road Initiative: Mongolia wishes to seize the opportunity of China Railway Express," Huanqiu Net. Retrieved February 15, 2018 from http://world.huanqiu.com/hot/2017-04/10446131.html
12 Qiu Haifeng, "The Belt and Road Initiative and the Steppe Road Plan," *People's Daily* (overseas edition), July 15, 2016, column 2.
13 "Joint declaration of China and Mongolia for establishing and developing a comprehensive strategic partnership," Xinhua Net. Retrieved February 17, 2018 from www.xinhuanet.com/world/2014-08/22/c_1112179283.htm
14 "The China–Mongolia transit RMB transaction center was formally established by the Agricultural Bank of China in Huhhot City (China)," *People's Daily Online*. Retrieved February 17, 2018 from http://nm.people.com.cn/n/2015/1022/c356223-26887351.html
15 "China–Mongolia Cultural Education Foundation and China-Mongolia Social Development Foundation were put into operation," *People's Daily Online*. Retrieved February 16, 2018 from http://world.people.com.cn/n/2014/0503/c1002-24967114.html
16 "Joint declaration of China and Mongolia for establishing and developing a comprehensive strategic partnership," Xinhua Net. Retrieved February 17, 2018 from www.xinhuanet.com/world/2014-08/22/c_1112179283.htm
17 "Outline for medium and long-term development of strategic partnership," Chinese Governments Portal. Retrieved February 17, 2018 from www.gov.cn/jrzg/2013-10/26/content_2515790.htm
18 "First translation and publication center of Chinese-theme books was formally established in Mongolia," *People's Daily Online*. Retrieved February 17, 2018 from http://edu.people.com.cn/n1/2016/1003/c1006-28755698.html

110
BRIGHT ROAD PLAN (KAZAKHSTAN)

Pang Jiaxin

Overview

After the financial crisis in 2008, Kazakhstan faced rigorous challenges and pronounced economic problems due to the following factors: slow, unclear recovery of the world economic; deterioration of the geopolitical environment; and change of global emerging markets. In December 2012, the "Kazakhstan Strategy 2050" was proposed by Nursultan Abishevich Nazarbayev (President of Kazakhstan): adhere to a slogan of "Strong commerce, strong country" and become one of the world's 30 largest economies by 2050 through a series of reform in society, economy and politics. In September 2013, during a visit to Kazakhstan, Xi Jinping (Chairman of China) proposed to jointly construct the Silk Road Economic Belt, which was actively responded by Kazakhstan. In 2014, due to the slump of international oil price, Kazakhstan entered a period of economic downturn because its economic growth excessively depended on the petroleum. On November 11, 2014, the annual speech and union address was made by President Nazarbayev in advance of 2 months to formally propose the "Bright Road Plan" (hereinafter "this plan").[1] By serving the "Kazakhstan Strategy 2050", this plan has the following objectives: guarantee continuous economic development and social stability; realise an upgrade and transformation of the economic structure; reduce the Kazakhstans economy's dependency on energy exports; and build Kazakhstan into a global transportation corridor connecting the major markets of China, Europe and the Middle East. Therefore, within the future 5 years, this plan will input US$9 billion of national foundation to various fields (e.g. infrastructure construction, industrialisation construction, construction of education and public service facilities and support of small and medium-sized enterprises).

As a new economic policy, this plan adheres to the core of infrastructure construction with road connectivity, so as to produce a multiplier effect of roads in economic fields and thus drive the rapid development in each economic field of Kazakhstan. The main contents of this plan are classified into 7 aspects.[2]

(1) Construct and perfect the traffic/logistic infrastructure. As the core of this plan, the following tasks are emphasised for the construction of traffic/logistic infrastructure: regard Astana (capital of Kazakhstan) as a central traffic hub; construct a traffic/logistic network of roads, railways and airways radiating to each regional centre of Kazakhstan; and realise interurban connectivity. The main construction projects of traffic facilities include: the China–Western Europe

route; the Astana–Almaty route; the Astana–UstKamenogorsk route; the Astana–Atone–Atyrau route; the Alme–UstKamenogorsk route; the Karagandy–Jezkazgan–Kyzylorda route; and the Atyrau–Astrakhan route. In addition, the following logistic facilities are constructed in this plan: a logistic pivot in the east of Kazakhstan and auxiliary marine infrastructure in the west of Kazakhstan as the main logistic transportation carrier for integration between China, Russia, Iran and the European Union countries.

(2) Develop and perfect the infrastructure of industries and service industry. In this plan, 3 types of infrastructure of industries and service industry are specified for construction: (a) accomplish infrastructure construction of 10 existing special economic zones and several industrial parks and promote their development by improving the investment environment and providing investors with relevant preferential policies: Astana Special Economic Zone is the largest one; and 33 projects are in operation. (b) establish and develop the new industrial areas to mainly provide the essential production facilities for small and medium-sized enterprises and provide the policy/funding support for their development. (c) Develop tourist infrastructure, exploit new tourism resources, boost the development of tourism resources, play the advantages of the tourist industry and create more employment opportunities.

(3) Boost an upgrading of energy infrastructure, and mainly perfect the infrastructure of power and natural gas. In the future 5 years, 2 high-voltage transmission routes will be laid to realise a balanced energy supply for all areas of Kazakhstan: the Ekibastuz–Semey–UstKamenogorsk route and the Semey–Aktogay–Taldykorgan–Almaty route. In addition, foreign capital and technologies will be introduced by Kazakhstan to construct an energy network of oil/gas pipeline.

(4) Realise the modernisation of public facilities and water/heat supply. By combining various financing channels (e.g. governmental funds, the Asian Development Bank, the Asian Infrastructure Investment Bank, the European Bank for Reconstruction and Development, the Islamic Development Bank and private investment), this plan accelerates the modernisation of the nationwide water/heat supply system and the perfection of public facilities.

(5) Strengthen construction of housing infrastructure. In order to solve the problem of incoordination between the urban population and the urban infrastructure, public rental houses are built using governmental funds to alleviate housing pressure on people at all levels.

(6) Perfect the social infrastructure. On the one hand, Kazakhstan develops its education by enlarging a fund input and properly introducing foreign capital: solving the long-term problems in deficiency and poor education modes/methods of preschool education institutions (e.g. kindergartens); providing high-competence workers for industrialisation construction; and appointing 10 higher-education institutions for integrating national industrialisation development. On the other hand, Kazakhstan perfects medical facilities, cultivates medical talents, introduces advanced medical facilities and overall improves the medical level.

(7) Continue to support and encourage the development of small and medium-sized enterprises. Through various financing channels (e.g. governmental funds, the Asian Development Bank, the Asian Infrastructure Investment Bank, the European Bank for Reconstruction and Development and the World Bank), small and medium-sized enterprises are developed into an important impetus for economic growth, which will account for more than 50% of GDP by 2050. Their advantages in labour absorption are fully played to provide more positions for Kazakhstan people and create more employment opportunities.

Alignment conditions with the Belt and Road Initiative

Kazakhstan lies in the central area of the Eurasian continent and is an important country along the Silk Road Economic Belt. A benefit fitness is enjoyed for the alignment between this plan and the Belt and Road Initiative. When the joint construction of the Silk Road Economic Belt was first proposed by Chairman Xi Jinping in 2013, President Nazarbayev expressed the wish to join China in its construction. On December 14, 2014, the "Memorandum of understanding on jointly boosting the construction of the Silk Road Economic Belt" was signed by both countries to boost a deep cooperation. In 2015, the "Joint communiqué" was signed by the premiers of both countries to accelerate a cooperation in the alignment between this plan and the Silk Road Economic Belt.[3] On September 2, 2016, the "Cooperation plan for integrating the Silk Road Economic Belt with the Bright Road Plan" was formally signed by both countries, which is the first bilateral cooperation plan under the Belt and Road framework, emphasising a substantial cooperation in various fields (e.g. infrastructure construction, production capacity, investment, agriculture and humanistic exchange).[4] So far, more than 10 governmental and interdepartmental cooperation agreements have been signed between China and Kazakhstan, whose responsibility is specially taken by their relevant departments. At present, the alignment work has been launched and made a plentiful achievement in various fields (e.g. traffic, production capacity, energy, finance and agriculture).

(1) Boost a construction of infrastructure connectivity. (a) Boost the construction of a transit railway transportation line: at present, 3 international railway transportation routes from China across Kazakhstan have been completed: the Eurasian Land Bridge (to Russia and Europe); the China–Kazakhstan–Turkmenistan route (to Iran and the Persian Gulf); and the China–Kazakhstan–Transcaucasian countries (Georgia, Azerbaijan and Armenia) (to European countries).[5] (b) Boost the construction of an international expressway transportation corridor connecting the west of Europe and the west of China: at the end of 2017, the Western Europe–Western China Expressway was wholly open to traffic (with a total length of more than 8000 km, of which more than 2000 km is in Kazakhstan territory), which becomes an important logistic transportation artery in the Central Asian area and greatly shortens transportation time from China to Europe.[6] (c) Construct a traffic logistic centre, including: a land port of the Khorgas–Eastern Portal Special Economic Zone and the China–Kazakhstan Khorgas International Border Cooperation Centre. (d) Integrate the construction of logistic ports: in 2015, the "Framework agreement on the strategic cooperation in jointly developing the Khorgas–Eastern Portal Special Economic Zone and the SCO International Logistic Park (Lianyungang City)" was signed by both countries. Then, the China–Kazakhstan Logistic Cooperation Base (Lianyungang) was established to integrate with the dry port at the eastern portal of Khorgas City and form an international trade logistic corridor via the China Railway Express (Lianyungang–Kazakhstan–Europe).

(2) Strengthen cooperation in production capacity. Kazakhstan is the largest investment target country of the Belt and Road construction. In August 2015, the "Framework agreement on strengthening cooperation in production capacity and investment" was signed by China and Kazakhstan, establishing a regular cooperation mechanism for production capacity cooperation and boosting overall cooperation in various fields (e.g. processing industry and power). Both countries enjoy a complementary advantage in production capacity cooperation. Up to 2017, 51 projects of production capacity cooperation had been signed by both countries, involving various fields (with a total investment amount of more than US$26 billion): manufacturing, metallurgy, petroleum chemicals, machine manufacturing, smelting of heavy/non-ferrous metals and food.[7] Several industrial blanks of Kazakhstan have been filled up by Chinese investment in Kazakhstan. The first electrolytic aluminium plant and the largest copper ore plant in Kazakhstan was constructed by the investment of China Non-ferrous Metal Industry's Foreign and Construction Engineering Co., Ltd; the first manufacturing enterprise of large-calibre steel pipe in Kazakhstan was established by the investment participation of China National

Petroleum Corporation; and plants in such products as polyacrylonitrile and edible oil have also been constructed by Chinese enterprises. As the largest project of non-resource cooperation between both countries, the Caspian Sea Asphalt Plant (a joint venture company of China and Kazakhstan) fills up the blank of asphalt production in Kazakhstan and meets the demand for asphalt for road construction in Kazakhstan. As largest pharmaceuticals plant in Kazakhstan, Kelun Pharmaceutical (Kazakhstan) Corporation (a joint venture company of China and Kazakhstan) also breaks the bottleneck in the development of Kazakhstan's pharmaceutical industry. In addition, the Production Capacity Cooperation Fund was established by both countries and is now in operation. After the Belt and Road Forum for International Cooperation, the "Cooperation framework agreement on supporting Chinese telecommunication enterprises for participating in the Digital Kazakhstan Plan (2020)" was signed by both countries.[8]

(3) Accelerate high-level development of energy cooperation. At present, the China National Petroleum Corporation owns 7 upstream projects (mainly oil/gas production) in Kazakhstan and has participated in the investment of 3 oil/gas pipelines between China and Central Asia (with a length of 1300 km in Kazakhstan territory). In April 2017, the southern route of the natural gas pipeline in Kazakhstan was wholly accomplished by China National Petroleum Corporation to connect with 4 main natural gas pipelines inside and outside Kazakhstan territory and optimise the energy structure of Kazakhstan, which is an extremely important project of people's livelihoods in Kazakhstan and a model of infrastructure connectivity along the Belt and Road. Meanwhile, 2 large-scale chemical projects are being constructed by the investment of China Petrochemical Corporation: the aromatics unit of the Atyrau Oil Refinery Plant and an integrated unit of petroleum deep-processing. The oil/gas business in Kazakhstan is also actively participated in by the investment of several Chinese private oil/gas enterprises: CEFC China Energy Company Limited, Guanghui Energy Co., Ltd, China Zhenhua Oil Co., Ltd and Geo-jade Petroleum Corporation. Besides traditional oil/gas, nuclear power and renewable energy are deeply cooperated by both countries. In December 2016, construction of the Nuclear Fuel Assembly Plant began (a joint venture company of CGNPC Uranium Resources Co., Ltd and Kazakhstan National Nuclear Energy Industry Corporation), which boosts an upgrading of the nuclear fuel industry in Kazakhstan (with a designed annual production capacity of up to 200 tons uranium). Several memorandums and implementation agreements have been signed by both countries for the projects of renewable energy, e.g. Kelbulak Hydropower Station (the first large hydropower station in Kazakhstan). Kazakhstan abounds in wind energy resources, which will be one of the key future investment fields for Chinese wind power enterprises.[9]

(4) Deepen financial cooperation. In May 2015, the "Memorandum of understanding for cooperation on the supervision of securities and futures" was signed by China and Kazakhstan to strengthen an exchange/cooperation in securities and futures and promote the healthy development of market capital. In December 2015, the Astana International Financial Centre was established by Kazakhstan to better align and cooperate with main international financial institutions (e.g. the Silk Road Foundation and CITIC Group). In 2016, the "Framework agreement on establishing the China–Kazakhstan Agricultural Development Fund" was signed by both countries to provide a fund support for expanding their agricultural cooperation. In June 2017, a cooperation agreement was signed between the Shanghai Stock Exchange and the Administrative Bureau of the Astana International Financial Centre to jointly invest in the construction of the Astana International Exchange. This exchange strives to become the RMB transaction centre in Central Asian areas and an important financial platform of the Belt and Road Initiative, providing a financing service for implementing the projects of the Belt and Road construction.[10]

(5) Expand agricultural cooperation. Among 51 projects signed between China and Kazakhstan, there are 3 agricultural projects, involving wheat production and grain/oil processing. In 2017, a safe grain transit channel was opened up by both countries, using Lianyungang (China) as the logistic transfer base and transporting Kazakhstan's grain to the South East Asian market. Meanwhile, by utilising Xi'an Port as a grain entry port, China boosts the entry of high-quality foreign grain into the Chinese market.

(6) Enhance understanding between people. On the one hand, education exchange is strengthened between both countries: besides the exchange of students, a Kazakhstan Centre is established in 4 colleges in Chinese cities (i.e. Beijing, Shanghai, Dalian and Xi'an). On the other hand, development of the tourist industry is reinforced: Kazakhstan has opened up more than 60 travel routes and simplified the formalities of visa granting to facilitate unofficial exchange.

As the bridgehead of the Belt and Road construction, Kazakhstan establishes a comprehensive strategic partnership with China. At present, the alignment cooperation between both countries is developing well and has made a phasic achievement with both cooperation plans and a perfect alignment mechanism. In the future, their alignment will be further deepened with a great potential and broad prospect.

Notes

1 Nyrly Zhol, "The Path to the Future," Official Site of the Republic of Kazakhstan. November 11, 2014. Retrieved January 21, 2018 from www.akorda.kz/en/addresses/the-address-of-president-of-the-republic-of-kazakhstan-nnazarbayev-to-the-people-of-kazakhstan-november-11–2014
2 Ibid.
3 "Joint communiqué of China and Kazakhstan," website of Ministry of Foreign Affairs of PRC. Retrieved January 28, 2018 from www.fmprc.gov.cn/web/ziliao_674904/1179_674909/t6938.shtml
4 "Cooperation plan for integrating the Silk Road Economic Belt with the Bright Road Plan," website of State Council Information Office of PRC. Retrieved January 28, 2018 from www.scio.gov.cn/31773/35507/htws35512/Document/1524812/1524812.htm
5 Kazakhstan ambassador in China, "Smooth integration between the Belt and Road Initiative and the Bright Road Plan," *People's Daily Online*. Retrieved January 28, 2018 from http://world.people.com.cn/n1/2017/0605/c1002-29318746.html
6 "The Belt and Road Initiative creates more opportunities for international cooperation," *People's Daily Online*. Retrieved January 28, 2018 from http://world.people.com.cn/n1/2017/1015/c1002-29587586.html
7 "Framework agreement on the strategic cooperation in the project of SCO International Logistic Park (Lianyungang City)," Lianyungang Media Net. Retrieved January 28, 2018 from http://2015v1.lyg1.com/news/political/2015/9/1/article_11379.shtml
8 "The Belt and Road makes China and Kazakhstan adjoin closer," Belt and Road Portal. Retrieved January 28, 2018 from www.china.com.cn/news/2017/06/09/content_40995093_2.htm
9 "Serial reports on the transit of the Belt and Road: Central Asia," Sina News Net. Retrieved January 28, 2018 from http://news.sina.com.cn/c/2017-07-17/doc-ifyiamif3138902.shtml
10 "Shanghai Stock Exchange and Kazakhstan jointly construct the Astana International Exchange," Belt and Road Portal. Retrieved January 29, 2018 from www.yidaiyilu.gov.cn/xwzx/gnxw/15629.htm

111
NEW NORTHWARD EXPANSION POLICY (SOUTH KOREA)

Pang Jiaxin

Overview

On September 7, 2017, in the keynote speech at the 3rd East Russia Economic Forum in Russia, the New Northward Expansion Policy was first proposed by Moon Jae-in (President of South Korea), which is developed on the basis of the Eurasia Initiative which was proposed by Park Geun-hye (former president of South Korea). Through various infrastructures between South Korea and Eurasian countries (e.g. traffic, logistic and energy), this policy realises the following objectives: create a new growth impetus for South Korea's economy, seek a common prosperity and realise peace/stability in the Korean Peninsula and even the Eurasian continent. This policy is new in the following aspects: preventing and overcoming contradiction in the age of a new Cold War; supporting North Korea in reforming, opening-up and merging into the international community; emphasising the active participation of the people and the main backup force of governments; boosting multilateral cooperation through such medium as combustible gas and power; and laying a peaceful foundation for Northeast Asia by expanding mutual dependence.

This policy lays a system foundation for South Korea to expand the economic cooperation with Eurasian countries. The cooperation countries of this policy involve all countries of the Commonwealth of Independent States (e.g. Russia, 5 Central Asian countries, Belarus and Ukraine) and other relevant countries (e.g. Mongolia and China). According to the strategic plan, a differentiation strategy is implemented by South Korea for 3 blocks of the Eurasian economic circle: (1) eastern economic circle (Far Eastern Russia and China): explore a cooperation potential for integrating with the China–Mongolia–Russia Economic Corridor and the Belt and Road Initiative through various platforms (e.g. 9-Bridge Strategic Plan and Asian Infrastructure Investment Bank); (2) central economic circle (5 Central Asian countries and Mongolia): strengthen cooperation in various fields stressed by South Korean enterprises (e.g. petrochemicals, manufacturing, road infrastructure and ICT) and utilise the support of Official Development Assistance in some fields (i.e. education training, medical care and public administration); and (3) western economic circle (Western Russia, Ukraine and Belarus): strengthen a cooperation in the technologies of high added value by combining the high-level basic technology (e.g. ICT, aerospace and aviation) and the application technology of South Korea and create a new growth mode.

Specifically, an orderly boosting system is established on the centre of the Northward Economic Cooperation Committee and through the working group responsible for the 9-Bridge Strategic Plan (i.e. natural gas, railway, port/harbour, power, Arctic route, shipbuilding, employment (industrial parks), agriculture and aquatic products). The following actions are taken by this policy: emphasise a combination of intergovernmental cooperation and unofficial exchange/cooperation; practically expand cooperation of South Korea with Eurasian countries in various fields (e.g. politics, economy, healthcare, medical treatment, culture, tourism and autonomous exchange); and strengthen a people intercourse through intergovernmental consultation/organisation (e.g. the expansion of advanced study for medical persons and support of medical facilities). Moreover, South Korea actively boosts the local cooperation forum between South Korea and Russia, which provides a good platform for South Korea's small and medium-sized enterprises to enter the Russian market.

Now, the Northward Economic Cooperation Committee has been initiated by South Korea to establish a normal alignment channel of high-level leaders among Eurasian cooperation countries. Subsequently, the following measures will be taken by South Korea: initiate and boost negotiation on the free trade area with the Eurasian Economic Union (EAEU); establish a linking channel of high-level leaders with some countries (e.g. Uzbekistan and Kazakhstan); boost the Far East Financial Cooperation Initiative between South Korea and Russia (with a scale of US$2 billion); and support relevant cooperation projects through financial institutions inside and outside South Korea (e.g. the Asian Development Bank and the Asian Infrastructure Investment Bank). In September 2017, at the Russia–SK Summit, both countries agreed to expand their exchange. At the 3rd East Russia Economic Forum, the 9-Bridge Strategic Plan was proposed by President Moon Jae-in during his keynote speech. In March 2018, at the 1st Russia–SK Joint Conference in Russia, a memorandum of understanding and a joint statement were released by both countries. According to this memorandum, the following actions are taken by both countries: jointly boost the 9-Bridge Strategic Plan; establish the Cooperation Group Committee of the 9-Bridge Strategic Plan; biannually hold the Russia–SK Joint Conference to jointly explore the cooperation topics; and support bilateral cooperation projects. At present, both countries select the aquatic products industry and energy as priority cooperation fields and enjoy substantial cooperation. In addition, South Korea actively launches the alignment work with the Belt and Road Initiative.

Alignment conditions with the Belt and Road Initiative

As a common wish, China and South Korea strive to realise economic prosperity in the Eurasian area and safeguard peace/stability in the Korean Peninsula. This policy possesses a very strong cooperation impetus to align with the Belt and Road Initiative. Their alignment work never leaves the Eurasia Initiative to this plan, and is mainly launched in the following areas.

(1) Stress policy coordination. In 2015, at the 70th Anniversary of Victory for the Chinese War of Resistance Against Japan and the World War of Resistance Against Fascist, Chairman Xi Jinping met President Moon Jae-in to state as follows: South Korea is welcomed to actively participate in the Belt and Road construction and the Eurasia Initiative coincides with the Belt and Road Initiative. Then, an important consensus was reached between China and South Korea on boosting the alignment between the Belt and Road Initiative and the Eurasia Initiative.[1] On October 31, 2015, the "Memorandum of understanding on the cooperation in the Belt and Road Initiative and the Eurasia Initiative" and other series of documents were signed under the witness of Li Keqiang (Premier of China) and President Park Geun-hye.[2] This memorandum is a guidance to strengthen the alignment between two initiatives and boost the cooperation

of both countries in the medium- and long-term outward development strategies. According to this memorandum, both countries expand a cooperation in the 5 long-term approaches (i.e. policy coordination, infrastructure connectivity, unimpeded trade, financial integration and understanding between people). Meanwhile, a series of cooperation agreements have been concluded by both countries with the following objectives: improve the international competitive power of their enterprises; combine the comparative advantages of their enterprises in various fields (e.g. infrastructure, urban construction, energy and ICT); strengthen the economic cooperation and market development in the countries involved in 2 initiatives; and adopt various main cooperation modes (e.g. tender invitation and joint investment of both countries; fund financing of the Asian Infrastructure Investment Bank and the Asian Development Bank; joint research on project cooperation; and sharing of third-country information). In December 2017, at the China–SK Forum for Industrial Cooperation in Chongqing (China), both countries agreed to actively explore the concrete protocols for the cooperation between this plan and the Belt and Road Initiative.

(2) Emphasise infrastructure connectivity. As the core of the Belt and Road Initiative, 6 economic corridors are constructed, which do not connect with the Korean Peninsula in the easternmost Eurasian continent. If the connection between the Trans-Korean Railway and Trans-Siberian Railway actively boosted by South Korea is further aligned with the China–Mongolia–Russia Economic Corridor, the transportation network of railway, airway and seaway will extend in all directions on the Eurasian continent. At present, the following actions are taken by both countries: integrate the traffic/logistic system; launch international cooperation in the high-speed railway; and boost the construction of the New Eurasian Land Bridge under the Belt and Road framework. As the plan of both countries, the Silk Road Express Train of South Korea will be integrated with more than 20 routes of the China Railway Express of China–Europe and China–Asia, so as to strengthen the connectivity from South Korea via China to Europe.[3] Six existing free economic zones of South Korea mostly lie in its western coast and face the Chinese areas around the Yellow Sea. By relying on their coastal areas, both countries jointly boost the construction of infrastructure network (e.g. pipeline, railway, port and logistic hub).[4] Meanwhile, both countries are discussing and studying the construction of a submarine tunnel, which will shorten the traffic distance between both countries, expand their people/trade intercourse and strengthen connectivity. Subsequently, both countries will strengthen/cultivate cooperation in the energy field (e.g. environment-friendly energy and cross-country power network integration) and construct the digital Silk Road through information technology.

(3) Boost unimpeded trade. This policy aims to reduce the regional trade barrier and circulate the investment, which is in line with the unimpeded trade proposed by the Belt and Road Initiative. On June 1, 2015, the Agreement on the Free Trade Area was formally signed by both countries to implement a zero tariff for most of their traded products.[5] Their enterprises also actively integrate the advantages, expand the cooperation projects in third-country markets and jointly enter the third-country market: infrastructure, industrial production capacity, industrial parks and emerging industries (e.g. marine economy, ecological protection and electronic commerce). On January 11, 2016, the "Future strategic cooperation agreement" was jointly signed by 41 entrepreneur representatives from South Korea and China in Lanzhou New Area (China), involving various industries: fine chemicals, new materials, equipment manufacturing, automobile, transit electronic commerce and modern agriculture. On January 11, 2016, the "Enterprise Headquarter Base of China–SK Industrial Park" was formally established in the Lanzhou New Area, which became the first China–SK Industrial Park in the north-western area of China.[6] According to this cooperation agreement, the following joint actions are taken

by both countries: build the Lanzhou New Area into a base of production capacity transfer and a logistic site of goods allocation; and strengthen cooperation in telecommunication field. In 2015, the China–SK Research Centre for Wireless Communication Technology was established in Shenzhen (China) to integrate Chinese enterprises (e.g. KONKA Group, Skyworth Group and TCL Group) with 8 mobile communication enterprises of South Korea: making full use of complementary advantage in their industries; forming a complete chain of information industry and innovative supply; rapidly transforming telecommunication technology into production achievements; and improving the competitive power of their telecommunication industry among Eurasian countries.[7]

(4) Promote financial integration. At present, the construction and development of infrastructure in Eurasian countries is served by various financing platforms (e.g. the Asian Infrastructure Investment Bank, the BRICS Development Bank, the Silk Road Foundation and the SCO Development Bank), which provides financing for an international cooperation in infrastructure construction between China and South Korea. Through various consultation channels (e.g. the China–SK Investment Cooperation Commission), both countries strive to lay a solid foundation for information exchange and financial support. In 2015, an agreement on financial cooperation was reached in their signed memorandum to facilitate the investment and financing of both countries: establish the over-the-counter market for WON to RMB at the China Foreign Exchange Trading Centre in Shanghai (China); and establish the over-the-counter pilot for RMB to WON in Shandong Province (China). In December 2017, at the China–SK Summit, the "Cooperation agreement on jointly providing a financial support for the enterprises of both countries to jointly enter the infrastructure market" was signed by Korea Trade Insurance Corporation and China Construction Bank. In addition, the "Emerging Asian Foundation" was established by the joint capital contribution of the Korea Development Bank and the Asian Infrastructure Investment Bank, further strengthening cooperation with multilateral development banks and actively supporting the enterprises of both countries in entering the third-country market.

(5) Emphasise a understanding between people. On one hand, an unofficial humanistic exchange is strengthened between both countries: actively launch various activities in both countries (e.g. cultural years, art festivals and tourist years); and create a good environment for unofficial exchange. On the other hand, cooperation and exchange is expanded in research/education between both countries: continuously increase the annual number of mutual overseas students and visiting scholars; and provide a sufficient fund and good condition for research cooperation.

Future prospect

With a benefit fitness and stronger complementarity, the alignment of 2 initiatives will certainly become a strong force to realise peace and common prosperity of both countries and in this region, and guide a double-win of human community. On one hand, 2 initiatives have many common points: (1) overlapped in geographical range; (2) common strategic objective (i.e. to realise regional economic prosperity and maintain regional peace/stability); (3) common benefit in particular fields (i.e. emphasise connectivity, accelerate the infrastructure construction of neighbouring countries and realise a common economic prosperity). A very great impetus for cooperation between both countries is exerted by these common points. On the other hand, the initiatives are strongly complementary. (1) Regional aspect: this plan attaches an importance to North Korea, Russia, Mongolia and 3 northern provinces of China, but the Belt and Road Initiative orients on common development and prosperity of the Belt and Road countries and their alignment can expand the radiation range to the whole Eurasian continent. (2) Infrastructure construction: the Belt and Road Initiative emphasises connectivity among the countries along the Belt and Road, but this policy dredges a route from South Korea to the Silk Road, and their integration can form an integral traffic logistic network in the Eurasian continent. (3) Industrial aspect: both countries have their own industrial advantages; a strengthening and innovation of industrial cooperation between their enterprises will realise a complementation of advantages and improve their competitive power in outward investment.

To sum up, the alignment of the 2 initiatives will connect the East Asian economic circle with other economic circles, activate the potential for economic growth in Eurasian countries and boost a better development of both countries at the direction of mutual benefit, double-win, joint contribution and benefit-sharing. In the future, the following actions will continue to be taken by both countries: expanding substantial cooperation in infrastructure, energy and the ICT industry; jointly striving to realise connectivity of the Eurasian continent and promoting the economic prosperity of Eurasian countries.

Notes

1 Guo Jiwen, "Organic integration between the China's Belt and Road Initiative and the South Korea's Eurasia Initiative," *China Reform Daily*, November 4, 2015, column 002.
2 Ibid.
3 Liu Ying, "Demonstration by China and South Korea: integration and cooperation between the Belt and Road Initiative and the Eurasia Initiative," Huanqiu Net. Retrieved January 25, 2018 from http://finance.huanqiu.com/br/focus/2015-12/8250776.html
4 Chi Fulin, "Practical boosting of economic cooperation between China and South Korea under the Belt and Road Initiative," China Development Net. Retrieved January 25, 2018 from www.chinadevelopment.com.cn/zk/yw/2017/07/1159948.shtml
5 Liu Ying, "Demonstration by China and South Korea: integration and cooperation between the Belt and Road Initiative and the Eurasia Initiative," Huanqiu Net. Retrieved January 25, 2018 from http://finance.huanqiu.com/br/focus/2015-12/8250776.html
6 "The Belt and Road Initiative boosts a deep economic and trade cooperation between China and South Korea," Xinhua Net. Retrieved January 25, 2018 from www.xinhuanet.com/fortune/2016-01/11/c_1117740167.htm
7 "China–SK Research Center for Wireless Communication Technology was formally established in Shenzhen City (China)," Shenzhen Special Zone Daily. Retrieved January 25, 2018 from www.aliyun.com/zixun/content/2_6_885156.html

PART XII

Case studies of BRI implementation and promotion

112
CASE STUDIES OF INFRASTRUCTURE CONNECTIVITY BUILDING

Zhang Zhongyuan

Improving people's livelihood constitutes an important content and a top priority in the BRI infrastructure construction

Case 1: E35 Expressway in Pakistan

The inauguration of the first and second sections of the Pakistani E35 Expressway, which was contracted by China Gezhouba Group Corporation (CGGC), was held on December 27, 2017 in Hazara, Khyber Pakhtunkhwa province in north-western Pakistan. Completed in April 2018, the E35 links the country's north–south traffic artery of Peshawar–Karachi Expressway with the northern Kala Kunlun Highway, which will greatly upgrade transportation and connectivity between the China–Pakistan border area and inland Pakistan and will drastically shorten the time needed for travel by land from Pakistan to China when it is completed.

The E35 Expressway is of great significance in strengthening the connectivity between Pakistan and China, promoting regional economic growth and driving the development of tourism in northern Pakistan, which has helped create 1500 local jobs and will benefit more than 100,000 locals.[1]

Case 2: China–Nepal trans-border optical fibre link

On January 12, 2018, the Nepal–China trans-border optical fibre link came into commercial operation in Kathmandu where China Telecom and Nepal Telecom jointly held an inauguration for celebration. The linkage provides Nepal an alternative route to receive internet services through China from major internet hubs, with Hong Kong included. This trans-border internet link project took 3.5 years of hard work, which is an impressive presentation of the deep friendship between the 2 countries.

The operation of the fibre link is a milestone for the development of internet infrastructure in Nepal, providing an alternative route through China for Nepal and will beef-up internet service quality in Nepal.[2]

Prior to the opening of the China–Nepal optical fibre link, the Nepalese internet was mainly connected to India through the southern towns of Siddharthanagar, Birganj, Biratnagar, etc., to obtain internet access services.

The opening of the optical fibre link and the broadband access of China Telecom have greatly improved internet service quality in Nepal, which will effectively meet the demand of network traffic growth and drastically improve the business environment in Nepal.

With the operation of the China–Nepal optical fibre link, Nepalese operators will have the opportunity to significantly cut internet broadband procurement costs, so that the mobile internet traffic costs paid by end users will be reduced by a large margin.

Infrastructure construction under the Belt and Road Initiative (BRI) should follow the principle of putting people's welfare first, to bring more tangible benefits to the people, which is an inherent content of the BRI. To be specific, landmark projects (such as transportation, electricity, communication and other infrastructure facilities) conducive to improving people's livelihoods along the Belt and Road are to be prioritised so as to ensure that people along the Belt and Road receive tangible benefits, build an indivisible people-to-people bond of mutual benefit and lay a solid foundation of public opinion for advancing the BRI.

Take the China–Nepal optical fibre link, for instance: the project not only built up the first direct network route between Nepal and China, but also reduced the network delay that Nepal has to suffer for accessing internet services through China to Europe, Central Asia and the greater Asia–Pacific region and promoted internet exit diversity and security of Nepal.

The operation of the China–Nepal cross-border optical fibre link will do good for reversing the weak development of the internet industry in Nepal caused by geography. Internet access from China will not only transform Nepal into a link connecting East Asia, South Asia, Central Asia, Russia and the Middle East, but will also offer a short-cut for internet access for China and East Asian countries to reach the Middle East and Africa.

While shortening the network delay between China and Nepal, the optical link will function as an economic driver for the 2 countries and will bring their people even closer, which provides a demonstration project for future bilateral collaboration under the BRI.

Promoting China standards and facilitating the BRI infrastructure construction

Case 3: Coal-fired power plant project at Port Muhhamad Bin Qasim (also known as Port Qasim), Pakistan

Port Qasim power plant is the first project implemented under the China–Pakistan Economic Corridor. The Power Construction Corporation of China groups Qatar's Al Mirqab Capital (AMC) in funding this project by a proportion of 51% and 49%, respectively, with a total investment of US$2.085 billion, of which the construction period is 36 months.

The first unit was put into use 3 months ahead of its scheduled time.

The project's 2 supercritical 660 MW generators was put into commercial operation in April 2018, with an average annual net electricity generation capacity of approximately 9 billion kWh, which can meet the household electricity demand of 4 million locals and hence ease the power shortfall in Pakistan by a great margin. It will also optimise Pakistan's energy structure and cut power generation costs.

The power plant project also facilitates China's standards, technologies and equipment to "go abroad", of which 99% of the equipment is of Chinese origin, including the steam turbine and 2 other core equipments, directly driving China's equipment in "going abroad" with a total value of more than 7 billion yuan.[3]

Case 4: The tunnelling work of the Gantas Tunnel, Algeria

The Gantas Tunnel is part of the coastal railway in the north of Algeria, connecting 9 ports and 22 provinces, home to over half the nation's population and described as the local strategic artery.

However, the coastal railway was built in the late nineteenth century, zig-zagging through the mountains. The fastest speed only reaches 80 km/h. It is of great significance to transform the northern part of the railway into one with high transportation capacity, which will facilitate Algeria's import and export.

To secure a speed-up, the rock must be tunnelled through.

The Gantas Tunnel is in the Mediterranean fold belt where the crustal stress in the surrounding rock is large. The main direction of the crustal stress there is almost vertical to the direction of the tunnel, which could trigger tunnel deformation. On the other hand, the tunnel's geological structure is very complex, mainly formed of marlstone and shale which could rapidly swell when it comes into contact with water. Therefore, the tunnel has very poor stability and is hence dubbed the "disaster for engineers".

The renovation of 55 km of railways and a double-track railway construction project (with the Gantas Tunnel included) has been conducted by China Civil Engineering Construction Corporation (CCECC). On the morning of October 30, 2017, the Gantas Tunnel project saw successful completion after 6.5 years of construction.

The Chinese solution successfully overcame the global engineering conundrum posed by the marlstone geological formation and presented the marvel of "Chinese Speed": the CCECC has hit new records with 520 m and 870 m excavated on a monthly basis, apart from a project delay caused by factors such as project supervision.[4]

Although many countries along the Belt and Road welcome Chinese capital and investment, they are more or less suspicious of Chinese standards. The Gantas Tunnel project was originally designed by European standards, but in the construction process, Chinese enterprises cannot only provide "Chinese solutions", but also adapt to "European standards". Chinese enterprises made the most of the innovation capability cultivated in domestic construction and hence obtained success in overseas practice, which fully demonstrated China's development philosophy of innovation and inclusiveness, terminated the global engineering conundrum posed by the marlstone geological formation and lifted the competitiveness of Chinese enterprises in competition with entities from developed markets.

Therefore, in advancing infrastructure construction under the BRI, Chinese enterprises should be determined and confident in competing with international standards backed by successful practices of "Chinese standards", to promote the application of the "Chinese standards" in the international market.

Improving passage-building, enhancing information connectivity and sharing, facilitating efficient logistics

Case 5: The China–Europe Railway Express

The China–Europe Railway Express has become a landmark achievement of the BRI. The cooperation agreement signed between China Railway Corporation and the railway departments of 6 countries along the Belt and Road is included in the list of deliverables of the Belt and Road Forum for International Cooperation, which advocates the establishment of the China–Europe railway express cooperation mechanism and a domestic transport coordination committee. Europe-bound cargo lines (standard gauge) would go through Bogie exchange (having containers reloaded to rail cars of a wider gauge, with 3 outbound trains reorganised into just 2). In this way, transportation cost is reduced and efficiency improved.

The year 2007 saw 3600 outbound trains under the China–Europe Railway Express, exceeding the total seen from 2011 to 2016.[5]

The Yiwu–Madrid Railway line is an important initiative undertaken by the Zhejiang provincial government to better integrate itself into the building of the BRI. In 2017, 168 train shifts (outbound and inbound) ran between Yiwu and Madrid with 14,910 TEUs delivered, an increase of 84.3% over 2016.

The Yiwu–Madrid Railway line now boasts the most railway routes with the highest level of market-based operating efficiency nationwide. Therefore, it spearheads the entire China–Europe Railway Express.

In 2007, a total of 1127 trips (55 inbounds included) were seen by the Yangtze River Delta–Europe (with Central Asia bound included) Train, registering an increase of 362 runs over 2016, or 47.32%. It hits a historic high in annual runs of the China–Europe Railway Express.

Since it started commercial operation, the Yangtze River Delta–Europe Train has run 2742 trips.[6]

In building the Silk Road Economic Belt, Xinjiang Autonomous Region enjoys evident geographical, cultural and policy advantages as it is situated in a core area.

The operation of west-bound trains brings commodities of Xinjiang by rail to Central Asia, Europe and other target markets, saving 30 days or more compared with traditional land and sea transportation.

On May 26, 2016, the Urumqi Assembly Centre witnessed the departure of the first China–Europe Railway Express train heading west. It began with a frequency of one trip per week as scheduled. It was not until November 30 that one trip per day was realised. A total of 135 trips was seen in 2016.

Seven hundred trips were sent out from the Urumqi Assembly Centre in 2017, which exceeded the annual goal of 500 set at the beginning of the year.[7]

Case 6: The LOGINK made logistics information sharing among the world's 31 international ports come true

The LOGINK, also known as the National Public Information Platform for Transportation & Logistics, is the main task and key project of the *State Council's Medium and Long Term Plan for the Development of Logistics Industry (2014–2020)* by the Ministry of Transport of China. It is a public, open, logistics-sharing information network sponsored by the Ministry of Transport and the National Development and Reform Commission, co-built by functional departments, research institutes, software developers, logistics companies and other parties concerned.

On November 8, 2017, the LOGINK signed a memorandum of understanding with the International Port Community Systems Association (IPCSA), Port Kelang (Malaysia), Port Abu Dhabi (UAE), Port of Antwerp (Belgium), among other parties. What's more, the LOGINK joined hands with Spanish Port Barcelona and Portuguese Port Sines (with which it had signed a similar MOU) in promoting connectivity and logistics information-sharing building among ports along the Belt and Road and forging a community of shared future for mankind under the BRI.

The LOGINK has so far established a logistics information-sharing and connectivity mechanism with 26 ports in northeast Asia. Coupled with 5 additional ports (with which it had signed an MoU), the number of signing ports reached 31.

Case 7: The China–ASEAN Port Cities Co-op Network

With Qinzhou (China) at its core, the China–ASEAN Port Cities Co-op Network is a major initiative to magnify China–ASEAN maritime connectivity. Progress has been made in terms of mechanism building, port connectivity, base construction and service support since 2013, with joint cooperation among parties concerned.

As of late 2017, there were 24 ports, cities and related port and shipping agencies joined the network, making major port-related institutions in China and ASEAN countries covered by the network.[8]

In the meantime, a Chinese secretariat was established and a consensus of holding a regular working conference annually was reached. Previously, cooperation between Chinese ports and those of Singapore, Malaysia, Thailand were conducted. With the construction of the Qinzhou base rolling out, comprehensive connectivity between China and Singapore is gaining momentum in its south wing.

In practice, driven by the aim to enhance docking capability for China–Europe cargo trains, countries and regions along the Belt and Road are building railway systems in order to improve the accessibility of domestic and foreign railways, ensuring trunk railways and branch railways become an international passage with greater reach, which is particularly important for countries and regions along the Silk Road Economic Belt.

Held on December 26, 2017, the second plenary meeting of the China–Europe Railway Express Transportation Coordination Committee announced that the number of China–Europe cargo trains would be increased to 4000 in 2018, to promote the building of the south passage of the west route and to run trial transportation on new passages through Lithuania, Latvia, Ukraine and on trans-sea transportation capability, so as to avoid traffic jams at land ports.

At present, the major congestion points are located at Brest of North Russia and Malaszewicze in Poland, the main reason for which being the designed capacity of the aforementioned stations not being big enough. Given that the number of China–Europe cargo trains is increasing year by year and stations are already running at full capacity, the frequent congestion in and out of stations has negatively affected the on-time rate of those trains.

Therefore, the BRI construction will contribute to the development of logistics service, the improvement of overseas business running network of international container shuttle trains, the optimisation of transportation and organisation of international container shuttle trains and the formation of regional and international competitive advantages.

Data show that enterprises can reduce the error rate of logistics business by 94%, improve efficiency of logistics cooperation by 80%, shorten logistics processing time by 95% and cut logistics operation period by 10%, through information sharing on the LOGINK.

We need to strengthen information connectivity and intelligent management capability, enhance the quality of the logistics service, intensify information exchange and connectivity among countries along the Belt and Road before we can see the BRI connectivity deliver performance and see the logistics resource allocation efficiency improved.

Notes

1 "Expressway in Pakistan Built by China is Opened to Traffic," People.cn, January 28, 2017, http://world.people.com.cn/n1/2017/1228/c1002-29733265-2.html
2 "The China–Nepal Cross-border Optical Fiber Link Came into Commercial Operation," *People's Daily*, January 15, 2018, http://world.people.com.cn/n1/2018/0115/c1002-29763761.html
3 "Port Qasim Power Plant Is Launched under the Build-Own-Operate (BOO) Mode," Xinhua Silk Road network, July 25, 2017, http://silkroad.news.cn/company/cases/zjqd/43094.shtml

4 "Longest tunnel in North Africa finished by Chinese company," Xinhua News Agency, http://news.xinhuanet.com/politics/2015-10/19/c_1116863718.htm
5 "China–Europe Cargo Trains Saw An Increase of 116% Year on Year in 2017," Xinhua net, January 22, 2018, www.xinhuanet.com/2018-01/22/c_1122297180.htm
6 "The Yangtze River Delta–Europe Cargo Trains Reached a New Annual Record This Year," Xinhua Net, January 3, 2018, www.xinhuanet.com/fortune/2018-01/03/c_1122202677.htm
7 "Xinjiang Saw 700 China–Europe Cargo Trains in 2007," Xinhuanet, January 11, 2018, www.xinhuanet.com/video/2018-01/11/c_129788257.htm
8 "The rollout of China–ASEAN Port Cities Co-op Network Facilitates Regional Connectivity," Xinhua Net. September 14, 2017, www.xinhuanet.com/2017-09/14/c_1121665452.htm

113
CASE STUDIES OF PRODUCTION CAPACITY COOPERATION

Zhang Zhongyuan

Increase complementarities of respective development strategies to boost coordinated development of production capacity

Long-term plan for China–Pakistan Economic Corridor (CPEC)

The CPEC is one of 6 major economic corridors under the BRI. For more than 4 years, the 2 sides have set up the "1+4" cooperation mode, namely, the 2 sides take CPEC as the core while prioritising Gwadar port, energy, transportation infrastructure and industrial cooperation, which has advanced the CPEC construction and delivered fruits.

On December 18, 2017, *Long-Term Plan for China–Pakistan Economic Corridor* (hereinafter "the Plan") was issued in Islamabad, the Pakistani capital. It is a national plan approved by both Chinese and Pakistani governments and will effectively match-make relevant national plans of China with *Pakistan Vision 2025*. The plan will be in effect until 2030 and will provide macro guidance for the CPEC implementation.

By 2020, the CPEC short-term projects will be done. By 2025, its medium-term projects will be accomplished.

The CPEC is clearly defined in the Plan, consisting of 7 key areas of cooperation, namely connectivity, energy-related fields, trade and industrial parks, agricultural development and poverty alleviation, cooperation in areas concerning people's livelihood and non-governmental exchanges.[1]

Case 2: China–Ukraine Agricultural Investment Cooperation Plan

In December 2017, the Ministry of Commerce and the Ministry of Agriculture of China signed the *China–Ukraine Agricultural Investment Cooperation Plan* with the Ministry of Agrarian Policy and Food and the Ministry of Economic Development and Trade of Ukraine. The plan was jointly drawn up by the Development Research Centre of the State Council (China) and the Academy of Agrarian Sciences (Ukraine), aiming to fully tap the 2 two countries' agricultural investment cooperation potential and direct their enterprises to adequately expand mutual investment in agriculture in order to complement each other's advantages and reach a mutual benefit and win–win result.

According to the plan, the two sides will encourage their enterprises to launch various kinds of agricultural investment cooperation guided by the principle of "being led by government, operating on market basis and the enterprises being the main players". They will push forward the key projects and constantly improve the level of their agricultural investment cooperation.[2]

Case 3: China–Myanmar Economic Corridor

In recent years, Myanmar's least-developed regions have had difficulty attracting foreign capital, mainly because of high logistics costs and a lack of infrastructure.

Apart from seeking peace and stability, people in Myanmar also hope that there will be major improvements in livelihoods, such as the problem of power shortages and a poor transportation infrastructure.

According to its Second Five-year Plan (2016/17–2020/21), Myanmar will reform parts of state-owned enterprises into public–private partnerships. Fields with a good prospect for such reform include: power industry, urban transportation, deep-water ports, restoration of inland ports and railways within the Asian Highway Network (AH, also known as the Great Asian Highway), railway transportation, inland waterway transportation, ports upgrade, etc.

In order to consolidate the comprehensive strategic cooperative partnership and deepen pragmatic cooperation between the 2 countries, China proposed on November 19, 2017 the construction of the China–Myanmar Economic Corridor according to the Myanmar national development plans and actual needs. Under the proposal, China and Myanmar have discussed the construction of an economic corridor which starts from south-west China's Yunnan province and extends to the central Myanmar city of Mandalay, and then east to Yangon and west to the Kyaukpyu Special Economic Zone (Myanmar).[3]

The China–Myanmar Economic Corridor will link the poorest areas in Myanmar with its richest ones, which can greatly accelerate local economic development, alleviate poverty, diffuse local conflicts, bring more peace and stability to Kyaukpyu and also facilitate the connectivity of major projects along the corridor, so as to push for more balanced development across the country.

Production capacity cooperation can best promote the economic growth of the countries concerned. Therefore, in accelerating such cooperation, attention should be paid to increasing the 2 countries' complementarities of national development strategies. Cooperation can be conducted in forms of inviting enterprise entry and investment with preferential supporting policies.[4]

For instance, the *Joint Declaration Between China and Laos* points out that the 2 should increase the complementarities of national development strategies and intensify production capacity cooperation, so as to advance the BRI and the strategy of Laos to transform itself from a land-locked to a land-linked country and align China's *13th Five-Year Plan* with *the 8th Five-Year National Socioeconomic Development Plan* of Laos. It also calls for the joint compilation of the outline of the plan for the BRI building cooperation, and practical measures to stimulate bilateral production capacity cooperation.[5]

In short, only through sufficient communication in terms of national policies can key national development strategies along the Belt and Road be aligned with the BRI, and China's national development strategy with that of other countries, so as to forge an industrial layout featuring economic complementarities.

Forge a demonstration project for international production capacity cooperation, accelerate cooperation in the real economy

Case 4: China provides Bangladesh with concessional loans to build a network infrastructure project

Chinese and Bangladeshi government representatives signed a framework agreement on September 10, 2017, which provides concessional loans for Bangladesh as a support for the Development of National ICTInfra-Network for Bangladesh Government Phase III (Info-Sarker Phase III) and Bangladeshi Modernisation of Telecommunication Network for Digital Construction of connectivity (MoTN) Project.

Built on the Info-Sarker Phase I and II, the Phase III project is to expand and extend the capacity of the Bangladeshi government's basic network, so as to give shape to a 100-G bandwidth network at municipal level, 10 G at county level, and 1 G at township level. The project scope includes the establishment of new networks for some townships, the enhancement of high-level administrative regional backbone networks and the design, supply, installation and training services needed for the deployment of a national network management platform.

The contract of the Info-Sarker Phase III accounts for US$169.6 million and is covered by concessional loans from the Chinese government.

The MoTN project budget totals US$231 million. The main objectives are to extend a reliable and affordable telecom facility and facilitate enhancement of teledensity, including building an IMS-based (IP Multimedia Subsystem) core network serving 1.6 million users, adding 350,000 new FTTX (Fibre-to-the-x, fibre access) broadband subscribers, upgrading and transforming copper cables on the existing network of 450,000 subscribers, 8t 100-G backbone fibre transmission and three 100-G metropolitan area transmission platforms, corresponding IP transmission platform, advanced billing system and network management system, laying of supporting backbone and access fibre.

The project covers the whole territory of Bangladesh and is a truly national broadband network, which can meet the needs of network development in Bangladesh for the next 10 years.[6]

With the progression of the BRI, China must attach great importance to promoting production capacity cooperation with other countries along the Belt and Road.

The international production capacity cooperation that China is for is a mutually beneficial and win–win international industrial investment cooperation centred on the building, transfer and promotion of new production capacity. Generally speaking, it is mainly about cooperation between China and host countries in building infrastructure and production lines, where China provides technologies, managerial and financial support and taps into local markets with host countries. It also includes co-developing a third-party market jointly with developed countries.

The production capacity cooperation we are talking about in this context is a market-oriented one that takes enterprises as the main body, focusing on developing the manufacturing industry, building infrastructure and developing resources and energy. Direct investment, project contracting, equipment trade and technical cooperation are the main forms of cooperation.

Create a new platform for production capacity cooperation, speed up the construction of overseas industrial parks

Case 5: China–Egypt TEDA Suez Economic and Trade Cooperation Zone to help upgrade the Egyptian manufacturing industry

The China–Egypt TEDA Suez Economic and Trade Cooperation Zone is located at the Northwest Special Economic Zone of the Gulf of Suez, 120 km from Cairo. It is divided into the starting area and the expansion zone, of which the construction and operation are led by Tianjin Teda Investment Holding Co., Ltd.

The construction of the starting area (of 1.34 km^2) began in 2007 and is now completed. It has attracted nearly 70 enterprises with agreed investment of US$1 billion.

About 700 million yuan has been invested in Phase I of the cooperation zone, facilitating service and manufacturing industries upgrading in Egypt, stimulating employment, bringing about more government revenue and promoting industrial restructuring. What's more, it also serves for Chinese enterprises' Going Abroad Strategy.

The expansion area was inaugurated in January 2016. With more than a year's construction, the phase I has delivered a road of 2 km^2 and completed water and electricity network infrastructure, boasting basic conditions for the arrival of projects.[7]

The construction of the third production line worth US$110 million invested by China Jushi Co., Ltd (a fibreglass business) officially started in late 2016. It was completed and put into operation in 2017. Driven by this project, Egypt has built the first fibreglass business in its history.

However, even a win–win project as such was confronted with many difficulties in the beginning. Firsty, China Jushi was struck by an energy shortfall. The project has a relatively large energy demand, electricity in particular, but the park was under huge pressure in terms of power supply, which led to a complete equipment shutdown. The cooperation zone administration referred this problem to the Egyptian government in different forms and ultimately helped China Jushi solve the problem.

Case 6: The Morowali Tsingshan Industrial Park, China–Indonesia Comprehensive Industrial Park

On October 3, 2013, during Chinese President Xi Jinping's state visit to Indonesia, the leaders witnessed the establishment of the Morowali Tsingshan Industrial Park in Jakarta and the signing ceremony of its first park.

On May 29, 2015, a delegation consisting of 5 ministers/governors/county magistrates headed by Indonesian President Joko Widodo visited the park, where he announced the commercial operation inauguration of its first project—a ferronickel smelter with 300,000 tons of estimated annual output (SMI Company)—and delivered a speech.

The Morowali Tsingshan Industrial Park passed through assessment and confirmation by the Commerce Ministry of China and COCE, Finance Ministry of China.

The Morowali Tsingshan Industrial Park is an industrial park comprehensively developing nickel, chromium and iron ores with an integrated "ferronickel + stainless steel" business model as its mainstay. A complete industrial chain has gradually taken place, from stainless steel upstream raw materials developing and processing such as ferronickel mining, ferronickel smelting and stainless steel smelting to downstream industries such as steel bar/wire/plate processing, steel pole production, fine wire processing, wharf transportation, international trade, etc.

The park is tailored to turn the advantages of the local ferronickel resource into wealth and gradually form an industrial chain integrating the production, processing and sales of ferronickel and stainless steel, an overseas ferronickel supply base, a stainless steel and stainless steel products production base, an international marketing base for stainless steel products, an important base for China's "ferronickel + stainless steel" enterprises to achieve global industrial layout and industrial clustering, a landmark project for China–Indonesia cooperation in mineral resource development, so as to give a strong boost to local and even the entire Indonesian economic growth and build a demonstration zone and an industrial cooperation platform for bilateral international production capacity and equipment manufacturing cooperation.[8]

Promoting international manufacturing cooperation through the industrial park construction constitutes an important component of the BRI.

Building industrial parks in countries along the Belt and Road comes from enterprises' own development demand. Industrial parks are built and operated according to market rules and related economic and trade cooperation is conducted based on resource endowment, market demand and development strategies of those countries.

Different from generic projects, the industrial park construction along the Belt and Road also demands additional overall services including but not limited to design, planning, financing, construction and operation, technology and personnel training.

The BRI building through industrial park construction can intensify China's production capacity cooperation with local ones while advancing the exportation of China's abundant and good-quality production capacity, in the course of advancing the exportation of China's abundant and good-quality production capacity. It not only provides necessary infrastructure facilities for the local manufacturing industry, but also accelerates the exportation of China's production capacity, capital and technical standards. It will bring to the locals a large number of technological innovations, unique product standards, advanced or original technology and standards and will expedite the localisation of technologies, managerial expertise and experienced workers, which can lend strong impetus to the industrial upgrade and the economic development of countries along the Belt and Road and deliver economic and social benefits, among other advantages.[9]

Notes

1 *Long Term Plan for China–Pakistan Economic Corridor*. Released in Pakistan, Xinhuanet, December 19, 2017, www.xinhuanet.com/world/2017-12/19/c_1122133903.htm
2 *China–Ukraine Agricultural Investment Cooperation Plan* Signed, Xinhua Silk Road Net, December 8, 2017, http://silkroad.news.cn/2017/1208/73631.shtml
3 "FM Wang Yi Proposes China–Myanmar Economic Corridor," website of China Foreign Ministry. Retrieved November 20, 2017 from www.fmprc.gov.cn/web/wjbzhd/t1512003.shtml
4 Zhao Jianglin, "How to Deepen the Complementarities Between the BRI and ASEAN Development Strategies," *Knowledge of the World*, 2016, Volume 8, pp. 17–19.
5 *The Joint Declaration Between the People's Republic of China and the Lao People's Democratic Republic* (full text), Xinhua net, May 4, 2016, www.xinhuanet.com/2016-05/04/c_1118803463.htm
6 "China and Bangladesh Signed a Framework Agreement for the Development of ICT Infrastructure in Bangladesh," September 11th, 2017, http://silkroad.news.cn/invest/tzzx/49974.shtml
7 "China–Egypt TEDA Suez Economic and Trade Cooperation Zone Has Attracted Investment of Nearly US$ 1 billion," May 23, 2017, www.tj.xinhuanet.com/jz/2017-05/23/c_1121021668.htm
8 "Morowali Tsingshan Industrial Park, China–Indonesia Comprehensive Industrial Park," January 6, 2017, www.cocz.org/news/content-262356.aspx
9 Shen Minghui, Zhang Zhongyuan, "COCZ: Production Capacity Cooperation Platform under the Belt and Road Initiative," *New Vision*, 2016, No. 3, pp. 110–115.

114
CASE STUDIES OF TRADE AND INVESTMENT FACILITATION

Zhang Zhongyuan

Free trade agreement
Case 1: The signing of the China–Georgia Free Trade Agreement

On November 28, 2017, both China and Georgia completed their respective domestic examination procedures stipulated in the *Free Trade Agreement Between the People's Republic of China and the Democratic Republic of Georgia* (hereinafter "the Agreement"), enabling the Agreement to come into effect on January 1, 2018.[1]

Negotiation on the Agreement began in December 2015 and was officially signed in May 2017.

The Agreement is the first of its kind ever signed between China and a Eurasian country. It is also the first free trade agreement initiated and completed by China after the BRI was proposed.

Since the Agreement came into effect, the 2 sides have cancelled tariffs on most of their traded goods, with 96.5% of Georgia's import tariffs on Chinese goods cut to zero (covering 99.6% of Georgia's total imports from China) and 93.9% of China's import tariffs on Georgian goods cut to zero (accounting for 93.8% of China's total imports from Georgia). Of China's import tariffs on Georgia, 90.9% was immediately dropped to zero, while 3% will be after 5 years.

In terms of trade in service, the two have committed to ensuring a high-quality market openness covering a wide range of the service sector, and perfecting the rules of intellectual property, environmental protection, e-commerce and competition.

The Agreement will further enhance bilateral trade liberalisation and facilitation, and will be in service of the formation of business-friendly environment where the market is more open, convenient and consumers enjoy greater affordability and higher quality of products.

Case 2: The China–Chile Free Trade Zone upgraded

The China–Chile Free Trade Agreement was signed in 2005 and came into effect in 2006. It is the first free trade agreement China has ever signed with a Latin American country.

In order to give a strong boost to bilateral cooperation in service and investment, the 2 sides signed supplementary agreements on trade in service and investment in 2008 and 2012, respectively.

In November 2016, during President Xi Jinping's state visit to Chile, the 2 sides signed a memorandum of understanding which began negotiations on upgrading the FTA, to further enhance bilateral trade and investment liberalisation and facilitation.

On November 11th, 2017, China and Chile signed a formal outcome document of negotiations on upgrading of the China–Chile FTA, the *Protocol to Amend the Free Trade Agreement Between the Government of the People's Republic of China and the Republic of Chile and the Supplementary Agreement on Trade in Services of the Free Trade Agreement Between the Government of the People's Republic of China and the Republic of Chile* (hereinafter "the Protocol").[2]

According to the Protocol, the customs procedures and the trade facilitation have been upgraded. Based on the FTA, new chapters on customs procedures and trade facilitation are added, mainly about the transparency of laws and regulations, further simplifying customs procedures, provision of fast and efficient customs clearance services with the use of risk management and information technology and joint maintenance of bilateral trade order, among other things.

The 2 sides have agreed to strengthen two-way exchanges and cooperation in customs, timely notification of trade-related customs matters, which will facilitate customs clearance and release of cargoes of both sides (perishable goods, in particular) to cut customs clearance costs, improve customs clearance efficiency and provide effective protection for the security and facilitation of two-way trade supply chain.

The Protocol is the second agreement of its kind signed by China following the upgrade of the China–ASEAN Free Trade Area, and the first signed by China with a Latin American country, which will lend a robust impetus to the reciprocity of bilateral economic cooperation and the enrichment of the China–Chile comprehensive strategic partnership.

Thanks to the FTAs signed, China and its trading partners now enjoy a relatively high level of liberalisation of trade in goods. Approximately 90% of China's imports (from its partners) is granted with zero-tariff treatment, covering over 8000 kinds of China's total imported products with zero tariff.

Under the framework of the Free Trade Agreement, nearly one-third of China's total imports of goods enjoy preferential tariff treatment, most of which is end-consumer goods; under the Free Trade Area project, products that enjoy zero-tariff treatment also include intermediate products and raw materials needed for the production of many end-consumer goods of China.

In 2018, China will advance 10 FTA negotiations and promote a joint feasibility study or upgrade joint research on free trade agreements with Panama, Palestine, Mongolia, Switzerland, Peru and other countries.

China is drawing up a globally oriented free trade area network map based on its periphery and radiating the BRI, to sketch out a framework of China's FTA strategy.

Deepen international tax cooperation

Case 3: China and Russia signed a new tax treaty

The new *Treaty between the Government of the People's Republic of China and the Government of the Russian Federation "On the avoidance of double taxation and prevention of fiscal evasion with respect to taxes on income"* and the *Protocol amending the treaty between the Government of the People's Republic of China and the Government of the Russian Federation "On the avoidance of double taxation and prevention of fiscal evasion with respect to taxes on income"* (hereinafter collectively referred to as "the new treaty") were formally signed in Moscow on October 13, 2014 and May 8, 2015, respectively.[3]

The new treaty has reduced the tax burden on cross-border investors on the original basis and made a number of major amendments, such as the separate provision of affiliated enterprises and the amendment in which dividend, interest and royalty income are added to the anti-treaty shopping provisions, which reflects the latest progress of international taxation jurisprudence, the will of competent tax authorities in the 2 countries to strengthen cooperation in taxation and management, jointly guard against fiscal evasion, and also conforms to the overall spirit of the G20 for promoting international cooperation, advancing international tax administration, and responding to the base erosion and profit shifting (BEPS).

Its signing will further promote trade and investment between the 2 countries and advance economic growth of both sides on the basis of current achievement.

China and Russia have completed their respective domestic legal procedures necessary for the new treaty's entry into force. The new treaty came into effect on April 9, 2016 and was enforced from January 1, 2017.

Since the BRI was proposed, the negotiation and signing process of China's tax treaties have speeded up significantly. As of May 2017, China has signed bilateral tax treaties, arrangements and agreements with 106 countries and regions, among which 54 countries are along the Belt and Road.

At present, prior to making any outbound investment, many Chinese enterprises often fail to pay due attention to tax-related issues in their due diligence. However, follow-up operation has found tax-related issues often constitute one of the underlying factors deciding whether their outbound investment can deliver.

The tax treaty is designed to avoid double taxation, which provides protection for Chinese enterprises when "going abroad" and helps reduce tax costs.

The progression of the BRI building urgently calls for in-depth tax cooperation. It is a pragmatic move to establish a long-term mechanism for tax cooperation among countries and regions along the Belt and Road, in order to efficiently and continuously facilitate trade and economic exchanges under the BRI.

Forge a convenient and efficient business environment

Case 4: Ramp up e-commerce cooperation

On November 10, 2017, built on the comprehensive strategic cooperative partnership that has been established, China and Cambodia signed the *Memorandum of Understanding between the Ministry of Commerce of the People's Republic of China and the Ministry of Commerce of the Kingdom of Cambodia on E-commerce Cooperation*. According to the MOU, both sides will ramp up trade facilitation and cooperation, strengthen policy communication, cooperation among enterprises, capability building, personnel training, joint research and other e-commerce exchanges and cooperation to further promote the sustainable and stable growth of bilateral trade, under the framework of the BRI and the "Four Angle Strategy" proposed by the Cambodian government and through intensifying e-commerce cooperation.[4]

On November 27, 2017, China and the Republic of Estonia signed the *Memorandum of Understanding on E-commerce Cooperation*. According to the MOU, both sides will establish a mechanism for e-commerce cooperation within the framework of the China–Estonia Joint Economic and Trade Committee to step up policy communication, encourage the promotion of national high-quality specialty products through e-commerce, actively support professional training, share best practices and innovative experience in e-commerce cooperation and lift the level of economic and trade cooperation between China and Estonia.[5]

Case 5: China signed agreements on AEO (authorized economic operator) mutual recognition with a number of economies[6]

In March 2017, China and New Zealand customs officially signed the *Customs of the People's Republic of China and the New Zealand Customs Department on the People's Republic of China Customs and Excise Department credit management system and the New Zealand Customs safety export plan mutual recognition arrangements*. The 2 sides decided to formally implement the mutual recognition arrangements since July 1, 2017.[7]

According to the mutual agreement, the two sides mutually recognised each other's customs "certified operators" ("AEO enterprises") for the import of goods from each other's AEO enterprises to provide customs clearance convenience. Among them, the New Zealand Customs recognised China Customs' senior certification enterprises for China's AEO enterprises; China Customs approved the New Zealand Customs'"safe export plan" members of the New Zealand AEO enterprises. The 2 sides, of the Customs and Excise Department in the import and export goods customs clearance, will give each other AEO enterprises following customs clearance measures: reduce the document audit and inspection; give inspection priority to goods needed for check; designate customs liaison responsible for communication to help out AEO enterprises encountering difficulties in customs clearance.

About 4000 Chinese enterprises can enjoy the bilateral customs clearance facilitation measures. Thanks to the achieved AEO mutual recognition, time for clearance alone can be reduced by about 50%. Therefore, enterprises with high credit can cut clearance and logistics costs by large margins.[8]

With the AEO mutual recognition achieved between the 2 countries, the import of goods from each other's AEO enterprises can enjoy customs clearance convenience, thus clearance and logistics costs of enterprises with high credit can be cut significantly.

The China–Switzerland Customs AEO mutual recognition agreement and its implementation started from September 1, 2017. The AEO enterprises of both sides will enjoy customs clearance convenience.

After the implementation of the AEO mutual recognition, the two customs administrations will offer 5 facilitation measures including lower inspection rate, status as secure trade partners, priority in clearance, appointment of an outreach officer and priority in clearance after recovery of trade.[9]

The enterprises, when exporting to the other country, will enjoy facilitation that can reduce inspection and clearance time by 30–50%, cutting port, insurance and logistics costs.

About 22,300 Chinese AEOs engage in trade with Swiss businesses, among which nearly 1000 are premium AEOs, with their import and export value accounting for about 20% of the China–Switzerland total.

2008 saw a rapid development of China's AEO system. To date, China has signed AEO mutual recognition agreements with over 30 countries and regions, among which are Singapore, South Korea, the EU, Switzerland and New Zealand. It is now talking with the USA, Japan, Australia, Brazil and Canada, among other countries and regions, on AEO mutual recognition.

The formal implementation of the customs AEO mutual recognition agreement has created a more open business environment of convenience and efficiency for both parties. Chinese AEO enterprises, when exporting to the other country, will enjoy facilitation that can reduce inspection by 60–80%, cutting clearance time and customs clearance cost by over 50%.

The Implementation Guideline of Mutual Recognition for Authorised Economic Operators (AEO) of the World Customs Organization (WCO), drafted by China Customs, was approved by the WCO. It is the first time Chinese customs successfully led the development of international rules in the field of AEO.

To better facilitate China's import and export enterprises in their "going abroad" endeavour, the next step is to align closely the implementation of the AEO system with that of important national strategies such as the BRI, Going Abroad Strategy, so as to intensify international mutual recognition and cooperation, and open up green channel for the BRI projects.

Notes

1 "China and Georgia Formally Signed the FTA," Xinhuanet, May 14, 2017, www.xinhuanet.com/world/2017-05/14/c_1120967865.htm
2 "China–Chile FTA Upgrading Negotiation Wrapped Up with A Protocol Signed," Retrieved from www.mofcom.gov.cn/article/b/e/200411/20041100306546.shtml
3 "China and Russia Interpret Treaty On the Avoidance of Double Taxation and Prevention of Fiscal Evasion with Respect to Taxes on Income, Which Will Be Enforced Next Year," August 1, 2016, www.xinhuanet.com/fortune/2016-08/01/c_129195892.htm
4 "China and Cambodia Signed *the Memorandum of Understanding on E-commerce Cooperation*," the Ministry of Commerce of the People's Republic of China, November 10, 2017, www.mofcom.gov.cn/article/ae/ai/201711/20171102668543.shtml
5 "China and Estonia Signed *the Memorandum of Understanding on E-commerce Cooperation*," the Ministry of Commerce of the People's Republic of China, November 28, 2017, www.mofcom.gov.cn/article/ae/ai/201711/20171102676927.shtml
6 Authorised economic operator (AEO) is an important system within the World Customs Organisation (WCO) Framework of Standards to Secure and Facilitate Global Trade, designed to authenticate enterprises with high degree of law observance, credit and security status to provide them with customs clearance convenience.
7 In 2017, the General Administration of Customs of the People's Republic of China (GACC) announced its 23rd announcement (on the implementation of the "Customs of the People's Republic of China and the New Zealand Customs Department on the People's Republic of China Customs and Excise Department credit management system and the New Zealand Customs safety export plan mutual recognition arrangements"), GACC, June 19, 2017, www.customs.gov.cn/publish/ Portal0/tab49661/info854193.htm
8 "China–New Zealand Customs AEO Mutual Recognition Will Be Implemented Next Month," *People's Daily*, June 28, 2017, http://world.people.com.cn/n1/2017/0628/c1002-29367027.html
9 "China–Switzerland AEO Mutual Recognition to be Implemented on September 1st," August 10, 2017, www.xinhuanet.com/2017-08/10/c_1121464351.htm

115
CASE STUDIES OF FINANCIAL COOPERATION

Zhang Zhongyuan

Promote financing connectivity and achieve win–win situation

Case 1. The establishment of the China–Central, Eastern Europe (CEE) InterBank Consortium

To promote multilateral financial cooperation under the framework of China–CEE "16+1 cooperation", the China Development Bank and financial institutions in the CEE jointly set up the China–CEE Interbank Consortium in November 2017.

The China–CEE Consortium consists of 14 members, all of which are state-owned policy banks, developmental financial institutions and commercial banks, including the China Development Bank, the Hungarian Development Bank, the Czech Export Bank, the EXIMBANKA SR, the Croatian Bank for Reconstruction and Development, the HBOR, the Bulgarian Development Bank, the Export–Import Bank of Romania, the Postal Savings Bank of Serbia, the Slovene Export and Development Bank, the Republic of Srpska Investment-Development Bank, the Macedonian Bank for Development Promotion, the Investment and Development Fund of the Republic of Montenegro, the Development Finance Institution ALTUM and the Public Investment Development Agency of the Republic of Lithuania.

According to the principles of "self management, independent decision making and risk taking", member banks cooperate in such fields as project financing, interbank credit, planning and consultation, training and communication, high-level dialogue, policy communication and information sharing.[1]

The China Development Bank will within 5 years provide a total of 2 billion euros of equivalent financial cooperation of development loans for the consortium member banks, to conduct trade cooperation with other member banks or future observers and jointly support investment and construction projects (such as infrastructure, electricity, telecommunications, industrial parks, agriculture, small and medium-sized enterprises, high and new technology) co-developed between Chinese and CEE companies.

Case 2: the Bank of China provides loans to the Shalkiya Zinc Project in Kazakhstan

In December 2017, the Bank of China Kazakhstan signed the participation agreement to provide US$120 million under the US$295 million syndicated loan for the expansion of Shalkiya zinc and lead mine arranged by the EBRD, which would provide US$175 million.

The project with JSC Shalkiya Zinc Ltd, a Kazakh mining company based in the Kyzylorda region, is currently owned by the Samruk-Kazyna (Kazakhstan's sovereign wealth fund).

JSC Shalkiya Zinc Ltd will dominate Kazakhstan's zinc mining market and rank among the world's top zinc mining companies when the expansion project is done. This project will not only give a robust boost to the local economy, but also bring about a series of positive effects on Kazakhstan's employment, the development of upstream and downstream industries.[2]

Case 3: China–UK bilateral investment to fund the BRI

On December 16, 2017, the 9th China–UK Economic and Financial Dialogue (EFD) published policy outcomes. A bilateral investment fund was set up, with an initial round of US$1 billion supporting projects under the BRI.

The fund, led by Chinese and British institutions, is built and operated on a commercial and market basis, and will be invested in innovative, sustainable and consumer-driven growth opportunities in the Chinese, British or third markets to create jobs, promote trade and support the BRI.

China and Britain will strengthen pragmatic cooperation in infrastructure connectivity, equipment manufacturing, finance and investment, explore cooperation in third markets along the Belt and Road, and forge a positive and sustainable trade, economic development and security gains within the framework the Sino-British Comprehensive Global Strategic Partnership for the 21st Century.[3]

Case 4: Guangxi–ASEAN BRI funds

In December 2017, the CDB Finance Co., Ltd (an investment arm of China's policy bank, the China Development Bank, CDB) partnered with the Guangxi Investment Group and established funds totaling 50 billion yuan (US$7.6 billion) to invest in Belt and Road projects in southern China's Guangxi Zhuang Autonomous Region and ASEAN countries. They will be used to support infrastructure and industrial projects along the Belt and Road.

In addition to those funds, the CDB and Guangxi also signed an agreement to strengthen comprehensive financial service, cooperation in the development of local and overseas financial institutions, over the next 5 years.

Besides setting up funds, the CDB also pledged more financing support to Guangxi through tools including loans, investments, bonds, leasing and securities, to help solve problems facing Guangzi such as uneven and insufficient development. It will render comprehensive financing, financial intelligence support for the optimisation of industrial structure, marine economy and international cooperation.[4]

The BRI projects require diverse, stable and low-cost funding. Currently, funding sources closely associated with the BRI mainly come from the following 5 categories: international financial institutions, development and policy financial institutions, commercial banks, special investment funds and emerging multilateral development financial institutions.

The BRI projects feature characteristics such as a long recovery cycle, a huge demand for funds, etc. Boasting multiple advantages, development finance business can not only connect to the government and the market, and integrate all resources, but also provides long- and medium-term credit support for those who have special needs. What's more, it can play a role model where development finance institutions play an important role, in terms of the utilisation of commercial capital.

For example, the China Development Bank, through planning, collaboration with think tanks, credit support, direct investment, multilateral financial cooperation, training exchange, etc., provides the BRI with long-term, stable, sustainable, risk-controllable financial support, making the most of its advantages (as a development bank) such as large sums of capital, wholesale and long-term financing. In this way, it funded a number of key projects such as Indonesia's Jakarta–Bandung High Speed Railway, Pakistan's Karot Hydropower Project, etc..

The BRI entails not only investment and financing cooperation, but also a large number of ancillary financial services.

Therefore, commercial banks are the market-oriented backbone of the BRI. Special investment funds, sovereign wealth funds, pension funds, insurance companies, investment institutions and other private sectors can also play a leading role in a variety of ways such as equity investment, debt financing in supporting the BRI projects.

Develop new business models to boost financing

Case 5: the China Export & Credit Insurance Corporation (SINOSURE) provides protection for BRI project financing

Risk assessment by banks of some countries along the Belt and Road is rather strict. Therefore, the cost of loans is relatively higher. The China Export Credit Insurance Corporation (hereinafter referred to as SINOSURE) match-makes the BRI construction and shares the risk of loans-lending banks, which enhances the banks' confidence and will. Consequently, the financing requirements needed for obtaining loans have also been optimised. The provision of risk protection and market-based measures has been used to leverage a large amount of commercial funds in "going abroad" and promoting the implementation of the BRI projects.

The Nam Ou River Basin Cascade Hydropower Plant Projects are important part of Laos' Renewable Energy Development Strategy, which turns its rich hydropower resource into wealth. In 2013, the SINOSURE issued an overseas investment insurance policy for the phase I of the Nam Ou River Basin Cascade Hydropower Plant, providing guarantee for the equity capital worth US$233 million and loans worth US$770 million injected into the project by Chinese companies and banks, respectively. This not only dispels the worries of Chinese companies and banks over fund safety, but also lends important support for the smooth implementation of the entire project.[5]

In 2017, the SINOSURE's insurance policy coverage further expanded. Its annual underwriting amount reached US$524.6 billion, of which medium- and long-term export credit insurance underwriting amount accounted for US$23.9 billion, overseas investment insurance underwriting US$48.9 billion and short-term export credit insurance underwriting US$412.8 billion. The SINOSURE has paid nearly US$1.4 billion of claims to customers.

Case 6: the CDB issued the Belt and Road Bond

On December 20, 2017, the China Development Bank issued a US$350 million 5-year Belt and Road bond via private placement (with 5 years of fixed interest rate) and will use the proceeds to support project construction along the Belt and Road. The Hong Kong Stock Exchange listed the bond.

This was the first Belt and Road bond the CDB issued. Dealers include the Bank of Communications (Hong Kong) Ltd, the China Construction Bank (Asia) and the HSBC Bank (Hong Kong) Ltd. Hong Kong is well-positioned for its advantages in attracting global quality investors and integrating global financial resources to support the BRI construction. The positive publicity and demonstration effect Hong Kong enjoys on the international financial market will help bring closer the financial cooperation between the mainland and Hong Kong, promote interconnection between the two markets, and better play a constructive role of Hong Kong in participating and assisting the BRI.[6]

Case 7: China's Hongshi Holding Group issued a Belt and Road Corporate Bond

On January 19, 2018, Hongshi Holding Group, a privately owned cement maker, printed the 300 million yuan (US$47 million) 3-year corporate bond on the Shanghai Stock Exchange. The bond was underwritten by Guotai Junan Securities Co., Ltd, with the interest rate at 6.34%, and the 3-year bond recorded a total of 2.67 times in subscription, with both the issuer and the bond rated AAA and the proceeds to be used in the purchase of relevant equipment for the Hongshi cement project in Vientiane, Laos. As one of the major Belt and Road construction projects involved in Zhejiang's enterprises, the project was included in the "Collection of Major Belt and Road Construction Projects Involved by Zhejiang Province" in June 2017. After completion, the project is expected to produce 2 million tons of high-grade cement annually, which will meet the demand for high-quality cement in construction of large-scale infrastructure in Laos and contribute to exporting China's advanced cement technology and equipment, so as to upgrade the overall development level of cement industry in Laos.

It was also the first Belt and Road construction corporate bond publicly offered by a Chinese enterprise, constituting an important initiative boosting financial connectivity of the BRI.[7]

Judging from the specific financing cases of "Going Abroad" by Chinese enterprises, we can tell that most companies prefer to adopt overseas loans under domestic guarantees, meaning domestic banks provide guarantees for affiliates of domestic enterprises or equity investment enterprises registered abroad, with loans provided for overseas investment companies by overseas banks.

The SINOSURE supports the export and investment of countries along the Belt and Road, thus has underwritten more than 1000 of various "going abroad" projects, such as the Central Asia–China gas pipeline, Jordan's Attarat Shale Oil-Fuelled Power Plant, the Pakistani Sahiwal Coal Power Project, the Malaysian steel coking plant with an annual output of 3.5 million tons, the Cambodian Sesan II hydropower project, etc., covering transportation, petroleum equipment, electric power engineering, housing construction, communications equipment and other fields.

With the support of the SINOSURE, China and countries along the Belt and Road have expanded cooperation in such areas as infrastructure connectivity, development and utilisation of energy resources, construction of trade and economic cooperation zones, and development of new and high-tech industries, which has greatly promoted economic and trade exchanges between China and its neighbours, lent a strong boost to the economic growth and people's livelihood of the countries along the Belt and Road, and lifted China's influence in the course of the BRI construction.

Steadily advance the internationalisation of the renminbi

Case 8: Pakistan approved renminbi as its settlement currency

On January 2, 2018, the State Bank of Pakistan took comprehensive policy-related measures to ensure that imports, exports and financing transactions can be denominated in Chinese yuan (CNY). Both public- and private-sector enterprises, Pakistani or Chinese, are free to choose CNY for bilateral trade and investment activities. It has created favourable conditions for renminbi's access into the Pakistani market. To date, Pakistan's import trade volume with China has exceeded US$10 billion a year and is expanding.

Under such circumstances, the renminbi settlement not only helps reduce the pressure on Pakistan's demand for US dollars, but also allows Pakistan to become an "experimental field" for advancing the internationalisation of the renminbi.[8]

As early as December 2011, the People's Bank of China (China's central bank) signed a 10-billion yuan (US$1.58 billion) currency swap deal with the State Bank of Pakistan, aiming at promoting bilateral financial cooperation and boosting trade and investment.

The use of renminbi in bilateral trade can further advance the building of the China–Pakistan Economic Corridor. As Chinese companies are actively entering the Pakistani market under the attraction of the CPEC, the renminbi settlement will make bilateral trade settlement more direct and simpler.

Case 9: the China Development Bank signed BRI loan deals with Egypt

In September 2017, the China Development Bank (CDB) signed 2 deals to provide loans to Egypt's SAIBANK, under which the CDB will provide the SAIBANK with a loan of US$40 million for small and medium-sized enterprises in Africa, and a special RMB denominated loan of 260 million yuan (US$ 40million) for infrastructure construction, power grid, energy, communication, transportation, agriculture, small and medium-sized enterprises, "going abroad" projects construction of Chinese enterprises.[9]

A growing demand for diversity in cross-border payments and settlement currencies is seen in countries along the Belt and Road. Currency diversity also helps expand the available sources of funds for the BRI construction. The demands of various fund users and projects will be met through the promotion of investment and financing diversity.

In particular, the promotion of cross-border RMB investment projects can make the international financial markets develop more value protection and hedging tools for the renminbi, which will bring more favourable overseas investment and financing conditions.

China is committed to providing more dedicated loans (funds) for countries along the Belt and Road, guiding domestic and foreign private capital in putting more renminbi funds into the BRI construction, and expanding the overseas capital pool and liquidity of the renminbi.

What's more, China also remains committed to speeding up the building of an RMB offshore centre, putting forth more innovative RMB products, increasing the connectivity between onshore and offshore markets, in order to realise the international application of the renminbi.

Notes

1 "China Development Bank-led China–CEE Interbank Consortium Established," Xinhua, November 29, 2017, www.xinhuanet.com/money/2017-11/29/c_129752150.htm
2 "Bank of China to provide US$120 mln as part of EBRD-arranged syndicated loan for Kazakhstan's ShalkiyaZinc," Xinhuanet, December 29, 2017, www.xinhuanet.com/world/2017-12/29/c_1122187208.htm

3 "China–UK bilateral investment fund with an initial round of $ 1 billion to support projects under the Belt and Road Initiative was set up," Xinhuanet, December 16, 2017, www.xinhuanet.com/world/2017-12/16/c_1122122062.htm
4 "China To Set Up 50 Billion Yuan Funds To Support BRI Projects In ASEAN, Guangxi," Xinhua, December 16, 2017, www.xinhuanet.com/local/2017-12/16/c_1122121613. htm
5 "SINOSURE Endorses the Belt and Road Initiative, says its president," Xinhua, May 4, 2017, www.xinhuanet.com/money/2017-05/04/c_1120919019.htm
6 "CDB Issued the First Belt and Road Bond," Xinhuanet, December 20, 2017, www.xinhuanet.com/money/2017-12/20/c_129771217.htm
7 "First Belt and Road construction corporate bond publicly offered by a Chinese enterprise issued," Xinhuanet, January 21, 2018, www.sh.xinhuanet.com/2018-01/21/c_136912094.htm
8 "State Bank of Pakistan allows use of yuan in bilateral trades," Xinhuanet, January 3, 2018, www.xinhuanet.com/world/2018-01/03/c_129781840.htm
9 "China Development Bank provides its first special RMB denominated loan for the BRI in Egypt," Xinhuanet, September 18, 2017, www.xinhuanet.com/money/2017-09/18/c_1121682726.htm

116
CASE STUDIES OF PEOPLE-TO-PEOPLE EXCHANGES

Zhang Zhongyuan

Strengthen vocational education and cultural exchange

Case 1: The construction of Lancang–Mekong vocational education base

In December 2014, the Chinese Ministry of Foreign Affairs, the Ministry of Education approved the establishment of the China–ASEAN Education and Training Centre by the Yunnan Minzu University. Built on the China–ASEAN Education and Training Centre, the Yunnan Minzu University set up the Lancang–Mekong International Vocational Institute in December 2016, which focuses on cultivating high-quality talents of practical skills that suit the needs of socio-economic development in the Lancang–Mekong region. The Lancang–Mekong alliance of vocational education was launched on January 15, 2017. To date, 3 universities, 19 higher-educational institutions and 30 other related organisations from Mekong countries have joined the Alliance.

The Yunnan Minzu University proposed the building of the Lancang–Mekong vocational education base consisting of 6 integral parts, i.e. the China–ASEAN Education and Training Centre, the Lancang–Mekong International Vocational Institute, the Lancang–Mekong alliance of vocational education, the Lancang–Mekong Institute of Vocational Education and Industrial Development, the Lancang–Mekong Integration Park of Education and Production, and the Lancang–Mekong International Cadres Institute.

Among them, the Lancang–Mekong International Cadres Institute has actively explored and carried out cadres training courses for political parties from South East Asian countries. In 2017, it sponsored 4 cadres training courses for international political parties and one Yunnan Provincial Party Organisation Department International Party Cadres Training Course, with 133 international trainees trained.

From the end of 2014 through 2017, the Yunnan Minzu University has successively trained 10,852 trainees in 7 training bases, namely the Border Economic Cooperation Zones of Ruili, Malipo, Mengla, Menglian, Lincang, plus Mangkang and Cangyuan. Trainees are mainly international workers to China from Myanmar, Laos, Vietnam, Thailand, Cambodia among other South East Asian countries.[1]

Case 2: the China–Malaysia Railway Talents Training Cooperation Programme

The training programme is jointly implemented by China Communications Construction Group (CCCG) with Malaysia Rail Link and Universiti Malaysia Pahang. It is funded by the CCCG, aiming at promoting CCCG's Malaysia East Coast Rail Line Project and the development of rail transportation in Malaysia.

The Malaysia East Coast Rail Line Project is to be built by the CCCG, with a total contract value of 55 billion ringgits (US$12.8 billion) and a 7-years contract period. The Malaysia East Coast Rail Line Project runs across Peninsular Malaysia, connecting the economically underdeveloped states of Pahang, Terengganu and Kelantan to one another and to economically developed Kuala Lumpur and its vicinity, which would significantly advance economic growth in the East Coast region and greatly improve the connectivity along the project.

According to the plan, the Malaysian government will vigorously develop railway transportation in the future. However, there is a certain shortfall of professionals for planning, construction and operation. Training local talents will help achieve a win–win outcome. Graduated trainees can participate in railway construction, thus local jobs are created. By 2022, this cooperation plan is expected to train 3600 trainees.[2]

Case 3: Bulgaria primary and secondary schools offer Chinese language courses

With the advancement of the BRI construction, Chinese and Chinese culture have received more popularity in Bulgaria. "Chinese fever" is heating up rapidly, with more and more students choosing to learn Chinese.

The Evlogi and Hristo Georgievi School was the first private school in Bulgaria to teach Chinese as its first foreign language. At the beginning of its establishment, the entire school had only 4 students. After only 2 years, the number of students studying Chinese in this school has increased to more than 40.

At present, 10 hours and 18 hours are scheduled per week for Chinese language and Chinese culture teaching in the school at the primary and secondary levels, respectively.

The development goal of the school is to develop Chinese and Chinese culture for a long period of time. It will offer Chinese language examination-related training courses, as well as follow-up training programmes for those who plan to study in China.

According to data of the Bulgarian Ministry of Education and Science, more than 20 primary and secondary schools in Bulgaria have offered Chinese language courses, and nearly 800 students are studying Chinese at school. Among them, the Sofia No. 18 Middle School, the first introducing the Chinese language curriculum into Bulgaria, has offered Chinese language courses for over 20 years.[3]

Vocational education boasts such characteristics as internationality and regionality. Different countries, regions may present huge differences in vocational education because of their distinctive industrial backgrounds and cultural differences.

Therefore, pilot work should be carried out in host countries to explore the road of localisation, prior to achieving the goal of "going abroad" for Chinese vocational education.

Only through combining the practical needs of host countries and achieving the localisation of vocational education standards, enterprise products and technology, can vocational education outcomes get a firm foothold in those countries, serving local socioeconomic development.

What the cooperation between China and South East Asia, South Asia and Central Asia enjoys is not only geographical advantage, but also their ongoing cooperation in such fields as agriculture, railways, etc. Built on these, vocational education and research institutes will drive vocational education cooperation and exchanges to a higher level.

Secondly, vocational education itself has a variety of social functions, such as talent training, social service, research and innovation. Extensive vocational education exchanges and cooperation between countries along the Belt and Road can not only fully mobilise the intellectual, human and technical resources owned by vocational education institutions along the Belt and Road to better support the BRI construction, but also give a bigger role to various types of vocational education institutions in terms of knowledge and professionalism, so as to enhance the international level of vocational education.

Health cooperation brings people along the Belt and Road closer

Case 4: The Chinese Red Cross Foundation carried out humanitarian relief projects

In 2017, the Chinese Red Cross Foundation (CRCF) set up the Silk Road Fraternity Fund designed to provide countries along the Belt and Road with humanitarian service.

Throughout 2017, it has funded a series of international humanitarian relief projects, with a total of 9 teams and 63 person-times dispatched.

Among them, the China–Pakistan Fraternity Emergency Care Centre, launched in Gwadar, welcomed the arrival of the Chinese Red Cross foreign aid medical team members to carry out a 2-year health service. The CRCF dispatched personnel for the first visit to Syria, providing large-scale mobile hospitals, vaccines and other humanitarian assistance; the CRCF's Angels Tour—the Belt and Road Humanitarian Rescue Afghanistan Action for Children with Severe Diseases—has taken 21 Afghan children and 53 Mongolian children with congenital heart disease (CHD) to China for free surgical treatment. The programme "Volunteers on Wheels" has raised funds for the first batch of 10,000 bicycles, and they would be fitted with equipment to assist in humanitarian services.[4]

Case 5: The Belt & Road Initiative: Loving Overseas Chinese-Brightness Action

This project is co-sponsored by the Oversea Chinese Charity Foundation of China, and the AIER Eye Hospital Group. The project has worked together with overseas Chinese and aims to provide sight restoration operations for free on impoverished cataract patients and help them to see the world again.

On November 19, 2017, the sight restoration project inauguration ceremony for Myanmar station under the Belt & Road Initiative: Loving Overseas Chinese-Brightness Action was held at the Thisan Eye Hospital, Sagaing province, Myanmar. The AIER Eye Hospital Group has dispatched an ophthalmic expert team of 6 from its Kunming hospital. They have participated in international medical assistance many times. The medical team has performed surgery on 200 Myanmar cataract patients, who trusted and praised its professionalism.[5]

The Belt & Road Initiative: Loving Overseas Chinese-Brightness Action came to Myanmar promoting the spirit of enabling everyone, rich or poor. It not only showcases the traditional Pauk-phaw friendship between Chinese and Myanmar people of mutual assistance, but also demonstrates the support for the BRI construction and aspiration for a win–win development of overseas Chinese.

This programme has also been launched in the Philippines, Cambodia and Malaysia among other South East Asian countries. In the near future, it will reach out to Europe and other regions, to see people-to-people connectivity really deliver.

Medical care, known as the most inclusively beneficial public goods and social undertaking of public interest, is crucially tied with human health. China is actively engaging with countries along the Belt and Road for health cooperation projects, which will gain the staunch support of those countries and give shape to a new picture of "people's livelihood diplomacy", jointly forging a road of health and eco-civilisation with countries along the Belt and Road.

In October 2015, the General office of National Health and Family Planning Commission of the People's Republic of China (NHFPC) issued the notice on the promotion of the Three-year Plan for Belt and Road Health Exchange and Cooperation (2015–2017), of which the key areas of cooperation include the provision of health assistance to some underdeveloped nations according to their health needs, building of medical and health infrastructure, donation of medicines and materials, dispatch of medical and health personnel and public health specialists to carry out technical assistance.

China should attach greater importance to the following areas: strengthening cooperation with countries along the Belt and Road in the training of health professionals, helping improve their capabilities in public health management and disease prevention and control, encouraging academic institutions, medical schools and NGOs to carry out teaching, research and personnel exchanges.

Therefore, medical aid team dispatch policies are to be improved in the future, so as to attract outstanding medical staff to work for the Belt and Road medical aid tasks.

Promote cultural exchange through building cultural facilities

Case 6: China offered restoration assistance to Nepal after an earthquake damaged the 9-tiered Basantapur Tower

The restoration project of the 9-tiered Basantapur Tower at Durbar Square in Kathmandu is the first large-scale cultural heritage aid project offered by China for Nepal.

The project, in which China has invested enormous energy in terms of technology and human resources, started in August 2017, with an expected duration of up to 5 years.

The Basantapur Tower is one of the landmark buildings in Nepal and is one of the 7 sites in the Kathmandu Valley which was inscribed by the UNESCO in 1979 as World Heritage.[6]

As an important palace building in Nepal's history, the tower boasts a high historical and architectural value.

Statistics have shown, amid the 8.1 magnitude earthquake rattling Nepal in April 2015, 14 ancient structures at the Durbar Square were damaged to varying degrees, of which 12 are UNESCO World Heritage sites.

After the earthquake, relevant agencies from the USA, Japan, South Korea and India have taken part in the restoration work in Nepal. China volunteered to assume one of the most challenging projects—the restoration of the 9-tiered Basantapur Tower, which was severely damaged, with some parts collapsed and severe overall deformation.

The restoration project is not only an assistance operation, but also a scientific investigation itself.

Prior to the start of the project, the 2 sides reached a consensus where they regarded the restoration as a systematic process of unveiling and classifying the historical value of the heritage, which is of far-reaching significance for studies on religions and history in South Asia and its surrounding areas.

Case 7: China and Jordan signed an agreement for the establishment of the Chinese Cultural Centre

The Agreement on the establishment of a Chinese cultural centre in Jordan between the Government of the People's Republic of the PRC and the Hashemite Kingdom of Jordan was signed on January 8, 2018.

According to the agreement, the Chinese Cultural Centre is an official non-profit cultural institution launched in Jordan by the Chinese government. Its functions include organising various cultural, artistic and educational activities, setting up libraries, reading rooms, film and television screening halls, introducing China and Chinese culture to the Jordanian public, presenting Chinese development experience, culture and arts.

The centre aims to promote more cultural exchanges between the 2 countries and deeper mutual understanding and friendship between the 2 peoples.

Jordan will provide partial tax exemption for the Chinese Cultural Centre and facilitate the permit-approval procedures for staff of the centre in line with its laws.[7]

Some countries along the Belt and Road are relatively closed and conservative in terms of economic development and their cultural development-related infrastructure is also relatively weak. Given that, China must work with them to achieving common progress if it wants to see the smooth progression of the BRI. China needs to help them establish a new type of cultural infrastructure and cultural industry with their distinctive characteristics, which entails the provision of financial, material, human and intellectual support they are in desperate need of. With proper aid and assistance, cultural exchange infrastructure in those countries could be built and cultural and economic development would both be advanced, which creates favourable material conditions for the smooth development of cultural exchange.

Cultural exchange is the bond connecting people along the Belt and Road and the lubricant of the BRI construction. It can attract people along the Belt and Road to know more about the BRI, so that the development of the BRI can transcend barriers of nationalities, languages, political systems and cultures. Therefore, the emotional bond among peoples will be consolidated.

Notes

1 "Serving the Belt and Road Initiative, promoting the Lancang–Mekong Cooperation—the Lancang–Mekong vocational education base becomes an important cooperation outcome under the Lancang–Mekong Cooperation," *Guangming daily*, January 16, 2018, http://epaper.gmw.cn/gmrb/html/2018-01/16/nw.D110000gmrb_20180116_5-08.htm
2 "China and Malaysia See Eye to Eye in Conducting Railway Personnel Training," Xinhuanet, November 12, 2017, www.xinhuanet.com/2017-11/12/c_1121942851.htm
3 "Bulgaria sees another round of 'Chinese Fever' with more than 20 primary and secondary schools offer Chinese language courses," Belt and Road net, January 15, 2018, www.yidaiyilu.gov.cn/xwzx/hwxw/43924.htm
4 "2017 has seen the Belt and Road Initiative humanitarian relief project take 74 international children to China for free treatment," Xinhuanet, December 29, 2017, www.xinhuanet.com/2017-12/29/c_1122187752.htm
5 "The Belt & Road Initiative: Loving Overseas Chinese-Brightness Action Brought Eyesight Back to 200 Myanmar Patients," Xinhuanet, November 19, 2017, www.xinhuanet.com/world/2017-11/19/c_1121979078.htm
6 "Chinese relics restoration aid project won praise in Nepal: Look forward to our the shining rebirth of our cultural treasure," *People's Daily*, October 30, 2017, http://world.people.com.cn/n1/2017/1030/c1002-29615294.html
7 "China and Jordan signed an agreement to establish a Chinese cultural center," Xinhuanet, January 8, 2018, www.xinhuanet.com/world/2018-01/08/c_1122228764.htm

117
THE CHINA INTERNATIONAL IMPORT EXPO

Zhang Zhongyuan

On May 14, 2017, Chinese President Xi Jinping attended the Belt and Road Forum for International Cooperation, during which he announced that China will hold the International Import Expo (CIIE) starting from 2018.

China will endeavour to build a win–win business partnership with other countries participating in the BRI, enhance trade and investment facilitation with them and build a Belt and Road free trade network. These efforts are designed to promote growth both in our respective regions and beyond.

On June 26, 2017, the Overall Plan of the CIIE was deliberated on and approved at the 36th meeting of the Central Leading Group for Deepening Overall Reform, which pointed out that the CIIE is an important decision to promote a new round of high-level opening-up and is a major initiative to open China's door wider to the world.

Chinese President Xi Jinping delivered a keynote speech at the Boao Forum for Asia (BFA) Annual Conference held on April 10, 2018, where he announced a series of new initiatives that will be taken for a greater opening-up, including the initiative to expand imports.

In 2018, China will significantly lower import tariffs for vehicles and reduce import tariffs for some other products. The country will work hard to import more products that are competitive and needed by the Chinese people. China will also seek faster progress towards joining the WTO Government Procurement Agreement.

The Chinese government has officially announced tariff reductions on all imported generic drugs, with zero import tariffs on pharmaceutical products containing alkaloids and which have anti-cancer properties as of May 1, 2018, to see all China's imported anti-cancer medications enjoy a zero-tariff treatment.

An introduction to the First China International Import Expo

From November 5 to 10, 2018 in Shanghai, the First China International Import Expo will be co-sponsored by the Chinese Ministry of Commerce (MoC) and the Shanghai Municipal People's Government, with the World Trade Organisation (WTO), the United Nations Conference on Trade and Development (UNCTAD) and the United Nations Industrial Development Organisation (UNIDO) among other international organisations as cooperative partners. The CIIE Bureau and the Shanghai National Exhibition and Convention Centre Co., Ltd will be the organisers.

1. Expo contents

The expo consists of 2 exhibitions, i.e. the Country Pavilion for Trade & Investment and the Enterprise & Business Exhibition.

Regarding the Country Pavilion for Trade & Investment, relevant countries and regions will be invited to participate in CIIE to showcase their trade and investment development achievements, including trade in goods and services, industries, investment and tourism, as well as representative products of the country or region with distinct features. It is exclusively reserved for country exhibitions, not for business transactions.

The Enterprise & Business Exhibition can be divided into 2 sections, i.e. trade in goods and trade in services. Relevant countries and regions will be invited to participate in the CIIE for exhibition and transaction.

Among them, the trade in goods section consists of 6 areas: high-end intelligent equipment, consumer electronics & appliances; automobiles; apparel; accessories & consumer goods; food & agricultural products; medical equipment & health care products, etc.; the trade in services section is divided into emerging technologies, service outsourcing, creative design, cultural & education, tourism service, logistics service and comprehensive service.

During the expo, the Hongqiao International Trade Forum, co-sponsored by the Chinese Ministry of Commerce and the Shanghai Municipal People's Government, will invite political leaders and ministers of exhibitors, and leaders of international organisations, as well as business leaders of world-famous enterprises and major multinational companies.

The Forum aims to promote economic globalisation in an open, inclusive, mutually beneficial, balanced and win–win direction, create an open world economy, and advance global trade growth.

This forum, including an opening ceremony and 3 parallel forums, will focus on such topics as "trade and opening", "trade and innovation", and "trade and investment", and mainly discuss, *inter alia*, the promotion of trade and investment liberalisation and facilitation, the construction of an open world economy, the boosting of trade innovation growth and the acceleration of sustainable development of trade and investment.

2. Preparatory meetings and implementation

The second meeting of the Preparatory Committee for the first China International Import Expo was held in Beijing on April 16, 2018. It was required at the meeting that preparatory work should be started at a higher level and implemented under stricter requirements to achieve the Expo's goals of "first-class enterprises, products, environment, services, and outcomes". Distinctive features of the expo as a national exhibition, an enterprise exhibition and a forum will be highlighted to make the Expo a good model of high-level opening-up, so as to enhance its influence and appeal and ensure that it is built into a landmark project boosting a new round of high-level opening up.

According to specific work programmes in the Overall Plan of the CIIE and the Implementation Scheme of China International Import Expo, such fields as clarifying the tasks, persons in charge, timetable and countdown schedule, as well as assisting in the works of exhibition invitation, investment attraction, foreign affairs reception, security, venue upgrading, city safeguard and media publicity should be prioritised in preparatory work.

3. The Expo is open to global exhibitors

The CIIE has offered its invitation to the whole world. It is open equally to global exhibitors, both from developed countries such as Europe and the USA and those of developing countries and the least-developed countries (LDCs).

As of late March, 2012, 10,584 companies and organisations from over 130 countries have submitted applications to the first CIIE, with more than 600 (including Fortune 500 and other leading enterprises) companies signed up.

To facilitate governments and companies fully understanding the Expo, the Chinese Ministry of Commerce launched an Expo column, while the CIIE's official website has also been opened.[1]

The Expo will provide the necessary support and assistance for exhibitors of developing countries and LDCs as appropriate, such as reduction or exemption of booth fees, the provision of 2 free standard booths for exhibitors from the LDCs and the provision of entry and exit facilitation for all international exhibitors and exhibits.

After the Expo, a one-stop online and offline trading platform will be established according to different characteristics and type of goods of countries, dedicated to providing long-term exhibition and trade service.

The significance of the China International Import Expo

1. The CIIE showcases China's confidence and determination in opening up

After the 2008 global financial crisis, the global economy has experienced a long and tortuous process of adjustment. As one of the engines driving economic growth, global trade presents a sign of recovery.

With the world economy undergoing an in-depth adjustment, economic globalisation encounters major setbacks. Global trade friction is intensifying. "Trade war" seems rampant. Global free trade is facing strong "headwinds".

Facing the big sticks of trade protectionism that some developed countries frequently wield, the world is more in need of openness, interconnection, inclusiveness, balance, and more in need of a China being a guardian of global governance and the torchbearer for the open trading system.

For this reason, China is firm in advocating, promoting and contributing to economic globalisation.

At the Boao Forum, the Chinese president Xi Jinping stressed that we should "keep an open mind", "stay committed to open regionalism", "significantly broaden market access". The 19th CPC National Congress Report also clearly stated "China will not close its door to the world; it will only become more and more open".

It is to convey China's determination and confidence in further expanding its opening up and spearheading the development of economic globalisation to the entire world.

Hosting the CIIE is an initiative China has taken to support trade liberalisation and economic globalisation, and open up its market to the world.

China will continue to benefit from global development. It will continue to contribute more dividends to the world, thereby promoting the common development of human civilisation, common prosperity. What's more, China remains committed to offering its wisdom through such concepts as economic globalisation and an open world.

2. The CIIE demonstrates China's sense of responsibility as a responsible major power, which is conducive to the formation of role model effect

The international community is showing stronger desire to expand the Chinese market and take the "express train" of China's development, with growing aspiration to participate in the BRI.

Through the CIIE, the world can share an open Chinese market. Therefore, international trade, market opening-up, in-depth economic globalisation and an open world economy can be promoted, all of which together will create friendly conditions for the construction of the community of a shared future.

China, the world's second largest economy, is a staunch advocate for trade liberalisation, the development of a global free trade system. China is committed to building a higher level of opening-up and cooperation system.

China will continue to increase imports and broaden market access to service industry market. Taking the initiative to expand imports demonstrates China is actively assuming more international responsibilities, reflecting a greater sense of responsibility as a major power. China is enabling people around the world to share its economic development achievements by letting more countries take full advantage of China's reform and opening-up, and its economic development dividends.

The CIIE mirrors China's determination to proceed with an in-depth integration into the world economy. It also tells the world that China will adopt more opening-up policies and China will open its door wider to the world.

It can be expected that China will open its door wider with the formation of a new comprehensive opening-up landscape. China pursues common development through win–win cooperation, which can advance the formation of a new comprehensive opening-up landscape.

3. The CIIE is setting up an exchange platform for promoting cooperation between international businesses

China, as a developing country hosting an expo with the theme of import, gives the world's countries at different development levels an opportunity to show their achievements in the field of trade and investment and builds a platform for advancing international trade exchange and for exploring major issues of international trade and global economy.

Worth particular mention is that supporting activities such as match-making meetings, negotiation sessions and investment briefings will be arranged based on the specific needs of exhibiting countries, in order to better help developing countries and LDCs enter the Chinese market. In this way, trade and industries can be accurately match-made to create new channels for trade and investment cooperation.

The Belt and Road countries boast diverse resources and industrial structures, thus having a lot to offer each other and enjoying huge potential for trade.

By cutting barriers, setting up platforms and perfecting import policies, China has actively expanded its imports from Belt and Road countries, to further optimise its trade structure.

Although led by government, the CIIE's floor is given to enterprises. As a trade platform, it is market-based, business-centred and project-oriented, and depends on the participation, innovation and creation of concerned parities (enterprises in particular). Market principles are followed on this platform, which presents market principles such as equality of subjects, free trade, fair competition and independent decision-making.

As a long-term decision and initiative, the CIIE will provide a first-class public platform for international cooperation for the Belt and Road countries, as well as the market cognition and cooperation opportunity essential for the interaction of a large-scale production community. The periodical holding of the CIIE can continuously develop and promote the convergence of China's interests and destiny with that of the rest of the world.

4. Continuously broadening international import channels to meet people's ever-growing needs for a better life

With the continuous development of China's economy, its middle-class ranks have gradually expanded and their purchasing power in the world has increased.

China's economy has shifted from a high-speed growth phase to a high-quality development stage. In the past, China was an important importer of intermediate products in the world. Today, China is becoming a major importer of consumer goods, with consumption as its fundamental driving force, with the position it takes in the national economy becoming more and more important. China has been witnessing a faster pace of consumption structure upgrade, new consumption highlights, high-quality products, with a growing appetite for well-known brands, high-quality products and featured products and services.

In terms of supply, however, the high-quality and diversified supply of goods still faces some weak areas. Therefore, people's ever-growing needs for a better life can be met through active expansion of imports.

Hosting the CIIE with imports as its theme not only meets the aspiration for common development, but also meets China's own development needs.

In addition, reform and opening-up is a powerful impetus for economic and social development. Only by promoting in-depth reform and high-level openness can quality development be materialised.

China's economy has been deeply integrated into the world. The CIIE is not only conducive to expanding imports and progressing balanced development of international trade, but more beneficial for improving the supply side structure and guiding domestic enterprises to pursue the innovation-driven development.

Note

1 Official CIIE website, www.shanghaiexpo.org.cn/zbh/index.html

Bibliography

1. "The ultimate goal of the Belt and Road Initiative: create a community of shared future for mankind," Xinhuanet. Retrieved January 19, 2018 from www.xinhuanet.com/globe/2017-08/14/c_13650036539.htm
2. "The Belt and Road Initiative, a splendid chapter of history and reality." Retrieved January 13, 2018 http://cpc.people.com.cn/n1/2017/1016/c414305-29588234.html
3. "Vision and Actions on Jointly Building Silk Road Economic Belt and 21st-Century Maritime Silk Road." Retrieved January 19, 2018 from http://zhs.mofcom.gov.cn/article/xxfb/201503/20150300926644.shtml
4. "Responding to the trend of the Times and promoting world peace and development—Xi Jinping's speech at the Moscow Institute of International Relations," the central Government portal. Retrieved January 19, 2018 from www.gov.cn/ldhd/2013-03/24/content_2360829.htm
5. Xi Jinping, "Secure a Decisive Victory in Building a Moderately Prosperous Society in All Respects and Strive for the Great Success of Socialism with Chinese Characteristics for a New Era—Delivered at the 19th National Congress of the Communist Party of China October 18, 2017." Retrieved January 26, 2018 from www.gov.cn/zhuanti/2017-10/27/content_5234876.htm

6. "Towards a Community of Common Destiny and A New Future for Asia—Keynote Speech by H.E. Xi Jinping, at the Boao Forum for Asia Annual Conference 2015," *People's Daily*. Retrieved January 26, 2018 from http://politics.people.com.cn/n/2015/0329/c1024-26765442.html
7. Xi Jinping, President of the People's Republic of China, "Working Together to Create a New Mutually Beneficial Partnership and Community of Shared Future for Mankind—Speech at the General Debate of the 70th Session of the UN General Assembly." Retrieved January 26, 2018 from http://politics.people.com.cn/n/2015/0929/c1024-27644905.html
8. "Work Together to Build the Silk Road Economic Belt and The 21st Century Maritime Silk Road—Speech by H.E. Xi Jinping, at the Opening Ceremony of The Belt and Road Forum for International Cooperation." Retrieved January 26, 2018 from http://world.people.com.cn/n1/2017/0515/c1002-29274975.html
9. Xi Jinping, "Build a community of shared future for mankind and achieve shared and win–win development." Retrieved February 2, 2018 from www.xinhuanet.com/mrdx/2017-01/20/c_135998532.htm
10. Wang Yi, "Build a community of shared future for mankind." Retrieved February 2, 2018 from http://opinion.people.com.cn/n1/2016/0531/c1003-28394300.html
11. Li Xiangyang, "Outstanding Problems Facing the Belt and Road Initiative and Way Out," *International Trade*, 2017, Volume 4, pp. 4–9.
12. He Weifang, "On the Chinese Solution to Building a Community of Shared Future for Mankind—based on the perspective of the Belt and Road construction," *Law and Society*, September 2017, Volume 2, pp. 119–121.
13. Zhao Jin, "The Belt and Road to a Community of Shared Future for Mankind," *Contemporary World*, June 2016, pp. 9–13.
14. Hu Angang, et al., "Xi Jinping's Thought on Building a Community of Shared Future for Mankind and Chinese Solution," *Journal of Xinjiang Normal University*, September 2018, 39th of Volume 5, pp. 1–8.
15. Wang Yin, "A Community of Shared Future for Mankind: Content and Construction Principles," *International Studies*, 2017, Volume 5.
16. "Xi Jinping on the Highest Goal of the Belt and Road Initiative," *Vanguard*, 1st of June 2017, pp. 6–7.
17. Wang Yuzhu, *Think Tank Report: the Belt and Road Initiative and the Reconstruction of Asian Integration Model*, Social Sciences Academic Press (China), May 2015.
18. Li Yongquan (Chief Editor), *Blue Paper of the Belt and Road Initiative: Belt and Road Construction and Development Report (2016)*, Social Sciences Academic Press, July 2016.

(Written by: Wang Yuzhu and Jiang Fangfei)

INDEX

21st Century Maritime Silk Road 61, 81, 89–92, 94, 101, 102, 111, 117, 120, 123, 127, 129, 130, 132, 134, 137, 138, 153, 154, 163, 190, 213, 337, 353, 368, 372, 416, 435, 441, 446, 454, 462, 475, 484, 490, 500, 522–524, 526, 527, 541, 551, 555; basic content 107
2030 Agenda *see* Agenda for Sustainable Development (2030)

Aborigines 530–532
Addis Ababa Action Agenda (AAAA) 363, 420–424; diversified financing mechanism in BRI 422–423; global framework for development financing after 2015 420–422
Aden 261, 269
affinity, sincerity, practical results and good faith 277–281
Afghanistan 57, 64, 66, 119, 147, 177, 374, 457, 474, 508–511, 595
Africa 53, 61, 70, 71, 77, 80, 82, 83, 92, 101, 103, 108, 109, 117, 123, 124, 127, 129, 148, 153, 155, 167, 178, 188, 194, 258, 260, 261, 267–269, 277–281, 291, 317, 391, 415, 425–428, 454, 455, 475, 524, 545–547, 572, 591
African Agenda 2063: alignment achievement and influence of BRI with 427–428; alignment of BRI with 426–427; with BRI 425–428; proposal and implementation 425–426
African Union (AU) 116, 121, 122, 268, 279, 285, 425, 426–428, 544, 545
Agenda for Sustainable Development (2030) 6, 132, 161, 163, 164, 183, 260, 353, 356, 363; with BRI 415–419; Chinese plan for sustainable development 415–416; development bonus of BRI 417–419; sustainable development in BRI 416–417

agriculture 166–167, 275, 278, 308, 332, 337, 360, 388, 395, 418, 448, 452, 470, 498, 514, 526, 527, 530, 532–533, 537, 549, 550, 552, 561, 565–566, 578, 587, 591, 595
airports 290, 307, 308, 337, 342, 464, 477, 488, 489, 490, 495, 506, 526, 532, 540, 544, 545
Akhtar, Shamshad 154, 294, 391
Aksu 57, 63
Albania 406, 448, 492, 493, 494, 495, 505
Amber Railway Freight Corridor (Poland) 535–539; background 535–536; future development prospects 537–538; main content 536–537
America 47, 78, 95, 117, 155, 208, 241, 291, 352, 454, 508, 509, 511, 530
amity, sincerity, mutual benefit and inclusiveness 272–276; elaboration and formation of concept 272–273; main content 273–274; sincerity 273; theoretical and practical significance 274–275
Amur (Darya Oxus) 200
Ancient Civilisations Forum 375; with BRI 430–434; founding of 430–431
Arabs 64, 84, 260
Arctic 176, 200, 474, 565
Argentina 121, 328, 367, 400, 422, 476, 477, 478, 479
Armenia 77, 460, 467–70, 505, 512, 561
ASEAN (Association of Southeast Asian Nations) 45, 80, 81, 89, 90, 92, 95, 103, 107, 116, 121, 130, 151, 180, 189, 193, 213–215, 223, 232, 262, 264, 266, 306–308, 313, 321, 322, 439–442, 444, 480–2, 531, 532, 550, 575, 588
ASEAN Community Vision 2025 with BRI 439–442; alignment 441–442; conceptual description and subject contents 439–441
ASEAN Plus China (10+1) 103, 118, 131, 133, 176

Index

Asia 53, 55, 61, 63, 77, 78, 80, 83, 92, 97, 101, 103, 106, 107, 109, 117, 123, 127, 129, 140, 148, 153, 155, 178, 198, 260, 261, 264, 269, 290, 291, 292, 301, 321, 329, 337, 367, 373, 374, 388, 391, 422, 443, 444, 454, 459, 473, 517, 535, 538, 540, 554
Asia Cooperation Dialogue (ACD) 104, 118, 176
Asia–Europe Meeting (ASEM) 104; and its connectivity working group with BRI 443–447; new starting point 445–446; origin and development 443–444; prospect and challenge of aligning 446–447
Asia–Pacific Economic and Social Council 154
Asia–Pacific Economic Circle 106
Asia–Pacific Economic Cooperation (APEC) 30; 25th Economic Leader' Meeting 176; Finance Ministers Meeting 328
Asia–Pacific region 154, 243, 244, 263–265, 274, 275, 328, 391, 407, 435–438, 446, 506, 519, 520, 531, 538, 572
Asian Development Bank (ADB) 50, 187, 189, 219, 291, 301, 400, 418, 419, 422, 517–519, 560, 565, 566
Asian Infrastructure Investment Bank (AIIB) 290–293; background for establishing 290–291; governance structure 292–293; preparations in progress for 291–292
astronomy 67, 82, 522
Atlantic 109, 490, 540
Australia 129, 263, 265, 266, 285, 286, 291, 321, 328, 396, 409, 530–533, 585
Austria 291, 316, 401, 492
authorized economic operator (AEO) 585–586
Azevedo, Robert 382, 395, 397

Bactria 59, 65
Bali 435, 498, 526
Baltic Sea 84, 89, 92, 102, 123, 127, 129, 448, 454, 455, 475, 490, 536
Bangladesh 13, 90, 102, 109, 119, 128, 133, 157, 162, 167, 176, 223–226, 291, 322, 454, 458, 505, 522–524; China provides with concessional loans to build network infrastructure project 579
Bangladesh–China–India–Myanmar Economic Corridor (BCIMEC) 13, 102, 223–227; concept explanation 223; details 224–225; latest development 225–226
Bank of China (BOC) 133, 152, 162, 188, 189, 205, 294, 296, 306, 398, 401, 528, 556, 557, 591; provides loans to Shalkiya Zinc Project, Kazakhstan 588
Beijing 71, 111, 132, 136, 137, 139, 140, 145, 150, 155, 160, 165, 176, 194, 199, 234, 242, 243, 252, 267, 272, 291, 292, 294, 312, 381, 382, 384, 385, 394, 398, 399, 403, 428, 432, 433, 435, 450, 477, 506, 523, 563, 599

Belarus 120, 152, 204, 286, 316, 343, 397, 400, 401, 422, 467, 469, 470, 474, 479, 512, 513, 536, 564
Belgium 394, 444, 465, 493, 574
Belt and Road Forum for International Cooperation (2017) 31, 39, 43, 379–411; background and major objectives 381–382; effects and responses 384–385; on Financial Connectivity 398–402; on Infrastructure Connectivity 390–393; Leaders Roundtable (2017) 125; main content 382–384; on People-to-People Connectivity 403–407; Thematic Sessions: on Connectivity of Development Policies and Strategies 386–389; on Think-Tank Exchanges 408–411; on Trade Connectivity 394–397
Belt and Road Initiative (BRI): Addis Ababa Action Agenda (AAAA) with 420–424; African Agenda 2063 with 425–428; Ancient Civilisations Forum with 430–434; ASEAN Community Vision 2025 with 439–442; ASEM and its connectivity working group with 443–447; background 94–98; background for proposing cooperation directions 128; basic contents 106–110; basic positioning and main purposes 123–125; basic principles 111–115; Bright Road Plan with 559–563; building four major Silk Roads 100–101; case studies of implementation and promotion 569–603; and China–EU connectivity platform 462–466; and China's responsibilities as major country 27–32; China–UK bilateral investment to fund 588; and confidence of major country 33–37; connectivity blueprint of Asia-Pacific economic cooperation with 435–438; continual evolvement of ideas of 91–93; cooperation between China and CEE countries with 448–452; cooperation mechanisms 103–104, 131–135; and deficit in development 38–42; and deficit in governance 47–51; and deficit in peace 43–46; and developing open economy and 9–14; development bonus of 417–419; directions of cooperation 127–130; diversified financing mechanism in 422–423; Eastern Partnership (EaP) with 467–471; economic cooperation corridors 13; and economic restructuring 15–20; Eurasian Economic Union (Russia) and 512–516; Eurasian Partnership Plan with 472–475; extensive consultation, joint contribution and shared benefits 111–115; facilitating infrastructure construction 572–573; five key cooperation directions 101–102; and five types of connectivity 102–103; formation 1–50; framework 99–105; general ideas 123–126; green action and direction 485–487; green commitment 484–485; IIRSA with 476–479; improving people's livelihood 571–572;

605

and innovation-driven development 21–26; international action plans relevant to 413–499; international plans similar to 501–567; Lamu Port–South Sudan–Ethiopia Transportation Corridor (Kenya) with 545–547; Leading Group for 91; innovative working mechanism and concept 139–140; Loving Overseas Chinese-Brightness Action 595–596; Master Plan on ASEAN Connectivity with 480–482; Mining Alliance 185; misunderstandings about 97–98; New Northward Expansion Policy with 565–567; organisational guarantee 104; organisational structure 136–141; Paris Agreement with 483–487; partners 116–122; paths to participate in 117–118; position in strategic decisions of central government and its tasks 137–139; process for proposing 89–93; Project Mausam Plan (India) 522–524; promoting formation of new pattern of regional economic integration 104–105; and Quality Infrastructure Partnership Plan (Japan) 518–519; and Road Connecting Different Civilisations 165–169; and Road of Innovation 160–164; and Road of Openness 155–159; and Road of Peace 145–149; and Road of Prosperity 150–154; Science, Technology and Innovation Cooperation Action Plan 161; Steppe Road Plan (Mongolia) 554–557; sustainable development in 416–417; Sustainable Development of the 2030 Agenda with 415–419; synergy with other development strategies 132–133; Trans-European Transport Networks (TEN-T) 488–491; Two Corridors and One Ring Plan (Vietnam) with 551–552; ultimate goal 125–126; upholding four concepts and building three communities 99–100; upholding principle of extensive consultation, joint contribution and shared benefits 101; Western Balkan 6 Connectivity Agenda whose strategies are aligned with BRI 118

Bilateral and Multilateral Cooperation Dialogue Mechanism for Macroeconomic Policies 327–331; dialogue mechanisms on bilateral economic policies 330–331; dialogue mechanisms on multilateral economic policies 327–329

biodiversity 163, 178, 191, 199

Black Sea 57, 65, 455

Boao Forum for Asia (BFA), China 104, 133, 153, 246, 286, 374, 598

Bolivia 375, 430, 431, 476, 478

Bosnia and Herzegovina 394, 395, 405, 448, 451, 492, 493, 495

Brazil 285, 291, 302, 303, 313, 328, 330, 331, 361, 367, 476, 477–479, 585

BRI *see* Belt and Road Initiative

BRICS 43, 47, 94, 234, 286, 288, 300–303, 321, 328, 373; Consultation on Peacekeeping Operations 44; Cooperation Mechanism 327, 328; Counter-Terrorism Working Group 44; Foreign Policy Planning Dialogue 44; Meeting of the Cybersecurity Working Group 44; New Development Bank 103, 161, 186, 187, 339, 383, 513, 567; Plus Cooperation Model 288

bridge development strategies 285–289, 337; concept 285–286; models and practices for 287–288; significance of in global era 286–287

bridges 129, 192, 290, 297, 307, 339, 369, 373, 409

Bright Road Plan (Kazakhstan) 559–563; alignment conditions with BRI 560–563; overview 559–560

Britain *see* Great Britain

Brunei 290, 291, 307, 406

Buddhism 61, 64, 67, 76, 192, 193, 375

Building the Belt and Road: Concept, Practice and China's Contribution 132, 136, 139, 288

Bukhara 504

Bulgaria 202, 448, 458, 505, 587; primary and secondary schools offer Chinese language courses 594–595

business environment 5, 11, 103, 174, 182, 184, 279, 323, 326, 348, 365, 366, 394, 418, 463, 464, 572; forge convenient and efficient 584–586

business models 25, 163, 307, 308, 333, 334, 347, 580; develop new to boost financing 589–590

Cambodia 119, 134, 166, 176, 192, 213, 216, 286, 288, 291, 294, 307, 317, 343, 401, 406, 442, 481, 482, 507, 514, 522, 584, 590, 593, 596

capitalism 3, 48, 239

Caribbean 117, 121, 156, 313, 477, 478

case studies: of BRI implementation and promotion 569–603; of infrastructure connectivity building 571–576; of production capacity cooperation 577–581; of trade and investment facilitation 582–586

Catholicism 76

Central America 478

Central and Eastern Europe (CEE) 129, 132, 162, 167, 188, 194, 202, 204, 286, 288, 301, 447–452, 453–455, 462, 468–469, 493–494, 535, 537, 538; *see also* China–Central and Eastern European (CEE) Countries

Central and Eastern European Investment Cooperation Fund 133, 205

Central Asia 13, 53–57, 60, 61, 63–67, 75, 76, 80, 92, 102, 104, 106, 108, 119, 123, 127–129, 132, 133, 148, 153, 162, 167, 177, 180, 202, 207–211, 298, 340, 342–344, 374, 454, 458–460, 473, 475, 504, 508–511, 514, 515, 561, 562, 564, 572, 574, 590, 595

Central Asia Regional Economic Cooperation (CAREC) 104, 118, 133, 177

Central China 13, 55
Central Plains of China 54, 59
Centre for Strategic and International Studies (CSIS) 93, 509
Chad 367, 498
Chang'an 59–61, 64, 77, 106
Cheshi 57, 60, 64
Chile 121, 286, 321, 322, 476, 477, 478, 479, 582–583
China: Centenary Goals 33; Communist Party see Communist Party of China (CPC); and economic restructuring 15–20; fields, contributions of responsibilities and obligations 29–30; five-year plans: 9th (1996–2000) 15; 10th (2001–05) 15; 11th (2006–10) 16; 12th (2011–15) 16; 13th (2016–20) 18; Foreign Exchange Trading Centre 188, 567; Free Trade Area (FTA) 319–322; and Jordan signed agreement for establishment of Chinese Cultural Centre 597; Ministry of Commerce 91, 138, 140, 156, 162, 185, 200, 205, 211, 214, 218, 221, 226, 296, 313, 315–317, 319, 338, 383, 394, 469, 472, 484, 513, 541, 542, 552, 555, 577, 584, 598–600; Ministry of Environmental Protection 162, 406, 485, 486; Ministry of Finance 140, 294, 296, 317, 331, 383, 398, 400, 401, 418, 422, 518; Ministry of Foreign Affairs 91, 138, 140, 162, 218, 296, 338, 406, 426, 448, 449, 484, 518, 541, 554, 555, 593; National Development and Reform Commission (China) 91, 104, 136, 138, 140, 162, 185, 218, 294, 296, 312, 353, 382, 383, 386, 387, 390, 391, 400, 410, 464, 483, 484, 486, 541, 555, 574; new contributions to world in response to deficit in peace 44–45; and obligations 31; offered restoration assistance to Nepal 596; principles, position of responsibilities and accountabilities 27–29; provides Bangladesh with concessional loans to build network infrastructure project 579; reform and opening up to world 1–50; responsibilities as major country 27–32; and Russia signed new tax treaty 583–584; signed agreements on AEO (authorized economic operator) 585–586; wisdom of, and Chinese concept for international order 48–49; as "world factory" 96; as "world market" 96–97; see also People's Republic of China (PRC)
China–Africa cooperation 121, 279–281, 428, 545
China–Africa Cooperation Forum 268, 270, 278, 428, 545, 546
China–Arab States Cooperation Forum (CASCF) 104, 118, 133, 165, 176, 177, 207
China–ASEAN Cooperation Fund (CAF) 306–309; founding of 305; investment and operation 307–308; operation progress 308
China–ASEAN Expo 104, 118, 133, 442, 551
China–ASEAN Interbank Association 103, 186

China–ASEAN Maritime Cooperation Fund 81, 90, 118
China–ASEAN Port Cities Co-op Network 575
China–Asia–Europe Expo 118, 133
China–Bangladesh Free Trade Area 157, 322
China Banking Regulatory Commission 152, 486
China–Belarus Industrial Park 151, 204, 316, 397, 513
China–CEE Fund 133, 162
China–Central and Eastern European (CEE) Countries: cooperation with BRI 448–452; Prague Declaration on Health Cooperation and Development 167
China–Central Asia–West Asia Economic Corridor 13, 102, 207–212; concept explanation 207–208; details 208–209; latest development 209–211
China Central Bank 140, 329, 339, 591
China–Central, Eastern Europe (CEE) InterBank Consortium 587
China–Chile Free Trade Zone upgraded 582–583
China Development Bank (CDB) 152, 188, 189, 295, 296, 401, 451, 542, 587–589; issued Belt and Road Bond 589–590; signed BRI loan deals with Egypt 591
China–Egypt TEDA Suez Economic and Trade Cooperation Zone 579–580
China–EU connectivity platform and BRI 462–466; multilateral effort in international cooperation 465–466; response of EU to BRI 462–463; strategic alignment 463–465
China–Eurasia Economic Cooperation Fund 118, 205
China–Europe Land–Sea Express Route 204, 433, 451, 491, 494, 495; with BRI 453–456; conceptual description and formation process of 453–454; significance of 455
China–Europe Railway Express 573–575
China Export & Credit Insurance Corporation (SINOSURE) 589–590; China–Georgia Free Trade Agreement 157, 582
China–Gulf Cooperation Council (GCC) 122, 211, 431; Free Trade Area 157, 322; Strategic Dialogue 104, 177
China–Indochina Peninsula Economic Corridor 13, 102, 109, 128, 130, 213–217; concept explanation 213–214; details 214–215; latest development 215–216
China–Indonesia Comprehensive Industrial Park 580–581
China International Import Expo (CIIE) 598–603; broadening international import channels 602; contents 599; demonstrates China's sense of responsibility as major power 601; First (2018) 598–600; open to global exhibitors 599; preparatory meetings and implementation 599; setting up exchange platform for promoting

cooperation between international businesses 601–602; showcases China's confidence and determination in opening up 600; significance 600–602
China–Israel Free Trade Area 157, 322
China–Laos railway 152, 215
China–Malaysia Railway Talents Training Cooperation Programme 594
China–Moldova free trade agreement 157, 322
China–Mongolia–Russia Economic Corridor (CMREC) 13, 102, 109, 128, 129, 152, 197–201, 554–556, 564, 566; concept explanation 197–198; details 198–199; latest developments 199–200
China–Myanmar Economic Corridor 13, 90, 102, 109, 119, 128, 226, 454, 458, 523, 524, 578
China–Nepal Free Trade Area 157, 322
China–Nepal trans-border optical fibre link 571–572
China NGO Network for International Exchanges 122, 383, 404
China Ocean Shipping Company (COSCO) 204, 209, 210, 453
China–Pakistan Economic Corridor (CPEC) 13, 90, 102, 109, 119, 128, 130, 152, 181, 189, 218–222, 454, 458–459, 524, 572, 591; concept explanation 218–219; details 219–220; latest development 220–221; Long-Term Plan for 577
China–Pakistan Free Trade Area 157, 322
China–Russia Expo 104, 133
China–South Asia Expo 104, 118, 133
China–Sri Lanka Free Trade Area 157, 322
China threat theory 241, 274
China–UK bilateral investment to fund BRI 588
China–Ukraine Agricultural Investment Cooperation Plan 577–578
Chinese characteristics 21–23, 27, 35, 45, 109, 111, 112, 124, 134, 325, 326; foreign affairs with 229–281; major country diplomacy with 231–235; socialism with 4, 5, 33, 34, 35, 36, 37, 40, 41, 232, 233, 247, 249, 253, 254, 270; theories and concepts of foreign affairs with 229–281; Thoughts on Socialist Economy with Chinese Characteristics for the New Era 10, 12, 34, 35
Chinese Cultural Centre 374, 597
Chinese Red Cross Foundation (CRCF) 193, 595
Chinese Social Organisations' Action Plan [...] 122, 404
Chipris, Brigitte 382, 396
Chongqing 107, 157, 319, 445, 566
Christianity/Christians 61, 76, 375, 459
climate change 28–31, 39, 103, 115, 163, 238, 243, 249–250, 261, 269, 301, 351, 353, 355–9, 362, 363, 415, 417, 418, 483–487; elaboration and formation of concept 355–356; main content for addressing 356–357; major progress and trends in global efforts against 357–359; tackling 355–359
Clinton, Hillary 508–511
coal-fired power plant project, Port Muhhamad Bin Qasim, Pakistan 572
Cold War 48, 49, 65, 113, 146, 232, 236–238, 244, 248, 257–259, 375, 443, 508, 564
Colombia 322, 476, 478
colonialism: new/neo- 12, 270
Communist Party of China (CPC) 16, 22–24, 27, 28, 35, 93, 124, 136–140, 158, 233, 236, 239, 240, 242–244, 252–255, 600; Central Committee 3, 4, 9–11, 15, 23, 33, 81, 90, 91, 111, 136–138, 140, 232, 247, 249, 274, 294, 321, 373, 382, 409; Central Economic Work Conference 90, 139; International Department 194, 383, 403; National Congress: 10th (1982) 236; 13th (1987) 252; 14th (1992) 3, 9; 15th (1997) 9, 252; 16th (2002) 9, 16; 17th (2005) 10; 18th (2012) 10, 22, 27, 33, 93, 231, 242, 243, 246, 249, 252, 253, 268; 19th (2017) 10, 16, 24, 28, 35, 112, 124, 139, 158, 236, 238–240, 244, 247, 253, 272, 600; 20th (2022) 253; Policy Research Office 91, 136, 137; Politburo 33, 81, 111
community 34, 94, 168, 178, 234, 244, 399, 417, 418, 439–441, 480, 522, 531, 545, 567; international 14, 27–31, 41, 45, 47–50, 82, 91, 92, 95, 126, 127, 139, 147, 174, 177, 180, 187, 192, 231, 233, 237–239, 244, 259, 270, 271, 351, 355–358, 360, 362, 387, 396, 419, 423, 430, 483, 506, 523, 564, 601, 602; of shared future for mankind 7, 28, 39, 44, 45, 48, 50, 81, 83, 96, 98, 100, 108, 111–114, 116, 125, 126, 128, 155, 174, 176, 194, 215, 231, 237, 240, 246–251, 258–261, 273, 275, 288, 320, 362, 371, 373, 376, 389, 403, 409, 412, 449, 451, 477, 574, 601; of shared interests 99–101, 108, 114, 126, 148, 156, 274, 285, 287, 320
Community of Latin American and Caribbean States 156, 313, 477
compass 67, 71, 76
competition 5, 9, 11, 22, 44, 48, 93, 96, 241, 320, 321, 326, 333, 348, 364, 497, 515, 519, 523, 573, 582, 601
Conference on Interaction and Confidence-Building Measures in Asia (CICA) 104, 118, 131 133, 176, 373
Confucius Institutes 166, 191–194, 370, 514, 547, 556, 557
Confusians/Confucianism 67, 259, 268
connectivity: blueprint of Asia-Pacific economic cooperation with BRI 435–438; of Development Policies and Strategies 386–389; facilities 178–181; Financial 398–402; five types of 102–103; information connectivity, enhancing 573–575; of infrastructure 178–181;

infrastructure case studies 571–576; Master Plan on ASEAN Connectivity 45; and pragmatic cooperation 445–446

cooperation: Belt and Road Forum for international 379–411; between China and CEE countries with BRI 448–452; directions of 127–130; energy efficiency 351–354; financial 451, 528; financial case studies 587–592; health 595–596; mechanisms 39, 44, 45, 47, 49, 103–104, 108, 112, 113, 115, 118, 121, 124, 131–135, 138, 140, 146, 162, 167, 174, 175, 176, 180, 187, 210, 213, 214, 263, 327–329, 335, 353, 355, 370, 392, 395–397, 403, 410, 411, 427, 442, 444, 449, 465, 514, 519, 520, 550, 556, 561, 573; new industrial innovation 332–336; people-to-people 368–371, 374, 403, 528; production capacity 129, 139, 151, 160, 162, 185, 202, 204, 210, 298, 308, 310–314, 442, 478, 541, 546, 551, 561, 562; production capacity case studies 577–581; win–win 10, 12, 27, 28, 31, 43–46, 49, 80, 81, 84, 89, 94, 95, 99, 100, 107, 108, 111, 124, 125, 126, 134, 146, 147, 160, 216, 236–238, 240–243, 246, 248, 249, 255, 257–262, 270, 275, 278, 279, 372, 397, 601

Cooperation between China and Central and Eastern European Countries 121–122, 448–452, 455

core concepts 283–377

cotton 71, 76, 498

cross-border industrial parks 315–318; experiences in developing overseas business cooperation zones 317–318; overseas business cooperation zones and their development 315–316; status quo of major overseas business cooperation zones 316–317

cultural and academic exchanges 103, 190, 192–193; promote through building cultural facilities 596–597; strengthen 593–595

cyber-(in)security 28, 248, 261

Czech Republic 167, 168, 202, 286, 383, 406, 448, 450, 451, 469

Davos 158, 239, 275, 335, 381, 470

Daxia (Bactria) 59, 65

Decision of the Central Committee [...] (2013) 4, 10, 11, 90, 140

deficit: China's new contributions to world in response to 44–45; in development 38–42; in governance and BRI 47–51; meaning and presentation 47–48; in peace 43–46

Deng Xiaoping 3, 34, 239

Ding Gong 381–397

disease control 190, 193

diversity 36, 48, 82, 94, 163, 168, 173, 174, 178, 187, 191, 199, 248, 250, 257, 261, 295, 305, 360, 372–374, 416, 485, 503, 572, 591

Doha Round Negotiations 497–498

Dong Xiangrong 53–85

double-track exchange between political parties and think tanks 194

drugs 598

Dubai 323–324

Dunhuang 59, 60, 64, 104, 133, 166

E35 Expressway, Pakistan 571

East Africa 107, 391, 454, 545–547

East Asia 19, 61, 74, 84, 89, 92, 101, 129, 130, 132, 167, 180, 202, 213–215, 223, 232, 265, 329, 354, 460, 473, 474, 568, 572; *see also* Northeast Asia; South East Asia

East Timor 119, 288, 531

Eastern Maritime Silk Road 68–70

Eastern Partnership (EaP): BRI and CEE countries under framework of 468–469; formation of 467–468; with BRI 467–471

e-commerce cooperation 584

economic globalisation 5–7, 10, 22, 28, 39, 48–50, 94, 99, 128, 153, 156–158, 163, 173, 183, 184, 209, 248, 250, 257, 265, 287, 311, 313, 329, 346–349, 383, 389, 396, 397, 409, 428, 535, 599–601

economic restructuring of China 15–20; and Belt and Road Initiative 18–19; characteristics and process 15–16; path and effectiveness 16–18

Ecuador 286, 476, 478, 479

education 3, 15, 21, 29, 41, 49, 132, 166, 167, 169, 178, 191–193, 199, 320, 333, 337, 363, 368–371, 383, 403–407, 427, 430, 436, 437, 444, 446, 448, 451, 452, 463, 480, 481, 503, 521, 550, 555, 557, 559, 560, 563, 564, 567, 593–595, 597, 599

"Education Action Plan for Jointly Building the Belt and Road" 166, 192

Egypt 53, 74, 151, 167, 176, 188, 189, 210, 211, 286, 291, 293, 313, 317, 374, 375, 401, 428, 430, 431, 473, 505, 514, 579, 580, 591; CDB signed BRI loan deals with 591; Suez Canal Economic Corridor 540–543

Elbegdorj, Tsakhiagiin 294, 555

electricity 18, 140, 180, 181, 187, 188, 198, 208, 219, 220, 224, 225, 260, 311, 317, 338, 339, 342, 352, 366, 572, 580, 587

energy 16, 19, 28, 92, 94, 109, 118, 122, 129, 133, 151, 162, 163, 166, 175, 178–181, 188, 189, 198, 200, 202, 207–210, 214, 216, 218–221, 223–225, 260, 270, 275, 280, 288, 295, 300–302, 307, 308, 312, 332, 334, 336–338, 340–343, 355, 382, 390–392, 396, 400, 415, 417–419, 432, 433, 436, 441, 446, 457–459, 463, 464, 468–470, 476–478, 480, 482–484, 486, 488, 491, 493, 495, 508–511, 514, 519, 526, 527, 530, 532, 533, 537, 541, 547, 554, 559–562, 564–566, 568, 572, 577, 579, 580, 589–591, 596; efficiency cooperation 351–354

England 120, 288

Erdogan, Recep 382, 457–460

Estonia 405, 448, 584
Ethiopia 121, 151, 181, 313, 316, 317, 343, 382, 420, 425–428, 544, 545, 547
Euphrates 53, 54, 70, 375
Eurasian Continental Bridge 107, 152, 202–205
Eurasian Economic Union (EEU) 45, 120, 129, 197, 198, 288, 472, 475, 512–516, 565; conditions for alignment with BRI 514; formation process 512; prospect and challenge alignment with BRI 515; strategic alignment with BRI 512–514
Eurasian Partnership Plan with BRI 472–475; alignment 474–475; based on equal, open and transparent principles 473–474; principles 473
Europe 19, 53–55, 58, 61, 63–65, 67, 70, 74, 75, 78, 80, 82, 83, 90, 92, 96, 97, 101–103, 106–109, 116, 117, 120–121, 123, 124, 127, 129, 148, 155, 178, 198, 202–204, 208, 233, 243, 255, 258, 261, 275, 288, 291, 298, 321, 324, 329, 337, 340, 344, 352, 367, 388, 391, 432, 443–448, 450, 453–455, 458, 459, 462–470, 473–475, 488–491, 493–495, 508, 509, 513, 519, 535–538, 540–542, 554–556, 559, 561, 566, 572–575, 596, 600
Europe 2020 Strategy 203, 255
European Bank for Reconstruction and Development 187, 189, 301, 400, 560
European Commission 331, 390, 391, 463, 464, 467, 468, 488, 489, 491, 492, 504, 535
European Economic Circle 92, 101, 106, 129, 202, 474
European Union (EU) 47, 116, 157, 194, 264, 285, 313, 328, 339, 421, 433, 439, 443, 444, 446–448, 452, 458, 459, 467–470, 473, 488, 489, 491–493, 512, 538, 560; China–EU connectivity platform (Juncker Plan) and BRI 462–466; response to BRI 462–463
exchanges and mutual learning among civilisations 372–377; concept interpretation and formation 372–373; main content and progress 373–375; significance of 375–377
Export–Import Bank of China (EIBC) 152, 205, 295, 401, 454, 528, 542, 546

facilities connectivity 178–181; concept of 178; implementation of 180–181; practical significance 179–180
Feng Weijiang 327–331, 364–367, 472–475, 488–491, 497–500
Ferghana 374
Fiji 167, 286, 322
financial connectivity 398, 400, 401, 587–589
financial cooperation 451, 528; case studies of 587–592
financial integration 103, 186–189, 556; concept 186–187; implementation progress 188–189; practical significance 187–188

First Silk Road NGO Cooperation Network Forum 122, 194
Five Principles of Peaceful Coexistence 49–50; Friendship Award 44; Scholarship of Excellence 44
five roads 143–169; Road of Peace and BRI 145–149
five types of connectivity 92, 171–193
foreign affairs with Chinese characteristics 229–281
foreign investment 9–11, 41, 150, 163, 211, 221, 226, 267, 270, 279, 281, 298, 313, 316, 317, 324, 365, 552
France 78, 120, 285, 291, 293, 328, 330, 343, 348, 388, 401, 443, 467, 492
free trade agreements 157, 174, 182, 184, 203, 263, 266, 319–321, 322, 396, 470, 512, 514, 532, 582–583
Free Trade Area (FTA): in China 319–322; concept of 319; progress in development 320–322
free trade ports (FTPs) 323–326; China's exploration on building 325; establishing free trade pilot areas 325; establishing Hainan Free Trade Pilot Zone and FTPs 325; international practices and experiences for building 323–324; significance for establishing Hainan Free Trade Pilot Zone and FTPs 325–326
friendship 31, 35, 36, 43, 44, 80, 81, 84, 89, 99, 105, 107, 110, 117, 124, 134, 146, 151, 175, 192, 237, 242, 259, 260, 267, 278, 279, 316, 368, 372, 373, 404, 409, 474, 518, 552, 571, 595, 597
Fu Jingjun 127–130
Fujian 4, 71, 72, 319, 325
Fur Road (aka Steppe Silk Road) 56, 65

G20 38, 132, 168, 207, 260, 327, 328, 335, 337, 339, 349, 354, 415, 416, 458, 485, 518, 584
Gansu 59, 61, 63
Gantas Tunnel, Algeria 573
Ge Cheng 131–135
Georgia 157, 188, 291, 293, 321, 396, 457, 467, 469, 470, 505, 561, 582
Germany 16, 55, 120, 244, 285, 286, 291, 328, 330, 348, 352, 358, 396, 446, 450, 463, 474, 488, 492, 493
global governance 29, 36, 46–50, 94, 99, 101, 109, 111–115, 156, 234, 237, 247–250, 255, 275, 285, 403, 410, 411, 600; meaning and presentation of deficit in 47–48
Global Maritime Axis Strategy (Indonesia) 526–529; conceptual description and main contents 526–527; conditions and progress in alignment with BRI 527–528
globalisation *see* economic globalisation
global value chain development and supply chain 346–350; characteristics 347–348; concept

346–347; development orientation 348–349; good faith 124, 268, 270, 277–281
Great Britain 78, 120, 244, 285, 348, 588
Greater Mekong Subregion (GMS) Economic Cooperation 104, 118, 133, 177, 549
Greece/Greeks 53–55, 134, 204, 343, 375, 404, 430–433, 453, 455, 462, 469, 505, 536
Green Silk Road 162–164, 485
Guangdong 71, 72, 77, 319, 325, 549
Guangxi 189, 213, 549, 551, 552
Guangxi–ASEAN BRI funds 588–589
Guangzhou 61, 64, 70–73, 77, 340, 394, 395
Gulf Cooperation Council 104, 122, 157, 177, 211, 431
gunpowder 67, 71, 75, 76
Guterres, Antonio 382, 386, 387, 417
Gwadar 152, 218–221, 458, 577, 595

Hainan 325–326, 549
Hami 294
Han 57–60, 63–70, 75–77, 80, 106
Hanoi 66, 215, 549–552
harmony 6, 35, 36, 38, 40, 46, 49, 81, 83, 112, 125, 165, 248, 250, 373, 441, 474
He Lifeng 386, 387
health 29, 41, 100, 132, 166, 167, 169, 178, 179, 190, 191, 219, 270, 307, 332, 336, 351, 363, 368, 369, 371, 383, 404, 407, 427, 448, 473, 545, 565, 599; cooperation 595–596
Hexi 58–60, 63–65, 77, 106
historic inheritance 51–86
Holland *see* Netherlands
Hong Kong 49, 319, 322–324, 498, 533, 571, 590; Monetary Authority 188
Hormuz 540
Hu Jintao 21, 33, 231, 241, 242, 457
Hungary 120, 152, 204, 205, 288, 448, 450, 451, 453, 455, 468, 469, 494, 535–538
Hungary–Serbia railway 152, 454, 455, 469, 494
Huns 58, 59, 64, 65, 78

inclusiveness 12, 37, 44, 80, 81, 99, 100, 108, 110, 112–114, 116, 124–128, 131, 155, 157, 168, 174, 191, 246–249, 260, 272–276, 280, 287, 294, 295, 349, 354, 372–374, 387, 399, 403, 404, 410, 416, 417, 420, 432, 441, 448, 473–475, 480, 573, 600
India 13, 53, 54, 56, 57, 60, 61, 63, 65–67, 71, 75, 77, 90, 94, 102, 109, 119, 128, 167, 189, 192, 205, 208, 223–226, 239, 263, 264, 266, 272, 285, 286, 291, 293, 300, 302, 328, 330, 331, 375, 430, 431, 454, 458, 472–474, 484, 498, 505, 509, 510, 514, 518, 519, 521–525, 531, 535, 571, 596
Indian Ocean 70, 92, 102, 107–109, 123, 127, 130, 174, 213, 223, 453, 454, 475, 521–523, 528, 540, 541
Indo-China 66, 107, 130

Indonesia 80, 89, 95, 119, 133, 137, 162, 192, 264, 285, 290, 291, 307, 328, 368, 401, 435, 442, 454, 481, 482, 498, 503, 505, 522, 526–528, 531, 580, 589
industrial development 96, 119, 121, 122, 151, 156, 162, 175, 198, 219, 224, 317, 332–333, 388, 401, 405, 406, 544, 593, 598
industrial revolution 75, 151, 163, 332–334, 346–348
infectious diseases 28, 190
information connectivity 342, 392, 573–575
infrastructure connectivity building, case studies 571–576
Inner Mongolia 107, 344, 556
innovation-driven development: and Belt and Road Initiative 21–26; concepts and features 21–22; path and achievements 22–24
International Civil Aviation Organisation 121, 122, 405, 431
International Committee of the Red Cross 122, 405
International Energy Agency (IEA) 219, 300, 352, 353, 484
international infrastructure network: categorisation of connotation for 338; concept 337–338; development 338–340; promoting 337–340
International Monetary Fund (IMF) 38, 187, 188, 232, 234, 328, 328, 329, 382, 383, 399, 401
international plans similar to BRI 501–567
international relations, new-type 236–240; formation of concept 236–238; main content 238–239; practical and theoretical significance 239–240
international tax cooperation 583–584
International Telecommunication Union 121, 344, 391, 392
International Think Tank Cooperation 122, 135, 370, 383, 406
International Trade Centre 121, 122, 405
Investment Plan for Europe (aka Juncker Plan) 450, 468; strategic alliance with BRI 463–465
Iran 57, 64, 74, 77, 106, 120, 147, 168, 176, 181, 207, 261, 286, 291, 374, 375, 401, 430, 431, 458–460, 472, 473, 504, 505, 508, 514, 524, 560, 561
Iraq 64, 70, 120, 375, 430, 431, 505, 522
Islam 67, 76, 375
Israel 120, 147, 157, 291, 322, 406, 505
Italy 120, 291, 328, 375, 397, 430, 431, 443, 445, 492, 503, 505

jade 58, 74
Jakarta–Bandung high-speed railway 152, 528
Japan 16, 56, 68–72, 119, 188, 208, 263–266, 285, 322, 327–331, 344, 503, 505, 517–520, 524, 532, 565, 585, 596
Java 70, 71, 526, 528

Jiang Fangfei 111–115, 123–126
Jiang Zemin 21, 237
Jordan 120, 291, 367, 498, 506, 590, 597
justice 267–271

Kashgar 57, 63, 330
Kazakhstan 80, 89, 92, 95, 106, 120, 137, 151, 152, 157, 162, 166, 168, 189, 193, 207, 208, 210, 226, 286, 288, 291, 298, 310, 312, 313, 329, 340, 342, 343, 368, 401, 405, 435, 457, 460, 474, 504, 505, 507, 510–514, 559–563, 565, 588
Kazan 199, 513
Kenya 82, 121, 134, 344, 401, 427, 544–548
Khiva 166, 504
Korea 64, 68, 69, 72, 77, 119, 147, 234, 261, 264, 285, 474; North 68, 69, 71, 119, 505, 564, 567; South 118, 192, 194, 263, 266, 269, 291, 321, 322, 327–329, 505, 523, 532, 564–568, 585, 596
Kotzias, Nikos 430–432
Kunming 65, 66, 213, 340, 549, 550, 595
Kushan 78
Kuwait 207, 291
Kyrgyzstan 120, 152, 157, 166, 207–210, 291, 293, 342, 505, 512, 514

Lamaism 76
Lamu Port–South Sudan–Ethiopia Transportation Corridor (Kenya) 544–548; alignment with BRI 545–547; overview 544–545
Lancang–Mekong International Waterway 130, 134, 213, 317, 549, 593
language cooperation and talent training 193–194
Laos 119, 134, 152, 192, 213, 215, 216, 226, 286, 288, 291, 307, 374, 401, 405, 442, 481, 578, 589, 590, 593
Latin America 19, 106, 117, 121, 148, 156, 176, 258, 260, 269, 313, 321, 415, 455, 475, 477–479, 582, 583
Latvia 448, 468, 469, 575
League of Arab States 122, 431
Lebanon 120, 288, 405
Li Keqiang 90, 132, 138, 188, 218, 225, 290, 310, 382, 426, 432, 445, 453, 457, 462, 478, 528, 552, 555, 565
Li Shicheng 99–105
Li Tianguo 178–181
Li Wei 386, 387
Li Zhifei 246–251, 272–276
Liaoning 69, 319
Lithuania 316, 448, 575, 587
Liu Jingye 517–520, 526–529, 549–553
Liu Junsheng 136–141, 236–260
Liu Qichen 383, 409
Liu Tianyi 439–442, 480–482
Liu Wei 420–424, 435–438, 443–447, 462–466, 512–516
LOGINK 574–575

logistics, facilitating efficient 573–575
Long Guoqiang 386, 388
Loving Overseas Chinese-Brightness Action 595–596

Macedonia 54, 448, 453–455, 492–494, 587
major country relations, new-type 241–245; formation of concept 241–242; main content 242–243; realistic and theoretical significance 243–244
Malacca 78, 102, 127, 213, 453, 454, 540
Malaya 401
Malaysia 70, 77, 119, 189, 213, 215, 216, 288, 291, 307, 342, 343, 390, 401, 574, 575, 590, 594, 596
Maldives 119, 157, 167, 291, 321
Manchuria 199
Manichaeism 61, 67, 76
Manila 72, 78, 189, 193, 329, 436
manufacturing 18, 19, 96, 110, 151, 153, 183, 185, 198, 205, 209, 214, 219, 224, 278, 290, 310–313, 316, 323–326, 332–334, 343, 346–348, 450, 470, 515, 522, 537, 543, 546, 556, 561, 564, 566, 579–581, 588
Mao Tse-Tung 21, 34
Maritime Silk Road 64, 65, 68–73, 76, 78, 80, 101, 127; Eastern 68–70; sea ban and decline of dominant power 72–73; Southern 68, 70–72; *see also* 21st Century Maritime Silk Road
Marshall Plan 93, 108, 234
Marxism 21, 34, 35, 247
Master Plan on ASEAN Connectivity with BRI 480–482; alignment 481–482; conceptual description and main contents 480–481
media 103, 110, 116, 175, 190–192, 232, 373, 374, 384, 406, 407, 450, 451, 482, 518, 555, 557, 599; cooperation and people-to-people exchange 194
medicine, 65, 67, 76, 82, 100, 167, 190, 193, 320, 427, 549, 550, 596
Mediterranean 57, 92, 102, 106, 123, 127, 129, 204, 207, 431–433, 453, 454, 458, 459, 467, 475, 490, 536, 540, 573
Mexico 72, 328, 375, 430, 431, 498
Miao Wei 390–392
Middle Corridor Initiative 46; with BRI 457–461; conceptual description and formation process 457–458; significance, favorable conditions and challenge of 459–460
Middle East 19, 120, 127, 148, 176, 207–209, 323, 431, 484, 509, 559, 572
Millennium Development Goals (MDGs) 6, 29, 361–363, 415
Ming 61, 67, 69–73, 82, 426
Minsk 151, 204, 316
Moldova 157, 322, 394, 467, 469, 470, 512
Mombasa 121, 428, 544, 546

Index

Mongolia 13, 65, 75, 78, 102, 107, 109, 119, 128, 129, 133, 152, 162, 167, 188, 192, 197–201, 272, 286, 288, 291, 294, 298, 322, 329, 340, 343, 344, 374, 406, 445, 454, 505, 518, 554–558, 564, 566, 567, 583, 595
Montenegro 448, 492–495, 587
Morowali Tsingshan Industrial Park 580–581
Moscow 197, 199, 237, 243, 246, 257, 258, 472, 512–514, 556, 583
Muslims 61, 76, 459
mutual benefit 272–276
mutual learning 28, 36, 37, 53, 80–83, 99, 100, 110, 114, 116, 124–127, 165, 168, 169, 191, 246, 248, 250, 261, 372–377, 387, 395, 398, 403, 407–410, 416, 432, 474
Myanmar 13, 66, 70, 90, 102, 109, 119, 128, 134, 147, 166, 167, 192, 193, 223–226, 263, 266, 288, 291, 307, 340, 342, 404, 454, 458, 523, 524, 578, 593, 595

Nepal 66, 119, 152, 157, 166–168, 176, 192, 288, 291, 322, 374, 524, 571, 572, 596
Nestorianism 67, 76
Netherlands 61, 69, 78, 121, 255, 291, 324
New Development Bank 300–305; background for founding 300–301; operation 302–303; positioning of 301–302; prospect of 303–305
New Eurasian Land Bridge Economic Corridor 13, 102, 202–206; concept explanation 202; details 203–204; latest developments 204–205
new industrial innovation cooperation 332–336; concept 332; correlations between new industrial development and scientific innovation 332–333; new content and new characteristics 333–334; pathways for 334–336
New Northward Expansion Policy (South Korea) 564–568; alignment conditions with BRI 565–567; future prospect 567–568; overview 564–565
New Silk Road Plan (USA) 508–511; background conditions 508–510; current situation and prospect 511; main contents 510–511
New Zealand 121, 263, 265, 266, 286, 291, 321, 322, 585
Ningbo 69, 71, 72
North Africa 53, 74, 107, 207, 298
North Atlantic Treaty Organisation (NATO) 460, 508, 509
North Korea 68, 69, 71, 119, 505, 564, 567
North–South cooperation 45, 109, 125, 133
Northeast Asia 61, 118, 129, 265, 444, 564, 574
Northeast China 55, 102, 127
Northern Australia Development Plan 530–534
Northern Territory, Australia 530, 530, 532
Norway 121, 291, 322, 406
nuclear weapons 44, 48, 147

Obama, Barack Hussein 242, 243, 460, 511
Oceania 117, 121, 291, 321
Oman 208, 210, 291, 367, 498
open economy 4, 6, 41, 101, 154, 156, 182, 183, 321, 473; achievements and prospects of building 10–12; developing, and BRI 9–14; formation and development of 9–10
openness 7, 11, 13, 30, 37, 81, 99, 110, 113, 116, 124–127, 135, 145, 146, 150, 155–158, 160, 165, 168, 239, 247, 248, 286, 287, 292, 293, 295, 297, 320, 321, 323–326, 337, 349, 366, 367, 384, 387, 404, 409, 410, 416, 432, 441, 448, 473–475, 582, 600, 602
Overland Silk Road 61, 63–67, 68, 70; historical significance 66–67
overseas business cooperation zones: development 315–316; experiences in developing 317–318; status quo of major 316–317

Pacific 12, 84, 89, 92, 95, 102, 103, 106, 107, 109, 122, 123, 127, 130, 133, 156, 157, 174, 176, 180, 213, 223, 232, 454, 475, 532, 540; *see also* Asia–Pacific region
Pakistan 13, 66, 90, 102, 109, 119, 128, 130, 133, 134, 152, 157, 162, 167, 168, 181, 189, 192, 205, 218, 219–221, 272, 286, 288, 291, 294, 298, 321, 322, 374, 382, 390, 395, 401, 404, 454, 457–460, 472, 474, 505, 510, 511, 522, 524, 571, 572, 577, 589–591, 595; approved renminbi as its settlement currency 591; *see also* China–Pakistan Economic Corridor (CPEC)
Panama 121, 213, 322, 478, 540, 583
Pang Jiaxin 530–9, 544–548, 559–568
Papua New Guinea 322, 526, 531
Paris Agreement 47, 358, 416, 419; with BRI: challenge of climate 483–484; green action and direction 485–487; green commitment 484–485
passage building, improving 573–575
peace 5–7, 38, 30, 31, 35–37, 48–50, 80, 81, 83, 84, 93, 94, 99–101, 105, 110, 112, 113, 116, 124, 125–128, 136, 150, 155, 160, 165, 168, 233, 237, 239, 243, 244, 247–249, 255, 257, 259–261, 268–270, 274, 275, 277, 279, 285, 348, 372–374, 387, 388, 395, 409, 416, 426, 427, 432, 439–441, 443, 474, 504, 505, 513, 515, 545, 564, 565, 567, 578; BRI and deficit in 43–47; BRI and Road of 145–149
people-to-people exchange 7, 66, 80, 109, 115, 132, 133, 160, 165, 166, 168, 175, 191–194, 199, 207, 219, 223, 225, 274, 315, 316, 373–375, 384, 387, 404, 405, 426, 449; case studies of 593–597; and cooperation 194, 368–371; guided by understanding of people 368–369; progress and outcomes 369–371
People's Representative Council of Indonesia 80, 89, 368

People's Republic of China (PRC) 11, 33, 43, 48, 137, 197, 232, 233, 252, 253, 274, 392, 418, 422, 426, 430, 448–451, 464, 469, 472, 483–486, 513, 541, 542, 550, 552, 555, 596, 597; *see also* China
Persia 61, 77, 535
Persian Gulf 61, 70, 77, 92, 102, 123, 127, 129, 207, 453, 454, 475, 561
Peru 286, 321, 322, 375, 430, 431, 476–479, 583
Philippines 71, 72, 119, 168, 188, 189, 291, 307, 329, 343, 436, 442, 481, 522, 596
Piraeus 152, 204, 432, 433, 453, 455
Pliny the Elder 54, 75, 77
Poland 120, 202, 205, 286, 291, 401, 448, 450, 451, 454, 467, 469, 474, 505, 535–539, 575
policy coordination 12, 13, 19, 24, 36, 84, 92, 96, 99, 102, 111, 114, 117, 121, 124, 128, 133, 173–177, 178, 190, 286, 327, 330, 331, 368, 382, 384, 387–389, 391, 398, 410, 416, 438, 441, 446, 448, 481, 485, 491, 526, 527, 537, 549, 551, 555, 565, 566; concept of 173–174; implementation progress of 175–177; practical significance 174–175
Polo, Marco 54–56
porcelain 65, 67, 70, 71, 74, 76, 78
Port Qasim, Pakistan 572
ports 4, 18, 61, 70–72, 102, 107, 127–129, 151, 152, 157, 199, 219, 220, 224, 290, 307, 308, 319, 323, 338–340, 342, 364, 393, 437, 452–454, 464, 475, 477, 488, 489, 491, 519, 526, 532, 535, 536, 540, 541, 544–546, 550, 556, 561, 573–575, 578; free trade 323–326
Portugal/Portuguese 69, 78, 244, 291, 313, 574
poverty 6, 7, 28, 29, 31, 33, 38, 41, 42, 49, 96, 146–149, 153, 154, 167, 179, 182, 191, 219, 286, 291, 301, 317, 360–363, 405, 410, 415, 417, 420, 421, 426, 427, 440, 545, 577, 578
practical results 268, 270, 277–281
printing 54, 67, 71, 76, 334
production 12, 16, 17, 24, 31, 40, 41, 43, 53, 69, 74, 76, 78, 96, 97, 107, 109, 110, 117, 125, 153, 156, 160–162, 169, 174, 183, 190, 191, 198–200, 202–204, 207, 209, 214–216, 224, 249, 265, 295, 317, 320, 324, 332–334, 337, 346–348, 360, 362, 388, 391, 396, 440, 452, 458, 472, 473, 480, 484, 485, 509, 515, 526, 531, 533, 545–547, 549, 552, 560–563, 566, 567, 583, 593, 602
production capacity cooperation 129, 139, 151, 160, 162, 185, 202, 204, 210, 298, 308, 310–314, 442, 478, 541, 546, 551, 561, 562; case studies of 577–581; create new platform for 579–581; forge demonstration project for international 579; initiation, connotations and meaning 310–311; major objectives and implementation approaches 311–312; progress on capacity cooperation 312–313

Project Mausam Plan (India) 521–525; current situation and problems of connection with BRI 522–524; origin, contents and development 521–522
Putin, Vladimir 330, 382, 472–474, 555

Qatar 120, 207, 208, 291, 521
Qin Sheng 173–177, 190–194
Qing Dynasty 61, 72, 73, 82
Quality Infrastructure Partnership Plan (Japan) 517–520; conceptual description and main contents 517–518; current description and prospect of alignment with BRI 518–519; future development direction 519–520
Quanzhou 61, 64, 70–72
Qu Caiyun 398–411

R&D 23, 25, 199, 316, 334–337, 347, 348, 351
rail 18, 61, 66, 102, 107, 121, 128–130, 151–153, 162, 180, 181, 197–199, 202–204, 209, 210, 215, 219, 220, 224, 225, 269, 290, 306, 307, 311, 313, 324, 337, 339–344, 366, 390, 391, 417, 426, 428, 441, 451–460, 464, 465, 468, 469, 474, 476–479, 482, 488–495, 510, 513, 518, 519, 528, 532, 533, 535–539, 542, 544–547, 549, 552, 554–556, 559, 561, 565, 566, 573–575, 578, 589, 594, 595
Red Sea 71, 78, 107, 453, 540
Regional Comprehensive Economic Partnership (RCEP) 157, 263–266; negotiation process and results 265; overview: proposals, contents and guiding principles 263–264; scale, economic benefits and impact 264–265; technical differences in integration 265–266
renewable energy 163, 302, 307, 417–419, 484, 562; basic connotation 351; development status 351–352; and energy efficiency cooperation 353–355; promoting energy efficiency cooperation 351–354
renminbi: Pakistan approved as its settlement currency 591; steadily advance internationalization of 591
Road Connecting Different Civilisations: and BRI 165–169; concept and origin 165; contribution to world 168–169; spirit of, reflected in BRI 165–168
Road of Innovation: and BRI 160–164; concept and origin 160; contribution to world 163–164; spirit of, reflected in BRI 160–163
Road of Openness: and BRI 155–159; concept and origin 155; contribution to world 157–159; spirit of, reflected in BRI 155–157
Road of Peace: and BRI 145–149; concept and origin 145; contribution to world 147–149; spirit of, reflected in BRI 146–147
Road of Prosperity: and BRI 150–154; concept and origin 150; contribution to world 153–154; spirit of, reflected in BRI 150–153

roads 33, 53, 63, 66, 74, 82, 100, 102, 107, 127, 129, 219, 224, 317, 324, 369, 409, 452, 457, 459, 464, 477–479, 488, 490, 532, 540, 546, 559; five 143–169

Roman Empire 54, 64, 75–77

Romania 448, 450, 453, 505, 587

Russia 13, 19, 45, 65, 78, 84, 92, 102, 104, 108, 109, 120, 123, 127–129, 133, 151, 152, 162, 167, 168, 176, 188, 189, 197–201, 202, 210, 232, 237, 243, 246, 257, 285, 286, 291, 298, 302, 303, 328, 330, 340, 343, 344, 367, 374, 375, 382, 390, 391, 400, 404, 405, 447, 454, 458, 467, 472–475, 493, 505, 507, 508, 512–516, 554–556, 560, 561, 564–567, 572, 575, 583, 584; and China signed new tax treaty 583–584

Rwanda 268, 367, 498

Samarkand 64, 503, 504

Saudi Arabia 120, 176, 181, 189, 207, 208, 210, 286, 288, 291, 328, 401, 406, 505

science and technology 7, 12, 21–25, 39, 41, 82, 161, 162, 166, 191, 192, 275, 326, 333, 369, 371, 383, 394, 403, 404, 406–408

scientific innovation, new industrial development and 332–333

Serbia 152, 168, 202, 204, 205, 286, 343, 390, 401, 448, 450, 451, 453–5, 469, 492–494, 536, 537, 587

Seres 53–55, 75, 77

Shaanxi 55, 319, 513

Shalkiya Zinc NV 189, 588

Shanghai 4, 71, 157, 258, 319, 325, 340, 423, 437, 563, 567, 598, 599

Shanghai Cooperation Organisation (SCO) 44, 84, 103, 118, 176, 186, 202, 286, 327, 329, 472, 514

Sharif, Mohamed Shabaz 294, 382, 404

Shen Minghui 182–189

ships 48, 61, 70–72, 145, 261, 269, 313, 521, 540, 542

Siberia 78

Sichuan 66, 107, 319

silk 53–5, 58, 60, 68–72, 74–78, 80, 145

Silk Road: brief history 57–62; commodity exchanges on 74–76; decline and rejuvenation 61; and exchanges among different countries 74–79; frequent flow of people on 76–78; of Green Development 100; of Health Cooperation 100; of Intelligence 100; naming of 53–56; of Peace 100; prosperity during Sui and Tang Dynasties 60–61; spirit 80–85; *see also* Maritime Silk Road; Overland Silk Road; Southern Silk Road; Steppe Silk Road

Silk Road Economic Belt 91; basic content 106–107

Silk Road Fund 294–299; business scope and governance structure 295–297; founding and positioning 294–295; operation principles and status quo 297–298

Silk Road International Arts Festival 166, 370

Silk Road International Film Festival 104, 133

Silk Road Tourism Programme (UN) 503–507; alignment with BRI and future development 506–507; concrete measures 505–506; overview 503–505

sincerity 124, 147, 260, 268, 270, 272, 369, 545; and amity, mutual benefit and inclusiveness 272–276; and practical results, affinity and good faith 277–281

Singapore 70, 119, 189, 213, 215, 286, 288, 291, 307, 321, 322, 324, 364, 366, 374, 410, 443, 473, 482, 497, 498, 522, 550, 575, 585

six economic corridors 195–227

Slovakia 202, 448, 450, 454, 535–538

Slovenia 448, 492, 493, 495, 535–538

socialism 3–5, 10, 12, 15, 17, 21–23, 27, 33–37, 40, 41, 232, 233, 239, 240, 247, 249, 252–255, 268, 270

Song Dynasty 67, 69, 71

South America initiative for integration of regional infrastructure (IIRSA) with BRI 476–479; alignment 477–478; IIRSA and COSIPLAN 476–477; prospect for participation 478–479

South Asia 63, 66, 67, 70, 71, 74, 84, 89, 92, 104, 107, 118, 119, 123, 127, 130, 132, 133, 162, 180, 213, 223, 225, 298, 340, 444, 454, 459, 473, 475, 508–511, 521, 524, 572, 595, 596

South China 3, 30, 55

South China Sea 92, 102, 107, 123, 127, 192, 193, 234, 243, 261, 275, 453, 454, 475, 541

South East Asia 61, 70, 71, 92, 108, 119, 123, 127, 129, 130, 132, 133, 153, 162, 176, 213, 223, 225, 265, 290, 291, 298, 324, 340, 442, 454, 473–475, 482, 484, 509, 524, 536, 563, 593, 595, 596

South Korea 118, 192, 194, 263, 266, 269, 291, 321, 322, 327–329, 505, 523, 532, 564–568, 585, 596

South–South Cooperation 13, 27, 29, 39, 45, 109, 125, 134, 260, 269, 405, 415, 416, 420, 485

Southern Europe 57, 448, 455

Southern Maritime Silk Road 68, 70–72

Southern Silk Road 63, 65–66

Southwest China 55, 65, 66, 102, 127, 130

Soviet Union, 64, 232, 244, 342, 508

Spain 61, 69, 72, 78, 244, 291, 505

spices 71, 74, 76, 77

Sri Lanka 70, 77, 119, 157, 167, 176, 192, 286, 291, 322, 374, 401, 404, 507, 522, 524

standard setting and institutional building for international infrastructure 341–345; concept 341–342; outcomes 343–344; pathway for forming international infrastructure standards and institutions 342–343

Steppe Road Plan (Mongolia) 554–558; overview 554; strategic alignment with BRI 554–557

Steppe Silk Road (aka China Road, Fur Road, Ironware Road, Northern Silk Road, Tea Road) 63, 65, 554

Suez 213; Economic Corridor (Egypt) 540–543; Economic Zone 151, 210, 317, 428, 579–580

Sui Dynasty 60–61, 64

Sumatra 70, 526

sustainable development 6, 11, 29, 38, 40, 41, 96, 118, 120, 125, 126, 128, 132, 148, 161–164, 174, 177, 178, 182–184, 187, 193, 203, 209, 211, 215, 220, 223, 224, 239, 249, 250, 254, 258, 260, 270, 275, 278, 281, 287, 290, 295, 297, 301–303, 307, 317, 329, 353, 356, 358–363, 367, 383, 384, 386–388, 394, 396, 397, 405, 408, 410, 411, 415–422, 426, 427, 438, 442, 464, 476, 485, 486, 503, 504, 506, 508, 526, 545, 551, 599; of 2030 Agenda and BRI 415–419; elaboration and formation of, as concept 360–361; new round of reform for 362–363; practices and connotation evolution if 361–362

Sweden 193, 291, 395, 467

Switzerland 121, 291, 321, 343, 387, 390, 470, 583, 585

Syria 58, 147, 167, 261, 450, 505, 595

Tajikistan 58, 120, 133, 157, 162, 207–210, 286, 288, 291, 514, 555

Tang Dynasty 60–61, 64, 67, 69–71, 75–78, 82

Tarim Basin 57, 77, 106

Tashkent 64, 197

tea , 65, 74, 76

Tea Road (aka Steppe Silk Road) 65, 167, 505, 554

telecommunications 178, 179, 185, 219, 224, 226, 307, 318, 337, 339, 341, 392, 399, 477, 587

terrorism 28, 30, 31, 43, 44, 100, 115, 145, 147–149, 238, 248–250, 261, 280, 395, 430, 447

Thailand 70, 119, 134, 151, 167, 168, 192, 213, 215, 216, 288, 290, 291, 307, 308, 317, 329, 374, 390, 392, 396, 401, 443, 482, 519, 522, 575, 593

Tian Feng 319–326, 332–350, 448–452

Tian Guangqiang 512–516, 540–543, 554–558

Tian Huifang 355–363, 483–487

Tibet 53, 66, 76

tourism 167, 169, 190, 193, 199, 219, 308, 326, 333, 369, 370, 371, 374, 383, 396, 403–406, 437, 446, 448, 452, 455, 480, 481, 503–507, 519, 522, 526, 527, 533, 538, 550, 551, 555, 560, 565, 571, 599

trade: and culture: and investment facilitation 364–367; and investment facilitation case studies 582–586; unimpeded 182–185

Trade Facilitation Agreement (TFA) of WTO: with BRI 497–500; main content and implementation 498–500; issuance and validation 497–488

Trans-European Transport Networks (TEN-T): with BRI 488–491; contents 489–490; formation process 488–489

Trans-Pacific (Economic) Partnership (TPP) 95, 157, 263–266, 520

transport 55, 58, 61, 70, 71, 77, 100, 102, 109, 128, 152, 153, 162, 178, 179, 184, 198, 199, 203, 204, 210, 214, 215, 218–220, 301, 306, 313, 318, 337, 339, 340, 342, 343, 355, 364–366, 392, 393, 490, 492, 573

Trump, Donald 47, 95, 238, 265, 330, 460, 511, 519

Turkey/Turks 45, 64, 207, 209–211, 288, 291, 328, 343, 401, 405, 457–460, 505

Turkmenistan 210, 343, 457–460, 474, 505, 510, 561

Two Centenary Goals 252–256; conceptual description and main contents 549–551; current conditions and progress of alignment with BRI 551–552; proposal and definition 252–253; theoretical and practical significance 253–255;

Two Corridors and One Ring Plan (Vietnam) 176, 549–553

Ukraine 396, 447, 467–470, 490, 493, 505, 564, 575, 577–578, 581

understanding between people 190–194; concept 190–191; cultural and academic exchanges 192–193; disease control and medical cooperation 193; double-track exchange between political parties and think tanks 194; implementation progress 192; language cooperation and talent training 193–194; people-to-people exchange and media cooperation 194; practical significance 191–192; tourism cooperation and sports exchanges 193

unimpeded trade 182–185; concept of 182–183; implementation progress 184–185; practical significance 183–184

United Arab Emirates (UAE) 120, 168, 189, 208, 210, 291, 323, 324, 388, 406, 574

United Kingdom (UK) 16, 47, 61, 69, 188, 192, 244, 286, 288, 291, 328, 330, 343, 358, 400, 588; see also Great Britain

United Nations (UN) 6, 14, 28, 30, 31, 38, 46, 47, 116, 146, 147, 154, 157, 162, 167, 168, 183, 237, 239, 246, 247, 250, 258, 260, 261, 358, 360–363, 373, 375, 382, 383, 386–8, 395, 396, 403, 415, 417, 418, 420, 421, 427, 430, 485, 518; Charter 28, 101, 154, 237, 246, 258; Children's Fund 121, 122; Conference on Trade and Development (UNCTAD) 121, 122, 224, 364, 365, 367, 395, 396, 405, 598; Development Programme (UNDP) 12, 121, 122, 137,